INTERNATIONAL NEGOTIATIONS:

A BIBLIOGRAPHY

About the Book and Author

The international system comprises a plurality of sovereign states often pursuing conflicting interests. One means of resolving or managing conflicts between those states is diplomatic bargaining or negotiation. In the last fifteen years, the study of negotiation has attracted researchers from various disciplines in the social sciences, and the volume of materials on negotiating behavior has grown dramatically. This bibliography systematically organizes all English-language materials on negotiation. Books, journal articles, doctoral dissertations, government documents, and conference reports are categorized by theories of negotiation, the psychological aspects of negotiating behavior, game theory, mediation studies, multilateral negotiations, arms control, diplomacy, and international trade. A complete author and title index is also included.

Amos Lakos is a librarian specializing in political science materials at the University of Waterloo. He is the author of *International Terrorism: A Bibliography* (Westview).

INTERNATIONAL NEGOTIATIONS:
A BIBLIOGRAPHY

AMOS LAKOS

WESTVIEW PRESS
BOULDER, SAN FRANCISCO, & LONDON

Westview Special Studies in International Relations

All rights reserved. No part of this publication may be reproduced or transmitted in any form or by any means, electronic or mechanical, including photocopy, recording, or any information storage and retrieval system, without permission in writing from the publisher.

Copyright © 1989 by Westview Press, Inc.

Published in 1989 in the United States of America by Westview Press, Inc., 5500 Central Avenue, Boulder, Colorado 80301, and in the United Kingdom by Westview Press, Inc., 13 Brunswick Centre, London WC1N 1AF, England

Library of Congress Cataloging-in-Publication Data
Lakos, Amos, 1946–
  International negotiations: a bibliography / by Amos Lakos.
    p. cm.—(Westview special studies in international relations)
  Includes index.
  ISBN 0-8133-7558-4
  1. Diplomatic negotiations in international disputes—Bibliography. I. Title. II. Series.
Z6464.Z9L32 1989
[JX4473]
016.3272—dc19   87-32600
                                                               CIP

Printed and bound in the United States of America

∞ The paper used in this publication meets the requirements of the American National Standard for Permanence of Paper for Printed Library Materials Z39.48-1984.

10   9   8   7   6   5   4   3   2   1

Table of Contents

Preface x
Acknowledgments xiii
I. Negotiation Processes and Theories 1
    1. Books 3
    2. Journal Articles 7
    3. Documents and Reports 21
II. Psychological & Sociological Aspects 29
    1. Books 31
    2. Journal Articles 33
    3. Documents and Reports 59
III. Game Theory 67
    1. Books 69
    2. Journal Articles 71
    3. Documents and Reports 91
IV. Mediation 99
    A. Mediation Theory 101
        1. Books 101
        2. Journal Articles 101
        3. Documents and Reports 107
    B. Mediation Case Studies 110
        1. Books 110
        2. Journal Articles 111
        3. Documents and Reports 113
V. Multilateral Negotiations 117
    A. General Works 119
        1. Books 119
        2. Journal Articles 119
        3. Documents and Reports 120
    B. United Nations 121
        1. Books 121
        2. Journal Articles 122
        3. Documents and Reports 125
    C. Conferences - General Works & Cases 127
        1. Books 127
        2. Journal Articles 128
        3. Documents and Reports 129
        c1. U.N. Disarmament Conferences 130
            1. Books 130
            2. Journal Articles 130
            3. Documents and Reports 131
        c2. World War II Conferences 131
            1. Books 131
            2. Journal Articles 132

        3. Documents and Reports 133
    D. Law of the Sea Conferences 135
        1. Books 135
        2. Journal Articles 135
        3. Documents and Reports 137
    E. North South Negotiations 139
        1. Books 139
        2. Journal Articles 140
        3. Documents and Reports 144
    F. Other Multilateral Negotiations 146
        1. Books 146
        2. Journal Articles 147
        3. Documents and Reports 149

VI. Arms Control Negotiations 153
    A. General Works 155
        1. Books 155
        2. Journal Articles 157
        3. Documents and Reports 167
    B. Test Ban Negotiations 173
        1. Books 173
        2. Journal Articles 173
        3. Documents and Reports 174
    C. SALT Negotiations 176
        1. Books 176
        2. Journal Articles 176
        3. Documents and Reports 179
    D. INF Negotiations 181
        1. Journal Articles 181
        2. Documents and Reports 182
    E. MBFR Negotiations 182
        1. Books 182
        2. Journal Articles 182
        3. Documents and Reports 184
    F. START Negotiations 185
        1. Journal Articles 185
        2. Documents and Reports 186
    G. Chemical Weapons Negotiations 186
        1. Books 186
        2. Journal Articles 186
        3. Documents and Reports 187
    H. Seabed Arms Control Negotiations 188
        1. Books 188
        2. Journal Articles 188
        3. Documents and Reports 188
    I. CSCE & CSBM Conferences 188
        1. Books 188
        2. Journal Articles 189
        3. Documents and Reports 191
    J. NPT Negotiations 193
        1. Books 193
        2. Journal Articles 193
        3. Documents and Reports 194
    K. Other Nuclear Negotiations 194
        1. Books 194

2. Journal Articles	195
3. Documents and Reports	196

VII. Summit Meetings 197
A. Superpower Summit Meetings 199
   1. Books 199
   2. Journal Articles 199
   3. Documents and Reports 202
B. Economic Summits 204
   1. Books 204
   2. Journal Articles 204
   3. Documents and Reports 205

VIII. International Trade Negotiations 207
A. General Works 209
   1. Books 209
   2. Journal Articles 209
   3. Documents and Reports 212
B. Cultural Aspects 214
   1. Books 214
   2. Journal Articles 214
   3. Documents and Reports 214
C. Oil Diplomacy 214
   1. Books 214
   2. Journal Articles 215
   3. Documents And Reports 215
D. Commodity Negotiations 216
   1. Books 216
   2. Journal Articles 216
   3. Documents and Reports 217
E. GATT Negotiations 218
   1. Books 218
   2. Journal Articles 218
   3. Documents and Reports 220
F. Canada - U.S. Trade Negotiations 221
   1. Books 221
   2. Journal Articles 221
   3. Documents and Reports 223
G. Soviet Trade Negotiations 224
   1. Books 224
   2. Journal Articles 224
   3. Documents and Reports 225
H. Chinese Trade Negotiations 225
   1. Books 225
   2. Journal Articles 225
   3. Documents and Reports 226
I. Japanese Trade Negotiations 226
   1. Books 226
   2. Journal Articles 226
   3. Documents and Reports 227
K. Other Trade Negotiations 227
   1. Books 227
   2. Journal Articles 228
   3. Documents and Reports 230

IX. Diplomacy 235
A. Diplomatic Methods 237

        1. Books 237
        2. Journal Articles 240
        3. Documents and Reports 249
    B. Diplomatic History 251
        1. Books 251
        2. Journal Articles 252
    C. Diplomatic Memoirs 253
        1. Books 253
        2. Journal Articles 254
    D. Unofficial Diplomacy 254
        1. Books 254
        2. Journal Articles 255
        3. Documents and Reports 257
    E. Public Diplomacy 257
        1. Books 257
        2. Journal Articles 258
        3. Documents and Reports 259

X. Soviet Diplomacy & Negotiating Behavior 261
    1. Books 263
    2. Journal Articles 264
    3. Documents and Reports 268

XI. American Diplomacy 273
    1. Books 275
    2. Journal Articles 278
    3. Documents and Reports 280

XII. Case Studies 283
    A. Middle East Negotiations 285
        1. Books 285
        2. Journal Articles 286
        3. Documents and Reports 290
    B. Vietnam War Negotiations 293
        1. Books 293
        2. Journal Articles 294
        3. Documents and Reports 297
    C. Korean Negotiations 298
        1. Books 298
        2. Journal Articles 298
        3. Documents and Reports 299
    D. Japanese Negotiations 299
        1. Books 299
        2. Journal Articles 300
        3. Documents and Reports 300
    E. Chinese Negotiations 301
        1. Books 301
        2. Journal Articles 301
        3. Documents and Reports 303
    F. African Negotiations 304
        1. Books 304
        2. Journal Articles 304
        3. Documents and Reports 305
    G. Latin American Negotiations 306
        1. Books 306
        2. Journal Articles 307
        3. Documents and Reports 308

H. Canada - U.S. Negotiations	310
1. Books	310
2. Journal Articles	311
3. Documents and Reports	311
I. Other Case Studies	312
1. Books	312
2. Journal Articles	313
3. Documents and Reports	316
Author Index	319
Subject Index	357

Preface

Our international system consists of a plurality of sovereign states, each pursuing its own interests and objectives. Diplomatic negotiation is the method by which conflicts between states are managed, resolved or terminated. The U.N. Charter recognizes negotiations as the best method for the peaceful resolution of conflicts. As long as there are conflicts between states, with the added spectre of nuclear proliferation and confrontation looming over, negotiations are the only sensible process of survival.

Lately, scholars have been attempting to lay the theoretical framework for the study of negotiations. This is a relatively new area of study, since strategies of war and battle have received much more systematic analysis. More efforts are being devoted to analyzing the problems inherent in peaceful coexistence, and attempts are made to clarify and define the nature of negotiations.

There exist a number of definitions to negotiations. I will just note here some of the elements common to all negotiations. The process of negotiation involves at least two parties who are engaged in a process of bringing differing viewpoints towards the achievement of a common agreement. The common interest is the achievement of an agreement. In the process, the parties undertake a redefinition of their interests. The parties engage in some sort of social interaction designed to influence each other's perceptions. The unifying element in all negotiation processes is that of problem solving. The aim of negotiations is to clarify and simplify complex issues and differences, so that resolution to the conflicts can be achieved. The nature of the subject to be negotiated, its framework and the behavioral strategies and tactics employed by the negotiators all contribute to the outcome of any given negotiation. Negotiators are always faced with tactical dilemmas concerning appropriate behavior in difficult situations. They cannot predict accurately the consequences of various behaviors, nor can they accurately predict all the potential solutions. Among the numerous factors influencing the outcome of negotiations, one can mention the personality of the negotiators, the nature or importance of the conflict, the setting of the negotiations, tactics employed by the parties and the pressures exerted on the negotiators to reach agreement. Negotiations have their own internal dynamics that influence the process and the outcome.

The primary focus of this bibliography is to identify and classify materials pertaining to the processes of diplomatic negotiations. The focus is on materials dealing with the process of negotiation, rather than with the content of specific negotiations. This presents certain difficulties, because the materials that deal with specific case studies also inevitably deal with policy issues. Invariably, studies of individual negotiations have to examine the issues being negotiated to be able to really study the negotiating strategies and tactics involved.

Much of the literature of negotiations is interdisciplinary. Researchers from various disciplines are contributing to the literature: labor relations, economics, psychology, sociology, international relations and law all have a contribution to make. Materials from these various disciplines have to be analyzed to see how they relate to the study of negotiations between states.

The bibliography is restricted to materials pertaining to the 20th century and published in the English language. It is classified into twelve major subject chapters and each subsection is arranged by form of material - monographs, journal articles, conference papers, government documents and dissertations. The bibliography excludes news magazine and newspaper articles.

The *Negotiation Theories and Processes* chapter lists materials of general nature which attempt to define and deal in a general way with negotiation theories and with negotiation processes. The *Psychological and Sociological Aspects* chapter covers materials dealing with behavioral aspects of negotiations, various psychological and sociological influences on the negotiation process with special emphasis on international negotiations. The chapter on *Game Theory* reflects the large literature of the theory of games - a mathematical discipline which investigates the optimal behavior of participants in games of strategy. This chapter is restricted to studies dealing with international interactions with particular emphasis on negotiations. The *Mediation* chapter covers the literature of peaceful settlement processes involving third parties. This chapter covers both theoretical works and case studies of international mediation. *Multilateral Negotiations* is a large chapter covering materials dealing with negotiations between more than two states, international bodies as forums of negotiations, conference diplomacy, north-south group negotiations, the Law of the Sea as an example of multilateral negotiations and other case studies. Materials dealing with *Arms Control* form another large chapter. Its focus is the processes of negotiating the various post World War II nuclear arms control agreements. It is made up of a large section on general materials dealing with the issues of negotiating arms control, and is further subclassified by the major nuclear arms control negotiations and conferences. The chapter on *Summit Meetings* focuses on the personal diplomacy of heads of state. This chapter is restricted to summit meetings and conferences between the United States and the Soviet Union and the multilateral economic conferences between the Western Powers. The next chapter deals with *International Trade Negotiations*. It covers bilateral and multilateral economic and trade negotiations, both through theoretical investigations and through case studies. Oil diplomacy, commodity negotiations, GATT issues, specific trade practices of the Soviet Union, China and Japan are highlighted, as well as the special aspects of trade between the U.S. and Canada. *Diplomacy* is a chapter which deals with diplomacy as a subset of negotiations between states. This may be a semantic difference, as most formal negotiations between states are negotiated by diplomats, using diplomatic protocols, customs and conventions. However, I found it impossible to completely integrate the large literature of diplomacy into the other chapters. Although the focus is on negotiation processes, the material included covers diplomatic methods, some diplomatic history, diplomatic memoirs, unofficial diplomacy and public diplomacy. Case studies of diplomatic negotiations are covered by the other chapter in the bibliography. The chapter on *Soviet Diplomacy and Negotiation Behavior* covers materials examining Soviet diplomacy and negotiating tactics and their evolution through time from the early Leninist foreign policy axioms to the Gorbachev changes. The chapter on *United States Diplomacy* examines materials dealing mainly with the processes of U.S. diplomacy. It includes materials on the State Department's role in the processes of international negotiations and examines U.S. diplomatic methods and case studies. The last chapter, *Case Studies*, attempts to list materials on particular negotiations. This chapter focuses on particular conflicts, such as the Middle East Conflicts and the Vietnam War negotiations and the Korean Conflict. Other case studies are highlighted because of their national characteristics, such as the Chinese and Japanese cases, while African and Latin American case studies are classified for geographical reasons. Canada - U.S. negotiation case studies are also highlighted.

The bibliography is organized around broad subject subdivisions. Each subsection is further subdivided by form of material. As a librarian, I believe this format eases the user's access to the materials. Entries are subdivided by form - books, journal articles and articles compiled in books, government documents and reports, dissertations. I have tried to include mostly post World War II materials. Each entry has a unique number which is used to identify it in the indexes.

The last part of the bibliography consists of an author and a subject index, which should greatly enhance the utility of this bibliography.

Amos Lakos
December 1988
Waterloo, Ontario

Acknowledgments

This work would not have been possible without the generous cooperation and encouragement of my colleagues and superiors at the University of Waterloo Library. I would like to single out Murray Shepherd, Head Librarian, who supported the project wholeheartedly and was very helpful in my quest for research support and study leave. I also wish to acknowledge the help of Joanne Hadley from the Research Office, who guided me through the grant proposals.

I wish to thank all those who graciously answered my bibliographic enquiries, and provided me with lists of their publications. I wish to single out the help of Margo Sweet who worked for the PIN Project at the American Academy of Arts and Sciences, and that of J. William Breslin, Director of Publications at the Program on Negotiation at the Harvard Law School.

I would like to thank the many librarians who helped my research at the following university libraries: University of Guelph, University of Toronto, Harvard University Library System, Cornell University, University of Wisconsin - Madison, SUNY at Buffalo, Georgetown University, Stanford University, Hebrew University in Jerusalem, the Centre for Applied Studies in International Negotiations in Geneva and the University of Waterloo.

On-line bibliographic research was supported through a grant from the University of Waterloo Social Sciences and Humanities General Research Grant Fund. Further research support was provided through a generous grant from the Canadian Institute for International Peace and Security.

The bibliography was organized and indexed with the help of the Foxbase data manager program. Final copy was produced with Wordperfect 5.0.

The contents and arrangement of this bibliography are my personal responsibility, as well as any omission, duplications, inaccuracies or mistakes. Any suggestions or corrections regarding this work will be most welcome.

Amos Lakos

I

Negotiation Processes and Theories

Negotiation is a form of social interaction through which individuals, organizations and governments try to arrange their conflicting interests. In peaceful contacts between sovereign states, negotiations are the technique used to achieve some kind of official arrangement. There is growing interest in understanding the workings of negotiation processes for the obvious utility of making the outcomes of negotiations more predictable. The increased efforts to understand the theories of the negotiating processes are reflected in the growth of the literature of negotiations between states.

This chapter covers materials dealing with the theoretical frameworks of international negotiations. The chapter includes materials dealing with the theoretical analysis of diplomatic negotiations, with the various types of negotiations focusing mainly on the processes of negotiations, with particular attention given to negotiations between sovereign states.

1. Books

1. Anand, R. P., ed. *Cultural Factors in International Relations.* New Delhi: Abhinav Publications, 1981. 291p.
2. Aron, Raymond. *Peace and War: A Theory of International Relations.* New York: Praeger, 1968. 820p.
3. Atwater, Elton, K. Foster and J. S. Prybyla. *World Tensions: Conflict and Accommodation.* New York: Appleton - Century - Crofts, 1967. 435p.
4. Axelrod, Robert. *Conflict of Interest: A Theory of Divergent Goal with Applications to Politics.* Chicago, IL.: Markham, 1970. 216p.
5. Azar, Edward E., and John W. Burton, eds. *International Conflict Resolution: Theory and Practice.* Boulder, CO.: Lynne Rienner, 1986. 159p.
6. _____. *International Events Interaction Analysis.* Beverly Hills, CA.: Sage, 1972. 80p.
7. _____., and Joseph D. Ben-Dak, eds. *Theory and Practice of Events Research: Studies in Inter-Nation Actions and Interactions.* New York: Gordon and Breach, 1975. 304p.
8. Bacharach, Samuel B., and Edward J. Lawler. *Bargaining: Power, Tactics and Outcomes.* San Francisco, CA.: Jossey-Bass, 1981. 234p.
9. Banks, Michael. *Conflict in World Society: A New Perspective on International Relations.* New York: St. Martin's Press, 1984. 234p.
10. Bar-Yaacov, Nissim. *The Handling of International Disputes by Means of Inquiry.* London: Oxford University Press, 1974. 370p.
11. Bartos, Otomar J. *The Process and Outcome of Negotiations.* New York: Columbia University Press, 1974. 451p.
12. Bazerman, Max H., and Roy J. Lewicki. *Negotiating in Organizations.* Beverly Hills, CA.: Sage, 1983. 392p.
13. Beckmann, Neal W. *Negotiations: Principles and Techniques.* Lexington, MA.: Lexington Books, 1977. 152p.
14. Bloomfield, Lincoln P., ed. *The Management of Global Disorder: Prospects for Creative Problem Solving.* Lanham, MD.: University Press of America, 1987. 547p.
15. Bok, Sissela. *Lying: Moral Choice in Public and Private Life.* New York: Vintage, 1978. 326p.
16. Boulding, Kenneth E. *Conflict and Defence: A General Theory.* New York: Harper & Row, 1962. 349p.
17. Bowett, D. W. *A Search for Peace.* London: Routledge & Kegan Paul, 1972. 236p.
18. Brecher, Michael, Jonathan Wilkenfeld and Sheila Moser. *Crises in the Twentieth Century, Volume I: Handbook of International Crises.* Elmsford, NY.: Pergamon Press, 1988. 346p.
19. Brown, William A. *Piecework Bargaining.* London: Heineman Educational, 1973. 176p.
20. Burns, E. L. M. *A Seat at the Table.* Toronto: Clarke, Irwin, 1972. 268p.
21. Burton, John W. *Conflict and Communication: The Use of Controlled Communications in International Relations.* London: Macmillan, 1969. 246p.
22. _____. *Resolving Deeprooted Conflict: A Handbook.* Lanham, MD.: University Press of America, 1987. 74p.
23. Butterworth, Robert L. *Managing Interstate Conflicts, 1945-1974.* Pittsburgh, PA.: University of Pittsburgh Press, 1976. 535p.
24. Callahan, Patrick, Linda P. Brady and Margaret G. Hermann, eds. *Describing Foreign Policy Behavior.* Beverly Hills, CA.: Sage, 1982. 364p.
25. Charell, Ralph. *How to Get the Upper Hand.* London: Stein & Day, 1978. 227p.

26. Charny, Israel W. *Strategies Against Violence: Design for Nonviolent Change.* Boulder, CO.: Westview Press, 1978. 417p.
27. Chesnut, H., ed. *Contributions of Technology to International Conflict Resolution.* London: Pergamon Press, 1987. 157p.
28. Cioffi-Revilla, Claudio A., et al. *Communication and Interaction in Global Politics.* Advances in Political Science, Vol 5. Beverly Hills, CA.: Sage, 1987. 271p.
29. Cohen, Herb. *You Can Negotiate Anything.* Secaucus, NJ.: Lyle Stuart, 1983. 264p.
30. Cohen, Raymond. *International Politics: The Rules of the Games.* London: Longman, 1981. 186p.
31. Curle, Adam. *Making Peace.* London: Tavistock, 1971. 301p.
32. Curwurah, A. O. *The Settlement of Boundary Disputes in International Law.* Dobbs Ferry, NY.: Oceana, 1967. 320p.
33. Davison, W. Phillips. *International Political Communication.* New York: Praeger, 1965. 404p.
34. De Waart, P. J. I. M. *The Element of Negotiation in the Pacific Settlement of Disputes Between States.* The Hague: Martinus Nijhoff, 1973. 229p.
35. Dedring, Juergen. *Recent Advances in Peace and Conflict Research: A Critical Survey.* Beverly Hills, CA.: Sage, 1976. 249p.
36. Doob, L. W. *The Pursuit of Peace.* Westport, CT.: Greenwood Press, 1981. Chapter 9. pp. 229-276.
37. Dunlop, John T. *Dispute Resolution: Negotiation and Consensus Building.* Dover, MA.: Auburn House, 1984. 296p.
38. Dunn, Frederick S. *Peaceful Change: A Study of International Procedures.* New York: Council of Foreign Relations, 1937. 156p.
39. Eldridge, Albert F. *Images of Conflict.* New York: St. Martin's Press, 1979. pp. 170-211.
40. Fisher, Glen H. *International Negotiation: A Cross-Cultural Perspective.* Chicago, IL.: Intercultural Press, 1980. 69p.
41. Fisher, Roger D. *Basic Negotiating Strategy: International Conflict for Beginners.* London: Allen Lane, 1971. 194p.
42. _____., and William L. Ury. *Getting to Yes: Negotiating Agreement Without Giving In.* Boston, MA.: Houghton Mifflin, 1981. 161p.
43. _____. *International Conflict and Behavioral Science: The Craigville Papers.* New York: Basic Books, 1964. 290p.
44. _____. *International Conflict for Beginners.* New York: Harper & Row, 1969. 231p.
45. Frei, Daniel, ed. *Managing International Crises.* Beverly Hills, CA.: Sage, 1981. 240p.
46. Greensburger, Francis, and Thomas Kiernan. *How to Ask for More and Get It: The Art of Creative Negotiation.* Garden City, NY: Doubleday, 1978. 173p.
47. Habeeb, William M. *Power and Tactics in International Negotiations: How Weak Nations Bargain with Strong Nations.* Baltimore, MD.: Johns Hopkins University Press, 1988. 168p.
48. Henkin, Louis. *How Nations Behave: Law and Foreign Policy.* New York: Praeger, 1968. 324p.
49. Hoglund, B., and J. W. Ulrich, eds. *Conflict Control and Conflict Resolution.* Copenhagen: Munksgard, 1972. 240p.
50. Holsti, K. J. *International Politics: A Framework for Analysis.* Ch. 8. Englewood Cliffs, N.J.: Prentice-Hall, 1983. 478p.
51. Ikle, Fred C. *Every War Must End.* New York: Columbia University Press, 1971. 160p.

52. _____. *How Nations Negotiate.* New York: Harper and Row, 1964. 274p.
53. Ilich, John. *The Art and Skill of Successful Negotiation.* Englewood Cliffs, NJ.: Prentice-Hall, 1973. 205p.
54. _____. *Power Negotiating: Strategies for Winning in Life and Business.* Reading, MA.: Addison-Wesley, 1980. 169p.
55. Isard, Walter, and Christine Smith. *Conflict Analysis and Practical Conflict Management Procedures: An Introduction to Peace Science.* Peace Science Studies Series. Cambridge, MA.: Ballinger, 1983. 611p.
56. _____., and Yoshimi Nagao. *International and Regional Conflict: Analytic Approaches.* Cambridge, MA.: Ballinger, 1983. 236p.
57. Jandt, Fred E. *Conflict Resolution Through Communication.* New York: Harper and Row, 1973. 473p.
58. _____., and Paul Gillette. *Win-Win Negotiating: Turning Conflict into Agreement.* New York: Wiley, 1985. 300p.
59. Jervis, Robert. *Perception and Misperception in International Politics.* Princeton, NY.: Princeton University Press, 1976. 445p.
60. Karrass, Chester L. *Give & Take: The Complete Guide to Negotiating Strategies and Tactics.* New York: Thomas Y. Crowell, 1974. 280p.
61. _____. *The Negotiating Game.* New York: World Pub., 1970. 234p.
62. Kissinger, Henry A. *Observations: Selected Speeches and Essays, 1982-1984.* Boston, MA.: Little Brown, 1986. 246p.
63. Lall, Arthur S. *Modern International Negotiation: Principles and Practice.* New York: Columbia University Press, 1966. 404p.
64. Lax, David A., and James K. Sebenius. *The Manager as Negotiator: Bargaining for Cooperation and Competitive Gain.* New York: Free Press, 1986. 395p.
65. Levin, Edward P. *Levin's Law: Tactics for Winning Without Intimidation.* Omaha, NE.: M. Evans, 1980. 193p.
66. Lewicki, Roy J., and Joseph A. Litterer. *Negotiation.* Homewood, IL.: R. D. Irwin, 1985. 365p.
67. _____. _____. *Negotiation: Readings, Exercises and Cases.* Homewood, IL.: R. D. Irwin, 1985. 633p.
68. Lewis, David V. *Power Negotiating Tactics and Techniques.* Englewood Cliffs, NJ.: Prentice-Hall, 1981. 243p.
69. Lockhart, Charles. *Bargaining in International Conflicts.* New York: Columbia University Press, 1979. 205p.
70. Luard, Evan, ed. *The International Regulation of Frontier Disputes.* London: Thames and Hudson, 1970. 247p.
71. Martinez, Oscar J. *Across Boundaries: Transborder Interaction in Comparative Perspective.* El Paso, TX.: Texas Western Press, 1986. 206p.
72. Miller, Linda B., comp. *Dynamics of World Politics: Studies in the Resolution of Conflict.* Englewood Cliffs, NJ.: Prentice-Hall, 1968. 294p.
73. Morgenthau, Hans J. *Politics Among Nations: The Struggle for Power and Peace.* 5th ed. New York: Knopf, 1973. 617p.
74. Mudd, Stuart D. *Conflict Resolution and World Education.* World Academy of Art and Science, No. 3. The Hague: Dr. W. Junk Pubs., 1966. 292p.
75. Neale, Margaret A., and Gregory B. Northcraft. *Bargaining and Dispute Resolution Curricula: A Sourcebook.* Durham, N.C.: Eno River Press, 1985. 237p.
76. Nierenberg, Gerald I. *Fundamentals of Negotiating.* New York: Hawthorn Books, 1973. 306p.
77. Northedge, F. S., and M. D. Donelan. *International Disputes: The Political Aspects.* London: David Davies Memorial Institute of International Studies, 1971, 349p.

78. O'Keefe, David, and Henry G. Schermers, eds. *Mixed Agreements.* Europa Institute Leiden. Deventer: Kluewer Law and Taxation, 1983. 148p.
79. Oliver, Robert T. *Culture and Communication; The Problem of Penetrating National and Cultural Boundaries.* Springfield, IL.: Thomas, 1962. 165p.
80. Opie, R., et al. *The Search for Peace Settlements.* Washington, D.C.: Brookings Institute, 1951. 366p.
81. Oren, Nissan, ed. *Termination of Wars: Processes, Procedures, and Aftermaths.* Jerusalem: Magnes Press, Hebrew University, 1982. 277p.
82. Osgood, C. E. *An Alternative to War or Surrender.* Urbana, IL.: University of Illinois Press, 1962. 183p.
83. Patchen, Martin. *Resolving Disputes Between Nations: Coercion or Conciliation.* Durham, NC.: Duke University Press, 1988. 396p.
84. Pillar, Paul R. *Negotiating Peace: War Termination as a Bargaining Process.* Princeton, NJ.: Princeton University Press, 1983. 282p.
85. Pirages, Dennis. *Managing Political Conflict.* New York: Praeger, 1975. 148p.
86. Pneuman, R. W., and M. E. Bruehl. *Managing Conflict: A Complete Process Centered Handbook.* Englewood Cliffs, NJ.: Prentice-Hall, 1982. 128p.
87. Posses, Frederick. *The Art of International Negotiation.* London: Business Books, 1978. 195p.
88. Pruitt, Dean G., and R. C. Snyder, eds. *Theory and Research on the Causes of War.* Englewood Cliffs, NJ.: Prentice-Hall, 1969. 314p.
89. Raiffa, Howard. *The Art and Science of Negotiation.* Cambridge, MA.: Harvard University Press, 1982. 373p.
90. Rangarajan, L. N. *The Limitation of Conflict: A Theory of Bargaining and Negotiation.* London: Croom Helm, 1985. 327p.
91. Roderick, Hilliard, and Ulla Magnusson, eds. *Avoiding Inadvertent War: Crisis Management.* Austin, TX.: The Lyndon B. Johnson School of Public Affairs, 1983. 184p.
92. Sandole, Dennis J. D., and Ingrid Sandole-Staroste, eds. *Conflict Management and Problem Solving: Interpersonal to International Applications.* London: Frances Pinter, 1987. 321p.
93. Schellenberg, James A. *The Science of Conflict.* New York: Oxford University Press, 1982. 291p.
94. Schelling, Thomas C. *The Strategy of Conflict.* Cambridge, MA.: Harvard University Press, 1963. 309p.
95. Scott, Bill. *The Skills of Negotiating.* Aldershot, Eng.: Gower, 1981. 230p.
96. Shea, Gordon F. *Creative Negotiating: Productive Tools and Techniques for Solving Problems, Resolving Conflicts and Settling Differences.* Boston, MA.: CBI Publications, 1983. 222p.
97. Smith, David S. *From War to Peace: Essays in Peacemaking and War Termination.* New York: Columbia University, 1974. 311p.
98. Smoke, Richard, and Willis Harman. *Paths for Peace: Exploring the Feasibility of Sustainable Peace.* Boulder, CO.: Westview Press, 1987. 112p.
99. Snyder, Glenn H., and Paul Diesing. *Conflict Among Nations: Bargaining, Decision-Making, and System Structure in International Crises.* Princeton, NJ.: Princeton University Press, 1977. 578p.
100. Sohn, Louis B. *Systematic Survey of Treaties for the Pacific Settlement of International Disputes, 1928-48.* Lake Success: United Nations Publications, 1948. 3 vols, 1202p.
101. Sparks, Donald B. *The Dynamics of Effective Negotiation.* Houston, TX.: Gulf Publishing, 1982. 162p.
102. Stevens, Carl M. *Strategy and Collective Bargaining Negotiation.* New York: McGraw-Hill, 1963. 192p.

103. Tabory, Mala. *Multilingualism in International Law and Institutions.* Amsterdam: Sijthoff, 1980. 283p.
104. Thakur, Ramesh, ed. *International Conflict Resolution.* Boulder, CO.: Westview Press, 1988. 309p.
105. Väyrynen, Raimo, Dieter Senghaas and Christian Schmidt. *The Quest for Peace: Transcending Collective Violence and War Among Societies, Cultures and States.* London: Sage, 1987.
106. Wainhouse, David W. *International Peace Observation: A History and Forecast.* Baltimore, MD.: Johns Hopkins University Press, 1966. 663p.
107. Wall, James A. *Negotiation: Theory and Practice.* Glenview, IL.: Scott, Foresman and Co., 1985. 182p.
108. Warschaw, Tessa A. *Winning by Negotiation.* New York: McGraw-Hill, 1980. 286p.
109. Wilkenfeld, Jonathan, Michael Brecher and Sheila Moser. *Crisis in the Twentieth Century: Volume II: Handbook of Foreign Policy Crisis.* Elmsford, NY.: Pergamon Press, 1988. 280p.
110. Williams, Philip Maynard. *Crisis Management: Confrontation and Diplomacy in the Nuclear Age.* New York: Wiley, 1976. 230p.
111. Winham, Gilbert R., ed. *New Issues in International Crisis Management.* Boulder, CO.: Westview Press, 1988. 258p.
112. Young, Oran R. *Bargaining: Formal Theories of Negotiation.* Urbana, IL.: University of Illinois Press, 1975. 412p.
113. _____. *The Politics of Force: Bargaining During International Crises.* Princeton, NJ.: Princeton University Press, 1968. 438p.
114. Zartman, I. William. *The 50% Solution: How to Bargain Successfully with Hijackers, Strikers, Bosses, Oil Magnates, Arabs, Russians, and Other Worthy Opponents in this Modern World.* Garden City, NY.: Anchor Press, 1976. 549p.
115. _____., ed. *The Negotiation Process: Theories and Applications.* Beverly Hills, CA.: Sage, 1978. 240p.
116. _____. *The Practical Negotiator.* New Haven, CT.: Yale University Press, 1982. 250p.

2. Journal Articles

117. Allen, Michael H. "Winning by Bargaining." *Development,* 3:4 (1983), 194-197.
118. Altfeld, Michael F., and Gary J. Miller. "Sources of Bureaucratic Influence: Expertise and Agenda Control." *Journal of Conflict Resolution,* 28:4 (December 1984), 701-730.
119. Arend, Anthony Clark. "The Obligation to Pursue Peaceful Settlement of International Disputes During Hostilities." *Virginia Journal of International Law,* 24:1 (Fall 1983), 97-126.
120. Avruch, K., and P. W. Black. "Expanding the Debate on Generic Theory of Conflict Resolution - Reply." *Negotiation Journal,* 3:1 (January 1987), 99-100.
121. _____. _____. "A Generic Theory of Conflict Resolution - A Critique." *Negotiation Journal,* 3:1 (January 1987), 87-96.
122. Axelrod, Robert, and Robert O. Keohane. "Achieving Cooperation Under Anarchy: Strategies and Institutions." *World Politics,* 38:1 (October 1985), 226-254.
123. _____. "Conflict of Interest: An Axiomatic Approach." *Journal of Conflict Resolution,* 11 (January 1967), 87-99.

124. Azar, Edward E. "The Conflict and Peace Data Bank (COPDAB) Project." *Journal of Conflict Resolution,* 24:1 (1980), 143-152.
125. Bacharach, Samuel B., and Edward J. Lawler. "Power Dependence and Power Paradoxes in Bargaining." *Negotiation Journal,* 2:2 (April 1986), 167-174.
126. Bacon, Francis. "Of Negotiating." In: *The Essay of Francis Bacon.* New York: Charles Scribner, 1908. pp. 225-227.
127. Bacon, Lawrence S., and M. Wheeler. "Negotiation: A Look at Decision Making." In: N. A. Huelsberg and W. F. Lincoln, eds. *Successful Negotiating.* Washington, D.C.: International City Management Association, 1985. pp. 124-142.
128. Ball, M. Margaret, and Hugh B. Killough. "Pacific Settlement of International Disputes." In: M. M. Ball and H. B. Killough, eds. *International Relations.* New York: Ronald, 1956. pp. 155-172.
129. Barston, Ronald P. "International Negotiation: The Development of Central Concepts." *European Journal of Political Research,* 11:2 (1983), 129-138.
130. Bartholdi, John J., C. Allen Butler and Michael A. Trick. "More on the Evolution of Cooperation." *Journal of Conflict Resolution,* 30:1 (March 1986), 129-140.
131. Bartos, Otomar J. "How Predictable are Negotiations." *Journal of Conflict Resolution,* 11:4 (1967), 481-496.
132. _____. "How Predictable are Negotiations?" In: I. W. Zartman, ed. *The 50% Solution.* Garden City, NY.: Anchor Press, 1976. pp. 485-509.
133. Bazerman, Max H., and Roy J. Lewicki. "Contemporary Research Directions in the Study of Negotiations in Organizations: A Selective Review." *Journal of Occupational Behavior,* 6 (1985), 1-17.
134. _____., and Margaret A. Neale. "Heuristics in Negotiation: Limitations to Effective Dispute Resolution." In: M. H. Bazerman and R. Lewicki, eds. *Negotiating in Organizations.* Beverly Hills, CA.: Sage, 1983. pp. 51-67.
135. Becker, Josef. "Communication and Peace: The Empirical and Theoretical Relations Between Two Categories in the Social Sciences." *Journal of Peace Research,* 19:3 (1982), 227-240.
136. Bell, David V. J. "Political Linguistics and International Negotiation." *Negotiation Journal,* 4:3 (July 1988), 233-246.
137. Benne, Kenneth D. "The Significance of Human Conflict." In: R. J. Lewicki and J. A. Litterer, eds. *Negotiation: Readings, Exercises and Cases.* Homewood, IL.: Irwin, 1985. pp. 26-32.
138. Bercovitch, Jacob. "Conflict, Peace and Peace Research: A Theoretical Orientation." *International Problems,* 19:1 (1980), 31-39.
139. _____. "Problems and Approaches in the Study of Bargaining and Negotiation." *Political Science,* 36:2 (December 1984), 125-144.
140. Bilder, Richard B. "Some Limitations of Adjudication as an International Dispute Settlement Technique." *Virginia Journal of International Law,* 23:1 (Fall 1982), 1-12.
141. Blix, H. "The Principle of Peaceful Settlement of Disputes." In: *The Legal Principles Governing Friendly Relations and Co-operation Among States.* Leyden: Sijthoff, 1966. pp. 45-68.
142. Brecher, Michael. "Toward a Theory of International Crisis Behavior." *International Studies Quarterly,* 21:1 (March 1977), 40-75.
143. Brody, Richard A. "International Events: Problems of Measurement and Analysis." In: E. E. Azar, ed. *International Events Interactions Analysis.* Beverly Hills, CA.: Sage, 1972. pp. 45-58.
144. Brown, E. H. P. "Bargaining." In: J. Gould and W. L. Kolb, eds. *A Dictionary of the Social Sciences.* Glencoe: Free Press, 1964. pp. 50-51.

145. Brown, S. N., D. Price and S. Raichur. "Public-Good Theory and Bargaining Between Large and Small Countries." *International Studies Quarterly*, 20:3 (1976), 393-414.
146. Brown, Winthrop A. "The Art of Negotiation" *Foreign Service Journal*, 45 (July 1968), 14-17.
147. Browne, E. C., and Peter Rice. "Bargaining Theory of Coalition Formation." *British Journal of Political Science*, 9 (January 1979), 67-87.
148. Burton, John W., and Dennis J. D. Sandole. "Expanding the Debate on Generic Theory of Conflict Resolution - A Response to a Critique." *Negotiation Journal*, 3:1 (January 1987), 97-98.
149. _____. _____. "Generic Theory: The Basis of Conflict Resolution." *Negotiation Journal*, 2:4 (October 1986), 333-344.
150. _____. "The History of International Conflict Resolution." In: E. E. Azar and J. W. Burton, eds. *International Conflict Resolution*. Boulder, Co.: Lynne Rienner, 1986. pp. 40-55.
151. _____. "The Procedures of Conflict Resolution." In: E. E. Azar and J. W. Burton, eds. *International Conflict Resolution*. Boulder, CO.: Lynne Rienner, 1986. pp. 92-116.
152. _____. "The Resolution of Conflict." *International Studies Quarterly*, 16:1 (1972), 5-29.
153. _____. "The Means to Agreement: Power of Values?" In: D. B. Bendahmane and J. W. McDonald, eds. *Perspectives on Negotiation*. Washington, D.C.: Foreign Service Institute, 1986. pp. 229-242.
154. _____. "Controlled Communication in the Resolution of Conflict." Paper Presented at the *Meeting of the American Political Science Association Proceedings*, held in 1969 in New York. Panel 2-F1. 26p.
155. Butterworth, Robert L. "Do Conflict Managers Matter? An Empirical Assessment of Interstate Security Disputes and Resolution Efforts, 1945-1974." *International Studies Quarterly*, 22:2 (June 1978), 195-214.
156. Callen, J. L., and L. L. Roos. "Political Coalition Bargaining Behavior." *Public Choice*, 32 (Winter 1977), 1-10.
157. Carroll, Berenice A. "How Wars End: An Analysis of Some Current Hypotheses." *Journal of Peace Research*, 4 (1969), 295-321.
158. Carter, Jimmy. "Principles of Negotiation." *Stanford Journal of International Law*, 23:1 (Spring 1987), 1-12.
159. Charney, Jonathan I. "Technology and International Negotiations." *American Journal of International Law*, 76:1 (1982), 78-118.
160. Cicourel, Aaron V. "Text and Context: Cognitive, Linguistic, and Organizational Dimensions in International Negotiations." *Negotiation Journal*, 4:3 (July 1988), 257-266.
161. Cohen, Raymond. "Rules of the Game in International Politics." *International Studies Quarterly*, 24 (March 1980), 129-150.
162. Colosi, Thomas. "A Core Model of Negotiation." In: R. J. Lewicki and J. A. Litterer, eds. *Negotiation: Readings, Exercises and Cases*. Homewood, IL.: Irwin, 1985. pp. 237-244.
163. _____. "A Model of Negotiation and Mediation." In: D. B. Bendahmane and J. W. McDonald, eds. *International Negotiation: Art and Science*. Washington, D.C.: Department of State, Foreign Service Institute, 1984. pp. 15-34.
164. _____. "A Model for Negotiation and Mediation." In: D. J. D. Sandole and I. Sandole-Staroste, eds. *Conflict Management and Problem Solving*. London: Francis Pinter, 1987. pp. 86-99.
165. _____. "The Iceberg Principle: Secrecy in Negotiation." In: D. B. Bendahmane and J. W. McDonald, eds. *Perspectives on Negotiation*. Washington, D.C.: Foreign Service Institute, 1986. pp. 243-262.

166. Cooper, C. L. "The Iron Law of Negotiations." *Foreign Policy,* 19 (1975), 94-98.
167. Coser, Lewis A. "The Termination of Conflict." *Journal of Conflict Resolution,* 5:4 (1961), 341-353.
168. Coulson, Robert. "What Can One Person Do to Support Dispute Resolution?" *Negotiation Journal,* 2:4 (October 1986), 329-331.
169. Crawford, Beverly K. "Stabilizing Factors in International Conflict Resolution." *Negotiation Journal,* 3:4 (October 1987), 333-346.
170. Croce, Cynthia. "Negotiation Instead of Confrontation." *EPA Journal,* 11:3 (April 1985), 23-24.
171. Dahl, Robert A. "Hierarchy, Democracy and Bargaining in Politics and Economics." In: R. A. Dahl, et al. *Research Frontiers in Politics and Government.* Washington, D.C.: Brookings Institute, 1955. pp. 45-69.
172. Darwin, H. G. "Methods of Peaceful Settlement: A: Negotiation." In: *International Disputes: The Legal Aspects.* London: David Davies Memorial Institute of International Studies, 1972. pp. 77-82.
173. de Felice, Fortune-Barthelemy. "Negotiations, or the Art of Negotiating." In: I. W. Zartman, ed. *The 50% Solution.* New York: Doubleday Anchor, 1976. pp. 47-65.
174. Dominick, Mary F. "Consultation." In: R. Bernhardt, ed. *Encyclopedia of Public International Law, 9: International Relations and Legal Cooperation in General Diplomacy and Consular Relations.* Amsterdam: North--Holland, 1986. pp. 45-49.
175. Donohue, William A. "Analyzing Negotiation Tactics: Development of a Negotiation Interact System." *Human Communication Research,* 7:3 (Spring 1981), 273-287.
176. _____. "Development of a Model of Rule Use in Negotiation Interaction." *Communication Monographs,* 48:2 (June 1981), 106-120.
177. _____., and Mary E. Diez. "Directive Use in Negotiation Interaction." *Communication Monographs,* 52:4 (December 1985), 305-318.
178. _____. "An Empirical Framework for Examining Negotiation Processes and Outcomes." *Communications Monographs,* 45:3 (1978), 247-257.
179. Dror, Yehezkel. "Rules for Negotiating Rules." *Jerusalem Quarterly,* 25 (Fall 1982), 46-53.
180. Druckman, Daniel. "Boundary Role Conflict: Negotiation as Dual Responsiveness." *Journal of Conflict Resolution,* 71:4 (1977), 639-662.
181. _____. "Boundary Role Conflict: Negotiation as Dual Responsiveness." In: I. W. Zartman, ed. *The Negotiation Process.* Beverly Hills, CA.: Sage, 1978. pp. 87-110.
182. _____., and Robert Mahoney. "Processes and Consequences of International Negotiations." *Journal of Social Issues,* 33:1 (1977), 60-87.
183. _____. "Four Cases of Conflict Management: Lessons Learned." In: D. B. Bendahmane and J. W. McDonald, eds. *Perspectives on Negotiation.* Washington, D.C.: Foreign Service Institute, Georgetown University, 1986. pp. 263-288.
184. Du Toit, Pierre. "Consociational Democracy and Bargaining Power." *Comparative Politics,* 19:4 (July 1987), 419-430.
185. Dugan, Maire A. "Conflict Resolution: Theory and Practice." *Peace and Change,* 8:2-3 (Summer 1982), 1-148.
186. Dulles, John Foster. "The Role of Negotiation." *Department of State Bulletin,* 38 (February 3, 1958), 159-168.
187. "The Essentials of Negotiation: An Interview with Sol Linowitz." *Foreign Service Journal,* 65:3 (March 1988), 36-39.

188. Faber, Jan. "Measuring Cooperation, Conflict, and the Social Network of Nations." *Journal of Conflict Resolution*, 3 (Summer 1987), 438-464.
189. Falk, Richard. "Conventional Statecraft Versus the Prospects for Global Reform." *New York University Journal of International Law and Politics*, 8:2 (1975), 129-152.
190. Farber, D. C. "Common-Sense Negotiation - How to Win Gracefully." *ABA Journal*, 73 (August 1, 1987), 92-99.
191. Farrands, C. "Perspectives on Negotiation: Diplomacy and Regime Change." In: B. Buzan and R. J. B. Jones, eds. *Change and the Study of International Relations*. London: Frances Pinter, 1981. pp. 85-99.
192. Fedder, Edwin A. "Negotiating Among Nations: A Review Article." *Background*, 9:4 (1966), 339-350.
193. Fisher, Roger D. "Constructing Rules that Affect Governments." In: D. G. Brennan, ed. *Arms Control, Disarmament and National Security*. New York: Braziller, 1961. pp.56-67.
194. _____. "Fractioning Conflict." *Daedalus*, (Summer 1964), 920-941.
195. _____. "Fractioning Conflict." In: R. Fisher, ed. *International Conflict and Behavioral Science: The Craigville Papers*. New York: Basic Books, 1964. pp. 91-109.
196. _____. "He Who Pays the Piper." *Harvard Business Review*, 63 (March-April 1988), 100-159.
197. _____. "How Theory Might Help." In: L. Sloss and M. Scott Davis, eds. *A Game for High Stakes*. Cambridge, MA.: Ballinger, 1986, pp. 141-154.
198. _____. "The Power of Theory." In: D. B. Bendahmane and J. W. McDonald, eds. *International Negotiations: Art and Science*. Washington, D.C.: U.S. Department of State. Foreign Service Institute, 1984. pp. 57-68.
199. _____. "The Structure of Negotiation: An Alternative Model." *Negotiation Journal*, 2:3 (July 1986), 233-235.
200. _____. "What About Negotiation as a Speciality?" *American Bar Association Journal*, 69 (1983), 1221-1224.
201. _____., and Scott Brown. "How Can We Accept Those Whose Conduct is Unacceptable?" *Negotiation Journal*, 4:2 (April 1988), 125-136.
202. Fitzmaurice, H., et al. "Val Victic or Woe to Negotiator! Your Treaty or Our "Interpretation" of It?" *American Journal of International Law*, 65 (1971), 358-373.
203. Fleischhauer, Carl August. "Negotiations." In: *Encyclopedia of Public International Law*. Amsterdam: North - Holland, 1981. pp. 152-154.
204. Fogg, Richard W. "Dealing with Conflict: A Repertoire of Creative, Peaceful Approaches." *Journal of Conflict Resolution*, 29:2 (June 1985), 330-358.
205. _____. "A Technical Equivalent of War." In: H. Chesnut, ed. *Contributions of Technology to International Conflict Resolution*. London: Pergamon Press, 1987. pp. 113-120.
206. Forkosch, Joel A. "The Negotiator's Art." In: R. J. Lewicki and J. A. Litterer, eds. *Negotiation: Readings, Exercises, and Cases*. Homewood, IL.: Irwin, 1985. pp. 186-189.
207. Francis, C. "The Art of Negotiation." *Public Management*, 65:1 (1983), 2-20.
208. Franck, Thomas M., and E. R. Chester. "Arms Length - Coming Law of Collective Bargaining in International Relations Between Equilibrated States." *Virginia Journal of International Law*, 15:3 (1975), 579-609.
209. Frei, Daniel. "Empathy in Conflict Management." *International Journal*, 40:4 (1985), 586-598.
210. _____., ed. *International Crises and Crisis Management*. New York: Praeger, 1978. 154p.

211. Fried, K. E., et al. "Bargaining Processes and Coalition Outcomes: An Integration." *Journal of Conflict Resolution,* 21 (June 1977), 267-298.
212. Gale, Stephen, and Basya Gale. "Language and Conflict: Towards a Semiotic Theory of "Harmonia Mundi"." *Journal of Peace Science,* 2:2 (1977), 215-230.
213. Galtung, Johan. "Institutionalized Conflict Resolution." *Journal of Peace Research (Oslo),* 4 (1965), 348-397.
214. Glenn, E.S., D. Witmeyer and V. A. Stevenson. "Cultural Styles of Persuasion." *International Journal of Intercultural Relations,* 1:3 (1977), 52-66.
215. Goodrich, L. M. "The Peaceful Settlement of Disputes." *Journal of International Affairs,* 9:2 (1955), 12-20.
216. Gorecki, H. "Negotiating Agreements, Multiobjective Approach." In: H. Chesnut, et al. *Supplemented Ways for Improving International Stability.* Elmsford, NY: Pergamon Press, 1984. pp. 189-198.
217. Gould, W. L. "Laboratory, Law and Anecdote: Negotiations and the Integration of Data." *World Politics,* 18:1 (1965), 92-104.
218. Greene, Fred. "The Peaceful Settlement of Disputes and Conflicts." In: F. Green, ed. *Dynamics of International Relations.* New York: Holt, Rinehart and Winston, 1964. pp. 553-579.
219. Greenhalgh, Leonard, and A. Neslin Scott. "Determining Outcomes of Negotiations: An Empirical Assessment." In: M. H. Bazerman and R. J. Lewicki, eds. *Negotiating in Organizations.* Beverly Hills, CA.: Sage, 1983. pp. 114-134.
220. Groom, A. J. R. "Problem Solving in International Relations." In: E. E. Azar and J. W. Burton, eds. *International Conflict Resolution.* Boulder, CO.: Lynne Rienner, 1986. pp. 85-91.
221. Gross Stein, Janice. "Detection and Defection: Security 'Regimes' and the Management of International Conflict." *International Journal,* 40:4 (1985), 599-627.
222. _____. "War Termination and Conflict Reduction, or How Wars Should End." *Jerusalem Journal of International Relations,* 1:1 (Autumn 1975), 1-27.
223. _____. "International Negotiation: A Multidisciplinary Perspective." *Negotiation Journal,* 4:3 (July 1988), 221-232.
224. Groux, Jean. "Mixed Negotiations." In: D. O'Keefe and H. G. Schermers, eds. *Mixed Agreements.* Deventer: Kluwer, 1983. pp. 87-96.
225. Guetzkow, H. "An Exploratory Empirical Study of the Role of Conflict in Decision-Making Conferences." *International Social Science Bulletin (UNESCO),* 5:2 (1953), 286-299.
226. Gulliver, Philip H. "Negotiations as a Mode of Dispute Settlement: Towards a General Model." *Law and Society Review,* 7 (1973), 667-691.
227. _____. "Anthropological Contributions to the Study of Negotiations." *Negotiation Journal,* 4:3 (July 1988), 247-255.
228. Haas, Ernst B. "Why Collaborate? Issue - Linkage and International Regimes." *World Politics,* 32:3 (April 1980), 357-405.
229. Haas, Michael. "Negotiations, Direct." In: E. Laszlo and Yong Youl Yoo, eds. *World Encyclopedia of Peace, Volume 2.* New York: Pergamon Press, 1986. pp. 21-22.
230. Haass, Richard N. "Ripeness and the Settlement of International Disputes." *Survival,* 30:3 (May/June 1988), 232-251.

231. Haines, Y. Y. "Hierarchical Multiobjective Risk Trade-Off Framework for Conflict Resolution Through Negotiation." In: H. Chestnut, ed. *Contributions of Technology to International Conflict Resolution.* London: Pergamon Press, 1987. pp. 105-110.
232. Hammond, Kenneth R. "New Directions in Research on Conflict Resolution." *Journal of Social Issues,* 11 (1965), 44-66.
233. Hansen, Richard E. "Professional Airman in International Negotiations: What Role? What Preparation?" *Air University Review,* 36:4 (May-June 1985), 67-73.
234. Harriman, W. Averell. "Observations on Negotiating: Informal Views of W. Averell Harriman." *Journal of International Affairs,* 29:1 (Spring 1975), 1-6.
235. Henderson, Bruce D. "The Non-Logical Strategy." In: R. J. Lewicki and Joseph A. Litterer, eds. *Negotiation: Readings, Exercises, and Cases.* Homewood, IL.: Irwin, 1985. pp. 149-155.
236. Hill, Barbara J. "An Analysis of Conflict Resolution Techniques: From Problem Solving Workshop to Theory." *Journal of Conflict Resolution,* 26:1 (1982), 109-138.
237. Hoedemaker, Edward D. "Distrust and Aggression: An Interpersonal - International Analogy". *Journal of Conflict Resolution,* 12 (May 1980), 69-81.
238. Holder, William E. "Towards Peaceful Settlement of International Disputes." *Australian Yearbook of International Law,* (1968-1969), 102-122.
239. Holsti, K. J. "Paths to Peace? Theories of Conflict Resolution and Realities of International Politics." In: R. Thakur, ed. *International Conflict Resolution.* Boulder, Co.: Westview Press, 1988. pp. 105-132.
240. Honeyman, Christopher. "In Defence of Ambiguity." *Negotiation Journal,* 3:1 (January 1987), 81-86.
241. Horowitz, Irving Lewis. "Deterrence Games: From Academic Casebook to Military Codebook." In P. Swingle, ed. *The Structure of Conflict.* New York: Academic Press, 1970. pp. 277-296.
242. Ikle, Fred C. "Bargaining and Communication." In J. de. S. Pool, et al. eds. *Handbook of Communication.* Chicago: Rand McNally, 1973. pp. 836-843.
243. _____. "Bargaining and Communication." In: J. R. Lewicki and J. A. Litterer, eds. *Negotiation: Readings, Exercises and Cases.* Homewood, IL.: Irwin, 1985. pp. 168-176.
244. _____. "Negotiating Effectively." In: E. Plischke, ed. *Modern Diplomacy: The Art and The Artisans.* Washington, D.C.: American Enterprise Institute, 1979. pp. 364-372.
245. _____. "Negotiating Effectively." In: D. S. McLellan, W. C. Olson and F. A. Sonderman, eds. *The Theory and Practice of International Relations.* 4th ed. Englewood Cliffs, N.J.: Prentice-Hall, 1974. pp. 203-206.
246. _____. "Negotiating Skill: East and West." In: L. B. Miller, ed. *Dynamics of World Politics: Studies in the Resolution of Conflict.* Englewood Cliffs, NJ.: Prentice-Hall, 1968. pp. 20-43.
247. _____. "Negotiation." In: *International Encyclopedia of the Social Sciences.* Vol.11. New York: McMillan and Free Press, 1968. pp. 117-120.
248. _____. "What Is Negotiation?" In: I. D. Duchacek, ed. *Discord and Harmony.* Hinsdale, IL.: Dryden Press, 1972. pp. 362-366.
249. "International Negotiations: Mechanisms for the Management of Complex Systems." *Conflict and Cooperation,* 23:2 (1988), 95-106.
250. Intriligator, Michael D. "Research on Conflict Theory: Analytical Approaches and Areas of Application." *Journal of Conflict Resolution,* 26 (June 1982), 302-327.

251. Isard, Walter, and Christine Smith. "Matching Conflict Situations and Conflict Management Procedures." *Conflict Management and Peace Science*, 5 (1980), 1-25.
252. Jacobs, David C. "The Concept of Adversary Participation." *Negotiation Journal*, 4:2 (April 1988), 137-142.
253. Janosik, Robert J. "Rethinking the Culture-Negotiation Link." *Negotiation Journal*, 3:4 (October 1987), 385-396.
254. Jervis, Robert. "Bargaining and Bargaining Tactics." In: J. R. Pennock and J. W. Chapman, eds. *Coercion*. Nomos XIV. Chicago, IL.: Aldine, Atherton, 1972. pp. 272-288.
255. Johnston, Robert W. "Negotiation Strategies: Different Strokes for Different Folks." In: R. J. Lewicki and J. A. Litterer, eds. *Negotiation: Readings, Exercises and Cases*. Homewood, IL.: Irwin, 1985. pp. 156-164.
256. Jönsson, Christer. "Interorganization Theory and International Organization." *International Studies Quarterly*, 30 (1986), 39-57.
257. _____. "Situation-Specific Versus Action-Specific Approaches to International Bargaining." *European Journal of Political Research*, 6:4 (1978), 381-398.
258. _____. "Bargaining Power: Notes on an Elusive Concept." *Cooperation and Conflict*, 16 (December 1981), 249-257.
259. Kaplan, Morton A. "Limited Retaliation as a Bargaining Process." In: K. Knorr and T, Read, eds. *Limited Strategic War*. London: Pall Mall, 1962. pp. 142-162.
260. Katz, Daniel. "Nationalism and Strategies of International Conflict Resolution." In: H. C. Kelman, ed. *International Behavior*. New York: Holt, Rinehart and Winston, 1965. pp. 354-390.
261. Katz, E., and M. Pilsworth. "Getting In and Getting Out - Notes on Method and Diplomacy in International Communication Research." *Communication*, 5:1 (1980), 135-153.
262. Katz, Neil, and Stuart Thorson. "Theory and Practice: A Pernicious Separation?" *Negotiation Journal*, 4:2 (April 1988), 115-118.
263. Kellerman, Barbara. "Commentary: Raising Issues of Style as Well as Substance." *Negotiation Journal*, 3:3 (July 1987), 275-278.
264. Kent, George. "Determinants of Bargaining Outcomes." *Peace Research Society (International) Papers*, 11 (1969), 23-42.
265. Kissinger, Henry A. *The Necessity of Choice*. New York: Harper & Row, 1961. 372p.
266. _____. "On Negotiation and Bargaining in the Modern World." In: *Modern Diplomacy: The Art and The Artisans*. Washington, D.C.: American Enterprise Institute, 1979. pp. 373-380.
267. _____. "On Negotiations." In: M. L. Rakove, ed. *Arms and Foreign Policy in the Nuclear Age*. New York: Oxford University Press, 1972. pp. 149-160.
268. Kochan, Thomas A., and Anil Verma. "Negotiations in Organizations: Blending Industrial Relations and Organizational Behavior Approaches." In: M. H. Bazerman and R. J. Lewicki, eds. *Negotiating in Organizations*. Beverly Hills, CA.: Sage, 1983. pp. 13-34.
269. Kremenyuk, Victor A. "The Emerging System of International Negotiations." *Negotiation Journal*, 4:3 (July 1988), 211-220.
270. Kriesberg, Louis. "International Decisionmaking." In: M. Haas, ed. *International Systems: A Behavioral Approach*. New York: Chandler, 1974. pp. 229-250.
271. _____. "Non-Coercive Inducements in International Conflict." In: C. M. Stephenson, ed. *Alternative Methods for International Security*. Washington, D.C.: University Press of America, 1982. pp. 105-120.

272. _____. "Timing and the Initiation of De-Escalation Moves." *Negotiation Journal*, 3:4 (October 1987), 375-384.
273. _____. "Non-coercive Inducements in International Conflict." In: B. H. Weston, ed. *Toward Nuclear Disarmament and Global Security: A Search for Alternatives.* Boulder, CO.: Westview Press, 1984. pp. 551-563.
274. Landi, Dale M., et al. "Improving the Means for Intergovernmental Communications in Crisis." *Survival*, 26 (1984), 200-214.
275. Laue, James H. "The U.S. Institute of Peace: A Federal Commitment to Dispute Resolution." *Negotiation Journal*, 1:2 (April 1985), 181-192.
276. Lauren, Paul G. "Theories of Bargaining with Threats of Force: Deterrence and Coercive Diplomacy." In: P. G. Lauren, ed. *Diplomacy.* New York: The Free Press, 1979. pp. 183-211.
277. Laver, Michael, and J. Underhill. "The Bargaining Advantages of Combining with Others." *British Journal of Political Science*, 12:1 (1982), 27-42.
278. _____. "Coalition Bargaining, Interest Representation and Government." *Political Studies*, 31:4 (1983), 650-655.
279. Lax, David A., and James K. Sebenius. "Interests: The Measure of Negotiation." *Negotiation Journal*, 2:1 (January 1986), 73-92.
280. _____. "Optimal Search in Negotiation Analysis." *Journal of Conflict Resolution*, 29:3 (September 1985), 456-472.
281. _____., and James K. Sebenius. "The Power of Alternatives or The Limits to Negotiation." *Negotiation Journal*, 1:2 (April 1985), 163-179.
282. _____. _____. "Three Ethical Issues in Negotiation." *Negotiation Journal*, 2:4 (October 1986), 363-370.
283. Lebow, Richard Ned. "Generational Learning and Conflict Management." *International Journal*, 40:4 (Autumn 1985), 555-585.
284. Leng, Russell J., and Stephen G. Walker. "Comparing Two Studies of Crisis Bargaining: Confrontation, Coercion and Reciprocity." *Journal of Conflict Resolution*, 26:4 (December 1982), 571-591.
285. _____., and C. S. Gochman. "Dangerous Disputes: A Study of Conflict Behavior and War." *American Journal of Political Science*, 26:4 (1982), 664-687.
286. _____., and H. G. Wheeler. "Influence Strategies, Success and War." *Journal of Conflict Resolution*, 23 (December 1979), 655-684.
287. _____. "When Will They Ever Learn? Coercive Bargaining in Recurrent Crises." *Journal of Conflict Resolution*, 27:3 (1983), 379-420.
288. Levi, A., and A. Benjamin. "Focus and Flexibility in a Model of Conflict Resolution." *Journal of Conflict Resolution*, 21:3 (1978), 405-425.
289. Levi, W. "On the Causes of War and the Conditions of Peace." *Journal of Conflict Resolution*, 4:4 (1960), 411-420.
290. Lewicki, Roy J. "Challenges of Teaching Negotiation." *Negotiation Journal*, 2:1 (January 1986), 15-27.
291. Lipsitz, Lewis, and Herbert M. Kritzer. "Unconventional Approaches to Conflict Resolution." *Journal of Conflict Resolution*, 19:4 (December 1975), 713-733.
292. Lockhart, Charles. "Conflict Actions and Outcomes: Long-Term Impacts." *Journal of Conflict Resolution*, 22:4 (1978), 565-598.
293. _____. "Problems in the Management and Resolution of International Conflicts." *World Politics*, 29 (April 1977), 370-403.
294. Lopez, George A. "In the Balance, Bringing People Together: The Literature on Dispute Settlement and Conflict Resolution." *Choice*, (November 1984), 383-392.

295. Luban, David. "Bargaining and Compromise: Recent Work on Negotiation and Informal Justice." *Philosophy and Public Affairs*, 14:4 (Fall 1985), 397-416.
296. Lukov, Vadim B. "International Negotiations of the 1980s: Features, Problems and Prospects." *Negotiation Journal*, 1:2 (April 1985), 139-148.
297. _____. Victor M. Sergeev and Ivan G. Tyulin. "Reflective Model of Negotiation Process." *IEEE Technology and Society*, 3:2 (June 1984), 20-27.
298. M'Bow, Amadou M. "The Practice and Consensus in International Relations." *International Social Science Journal*, 30:4 (1978), 893-903.
299. Mabry, Bebars DuPre. "The Pure Theory of Bargaining." *Industrial and Labor Relations Review*, 18:4 (July 1965), 479-502.
300. Mainland, Edward A., and David C. McGaffey. "An Appraisal of Some Books on the Art of Negotiating." *State*, (June 1982), 36-38.
301. Malitza, Mircea. "Small States and the Peaceful Settlement of Disputes." In: A. Lall, ed. *Multilateral Negotiation and Mediation*. New York: Pergamon Press, 1985. pp. 77-92.
302. Mandel, Robert. "Adversaries' Expectations and Desires about War Termination." In: S. J. Cimbala, ed. *Strategic War Termination*. New York: Praeger, 1986. pp. 174-189.
303. Marshall, Charles Burton. "The Problem of Incompatible Purposes." In: I. D. Duchacek, ed. *Conflict and Cooperation Among Nations*. New York: Holt, Rinehart and Winston, 1960. pp. 518-521.
304. Martin, Geoffrey R. "The "Practical" and the "Theoretical" Split in Modern Negotiation Literature." *Negotiation Journal*, 4:1 (January 1988), 45-54.
305. Martz, M. J. R. "Conflict Resolution and Peaceful Settlement of Disputes." In: *Governance in the Western Hemisphere*. New York: Aspen Institute for Humanistic Studies, 1982. pp. 151-178.
306. Mastenbrock, Willem F. G. "Negotiating: A Conceptual Model." *Group and Organization Studies*, 5:3 (September 1980), 324-339.
307. McClintock, Robert. "On the Manner of Negotiating with Princes." In: N.J. Padelford and S.L. Kriner, eds. *Contemporary International Relations Readings, Third Series*. Cambridge, MA.: Harvard University Press, 1954. pp. 294-300.
308. McCullough, George B. "Transnational Bargaining - Problems and Prospects." *Monthly Labor Review*, 101:3 (March 1978), 33-34.
309. McGinnis, Michael D. "Issue Linkage and the Evolution of International Cooperation." *Journal of Conflict Resolution*, 30:1 (March 1986), 141-191.
310. McKersie, Robert B. "Tis Better to Confer than to Decide." *Negotiation Journal*, 3:4 (October 1987), 329-332.
311. Meeks, Kenneth W. "Foreign Negotiations Require Tact, Diplomacy, Know--How." *Naval Civil Engineering*, 24:1 (Spring 1984), 19-23.
312. Midgaard, Knut. "Cooperative Negotiations and Bargaining: Some Notes on Power and Powerlessness." In: B. Barry, ed. *Power and Political Theory: Some European Perspectives*. London: Wiley, 1976. pp. 117-138.
313. _____. "Theory of International Negotiations." *International Politics (Norway)*, 4 (October 1973), 923-946.
314. Millhauser, M. "The Unspoken Resistance to Alternative Dispute Resolution." *Negotiation Journal*, 3:1 (January 1987), 29-36.
315. Mitchell, C. R. "Conflict Resolution and Controlled Communication." *Journal of Peace Research*, 10:1 (1973), 123-132.
316. _____. "Evaluating Conflict." *Journal of Peace Research*, 17:1 (1980), 61-76.

317. Morgenthau, Hans J. "The Art of Diplomatic Negotiation." In: D. S. McLellan, W. C. Olson and F. A. Sondermann, eds. *The Theory and Practice of International Relations*. Englewood Cliffs, NJ.: Prentice-Hall, 1960. pp. 217-219.
318. _____. "The Art of Diplomatic Negotiation." In: L. White, ed. *The State of the Social Sciences*. Chicago, IL.: University of Chicago Press, 1956. pp. 404-414.
319. Morse, Oliver. "Methods of Pacific Settlement of International Disputes: Difficulties and Revision." *Brooklyn Law Review*, 25 (December 1958), 21-32.
320. Murray, John S. "Understanding Competing Theories of Negotiation." *Negotiation Journal*, 2:2 (April 1986), 179-186.
321. Newsom, David D. "Domestic Models of Conflict Resolution: Are They Relevant in the International Context?" In: D. B. Bendahmane and J. W. McDonald, eds. *International Negotiations: Art and Science*. Washington, D.C.: U.S. Dept. of State. Foreign Service Institute, 1984. pp. 35-38.
322. Nicholson, M. B. "The Resolution of Conflict." In: D. R. Young, ed. *Bargaining*. Urbana, IL.: University of Illinnois Press, 1975. pp. 231-244.
323. _____. "The Resolution of Conflict." *Journal of the Royal Statistical Society, Series A*, (1967), 529-540.
324. Nierenberg, Gerald I. "Negotiating Strategies and Counter Strategies: How to Develop Win/win Techniques." *Management Review*, 72 (February 1983), 48-49.
325. _____. "The Use of Questions in Negotiating." In: R. J. Lewicki and J. A. Litterer, eds. *Negotiation: Readings, Exercises and Cases*. Homewood, IL.: Irwin, 1985. pp. 99-110.
326. Northedge, F. S. "Negotiation." In: J. Gould and W. L. Kolb, eds. *A Dictionary of Social Science*. Glencoe, NY.: The Free Press, 1964. pp. 463-464.
327. Nyerges, Janos. "10 Commandments for a Negotiator." *Negotiation Journal*, 3:1 (January 1987), 21-28.
328. Orion, White, Jr. "The Dynamics of Negotiations." In: N. A. Huelsberg and W. F. Lincoln, eds. *Successful Negotiating*. Washington, D.C.: International City Management Association, 1985. pp. 143-160.
329. Pedler, Mike J. "Negotiation Skills Training - Part 1." *Journal of European Industrial Training*, 1:4 (1977), 18-21.
330. _____. "Negotiation Skills Training: Part 2." *Journal of European Industrial Training*, 1:5 (1977a), 12-16.
331. _____. "Negotiation Skills Training, Part 3." *Journal of European Industrial Training*, 1:6 (1977b), 25-27.
332. _____. "Negotiation Skills Training - Part 4: Learning to Negotiate." *Journal of European Industrial Training*, 2:1 (1978), 20-25.
333. Plantey, A. "A Cultural Approach to International Negotiation." *International Social Science Journal*, 34:3 (1982), 535-544.
334. Porshalt, Lars. "On Methods of Conflict and Prevention." *Journal of Peace Research*, 3:2 (1966), 178-193.
335. Pruitt, Dean G. "Achieving Integrative Agreements in Negotiation." Paper Presented at the *PARC Conflict Forum Speaker Series*, held on April 9, 1987, at the Maxwell School of Citizenship and Public Affairs, Syracuse University.
336. _____. "Creative Approaches to Negotiation." In: D. J. D. Sandole and I. Sandole-Staroste, eds. *Conflict Management and Problem Solving*. London: Frances Pinter, 1987. pp. 62-76.

337. _____. "Foreign Policy Decisions, Threats and Compliance to International Law." *Proceedings of the American Society of International Law*, (1964), 54-60.
338. Raiffa, Howard. "Post-Settlement Settlements." *Negotiation Journal*, 1:1 (January 1985), 9-12.
339. _____. "Teaching the Art and Science of Negotiation." In: D. B. Bendahmane and J. W. McDonald, eds. *International Negotiation: Art and Science*. Washington, D.C.: U.S. Department of State. Foreign Service Institute, 1984. pp. 39-46.
340. Ramsey, James A. "Negotiating with Friends: Nature and Techniques of Negotiations among Friendly Powers." *Foreign Service Journal*, 36 (March 1959), 23-26.
341. Randolph, Lillian L. "A Suggested Model of International Negotiation." *Journal of Conflict Resolution*, 10:3 (1966), 344-353.
342. Rao, G. A., and M. F. Shakun. "A Normative Model for Negotiations." *Management Science*, 20 (1974), 1364-1375.
343. Raven, Bertram H., and Arie W. Kruglanski. "Conflict and Power." In: P. Swingle, ed. *The Structure of Conflict*. New York: Academic Press, 1970. pp. 69-110.
344. Reiches, N. A., and H. B. Harral. "Argument in Negotiation: A Theoretical and Empirical Approach." *Speech Monographs*, 41 (1974), 36-48.
345. Rohrl, Vivian J. "International Relations Revisited: Cross-Cultural Analysis and Application." In: P. J. Magnarella, ed. *Anthropological Diplomacy*. Williamsburg, VA.: Dept. of Anthropology, College of William and Mary, 1982. pp. 13-22.
346. "The Role of Secrecy in the Conduct of Foreign Policy." *American Journal of International Law, Proceedings*, 66 (September 1972), 61-78.
347. Rosencrance, Richard N. "Reward, Punishment, and Interdependence." *Journal of Conflict Resolution*, 25:1 (March 1981), 31-46.
348. Rosenthal, Donald B. "Bargaining Analysis in Intergovernmental Relations." *Publius*, 10:3 (Summer 1980), 5-44.
349. Rothschild, K. W. "Approaches to the Theory of Bargaining." In: J. T. Dunlop, ed. *The Theory of Wage Determination*. London: MacMillan, 1964. pp. 281-291.
350. Ruloff, Dieter, and Daniel Frei. "Forecasting East-West Diplomatic Climate: A Politometric Approach." In: V. Luterbacher and M. D. Ward, eds. *Dynamic Models of International Conflict*. Boulder, CO.: Lynne Rienner, 1985. pp. 489-516.
351. Rummel, R. J. "Dimensions of Conflict Behavior Within Nations, 1946-59." *Journal of Conflict Resolution*, 10 (1966), 65-73.
352. _____. "Testing Some Possible Predictors of Conflict Behavior Within and Between Nations." *Parliamentary Papers of Peace Research Society*, 1 (1964), 79-111.
353. Rush, Thomas A. "Comparative Conflict Analysis of Violent and Non-Violent Methods' Impact on Conflict Resolution." In J. P. Maas and R. A. L. Stewart, eds. *Toward a World of Peace*. Suva, Fiji: University of the South Pacific, 1986. pp. 68-75.
354. Salleh Bin Abas, Haji Mohammed Tan. "Cultural Problems in Treaty Negotiations: A Case Study." In: R. P. Anand, ed. *Cultural Factors in International Relations*. New Delhi: Abhinav Publications, 1981. pp. 149-162.
355. Sampson, Martin W. III. "Some Necessary Conditions for International Policy Coordination." *Journal of Conflict Resolution*, 26:2 (June 1982), 359-384.

356. Sander, Frank E. A., and Jeffrey Z. Rubin. "The Janus Quality of Negotiation: Dealmaking and Dispute Resolution." *Negotiation Journal*, 4:2 (April 1980), 109-114.
357. Saunders, Harold H. "International Relationships - It's Time to Go Beyond "We" and "They"." *Negotiation Journal*, 3:3 (July 1987), 245-274.
358. _____. "The Pre-Negotiation Phase." In: D. B. Bendahmane and J. W. McDonald, eds. *International Negotiation: Art and Science.* Washington, D.C.: U.S. Department of State, Foreign Service Institute, 1984. pp. 47-56.
359. _____. "We Need a Larger Theory of Negotiation: The Importance of Pre-Negotiating Phases." *Negotiation Journal*, 1:3 (July 1985), 249-262.
360. Schelling, Thomas C. "Arrangements of Reciprocal Assurance." In: H. Roderick and U. Magnusson, eds. *Avoiding Inadvertent War: Crisis Management.* Austin, TX.: The University of Texas, 1983. pp. 123-130.
361. _____. "Bargaining, Communication and Limited War." *Journal of Conflict Resolution*, 1:1 (1957), 19-36.
362. _____. "Tacit Coordination of Expectations and Behavior." In: I. D. Duchacek, ed. *Discord and Harmony.* Hinsdale, IL.: Dryden Press, 1972. pp. 378-394.
363. Schwartz, H., et al. "An Interview with Theodore Von Laue: The Semantic Curtain of 'Negotiations'." *Minority of One*, 8 (November 1966), 2-6.
364. Scott, Andrew M. "Bargaining and Negotiation." In: A. M. Scott, ed. *The Functioning of the International Political System.* New York: MacMillan, 1967. pp. 172-182.
365. _____. "The Logic of International Interaction." *International Studies Quarterly*, 21:3 (1977), 429-460.
366. Sebenius, James K. "Negotiating Arithmetic: Adding and Subtracting Issues and Parties." *International Organization*, 37:2 (Spring 1983), 281-316.
367. Shea, Gregory P. "The Study of Bargaining and Conflict Behavior: Broadening the Conceptual Arena." *Journal of Conflict Resolution*, 24:4 (December 1980), 706-741.
368. Slusher, E. Allen, G. L. Ross and K. Y. Roering. "Commitment to Future Interaction and Relative Power Under Conditions of Interdependence." *Journal of Conflict Resolution*, 22:2 (1978), 282-298.
369. Snyder, Glenn H., and Paul Diesing. "External Bargaining and Internal Bargaining." In: R. D. Matthews, A. G. Rubinoff and J. Gross Stein, eds. *International Conflict and Conflict Management.* Scarborough, Ont.: Prentice-Hall, 1984. pp. 128-136.
370. Suefeld, Peter, and Philip Tetlock. "Integrative Complexity of Communications in International Crises." *Journal of Conflict Resolution*, 21:1 (1977), 169-184.
371. Susskind, Lawrence. "Scorable Games: A Better Way to Teach Negotiation?" *Negotiation Journal*, 1:3 (July 1985), 205-209.
372. Suttmeier, R. P. "Domestic Origins of An International Negotiating Position." *Orbis*, 22:3 (1978), 651-680.
373. Swingle, Paul G. "Dangerous Games." In: P. Swingle, ed. *The Structure of Conflict.* New York: Academic Press, 1970. pp. 235-276.
374. Teja, J. S. "Decision Making Through Negotiations." *International Studies*, 22:3 (July-September 1985), 239-264.
375. Tobias, Andrew. "Winning Through Negotiation." In: R. J. Lewicki and J. A. Litterer, eds. *Negotiation: Readings, Exercises, and Cases.* Homewood, IL.: Irwin, 1985. pp. 6-18.
376. Tollison, Robert D., and Thomas D. Willett. "An Economic Theory of Mutually Advantageous Issue Linkages in International Negotiations." *International Organization*, 33 (Autumn 1979), 425-449.

377. Touval, Saadia. "Managing the Risks of Accommodation." In: N. Oren, ed. *Termination of Wars.* Jerusalem: The Magnes Press, Hebrew University, 1982. pp. 17-39.
378. Underdal, Arild. "Causes of Negotiation Failure." *European Journal of Political Research,* 11:2 (1983), 183-196.
379. Unterman, Israel. "Negotiation and Cross-Cultural Communication." In: D. B. Bendahmane and J. W. McDonald, eds. *International Negotiation: Art and Science.* Washington, D.C.: U.S. Department of State. Foreign Service Institute, 1984. pp. 69-75.
380. Van de Velde, Kenneth J. "Treaty Interpretation from a Negotiator's Perspective." *Vanderbilt Journal of Transnational Law,* 21:2 (1988), 281-311.
381. Varis, Tapio. "Peace and Communication: An Approach by Flow Studies." *Journal of Peace Research,* 19:3 (1982), 241-250.
382. Wagner, R. Harrison. "Economic Interdependence, Bargaining Power and Political Influence." *International Organization,* 42:3 (Summer 1988), 461-484.
383. Ways, Max. "Virtues, Dangers and Limits of Negotiation." *Fortune,* 99:1 (1979), 86-90.
384. _____. "The Virtues, Dangers, and Limits of Negotiation." In: R. J. Lewicki and J. A. Litterer, eds. *Negotiation: Readings, Exercises, and Cases.* Homewood, IL.: Irwin: 1985. pp. 19-25.
385. _____. "The Virtues, Dangers, and Limits of Negotiation." *Fortune,* 99:1 (1979), 86-90.
386. Williams, Philip Maynard. "Crisis Management." *Towson State Journal of International Affairs,* 8:1 (Fall 1973), 11-22.
387. Williams, R. M. "Resolving and Restricting International Conflicts." *Armed Forces and Society,* 7:3 (1981), 367-382.
388. Winham, Gilbert R. "International Negotiation in an Age of Transition." *International Journal,* 5:1 (1980), 1-20.
389. _____. "Negotiation as a Management Process." In: R. D. Matthews, A. G. Rubinoff, and J. Gross Stein, eds. *International Conflict and Conflict Management.* Scarborough, Ont.: Prentice-Hall of Canada, 1984. pp. 465-479.
390. _____. "Negotiation as a Management Process." *World Politics,* 30 (October 1977), 87-114.
391. _____. "Negotiation as Art and Science." *International Perspectives,* (March 1980), 24-27.
392. _____. "Practitioners' Views of International Negotiation." *World Politics,* 32:1 (1979), 111-135.
393. Wittman, Donald. "How War Ends: A Rational Model Approach." *Journal of Conflict Resolution,* 23 (December 1979), 743-763.
394. Wolfers, Arnold. "Peace Strategies of Deterrence and Accommodation." In: L. B. Miller, ed. *Dynamics of World Politics.* Englewood Cliffs, NJ.: Prentice-Hall, 1968. pp. 10-19.
395. Young, Oran R. "Strategic Interaction and Bargaining." In: O. R. Young, ed. *Bargaining.* Urbana, IL.: University of Illinois Press, 1975. pp. 3-22.
396. Zartman, I. William. "Alternative Attempts at Crisis Management: Concept and Processes." In: G. R. Winham, ed. *New Issues in International Crisis Management.* Boulder, CO.: Westview Press, 1988. pp. 199-224.
397. _____. "The Analysis of Negotiation." In: I. W. Zartman, ed. *The 50% Solution...* Garden City, N.Y.: Anchor Press, 1976. pp. 1-42.
398. _____. "Common Elements in the Analysis of Negotiating Process." *Negotiating Journal,* 4:1 (January 1988), 31-44.

399. _____. "Negotiation: Theory and Reality." In: D. B. Bendahmane and J. W. McDonald Jr., eds. *International Negotiation: Art and Science.* Washington, D.C.: Foreign Service Institute, U.S. Department of State, 1984. pp. 1-8.
400. _____. "Negotiation as a Joint Decision-Making Process." In: J. W. Zartman, ed. *The Negotiation Process.* Beverly Hills, CA.: Sage, 1978. pp. 67-86.
401. _____. "Negotiation as a Joint Decision-Making Process." *Journal of Conflict Resolution,* 21:4 (1977), 619-638.
402. _____. "Negotiations: Theory and Reality." *Journal of International Affairs,* 29:1 (Spring 1975), 69-78.
403. _____. "The Political Analysis of Negotiation: How Who Gets What and When." *World Politics,* 26:3 (1974), 385-399.
404. Zemke, Ron. "Negotiation Skills Training: Helping Others Get What They Want Gracefully." *Training/HDR,* (February 1980), 25-28.

3. Documents and Reports

405. Aggarwal, V. K., and Allan Pierre. "Evolution of Bargaining Theories: Toward an Integrated Approach to Explain Strategies of the Weak." Paper Presented at the *79th Annual Meeting of the American Political Science Association,* held on September 1-4, 1983, in Chicago, IL.
406. Allan, Pierre. *Dynamics of Bargaining in International Conflict.* Ph.D. Dissertation. Geneva: The Graduate Institute of International Studies, 1980.
407. Antrim, Lance. "Future Needs for Negotiation Support Systems: A Practitioner's View." Paper Presented at the *Annual Meeting of the Operations Research Society of America,* held in October 1986, in Miami, FL.
408. Babbitt, Eileen. *The Development of Teaching and Research Materials for the Study of Processes of International Negotiation.* Working Paper Series 1. Cambridge, MA.: The Program on the Processes of International Negotiation, American Academy of Arts and Sciences, 1987. 11p.
409. _____., and Alan McDonald. *Negotiations Analysis as a Tool in the Management of Large International Rivers.* Working Papers Series 3. Cambridge, MA.: The Program on the Processes of International Negotiations. American Academy of Arts and Sciences, 1987. 27p.
410. Bachner, Dave, and Michael R. Paige. "Managing Intercultural Conflict: Applications from Intergroup and Interorganizational Relations." Papers Presented at the *Tenth SIETAR International Conference,* held on May 21-25, 1984, at the George Mason University, Washington, D.C.
411. Bass, B. M. *Effects on Negotiators of Their Prior Experience in Strategy or Study Groups.* Technical Report No. 1. Pittsburgh, PA.: University of Pittsburgh, 1963.
412. Behue, August. *The Cognitive Structure of International Bargaining: A Cognitive Mapping Analysis of the Pre-Munich Talks Between Hitler and Chamberlain.* M.A. Thesis. Ottawa: Carleton University, 1980.
413. Bendahmane, Diane B., and John W. McDonald, eds. *International Negotiation: Art and Science: Report of a Conference on International Negotiation, June 9-10, 1983.* Washington, D.C.: U.S. Government Printing Office, 1984. 85p.
414. Bercovitch, Jacob, and H. Ohlman. *Computers in the Settlement of International Disputes.* Research Report No. 6. Geneva: International Peace Research Institute, 1984. 64p.

415. _____. *Managing International Conflicts: The Structure and Process of International Negotiation.* Christchurch, New Zealand: Department of Political Science Monograph, Canterbury University, 1982. 97p.
416. Binnendijk, Hans, ed. *National Negotiating Styles.* Washington, D.C.: Department of State, Foreign Service Institute, 1987. 147p.
417. Blass, Asher, and Howard Raiffa. *On Computing the Efficient Frontier: A Computer Program for Investigating the Efficient Solutions for Two - Party Multiple - Issue Negotiations.* Working Paper Series. 7. Cambridge, MA.: The Program on the Processes of International Negotiations, American Academy of Arts and Sciences, 1987. 43p.
418. Bontadini, Pier Luigi. "Negotiation for Results: How to Develop Related Executive Skills." Paper Presented at the *Conference on the Processes of International Negotiations,* held on May 18-22, 1987, at the International Institute for Applied Systems Analysis (IIASA), Laxenburg, Austria.
419. Buchan, Alastair. *Crisis Management: The New Diplomacy.* Atlantic Papers; NATO Series II. Boulogne-sur-Seine: The Atlantic Institute, 1966. 63p.
420. Burton, John W., et al. "Problem Solving Approaches to the Resolution of International Conflict." Paper Presented at the *Annual Meeting of the International Studies Association,* held on March 21-24, 1979, in Toronto.
421. Carter, Jimmy. *Negotiation: The Alternative to Hostility.* Macon, GA.: Mercer University Press, 1984. 57p.
422. Casse, Pierre, and Surinder Deol. *Managing Intercultural Negotiations: Guidelines for Trainers and Negotiators.* Washington, D.C.: SIETAR International, 1985. 160p.
423. _____. *Training for the Cross - Cultural Mind: A Handbook for Cross - Cultural Trainers and Consultants.* Washington, D.C.: SIETAR, 1981. 260p.
424. Coffin, Royce A. *The Negotiator: A Manual for Winners.* New York: AMACOM, 1973. 160p.
425. Cohen, Stephen. "Communication Structures in Bargaining." Paper Presented at the *17th Annual Convention of the International Studies Association,* held on February 25-29, 1976, in Toronto.
426. *Computer Assisted Negotiation at the American Academy of Arts and Sciences: A Program of Research.* Cambridge, MA.: The Program on the Processes of International Negotiations, The American Academy of Arts and Sciences, 1987. 24p.
427. Contini, Bruno. *The Value of Time in Bargaining Negotiations: Part 1, A Dynamic Model of Bargaining.* Working Paper 207. Berkeley, CA.: Center of Research in Management Science, University of California, 1967.
428. Cottam, Richard W. *Understanding Negotiations: The Academic Contribution.* PEW Case Studies, 413.0-D-88-P. Pittsburgh. PA.: Graduate School of Public and International Affairs, 1988.
429. Cross, John G. "Obstacles to International Agreements: Perspectives from Negotiation Theory." Paper Presented at the *28th Annual Convention of the International Studies Association,* held on April 14-18, 1987, in Washington, D.C.
430. Druckman, Daniel. "Processes and Influences of East-West Negotiations." Paper Presented at the *23rd Annual Convention of the International Studies Association,* held on March 24-27, 1982, in Cincinnati, OH.

431. Dupont, Christophe. "Negotiating a Research Project on Negotiation: The Fixed Link (Transchannel) Pre-Negotiations." Paper Presented at the *Conference on the Processes of International Negotiations*, held on May 18-22, 1987, at the International Institute for Applied Systems Analysis (IIASA) in Laxenburg, Austria.
432. Fisher, Glen H. "Mindsets in Cultural Lens." Paper Presented at the *28th Annual Convention of the International Studies Association*, held on March 14-18, 1987 in Washington, D.C.
433. Fisher, Roger D. "Future Prospects for Negotiations and How to Negotiate." Paper Presented at the *American Association for the Advancement of Science*, held on January 3-8,1981, in Toronto.
434. _____. "Issues of an Emerging Field." Paper Presented at the *National Conference on Peacemaking and Conflict Resolution*, held on September 18-20, 1984, at the University of Missouri, St. Louis.
435. Fitzgerald, Mark, and William A. Lechy. *Conference on Bargaining under Economic Challenge: Proceedings.* Notre Dame, IN.: University of Notre Dame, Department of Economics, 1976. 69p.
436. Grunert, Horst. "Negotiations in Our Time." Paper Presented at the *Conference on the Processes of International Negotiations*, held on May 18-22, 1987, at the International Institute for Applied Systems Analysis (IIASA), at Laxenburg, Austria.
437. Gumpert, P. *Some Antecedents and Consequences of the Use of Punitive Power by Bargainers.* Ph.D. Dissertation. New York: Columbia University Teachers College, 1967. 169p.
438. Habeeb, William M. *Power and Tactics in Asymmetrical Negotiation.* Ph.D. Dissertation. Baltimore, MD.: Johns Hopkins University, 1986. 329p.
439. Handel, Michael I. *War Termination: A Critical Survey.* Jerusalem Papers on Peace Survey, 24. Jerusalem: Leonard Davis Institute for International Relations, 1978. 50p.
440. Hassner, Pierre. *Europe in the Age of Negotiations.* Washington Papers; Vol. I, 8. Beverly Hills, CA.: Sage, 1973. 82p.
441. Hayles, Robert, and Eileen Newmark. "Needs Assessment for Designing Conflict Resolution and Negotiation Activities." Paper Presented at the *Tenth SIETAR International Conference*, held on May 21-25, 1984, at George Mason University, Washington, D.C.
442. Hofstede, Geert. "Cultural Predictors of National Negotiation Style." Paper Presented at the *Conference on the Processes of International Negotiations*, held on May 18-22, 1987, at the International Institute for Applied Systems Analysis (IIASA), in Laxenburg, Austria.
443. Hopmann, P. Terrence. "Cumulation in International Relations Research: Conflict Resolution." Paper Presented at the *Annual Meeting of the International Studies Association*, held on March 21-24, 1979, in Toronto.
444. Hurwitz, Alan. "The Elements of the Negotiating Process - A Cross-Cultural Perspective." Papers Presented at the *Tenth SIETAR International Conferen*, held on May 21-25, 1984, at George Mason University, Washington, D.C.
445. Iaquinta, Leonard. "Experimental Research and the Negotiation of International Disputes." Paper presented at the *Academy for Educational Development Conference on Mediation and Negotiation*, held in July 1973 at Villa Servelloni, Bellagio, Italy.
446. Janosik, Robert J. *Negotiation Theory: Considering the Cultural Variable in the Japanese and American Cases.* Ph.D. Dissertation. New York: New York University, 1983. 312p.

447. _____. "Negotiations and the Experienced Practitioner: Adding a Culture Variable." Paper Presented at the *17th Annual Convention of the International Studies Association*, held on February 25-29, 1976, in Toronto.
448. Joiner, Harry. *A Theoretical Model of International Negotiation*. Ph.D. Dissertation. Geneva: The Institute of International Studies, 1969.
449. Kambalov, S. "New Political Thinking and International Negotiations." Paper Presented at the *Conference on the Processes of International Negotiations*, held on May 18-22, 1987, at the International Institute for Applied Systems Analysis (IIASA), in Laxenburg, Austria.
450. Kaufmann, Johan. "Towards an Integral Analysis of International Negotiations." Paper Presented at the *Conference on the Processes of International Negotiations*, held on May 18-22, 1987, at the International Institute for Applied Systems Analysis (IIASA), at Laxenburg, Austria.
451. Kimmel, Paul R. "Multicultural Analysis of International Negotiations." Paper Presented at the *Conference on the Processes of International Negotiations*, held on May 18-22, 1987, at the International Institute for Applied Systems Analysis (IIASA), in Laxenburg, Austria.
452. Kloepzig, R., and V. A. Richardson. "From Negotiations to Consultations." Paper Presented at the *Conference on the Processes of International Negotiations*, held on May 18-22, 1987, at the International Institute for Applied Systems Analysis (IIASA), in Laxenburg, Austria.
453. Kremenyuk, Victor A. "The System of International Negotiations and its Impact on the Processes of Negotiation." Paper Presented at the *Conference on the Processes of International Negotiations*, held on May 18-22, 1987, at the International Institute for Applied Systems Analysis, at Laxenburg, Austria.
454. Kriesberg, Louis. ""Ripeness" and the De-Escalation of International Conflict." Paper Presented at the *28th Annual Convention of the International Studies Association*, held on April 14-18, 1987, in Washington, D.C.
455. Landi, Dale M., et al. *Improving the Means for Intergovernmental Communications in Crisis*. RAND R-3157-FF. Santa Monica, CA.: Rand Corporation, 1984. 29p.
456. Laue, James H. "Nonviolent Alternatives for the Resolution of International Conflict." Paper Presented at the *Meeting at the Centre for International Understanding*, held in February 1985, in Bellagio, Italy.
457. _____. *Peacemaking Behavior: Major Research Areas, with Special Reference to International and Intercultural Applications*. Washington, D.C.: National Peace Institute Foundation, 1986. 14p.
458. Lax, David A. *Optional Search In Negotiation Analysis*. Boston, MA.: Division of Research, Graduate School of Business Administration, Harvard University, 1983. 14p.
459. _____., and James K. Sebenius. *The Power of Alternatives, or, the Limits to Negotiation*. Boston, MA.: Division of Research, Graduate School of Business Administration, Harvard University, 1983. 14p.
460. _____. _____. *Negotiation and Management: Some Analytic Theories*. Cambridge, MA.: Division of Research, Graduate School of Business Administration, Harvard University, June 1983. 23p.
461. Livne, Zvi. *The Role of Time in Negotiations*. Ph.D. Dissertation. Cambridge, MA.: MIT, 1979.
462. Mandel, Robert, and Sarah Clarke. "Intractability in International Bargaining." Paper Presented at the *22nd Annual Convention of the International Studies Association*, held on March 18-21, 1981 in Philadelphia, PA.

463. Mandell, Brian S. "Conflict Resolution and Conflict Resolution Studies: A Synopsis." Paper Presented at the *Canadian Institute for International Peace and Security,* held on May 1, 1986, in Ottawa.
464. Marais, N. *The Political Dimension of the Settlement Phase During a Revolutionary War.* Pretoria: Institute for Strategic Studies, University of Pretoria, 1982. 32p.
465. Mastenbrock, Willem F. G. "Training in International Negotiating: A Learning Instrument." Paper Presented at the *Conference on the Processes of International Negotiations,* held on May 18-22, 1987, at the International Institute for Applied Systems Analysis (IIASA), in Laxenburg, Austria.
466. Mayer, Andrew C. "Renegotiation." In: *Major Studies and Issue Briefs of the Congressional Research Service,1976-78 Supplement.* Washington, D.C.: University Publications of America, 1978. Reel IX. 58p.
467. McDonald, John W. "Negotiating Styles of Different Countries." Paper Presented at the *28th Annual Convention of the International Studies Association,* held April 14-18, 1987, in Washington, D.C.
468. Merle, Mercel. "International Negotiation: A Process Worthy of Reexamination." Paper Presented at the *Conference on the Processes of International Negotiations,* held on May 18-22, 1987, at the International Institute for Applied Systems Analysis (IIASA), in Laxenburg, Austria.
469. Nyerges, Janos. "The Negotiating Process." Paper Presented at the *20th Anniversary Symposium of UNCTAD,* held in November 1984, in Geneva.
470. Osgood, C. E. *Graduated Reciprocation in Tension Reduction: A Key to Initiative in Foreign Policy.* Urbana, IL.: Institute of Communications Research, University of Illinois, 1960. 82p.
471. Pantev, Plamen. "The Role of Forecasting Of International Relations in the Process of International Negotiations." Paper Presented at the *Conference on the Processes of International Negotiations,* held on May 18-22, 1987, at the International Institute for Applied Systems Analysis (IIASA), in Laxenburg, Austria.
472. Paone, Rocco M. "Research Approaches to Understanding International Negotiations Related to Environmentalism." Paper Presented at the *15th Annual Convention of the International Studies Association,* held on March 20-23, 1974, in St.Louis.
473. Phillips, James L., and Thomas L. Conner. *Studies of Conflict, Conflict Resolution and Alliance Formation.* AFOSR-70-1223TR. East Lansing, MI.: Michigan State University, Computer Institute for Social Science Research, 1970. 275p.
474. Pillar, Paul R. *Negotiating Peace: The Making of Armistice Agreements.* Ph.D. Dissertation. Princeton, NJ.: Princeton University, 1978.
475. Raiffa, Howard, and James K. Sebenius. "Synthesizing Themes of the PIN-US Program." Paper Presented at the *Conference on the Processes of International Negotiations,* held on May 18-21, 1987, at the International Institute for Applied Systems Analysis (IIASA), in Laxenburg, Austria.
476. Randolph, Lillian L. *Process and Outcome of International Negotiations.* Ph.D. Dissertation. Berkeley, CA.: University of California, 1966. 338p.
477. *Report of the United States Program on the Processes of International Negotiation, December, 1985 - June, 1987.* Cambridge, MA.: The Program on the Processes of International Negotiations, The American Academy of Arts and Sciences. 1987. 31p.
478. Sandole, Dennis J. D. "Conflict Resolution and Culture." Paper Presented at the *28th Annual Convention of the International Studies Association,* held on April 14-18, 1987, in Washington, D.C.

479. Saner, Raymond, and Chia Yiu Li. "Influence of Culture and Power Distribution on Negotiation Theory and Negotiation Practice: A Historical-Developmental Perspective II." Paper Presented at the *Tenth SIETAR International Conference*, held on May 21-25, 1984, at George Mason University, Washington.
480. Schuler, Douglas. *Some Prospects for Computer Aided Negotiation.* Unpublished Manuscript. Knowledge Systems Laboratory, M/S 7L-64. Seattle, WA.: Advanced Technology Centre, Boeing Computer Services.
481. Sebenius, James K. "New Concepts and Theories of International Negotiation." Paper Presented at the *Annual Meeting of the International Studies Association*, held in April 1987, in Washington, D.C.
482. Serguiev, A. "On a Programme of Scientific Research in the Realization of the Project 'Process of International Negotiation'." Paper Presented at the *Conference on the Processes of International Negotiations*, held on May 18-22, 1987, at the International Institute for Applied Systems Analysis (IIASA), in Laxenburg, Austria.
483. Singer, J. David. "The Management of Serious Disputes: Historical Patterns Since the Congress of Vienna." Paper Presented at the *11th World Congress of the International Political Science Association*, held on August 12-18, 1979, in Moscow.
484. Smart, Reginald, and Ellen Raider. "Needed Empirical Research on International Negotiation." Papers Presented at the *Tenth SIETAR International Conference*, held on May 21-25, 1984, at George Mason University, Washington, D.C.
485. Snyder, Glenn H. *Crisis Bargaining.* Special Studies Series 1. Buffalo, NY.: Council on International Studies, State University of New York, 1971. 74p.
486. Trubowitz, Peter. "Military Capabilities and Bargaining Power in International Crises." Paper Presented at the *23rd Annual Convention of the International Studies Association*, held on March 24-27, 1982, in Cincinnati, OH.
487. United States. Congress. Senate. Committee on Government Operations. Permanent Subcommittee on Investigations. *Negotiation and Statecraft: Hearings, Part 1: with Walter Laqueur.* 93rd Cong., 1st sess. Washington, D.C.: U.S. Government Printing Office, 1973. 50p.
488. _____._____._____._____._____. *Negotiation and Statecraft: Hearings. Part 2: with Leopold Labedz.* 93rd Cong., 1st sess. Washington, D.C.: U.S. Government Printing Office, 1973. pp. 51-122.
489. _____._____._____._____._____. *Negotiation and Statecraft: Hearings. Part 3: with Bernard Lewis.* 93rd Cong., 2nd sess. Washington, D.C.: U.S. Government Printing Office, 1974. pp. 123-149.
490. _____._____._____._____._____. *Negotiation and Statecraft: Hearing with Panel on International Freedom to Write and Publish. Part 4.* 94th Cong., 1st sess. Washington, D.C.: U.S. Government Printing Office, 1975. pp. 151-299.
491. _____._____._____.Subcommittee on National Security and International Operations. *International Negotiations: Great Power Triangle.* 92nd Cong., 1st sess. Washington, D.C.: U.S. Government Printing Office, 1971. 34p.
492. _____._____._____._____._____. *Negotiation and Statecraft: Selection of Readings.* 91st Cong., 2nd sess. Washington, D.C.: U.S. Government Printing Office, 1970. 59p.
493. Vetschera, Rudolf. "Group Decision and Negotiation Support in Long Range Planning." Paper Presented at the *31th Annual Meeting of the International Society for General Systems Research*, held on June 1-5, 1987, in Budapest, Hungary.

494. Weiss-Wik, Stephen. "Conflict Regulation as Communicative Procedure." Paper Presented at the *Peace Science Society (International) Seminars*, held on November 19, 1979, at Cornell University, in Ithaca, N.Y.
495. Winham, Gilbert R. "The Relevance of Clausewitz to a Theory of International Negotiations." Paper Presented at the *Annual Meeting of the American Political Science Association*, held on September 5, 1987 in Chicago.
496. Zartman, I. William. "Alternative Attempts at Crisis Management: Concepts and Processes." Paper Presented at the *13th World Congress of the International Political Science Association*, held on July 15-20, 1985 in Paris, France.
497. _____. "In Search of Common Elements in the Analysis of the Negotiation Process." Paper Presented at the *Conference on the Processes of International Negotiations*, held on May 18-22, 1987, at the International Institute for Applied Systems Analysis (IIASA), in Laxenburg, Austria.
498. _____. "Convergence and Power: An Approach to the Analysis of Negotiations." Paper presented to the *1969 Annual Meeting of the American Political Science Association*, held in 1965, in New York. Panel 2-F1. 24p.
499. _____. "New Concepts and Theories of International Negotiations." Paper Presented at the *28th Annual Convention of the International Studies Association*, held on April 14-18, 1987, in Washington, D.C.

II
Psychological and Sociological Aspects

The common factor in all negotiations is the human presence. Persons, in their roles as negotiators, are required to communicate, responde to various signals, achieve certain outcomes. This personal level of behavioral interaction in negotiation situations is the focus of much psychological research.

During the last two decades, a large body of literature emerged which examines bargaining situations using psychological and sociological tools. The majority of studies examine psychological aspects of bargaining behavior, focusing mainly on behavioral aspects of individual players. These psychological and sociological investigations of bargaining behaviors have serious implications for the better understanding of the processes of negotiations between states.

This chapter is an inclusive list of psychological and sociological investigations into the negotiation process with particular focus on international negotiation processes. It subjects such as prenegotiation procedures, formulation of agenda preferences, communication, persuasion, threats, promises, psychological and physical stress, time pressure and decision making aspects among the many parameters covered by these disciplines.

1. Books

500. Abdennur, Alexander. *The Conflict Resolution Syndrome: Volunteerism, Violence and Beyond.* Ottawa: University of Ottawa Press, 1987. 154p.
501. Andersen, Kenneth E. *Persuasion: Theory and Practice.* Boston, MA.: Allyn and Bacon, 1971. 386p.
502. Argyle, Michael. *The Psychology of Interpersonal Behaviour.* London: Pelican, 1967. 223p.
503. Bacharach, Samuel B., and Edward J. Lawler. *Power and Politics in Organizations: The Social Psychology of Conflict, Coalitions, and Bargaining.* San Francisco, CA.: Jossey-Bass, 1980. 249p.
504. Bilder, Richard B. *Managing the Risk of International Agreement.* Madison, WI.: University of Wisconsin Press, 1981. 302p.
505. Brockner, Joel, and Jeffrey Z. Rubin. *The Entrapment in Escalating Conflicts: A Social Psychological Analysis.* New York: Springer-Verlag, 1985. 275p.
506. Cohen, Raymond. *Threat Perception in International Crisis.* Madison, WI.: University of Wisconsin Press, 1979. 229p.
507. Cottam, Martha L. *Foreign Policy Decision Making: The Influence of Cognition.* Boulder, CO.: Westview Press, 1986. 262p.
508. De Rivera, Joseph H. *The Psychological Dimensions of Foreign Policy.* Columbus, OH.: C. E. Merrill, 1968. 441p.
509. Deutsch, Morton. *The Resolution of Conflict: Constructive and Destructive Processes.* New Haven, CT.: Yale University Press, 1973. 420p.
510. Doob, L. W. *Resolving Conflict in Africa: The Fermeda Workshop.* New Haven, CT.: Yale University Press, 1970. 209p.
511. Druckman, Daniel. *Human Factors in International Negotiations: Social Psychological Aspects of International Conflict.* Sage Professional Paper in International Studies, 02-020. Beverly Hills, CA.: Sage, 1973. 96p.
512. _____. *Negotiations: Social-Psychological Perspectives.* Beverly Hills, CA.: Sage, 1977. 416p.
513. Haas, Michael. *International Systems: A Behavioral Approach.* New York: Chandler Publishers, 1974. 433p.
514. Harnett, D. L., and L. L. Cummings. *Bargaining Behavior: An International Study.* Houston, TX.: Dame, 1980. 307p.
515. Herman, Charles F., ed. *International Crises: Insights From Behavioral Research.* New York: Free Press, 1972. 334p.
516. Hermann, Margaret G., ed. *A Psychological Examination of Political Leaders.* New York: Free Press, 1976. 516p.
517. Himes, J. S. *Conflict and Conflict Management.* Athens, GA.: University of Georgia Press, 1980. 333p.
518. Hopple, Gerald W. *Political Psychology and Biopolitics: Assessing and Predicting Elite Behavior in Foreign Policy Crises.* Boulder, CO.: Westview Press, 1980. 218p.
519. Janis, Irving L. *Victims of Groupthink: A Psychological Study of Foreign--Policy Decisions and Fiascos.* 2nd ed. Boston, MA.: Houghton Mifflin, 1982. 349p.
520. Jönsson, Christer. *Cognitive Dynamics and International Politics.* London: Frances Pinter, 1982. 210p.
521. Kelman, Herbert C., ed. *International Behavior: A Social Psychological Analysis.* New York: Holt, Rinehart and Winston, 1965. 626p.
522. Kent, George. *The Effects of Threats.* Columbus, OH.: Ohio State University Press, 1967. 113p.
523. Klineberg, Otto. *The Human Dimension of International Relations.* New York: Holt, Rinehart & Winston, 1964. 173p.

524. Kofoed-Hansen, Otto. *The Negotiations: The Challenge of the Atomic Age.* Copenhagen: Munsgaard, 1964. 155p.
525. Kriesberg, Louis, ed. *Social Processes in International Negotiations: A Reader.* New York: Wiley, 1968. 577p.
526. Lockhart, Charles. *The Efficacy of Threats in International Interaction Strategies.* Sage Professional Papers. International Studies, Vol. 2. No. 023. Beverly Hills, Ca.: Sage, 1973. 50p.
527. Merritt, Richard L., ed. *Communication in International Politics.* Chicago, IL.: University of Illinois Press, 1972. 461p.
528. Milburn, Thomas W., and Kenneth H. Watman. *On the Nature of Threat: A Social Psychological Analysis.* New York: Praeger, 1981. 148p.
529. Miller, Clyde R. *The Process of Persuasion.* New York: Crown, 1946. 234p.
530. Morley, Ian E. *The Social Psychology of Bargaining.* London: Allen & Unwin, 1977. 317p.
531. Nierenberg, Gerald I. *The Art of Negotiating: Psychological Strategies for Gaining Advantageous Bargains.* New York: Hawthorn Books, 1968. 195p.
532. ____. *The Complete Negotiator.* New York: Nierenberg & Zeif, 1986. 345p.
533. Patton, Bobby R., and K. Giffin. *Problem-Solving Group Interaction.* New York: Harper & Row, 1973. 264p.
534. Pruitt, Dean G. *Negotiation Behavior.* New York: Academic Press, 1981. 263p.
535. ____., and Jeffrey Z. Rubin. *Social Conflict: Escalation, Stalemate and Resolution.* New York: Random House, 1986. 213p.
536. Reychler, Luc. *Patterns of Diplomatic Thinking: A Cross National Study of Structural and Social Psychological Determinants.* New York: Praeger, 1979. 295p.
537. Rubin, Jeffrey Z., and B. R. Brown. *The Social Psychology of Bargaining and Negotiation.* New York: Academic Press, 1975. 357p.
538. Singer, J. David, ed. *Human Behavior and International Politics: Contributions from the Social Psychological Sciences.* Chicago, IL.: Rand McNally, 1965. 466p.
539. Smith, Clagett G., ed. *Conflict Resolution: Contributions of the Behavioral Sciences.* Bloomington, IN.: Indiana University Press, 1971. 553p.
540. Strauss, Anselm. *Negotiations: Varieties, Contexts, Processes and Social Order.* San Francisco, CA.: Jossey-Bass, 1978. 275p.
541. Swingle, Paul G., ed. *The Structure of Conflict.* New York: Academic Press, 1970. 305p.
542. Walther, Regis. *Orientations and Behavioral Styles of Foreign Service Officers.* New York: Carnegie Endowment, 1965. 52p.
543. Walton, Richard E., and Robert B. McKersie. *A Behavioral Theory of Labor Negotiations: An Analysis of Social Interaction System.* New York: McGraw-Hill, 1965. 437p.
544. ____. *Interpersonal Peacemaking: Confrontation and Third Party Consultation.* Reading, MA.: Addison-Wesley, 1969. 151p.
545. ____. *Managing Conflict - Interpersonal Dialogue and Third Party Roles.* 2nd ed. Reading, MA.: Addison-Wesley, 1987. 160p.
546. White, Ralph K., ed. *Psychology and the Prevention of Nuclear War.* New York: New York University Press, 1986. 591p.
547. Wollman, Neil, ed. *Working for Peace: A Handbook of Practical Psychology and Other Tools.* San Luis Obispo, CA.: Impact Publishers, 1985. 270p.

2. Journal Articles

548. Acuff, Frank L., and Maurice Villere. "Game Negotiators Play." In: R. J. Lewicki and J. A. Litterer, eds. *Negotiation: Readings, Exercises, and Cases.* Homewood, IL.: Irwin, 1985. pp. 177-185.
549. Alcock, James E. "Motivation in an Asymmetric Bargaining Situation: Cross-Cultural Study." *International Journal of Psychology,* 10:1 (1975), 69-81.
550. _____., and Diana Mansell. "Predisposition and Behavior in a Collective Dilemma." *Journal of Conflict Resolution,* 21:3 (September 1977), 443-458.
551. Alevy, Daniel I. "Rationale, Research, and Role Relations in the Stirling Workshop." *Journal of Conflict Resolution,* 18:2 (June 1974), 276-284.
552. Alexander, Elmore R. "The Reduction of Cognitive Conflict." *Journal of Conflict Resolution,* 23:1 (March 1979), 102-119.
553. Alger, Chadwick F. "Personal Contact in Intergovernmental Organizations." In: H. C. Kelman, ed. *International Behavior: A Social Psychological Analysis.* New York: Holt, Rinehart & Winston, 1965. pp. 521-547.
554. Anderson, R. E. "Status Structures in Coalition Bargaining Games." *Sociometry,* 30 (1967), 393-403.
555. Apfelbaum, E. "On Conflict and Bargaining." *Advances in Experimental Social Psychology,* 7 (1974), 103-156.
556. Argyle, Michael, and Jonathan Dean. "Eye Contact, Distance and Affiliation." *Sociometry,* 28 (1965), 289-304.
557. Atthowe, J. M. "Interpersonal Decision Making: The Resolution of Dyadic Conflict." *Journal of Abnormal and Social Psychology,* 62 (1961), 114-119.
558. Bartos, Otomar J. "Concession-Making in Experimental Negotiations." In: J. Berger, et al. *Sociological Theories in Progress.* Vol. 1. Boston, MA.: Houghton Mifflin, 1966. pp. 3-28.
559. _____. "Determinants and Consequences of Toughness." In: P. Swingle, ed. *The Structure of Conflict.* New York: Academic Press, 1970. pp. 45-68.
560. _____. "Foundations for a Rational-Empirical Model of Negotiation." In: J. Berger, M.Zelditch and B. Anderson, eds. *Sociological Theories in Progress. Vol. 2.* Boston, MA.: Houghton Mifflin, 1972. pp. 20-30.
561. _____. "Personality and Style in Negotiations." In: L. Kriesberg, ed. *Research in Social Movements, Conflicts and Change: A Research Annual. Vol. 3.* Greenwich, CT.: JAI Press, 1980. pp. 69-97.
562. _____. "Simple Model in Negotiation: A Sociological Point." In: I. W. Zartman, ed. *The Negotiation Process.* Beverly Hills, CA.: Sage, 1978. pp. 13-28.
563. Bass, B. M. "Effects on the Subsequent Performance of Negotiators of Studying Issues or Planning Strategies Alone or in Groups." *Psychological Monographs: General and Applied,* 80:614 (1966), 1-31.
564. Bazerman, Max H., and Margaret A. Neale. "Improving Negotiation Effectiveness Under Final Offer Arbitration: The Role of Selection and Training." *Journal of Applied Psychology,* 67 (1982), 543-548.
565. _____. "Negotiator Judgement: A Critical Look at the Rationality Assumption." *American Behavioral Scientist,* 27:2 (1983), 211-228.
566. _____. Lee E. Russ and Elaine Yakurra. "Post-Settlement Settlements in Two-Party Negotiations." *Negotiation Journal,* 3:3 (July 1987), 283-292.
567. _____. "Why Negotiations Go Wrong." *Psychology Today,* 20 (June 1986), 54-58.

568. _____., and John S. Carroll. "Negotiator Cognition." In: B. M. Stall and L. L. Cummings, eds. *Research in Organizational Behavior. Vol IX.* Greenwich, CT.: JAI Press, 1987. pp. 247-288.
569. _____., and Harris Sondak. "Judgmental Limitations in Diplomatic Negotiations." *Negotiation Journal,* 4:3 (July 1988), 303-317.
570. Ben Yoav, Orly, and Dean G. Pruitt. "Accountability to Constituents: A Two-Edged Sword." *Organizational Behavior and Human Performance,* 34 (1984), 282-295.
571. _____. _____. "Resistance to Yielding and the Expectation of Cooperative Future Interaction in Negotiation." *Journal of Experimental Social Psychology,* 20:4 (July 1984), 323-353.
572. Benton, A. A. "Bargaining Visibility and the Attitudes and Negotiation Behavior of Male and Female Group Representatives." *Journal of Personality,* 43 (1975), 661-675.
573. _____., and Daniel Druckman. "Constituent's Bargaining Orientation and Intergroup Negotiation." *Journal of Applied Social Psychology,* 4 (1974), 141-150.
574. _____. H. H. Kelley and B. Liebling. "Effects of Extremity of Offers and Concession Rate on the Outcome of Bargaining." *Journal of Personality and Social Psychology,* 24 (1972), 73-83.
575. _____., and Daniel Druckman. "Salient Solutions and the Bargaining Behavior of Representatives and Non-Representatives." *International Journal of Group Tensions,* 3 (1973), 23-39.
576. Bixenstine, V. E., H. M. Potash and K. V. Wilson. "Effects of Level of Cooperative Choice by the Other Player on Choices in a Prisoner's Dilemma Game, Part I." *Journal of Abnormal and Social Psychology,* 66 (1963), 308-313.
577. _____., and K. V. Wilson. "Effects of Level of Cooperative Choice by the Other Player on Choices in a Prisoner's Dilemma Game, Part II." *Journal of Abnormal and Social Psychology,* 67 (1963), 139-147.
578. _____., and J. W. Gaebelein. "Strategies of "Real" Opponents in Eliciting Cooperative Choice in a Prisoner's Dilemma Game." *Journal of Conflict Resolution,* 15 (1971), 157-166.
579. Blake, Robert R. "Psychology and the Crisis of Statemanship." *American Psychologist,* 14 (1959), 87-94.
580. Boehringer, G. H., et al. "Stirling: Destructive Application of Group Techniques to a Conflict." *Journal of Conflict Resolution,* 18:2 (June 1974), 257-275.
581. Bonham, Matthew G., et al. "Cognition and International Negotiation: The Historical Recovery of Discursive Space." *Cooperation and Conflict,* 22:1 (March 1987), 1-20.
582. Bonoma, Thomas V. "The Relative Efficacies of Escalation and Deescalation for Compliance-Gaining in Two Party Conflicts." *Social Behavior and Personality,* 2 (1974), 212-218.
583. Borah, L. A.,Jr. "The Effects of Threat in Bargaining: Critical and Experimental Analysis." *Journal of Abnormal and Social Psychology,* 66 (1963), 37-44.
584. Borgatta, M. L., and E. F. Borgatta. "Coalitions in Three-Person Groups." *Journal of Social Psychology,* 60 (1963), 319-326.
585. _____. "Power Structure and Coalitions in Three Person Groups." *Journal of Social Psychology,* 55 (1961), 287-300.

586. Brandstatter, H., G. Kette and J. Sageder. "Expectations, Attributions, and Behavior in Bargaining with Liked and Disliked Partners." In: R. Tietz, ed. *Aspiration Levels in Bargaining and Economic Decision Making.* Berlin: Springer-Verlag, 1983. pp. 136-152.
587. Breaugh, James A., and Richard J. Klimoski. "The Choice of a Group Spokesman in Bargaining: Member or Outsider?" *Organizational Behavior and Human Performance,* 19:2 (1977), 325-336.
588. _____. _____. and Mitchell B. Shapiro. "Third-Party Characteristics and Intergroup Conflict Resolution." *Psychological Reports,* 47:2 (October 1980), 447-451.
589. Brehmer, Berndt, and Kenneth R. Hammond. "Cognitive Factors in Interpersonal Conflict." In: D. Druckman, ed. *Negotiations: Social-Psychological Perspectives.* Beverly Hills, CA.: Sage, 1977. pp. 79-104.
590. Brockner, Joel, Jeffrey Z. Rubin and E. Lang. "Face-Saving and Entrapment." *Journal of Experimental Social Psychology,* 17 (1981), 68-79.
591. _____., et al. "Factors Affecting Entrapment in Escalating Conflicts: The Importance of Timing." *Journal of Research in Personality,* 16 (1982), 247-266.
592. _____. M. C. Shaw and Jeffrey Z. Rubin. "Factors Affecting Withdrawal from an Escalating Conflict: Quitting Before It's Too Late." *Journal of Experimental Social Psychology,* 15 (1979), 492-503.
593. Brohmer, B., et al. "A Cross-National Comparison of Cognitive Conflict." *Journal of Cross-Cultural Psychology,* 1 (1970), 5-20.
594. Brown, B. R. "The Effects of Need to Maintain Face in Interpersonal Bargaining." *Journal of Experimental Social Psychology,* 4 (1968), 107-122.
595. _____. "Face-Saving and Face-Restoration in Negotiation." In: D. Druckman, ed. *Negotiation: Social-Psychological Perspectives.* Beverly Hills, CA.: Sage, 1977. pp. 275-300.
596. _____. "Face-Saving Following Experimentally Induced Embarrassment." *Journal of Experimental Social Psychology,* 6 (1970), 255-271.
597. _____. "Saving Face." In: R. J. Lewicki and J. A. Litterer, eds. *Negotiation: Readings, Exercises, and Cases.* Homewood, IL.: Irwin, 1985. pp. 250-261.
598. Cann, Arnie, Steven J. Sherman and Roy Elkes. "Effects on Initial Size and Timing of a Second Request on Compliance: The Foot in the Door and the Door in the Face." *Journal of Personality and Social Psychology,* 32 (November 1975), 774-782.
599. Carnevale, Peter J. "Accountability of Group Representatives and Intergroup Relations." In: E. J. Lawler, ed. *Advances in Group Processes: Theory and Research, Vol. 2.* Greenwich, CT.: JAI Press, 1985. pp. 227-248.
600. _____., and Alice M. Isen. "Communication Processes in Bilateral Negotiation." Paper Presented at the *Meeting of the Academy of Management Proceedings,* held in 1983, in Dallas, TX. pp. 203-208.
601. _____. _____. "The Influence of Positive Affect and Visual Access on the Discovery of Integrative Solutions in Bilateral Negotiations." *Organizational Behavior and Human Decision Processes,* 37:1 (February 1986), 1-13.
602. _____. Dean G. Pruitt and S. D. Seilheinner. "Looking and Competing: Accountability and Visual Access in Integrative Bargaining." *Journal of Personality and Social Psychology,* 40:1 (January 1981), 111-120.
603. _____. _____. and S. D. Britton. "Looking Tough: The Negotiator Under Constituent Surveillance." *Personality and Social Psychology Bulletin,* 5 (1979), 118-121.
604. _____., and Edward J. Lawler. "Time Pressure and the Development of Integrative Agreements in Bilateral Negotiations." *Journal of Conflict Resolution,* 30 (December 1986), 636-659.

605. Carroll, John S., Max H. Bazerman and Robin Maury. "Negotiator Cognitions: A Descriptive Approach to Negotiators' Understanding of Their Opponents." *Organizational Behavior and Human Decision Processes*, 41:3 (June 1988), 352-370.
606. Cheney, John, Thomas Hardford and Leonard Solomon. "The Effects of Communicating Threats and Promises upon the Bargaining Process." *Journal of Conflict Resolution*, 16 (1972), 99-108.
607. Chertkoff, J. M., and S. L. Baird. "The Application of the Big Lie Technique and the Last Clear Chance Doctrine to Bargaining." *Journal of Personality and Social Psychology*, 20 (1971), 298-303.
608. _____. _____. "The Effects of Probability of Future Success on Coalition Formation." *Journal of Experimental Psychology*, 2 (1966), 265-277.
609. _____., and M. Cowley. "Opening Offer and Frequency of Concession on Bargaining Strategies." *Journal of Personality and Social Psychology*, 7 (1967), 181-187.
610. _____., and James K. Esser. "A Review of Experiments in Explicit Bargaining." *Journal of Experimental and Social Psychology*, 12 (September 1976), 464-486.
611. Cialdini, R. B., et al. "Reciprocal Concessions Procedure for Inducing Compliance: The Door-in-the-Face Technique." *Journal of Personality and Social Psychology*, 31 (1979), 12-24.
612. Clark, R. D., and L. B. Sechrest. "The Mandate Phenomenon." *Journal of Personality and Social Psychology*, 34 (1976), 1057-1061.
613. Cohen, Stephen, et al. "Evolving Intergroup Techniques for Conflict Resolution: An Israeli - Palestinian Pilot Workshop." *Journal of Social Issues*, 33:1 (1977), 165-188.
614. Cole, Steven G., and P. Nail. "Social-Learning vs. Direct Experience as Determinants of Aspiration Level and Bargaining Behavior." In: R. Tietz, ed. *Aspiration Levels in Bargaining and Economic Decision Making*. Berlin: Springer-Verlag, 1983. pp. 231-242.
615. Cottam, Martha L. "The Impact of Psychological Images on International Bargaining: The Case of Mexican Natural Gas." *Political Psychology*, 6:3 (September 1985), 413-440.
616. Crott, Helmut W., E. Kayser and Helmut Lamm. "The Effects of Information Exchange and Communications in an Asymmetrical Negotiation Situation." *European Journal of Social Psychology*, (1980), 149-163.
617. Crow, W. J., and R. C. Noel. "An Experiment in Simulated Historical Decision Making." In: M. G. Herman, ed. *A Psychological Examination of Political Leaders*. New York: Free Press, 1976. pp. 385-405.
618. Crowne, D. P. "Family Orientation, Level of Aspirations and Interpersonal Bargaining." *Journal of Personal and Social Psychology*, 3 (1966), 641-645.
619. Crumbaugh, C., and G. Evans. "Presentation Format, Other Person Strategies and Cooperative Behavior in the Prisoner's Dilemma." *Psychological Reports*, 20 (1967), 895-902.
620. Daniels, W. "Communication, Incentive and Structural Variables in Interpersonal Exchange and Negotiation." *Journal of Experimental Social Psychology*, 3 (1967), 47-74.
621. Day, R., and J. Day. "A Review of the Current State of Negotiated Order Theory." *Sociological Quarterly*, 18 (1977), 126-142.
622. Derakhshani, S. "Models of Negotiations - A Behavioral Assessment." In: H. Chesnut, et al. *Supplemental Ways for Improving International Stability*. Elmsford, NY.: Pergamon Press, 1986. pp. 179-182.

623. Deutsch, Morton. "Cooperation and Trust: Some Theoretical Notes." In: M. R. Jones, ed. *Nebraska Symposium on Motivation, 1962.* Lincoln, NB.: University of Nebraska Press, 1962. pp. 275-318.
624. _____. D. Canavan and Jeffrey Z. Rubin. "The Effects of Size of Conflict and Sex of Experimenter Upon Interpersonal Bargaining." *Journal of Experimental Social Psychology,* 7 (1971), 258-267.
625. _____., and Robert M. Krauss. "The Effects of Threat Upon Interpersonal Bargaining." *Journal of Abnormal and Social Psychology,* 61 (1980), 181-189.
626. _____. _____. "The Effects of Threat Upon Interpersonal Bargaining." In: R. A. Baron and R. M. Liebert, ed. *Human Social Behavior.* Homewood, IL.: The Dorsey Press, 1971. pp. 405-420.
627. _____. "Recurrent Themes in the Study of Social Conflict." *Journal of Social Issues,* 33:1 (1977), 222-225.
628. _____., et al. "Strategies of Inducing Cooperation: An Experimental Study." *Journal of Conflict Resolution,* 11 (1967), 345-360.
629. _____. "A Theoretical Perspective on Conflict and Conflict Resolution." In: D. J. D. Sandole and I. Sandole-Staroste, eds. *Conflict Management and Problem Solving.* London: Frances Pinter, 1987. pp. 38-49.
630. _____. "Trust and Suspicion." *Journal of Conflict Resolution,* 2 (1958), 265-279.
631. _____. "Trust, Trustworthiness, and the F-Scale." *Journal of Abnormal and Social Psychology,* 61 (1960), 138-140.
632. Doob, L. W., and W. J. Foltz. "The Belfast Workshop: An Application of a Group Technique to a Destructive Conflict." *Journal of Conflict Resolution,* 17:4 (1973), 237-256.
633. _____. "A Cyprus Workshop: An Exercise in Intervention Methodology." *Journal of Social Psychology,* 94 (1974), 161-178.
634. _____. "A Cyprus Workshop: Intervention Methodology During a Continuing Crisis." *Journal of Social Psychology,* 98 (1976), 143-144.
635. _____. W. J. Foltz and R. B. Stevens. "The Fermeda Workshop: A Different Approach to Border Conflicts in Eastern Africa." *Journal of Psychology,* 73 (1968), 249-266.
636. _____. _____. "The Impact of a Workshop of Grass Roots Leaders in Belfast." *Journal of Conflict Resolution,* 18:2 (June 1974), 237-256.
637. _____. "The Impact of the Fermeda Workshop on the Conflicts in the Horn of Africa." *International Journal of Group Tensions,* 1:1 (1971), 91-98.
638. _____. "The Analysis and Resolution of International Disputes." *Journal of Psychology,* 86 (1974), 316-326.
639. _____. "Fermeda Workshop: A Different Approach to Border Conflicts in Eastern Africa." *Mental Health Digest,* 2:3 (March 1970), 33-36.
640. Driver, M. J. "Individual Differences as Determinants of Aggression in the Inter-Nation Simulation." In: M. G. Hermann, ed. *A Psychological Examination of Political Leaders.* New York: Free Press, 1976. pp. 337-353.
641. Druckman, Daniel, and Kathleen Zechmeister. "Conflict of Interest and Value Dissensus." *Human Relations,* 23 (1970), 431-438.
642. _____. _____. "Conflict of Interest and Value Dissensus: Propositions in the Sociology of Conflict." *Human Relations,* 26 (1976), 449-466.
643. _____. Richard Rozelle and Kathleen Zechmeister. "Conflict of Interest and Value Dissensus: Two Perspectives." In: D. Druckman, ed. *Negotiations: Social-Psychological Perspectives.* Beverly Hills, CA.: Sage, 1977. pp. 105-132.

644. _____, and L. D. Ludwig. "Consensus and Evaluative Descriptions of One's Own Nation, Its Allies, and Its Enemies." *Journal of Social Psychology*, 81 (1970), 223-234.
645. _____. Kathleen Zechmeister and Daniel Solomon. "Determinants of Bargaining Behavior in a Bilateral Monopoly Situation: Opponent's Concession Rate and Relative Defensibility." *Behavioral Science*, 17 (1972), 514-531.
646. _____, and Thomas V. Bonoma. "Determinants of Bargaining Behavior in a Bilateral Monopoly Situation II: Opponent's Concession Rate and Similarity." *Behavioral Science*, 21 (1976), 252-262.
647. _____. "Dogmatism, Prenegotiation Experience and Simulated Group Representation as Determinants of Dyadic Behavior in a Bargaining Situation." *Journal of Personality and Social Psychology*, 6 (1967), 279-290.
648. _____. D. Karis and E. Douchin. "Information-Processing in Bargaining: Reactions to an Opponents Shift in Concession Strategy." In: R. Tietz, ed. *Aspiration Levels in Bargaining and Economic Decision Making*. Berlin: Springer-Verlag, 1983. pp. 153-169.
649. _____. "New Directions for a Social Psychology of Conflict." In: D. J. D. Sandole and I. Sandole-Staroste, eds. *Conflict Management and Problem Solving*. London: Frances Pinter, 1987. pp. 50-56.
650. _____. "On the Effects of Group Representation." *Journal of Personality and Social Psychology*, 18 (1971), 523-554.
651. _____. "The Person, Role and Situation in International Negotiations." In: M. G. Herman and T. W. Milburn, eds. *A Psychological Examination of Political Leaders*. New York: Free Press, 1976. pp. 409-456.
652. _____. "Prenegotiation Experience and Dyadic Conflict Resolution in a Bargaining Situation." *Journal of Experimental Social Psychology*, 4 (1968), 367-383.
653. _____., and Robert Mahoney. "Processes and Consequences of International Negotiations." *Journal of Social Issues*, 33:1 (1977), 60-87.
654. _____. "Social Psychological Approaches to the Study of Negotiations." In: D. Druckman, ed. *Negotiations: Social-Psychological Perspectives*. Beverly Hills, CA.: Sage, 1977. pp. 15-44.
655. _____. "Social Psychology and International Negotiations: Processes and Influences." In: R. F. Kidd and M. J. Saks, eds. *Advances in Applied Social Psychology, Vol. 2*. Hillsdale, NJ.: Lawrence Erlbaum, 1984. pp. 51-82.
656. _____. "The Influence of the Situation in Inter-Party Conflict." *Journal of Conflict Resolution*, 15 (1971), 523-554.
657. Duffy, John F., and Michael J. Kavanagh. "Video Tape Modeling of Negotiating Styles." *Northeast Peace Science Review*, 1 (1978), 160-170.
658. _____. _____. "Confounding the Creation of Social Forces: Laboratory Studies of Negotiation Behavior." *Journal of Conflict Resolution*, 27:4 (1983), 635-647.
659. Dugan, Maire A. "Intervenor Roles and Conflict Pathologies." In: D. J. D. Sandole and I. Sandole-Staroste, eds. *Conflict Management and Problem Solving*. London: Frances Pinter, 1987. pp. 57-61.
660. Eisenberg, M. A., and M. E. Patch. "Prominence as a Determinant of Bargaining Outcome." *Journal of Conflict Resolution*, 20:3 (1976), 523-538.
661. Emerson, R. M., and S. L. Messinger. "Micro-Politics of Trouble." *Social Problems*, 25 (December 1977), 121-134.
662. Esser, James K., and S. S. Komorita. "Reciprocity and Concession Making in Bargaining." *Journal of Personality and Social Psychology*, 31 (1975), 864-872.

663. Etheredge, Lloyd S. "Personality and Foreign Policy." *Psychology Today*, 8 (March 1975), 37-41.
664. ____. "Personality Effects on American Foreign Policy, 1898-1968: A Test of Interpersonal Generalization Theory." *America Political Science Review*, 72 (June 1978), 434-451.
665. Etzioni, Amitai. "Social Psychological Aspects of International Relations." In: G. Lindzey and E. Aronson, eds. *Handbook of Social Psychology*. Vol. 5. New York: Addison - Wesley, 1969. pp. 538-601.
666. Evans, G. "Effects of Unilateral Promise and Value of Rewards Upon Cooperation and Trust." *Journal of Abnormal and Social Psychology*, 69 (1964), 587-590.
667. ____., and C. Crumbaugh. "Effects of Prisoner's Dilemma Format on Cooperative Behavior." *Journal of Personality and Social Psychology*, 3 (1966), 486-488.
668. Faley, T., and J. T. Tedeschi. "Status and Reaction to Threats." *Journal of Personality and Social Psychology*, 17 (1971), 192-199.
669. Fells, R. E., and L. K. Savery. "Leadership as a Productive Strategy in Negotiation." *Leadership and Organization Development Journal*, 5:1 (1984), 21-24.
670. Fine, Gary A. "Negotiated Orders and Organizational Cultures." *Annual Review of Sociology*, 10 (1984), 239-262.
671. Fisher, Glen H. "Behavioral Science and the Foreign Affairs Specialist." *Foreign Area Research Horizons*, 4:6 (Nov 1971), 6-7.
672. Fisher, M. L. "Evaluating Negotiation Behavior and Results: Can We Identify What We Say We Know." *Catholic University Law Review*, 36:2 (1987), 395-453.
673. Fisher, Roger D. "Dealing with Conflict Among Individuals and Nations: Are There Common Principles?." *Psychoanalytic Inquiry*, 6:2 (1986), 143-153.
674. ____. "Negotiating Power: Getting and Using Influence." *American Behavioral Scientist*, 27:2 (November/December 1983), 149-166.
675. Foddy, Margaret. "Patterns of Gaze in Cooperation and Competitive Negotiation." *Human Relations*, 31:11 (1978), 925-938.
676. Ford, David L. "Effects of Personal Control Beliefs: An Explanatory Analysis on Bargaining Outcomes in Intergroup Negotiations." *Group and Organization Studies*, 8:1 (March 1983), 113-125.
677. Frank, Jerome D. "Psychological Aspects of International Negotiations." *American Journal of Psychotherapy*, 23:4 (1969), 569-583.
678. ____. "Psychological Aspects of Disarmament and International Negotiations." In: B. H. Weston, ed. *Toward Nuclear Disarmament and Global Security: A Search for Alternatives*. Boulder, CO.: Westview Press, 1984. pp. 324-336.
679. Frey, Robert L., and J. S. Adams. "The Negotiator's Dilemma: Simultaneous In-Group and Out-Group Conflict." *Journal of Experimental Psychology*, 8 (1972), 331-346.
680. Friedland, Nehemia. "Weakness as Strength: The Use and Misuse of a "My Hands Are Tied" Ploy in Bargaining." *Journal of Applied Social Psychology*, 13:5 (September - October 1983), 422-426.
681. Friedman, Myles I., and M. E. Jacks. "The Negative Effect of Group Cohesiveness on Intergroup Negotiation." *Journal of Social Issues*, 25:1 (1969), 181-194.
682. Froman, L. A., Jr., and M. D. Cohen. "Compromise and Logroll: Comparing the Efficiency of Two Bargaining Processes." *Behavioral Science*, 15 (1970), 180-183.

683. _____. _____. "Threats and Bargaining Efficiency." *Behavioral Science*, 14 (1969), 147-153.
684. Fry, William R. "The Effect of Dyad Machiavellianism and Visual Access on Integrative Bargaining Outcomes." *Personality and Social Psychology Bulletin*, 11 (March 1985), 51-62.
685. Gahagan, J. P., et al. "Patterns of Punishment and Reactions to Threats." *Journal of Social Psychology*, 80 (1970), 115-116.
686. Gallo, Philip S. "Effects of Increased Incentives Upon the Use of Threat in Bargaining." *Journal of Personality and Social Psychology*, 4 (1966), 14-21.
687. Garner, Katherine, and Morton Deutsch. "Cooperative Behavior in Dyads: Effects of Dissimilar Goal Orientations and Differing Expectations About the Partner." *Journal of Conflict Resolution*, 18:4 (December 1974), 634-645.
688. Geis, Florence. "Bargaining Tactics in the Con Game." In: R. Christie and F. L. Geis, eds. *Studies in Machiavellianism*. New York: Academic Press, 1970. pp. 130-160.
689. Gilkey, Roderick W., and Leonard Greenhalgh. "The Role of Personality in Successful Negotiating." *Negotiation Journal*, 2:3 (July 1986), 245-256.
690. Gladwin, T. N., and R. Kumar. "The Social Psychology of Crisis Bargaining: Toward a Contingency Model." *Columbia Journal of World Business*, 22 (Spring 1987), 23-31.
691. Gray, S. H. "Model Predictability in Bargaining." *Journal of Psychology*, 97 (November 1977), 171-178.
692. Greenhalgh, Leonard, Scott A. Neslin and Roderick W. Gilkey. "The Effects of Negotiator Preferences, Situational Power and Negotiator Personality on Outcomes of Business Negotiations." *Academy of Management Journal*, 28 (March 1985), 9-33.
693. _____. "Relationships in Negotiations." *Negotiation Journal*, 3:3 (July 1987), 235-244.
694. _____., and Scott A. Neslin. "Conjoint Analysis of Negotiator Preferences." *Journal of Conflict Resolution*, 25:2 (1981), 301-328.
695. Grigsby, D. W., and W. J. Bigoness. "Effects of Mediation and Alternative Forms of Arbitration on Bargaining Behavior - A Laboratory Study." *Journal of Applied Psychology*, 67 (1982), 549-554.
696. Gruder, C. L., and N. Rosen. "Effects of Intergroup Relations on Intergroup Bargaining." *International Journal of Group Tensions*, 1 (1971), 301-317.
697. _____. "Social Power in Interpersonal Negotiations." In: P. Swingle, ed. *The Structure of Conflict*. New York: Academic Press, 1970. pp. 111-154.
698. _____. "Relationship with Opponent and Partner in Mixed-Motive Bargaining." *Journal of Conflict Resolution*, 15:3 (1971), 403-416.
699. Gumpert, P., Morton Deutsch and Y. Epstein. "The Effect of Incentive Magnitude on Cooperation in the Prisoner's Dilemma Game." *Journal of Personality and Social Psychology*, 11 (1969), 66-69.
700. Haccoun, R. R., and R. J. Klimoski. "Negotiator Status and Accountability Source: A Study of Negotiator Behavior." *Organizational Behavior and Human Performance*, 14 (1975), 342-359.
701. Hagva, V. "Psychological Elements in International Mediation." *Revue Roumaine d'Etudes Internationales*, 3:13 (1971), 89-94.
702. Hamblin, Robert L. "Group Interaction During a Crisis." *Human Relations*, 11 (1958), 67-76.
703. _____. "Group Interaction During a Crisis." In: J. D. Singer, ed. *Human Behavior and International Relations: Contributions from the Social--Psychological Sciences*. Chicago, IL.: Rand McNally, 1965. pp. 220-230.

704. Hamilton, T., W. C. Swap and Jeffrey Z. Rubin. "Anticipated Third-Party Intervention: The Effects of Dependence and Personality." *Journal of Personality and Social Psychology,* 41 (1981), 1141-1152.
705. Hammond, Kenneth R., and Berndt Brehmer. "Quasi-Rationality and Distrust: Implications for International Conflict." In: L. Rapoport and S. Summers, eds. *Human Judgement and Social Interaction.* New York: Holt, Rinehart and Winston, 1973. pp. 338-392.
706. _____. "The Cognitive Side of Conflict: From Theory to Resolution of Policy Disputes." In: S. Oskamp, ed. *International Conflict and National Public Policy Issues.* Beverly Hills, CA.: Sage, 1985. pp. 233-254.
707. Hamner, W. C. "Effects of Bargaining Strategy and Pressure to Reach Agreement in a Stalemated Negotiation." *Journal of Personality and Social Psychology,* 30 (1974), 458-467.
708. _____., and D. L. Harnett. "The Effect of Information and Aspiration Level on Bargaining Behavior." *Journal of Experimental Psychology,* 11 (1975), 329-342.
709. _____. "The Influence of Structural, Individual and Strategic Differences." In: D. L. Harnett and L. L. Cummings, ed. *Bargaining Behavior: An International Study.* Houston, TX.: Dame Pubs, 1980. pp. 21-80.
710. _____., and Garry A. Yukl. "The Effectiveness of Different Offer Strategies in Bargaining." In: D. Druckman, ed. *Negotiations: Social-Psychological Perspectives.* Beverly Hills, CA.: Sage, 1977. pp. 137-160.
711. Hare, Paul, and David Naveh. "Creative Problem Solving: Camp David Summit, 1978." *Small Group Behavior,* 16:2 (May 1985), 123-138.
712. Harf, J. E. "A Model of Inter-Nation Conflict Resolution." *International Journal of Group Tensions,* 3:1 (1971), 91-122.
713. Harnett, D. L., L. L. Cummings and G. D. Hughes. "The Influence of Risk-Taking Propensity on Bargaining Behavior." *Behavioral Science,* 13 (1968), 91-101.
714. _____. _____. and W. C. Hamner. "Personality Bargaining Style and Payoff in International Bargaining." *Sociometry,* 36 (1973), 325-345.
715. Harsanyi, John C. "Measurement of Social Power in In-Person Reciprocal Power Situations." *Behavioral Science,* 7 (1962), 81-91.
716. _____. "Measurement of Social Power, Opportunity Costs and the Theory of Two-Person Bargaining Games." In: J. D. Singer, ed. *Human Behavior and International Politics: Contributions from the Social-Psychological Sciences.* Chicago, IL.: Rand McNally, 1965. pp. 378-385.
717. Harvey, Jerry. "Some Dynamics of Intergroup Competition." In: R. J. Lewicki and J. A. Litterer, eds. *Negotiation: Readings, Exercises, and Cases.* Homewood, IL.: Irwin, 1985. pp. 53-60.
718. Heckathorn, Douglas. "A Paradigm for Bargaining and a Test of Two Bargaining Models." *Behavioral Science,* 23:2 (1978), 73-85.
719. _____. "A Unified Model for Bargaining and Conflict." *Behavioral Science,* 25:4 (July 1980), 261-289.
720. Herman, Charles F., and Linda P. Brady. "Alternative Models of International Crisis Behavior." In: C. F. Herman, ed. *International Crisis: Insights from Behavioral Research.* New York: Free Press, 1972. pp. 281-320.
721. Hermann, Margaret G., and Nathan Kogan. "Effects of Negotiator's Personalities on Negotiating Behavior." In: D. Druckman, ed. *Negotiations: Social-Psychological Perspectives.* Beverly Hills, CA.: Sage, 1977. pp. 247-274.
722. _____. _____. "Negotiation in Leader and Delegate Groups." *Journal of Conflict Resolution,* 7:3 (1968), 332-344.
723. Hessel, Marek. "Mutual Perceptions in Bargaining: A Quantitative Approach." *Behavioral Science,* 29:4 (October 1984), 221-232.

724. Hickman, James L., and James L. Garrison. "Psychological Principles of Citizen Diplomacy." In: D. D. Newsom, ed. *Private Diplomacy with the Soviet Union*. Lanham, MD.: University Press of America, 1987. pp. 129-144.
725. Hiltrop, Jean M., and Jeffrey Z. Rubin. "Effects of Intervention Mode and Conflict of Interest on Dispute Resolution." *Journal of Personality and Social Psychology*, 42 (1982), 665-672.
726. ___. ___. "Position Loss and Image in Bargaining." *Journal of Conflict Resolution*, 25:3 (1981), 521-534.
727. Hoffman, P. J., L. Festinger and D. Lawrence. "Tendencies Toward Group Comparability in Competitive Bargaining." *Human Relations*, 7 (1954), 141-159.
728. Holmes, J. G., W. F. Thorp and L. H. Strickland. "The Effects of Prenegotiation Expectations on the Distributive Bargaining Process." *Journal of Experimental Social Psychology*, 7 (1971), 582-599.
729. Holsti, K. J. "Resolving International Conflicts: A Taxonomy of Behavior and Some Figures and Procedures." *Journal of Conflict Resolution*, 10:3 (1966), 272-296.
730. ___. "Resolving International Conflicts: A Taxonomy of Behavior and Some Figures on Procedures." In: L. Kriesberg, ed. *Social Processes in International Relations*. New York: Wiley, 1968. pp. 540-564.
731. Holsti, Ole R. "Perceptions of Time, Perceptions of Alternatives, and Patterns of Communication as Factors in Crisis Decision-Making." *Peace Research Society Papers*, 3 (1965), 79-120.
732. ___. "Theories of Crisis Decision Making." In: P. G. Lauren, ed. *Diplomacy*. New York: The Free Press, 1979. pp. 99-136.
733. Hopmann, P. Terrence, and Charles Walcott. "The Impact of External Stresses and Tensions on Negotiations." In: D. Druckman, ed. *Negotiations: Social-Psychological Perspectives*. Beverly Hills, CA.: Sage, 1977. pp. 301-324.
734. Horai, J., and J. T. Tedeschi. "Effects of Credibility and Magnitude of Punishment on Compliance to Threats." *Journal of Personality and Social Psychology*, 12 (1969), 164-169.
735. Hornstein, H. A. "The Effects of Different Magnitudes of Threat Upon Interpersonal Bargaining." *Journal of Experimental Social Psychology*, 1 (1965), 282-293.
736. ___., and D. W. Johnson. "The Effects of Process Analysis and Ties to His Group Upon a Negotiator's Attitudes Toward the Outcomes of Negotiations." *Journal of Applied Behavioral Science*, 2 (1966), 449-463.
737. Houlden, P., et al. "Preference for Models of Dispute Resolution as a Function of Process and Decision Control." *Journal of Experimental and Social Psychology*, 14 (January 1978), 13-30.
738. Huber, Vandra L., and Margaret A. Neale. "Effects of Cognitive Heuristics and Goals on Negotiator Performance and Subsequent Goal Setting." *Organizational Behavior and Human Decision Processes*, 38:3 (December 1986), 342-365.
739. ___. ___. "Effects of Self and Competitor Goals on Performance in an Independent Bargaining Task." *Journal of Applied Psychology*, 72 (May 1987), 197-203.
740. Janis, Irving L. "Decisional Conflicts: A Theoretical Analysis." *Journal of Conflict Resolution*, 3:1 (March 1959), 6-27.
741. Jefferson, Gail. "What is a 'Niem'?" *Sociology*, 12:1 (January 1978), 135-139.
742. Jensen, Lloyd. "Military Capabilities and Bargaining Behavior." *Journal of Conflict Resolution*, 9:2 (1965), 155-163.

743. Jervis, Robert. "Hypotheses on Misperception." *World Politics*, 20 (1968), 454-479.
744. _____. "Hypotheses on Misperception." In: J. Rosenau, ed. *International Politics and Foreign Policy*. New York: Free Press, 1969. pp. 239-254.
745. Johnson, David W., Kenneth McCarthy and Thomas Allen. "Congruent and Contradictory Verbal and Nonverbal Communications of Cooperativeness and Competitiveness in Negotiations." *Communication Research*, 3:3 (July 1976), 275-292.
746. Jönsson, Christer. "A Cognitive Approach to International Negotiations." *European Journal of Political Research*, 11:2 (1983), 139-150.
747. Joseph, M. L., and R. H. Willis. "An Experimental Analog to Two-Party Bargaining." *Behavioral Science*, 8 (1963), 117-127.
748. Kahan, James P. "Effects of Level of Aspiration on an Experimental Bargaining Situation." *Journal of Personality and Social Psychology*, 8 (1968), 154-159.
749. Kahn, A. S., and J. W. Kohls. "Determinants of Toughness in Dyadic Bargaining." *Sociometry*, 35 (1972), 305-315.
750. Kaplowitz, Noel. "Psychological Dimensions of the Middle East Conflict: Policy Implications." *Journal of Conflict Resolution*, 20:2 (1976), 279-318.
751. Kee, Herbert W., and Robert E. Knox. "Conceptual and Methodological Considerations in the Study of Trust and Suspicion." *Journal of Conflict Resolution*, 14:3 (September 1970), 357-366.
752. Kelley, Harold H., and D. P. Scheinitzki. "Bargaining." In: C. G. McClintock, ed. *Experimental Social Psychology*. New York: Holt, Rinehart and Winston, 1972. pp. 298-337.
753. _____. "A Comparative Experimental Study of Negotiation Behavior." *Journal of Personality and Social Psychology*, 16 (1970), 411-438.
754. _____., et al. "The Development of Cooperation in the 'Minimal Social Situation'." *Psychological Monographs, No. 538.*, 76:19 (1962), 1-19.
755. _____., and A. J. Stahelski. "Errors in Perception of Intentions in a Mixed-Motive Game." *Journal of Experimental Social Psychology*, 16 (1970), 379-400.
756. _____. "Experimental Studies of Threats in International Negotiations." *Journal of Conflict Resolution*, 9:1 (1965), 79-105.
757. _____. L. L. Beckman and C. S. Fisher. "Negotiating the Division of Reward Under Incomplete Information." *Journal of Experimental Social Psychology*, 3 (1967), 361-398.
758. _____., and A. J. Stahelski. "Social Interaction Basis of Cooperators' and Competitors' Beliefs About Others." *Journal of Personality and Social Psychology*, 16 (1970), 66-91.
759. _____. "The Inference if Intentions from Moves in the Prisoner's Dilemma Game." *Journal of Experimental Social Psychology*, 7 (1970), 401-419.
760. Kelman, Herbert C. "International Interchanges: Some Contributions from Theories of Attitude Change." *Studies in Comparative International Development*, 10:1 (Spring 1975), 83-99.
761. _____. "Israelis and Palestinians: Psychological Prerequisites for Mutual Acceptance." *International Security*, 5:1 (1978), 162-186.
762. _____. "Overcoming the Psychological Barrier: An Analysis of the Egyptian-Israeli Peace Process." *Negotiation Journal*, 1:3 (July 1985), 213-234.
763. _____. "The Political Psychology of the Israeli-Palestinian Conflict - How Can We Overcome the Barriers to a Negotiated Solution?" *Political Psychology*, 8:3 (September 1987), 347-364.

764. _____. "The Problem-Solving Workshop: A Social-Psychological Contribution to the Resolution of International Conflicts." *Journal of Peace Research,* 13 (1976), 79-90.
765. _____. "The Problem-Solving Workshop in Conflict Resolution." In: A. L. Merritt, ed. *Communication in International Politics.* Hobson, IL.: University of Illinois Press, 1972. pp. 168-204.
766. _____., and S. P. Cohen. "Reduction in International Conflict: An International Approach." In: W. G. Austin and W. Worchel, eds. *The Social Psychology of Intergroup Relations.* Monterey, CA.: Brooks, Cole, 1979. pp. 288-303.
767. _____. "Societal, Attitudinal and Structural Factors in International Relations." *Journal of Social Issues,* 11:1 (1955), 42-56.
768. Kilmann, R. H., and K. W. Thomas. "Developing a Forced-Choice Measure of Conflict-Handling Behavior: The MODE Instrument." *Educational and Psychological Measurement,* 37 (1977), 309-325.
769. Kimmel, M. J., et al. "Effects of Trust, Aspiration and Gender on Negotiation Tactics." *Journal of Personality and Social Psychology,* 38:1 (1980), 9-22.
770. Kinder, D., and J. Weiss. "In Lieu of Rationality: Psychological Perspectives on Foreign-Policy Decision Making." *Journal of Conflict Resolution,* 22 (1978), 707-735.
771. Klauss, R. "Structural and Attitudinal Factors in Interpersonal Bargaining." *Journal of Experimental Social Psychology,* 2 (1966), 42-55.
772. Kleinke, C., and P. D. Pohlan. "Effective and Emotional Responses as a Function of Other Person's Gaze and Cooperativeness in Two Person Games." *Journal of Personality and Social Psychology,* 17 (1971), 308-313.
773. Klimoski, Richard J., and Ronald A. Ash. "Accountability and Negotiation Behavior." *Organizational Behavior and Human Performance,* 11 (1974), 409-425.
774. _____. "The Effects of Intragroup Forces on Intergroup Conflict Resolution." *Organizational Behavior and Human Performance,* 8 (1972), 363-383.
775. _____., and R. R. Haccoun. "Negotiator Status and Accountability Sources: A Study of Negotiator Behavior." *Organizational Behavior and Human Performance,* 14 (1975), 342-359.
776. Kogan, Nathan, Helmut Lamm and G. Trommsdorff. "Negotiation Constraints in the Risk-Taking Domain: Effects of Being Observed by Partners of Higher or Lower Status." *Journal of Personality and Social Psychology,* 23 (1972), 143-156.
777. Komorita, S. S., and A. R. Brenner. "Bargaining and Concession-Making Under Bilateral Monopoly." *Journal of Personality and Social Psychology,* 9 (May 1968), 15-20.
778. _____., and C. E. Miller. "Bargaining Strength as a Function of Coalition Alternatives." *Journal of Personality and Social Psychology,* 51 (August 1986), 325-332.
779. _____., and J. M. Chertkoff. "A Bargaining Theory of Coalition Formation." *Psychological Review,* 80 (1973), 149-162.
780. _____., and J. Mechling. "Betrayal and Reconciliation in a Two Person Game." *Journal of Personality and Social Psychology,* 6 (1967), 349-353.
781. _____. "Concession-Making and Conflict Resolution." *Journal of Conflict Resolution,* 17 (December 1973), 745-762.
782. _____., and D. A. Kravitz. "Effects of Alternatives in Bargaining." *Journal of Experimental Social Psychology,* 15 (March 1979), 147-157.

783. _____. R. Lange and T. Hamilton. "The Effects of Level of Aspiration in Coalition Bargaining." In: R. Tietz, ed. *Aspiration Levels in Bargaining and Economic Decision Making.* Berlin: Springer-Verlag, 1983. pp. 291-305.
784. _____., and M. Barnes. "Effects of Pressures to Reach Agreement in Bargaining." *Journal of Personality and Social Psychology,* 13 (1969), 245-252.
785. _____., and James K. Esser. "Frequency of Reciprocated Concessions in Bargaining." *Journal of Personality and Social Psychology,* 32 (October 1975), 699-705.
786. _____. "Negotiating from Strength and the Concept of Bargaining Strength." *Journal for the Theory of Social Behavior,* 7:1 (1977), 49-69.
787. _____., and C. William Lupworth. "Alternative Choices in Social Dilemmas." *Journal of Conflict Resolution,* 26:4 (December 1982), 642-708.
788. _____. "Cooperative Choice in a Prisoner's Dilemma Game." *Journal of Personality and Social Psychology,* 2 (1965), 741-745.
789. _____. J. P. Sheposh and L. S. Braver. "Power, the Use of Power and Cooperative Choice in a Two-Person Game." *Journal of Personality and Social Psychology,* 8 (1968), 134-142.
790. _____., and James K. Esser. "Frequency of Reciprocated Concessions in Bargaining." *Journal of Personality and Social Psychology,* 32 (1975), 699-705.
791. _____., and C. E. Miller. "Changes in Outcomes in Coalition Bargaining." *Journal of Personality and Social Psychology,* 51 (1986), 721-729.
792. Krauss, Robert M., and Morton Deutsch. "Communication in International Bargaining." *Journal of Personality and Social Change,* 4 (1966), 572-577.
793. _____. "Structural and Attitudinal Factors in Interpersonal Bargaining." *Journal of Experimental Social Psychology,* 2 (1966), 42-55.
794. Kriesberg, Louis. "Social Theory and the De-Escalation of International Conflict." *Sociological Review,* 32:3 (August 1984), 471-491.
795. _____. "Clinical Sociology and Preventing Nuclear War." *Clinical Sociology Review,* (August 1986), 91-106.
796. Kuhlman, D. M., and A. F. J. Marshello. "Individual Differences in Game Motivation as Moderators of Preprogrammed Strategy Effects in Prisoner's Dilemma." *Journal of Personality and Social Psychology,* 32 (1975), 922-931.
797. Kuhn, Alfred. "Bargaining Power in Transaction: Basic Model of Interpersonal Relationships." *American Journal of Economics and Sociology,* 23:1 (1964), 49-63.
798. Lacy, William S. B. "Assumptions of Human Nature, and Initial Expectations and Behavior as Mediators of Sex Effects in Prisoner's Dilemma Research." *Journal of Conflict Resolution,* 22:2 (June 1978), 269-281.
799. Lamm, Helmut, and E. Kayser. "Analysis of Negotiation Concerning the Allocation of Jointly Produced Profit or Loss-Roles of Justice Norms, Politeness, Profit Maximization and Tactics." *International Journal of Group Tensions,* 8:1-2 (1978), 64-80.
800. _____., and C. Sauer. "Discussion-Induced Shift Towards Higher Demands in Negotiation." *European Journal of Social Psychology,* 4 (1974), 85-88.
801. _____. "Dyadic Negotiations Under Asymmetric Conditions: Comparing the Performance of the Uninformed and of the Informed Party." *European Journal of Social Psychology,* 6:2 (1976), 255-259.
802. _____. E. Kayser and Helmut W. Crott. "The Effects of Information Exchange and Communication in an Asymmetrical Negotiation Situation." *European Journal of Social Psychology,* 10:2 (1980), 149-163.

803. _____. "Group-Related Influences on Negotiation Behavior: Two-Person Negotiation as a Function of Representation and Election." In: H. Sauermann, ed. *Bargaining Behavior.* Tübingen: Mohr, 1978. pp. 284-309.
804. _____., and E. Rosch. "Information and Competitiveness of Incentive Structure as Factors in Two Person Negotiation." *European Journal of Social Psychology,* 2 (1972), 459-462.
805. _____. "Intragroup Effects on Intergroup Negotiations." *European Journal of Social Psychology,* 3 (1973), 179-192.
806. _____., and Nathan Kogan. "Risk-Taking in the Context of Intergroup Negotiations." *Journal of Experimental Social Psychology,* 6 (1970), 357-363.
807. _____. "A Review of Our Research on Group Polarization: 11 Experiments on the Effects of Group Discussion on Risk Acceptance, Probability Estimation, and Negotiation Positions." *Psychological Reports,* 62:3 (1988), 807-813.
808. Larson, Deborah W. "The Psychology of Reciprocity in International Relations." *Negotiation Journal,* 4:3 (July 1988), 281-301.
809. Latour, Stephen, et al. "Some Determinants of Preference for Modes of Conflict Resolution." *Journal of Conflict Resolution,* 20:2 (1976), 319-356.
810. Laue, James H. "Getting to the Table." *Clinical Sociology Newsletter,* 8:3 (Summer 1986), 6-7.
811. Lave, Lester B. "Factors Affecting Cooperation in the Prisoner's Dilemma Game." *Behavioral Science,* 10 (1965), 26-38.
812. Lawler, Edward J., and B. K. MacMurray. "Bargaining Toughness: A Qualification of Level of Aspiration and Reciprocity Hypotheses." *Journal of Applied Social Psychology,* 10 (1980), 416-430.
813. _____. "Bilateral Deterrence and Conflict Spiral: A Theoretical Analysis." In: E. J. Lawler, ed. *Advances in Group Processes. Vol 3.* Greenwich, CT.: JAI Press, 1986. pp. 107-130.
814. Leung, K. "Some Determinants of Reactions to Procedural Models for Conflict Resolution: A Cross National Study." *Journal of Personality and Social Psychology,* 53 (November 1987), 898-908.
815. _____. "Some Determinants of Conflict Avoidance." *Journal of Cross-Cultural Psychology,* 19:1 (1988), 125-136.
816. Lewicki, Roy J. "Lying and Deception: A Behavioral Model." In: M. H. Bazerman and R. J. Lewicki, eds. *Negotiating in Organizations.* Beverly Hills, CA.: Sage, 1983. pp. 68-90.
817. Lewis, S. A., and W. R. Fry. "Effects of Visual Access and Orientation on the Discovery of Integrative Bargaining Alternatives." *Organizational Behavior and Human Performance,* 20 (1977), 75-92.
818. Lieberman, B. "I-Trust: A Notion of Trust in Three-Person Games and International Affairs." *Journal of Conflict Resolution,* 8 (1964), 271-280.
819. _____. "Human Behavior in a Strictly Determined 3x3 Matrix Game." *Behavioral Science,* 5 (1960), 317-322.
820. Liebert, Robert M., et al. "The Effects of Information and Magnitude of Initial Offer in Interpersonal Negotiation." *Journal of Experimental Social Psychology,* 4 (1968), 431-441.
821. _____., et al. "The Effects of Information and Magnitude of Initial Offer on Interpersonal Negotiations." In: R. A. Baron and R. M. Liebert, eds. *Human Social Behavior.* Homewood, IL.: The Dorsey Press, 1971. pp. 434-443.
822. Liebrand, Wim B. G., et al. "Value Orientation and Conformity: A Study Using Three Types of Social Dilemma Games." *Journal of Conflict Resolution,* 30:1 (March 1986), 77-98.

Psychological Aspects

823. Lifshitz, Michaela N. "Internal-External Locus of Control and Negotiation." In: H. B. Pepinsky and M. J. Patton, eds. *The Psychological Experiment: A Practical Accomplishment.* New York: Pergamon Press, 1971. pp. 89-112.
824. Lind, E. A., et al. "Procedure and Outcome Effects on Reactions to Abjudicated Resolutions of Conflict of Interest." *Journal of Personality and Social Psychology,* 39:4 (1980), 643-653.
825. Lindskold, S., and R. Bennett. "Attributing Trust and Conciliatory Intent from Coercive Power Capability." *Journal of Personality and Social Psychology,* 28 (1973), 180-186.
826. _____., et al. "Developmental Aspects of Reaction to Positive Inducements." *Developmental Psychology,* 3 (1970), 277-284.
827. _____., and M. G. Collins. "Inducing Cooperation by Groups and Individuals: Applying Osgood's GRIT Strategy." *Journal of Conflict Resolution,* 22 (1978), 678-690.
828. _____., et al. "Reward Power and Bilateral Communication in Conflict Resolution." *Psychonomic Science,* 23 (1971), 415-416.
829. _____., and M. L. Finch. "Styles in Announcing Conciliation." *Journal of Conflict Resolution,* 25:1 (1981), 145-155.
830. _____. "Trust Development, the GRIT Proposal, and the Effect of Conciliatory Acts on Conflict and Cooperation." *Psychology Bulletin,* 85 (1978), 772-793.
831. _____. "Conciliation with Simultaneous or Sequential Interaction: Variations in Trustworthiness and Vulnerability in Prisoner's Dilemma." *Journal of Conflict Resolution,* 23:4 (December 1979), 704-714.
832. Lindskold, Svenn, Thomas V. Bonoma and James T. Tedeschi. "Relative Costs and Reactions of Threats." *Psychonomic Science,* 15 (1969), 303-304.
833. _____., and James T. Tedeschi. "Reward Power and Attraction in Interpersonal Conflict." *Psychonomic Science,* 22 (1971), 211-213.
834. _____., and Gyuseog Han. "GRIT as a Foundation for Integrative Bargaining." *Personality and Social Psychology Bulletin,* 14:2 (June 1988), 335-345.
835. Lipe, Dewey. "Prior Arousal and Disconfirmation of Expectancy in Negotiation." In: H. B. Pepinski and M. J. Patton, eds. *The Psychological Experiment: A Practical Accomplishment.* New York: Pergamon Press, 1971. pp. 113-130.
836. Lockhart, Charles. "Flexibility and Commitment in International Conflicts." *International Studies Quarterly,* 22:4 (1978), 545-568.
837. Loomis, J. L. "Communication, the Development of Trust and Cooperative Behavior." *Human Relations,* 12 (1959), 305-315.
838. Magenau, J. M., and Dean G. Pruitt. "The Social Psychology of Bargaining: A Theoretical Synthesis." In: G. M. Stephenson and C. J. Brotherton, eds. *Industrial Relations: A Social Psychological Approach.* New York: Wiley, 1978. pp. 181-210.
839. Malcolm, D., and B. Lieberman. "The Behavior of Responsive Individuals Playing a Two-Person Zero-Sum Game Requiring the Use of Mixed Strategies." *Psychonomic Games,* 2 (1965), 373-374.
840. Maoz, Zeev, and Dan S. Felsenthal. "Self-Binding Commitment, the Inducement of Trust, Social Choice, and the Theory of International Cooperation." *International Studies Quarterly,* 31:2 (June), 177-200.
841. Marlowe, D., K. J. Gergen and A. N. Doob. "Opponent's Personality, Expectation of Social Interaction and Interpersonal Bargaining." *Journal of Personality and Social Psychology,* 3 (1966), 206-213.
842. Matthews, Byron A., William M. Kordonski and Eliot Shimoff. "Temptation and the Maintenance of Trust; Effects of Bilateral Punishment and Capability." *Journal of Conflict Resolution,* 27:2 (June 1983), 255-278.

843. Mazur, Allan. "A Non-Rational Approach to Theories of Conflict and Coalitions." *Journal of Conflict Resolution,* 12:2 (1968), 196-205.
844. McClintock, Charles G., and S. P. McNeel. "Reward Level and Game Playing Behavior." *Journal of Conflict Resolution,* 10 (1966), 98-102.
845. _____. "Social Motivation in Settings of Outcome Interdependence." In: D. Druckman, ed. *Negotiations: Social-Psychological Perspectives.* Beverly Hills, CA.: Sage, 1977. pp. 49-78.
846. _____., et al. "Internationalism-Isolationism, Strategy of the Other Player and Two Person Game Behavior." *Journal of Abnormal and Social Psychology,* 67 (December 1963), 631-636.
847. _____. Frank J. Stech and J. K. Beggan. "The Effects of Commitment to Threats and Promises Upon Bargaining Behavior and Outcomes." *European Journal of Social Psychology,* 17:4 (October-December 1987), 447-464.
848. _____. Frank J. Steach and Linda J. Keil. "The Influence of Communication Upon Bargaining." In P. B. Paulus, ed. *Basic Group Processes,*
849. McGillicuddy, N. B., Dean G. Pruitt and Helena Syna. "Perceptions of Firmness and Strength in Negotiations." *Personality and Social Psychology Bulletin,* 10:3 (September 1984), 402-409.
850. McGrath, J. E., and N. J. Vidmar. "Forces Affecting Success in Negotiation Groups." *Behavioral Sciences,* 15:2 (1970), 154-163.
851. _____., and J. W. Julian. "Interaction Process and Task Outcome in Experimentally Created Negotiation Groups." *Journal of Psychological Studies,* 14 (1963), 117-138.
852. _____. "A Social Psychological Approach to the Study of Negotiation." In: R. V. Bowers, ed. *Studies on Behavior in Organizations: A Research Symposium.* Athens, GA.: University of Georgia Press, 1966. pp. 101-134.
853. Mese, L. A. "Equity in Bilateral Bargaining." *Journal of Personality and Social Psychology,* 17 (1971), 287-291.
854. Michener, H. A., and E. D. Cohen. "Effects of Punishment Magnitude in the Bilateral Threat Situation: Evidence for the Deterrence Hypothesis." *Journal of Personality and Social Psychology,* 26 (1973), 427-438.
855. _____., et al. "Factors Affecting Concession Rate and Threat Usage in Bilateral Conflict." *Sociometry,* 38 (1975), 62-80.
856. _____. E. J. Lawler and S. B. Badirach. "Perception of Power in Conflict Situations." *Journal of Personality and Social Psychology,* 28 (1973), 155-162.
857. _____. J. A. Fleishman and J. J. Vaske. "A Test of the Bargaining Theory of Coalition Formation in Four-Person Groups." *Journal of Personality and Social Psychology,* 34 (1976), 1114-1126.
858. _____. J. Griffith and R. L. Palmer. "Threat Potential and Rule Enforceability as Sources of Normative Emergence in a Bargaining Situation." *Journal of Personality and Social Psychology,* 20 (1971), 230-239.
859. Miller, G. H., and S. W. Pyke. "Sex, Matrix Variations, and Perceived Personality Effects in Mixed Motive Games." *Journal of Conflict Resolution,* 17:2 (June 1973), 335-350.
860. Miller, Ralph R. "No Play, A Means of Conflict Resolution." *Journal of Personality and Social Psychology,* 6 (June 1967), 150-156.
861. Mitchell, Ted J., and Roger Heeler. "Toward a Theory of Acceptable Outcomes." *Behavioral Science,* 26:2 (April 1981), 163-176.
862. Mitchell, Terence R. "Review and Evaluation of Research Studies on Negotiation Behavior." *Journal of Occupational Behavior,* 6:1 (1985), 85-91.
863. Mogy, R. B., and Dean G. Pruitt. "The Effects of a Threatener's Enforcement Costs on Threat Credibility and Compliance." *Journal of Personality and Social Psychology,* 29 (1974), 173-180.

864. Molander, Peter. "The Optimal Level of Generosity in a Selfish, Uncertain Environment." *Journal of Conflict Resolution,* 29:4 (December 1985), 611-618.
865. Moore, Sally F. "Dividing the Pot of Gold: Social and Symbolic Elements in an Instrumental Negotiation." *Negotiation Journal,* 1:1 (1985), 29-43.
866. Morgan, W. R., and J. Sawyer. "Bargaining, Expectations and the Preference for Equality over Equity." *Journal of Personality and Social Psychology,* 6 (1967), 139-149.
867. Morley, Ian E. "Formality in Experimental Negotiations: A Validation Study." *British Journal of Psychology,* 61 (1970), 383-384.
868. _____. "Preparation for Negotiation: Conflict, Commitment, Choice." In: H. Brandstatter, et al. *Group Decision Making.* New York: Academic Press, 1982. pp. 387-419.
869. _____., and G. M. Stephenson. "Strength of Case, Communication Systems and the Outcomes of Simulated Negotiations: Some Special Social Psychological Aspects of Bargaining." *Industrial Relations Journal,* 1 (1970), 19-20.
870. Morrison, Bruce J., et al. "The Effect of Electrical Shock and Warning on Cooperation in a Non-Zero-Sum Game." *Journal of Conflict Resolution,* 15:1 (March 1971), 105-108.
871. Mugny, Gabriel. "Negotiations, Image of the Other and the Process of Minority Influence." *European Journal of Social Psychology,* 5:2 (1975), 209-228.
872. Muney, B. F., and Morton Deutsch. "The Effects of Role-Reversal During the Discussion of Opposing Viewpoints." *Journal of Conflict Resolution,* 12 (1968), 345-356.
873. Murdoch, P. "Exploitation-Accommodation and Social Responsibility in a Bargaining Game." *Journal of Personality,* 36 (1968), 440-453.
874. Murnighan, J. K., and E. Szajkowski. "Coalition Bargaining in Four Games That Include a Veto Player." *Journal of Personality and Social Psychology,* 37 (1979), 1933-1946.
875. Myers, A. E., and F. P. King. "Experience as an "Instructional Set" in Negotiation." *Journal of Social Psychology,* 68 (1966), 331-345.
876. Nardin, T. "Communication and the Effects of Threats in Strategic Interaction." *Peace Research Society Papers,* 9 (1968), 69-85.
877. Neale, Margaret A., and Max H. Bazerman. "The Effects of Framing and Negotiator Overconfidence on Bargaining Behaviors and Outcomes." *Academy of Management Journal,* 28 (March 1985), 34-49.
878. _____. "The Effects of Negotiation and Arbitration Cost Salience on Bargainer Behavior: The Role of the Arbitration and Constituency on Negotiator Judgment." *Organizational Behavior & Human Performance,* 34:1 (1984), 97-111.
879. _____., and Gregory B. Northcraft. "Experts, Amateurs and Refrigerators: Comparing Expert and Amateur Negotiators in a Novel Task." *Organizational Behavior and Human Decision Processes,* 38:3 (December 1986), 305-317.
880. _____. Vandra L. Huber and Gregory B. Northcraft. "The Framing of Negotiations: Contextual Versus Task Frames." *Organizational Behavior and Human Decision Processes,* 39:2 (April 1987), 228-241.
881. _____., and Max H. Bazerman. "Perspectives for Understanding Negotiation: Viewing Negotiation as a Judgmental Process." *Journal of Conflict Resolution,* 29:1 (March 1985), 33-55.
882. Nemeth, C. "Bargaining and Reciprocity." *Psychological Review,* 74 (1970), 297-308.

883. _____. "A Critical Analysis of Research Using the Prisoner's Dilemma Paradigm for the Study of Bargaining." In: L. Berkowitz, ed. *Advances in Experimental Social Psychology. Vol. 6.* New York: Academic Press, 1972. pp. 203-234.
884. Newcomb, T. M. "Communicative Behavior." In: R. Young, ed. *Approaches to the Study of Politics.* Evanston, IL.: Northwestern University Press, 1958. pp. 244-264.
885. Ofshe, Richard, and S. L. Ofshe. "Choice Behavior in Coalition Games." *Behavioral Science,* 15 (1970), 337-349.
886. Oliver, Pamela. "Rewards and Punishment as Selective Incentives." *Journal of Conflict Resolution,* 28:1 (March 1984), 123-148.
887. Olivia, T. A., and T. L. Leap. "Taxonomy of Bargaining Models." *Human Relations,* 34:11 (November 1981), 935-946.
888. Oskamp, Stuart. "Introduction: Social Psychology, International Affairs, and Public Policy." In: S. Oskamp, ed. *International Conflict and National Public Policy Issues.* Beverly Hills, CA.: Sage, 1985. pp. 7-18.
889. _____., and C. Kleinke. "Amount of Reward as a Variable in the Prisoner's Dilemma Game." *Journal of Personality and Social Psychology,* 16 (1970), 133-140.
890. _____. "Effects of Programmed Initial Strategies in a Prisoner's Dilemma Game." *Psychonomic Science,* 19 (1970), 195-196.
891. _____. "Effects of Programmed Strategies on Cooperation in Prisoner's Dilemma and Other Mixed Games." *Journal of Conflict Resolution,* 15 (1971), 225-259.
892. _____. "Comparison of Sequential and Simultaneous Responding, Matrix, and Strategy Variables in a Prisoner's Dilemma Game." *Journal of Conflict Resolution,* 18:1 (March 1974), 107-116.
893. Overstreet, R. E. "Social Exchange in a Three-Person Game." *Journal of Conflict Resolution.,* 16:1 (March 1972), 109-124.
894. Patchen, Martin. "Models of Cooperation and Conflict: A Critical Review." *Journal of Conflict Resolution,* 14 (1970), 389-407.
895. _____. "Strategies for Eliciting Cooperation from an Adversary: Laboratory and International Findings." *Journal of Conflict Resolution,* 31 (March 1987), 164-185.
896. Peay, Marilyn Y. "Changes in Attitudes and Beliefs in Two-Person Interaction Situations." *European Journal of Social Psychology,* 10:4 (October-December 1980), 367-377.
897. Perry, S. E. "Notes on the Role of the National: A Social-Psychological Concept for the Study of International Relations." *Journal of Conflict Resolution,* 1 (1957), 346-363.
898. Phillips, James L., and Lawrence H. Nitz. "Social Contacts in a Three-Person 'Political Convention' Situation." *Journal of Conflict Resolution,* 12 (1968), 206-214.
899. Phillips, Thomas E. "Resolving 'Hopeless Conflicts'." *Journal of Conflict Resolution,* 5:3 (1961), 274-278.
900. Phillips, Warren R. "International Communications." In: M. Haas, ed. *International Systems: A Behavioral Approach.* New York: Chandler, 1974. pp. 177-202.
901. Pilisuk, Mark. "Inducing Trust: A Test of the Osgood Proposal." *Journal of Personality and Social Psychology,* 8 (1968), 121-133.
902. _____., and Emmanuel Uren. "Devising a Language for Interaction Sequences." *Journal of Conflict Resolution,* 19:3 (September 1975), 484-502.

903. Powell, G. B., and R. P. Stifbold. "Anger, Bargaining and Mobilization as Middle-Range Theories of Elite Behavior." *Comparative Politics*, 9 (July 1977), 379-398.
904. Pruitt, Dean G. "Achieving Integrative Agreements." In: M. H. Bazerman and R. Lewicki, eds. *Negotiating in Organizations*. Beverly Hills, CA.: Sage, 1983. pp. 35-50.
905. _____. "Achieving Integrative Agreements in Negotiation." In: R. K. White, ed. *Psychology and the Prevention of Nuclear War*. New York: New York University Press, 1986. pp. 463-478.
906. _____. "Definition of the Situation as a Determinant of International Action." In: H. C. Kelman, ed. *International Behavior: A Social-Psychological Analysis*. New York: Holt, Rinehart & Winston, 1965. pp. 391-432.
907. _____, and Peter J. Carnevale. "The Development of Integrative Agreements in Social Conflict." In: V. J. Derlega and J. Grzelak, eds. *Living With Other People*. New York: Academic Press, 1982. pp. 151-181.
908. _____, and Steven A. Lewis. "Developments of Integrative Solutions in Bilateral Negotiations." *Journal of Personality and Social Psychology*, 31 (1975), 621-633.
909. _____, and R. B. Mogy. "Effects of a Threatener's Enforcement Costs on Threat Credibility and Compliance." *Journal of Personality and Social Psychology*, 29 (1974), 73-180.
910. _____, and J. L. Drecos. "The Effects of Time Pressure, Time Elapsed, and the Opponent's Concession Rate on Behavior in Negotiation." *Journal of Experimental Social Psychology*, 5 (1969), 43-60.
911. _____, et al. "Gender Effects in Negotiation: Constituent Surveillance and Contentious Behavior." *Journal of Experimental Social Behavior*, 22 (1986), 264-275.
912. _____, and D. L. Smith. "Impression Management in Bargaining: Image of Firmness and Trustworthiness." In: J. T. Tedeschi, ed. *Impression Management Theory and Social Psychological Theory*. New York: Academic Press, 1981. pp. 247-267.
913. _____. "Indirect Communication and the Search for Agreement in Negotiations." *Journal of Applied Social Psychology*, 1:3 (1971), 205-239.
914. _____. Peter J. Carnevale and S. D. Britton. "Looking Tough - Negotiator Under Constituent Surveillance." *Personality and Social Psychology Bulletin*, 5 (1979), 118-121.
915. _____. "Methods for Resolving Differences of Interest: A Theoretical Analysis." *Journal of Social Issues*, 20 (1972), 133-154.
916. _____, and Helena Syna. "Mismatching the Opponent's Offer in Negotiation." *Journal of Experimental Social Psychology*, 21:2 (March 1985), 103-113.
917. _____. "Motivational Processes in the Decomposed Prisoner's Dilemma Game." *Journal of Personality and Social Psychology*, 14 (1970), 227-238.
918. _____. "National Power and International Responsiveness." *Background*, 7 (1964), 165-178.
919. _____. "Power and Bargaining." In: B. Seidenberg and A. Snadowsky, eds. *Social Psychology: A Textbook*. New York: The Free Press, 1976. pp. 343-375.
920. _____, and Steven A. Lewis. "The Psychology on Integrative Bargaining." In: D. Druckman, ed. *Negotiations: Social-Psychological Perspectives*. Beverly Hills, CA.: Sage, 1977. pp. 161-192.
921. _____. "Reaction Systems and Instability in Interpersonal and International Affairs." In: G. H. Snyder, ed. *Studies in International Conflict*. Buffalo Studies No. 4. Buffalo, NY.: State University of New York in Buffalo, Center for International Security and Conflict Studies, 1968. pp. 3-28.

922. ____. "Reciprocity and Credit Building in Dyads." *Journal of Personality and Social Psychology,* 8 (1968), 143-147.
923. ____. "Reward Structure and Cooperation: The Decomposed Prisoner's Dilemma Game." *Journal of Personality and Social Psychology,* 7 (1967), 21-27.
924. ____. "Stability and Sudden Change in Interpersonal and International Affairs." *Journal of Conflict Resolution,* 13 (1969), 18-38.
925. ____. "Stability and Sudden Change in Interpersonal and International Affairs." In: J. Rosenau, ed. *International Politics and Foreign Policy.* New York: The Free Press, 1969. pp. 392-408.
926. ____. "Strategic Choice in Negotiation." *American Behavioral Scientists,* 27:2 (1983), 167-194.
927. ____., and Helena Syna. "Successful Problem Solving." In: D. Tjosvold and D. W. Johnson, eds. *Conflicts in Organization.* New York: Irvington, 1983. pp. 62-81.
928. ____. "Negotiation." In: R. Hare & R. Lamb, eds. *The Encyclopedia Dictionary of Psychology.* Oxford: Blackwell, 1983. pp. 409-410.
929. ____. "Negotiation." In: R. Hare & R. Lamb, eds. *The Dictionary of Personality and Social Psychology.* Oxford: Blackwell, 1986. pp. 229-231.
930. ____., and M. J. Kimmel. "Twenty Years of Experimental Gaming: Critique, Synthesis and Suggestions for the Future." *Annual Review of Psychology,* 28 (1977), 363-392.
931. Psathas, G., and S. Stryker. "Bargaining Behavior and Orientations in Coalition Formation." *Sociometry,* 28 (1965), 124-144.
932. Putnam, L., and T. Jones. "The Role of Communication in Bargaining." *Human Communications Research,* 8 (1982), 262-280.
933. Rabbie, Jacob M., and Lieuwe Visser. "Bargaining Strength and Group Polarization in Intergroup Negotiations." *European Journal of Social Psychology,* 2:4 (1972), 410-416.
934. Racklam, N., and J. Carlisle. "The Effective Negotiator: Part I: The Behavior of Successful Negotiations." *Journal of European Industrial Training,* 2:6 (1978), 6-11.
935. Raven, Bertram H., and Jeffrey Z. Rubin. "The Interdependence of Persons." In: R. J. Lewicki and J. A. Lewicki, eds. *Negotiation: Readings, Exercises, and Cases.* Homewood, IL.: Irwin, 1985. pp. 35-52.
936. Reychler, Luc. "The Effectiveness of Pacific Strategy in Conflict Resolution: An Experimental Study." *Journal of Conflict Resolution,* 23:2 (1979), 228-260.
937. Rogers, Rita M. "Can Psychiatry Contribute to International Conciliation?." *Comprehensive Psychiatry,* 12:6 (1971), 511-519.
938. ____. "Psychological Aspects of Diplomatic Contacts in a Multi-Cultural Setting." *Coexistence,* 23:3 (1986), 283-302.
939. Roloff, Michael E., and Douglas E. Campion. "On Alleviating the Debilitating Effects of Accountability on Bargaining: The Authority and Self-Monitoring." *Communication Monographs,* 54:2 (June 1987), 145-164.
940. Roos, L. L. "Toward a Theory of Cooperation, Experiments Using Non Zero Sum Games." *Journal of Social Psychology,* 69 (1966), 277-289.
941. Rosenthal, Robert W. "Interpersonal Expectancies, Nonverbal Communication, and Research on Negotiation." *Negotiation Journal,* 4:3 (July 1988), 267-279.
942. Roucek, Joseph S. "Some Sociological Aspects of Diplomacy." *Journal of Human Relations,* 8 (Winter 1960), 209-242.

943. Rubin, Jeffrey Z., and M. R. Di Matteo. "Factors Affecting the Magnitude of Subjective Utility Parameters in a Tacit Bargaining Game." *Journal of Experimental Social Psychology*, 8 (1972), 412-426.
944. _____. "The Nature and Success of Influence Attempts in a Four-Party Bargaining Relationship." *Journal of Experimental Social Psychology*, 7 (1971), 17-35.
945. _____. "Negotiation: An Introduction to Some Issues and Themes." *American Behavioral Scientist*, 27:2 (November/December 1983), 135-147.
946. _____., and Roy J. Lewicki. "A Three-Factor Experimental Analysis of Promises and Threats." *Journal of Applied Social Psychology*, 3 (1973), 240-257.
947. _____., et al. "Factors Affecting Entry into Psychological Traps." *Journal of Conflict Resolution*, 24:3 (September 1980), 405-426.
948. _____. "Psychological Traps." In: R. J. Lewicki and J. A. Litterer, eds. *Negotiation: Readings, Exercises, and Cases*. Homewood, IL.: Irwin, 1985. pp. 69-78.
949. _____., et al. "Weakness as Strength: Test of a "My Hands Are Tied" Play in Bargaining." *Personality and Social Psychology Bulletin*, 6 (1980), 216-221.
950. Saunders, Harold H. "The Psychology of Negotiation." *American - Arab Affairs*, 15 (Winter 1985-86), 10-18.
951. Sawyer, J., and H. Guetzkow. "Bargaining and Negotiation in International Relation." In: H. C. Kelman, ed. *International Behavior: A Social-Psychological Analysis*. New York: Holt, Rinehart & Winston, 1965. pp. 466-520.
952. Scheff, T. "Negotiating Reality: Notes on Power in the Assessment of Responsibility." *Social Problems*, 16 (1968), 3-17.
953. Schlenker, Barry R., et al. "Compliance to Threats as a Function of the Wording of the Threat and the Exploitativeness of the Threatener." *Sociometry*, 33 (1970), 394-408.
954. Schofield, Norman. "The Bargaining Set in Voting Games." *Behavioral Science*, 25:2 (March 1980), 120-129.
955. Sermat, V. "Cooperative Behavior in a Mixed-Motive Game." *Journal of Social Psychology*, 62 (1964), 217-239.
956. _____. "The Effect of Initial Cooperative or Competitive Treatment Upon a Subject's Response to Conditional Cooperation." *Behavioral Science*, 12 (1967), 301-313.
957. Shaw, Jerry I. "Situational Factors Contributing to a Psychological Advantage in Competitive Negotiations." *Journal of Personality and Social Psychology*, 19 (1971), 251-260.
958. _____., and Christer Thorslund. "Varying Patterns of Reward Cooperation: The Effects in a Prisoner's Dilemma Game." *Journal of Conflict Resolution*, 19:1 (March 1975), 108-122.
959. Sheposh, J. P., and P. S. Gallo. "Asymmetry of Payoff Structure and Cooperative Behavior in the Prisoner's Dilemma Game." *Journal of Conflict Resolution*, 17:2 (June 1973), 321-334.
960. Sher, Jordan M. "Conflict, Negotiation and Cooperation - Analysis of these Parameters in International Relations." *Mental Health and Society*, 2:3-6 (1975), 196-204.
961. Short, J. A. "Effects of Medium of Communication on Experimental Negotiation." *Human Relations*, 27 (1974), 225-234.
962. Shure, G. H., R. J. Meeker and E. A. Hansford. "The Effectiveness of Pacifist Strategies in Bargaining Games." In: M. Wertheimer, ed. *Psychology and Social Problems*. Chicago, IL.: Scott, Foresman, 1970.

963. _____. _____. _____. "The Effectiveness of Pacifist Strategies in Bargaining Games." In: J. E. Mueller, ed. *Approaches to Measurement in International Relations: A Nonevangelical Survey.* New York: Appleton - Century - Crofts, 1969.
964. Singer, J. David, and P. Ray. "Decision-Making in Conflict: From Inter-Personal to Inter-National Relations." *Menninger Clinic Bulletin,* 30 (1966), 300-312.
965. _____. "Threat-Perception and the Armament-Tension Dilemma." *Journal of Conflict Resolution,* 2 (1958), 90-105.
966. Sirois, P., and B. Douval. "The Role of Returns to a Prior Topic in the Negotiation of Topic Change: A Developmental Investigation." *Journal of Psycholinguistic Research,* 17:3 (1988), 185-210.
967. Slack, B. D., and J. D. Look. "Authoritarian Behavior in a Conflict Situation." *Journal of Personality and Social Psychology,* 25 (1973), 130-136.
968. Slusher, E. Allen. "Counterpart Strategy, Prior Relations, and Constituent Pressure in a Bargaining Simulation." *Behavioral Science,* 23:6 (1978), 470-477.
969. Smith, Clagett G. "Studies in International Conflict: Recent Contributions of the Behavioral Sciences." *International Journal of Group Tensions,* 11:1 (1979), 86-109.
970. Smith, D. F., and D. J. Turkington. "Testing a Behavioral Theory of Bargaining: An International Comparative Study." *British Journal of Industrial Relations,* 19:3 (1981), 361-369.
971. Smith, D. Leasel, Dean G. Pruitt and Peter J. Carnevale. "Matching and Mismatching the Effect of Own Limit, Other's Toughness and Time Pressure on Concession Rate in Negotiation." *Journal of Personality and Social Psychology,* 42:5 (May 1982), 876-883.
972. Smith, David H. "Communication and Negotiation Outcome." *Journal of Communication,* 19 (1969), 248-256.
973. _____. "Communication, Minimum Disposition, and Negotiation." In: H. B. Pepinsky and M. J. Patton, eds. *The Psychological Experiment: A Practical Accomplishment.* New York: Pergamon Press, 1971. pp. 131-148.
974. Smith, William P., and W. A. Leginski. "Magnitude and Precision of Primitive Power in Bargaining Strategy." *Journal of Experimental Social Psychology,* 6 (1963), 57-76.
975. _____., and A. J. Anderson. "Threats, Communication and Bargaining." *Journal of Personality and Social Psychology,* 32 (1975), 76-82.
976. _____., and Timothy D. Emmons. "Outcome Information and Competitiveness in Interpersonal Bargaining." *Journal of Conflict Resolution,* 13 (1969), 262-270.
977. _____. "Conflict and Negotiation: Trends and Emerging Issues." *Journal of Applied Social Psychology,* 17 (July 1987), 641-677.
978. Snyder, C. R., and R. C. Higgins. "Excuses - Their Effective Role in the Negotiation of Reality." *Psychological Bulletin,* 104:1 (1988), 23-35.
979. Snyder, Glenn H. "Crisis Bargaining." In: C. F. Hermann, ed. *International Crises: Insights from Behavioral Research.* New York: The Free Press, 1972. pp. 217-256.
980. _____. "Prisoner's Dilemma and 'Chicken' Models in International Politics." *International Studies Quarterly,* 15 (1971), 66-103.
981. Snyder, Jack L. "Rationality at the Brink: The Role of Cognitive Processes in Failures of Deterrence." *World Politics,* 30 (April 1978), 345-365.
982. Spector, Bertram I. "Negotiation as a Psychological Process." *Journal of Conflict Resolution,* 21:4 (1977), 607-618.

Psychological Aspects

983. _____. "Negotiation as a Psychological Process." In: I. W. Zartman, ed. *The Negotiation Process.* Beverly Hills, CA.: Sage, 1978. pp. 55-66.
984. _____. "A Social-Psychological Model of Position Modification: Aswan." In: I. W. Zartman, ed. *The 50% Solution.* New York: Doubleday, 1976. pp. 343-371.
985. Stagner, Ross. *Psychological Aspects of International Conflict.* Belmont, CA.: Brooks-Cole, 1967. 234p. Chapter 11. pp. 157-172.
986. Starbuck, W., and D. F. Grant. "Bargaining Strategies with Asymmetric Initiation." *Journal of Applied Social Psychology,* 1 (1971), 344-363.
987. Stech, Frank J., Charles G. McClintock and Barry F. Moss. "The Effectiveness of the Carrot and the Stick in Increasing Dyadic Outcomes During Duopolistic Bargaining." *Behavioral Science,* 29:1 (June 1984), 1-12.
988. Stephenson, G. M., M. Skinner and C. J. Brotherton. "Group Participation and Intergroup Relations: An Experimental Study of Negotiation Groups." *European Journal of Social Psychology,* 6:1 (1976), 51-70.
989. _____. "Inter-Group Relations and Negotiating Behavior." In: P. B. Warr, ed. *Psychology at Work.* Harmondsworth, England: Penguin Books, 1971. pp. 347-373.
990. _____., and B. K. Kniveton. "Interpersonal and Interparty Exchange: An Experimental Study of the Effects of Seating Position on the Outcome of Negotiations Between Teams Representing Parties in Dispute." *Human Relations,* 31 (June 1979), 555-556.
991. _____. K. Ayling and D. R. Rutter. "The Role of Visual Communication in Social Exchange." *British Journal of Social & Clinical Psychology,* 15:2 (June 1976), 113-120.
992. Sternberg, R. J., and L. J. Soriano. "Styles of Conflict Resolution." *Journal of Personality and Social Psychology,* 47:1 (July 1984), 115-126.
993. Streufert, S., S. C. Streufert and C. H. Castore. "Leadership in Negotiations and the Complexity of Conceptual Structure." *Journal of Applied Psychology,* 52 (1968), 218-223.
994. _____., and S. I. Sandler. "Perceived Success and Competence of Opponent or the Laboratory Dien Bien Phu." *Journal of Applied Social Psychology,* 3:1 (1973), 84-93.
995. _____., et al. "Tactical and Negotiations Game for Analysis of Decision Integration Across Decision Areas." *Psychological Reports,* 20 (1967), 155-157.
996. Sullivan, Michael P. "International Bargaining Behavior." *International Studies Quarterly,* 15:3 (1971), 359-382.
997. Summers, D. A. "Conflict, Compromise, and Belief Change in a Decision Making Task." *Journal of Conflict Resolution,* 12 (1968), 215-221.
998. Susskind, Lawrence, and Jeffrey Z. Rubin. "Negotiation: Behavioral Perspectives." *American Behavioral Scientist,* 27 (1983), 133-279.
999. Swingle, Paul G., and H. Coady. "Effects of the Partner's Abrupt Strategy Change Upon Subject's Responding in Prisoner's Dilemma." *Journal of Personality and Social Psychology,* 5 (1967), 357-363.
1000. _____. "Ethnic Factors in Interpersonal Bargaining." *Journal of Psychology,* 23 (1969), 136-146.
1001. _____. "The Effects of Game Structure and S's Behavior on Attitudes Toward Cooperative Opponents." *Journal of Conflict Resolution,* 18:4 (December 1974), 714-726.
1002. _____. "The Effect of Illusory Power in Non-Zero-Sum Games." *Journal of Conflict Resolution,* 15:4 (December 1971), 513-522.
1003. _____. "Exploitative Behavior in Non-Zero-Sum Games." *Journal of Personality and Social Psychology,* 16 (1970), 121-132.

1004. Swinth, R. L. "The Establishment of the Trust Relationship." *Journal of Conflict Resolution*, 11 (1967), 335-344.
1005. Tedeschi, James T., and P. Rosenfeld. "Communication in Negotiation and Bargaining." In: M. E. Roloff and G. R. Miller, eds. *Persuasion: New Directions in Theory and Research*. Beverly Hills, CA.: Sage, 1980. pp. 225-248.
1006. _____., and Thomas V. Bonoma. "Measures or Last Resort: Coercion and Aggression in Bargaining." In: D. Druckman, ed. *Negotiations: Social-Psychological Perspectives*. Beverly Hills, CA.: Sage, 1977. pp. 213-242.
1007. _____. _____. and Svenn Lindskold. "Threatener's Reactions to Prior Announcement of Behavioral Compliance or Defiance." *Behavioral Science*, 15 (1970), 171-179.
1008. _____. "Threats and Promises." In: P. Swingle, ed. *The Structure of Conflict*. New York: Academic Press, 1970. pp. 155-192.
1009. _____. Thomas V. Bonoma and N. Novison. "Behavior of a Threatener: Relation vs. Fixed Opportunity Costs." *Journal of Conflict Resolution*, 14 (1970), 69-76.
1010. _____. _____. and R. C. Brown. "A Paradigm for the Study of Coercive Power." *Journal of Conflict Resolution*, 15 (1971), 197-223.
1011. Teger, A. I. "The Effects of Early Cooperation on the Escalation of Conflict." *Journal of Experimental Social Psychology*, 6 (1970), 187-204.
1012. Terhune, Kenneth W. "The Effects of Personality in Cooperation and Conflict." In: P. Swingle, ed. *The Structure of Conflict*. New York: Academic Press, 1970. pp. 193-234.
1013. _____. "Motives, Situation and Interpersonal Conflict Within the Prisoner's Dilemma." *Journal of Personal and Social Psychology*, Monograph Supplement, 8. 3:2 (1968), 1-24.
1014. _____. "Studies of Motives, Cooperation and Conflict Within Laboratory Microcosms." In: G. H. Snyder, ed. *Studies in International Conflict*. Research Monograph No. 1. Buffalo, NY.: Center for International Security and Conflict Studies, University of NY at Bufallo, 1968. pp. 29-58.
1015. Tetlock, Philip. "Integrative Complexity of American and Soviet Foreign Policy Rhetoric: A Time-Series Analysis." *Journal of Personality and Social Psychology*, 49:6 (1985), 1565-1585.
1016. Thibault, J., and C. Faucheux. "The Development of Contractual Norms in a Bargaining Situation Under Two Types of Stress." *Journal of Experimental Social Psychology*, 1 (1965), 89-105.
1017. _____. "The Development of Contractual Norms in Bargaining: Replication and Variation." *Journal of Conflict Resolution*, 12:1 (1968), 102-112.
1018. _____., and C. L. Gruder. "Formation of Contractual Agreements Between Parties of Unequal Power." *Journal of Personality and Social Psychology*, 11 (1969), 59-65.
1019. Thompson, L. L., E. A. Mannix and Max H. Bazerman. "Group Negotiation - Effects of Decision Rule, Agenda and Aspiration." *Journal of Personality and Social Psychology*, 54:1 (January 1988), 86-95.
1020. Tjosvold, Dean. "The Effects of the Constituent's Affirmation and the Opposing Negotiator's Self-Presentation in Bargaining Between Unequal Status Groups." *Organizational Behavior & Human Performance*, 18:1 (February 1977), 146-157.
1021. _____. David W. Johnson and Roger Johnson. "Influence Strategy, Perspective-Taking, and Relationships Between High and Low Power Individuals in Cooperative and Competitive Contexts." *Journal of Psychology*, 116:2 (March 1984), 187-202.

1022. _____. "Low Power Persons Strategies in Bargaining Negotiability of Demand, Maintaining Face and Race." *International Journal of Group Tensions*, 7:1-2 (1977), 29-41.
1023. _____., and T. L. Huston. "Social Face and Resistance to Compromise in Bargaining." *Journal of Social Psychology*, 104 (February 1978), 57-68.
1024. Tornatzky, L., and P. J. Geiwitz. "The Effects of Threat and Attraction on Interpersonal Bargaining." *Psychonomic Science*, 13 (1968), 125-126.
1025. Torre, Motram. "How Does Physical and Mental Illness Influence Negotiations Between Diplomats." *International Journal of Social Psychiatry*, 10:2 (1964), 170-176.
1026. Turnbull, Allen A., Lloyd H. Strickland and Kelly G. Shaver. "Medium of Communication, Differential Power and Phasing of Concessions: Negotiating Success and Attribution to the Opponent." *Human Communication Research*, 2:3 (1976), 262-270.
1027. _____. _____. _____. "Phasing of Concessions, Differential Power, and Medium of Communication: Negotiating Success and Attributions of the Opponent." *Personality and Social Psychology Bulletin*, 1:1 (1974), 228-230.
1028. Tutzauer, Frank. "Bargaining as a Dynamical System." *Behavioral Science*, 31 (April 1986), 65-81.
1029. Tysoe, Maryon. "Social Cues and the Negotiation Process." *British Journal of Social Psychology*, 23:1 (1984), 61-67.
1030. Vidmar, N. J. "Effects of Representational Roles and Mediators on Negotiation Effectiveness." *Journal of Personality and Social Psychology*, 17:1 (1971), 48-58.
1031. _____. "Forces Affecting Success in Negotiating Groups." *Behavioral Science*, 15 (1970), 154-163.
1032. Vinacke, W. Edgar, et al. "Accommodative Strategy and Communication in a Three-Person Matrix Game." *Journal of Personality and Social Psychology*, 29:4 (April 1974), 509-525.
1033. _____. "Negotiations and Decision in a Political Game." In: B. Lieberman, ed. *Social Choice*. New York: Gordon & Bach, 1971. pp. 5-82.
1034. Vitz, P. C., and W. R. Kite. "Factors Affecting Conflict and Negotiation Within an Alliance." *Journal of Experimental Social Psychology*, 6 (1970), 233-247.
1035. Volkan, Vanik D. "Psychological Concepts Useful in the Building of Political Foundations Between Nations: Track II Diplomacy." *Journal of the American Psychoanalytic Association*, 35:4 (1987), 903-936.
1036. Wade, L. L., and R. L. Curry. "An Economic Model of Socio-Political Bargaining." *American Journal of Economics and Sociology*, 30 (1971), 383-393.
1037. Wadington, J. "Social Decision Schemes and Two-Person Bargaining." *Behavioral Science*, 20:3 (1975), 157-165.
1038. Walcott, Charles, and P. Terrence Hopmann. "Interaction Analysis and Bargaining Behavior." *Experimental Study of Politics*, 4 (February 1975), 1-19.
1039. Wall, James A. "Effects of Constituent Trust and Representative Bargaining Orientation on Intergroup Bargaining." *Journal of Personality and Social Psychology*, 31 (1975), 1004-1012.
1040. _____. "Effects of Mediator Rewards and Suggestions Upon Negotiations." *Journal of Personality and Social Psychology*, 37 (1979), 1554-1560.
1041. _____. "Effects of Opposing Constituent Stances, Opposing Representative's Locus of Control." *Journal of Conflict Resolution*, 21 (September 1977), 459-474.

1042. _____. "Effects of Sex and Opposing Representative's Bargaining Orientation on Intergroup Bargaining." *Journal of Personality and Social Psychology*, 33 (1976), 55-61.
1043. _____. "Intergroup Bargaining: Effects of Opposing Constituent Stances, Opposing Representative's Bargaining and Representative's Locus of Control.' *Journal of Conflict Resolution*, 21:3 (1977), 459-474.
1044. _____. "Operantly Conditioning a Negotiator's Concession Making." *Journal of Experimental Social Psychology*, 13 (September 1977), 431-440.
1045. Wallace, Donnel, and Paul Rothaus. "Communication, Group Loyalty and Trust in the Prisoner's Dilemma Game." *Journal of Conflict Resolution*, 13 (1969), 370-380.
1046. Walsh, J. P., and Leonard Greenhalgh. "Age-Based Status Group Membership and Bargaining Behavior." *Journal of Social Psychology*, 127 (April 1987), 117-128.
1047. Walton, Richard E. "A Problem Solving Workshop on Border Conflicts in Eastern Africa." *Journal of Applied Behavioral Science*, 6:4 (1970), 433-489.
1048. Ward, Hugh D. "A Behavioral Model of Bargaining." *British Journal of Political Science*, 9:2 (1979), 201-218.
1049. Ward, M. D. "Cooperation and Conflict in Foreign Policy Behavior: Reaction and Memory." *International Studies Quarterly*, 26 (1982), 87-126.
1050. Wedge, Bryant, and Cyril Muromcew. "Psychological Factors in Soviet Disarmament Negotiation." *Journal of Conflict Resolution*, 9:1 (1965), 18-36.
1051. Weiss-Wik, Stephen. "Enhancing Negotiator's Successfulness: Self-Help Books and Related Empirical Research." *Journal of Conflict Resolution*, 27:4 (1983), 706-739.
1052. White, Ralph K. "Ten Psychological Contributions to the Prevention of Nuclear War." In: S. Oskamp, ed. *International Conflict and National Public Policy Issues*. Beverly Hills, CA.: Sage, 1985. pp. 45-62.
1053. Wichman, H. "Effects of Isolation and Communication in a Two-Person Game." *Journal of Personality and Social Psychology*, 16 (1970), 114-120.
1054. Willis, Richard H., and Myron L. Joseph. "Bargaining Behavior I: 'Prominence' as a Predictor of the Outcome of Games of Agreement." *Journal of Conflict Resolution*, 3:2 (1959), 102-113.
1055. Wilson, W., and J. Wong. "Intergroup Attitudes Towards Cooperative vs. Competitive Opponents in a Modified Prisoner's Dilemma Game." *Perceptual and Motor Skills*, 27 (1968), 1059-1066.
1056. Winham, Gilbert R. "Complexity in International Negotiation." In: D. Druckman, ed. *Negotiations: Social-Psychological Perspectives*. Beverly Hills, CA.: Sage, 1977. pp. 347-366.
1057. Worchel, Stephen, et al. "Determinants of the Effect of Intergroup Cooperation on Intergroup Attraction." *Journal of Conflict Resolution*, 22:3 (September 1978), 429-440.
1058. Wyer, R. "Prediction of Behavior in Two-Person Games." *Journal of Personality and Social Psychology*, 13 (1969), 222-238.
1059. _____. "Effects of Outcome Matrix and Partner's Behavior in Two-Person Games." *Journal of Experimental Social Psychology*, 7 (1971), 190-210.
1060. Yalem, R. "Controlled Communication and Conflict Resolution." *Journal of Peace Research*, 8:3 (1971), 263-272.
1061. Yukl, Gary A. "Effects of Situational Variables and Opponent Concessions on a Bargainer's Perception, Aspirations and Concessions." *Journal of Personality and Social Psychology*, 29 (1974), 227-236.

1062. _____. "The Effects of the Opponent's Initial Offer and Concession Magnitude and Concession Frequency on Bargaining Behavior." *Journal of Personality and Social Psychology*, 29 (1974), 327-330.
1063. _____., et al. "The Effects of Time Pressure and Issue Settlement Order on Integrative Bargaining." *Sociometry*, 19:3 (September 1976), 277-281.
1064. Zimbardo, Phillip G. "The Tactics and Ethics of Persuasion." In: R. J. Lewicki and J. A. Litterer, eds. *Negotiation: Readings, Exercises, and Cases*. Homewood, IL.: Irwin, 1985. pp. 200-215.

3. Documents and Reports

1065. Axelrod, Robert. *Framework for a General Theory of Cognition and Choice*. Berkeley, CA.: Institute of International Studies, University of California, 1972. 55p.
1066. Ben Yoav, Orly, and Dean G. Pruitt. "Level of Aspiration and Expectation of Future Interaction in Negotiation." Paper Presented at the *Annual Convention of the American Psychological Association*, held in August 1982, in Washington, D.C.
1067. _____. *Accountability to Constituents and Constituent Surveillance as Antecedents of Negotiation Behavior in Boundary Positions*. Ph.D. Dissertation. Buffalo, NY.: State University of New York at Buffalo, 1984.
1068. _____., and Dean G. Pruitt. "Accountability, a Two Edged Sword: Friend and Foe of Integrative Agreements." Paper Presented at the *Annual Convention of the Eastern Academy of Management*, held in May 1983, in Pittsburgh.
1069. Benson, J., and R. Day. "On the Limits of Negotiation: A Critique of the Theory of Negotiated Order." Paper Presented at the *Annual Meeting of the American Sociological Association*, held in 1976, in New York.
1070. Benton, A. A. "Accountability and Negotiations Between Group Representatives." Paper Presented at the *Proceedings of the 80th Annual Convention of the American Psychological Association*, held in 1972 in Hawaii. pp. 227-228.
1071. Bonoma, Thomas V. "Theories of Escalation and Deescalation from an Influence Perspective." Paper Presented at the *15th Annual Convention of the International Studies Association*, held on March 20-23, 1974 in St.Louis.
1072. Borah, L. A.,Jr. *An Investigation of the Effect of Threat Upon Interpersonal Bargaining*. Ph.D. Dissertation. Minneapolis, MN.: University of Minnesota, 1961. 102p.
1073. Boyd, Norman K. *Negotiation Behavior of Elected and Appointed Representatives Serving as Group Leaders or Spokesmen Under Different Cooperative Group Expectation*. Ph.D. Dissertation. Adelphi, MD.: University of Maryland, 1972. 125p.
1074. Broskowski, A. T. *The Effects of Reciprocity Relationship on the Bargaining Behavior of the Dyad*. Ph.D. Dissertation. Bloomington, IN.: Indiana University, 1967.
1075. Brown, B. R., H. Garland and S. Freedman. "The Effects of Constituency Feedback, Representational Role, and Strategy of the Other on Concession-Making in a Bilateral Monopoly Bargaining Task." Paper Presented at the *Annual Meeting of the Eastern Psychological Association*, held on May 1973, in Washington, D.C.
1076. Caldarelli, Cesare. *A Descriptive Case Study of Behavior and Attitudes in Open Negotiations*. Ph.D. Dissertation. Nashville, TE.: George Peabody College for Teachers of Vanderbilt University, 1984. 120p.

1077. Cann, Arnie, James K. Esser and S. S. Komorita. "Equity and Concession Strategies in Bargaining." Paper Presented at the *Annual Meeting of the Midwestern Psychological Association*, held on May 12, 1973, in Chicago, IL.
1078. Carnevale, Peter J. "Effects of Cooperative and Competitive Expectations on Facial Affect." Paper Presented at the *Meeting of the Eastern Psychological Association*, held in 1984, in Baltimore, MD.
1079. _____. Dean G. Pruitt and S. D. Seilheinner. "Negotiator Accountability and Nonverbal Communication as Determinants of Bargaining Outcome." Paper Presented at the *Annual Meeting of the Eastern Psychological Association*, held in 1979, in Philadelphia, PA.
1080. _____., and Alice M. Isen. "Negotiator Mood Moderates the Barrier Effect." Paper Presented at the *Annual Meeting of the Eastern Psychological Association*, held in 1981, in New York.
1081. _____. P. Sherer and Dean G. Pruitt. "Some Determinants of Concession Rate and Distributive Tactics in Negotiation." Paper Presented at the *87th Annual Convention of the American Psychological Association*, held in September 1979, in New York.
1082. _____., et al. "Visual Interaction in Integrative Bargaining." Paper Presented at the *Annual Meeting of the American Psychological Association*, held in 1981, in Los Angeles, CA.
1083. Castles, Alex. *Social Psychological Techniques and the Peaceful Settlement of International Disputes: A Report Based on Proceedings of a Workshop at Lake Mohonk, NY, May 1970.* UNITAR Research Reports No. 1. New York: United Nations Institute for Training and Research, 1970. 39p.
1084. Cheney, John. *The Effects Upon the Bargaining Process of Positive and Negative Communication Options in Equal and Unequal Power Relationships.* Ph.D. Dissertation. Boston, MA.: Boston University, 1967.
1085. Clark, Marian F. *Contextual Variation Effect on Influence Choice in a Negotiation Situation.* Ph.D. Dissertation. Tempe, AZ.: Arizona State University, 1983. 268p.
1086. Cohen, Eugene D. *The Effects of Punishment Magnitude and Threat Usage on Interpersonal Negotiations in a Bilateral Situation.* M.S.Thesis. Madison, WI.: University of Wisconsin, 1972. 90p.
1087. Cottam, Martha L. *Cognitive Limitations and Foreign Policy Decision Making.* Ph.D. Dissertation. Los Angeles, CA.: University of California at Los Angeles, 1983. 426p.
1088. Coudry, S. C. *The Effects of Situational Power and Personality Upon the Decision to Negotiate or Not in a Two Person Bargaining Situation.* Ph.D. Dissertation. Los Angeles, CA.: University of California at Los Angeles, 1966.
1089. Davis, Diana K. *Strategic Behavior in Mixed Motive Problems.* Ph.D. Dissertation. Philadelphia, PA.: University of Pennsylvania, 1978. 207p.
1090. Davis, Earl E., and Stuart P. Fischoff. "Measures of Interpersonal Attitudes as Predictors of Outcomes of Intergroups Negotiations: A Theoretical Interpretation of Contradictory Findings." Paper Presented at the *81st Annual Convention of the American Psychological Association, Proceedings*, held in 1973, in Montreal. Vol. 8. pp. 255-256.
1091. Davis, Lillian J. *An Experimental Investigation of Tolerance of Ambiguity and Information in Interpersonal Bargaining.* Ph.D. Dissertation. Austin, TX.: University of Texas, 1975. 179p.

1092. De Renck, Anthony. "Controlled Communication: Rationale and Dynamics." Paper Presented at the *UNITAR Workshop on Social Psychological Aspects of Peaceful Settlement*, held on May 15-17, 1970, in New Paltz, NY.
1093. Delano, Juno Lee. *Gender Effects in Values and Negotiation Outcomes.* Ph.D. Dissertation. Gainesville, FL.: University of Florida, 1983. 164p.
1094. Diez, Mary E. *Negotiation Competence: Interpreting Situational Differences in Code Choice.* Ph.D. Dissertation. East Lansing, MI.: Michigan State University, 1983. 117p.
1095. Druckman, Daniel. "Behavioral Aspects of International Negotiation." Paper Presented at the *28th Annual Convention of the International Studies Association*, held on April 14-18, 1987, in Washington, D.C.
1096. Ellis, William F. *The Effects of Differing Third Party Roles and Behaviors on Conciliatory and Retaliatory Negotiator Behavior Involved in a Simulated Intergroup Conflict.* Ph.D. Dissertation. Columbia, SC.: University of South Carolina, 1983. 155p.
1097. Engram, P. S. *Dyadic Interaction Patterns in an Integrative Bargaining Setting.* Ph.D. Dissertation. Buffalo, NY.: State University of New York at Buffalo, 1981.
1098. Faerstein, Paul H. *Negotiating Skills: Examining Behaviors, Processes and Outcomes.* Ph.D. Dissertation. New York: New York University, 1979. 203p.
1099. Fischoff, Stuart P. *The Effects of Ego-Involvement, Pre-Negotiation Experience and Reference Group Influence on Outcomes in an Experimental Simulation of Inter-Group Negotiation.* Ph.D. Dissertation. New York: New School of Social Research, 1972. 418p.
1100. Forcey, B., et al. "Effects of a Prior Helping Experience on Negotiation Outcome." Paper Presented at the *Annual Meeting of the Eastern Psychological Association*, held in 1982, in Baltimore, MD.
1101. Freedman, Stuart C. *The Effects of Motive Attribution and Perceived Tactical Alternatives on Compliance to Threats and Promises in a Negotiation Task.* Ph.D. Dissertation. Ithaca, NY.: Cornell University, 1977. 165p.
1102. Graeven, D. B. *Intergroup Conflict and the Group Representative: The Effects of Power and the Legitimacy of the Power Relations on Negotiations in an Experimental Setting.* Ph.D. Dissertation. Iowa City, IA.: University of Iowa, 1970.
1103. Gruder, C. L. *Effects of Perception of Opponent's Bargaining Style and Accountability to Opponent and Partner on Interpersonal Mixed-Motive Bargaining.* Ph.D. Dissertation. Chapell Hill, NC.: University of North Carolina, 1968.
1104. Haccoun, R. R. *Mandate Base and Evaluation Source as Determiners of Negotiator Behavior.* Ph.D. Dissertation. Columbus, OH.: Ohio State University, 1973. 173p.
1105. Hamner, W. C. *The Effects of Bargaining Strategy and Pressure to Reach Agreement on Behavior in a Stalemated Negotiation.* Ph.D. Dissertation. Bloomington, IN.: Indiana University, 1972. 193p.
1106. Hopple, Gerald W., and Jonathan Winkenfeld. *International Behavior Analysis: The Operationalization Task.* College Park, MD.: Department of Political Science, University of Maryland, 1976. 58p.
1107. Jackson, Conrad N. *The Effects of a Representative's Power Within His/Her Own Organization on the Outcome of a Negotiation.* West Lafayette, IN.: Institute for Research in the Behavioral, Economic and Management Sciences, Purdue University, 1981. 17p.

1108. Jönsson, Christer. "International Negotiations and Cognitive Theory: A Research Project." Paper Presented at the *Conference on the Processes of International Negotiations*, held on May 18-22, 1987, at the International Institute for Applied Systems Analysis (IIASA), in Laxenburg, Austria.
1109. Karrass, Chester L. *A Study of the Relationship of Negotiator Skill and Power as Determinants of Negotiation Outcome.* Ph.D. Dissertation. Los Angeles, CA.: University of Southern California, 1968.
1110. Katz, Neil. "Communication and Conflict Management Workshop." Paper Presented at the *National Conference of Peacemaking and Conflict Resolution*, held in June 1986, in Denver, CO.
1111. Kee, Herbert W. *The Development and Effects Upon Bargaining, of Trust and Suspicion.* Ph.D. Dissertation. Vancouver, BC.: University of British Columbia, 1969.
1112. Keiffer, M. G. *The Effect of Availability and Precision of Threat on Bargaining Behavior.* Ph.D. Dissertation. New York: Columbia University, 1968.
1113. Klimoski, Richard J., and Stephen B. Knouse. "An Operant Conditioning Investigation of Negotiation Behavior." Paper Presented at the *19th Conference of the Midwest Division of the Academy of Management*, held in 1976, in St.Louis, MO.
1114. Knouse, Stephen B. *An Analysis of the Processes of Accountability in Negotiating Behavior.* Ph.D. Dissertation. Columbus, OH.: Ohio State University, 1977. 172p.
1115. Komorita, S. S., and R. Koziej. "Tacit Communication in the Prisoner's Dilemma Game." Paper Presented at the *Annual Meeting of the Midwestern Psychological Association*, held in April 1970, in Cincinnati, OH.
1116. Lake, D. G. *Impression Formation, Machiavellianism and Interpersonal Bargaining.* Ph.D. Dissertation. New York: Columbia University, 1967.
1117. Lanto, S., and G. H. Shure. "Effects of Size of Payoff and Real Versus Imaginary Rewards on Prebargaining Perceptions." Paper Presented to the *Proceedings of the 80th Annual Convention of the American Psychological Association*, held in 1972, in Honolulu, HI. pp. 231-232.
1118. Lewicki, Roy J., and Jeffrey Z. Rubin. "Effects of Variations in the Informational Clarity of Promises and Threats Upon Interpersonal Bargaining." Paper Presented at the *81st Annual Convention of the American Psychological Association*, held in 1973. pp. 137-138.
1119. Lifshitz, Michaela N. *Internal-External Locus of Control and Negotiation Behavior.* Ph.D. Dissertation. Columbus, OH.: Ohio University, 1966.
1120. Lindskold, Svenn. *Threatening and Conciliatory Influence Attempts as a Function of Source's Perception of Own Competence in a Conflict Situation.* Ph.D. Dissertation. Miami, FL.: University of Miami, 1970.
1121. Magenau, J. M. *A Laboratory Investigation of Alternative Dispute Resolution Procedures in Bargaining.* Ph.D. Dissertation. Buffalo, NY.: State University of New York at Buffalo, 1980.
1122. McGrath, J. E., and J. W. Julian. *The Influence of Leader and Member Behavior on the Adjustment and Task Effectiveness of Negotiation Groups.* Technical Report No. 17. Urbana, IL.: Group Effectiveness Research Laboratory, University of Illinois, 1963.
1123. _____. _____. *Negotiation and Conflict: An Experimental Study.* Technical Report No. 16. Urbana, IL.: Group Effectiveness Research Laboratory, University of Illinois, 1967. 80p.
1124. McLaren, Virginia. "Conflict Management and Learning in a Multi-Objective Two-Participant Situation." Paper Presented at the *International Peace Science Society*, held on November 9-11, 1981, in Philadelphia, PA.

Psychological Aspects

1125. Medford, Robert E. *The Professional Negotiator: Role Conflict, Role Ambiguity and Motivation to Work.* Ph.D. Dissertation. Lawrence, KA.: University of Kansas, 1973. 115p.
1126. Mitchell, Ted J. "Necessary Conditions for Bluffing: Some Experimental Results." Paper Presented at the *23rd Annual Convention of the International Studies Association,* held on March 25, 1982, in Cincinnati, Ohio.
1127. Mittelmark, M., Richard Rozelle and Daniel Druckman. "Accountability and Role Behavior of Bargainers." Paper Presented at the *Annual Meeting of the American Psychological Association,* held in 1977, in San Francisco, CA.
1128. Morley, Ian E. "Social Interaction in Experimental Negotiations." Paper Presented at the *Symposium on Experimental Studies of Negotiation Groups,* held on August 21, 1973, at the Annual Conference of the British Association for the Advancement of Science, in Canterbury.
1129. _____. *Social Interaction in Experimental Negotiations.* Ph.D. Dissertation. Nottingham: University of Nottingham, 1974.
1130. Neale, Margaret A. *Improving Negotiation: A Decision Making Perspective.* Ph.D. Dissertation. Austin, TX.: University of Texas, 1982.
1131. _____., and Gregory B. Northcraft. "Strategic Conceptualization and Feedback in Bargaining: An Examination of the Essence of Expertise." Paper Presented at the *Third Annual Research Conference on Negotiation,* held on April 23-25, 1987, at Ohio State University.
1132. Nochajski, T. H., et al. "Positive Mood, Aspirations and Negotiation Behavior." Paper Presented at the *Annual Convention of the Eastern Psychological Association,* held on March 1982, in Baltimore, MD.
1133. O'Brien, G. M. *The Effects of Information Accessibility and Machiavelianism in Interpersonal Perception and Bargaining Behavior.* Ph.D. Dissertation. Boston, MA.: Boston University, 1970.
1134. Pace, Roger C. *The Role of Communication in Consensus Formation: A Descriptive Analysis of Interaction Differences Between High and Low Consensus Groups.* Ph.D. Dissertation. University Park, PA.: Pennsylvania State University, 1984. 206p.
1135. Pepinsky, Harold B., U. Kumar and Michaela N. Lifshitz. "Effects of Trust and Approval Motive Upon Negotiation Behavior." Paper Presented at the *Midwestern Psychological Association Convention,* held in May 1966, in Chicago, IL.
1136. Poortinga, Ype H., and Erwin C. Hendriks. "Culture as a Factor in International Negotiations: A Proposed Research Project from a Psychological Perspective." Paper Presented at the *Conference on the Processes of International Negotiations,* held on May 18-22, 1987, at the International Institute for Applied Systems Analysis (IIASA), in Laxenburg, Austria.
1137. Pruitt, Dean G., et al. "International Negotiations." Paper Presented at the *Annual Meeting of the International Studies Association,* held on March 21-24, 1979, in Toronto.
1138. _____. *Problem Solving in the Department of State.* Social Science Foundation and Department of International Relations Monograph Series in World Affairs. Denver, CO.: University of Denver, 1964. 56p.
1139. _____., and Julie L. Drews. *The Effects of Time Pressure, Time Elapsed, and the Opponent's Concession Rate on Behavior in Negotiations.* Technical Report No. 3. Buffalo, NY.: Department of Psychology, SUNY at Buffalo, 1968.
1140. _____. *Negotiations as a Form of Social Behavior.* Technical Report No. 6. Buffalo, NY.: Department of Psychology, SUNY at Buffalo, 1971. 31p.

1141. _____. *Reaction Systems and Instability in Interpersonal and International Affairs.* Technical Report No. 2. Buffalo, NY.: Department of Psychology, SUNY at Buffalo, 1967. 34p.
1142. _____. *Reward Structure and Cooperation, Part II: International Processes in the Decomposed Prisoner's Dilemma Game.* Technical Report No. 8. Buffalo, NY.: Department of Psychology, SUNY at Buffalo, 1969. 27p.
1143. _____. *Reward Structure and Cooperation: The Decomposed Prisoner's Dilemma Game.* Technical Report No. 14. Newark, DE.: Center for Research on Social Behavior, University of Delaware, 1965. 52p.
1144. Ramsey, George H. Jr. *Social Psychological Threat Research: A Review and Assessment.* TR/A Technical Paper -11. Los Angeles, CA.: University of Southern California Los Angeles, International Relations Research Institute, 1974. 17p.
1145. Rogers, John P. *The Crisis Bargaining Code Model: The Influence of Cognitive Beliefs and Processes on U.S. Policy-Making During Crises.* Ph.D. Dissertation. Austin, TX.: University of Texas, 1986. 1019p.
1146. Rubin, Jeffrey Z., Roy J. Lewicki and L. Dunn. "Perceptions of Promisors and Threateners." Paper Presented at the *81st Annual Convention of the American Psychological Association Proceedings,* held in 1973. pp. 141-142.
1147. _____., et al. "Perception of Attempts at Interpersonal Influence." Paper Presented at the *79th Annual Convention of the American Psychological Association,* held in 1979. pp. 391-392.
1148. Schemitzki, D. P. *Bargaining, Group Decision Making and the Attainment of Maximum Joint Outcome.* Ph.D. Dissertation. Minneapolis, MN.: University of Minnesota, 1962.
1149. Shapiro, Debra L. *Deceptive Communication in the Bargaining Context: Does Hedging Enhance the Bluffer's Chance of Gaining Trust, Pardon, and Integrative Agreements.* Ph.D. Dissertation. Evanston, IL.: Northwestern University, 1986. 195p.
1150. Shaw, Jerry I. *Situational Factors Leading to the Acquisition of a "Psychological Advantage" in Competitive Negotiations.* Ph.D. Dissertation. Los Angeles, CA.: University of California at Los Angeles, 1969.
1151. Sherman, Allen W. *The Social Psychology of Bilateral Negotiations.* M.A. Thesis. Evanston, IL.: Northwestern University, 1963.
1152. Silver, R. B. *Reactions to Commitment to Relinquish an Alternative and Power in a Bargaining Game.* Ph.D. Dissertation. Nashville, TN.: Vanderbilt University, 1969.
1153. Smith, David H. *An Experimental Study of Communication Restriction and Knowledge of the Opponent's Minimum Dispositions as Variables Influencing Negotiation Outcomes.* Ph.D. Dissertation. Columbus, OH.: Ohio State University, 1966. 105p.
1154. Snyder, Glenn H. *Studies in International Conflict.* Research Monograph No. 1. Buffalo, NY.: Center for International Security and Conflict Studies, State University of New York in Buffalo, 1968. 132p.
1155. Solomon-Ravich, Rachel. *The Effects of Alternatives and Motivational Orientation on Negotiation Behavior.* Ph.D. Dissertation. New York: Columbia University, 1985. 264p.
1156. Spector, Bertram I. "Negotiation as a Psychological Process." Paper Presented at the *Annual Meeting of the American Political Science Association,* held on September 1976, in Chicago, IL.
1157. _____. "Psychological Impacts on Negotiations: An Empirical Analysis." Paper Presented at the *Annual Meeting of the International Studies Association,* held in 1977, in St.Louis, MI.

1158. _____. *The Effects of Personality, Perception and Power on the Bargaining Process and Outcome: A Field Theory and Political Analysis of a Negotiation Simulation.* Ph.D. Dissertation. New York: New York University, 1976. 276p.
1159. Stech, Frank J. *Communicated Influence Effects on Duopoly Bargaining Behavior.* Ph.D. Dissertation. Santa Barbara, CA.: University of California at Santa Barbara, 1977. 375p.
1160. Stephenson, G. M. "Experimental Studies of Negotiation Groups." Paper Presented at the *Annual Conference of the British Psychological Society*, held in 1975, at the University of Nottingham, Nottingham.
1161. Swingle, Paul G. "Incantation of the Operational Definition." Paper Presented at the *17th Annual Convention of the International Studies Association*, held on February 25-29, 1976, in Toronto.
1162. Terhune, Kenneth W. *Personality Factors in Experimental Studies of Cooperation and Conflict.* Buffalo, NY.: Cornell Aeronautical Laboratory, (1966), 30p.
1163. _____., and J. M. Firestone. *Psychological Studies in Social Interaction and Motives (SIAM).* CAL Report VX-2018-G-1. Buffalo, NY.: Cornell Aeronautical Laboratory, 1965-1967. 2 Vols.
1164. United States. Congress. Senate. Committee on Foreign Relations. *Psychological Aspects of International Relations: Hearings.* 89th Cong., 2nd sess. Washington, D.C.: U.S. Government Print Office, 1966. 79p.
1165. Van Slyck, M. R., Dean G. Pruitt and Peter J. Carnevale. "Impact of Limit Salience on Demand Level and Bargainer Outcome." Paper Presented at the *Annual Meeting of the Eastern Psychological Association*, held in April 1981, in New York.
1166. _____. _____. _____. "Effects of Self-Awareness and Limit Salience on Negotiation Behavior." Paper Presented at the *Annual Meeting of the Eastern Psychological Association*, held in 1982, in Baltimore, MD.
1167. _____., et al. "Focus of Attention in Negotiation." Paper Presented at the *Annual Meeting of the Eastern Psychological Association*, held in 1984, in Baltimore, MD.
1168. _____. Dean G. Pruitt and Peter J. Carnevale. "Objective Selfawareness Moderates the Impact of Limit Salience in Negotiation." Paper Presented at the *Annual meeting of the Eastern Psychological Association*, held in 1983, in Philadelphia, PA.
1169. Vidmar, N. J. *Leadership and Role Structure in Negotiations and Other Decision-Making Groups.* Ph.D. Dissertation. Urbana, IL.: University of Illinois, 1967.
1170. _____., and J. E. McGrath. *Role Assignment and Attitudinal Commitment as Factors in Negotiation.* Technical Report, No. 3. Urbana, IL.: Department of Psychology, University of Illinois, 1965.
1171. _____. _____. *Role Structure, Leadership and Negotiation Effectiveness.* Technical Report, No. 6. Urbana, IL.: Department of Psychology, 1967.
1172. Wallace, Samuel P. *An Examination of the Influence of Interaction Involvement on Outcome and Persuasion Strategy in Dyadic Negotiation Sessions.* Ph.D. Dissertation. Columbus, OH.: Ohio State University, 1985. 125p.
1173. Ward, Hugh D. *Behavioral Models of Bargaining: The Dynamics of Subjective Power and Bargaining Goals in Situations of Conflict.* Ph.D. Dissertation. Essex: University of Essex, 1979.
1174. Weiss, Stephen E. *The Language of Successful Negotiators: A Study of Communicative Competence in Intergroup Negotiation Simulations.* Ph.D. Dissertation. Philadelphia, PA.:University of Pennsylvania, 1985. 350p.

1175. ____. "The Language of Successful Negotiators: A Study of Communicative Competence in Intergroup Negotiation Simulation." Paper Presented at the *National Conference on Peacemaking and Conflict Resolution,* held on September 18-23, 1984, at University of Missouri, St.Louis.
1176. Weiss-Wik, Stephen. "Linguistic Structure and Creative Response in Direct Negotiations." Paper Presented at the *International Peace Science Society,* held on November 9-11, 1981, in Philadelphia, PA.
1177. Wells, R. B. *The Control of Disruptive Behavior in a Bargaining Game.* Ph.D. Dissertation. Chapel Hill, NC.: University of North Carolina, 1967.
1178. Womack, Deanna F. *Orientations to Conflict and Their Consequences in Negotiating Behavior.* Ph.D. Dissertation. Lawrence, KA.: University of Kansas, 1982. 261p.
1179. Young, Allan R. *Bargaining Under Incomplete Information: Attitudes Towards Risk and Strategic Behavior.* Ph.D. Dissertation. San Diego, CA.: University of California, 1983. 105p.
1180. Yukl, Gary A. "The Effect of Opponent Concessions on a Bargainer's Perception and Concessions." Paper Presented at the *80th Annual Convention of the American Psychological Association,* held in 1972, in Honolulu, HI. pp. 229-230.
1181. Zagare, Frank C. *Deception in 3-Person Games: An Analysis of Strategic Misrepresentation in Vietnam.* Ph.D. Dissertation. New York: New York University, 1977.

III

Game Theory

Game theory is a method for the study of decision making in situations of conflict. It addresses problems involving conflict, cooperation or both. The decision making unit may be an individual, a group of people, an organization or a governmental body. Conflicts may be reflective of political, social, psychological or economic aspects of human affairs.

This chapter, although primarily restricted to materials dealing with studies of international negotiations, also includes general game theoretic investigations of negotiations. The activities of diplomats engaged in international negotiations may be usefully examined with game theoretic methods of analysis and simulation. By nature, games and simulations are restricted by types of variables, numbers of players, types of available options for analysis. In analysing diplomatic negotiations, the characteristics of players have to be taken account of, goals have to be evaluated, and variables have to be restricted. In this sense, game theoretic analysis, is restricted by the input variables and assumptions. Outcomes of games depends on the number of players, the payoffs and the rules which control the game environment. Game theoretic analysis of negotiations and in this case of international negotiations have contributed new insights into the theory of bargaining and to the processes of negotiations.

This chapter is an inclusive English language listing of game theoretic literature dealing with situations of international negotiations.

1. Books

1182. Archibald, Kathleen, ed. *Strategic Interaction and Conflict: Original Papers and Discussion*. Berkeley, CA.: Institute of International Studies, University of California, 1966. 227p.
1183. Aumann, R. J., et al. *The Indirect Measurement of Utility*. Princeton, NJ.: Mathematica Inc.,1968. 2 Vols.
1184. Avenhaus, Rudolf, and Reiner K. Huber. *Quantitative Assessment in Arms Control: Mathematical Modeling and Simulation in the Analysis of Arms Control Problems*. New York: Plenum Press, 1984. 480p.
1185. _____. _____. and John D. Kettelle, eds. *Modelling and Analysis in Arms Control*. NATO ASI Series F: Computer and Systems Sciences, Vol. 26. Berlin: Springer Verlag, 1986. 488p.
1186. Axelrod, Robert. *The Evolution of Cooperation*. New York: Basic Books, 1984. 241p.
1187. _____., ed. *The Structure of Decision: The Cognitive Maps of Political Elite*. Princeton, NJ.: Princeton University Press, 1976. 404p.
1188. Beal, Richard S. *Systems Analysis of International Crises*. Washington, D.C.: University Press of America, 1979. 407p.
1189. Bennett, P. G., ed. *Analysing Conflict and Its Resolution: Some Mathematical Contributions*. Oxford: Clarendon Press, 1987. 349p.
1190. Binmore, K. G., and Partha Dasgupta. *The Economics of Bargaining*. Oxford: Basil Blackwell, 1987. 260p.
1191. Brams, Steven J. *Game Theory and Politics*. New York: Free Press, 1975. 312p.
1192. _____. *Superpower Games: Applying Game Theory to Superpower Conflicts*. New Haven, CT.: Yale University Press, 1985. 176p.
1193. _____., and D. Marc Kilgour. *Game Theory and National Security*. New York: Basil Blackwell, 1988. 199p.
1194. _____. *Rational Politics*. Washington, D.C.: Congressional Quarterly, 1985. 214p.
1195. Coddington, Alan H. *Theories of the Bargaining Process*. Chicago, IL.: Aldine, 1968. 106p.
1196. Colman, Andrew M. *Game Theory and Experimental Games: The Study of Strategic Interaction*. New York: Pergamon Press, 1982. 301p.
1197. Cross, John G. *The Economics of Bargaining*. New York: Basic Books, 1969. 247p.
1198. Davis, Morton D. *Game Theory: A Nontechnical Introduction*. New York: Basic Books, 1983. 252p.
1199. Dutton, William B., and Kenneth L. Kraemer. *Modeling as Negotiating: The Political Dynamics of Computer Models in the Policy Process*. Norwood, NJ.: Ablex, 1985. 261p.
1200. Festinger, Leon. *The Theory of Cognitive Dissonance*. New York: Row Peterson, 1957. 291p.
1201. Fouraker, Lawrence E., and Sidney Siegel. *Bargaining Behavior*. New York: McGraw-Hill, 1963. 309p.
1202. Fraser, Niall M., and Keith W. Hipel. *Conflict Analysis: Models and Resolutions*. New York: North-Holland, 1984. 377p.
1203. Harsanyi, John C. *Papers in Game Theory*. Dordrecht: D. Reidel, 1982. 258p.
1204. _____. *Rational Behavior and Bargaining Equilibrium in Games and Social Situations*. Cambridge: Cambridge University Press, 1977. 314p.
1205. Jones, A. J. *Game Theory: Mathematical Theory in Conflict*. Chichester, England: Ellis Horwood, 1980. 309p.

1206. Keeney, Ralph L, and Howard Raiffa. *Decisions with Multiple Objectives: Preferences and Value Tradeoffs.* New York: John Wiley & Sons, 1976. 569p.
1207. Luce, R. Duncan ____. *Games and Decisions: Introduction and Critical Survey.* New York: John Wiley, 1957. 509p.
1208. McDonald, John D. *Strategy in Poker, Business & War.* New York: McGraw-Hill, 1953. 128p.
1209. Munier, Bertrand R., and Melvin F. Shakun, eds. *Compromise Negotiation and Group Decision.* Dordrecht: D. Reidel, 1988. 300p.
1210. Ordeshook, Peter C. *Game Theory and Political Theory: An Introduction.* Cambridge: Cambridge University Press, 1986. 511p.
1211. Rapoport, Amnon, et al. *Coalition Formation by Sophisticated Players.* Berlin: Springer-Verlag, 1979. 170p.
1212. Rapoport, Anatol. *Fights, Games and Debates.* Ann Arbor, MI.: University of Michigan Press, 1960. 400p.
1213. ____., ed. *Game Theory as a Theory of Conflict Resolution.* Dordrecht: D. Reidel, 1974. 283p.
1214. ____. *N-Person Game Theory: Concepts and Applications.* Ann Arbor, MI.: University of Michigan Press, 1970. 331p.
1215. ____., and Albert M. Chammah. *Prisoner's Dilemma: A Study in Conflict and Cooperation.* Ann Arbor, MI.: University of Michigan Press, 1965. 258p.
1216. ____. Melvin J. Guyer and David G. Gordon. *The 2x2 Game.* Ann Arbor, MI.: University of Michigan Press, 1976. 461p.
1217. ____. *Two-Person Game Theory: The Essential Ideas.* Ann Arbor, MI.: University of Michigan Press, 1966. 229p.
1218. Roth, Alvin E. *Axiomatic Models of Bargaining.* New York: Springer-Verlag, 1979. 121p.
1219. ____., ed. *Game-Theoretic Models of Bargaining.* Cambridge: Cambridge University Press, 1985. 390p.
1220. Saaty, Thomas. *Mathematical Models of Arms Control and Disarmament.* New York: John Wiley, 1968. 190p.
1221. Sauermann, Heinz, ed. *Bargaining Behavior.* Tübingen: Mohr, 1978. 383p.
1222. Shubik, Martin, ed. *Game Theory and Related Approaches to Social Behavior.* New York: John Wiley, 1964. 390p.
1223. ____. *Games for Society, Business and War: Towards a Theory of Gaming.* New York: Elsevier, 1975. 371p.
1224. Siegel, Sidney, and Lawrence E. Fouraker. *Bargaining and Group Decision Making: Experiments in Bilateral Monopoly.* New York: McGraw-Hill, 1960. 132p.
1225. Stahl, Ingolf. *Bargaining Theory.* Stockholm: Stockholm School of Economics, Economic Research Institute, 1972. 313p.
1226. Taylor, Michael. *The Possibility of Cooperation.* Cambridge: Cambridge University Press, 1987. 205p.
1227. Thomson, William, and Terje Lensberg. *Axiomatic Theory of Bargaining with a Variable Number of Agents.* Cambridge: Cambridge University Press, 1988. 230p.
1228. Tietz, Reinhard, ed. *Aspirative Levels in Bargaining and Economic Decision Making: Proceedings of the Third Conference on Experimental Economics, Winzenhohl, Germany, August 29 - September 3, 1982.* Berlin: Springer-Verlag, 1983. 406p.
1229. Von Neumann, John, and Oskar Morgenstern. *Theory of Games and Economic Behavior.* 3rd ed. Princeton, NJ.: Princeton University Press, 1953. 641p.

2. Journal Articles

1230. Albers, Wulf. "Two-Person Bargaining Between Threat and Fair Solution." In: R. Avenhaus, R. K. Huber and J. D. Kettelle, eds. *Modelling and Analysis in Arms Control.* Berlin: Springer-Verlag, 1986. pp. 295-306.
1231. _____. "Bloc Forming Tendencies as Characteristics of Bargaining Behavior in Different Versions of Apex Games." In: H. Sauermann, ed. *Coalition Formation Behavior.* Tübingen: Mohr, 1978. pp. 172-206.
1232. Alexander, C. N., and H. G. Weil. "Players, Persons and Purposes: Situational Meaning and Prisoner's Dilemma Game." *Sociometry,* 32 (1969), 121-144.
1233. Alker, H. R., and R. D. Brunner. "Simulating International Conflict: A Comparison of Three Approaches." *International Studies Quarterly,* 13:1 (1969), 70-110.
1234. Axelrod, Robert. "Effective Choice in Prisoner's Dilemma." *Journal of Conflict Resolution,* 24:1 (March 1980), 3-26.
1235. _____. "More Effective Choice in the Prisoner's Dilemma." *Journal of Conflict Resolution,* 24:3 (1980), 379-403.
1236. _____., and Robert O. Keohane. "Achieving Cooperation Under Anarchy: Strategies and Institutions." In K. A. Oye, ed. *Cooperation Under Anarchy.* Princeton, NY.: Princeton University Press, 1986. pp. 226-254.
1237. _____. "The Emergence of Cooperation Among Egoists." *American Political Science Review,* 75 (June 1981), 306-318.
1238. _____. "Argumentation in Foreign Policy Settings: Britain in 1918, Munich in 1938, and Japan in 1970." In: I. W. Zartman, ed. *The Negotiation Process.* Beverly Hills, CA.: Sage, 1978. pp. 175-192.
1239. _____., and William D. Hamilton. "The Evolution of Cooperation." *Science,* 211 (1981), 1390-1396.
1240. _____. "Argumentation in Foreign Policy Settings: Britain in 1918, Munich in 1938, and Japan in 1970." *Journal of Conflict Resolution,* 21:4 (1977), 727-744.
1241. Baldwin, Robert E., and Richard N. Clarke. "Game Modeling Multilateral Trade Negotiations." *Journal of Policy Modeling,* 9:2 (Summer 1987), 257-284.
1242. Banks, M. H., A. J. R. Gwom and A. N. Oppenheim. "Gaming and Simulation in International Relations." *Political Studies,* 16 (1968), 1-17.
1243. Bartos, Otomar J. "Is Toughness Profitable?" In: H. Sauermann, ed. *Contributions to Experimental Economics, Vol. 3.* Tübingen: Mohr, 1972. pp. 166-219.
1244. _____. "A Model of Negotiation and the Recent Effect." *Sociometry,* 27 (1964), 311-326.
1245. _____. "Negotiation and Justice." In: H. Sauermann, ed. *Bargaining Behavior.* Tübingen: Mohr, 1978. pp. 103-126.
1246. _____. Reinhard Tietz and C. McLean. "Toughness and Fairness in Negotiations." In: R. Tietz, ed. *Aspiration Levels in Bargaining and Economic Decision Making.* Berlin: Springer-Verlag, 1983. pp. 35-51.
1247. Baudier, Edmond. "Negotiation Procedure in a Coherent Game." In: B. R. Munier and M. F. Shakun, eds. *Compromise, Negotiation and Group Decision.* Dordrecht: D. Reidel, 1987. pp. 103-118.
1248. Bazerman, Max H., and William F. Samuelson. "The Winner's Curse: An Empirical Investigation." In: R. Tietz, ed. *Aspiration Levels in Bargaining and Economic Decision Making.* New York: Springer Verlag, 1983. pp. 186-200.

1249. Becker, Otwin, and Stephan Huschens. "Bounded Rational Strategies in Sequential Bargaining: An Experiment and a Learning by Evolution Strategy." In: R. Tietz, W. Albers and R. Selten, eds. *Bounded Rational Behavior in Experimental Games and Markets.* Berlin: Springer Verlag, 1988. pp. 129-141.
1250. Ben-Dak, Joseph D. "Social Exchange in Simulation Gaming: Strategic Linkages in Research on Conflict Resolution." In: *2nd Pugwash International Summer School on Disarmament and Arms Control.* Pavia, Italy: (Pugwash), 1968. pp. 261-290.
1251. Benson, Oliver. "Simulation of International Relations and Diplomacy." In: H. Borko, ed. *Computer Applications in the Behavioral Science.* Englewood Cliffs, NJ.: Prentice Hall, 1962. pp. 574-595.
1252. _____. "A Simple Diplomatic Game." In: J. N. Rosenau, ed. *International Politics and Foreign Policy.* New York: The Free Press, 1961. pp. 504-511.
1253. Berl, Janet E., et al. "An Experimental Test of the Core in a Simple N-Person Cooperative Nonsidepayment Game." *Journal of Conflict Resolution,* 20:3 (September 1976), 453-480.
1254. Bernhardt, R. G. "Four Way Decision Making." *Simulation and Games,* 9 (June 1978), 227-233.
1255. Bigoness, W. J., and D. W. Grigsby. "The Effects of Need for Achievement and Alternative Forms of Arbitration upon Bargaining Behavior." In: R. Tietz, ed. *Aspiration Levels in Bargaining and Economic Decision Making.* Berlin: Springer-Verlag, 1983. pp. 122-135.
1256. Binmore, K. G., Ariel Rubinstein and A. Wolinsky. "The Nash Bargaining Solution in Economic Modelling." *RAND Journal of Economics,* 17 (Summer 1986), 176-188.
1257. _____. A. Shaked and John Sutton. "Testing Noncooperative Bargaining Theory: A Preliminary Study." *American Economic Review,* 75 (December 1985), 1178-1180.
1258. _____., and M. J. Herrero. "Security Equilibrium." *Review of Economic Studies,* 55 (January 1988), 33-48.
1259. Bishop, Robert L. "Game Theoretic Analyses of Bargaining." In: O. R. Young, ed. *Bargaining.* Urbana, IL.: University of Illinois Press, 1975. pp. 85-130.
1260. _____. "Game Theoretic Analysis of Bargaining." *Quarterly Journal of Economics,* 77:4 (1963), 559-602.
1261. _____. "A Zeuthen-Hicks Theory of Bargaining." In: O. R. Young, ed. *Bargaining.* Urbana, IL.: University of Illinois Press, 1975. pp. 183-190.
1262. _____. "A Zeuthen-Hicks Theory of Bargaining." *Econometrica,* 32 (1964), 410-417.
1263. Bixenstine, V. E., C. A. Levitt and K. V. Wilson. "Collaborating Among Six Persons in a Prisoner's Dilemma Game." *Journal of Conflict Resolution,* 10 (1966), 488-496.
1264. _____., and H. Blundell. "Control of Choice Exerted by Structural Factors in Two-Person, Non-Zero-Sum Games." *Journal of Conflict Resolution,* 10 (1966), 478-487.
1265. Black, J., and G. Buckley. "The Role of Strategic Information Transmission in a Bargaining Model." *Economic Journal,* 98:Supplement (1988), 50-57.
1266. Bloomfield, Lincoln P. "Bellex - the Bellagio 'Mini-Game'." In: M. R. Berman and J. E. Johnson, eds. *Unofficial Diplomats.* New York: Columbia University Press, 1977. pp. 222-240.
1267. _____. "Computerizing Conflicts." *Foreign Service Journal,* 65:6 (June 1988), 46-49.

1268. Bobrow, Davis B. "Ecology of International Games: Requirement for a Model of the International System." *Peace Research Society (International) Papers*, 11 (1968), 67-88.
1269. Bonacich, Phillip, et al. "Cooperation and Group Size in the N-Person Prisoner's Dilemma." *Journal of Conflict Resolution*, 20:4 (December 1976), 687-706.
1270. ____. "Putting the Dilemma Back into Prisoner's Dilemma." *Journal of Conflict Resolution*, 14:3 (September 1970), 379-388.
1271. Bonham, Matthew G. "Simulating International Disarmament Negotiations." *Journal of Conflict Resolution*, 15:3 (1971), 299-316.
1272. Boulding, Kenneth E. "Towards a Pure Theory of Threat Systems." *American Economic Review*, 52 (1963), 424-434.
1273. Brams, Steven J. "Deception in a 2x2 Games." *Journal of Peace Science*, 2 (1977), 171-203.
1274. ____., and Donald Wittman. "Nonmyopic Equilibria in 2x2 Games." *Conflict Management and Peace Science*, 6:1 (Fall 1981), 39-62.
1275. ____. "Newcomb's Problem and Prisoner's Dilemma." *Journal of Conflict Resolution*, 19:4 (December 1975), 596-612.
1276. ____., and D. Marc Kilgour. "Winding Down If Preemption and Escalation Occurs: A Game Theoretic Analysis." *Journal of Conflict Resolution*, 31:4 (December 1987), 547-572.
1277. Braunstein, Yale, and Andrew Schotter. "An Experimental Study of the Problem of "Theory Absorbtion" in N-Person Bargaining Situations or Games." In: H. Sauermann, ed. *Coalition Formation Behavior*. Tübingen: Mohr, 1978. pp. 1-25.
1278. Braver, Sanford, and Bruce Barnett. "Perception of Opponent's Motives and Cooperation in a Mixed-Motive Game." *Journal of Conflict Resolution*, 18:4 (December 1974), 686-699.
1279. Bredemeier, M. E. "Policy Negotiations." *Simulation and Games*, 11 (June 1980), 243-247.
1280. Brenenstuhl, Daniel C., and Richard Blalack. "Role Preference and Vested Interest in a Bargaining Environment." *Simulation and Games*, 9:1 (March 1978), 53-65.
1281. Brew, J. S. "An Altruism Parameter for Prisoner's Dilemma." *Journal of Conflict Resolution*, 17:2 (June 1973), 351-367.
1282. Brown, Scott. "The Superpowers' Dilemma: Can Game Theory Improve the U.S. - Soviet Negotiation Relationship?." *Negotiation Journal*, 2:4 (October 1986), 371-384.
1283. Bryant, Jim. "Modelling Alternative Realities in Conflict and Negotiation." *Journal of Operational Research Society*, 35 (November 1984), 985-993.
1284. Buckley, James J., and T. Edward Westen. "Bargaining Set Theory and Majority Rule." *Journal of Conflict Resolution*, 20:3 (1976), 481-496.
1285. ____. ____. "The Symmetric Solution to a Five Person Constant-Sum Game as a Description of Experimental Outcomes." *Journal of Conflict Resolution*, 17:4 (December 1973), 703-718.
1286. Burns, T., and L. D. Meeker. "Structural Properties and Resolutions of the Prisoner's Dilemma Game." In: A. Rapoport, ed. *Game Theory as a Theory of Conflict Resolution*. Dordrecht: D. Reidel, 1974. pp. 35-62.
1287. Carling, Alan H. "The Unified Solution of the Cross/Coddington Model of the Bargaining Process." *Public Choice*, 32 (Winter 1977), 11-38.
1288. Carment, D. W., and James E. Alcock. "Indian and Canadian Behavior in Two-Person Power Games." *Journal of Conflict Resolution*, 28:3 (1984), 507-521.

1289. Carnevale, Peter J. "Modeling Mediator Behavior in Experimental Games." In: R. Tietz, W. Albers and R. Selten, eds. *Bounded Rational Behavior in Experimental Games and Markets*. New York: Springer Verlag, 1988. pp. 160-172.
1290. Chatterjee, Kalyan. "Bargaining Under Incomplete Information." *Operational Research*, 31 (September-October 1983), 835-851.
1291. _____., and L. Samuelson. "Bargaining with Two-Sided Incomplete Information: An Infinite Horizon Model with Alternating Offers." *Review of Economic Studies*, 54 (April 1987), 175-192.
1292. _____., and Gary L. Lilien. "Efficiency of Alternative Bargaining Procedures: An Experimental Study." *Journal of Conflict Resolution*, 28:2 (June 1984), 270-295.
1293. _____. "Incentive Compatibility in Bargaining Under Uncertainty." *Quarterly Journal of Economics*, 97 (November 1982), 717-726.
1294. Chertkoff, J. M., and Lynn L. Laue. "The Interaction and Perceptions of Cooperators and Competitors in a Prisoner's Dilemma Game Versus an Expanded Prisoner's Dilemma Game." In: H. Sauermann, ed. *Bargaining Behavior*. Tübingen: Mohr, 1978. pp. 1-19.
1295. Coddington, Alan H. "Bargaining as a Decision Process." *Swedish Journal of Economics*, 75 (1973), 397-405.
1296. _____. "Game Theory, Bargaining Theory and Strategic Reasoning." *Journal of Peace Research*, 4 (1967), 39-44.
1297. _____. "A Theory of the Bargaining Process: Comments." *American Economic Review*, 56 (1966), 522-530.
1298. _____. "On the Theory of Bargaining." In: C. F. Carter and J. L. Ford, eds. *Uncertainty and Expectations in Economics*. Oxford: Blackwells, 1972. pp. 43-57.
1299. Cole, Steven G., and Lester W. Barnett. "The Subjective Distribution of Achieved Power and Associated Coalition Formation Behavior." In: H. Sauermann, ed. *Coalition Formation Behavior*. Tübingen: Mohr, 1978. pp. 40-54.
1300. Conrath, David W. "Experience as a Factor in Experimental Gaming Behavior." *Journal of Conflict Resolution*, 14:2 (June 1970), 195-202.
1301. _____., and Thomas J. Price. "Sex Role and "Cooperation" in the Game of Chicken." *Journal of Conflict Resolution*, 16:3 (September 1972), 433-444.
1302. Contini, Bruno. "Value of Time in Bargaining Negotiations: Some Experimental Evidence." *American Economic Review*, 48 (1958), 374-393.
1303. Coplin, William D. "Inter-Nation Simulation and Contemporary Theories of International Relations." *American Political Science Review*, 60 (September 1966), 562-578.
1304. Crampton, Peter C. "Bargaining with Incomplete Information: An Infinite-Horizon Model with Two-Sided Uncertainty." *Review of Economic Studies*, 51 (October 1984), 579-593.
1305. Crawford, Vincent P. "Dynamic Games and Dynamic Contract Theory." *Journal of Conflict Resolution*, 29:2 (June 1985), 195-224.
1306. _____. "A Note on the Zeuthen - Harsanyi Theory of Bargaining." *Journal of Conflict Resolution*, 24 (September 1980), 525-535.
1307. _____. "A Theory of Disagreement in Bargaining." *Econometrica*, 50:3 (May 1982), 607-637.
1308. Cross, John G. "Negotiations as a Learning Process." *Journal of Conflict Resolution*, 21:4 (1977), 581-606.
1309. _____. "Negotiation as a Learning Process." In: I. W. Zartman, ed. *The Negotiation Process*. Beverly Hills, CA.: Sage, 1978. pp. 29-54.

1310. _____. "A Theory of the Bargaining Process." In: O. R. Young, ed. *Bargaining*. Urbana, IL.: University of Illinois Press, 1975. pp. 191-218.
1311. _____. "A Theory of the Bargaining Process." *American Economic Review*, 55:1 (1965), 66-94.
1312. _____. "A Theory of the Bargaining Process: Reply." *American Economic Review*, 56:3 (1966), 530-533.
1313. Crott, Helmut W., R. Luhr and C. Rombach. "The Effects of Level of Aspiration and Experience in 3-Person Bargaining Games." In: R. Tietz, ed. *Aspiration Levels in Bargaining and Economic Decision Making*. Berlin: Springer-Verlag, 1983. pp. 276-290.
1314. _____. Günter F. Muller and Peter L. Hamel. "The Influence of Aspiration Level, of the Level of Information and Bargaining Experience on the Process and Outcome in a Bargaining Situation." In: H. Sauermann, ed. *Bargaining Behavior*. Tübingen: Mohr, 1978. pp. 211-230.
1315. Dagnino, Aldo, Keith W. Hipel and Niall M. Fraser. "Game Theory Analysis of a Ground Water Contamination Dispute." *Journal of the Geological Society of India*, 29 (January 1987), 6-22.
1316. Deutsch, Karl W. "Game Theory and Politics: Some Problems of Application." *Canadian Journal of Economics and Political Science*, 120 (1954), 76-83.
1317. Deutsch, Morton. "The Face of Bargaining." *Operations Research*, 9 (1961), 886-897.
1318. _____., and Roy J. Lewicki. "'Locking-in' Effects During a Game of Chicken." *Journal of Conflict Resolution*, 14 (September 1970), 367-378.
1319. _____., and Robert M. Krauss. "Studies in Interpersonal Bargaining." In: M. Shubik, ed. *Game Theory and Related Approaches to Social Behavior*. New York: John Wiley, 1964. pp. 324-337.
1320. _____., and Paul Kotik. "Altruism and Bargaining." In: H. Sauermann, ed. *Bargaining Behavior*. Tübingen: Mohr, 1978. pp. 20-40.
1321. _____. "Bargaining, Threat and Communication: Some Experimental Studies. In: K. Archibald, ed. *Strategic Interaction and Conflict: Original Papers and Discussion*. Berkeley, CA.: Institute of International Studies, 1966. pp. 19-48.
1322. _____., and Robert M. Krauss. "Studies in Interpersonal Bargaining." *Journal of Conflict Resolution*, 6:1 (1962), 52-76.
1323. Dolbear, F. Trenery, et al. "Collusion in the Prisoner's Dilemma: Number of Strategies." *Journal of Conflict Resolution*, 13:2 (June 1969), 252-261.
1324. _____., and Lester B. Lave. "Risk Orientation as a Predictor in the Prisoner's Dilemma." *Journal of Conflict Resolution*, 10:4 (December 1966), 506-515.
1325. Downs, George W., and David M. Rocke. "Tacit Bargaining and Arms Control." *World Politics*, 39:3 (April 1987), 297-325.
1326. Druckman, Daniel. "The Monitoring Function in Negotiation: Two Models of Responsiveness." In: H. Sauermann, ed. *Bargaining Behavior: Contributions to Experimental Economics, No. 7*. Tübingen: Mohr, 1978. pp. 344-375.
1327. _____. "Understanding the Operation of Complex Social Systems: Some Uses of Simulation Design." *Simulation and Games*, 2 (1971), 173-195.
1328. Ells, J. G., and V. Sermat. "Motivational Determinants of Choice in Chicken and Prisoner's Dilemma." *Journal of Conflict Resolution*, 12 (1968), 374-380.
1329. Ellsberg, Daniel. "The Theory and Practice of Blackmail." In: O. R. Young, ed. *Bargaining*. Urbana, IL.: University of Illinois Press, 1975. pp. 343-363.

1330. _____. "Theory of the Reluctant Duelist." In: O. R. Young, ed. *Bargaining.* Urbana, IL.: University of Illinois Press, 1975. pp. 38-52.
1331. _____. "Theory of the Reluctant Duelist." *American Economic Review,* 46 (1956), 909-923.
1332. Emshoff, J. R., and Russell L. Ackoff. "Explanatory Models of Interactive Choice Behavior." *Journal of Conflict Resolution,* 14:1 (March 1970), 77-90.
1333. England, J. Lynn. "The Bargaining Automata: Linear and Nonlinear Models." *Journal of Conflict Resolution,* 23:2 (June 1979), 296-325.
1334. _____. "Linear Learning Models for Two-Party Negotiations." *Journal of Conflict Resolution,* 19 (December 1975), 682-707.
1335. _____. "Mathematical Models of Two-Party Negotiations." *Behavioral Science,* 18 (May 1973), 189-197.
1336. _____. "Two Bargaining Automata: Linear and Nonlinear Models." *Journal of Conflict Resolution,* 23:2 (June 1979), 296-325.
1337. Fang, L., Keith W. Hipel and D. Marc Kilgour. "A Comprehensive Decision Support System for Two Player Conflicts." *Large Scale Systems,* 11:1 (1986), 19-29.
1338. Felsenthal, Dan S., and Abraham Diskin. "The Bargaining Problem Revisited: Minimum Utility Point, Restricted Monotomicity Axiom, and the Mean as an Estimate of Expected Utility." *Journal of Conflict Resolution,* 26:4 (1982), 664-691.
1339. _____. "Bargaining Behavior When Profits are Unequal and Loses are Equal." *Behavioral Science,* 22:5 (1977), 334-340.
1340. Fogelman, S. F., Bertrand R. Munier and Melvin F. Shakun. "Bivariate Negotiations as a Problem of Stochastic Terminal Control." *Management Science,* 29:7 (July 1983), 840-855.
1341. Fox, John, and Melvin J. Guyer. "Equivalence and Stooge Strategies in Zero-Sum Games." *Journal of Conflict Resolution,* 17 (1973), 513-533.
1342. _____. "The Learning of Strategies in a Simple, Two-Person Zero-Sum Game Without Saddle Point." *Behavioral Science,* 17 (1972), 300-308.
1343. _____., and Melvin J. Guyer. "Group Size and Other's Strategy in an N-Person Game." *Journal of Conflict Resolution,* 21:2 (June 1977), 323-338.
1344. _____. _____. ""Public" Choice and Cooperation in N-Person Prisoner's Dilemma." *Journal of Conflict Resolution,* 22:3 (September 1978), 469-482.
1345. Fraser, Niall M. "General Ordinal 2x2 Games in Arms Control Negotiations." In: R. Avenhaus, R. K. Huber and J. D. Kettelle, eds. *Modelling and Analysis in Arms Control.* Berlin: Springer-Verlag, 1986. pp. 307-318.
1346. _____. Keith W. Hipel and J. R. Del Monte. "Algorithmic Approaches to Conflict Modelling." In: J. H. P. Paelinck and P. H. Vossen, eds. *Axiomatic and Pragmatics of Conflict Analysis.* Aldershot, England: Gower, 1986. pp. 53-79.
1347. _____. _____. _____. "Approaches to Conflict Modelling: A Study of Possible USA-USSR Nuclear Confrontation." *Journal of Policy Modeling,* 5:3 (1983), 397-417.
1348. _____. _____. "Conflict Analysis Techniques in Strategic Choice." In: L. Wilkin and A. Sutton, eds. *The Management of Uncertainty: Approaches, Methods, and Applications.* Dordrecht: Nijhoff, 1986. pp. 264-274.
1349. _____. _____. "Conflict Analysis as a Negotiation Support System." In: B. R. Munier and M. F. Shakun, eds. *Compromise, Negotiation and Group Decision.* Dordrecht: D. Reidel, 1987. pp. 225-244.

1350. Freimer, M., and P. L. Yu. "The Application of Compromise Solutions to Reporting Games." In: A. Rapoport, ed. *Game Theory as a Theory of Conflict Resolution.* Dordrecht: D. Reidel, 1974. pp. 235-260.
1351. Friend, Kenneth E., James D. Laing and Richard J. Morrison. "Bargaining Processes and Coalition Outcomes: An Integration." *Journal of Conflict Resolution*, 21:2 (June 1977), 267-298.
1352. Fudenberg, Drew, and Jean Tirole. "Sequential Bargaining with Incomplete Information." *Review of Economic Studies*, 50 (April 1983), 221-247.
1353. Gahagan, J. P., and J. T. Tedeschi. "Strategy and Credibility in the Prisoner's Dilemma Game." *Journal of Conflict Resolution*, 12 (1968), 224-234.
1354. Gallo, Philip S. "Personalizing Impression Formation in a Maximizing Difference Game." *Journal of Conflict Resolution*, 13:1 (March 1969), 118-122.
1355. Gentile, Ralph. "Modeling Negotiations: Assertion, Argument, Agreement." *Northeast Peace Science Review*, 1 (1978), 139-159.
1356. Gillis, John S., and George T. Woods. "The 16 PF as an Indicator of Performance in the Prisoner's Dilemma Game." *Journal of Conflict Resolution*, 15:3 (September 1971), 393-402.
1357. Goehring, Dwight J., and James P. Kahan. "The Uniform N-Person Prisoner's Dilemma Game: Construction and Test of an Index of Cooperation." *Journal of Conflict Resolution*, 20:1 (March 1976), 111-128.
1358. Goldberg, Andrew, and Debra Van Opstal. "Why Play Games." *Foreign Service Journal*, 65:6 (June 1988), 34-36.
1359. Goldhamer, H., and H. Speier. "Some Observations on Political Gaming." In: M. Shubik, ed. *Game Theory and Related Approaches to Social Behavior.* New York: John Wiley, 1964. pp. 261-272.
1360. _____. _____. "Some Observations on Political Gaming." *World Politics*, 12 (1959), 71-83.
1361. Goryachev, A., and V. Sergeev. "On Mathematical Models of Bargaining." In: H. Chesnut, et al. *Supplemental Ways for Improving International Stability.* Elmsford, NY.: Pergamon Press, 1984. pp. 183-188.
1362. Griesinger, D., and D. Livingston. "Towards a Model of International Motivation in Experimental Games." *Behavioral Science*, 18 (1973), 173-188.
1363. Grossman, Sanford J., and Motty Perry. "Sequential Bargaining Under Asymmetric Information." *Journal of Economic Theory*, 39 (June 1986), 120-154.
1364. Gruder, George W. "Elicitation of Cooperation by Retaliatory and Nonretaliatory Strategies in a Mixed Motive Game." *Journal of Conflict Resolution*, 17:1 (March 1973), 162-174.
1365. Guetzkow, H. "A Use of Simulation in the Study of International Relations." In: M. Shubik, ed. *Game Theory and Related Approaches to Social Behavior.* New York: John Wiley, 1964. pp. 273-282.
1366. _____. "A Use of Simulation in the Study of International Relations." *Behavioral Science*, 4:3 (July 1959), 183-191.
1367. Güth, Werner, and Reinhard Tietz. "Ultimatum Bargaining for a Shrinking Cake: An Experimental Analysis." In: R. Tietz, W. Albers and R. Selten, eds. *Bounded Rational Behavior in Experimental Games and Markets.* Berlin: Springer Verlag, 1988. pp. 111-128.
1368. _____. R. Schmittberger and B. Schwarze. "An Experimental Analysis of Ultimatum Bargaining." *Journal of Economic Behavior and Organization*, (1982), 367-388.
1369. Guyer, Melvin J. "An Analysis of Duopology Bargaining." *General Systems*, 11 (1966), 215-224.

1370. _____., and Anatol Rapoport. "Information Effects in Two Mixed Motive Games." *Behavioral Science*, 14 (1969), 467-482.
1371. _____. _____. "2x2 Games Played Once." *Journal of Conflict Resolution*, 16 (1972), 409-431.
1372. _____. John Fox and Henry Hamburger. "Format Effects in the Prisoner's Dilemma Game." *Journal of Conflict Resolution*, 17:4 (December 1973), 719-744.
1373. Hamner, W. C., and S. L. Baird. "The Effects of Strategy, Pressure to Reach Agreement and Relative Power on Bargaining Behavior." In: H. Sauermann, ed. *Bargaining Behavior*. Tübingen: Mohr, 1978. pp. 247-269.
1374. Harbottle, Michael. "Simulating Peace-Making in the Middle East: An Exercise in Reality." In: M. R. Berman and J. E. Johnson, eds. *Unofficial Diplomats*. New York: Columbia University Press, 1977. pp. 241-249.
1375. Harford, J. C., and Leonard Solomon. "'Reformed Sinner' and 'Lapsed Saint' Strategies in the Prisoner's Dilemma Game." *Journal of Conflict Resolution*, 11 (1967), 104-109.
1376. Harnett, D. L., and James A. Wall. "Aspiration Competitive Effects on the Mediation of Bargaining." In: R. Tietz, ed. *Aspiration Levels in Bargaining and Economic Decision Making*. Berlin: Springer-Verlag, 1983. pp. 8-21.
1377. _____. "Bargaining and Negotiation in a Mixed-Motive Game: Price Leadership Bilateral Monopoly." *Social Economic Journal*, 33 (1967), 479-487.
1378. _____., and B. L. Cummings. "Bilateral Monopoly Bargaining: An International Study." In: H. Sauermann, ed. *Contributions to Experimental Economics, Vol 3*. Tübingen: Mohr, 1972. pp. 100-129.
1379. _____., and L. P. Vincelette. "Strategic Influences on Bargaining Effectiveness." In: H. Sauermann, ed. *Bargaining Behavior: Contributions to Experimental Economics, Vol 7*. Tübingen: Mohr, 1978. pp. 231-246.
1380. _____., and W. C. Hamner. "The Value of Information in Bargaining." *Western Economic Journal*, 11 (1973), 81-88.
1381. Harsanyi, John C. "Approaches to the Bargaining Problem Before and After the Theory of Games." In: O. R. Young, ed. *Bargaining*. Urbana, IL.: University of Illinois Press, 1975. pp. 253-266.
1382. _____. "Approaches to the Bargaining Problem Before and After the Theory of Games." *Econometrica*, 24:2 (1956), 144-157.
1383. _____. "Bargaining and Conflict Situations in the Light of a New Approach to Game Theory." In: O. R. Young, ed. *Bargaining*. Urbana, IL.: University of Illinois Press, 1975. pp. 74-84.
1384. _____. "Bargaining and Conflict Situations in the Light of a New Approach to Game Theory." *American Economic Review*, 55 (1965), 447-457.
1385. _____. "Bargaining in Ignorance of the Opponent's Utility Function." *Journal of Conflict Resolution*, 6:1 (1962), 29-38.
1386. _____. "Bargaining Model for the Cooperative In-Person Game." In: A. W. Tucker and R. D. Luce, eds. *Contributions to the Theory of Games*. Vol. 4. Princeton, NJ.: Princeton University Press, 1959. pp. 325-356.
1387. _____. "A Bargaining Model of Social Status in Informal Groups and Organizations." *Behavioral Science*, 11 (1966), 357-369.
1388. _____. "Game Theory and the Analysis of International Conflict." *The Australian Journal of Politics and History*, 11 (1955), 292-304.
1389. _____. "A General Theory of Rational Behavior in Game Situations." *Econometrica*, 34 (1966), 613-634.
1390. _____., and R. Selten. "A Generalized Nash Solution for Two-Person Bargaining Games with Incomplete Information." *Management Science*, 18 (1972), 80-106.

1391. ____. "Measurement of Social Power, Opportunity Costs and the Theory of Two-Person Bargaining Games." *Behavioral Science*, 7 (January 1962), 67-80.
1392. ____. "Notes on the Bargaining Problem." *Southern Economic Journal*, 24 (1958), 471-476.
1393. ____. "On the Rationality Postulates Underlying the Theory of Cooperative Games." *Journal of Conflict Resolution*, 5:2 (1961), 179-196.
1394. ____. "Rationality Postulates for Bargaining in Cooperative and in Non-Cooperative Games." *Management Science*, 9 (1962), 141-153.
1395. ____. "A Simplified Bargaining Model for the N-Person Cooperative Game." *International Economic Review*, 4 (1963), 194-220.
1396. ____. "Some Social-Science Implications of a New Approach to Game Theory." In: K. Archibald, ed. *Strategic Interaction and Conflict: Original Papers and Discussion*. Berkeley, CA.: Institute of International Studies, University of California, 1966. pp. 1-18.
1397. Hartman, E. Alan, Steven G. Cole and James L. Phillips. "Bargaining as a Function of Power Structure, Position and Divisibility of Payoff." In: H. Sauermann, ed. *Coalition Formation Behavior*. Tübingen: Mohr, 1978. pp. 55-74.
1398. Hazleton, William A., and James E. Jacob. "Simulating International Diplomacy: The National Model United Nations Experience." *Teaching Political Science*, 10:2 (1982-83), 89-99.
1399. Henss, Ronald. "Bargaining Strength in Three-Person Characteristic-Function Games with v(i)>0: A Reanalysis of Kahan and Rapoport." *Theory and Decision*, 21:3 (November 1986), 267-282.
1400. Herman, Charles F. "Validation Problems in Grass and Simulations with Special Reference to Models of International Politics." *Behavioral Science*, 12 (1967), 216-231.
1401. Hessel, Marek. "Bargaining Costs and Rational Behavior: A Simple Model." *Journal of Conflict Resolution*, 25:3 (1981), 535-558.
1402. Hinton, B. L., W. C. Hamner and M. F. Pohlen. "The Influence of Reward Magnitude, Opening Bid and Concession Rate on Profit Earned in a Managerial Negotiation Game." *Behavioral Science*, 19 (1974), 197-203.
1403. Hipel, Keith W., and Niall M. Fraser. "Modelling Political Uncertainty Using the Improved Metagame Analysis Algorithm." In: L. Wilkin and A. Sutton, eds. *The Management of Uncertainty: Approaches,Methods and Applications*. Dordrecht: Nijhoff, 1986. pp. 138-157.
1404. ____. ____. "Systems Management: Conflict Analysis." In: M. G. Singh, ed. *Encyclopedia of Systems and Control*. Oxford: Pergamon Press, 1987. pp. 4793-4799.
1405. ____. Muhong Wang and Niall M. Fraser. "Hypergame Analysis of the Falkland/Malvinas Conflict." *International Studies Quarterly*, 32:3 (September 1988), 335-358.
1406. Hoggatt, Austin, et al. "Bargaining Experiments with Incomplete Information." In: H. Sauermann, ed. *Bargaining Behavior*. Tübingen: Mohr, 1978. pp. 127-178.
1407. ____., et al. "Robots as Instrumental Functions in the Study of Bargaining Behavior." In: H. Sauermann, ed. *Bargaining Behavior*. Tübingen: Mohr, 1978. pp. 179-210.
1408. Horowitz, Abraham D. "The Competitive Bargaining Set for Cooperative N-Person Games." *Journal of Mathematical Psychology*, 10 (1973), 265-289.

1409. _____., and Amnon Rapoport. "Test of the Kernel and Two Bargaining Set Models in Four and Five-Person Games." In: A. Rapoport, ed. *Game Theory as a Theory of Conflict Resolution.* Dordrecht: D. Reidel, 1974. pp. 161-192.
1410. Howard, Nigel. "'General' Metagames: An Extension of the Metagame Concept." In: A. Rapoport, ed. *Game Theory as a Theory of Conflict Resolution.* Dordrecht: D. Reidel, 1974. pp. 261-283.
1411. Hunsaker, J. S., G. G. Whitney and P. L. Hunsaker. "Learning Negotiation Skills Through Simulation." *Simulation and Games,* 14:4 (1983), 391-400.
1412. Ikle, Fred C., and Nathan C. Leites. "Negotiations: A Device for Modifying Utilities." In: M. Shubik, ed. *Game Theory and Related Approaches to Social Behavior.* New York: John Wiley, 1964. pp. 243-258.
1413. _____. _____. "Political Negotiation as a Process of Modifying Utilities." *Journal of Conflict Resolution,* 6:1 (1962), 19-28.
1414. Jenkins, Frank W. "The Use of Arms Control Negotiations Simulation as a Bridge Between Policy and Analysis." In: R. Avenhaus, R. K. Huber and J. D. Kettelle, ed. *Modelling and Analysis in Arms Control.* Berlin: Springer-Verlag, 1986. pp. 143-152.
1415. Jervis, Robert. "Realism, Game Theory and Cooperation." *World Politics,* 40:3 (April 1988), 317-349.
1416. Kahan, James P., and Amnon Rapoport. "Matrix Experiments and Theories of N-Person Games." *Journal of Conflict Resolution,* 25:4 (1981), 725-732.
1417. _____. _____. "Test of the Bargaining Set and Kernel Models in Three-Person Games." In: A. Rapoport, ed. *Game Theory as a Theory of Conflict Resolution.* Dordrecht: D. Reidel, 1974. pp. 119-160.
1418. _____. _____. "When You Don't Need To Join: The Effects of Guaranteed Payoffs on Bargaining in Three-Person Cooperative Games." *Theory and Decision,* 8 (1977), 97-126.
1419. Kalai, Ehud. "Proportional Solutions to Bargaining Situations: Interpersonal Utility Comparisons." *Econometrica,* 45 (1977), 1623-1630.
1420. _____., and M. Smorodinsky. "Other Solutions to Nash's Bargaining Problem." *Econometrica,* 43 (1957), 513-518.
1421. _____. "Preplay Negotiations and the Prisoner's Dilemma." *Mathematical Social Sciences,* 1 (1981), 375-379.
1422. Kaplan, Morton A. "A Note on Game Theory and Bargaining." In: M. A. Kaplan, ed. *New Approaches to International Relations.* New York: St. Martin's. 1968. pp. 483-518.
1423. Katz, Marsha. "Trivial Games as Predictors of a Mixed Motive Game." *Journal of Conflict Resolution,* 18:4 (December 1974), 700-706.
1424. Kelley, Harold H. "A Classroom Study of the Dilemma in Interpersonal Negotiations." In: K. Archibald, ed. *Strategic Interaction and Conflict: Original Papers and Discussion.* Berkeley, CA.: Institute of International Studies, University of California, 1966. pp. 49-73.
1425. Kersten, Gregory E., and Tomasz Szapiro. "Generalized-Approach to Modeling Negotiations." *European Journal of Operational Research,* 26:1 (1986), 142-149.
1426. _____. "Generating and Editing Compromise Proposals for Negotiations." In: B. R. Munier and M. F. Shakun, eds. *Compromise, Negotiation and Group Decision.* Dordrecht: D. Reidel, 1987. pp. 195-212.
1427. _____., and Tomasz Szapiro. "A Redescription of a Negotiation Problem with Decision Makers Under Pressure." In: B. R. Munier and M. F. Shakun, eds. *Compromise, Negotiation and Group Decision.* Dordrecht: D. Reidel, 1987. pp. 177-194.

1428. _____. "On The Roles Decision Support Systems Can Play in Negotiations." *Information Processing and Management*, 23:6 (1987), 605-614.
1429. _____. "Negotiation Group Decision Support System." *Information and Management*, 8:5 (1985), 237-246.
1430. Kilgour, D. Marc. "On 2x2 Games and Braithwaite's Arbitration Scheme." In: A. Rapoport, ed. *Game Theory as a Theory of Conflict Resolution.* Dordrecht: D. Reidel, 1974. pp. 63-74.
1431. _____. "A Shapley Value for Cooperative Games with Quarrelling." In: A. Rapoport, ed. *Game Theory as a Theory of Conflict Resolution.* Dordrecht: D. Reidel, 1974. pp. 193-206.
1432. _____. Keith W. Hipel and L. Fang. "The Graph Model of Conflicts." *Automatica*, 23:1 (1987), 41-55.
1433. _____., and Marc A. Zagare. "Holding Power in Sequential Games." *International Interactions*, 13:2 (1987), 91-114.
1434. Kivikari, Urpo, and Harmu Nurmi. "A Game-Theoretic Approach to Political Characteristics of East-West Trade." *Cooperation and Conflict*, 21 (1986), 65-78.
1435. Klimoski, Richard J. "Simulation Methodologies in Experimental Research on Negotiations by Representatives." *Journal of Conflict Resolution*, 22:1 (1978), 61-78.
1436. Komorita, S. S., and David A. Kravitz. "Some Test of Four Descriptive Theories of Coalition Formation." In: H. Sauermann, ed. *Coalition Formation Behavior.* Tübingen: Mohr, 1978. pp. 207-230.
1437. Kraemer, Kenneth L. "Modeling as Negotiating - the Political Dynamics of Computer Models in Policy Making." In: R. F. Conlam and R. A. Smith, eds. *Advances in Information Processing in Organizations, Vol 2.: Research on Public Organizations.* Greenwich, CT.: JAI Press, 1985. pp. 275-308.
1438. Kuhn, Harold W. "Game Theory and Models of Negotiations." *Journal of Conflict Resolution*, 6:1 (1962), 1-4.
1439. Ladner, Robert. "Strategic Interaction and Conflict - Negotiating Expectations in Accounting for Actions." *Journal of Conflict Resolution*, 17:1 (March 1973), 175-184.
1440. Laing, James D., and Richard J. Morrison. "Coalitions and Payoffs in Three-Person Super Games Under Multiple-Trial Agreements." In: A. Rapoport, ed. *Game Theory as a Theory of Conflict Resolution.* Dordrecht: D. Reidel, 1974. pp. 207-234.
1441. Leng, Russell J. "Crisis Learning Games." *American Political Science Review*, 82:1 (March 1988), 179-194.
1442. Levinsohn, Jay R., and Amnon Rapoport. "Coalition Formation in Multistage Three-Person Cooperative Games." In: H. Sauermann, ed. *Coalition Formation Behavior.* Tübingen: Mohr, 1978. pp. 107-143.
1443. Light, Margot. "Problem-Solving Workshops: The Role of Scholarship in Conflict Resolution." In: M. Banks, ed. *Conflict in World Society.* Brighton: Wheatsheaf Books, 1984. pp. 146-160.
1444. Livne, Zvi. "The Bargaining Problem with an Uncertain Conflict Outcome." *Mathematical Social Sciences*, 15:3 (June 1988), 287-302.
1445. Lumsden, Malvern. "The Cyprus Conflict as a Prisoner's Dilemma Game." *Journal of Conflict Resolution*, 17:1 (March 1973), 7-32.
1446. Lupfer, Michael, et al. "Risk Taking in Cooperative and Competitive Dyads." *Journal of Conflict Resolution*, 15:3 (September 1971), 385-392.
1447. Lutzker, D. R. "Internationalism as a Prediction of Cooperative Behavior." *Journal of Conflict Resolution*, 4 (1960), 426-430.

1448. Malouf, Michael W. K., and Alvin E. Roth. "Disagreement in Bargaining: An Experimental Study." *Journal of Conflict Resolution*, 25:2 (1981), 329--348.
1449. Maoz, Zeev. "Decision-Theoretic and Game-Theoretic Models of International Conflict." In: V. Luterbacher and M. D. Ward, eds. *Dynamic Models of International Conflict*. Boulder, CO.: Lynne Rienner, 1985. pp. 76-111.
1450. Marin, Gerardo. "Cooperation in the Prisoner's Dilemma and Personality Correlates: A Non-Existent Relationship." *Peace Research*, 5:6 (1973), 29-32.
1451. Maschler, Michael. "Playing an N-Person Game - An Experiment." In: H. Sauermann, ed. *Coalition Formation Behavior*. Tübingen: Mohr, 1978. pp. 231-238.
1452. Meeker, R. J., and G. H. Shure. "Pacifist Bargaining Tactics: Some "Outsider" Influences." *Journal of Conflict Resolution*, 13 (1969), 487-493.
1453. Michelini, Ronald L. "Effects of Prior Interaction, Contact, Strategy, and Expectation of Meeting on Game Behavior and Sentiment." *Journal of Conflict Resolution*, 15:1 (1971), 97-104.
1454. Michener, H. A., et al. "Competitive Test of the MI(i) and MI(im) Bargaining Sets." *Journal of Conflict Resolution*, 23 (March 1979), 102-119.
1455. _____., and K. Potter. "Generalizability of Tests in N-Person Sidepayment Games." *Journal of Conflict Resolution*, 25:4 (1981), 733-749.
1456. _____. "Mollifier Representation in Non-Constant-Sum Games: An Experimental Test." *Journal of Conflict Resolution*, 30:2 (June 1986), 361-382.
1457. _____., and K. Yuen. "A Test of MI(im) Bargaining Sets in Sidepayment Games." *Journal of Conflict Resolution*, 27:1 (March 1983), 109-135.
1458. _____. _____. and I. J. Ginsberg. "A Competitive Test of the MI Bargaining Set, Kernel and Equal Share Models." *Behavioral Science*, 22 (1977), 341-355.
1459. _____. _____. and Stephen B. Geisleker. "Nonsymmetry and Core Size in N-Person Sidepayment Games." *Journal of Conflict Resolution*, 24:3 (September 1980), 495-524.
1460. Midgaard, Knut. "Bargaining and Rationality: A Discussion of Zeuthen's Principle and Some Other Decision Rules." In: B. P. Stigun and F. Wenstop, eds. *Foundations of Utility Theory with Applications*. Dordrecht: D. Reidel, 1983. pp. 311-328.
1461. _____. "Co-ordination in 'Tacit' Games: Some New Concepts." *Cooperation and Conflict*, 2 (1965), 39-52.
1462. Minas, J. Sayer. "Some Descriptive Aspects of Two-Person Non-Zero-Sum--Games II." *Journal of Conflict Resolution*, 4:2 (June 1960), 193-197.
1463. Moreaux, Michel, Jean-Pierre Poussard and Patrick Rey. "Cooperation in Finitely Repeated Non-Cooperative Games." In: B. R. Munier and M. F. Shakun, eds. *Compromise, Negotiation and Group Decision*. Dordrecht: D. Reidel, 1987. pp. 159-174.
1464. Morehouse, L. G. "One-Play, Two-Play, Five-Play and Ten-Play Runs of Prisoner's Dilemma." *Journal of Conflict Resolution*, 10:3 (1966), 363--366.
1465. Morgan, Thomas C. "A Spatial Model of Crisis Bargaining." *International Studies Quarterly*, 28:4 (December 1984), 407-425.
1466. Munier, Bertrand R., and Marcel Egea. "Repeated Negotiation Sessions: A Generalized Gametheoretic Approach." In: B. R. Munier and M. F. Shakun, eds. *Compromise, Negotiation and Group Decision*. Dordrecht: D. Reidel, 1987. pp. 213-224.

1467. Murnighan, J. K., and Alvin E. Roth. "The Effects of Communication and Information Availability in an Experimental Study of a Three Person Game." *Management Science*, 23 (August 1977), 1336-1348.
1468. _____. _____. "Effects of Group Size and Communication Availability on Coalition Bargaining in a Veto Game." *Journal of Personality and Social Psychology*, 39 (1980), 92-103.
1469. _____. _____. "Expecting Continued Play in Social Dilemmas Games." *Journal of Conflict Resolution*, 27:2 (June 1983), 279-300.
1470. _____. _____. "Large Group Bargaining in a Characteristic Function Game." *Journal of Conflict Resolution*, 22 (1978), 299-317.
1471. Murphy, J. L. "Effects of the Threat of Losses on Duopoly Bargaining." *Quarterly Journal of Economics*, 80 (1966), 296-313.
1472. Myerson, R. M. "Incentive Compatibility and the Bargaining Problem." *Econometrica*, 47 (1979), 61-74.
1473. _____. "Two-Person Bargaining Problems and Comparable Utility." *Econometrica*, 45 (1977), 1631-1637.
1474. _____. "Two-Person Bargaining Problems with Incomplete Information." *Econometrica*, 52:2 (March 1984), 461-487.
1475. Mytelka, Lynn K. "Fiscal Politics and Regional Redistribution: Bargaining Strategies in Asymmetrical Integrative Bargaining." *Journal of Conflict Resolution*, 19:1 (1975), 138-160.
1476. Nash, John F. "The Bargaining Problem." *Econometrica*, 18 (April 1950), 155-162.
1477. _____. "The Bargaining Problem." In: O. R. Young, ed. *Bargaining*. Urbana, IL.: University of Illinois Press, 1975. pp. 63-60.
1478. _____. "Two-Person Cooperative Game." In: O. R. Young, ed. *Bargaining*. Urbana, IL.: University of Illinois Press, 1975. pp. 61-73.
1479. _____. "Two-Person Cooperative Games." *Econometrica*, 21:1 (1953), 268-295.
1480. Nitz, Lawrence H., and James L. Phillips. "The Effects of Divisibility of Payoff on Confederate Behavior." *Journal of Conflict Resolution*, 13:3 (September 1969), 381-387.
1481. Nydegger, Rudy V. "Independent Utility Scaling and the Nash Bargaining Model." *Behavioral Science*, 22:4 (1977), 283-239.
1482. _____., and G. Owen. "Two-Person Bargaining: An Experimental Test of Nash's Axioms." *International Journal of Game Theory*, 3 (1975), 239-249.
1483. Ofshe, Richard. "The Effectiveness of Pacifist Strategies: A Theoretical Approach." *Journal of Conflict Resolution*, 15:2 (June 1971), 261-270.
1484. Oliva, Terence A., and Terry L. Leap. "A Taxonomy of Bargaining Models." *Human Relations*, 34:1 (November 1981), 935-946.
1485. Orkin, Michael. "Balanced Strategies for Prisoner's Dilemma." *Journal of Conflict Resolution*, 31:1 (March 1987), 186-191.
1486. Orwant, Carol J., and Jack E. Orwant. "A Comparison of Interpreted and Abstract Versions of Mixed-Motive Games." *Journal of Conflict Resolution*, 14:1 (March 1970), 91-98.
1487. Pen, Jan. "Comments on the Bargaining Problem." In: O. R. Young, ed. *Bargaining*. Urbana, IL.: University of Illinois Press, 1975. pp. 267-269.
1488. _____. "A General Theory of Bargaining." In: O. R. Young, ed. *Bargaining*. Urbana, IL.: University of Illinois Press, 1975. pp. 164-182.
1489. _____. "A General Theory of Bargaining." *America Economic Review*, 1 (1952), 29-42.
1490. Picard, Louis A. "The SALT I Negotiations: A Game Theory Paradigm." *Policy Studies Journal*, 8:1 (Autumn 1979), 120-127.

1491. Pilisuk, Mark. "Experimenting with the Arms Race." *Journal of Conflict Resolution*, 28:2 (June 1984), 296-315.
1492. _____., and Anatol Rapoport. "Stepwise Disarmament and Sudden Destruction in a Two-Person Game: A Research Tool." *Journal of Conflict Resolution*, 8 (1964), 36-49.
1493. _____., et al. "War Hawks and Peace Doves: Alternative Resolutions of Experimental Conflicts." *Journal of Conflict Resolution*, 9 (1965), 491-508.
1494. Pincus, J., and V. E. Bixenstine. "Cooperation in the Decomposed Prisoner's Dilemma Game." *Journal of Conflict Resolution*, 21 (1977), 519-530.
1495. Powell, Robert. "Nuclear Brinkmanship with Two-Sided Incomplete Information." *American Political Science Review*, 82 (March 1988), 155-178.
1496. Pruitt, Dean G., et al. "The Effect of Accountability and Surveillance on Integrative Bargaining." In: H. Sauermann, ed. *Bargaining Behavior*. Tübingen: Mohr, 1978. pp. 310-343.
1497. _____., et al. "Incentives for Cooperation in Integrative Bargaining." In: R. Tietz, ed. *Aspiration Levels in Bargaining and Economic Decision Making*. Berlin: Springer-Verlag, 1983. pp. 22-34.
1498. _____. "An Analysis of Responsiveness Between Nations." *Journal of Conflict Resolution*, 6 (1962), 5-18.
1499. Quandt, R. E. "On the Use of Game Models in Theories of International Relations." In: K. Knorr and S. Verba, eds. *The International System: Theoretical Essays*. Princeton, NJ.: Princeton University Press, 1961. pp. 69-76.
1500. Radlow, Robert. "An Experimental Study of 'Cooperation' in the Prisoner's Dilemma Game." *Journal of Conflict Resolution*, 9:2 (June 1965), 221-227.
1501. _____., and Marianna F. Weidner. "A Two-Person Game with Unenforced Commitments in 'Cooperative' and 'Noncooperative' Non-Constant-Sum Game." *Journal of Conflict Resolution*, 10:4 (December 1966), 497-505.
1502. Raiffa, Howard. "Mock Pseudo-Negotiations with Surrogate Disputants." *Negotiation Journal*, 1:2 (April 1985), 111-115.
1503. Rapoport, Amnon, and A. Mowshovitz. "Experimental Studies of Stochastic Models for the Prisoner's Dilemma." *Behavioral Science*, 11 (1966), 444-458.
1504. _____., and James P. Kahan. "The Power of a Coalition and Payoff Disbursement in Three-Person Negotiable Conflicts." *Journal of Mathematical Sociology*, 8:2 (1981), 193-224.
1505. _____. _____. and Thomas S. Wallsten. "Sources of Power in Four-Person Apex Games." In: H. Sauermann, ed. *Coalition Formation Behavior*. Tübingen: Mohr, 1978. pp. 75-106.
1506. Rapoport, Anatol. "The Application of Game Theory to Peace Research." In: C. Schaerf and E. Barnaby, eds. *Disarmament and Arms Control: Proceedings*. London: Gordon and Breach, 1972. pp. 253-272.
1507. _____. "Conflict Resolution in the Light of Game Theory and Beyond." In: P. Swingle, ed. *The Structure of Conflict*. New York: Academic Press, 1970. pp. 1-44.
1508. _____. "Experimental Games: A Review." *Behavioral Science*, 7:1 (January 1962), 1-37.
1509. _____., and Carol J. Orwant. "Experimental Games." In: M. Shubik, ed. *Game Theory and Related Approaches to Social Theory*. New York: John Wiley, 1964. pp. 283-310.

1510. _____. "Formal Games as Probing Tools for Investigating Behavior Motivated by Trust and Suspicion." *Journal of Conflict Resolution*, 7 (1963), 570-579.
1511. _____., and Albert M. Chammah. "The Game of Chicken." *American Behavioral Scientist*, 10 (1966), 10-28.
1512. _____. _____. "The Game of Chicken." In: I. R. Buchler and H. G. Nutini, eds. *Game Theory in the Behavioral Sciences*. Pittsburgh, PA.: University of Pittsburgh Press, 1969. pp. 151-178.
1513. _____., and Phillip S. Dale. "The 'End' and 'Start' Effects in Iterated Prisoner's Dilemma." *Journal of Conflict Resolution*, 10:3 (1966), 363-366.
1514. _____. "Games Which Simulate Deterrence and Disarmament." *Peace Research Reviews*, 1 (1967), 1-76.
1515. _____. "Prisoner's Dilemma: Recollections and Observations." In: A. Rapoport, ed. *Game Theory as a Theory of Conflict Resolution*. Dordrecht: D. Reidel, 1974. pp. 17-34.
1516. _____. "Strategic and Non-Strategic Approaches to Problems of Security and Peace." In: K. Archibald, ed. *Strategic Interaction and Conflict*. Berkeley, CA.: Institute of International Studies, 1966. pp. 88-101.
1517. _____., and Melvin J. Guyer. "A Taxonomy of 2x2 games." *General Systems*, 11 (1966), 203-214.
1518. _____., and J. Perner. "Testing Nash's Solution of the Cooperative Game." In: A. Rapoport, ed. *Game Theory as a Theory of Conflict Resolution*. Dordrecht: D. Reidel, 1974. pp. 103-118.
1519. _____., et al. "Three Person Non-Zero-Sum Non-Negotiable Games." *Behavioral Science*, 7 (1962), 38-58.
1520. _____. "Comment on Bram's Discussion of Newcomb's Paradox." *Journal of Conflict Resolution*, 19:4 (December 1975), 613-619.
1521. _____., and Phillip S. Dale. "The "End" and "Start" Effects in Iterated Prisoner's Dilemma." *Journal of Conflict Resolution*, 10:3 (September 1966), 363-366.
1522. _____. "Formal Games as Probing Tools for Investigating Behavior Motivated by Trust and Suspicion." *Journal of Arms Control*, 1:4 (1963), 664-673.
1523. Rice, Peter. "The Finite Negotiation Problem: A Solution Theory." *Journal of Conflict Resolution*, 23:3 (1979), 561-576.
1524. Rieger, Hans Christoph. "Game Theory and the Analysis of Protectionist Trends." *The World Economy: A Quarterly Journal of International Economic Affairs*, 9:2 (June 1986), 171-192.
1525. Riker, W. H. "Bargaining in a Three-Person Game." *American Political Science Review*, 61 (1967), 642-656.
1526. Rochet, J. C. "Some Recent Results in Bargaining Theory." *European Economic Review*, 31 (February - March, 1987), 326-335.
1527. Rosenthal, Robert W. "Repeated Bargaining with Opportunities for Learning." *Journal of Mathematical Sociology*, 8:1 (1981), 61-74.
1528. Roth, Alvin E. "Bargaining Ability, the Utility of Playing a Game, and Models of Coalition Formation." *Journal of Mathematical Psychology*, 16 (October 1977), 153-160.
1529. _____., and F. Schoumaker. "Expectations and Reputations in Bargaining: An Experimental Study." *American Economic Review*, 73 (June 1983), 362-372.
1530. _____., and M. W. K. Malouf. "Game-Theoretic Models and the Role of Information in Bargaining." *Psychological Review*, 86 (November 1979), 574-594.

1531. _____. "An Impossibility Result Concerning N-Person Bargaining Games." *International Journal of Game Theory*, 8 (1980), 129-132.
1532. _____. "Independence of Irrelevant Alternatives and Solutions to Nash's Bargaining Problem." *Journal of Economic Theory*, 16:2 (1977), 247-251.
1533. _____. "Individual Rationality and Nash's Solution to the Bargaining Problem." *Mathematics of Operations Research*, 2:1 (1977), 64-65.
1534. _____, and J. K. Murnighan. "Information and Aspirations in 2-Person Bargaining." In: R. Tietz, ed. *Aspiration Levels in Bargaining and Economic Decision Making*. Berlin: Springer-Verlag, 1983. pp. 91-103.
1535. _____. "The Nash Solution and the Utility of Bargaining." *Econometrica*, 46 (1978), 587-594.
1536. _____. "The Nash Solution as a Model of Rational Bargaining." In: A. V. Fiaco and K. O. Kortanek, eds. *External Methods and Systems Analysis*. New York: Springer-Verlag, 1980. pp. 306-311.
1537. _____. "Proportional Solutions to the Bargaining Problem." *Econometrica*, 47 (1979), 775-778.
1538. _____. "Risk Aversion and Nash's Solution for Bargaining Games with Risky Outcomes." *Econometrica*, 50 (1982), 639-647.
1539. _____, and J. K. Murnighan. "The Role of Information in Bargaining: An Experimental Study." *Econometrica*, 50 (1982), 1123-1142.
1540. _____, and M. W. K. Malouf. "Scale Changes and Shared Information in Bargaining: An Experimental Study." *Mathematical Social Sciences*, 3 (1982), 157-177.
1541. _____. "Toward a Focal-Point Theory of Bargaining." In: A. E. Roth, ed. *Game-Theoretic Models of Bargaining*. Cambridge: Cambridge University Press, 1985. pp. 259-268.
1542. _____. "Towards a Theory of Bargaining: An Experimental Study in Economics." *Science*, 220 (Nay 13, 1983), 687-691.
1543. _____. "Values for Games Without Side Payments: Some Difficulties with Current Concepts." *Econometrica*, 48 (March 1980), 457-465.
1544. _____. M. W. K. Malouf and J. K. Murnighan. "Sociological Versus Strategic Factors in Bargaining." *Journal of Economic Behavior and Organization*, 2 (1981), 153-177.
1545. _____. "Toward a Focal-Point Theory of Bargaining." In: A. E. Roth, ed. *Game-Theoretic Models of Bargaining*. Cambridge: Cambridge University Press, 1985. pp. 259-268.
1546. _____. "Some Additional Thoughts on Post-Settlement Settlements." *Negotiation Journal*, 1:3 (July 1985), 245-247.
1547. Rubinstein, Ariel. "A Bargaining Model with Incomplete Information About Time Preferences." *Econometrica*, 63 (September 1985), 1151-1172.
1548. _____. "Perfect Equilibrium in a Bargaining Model." *Econometrica*, 50 (1982), 97-109.
1549. Samuelson, William F. "Bargaining Under Asymmetric Information." *Econometrica*, 52 (July 1984), 995-1005.
1550. _____, and Max H. Bazerman. "The Winner's Curse in Bilateral Negotiations." In: V. L. Smith, ed. *Research in Experimental Economics: A Research Annual, Vol. III*. Greenwich, CT.: JAI Press, 1985. pp. 105-138.
1551. Saraydar, Edward. "A Certainty-Equivalent Model of Bargaining." *Journal of Conflict Resolution*, 15:3 (1971), 281-298.
1552. _____. "Modeling the Role of Conflict and Conciliation in Bargaining." *Journal of Conflict Resolution*, 28:3 (September 1984), 420-450.
1553. _____. "Zeuthen's Theory of Bargaining: A Note." *Econometrica*, 33 (1965), 802-813.

1554. Savich, P., Keith W. Hipel and Niall M. Fraser. "The Alaskan Gas Pipeline Conflict." *Energy - The International Journal,* 8:3 (1983), 213-224.
1555. Schellenberg, James A., and Daniel Druckman. "Bargaining and Gaming." *Social Science and Modern Society,* 23:6 (September/October 1986), 65-71.
1556. _____. "A Comparative Test of 3 Models for Solving the Bargaining Problem." *Behavioral Science,* 33:2 (April 1988), 81-96.
1557. Schelling, Thomas C. "An Essay on Bargaining." In: O. R. Young, ed. *Bargaining.* Urbana, IL.: University of Illinois Press, 1975. pp. 319-342.
1558. _____. "Experimental Games and Bargaining Theory." *World Politics,* 14:1 9 (October 1961), 47-68.
1559. _____. "An Essay on Bargaining." *American Economic Review,* 46:3 (1956), 281-306.
1560. _____. "Experimental Games and Bargaining Theory." In: M. Shubik, ed. *Game Theory and Related Approaches to Social Behavior.* New York: John Wiley, 1964. pp. 311-323.
1561. _____. "The Strategy of Conflict: Prospectus for a Reorientation of Game Theory." *Journal of Conflict Resolution,* 2 (1958), 203-264.
1562. _____. "Uncertainty, Brinkmanship and the Game of 'Chicken'." In: K. Archibald, ed. *Strategic Interaction and Conflict.* Berkeley, CA.: Institute of International Studies, 1966. pp. 74-87.
1563. _____. "Experimental Games and Bargaining Theory." In: K. Knorr and S. Verba, eds. *The International System: Theoretical Analysis.* Princeton, NJ.: Princeton University Press, 1961. pp. 47-68.
1564. Schleicher, Heinz. "A Fair Division Process in a Cooperative N-Person Context Where Side-Payments are Allowed." In: R. R. Munier and M. F. Shakun, eds. *Compromise, Negotiation and Group Decision.* Dordrecht: D. Reidel, 1987. pp. 133-144.
1565. Schlenker, Barry R., and Thomas V. Bonoma. "Fun and Games: The Validity of Games for the Study of Conflict." *Journal of Conflict Resolution,* 22:1 (March 1978), 7-38.
1566. Schofield, Michael. "Modeling Crises." *Foreign Service Journal,* 65:6 (June 1988), 37-45.
1567. Schofield, Norman. "Generalized Bargaining Sets for Cooperative Games." *International Journal of Games Theory,* 7 (1978), 183-199.
1568. Scholz, R. W., A. Fleischer and A. Bentrup. "Aspiration Forming and Predictions Based on Aspiration Levels Compared Between Professional and Nonprofessional Bargainers." In: R. Tietz, ed. *Aspiration Levels in Bargaining and Economic Decision Making.* Berlin: Springer-Verlag, 1983. pp. 104-121.
1569. Scodel, A. "Induced Collaboration in Some Non-Zero-Sum Games." *Journal of Conflict Resolution,* 6 (1962), 335-340.
1570. _____., et al. "Some Descriptive Aspects of Two-Person, Non-Zero-Sum Games." *Journal of Conflict Resolution,* 3 (1959), 114-119.
1571. Seitz, Steven T. "Fuzzy Modelling and Conflict Analysis." *Conflict Management and Peace Science,* 9:1 (Fall 1985), 53-67.
1572. Shubik, Martin. "Cooperative Game Solutions: Australian, Indian and U.S. Opinions." *Journal of Conflict Resolution,* 30:1 (March 1986), 63-76.
1573. _____. "The Dollar Auction Game: A Paradox in Non Cooperative Behavior and Escalation." *Journal of Conflict Resolution,* 15 (1971), 109-111.
1574. _____. "Information, Risk, Ignorance and Indeterminacy." *Quarterly Journal of Economics,* 8 (1959), 1-21.
1575. _____. "Some Experimental Non-Zero-Sum Games with Lack of Information About the Rules." *Management Science,* 8 (1962), 215-233.

1576. _____. "Some Reflections on the Design of Game Theoretic Models for the Study of Negotiations and Threats." *Journal of Conflict Resolution*, 7 (1963), 1-12.
1577. _____. "On the Study of Disarmament and Escalation." *Journal of Conflict Resolution*, 12 (1968), 83-101.
1578. _____. "Game Theory, Behavior, and the Paradox of Prisoner's Dilemma: Three Solutions." *Journal of Conflict Resolution*, 14:2 (June 1970), 181-194.
1579. _____. Gerrit Wolf and Byron Poon. "Perception of Payoff Structure and Opponent's Behavior in Related Matrix Games." *Journal of Conflict Resolution*, 18:4 (December 1974), 646-655.
1580. Shure, G. H., R. J. Meeker and E. A. Hansford. "The Effectiveness of Pacifist Strategies in Bargaining Games." In: J. E. Mueller, ed. *Approaches to Measurement in International Relations: A Nonevangelical Survey*. New York: Appleton-Century-Crofts, 1969. pp. 99-112.
1581. _____. _____. "Bargaining Processes in Experimental Territorial Conflict Situations." *Peace Research Society (International) Papers*, 11 (1968), 109-122.
1582. Siegel, Sidney, and Lawrence E. Fouraker. "The Effects of Level of Aspiration on the Differential Payoff in Bargaining by Bilateral Monopolies." In: S. Messick and A. H. Brayfield, eds. *Decision and Choice: Contributions of Sidney Siegel*. New York: McGraw-Hill, 1964. pp. 135-143.
1583. Skotko, Vincent, David Langmeyer and David Lundgren. "Sex Differences as Artifact in the Prisoner's Dilemma Game." *Journal of Conflict Resolution*, 18:4 (December 1974), 707-713.
1584. Snidal, Duncan J. "The Game of "Theory" of International Politics." *World Politics*, 38:1 (October 1985), 25-57.
1585. _____. "The Game Theory of International Politics." In: K. A. Oye, ed. *Cooperation Under Anarchy*. Princeton, NY.: Princeton University Press, 1986. pp. 25-57.
1586. Sobel, Joel, and Ichiro Takahashi. "A Multistage Model of Bargaining." *The Review of Economic Studies*, 50 (July 1983), 411-426.
1587. Steele, M. W., and J. T. Tedeschi. "Matrix Indices and Strategy Choice in Mixed-Motive Games." *Journal of Conflict Resolution*, 11 (1967), 198-205.
1588. Stevens, Carl M. "On the Theory of Negotiation." *Quarterly Journal of Economics*, 72 (1958), 77-97.
1589. Stoecker, Rolf. "Altruism and Performance in Bertrand-Duopoly-Experiments." In: H. Sauermann, ed. *Bargaining Behavior*. Tübingen: Mohr, 1978. pp. 41-59.
1590. Stokes, N. W., and Keith W. Hipel. "Conflict Analysis of an Export Credit Trade Dispute." *OMEGA: The International Journal of Management Science*, 11:4 (1983), 365-376.
1591. _____. _____. and P. H. Roe. "The New York Subway Car Dispute." *INFOR*, 23:2 (1985), 51-68.
1592. _____. _____. "Simultaneous Sanctioning in Non-Cooperative Games." *Journal of Operational Research Society*, 37:6 (1986), 637-641.
1593. Stone, Jeremy J. "An Experiment in Bargaining Games." *Econometrica*, 26 (1958), 286-296.
1594. Stover, William J., and Jawad Adra. "Models of International Crisis Bargaining and Middle East Conflict: Applications and Limitations." *International Review of History and Political Science*, 18 (August 1981), 1-29.

1595. Sugden, Robert. "Evolutionary Stable Strategies in the Prisoner's Dilemma and Chicken Games." In: B. R. Munier and M. F. Shakun, eds. *Compromise, Negotiation and Group Decision.* Dordrecht: D. Reidel, 1987. pp. 145-158.
1596. Sutton, John. "Bargaining Experiments." *European Economic Review,* 31 (February-March 1987), 372-384.
1597. _____. "Non-Cooperative Bargaining Theory: An Introduction." *Review of Economic Studies,* 53 (October 1986), 709-724.
1598. Swenson, R. G. "Cooperation in the Prisoner's Dilemma Game: I. The Effects of Asymmetric Payoff Information and Explicit Communication." *Behavioral Science,* 12 (1967), 314-322.
1599. Swinth, R. L. "Artifacts in the Siegel-Fouraker Study of Bargaining and Group Decision Making." *Management Science,* 16 (1969), 85-93.
1600. Talbot, Phillips. "The Cyprus Seminar." In: M. R. Berman and J. E. Johnson, eds. *Unofficial Diplomats.* New York: Columbia University Press, 1977. pp. 159-167.
1601. Terhune, Kenneth W. ""Wash-In", Wash-Out" and Systemic Effects in Extended Prisoner's Dilemma." *Journal of Conflict Resolution,* 18:4 (December 1974), 656-685.
1602. Tietz, Reinhard, and Hans-Jurgen Weber. "Decision Behavior in Multivariable Negotiations." In: H. Sauermann, ed. *Bargaining Behavior.* Tübingen: Mohr, 1978. pp. 60-87.
1603. _____., et al. "On Aspiration-Forming Behavior in Repetitive Negotiations." In: H. Sauermann, ed. *Bargaining Behavior.* Tübingen: Mohr, 1978. pp. 88-102.
1604. _____., and Hans-Jurgen Weber. "On the Nature of the Bargaining Process in the KRESKO-Game." In: H. Sauermann, ed. *Contributions to Experimental Economy, Vol. 3.* Tübingen: Mohr, 1972. pp. 305-334.
1605. _____., and Otomar J. Bartos. "Balancing of Aspiration Levels as Fairness Principle in Negotiations." In: R. Tietz, ed. *Aspiration Levels in Bargaining and Economic Analysis.* Berlin: Springer-Verlag, 1983. pp. 52-66.
1606. _____., et al. "Semi-Normative Properties of Bounded Rational Bargaining Theories." In: R. Tietz, W. Albers and R. Selten, eds. *Bounded Rational Behavior in Experimental Games and Markets.* Berlin: Springer Verlag, 1988. pp. 142-159.
1607. Toda, Masanao, and Hiromi Shinotsuka. "Three Person Bargaining for Coalition Formation." In: H. Sauermann, ed. *Coalition Formation Behavior.* Tübingen: Mohr, 1978. pp. 144-171.
1608. Tyszka, Tadeusz, and Janusz Grzelak. "Criteria of Choice in Non-Constant--Sum Games." *Journal of Conflict Resolution,* 20:2 (June 1976), 357-376.
1609. Ulvila, Jacob W., and Warren D. Snider. "Negotiation of International Oil Tanker Standards - Application of Multiattribute Value Theory." *Operations Research,* 28:1 (1980), 81-96.
1610. _____. _____. "Negotiations on Tanker Standards: An Application of Multi--Attribute Value Theory." *Operations Research,* 28 (June-February 1980), 81-95.
1611. Umeoka, Yoshitaka. "A 2x2 Non-Constant-Sum Game with a Coordination Problem." *Journal of Conflict Resolution,* 14:1 (March 1970), 99-100.
1612. Valavanis, Stephan. "The Resolution of Conflict When Utilities Interact." *Journal of Conflict Resolution,* 2 (June 1958), 156-169.
1613. Van Damme, Eric. "The Nash Bargaining Solution is Optimal." *Journal of Economic Theory,* 38 (February 1986), 78-100.
1614. Vincent, Jack E., and J. O. Tindell. "Alternative Cooperative Strategies in a Bargaining Game." *Journal of Conflict Resolution,* 13 (1969), 494-510.

1615. _____., and E. W. Schwerin. "Ratios of Force and Escalation in a Game Situation." *Journal of Conflict Resolution*, 15 (1971), 489-511.
1616. Wagner, Harvey M. "Rejoinder on the Bargaining Problem." *Southern Economic Journal*, 24 (1958), 476-482.
1617. _____. "A Unified Treatment of Bargaining Theory." In: O. R. Young, ed. *Bargaining*. Urbana, ILL.: University of Illinois Press, 1975. pp. 270-287.
1618. _____. "A Unified Treatment of Bargaining Theory." *Southern Economic Journal*, 23 (1957), 380-397.
1619. Wagner, R. Harrison. "On the Unification of Two-Person Bargaining Theory." *Journal of Conflict Resolution*, 23:1 (1979), 71-101.
1620. _____. "Deterrence and Bargaining." *Journal of Conflict Resolution*, 26:2 (June 1982), 329-358.
1621. _____. "A Noncooperative Solution to a Two-Person Bargaining Game." *Theory and Decision*, 21:3 (November 1986), 311-335.
1622. _____. "The Theory of Games and the Balance of Power." *World Politics*, 38:4 (July 1986), 546-576.
1623. _____. "The Theory of Games and the Problem of International Cooperation." *American Political Science Review*, 77:2 (1983), 330-346.
1624. Wall, James A. "A Negotiator's Bargaining: The Effects of Representation and the Opponent's Sex." In: H. Sauermann, ed. *Bargaining Behavior*. Tübingen: Mohr, 1978. pp. 270-283.
1625. Weber, Hans-Jürgen, and Reinhard Tietz. "Third Party Influences on Negotiation Behavior." In: H. Sauermann, ed. *Coalition Formation Behavior*. Tübingen: Mohr, 1978. pp. 26-39.
1626. Werner, T. _____. "The Search Process in Bilateral Negotiations." In: R. Tietz, ed. *Aspiration Levels in Bargaining and Economic Decision Making*. Berlin: Springer-Verlag, 1983. pp. 67-79.
1627. Wiberg, Hakan. "Some Comments on the Functions and Meaning of Game Theory." *Cooperation of Conflict*, 4 (1968), 247-253.
1628. Wierzbicki, Andrzej P. "Negotiation and Mediation in Conflicts II: Plural Rationality and Interactive Decision Process." In: M. Grauer, M. Thompson and A. Wierzbicki, eds. *Lecture Notes in Economics and Mathematical Systems. 248*. Berlin: Springer Verlag, 1985. pp. 114-131.
1629. Wilson, Kellog V., and V. E. Bixenstine. "Forms of Social Control in Two-Person, Two-Choice Games." In: M. Shubik, ed. *Game Theory and Related Approaches to Social Behavior*. New York: John Wiley, 1986. pp. 338-358.
1630. _____. _____. "Forms of Social Control in Two-Person, Two-Choice Games." *Behavioral Science*, 7:1 (January 1962), 92-102.
1631. Wilson, W. "Cooperation and the Cooperativeness of the Other Player." *Journal of Conflict Resolution*, 13 (1969), 110-117.
1632. _____. "Reciprocation and Other Techniques for Inducing Cooperation in the Prisoner's Dilemma Game." *Journal of Conflict Resolution*, 15 (1971), 167-196.
1633. Winham, Gilbert R., and H. E. Bovis. "Agreement and Breakdown in Negotiations: Report on a State Department Training Simulation." *Journal of Peace Research*, 15:4 (1978), 285-303.
1634. _____. _____. "Distribution of Benefits in Negotiation: Report on a State Department Training Simulation." *Journal of Conflict Resolution*, 23 (1979), 408-424.
1635. Worchel, Philip. "Temptation and Threat in Non-Zero-Sum Games." *Journal of Conflict Resolution*, 13 (1969), 103-109.

1636. Young, Jerald W. "Behavioral and Perceptual Differences Between Structurally Equivalent, Two-Person games: A Rich Versus Poor Context Comparison." *Journal of Conflict Resolution,* 21:2 (June 1977), 299-322.
1637. Young, Oran R. "The Analysis of Bargaining: Problems and Prospects." In; O. R. Young, ed. *Bargaining.* Urbana, IL.: University of Illinois Press, 1975. pp. 391-408.
1638. ____. "The Bargainer's Calculus." In: O. R. Young, ed. *Bargaining.* Urbana, IL.: University of Illinois Press, 1975. pp. 364-390.
1639. Zagare, Frank C. "A Game Theoretic Analysis of the Vietnam Negotiations: Preferences and Strategies 1968-1973." *Journal of Conflict Resolution,* 21:4 (1977), 663-684.
1640. ____. "A Game Theoretic Evaluation of the Cease-Fire Alert Decision of 1973." *Journal of Peace Research,* 20:1 (1983), 73-86.
1641. ____. "A Game-Theoretic Analysis of the Vietnam Negotiations: Preferences and Strategies 1968-1973." In: I. W. Zartman, ed. *The Negotiation Process.* Beverly Hills, CA.: Sage, 1978. pp. 111-132.
1642. ____. "Limited Move Equilibria in 2x2 Games." *Theory and Decision,* 16 (January 1984), 1-19.
1643. ____. "Nonmyopic Equilibria and the Middle East Crisis of 1967." *Conflict Management and Peace Science,* 5 (Spring 1981), 139-162
1644. Zechmeister, Kathleen, and Daniel Druckman. "Determinants of Resolving a Conflict of Interest: A Simulation of Political Decision Making." *Journal of Conflict Resolution,* 17 (1973), 63-88.
1645. Zellner, A. "War and Peace: A Fantasy in Game Theory." *Journal of Conflict Resolution,* 6 (1962), 39-41.
1646. Zeuthen, Frederick. "Economic Warfare." In: O. R. Young, ed. *Bargaining.* Urbana, IL.: University of Illinois Press, 1975. pp. 145-163.

3. Documents and Reports

1647. Aggarwal, Lalit. "Effects of Costs and Resources in Bargaining Processes." Paper Presented at the *International Peace Science Society,* held on November 14-16, 1977, at the University of Pennsylvania in Philadelphia.
1648. Albers, Wulf. "Aspirations and Aspiration Adjustment in Location Games." Paper Presented at the *First Annual Conference on the Processes of International Negotiations,* held on May 18-22, 1987, at the International Institute for Applied Systems Analysis (IIASA), in Laxenburg, Austria.
1649. Alker, H. R. *Games Foreign Policy Experts Play: The Political Exercises Come of Age.* Cambridge, MA.: Massachusetts Institute of Technology, Center for International Studies, 1971.
1650. Antrim, Lance, David A. Lax and J. Daniel Nyhart. *Contributions to the Conference on Problems of Constancy and Change of the International Society for General Systems Research.* Working Paper-10. Cambridge, MA.: The Program on the Processes of International Negotiations, American Academy of Arts and Sciences, 1987.
1651. Barclay, S., and C. Peterson. *Multi-Attribute Utility Model for Negotiations.* Technical Report 76-1. Mc Lean, VA.: Decisions and Designs, 1976.
1652. Bartos, Otomar J. *Predictive Model for Intergroup Negotiations: Final Report.* Springfield, VA.: Clearinghouse for Federal Scientific and Technical Information, 1968. 12p.
1653. Benjamin, Charles. "The Iranian Hostage Negotiations: A Metagame Analysis of the Crisis." Paper Presented at the *Annual Meeting of the International Studies Association,* held on May 25, 1982, in Cincinnati, OH.

1654. Benson, Oliver. "A Simple Diplomatic Game or Putting One and One Together." Paper Presented at the *55th Annual meeting of the American Political Science Association*, held on September 10-12, 1959, in Washington, D.C.
1655. Benton, A. A. "Application of Gaming Studies to International Negotiations." Paper Presented at the *15th Annual Convention of the International Studies Association*, held on March 20-23, 1974, in St.Louis.
1656. Betts, George C. *The Lancaster House Conference: A Game Theoretical Explanation of The Outcome.* M.A. Thesis. Ottawa: Carleton University, 1984.
1657. Brams, Steven J. "Deception in 2 x 2 Games." Paper Presented at the *17th Annual Convention of the International Studies Association*, held on February 25-29, 1976, in Toronto.
1658. Bronisz, Piotr, and Lech Krus. "An Experimental System Supporting Negotiation on Joint Development Program." Paper Presented at the *First Annual Conference on the Processes of International Negotiations*, held on May 18-22, 1987, at the International Institute for Applied Systems Analysis (IIASA), in Laxenburg, Austria.
1659. _____. _____. "A Dynamic Solution of Two-Person Bargaining Game." Paper Presented at the *First Annual Conference on the Processes of International Negotiations*, held on May 18-22, 1987, at the International Institute for Applied Systems Analysis (IIASA), in Laxenburg, Austria.
1660. Cave, J. K. *Introduction to Game Theory.* RAND P-7336. Santa Monica, CA.: RAND Corporation, 1987. 23p.
1661. Chatterjee, Kalyan. *A One-Stage Distributive Bargaining Game.* Working Paper 78-13. Cambridge, MA.: Graduate School of Business Adminstration, Harvard University, 1978.
1662. Cook, D. L. *Korean Unification: A Game Theoretical and Bargaining Analysis.* M.A. Thesis. Monterey, CA.: Naval Postgraduate School, 1984. 174p.
1663. Crampton, Peter C. *Bargaining with Incomplete Information: An Infinite Horizon-Model with Continuous Uncertainty.* Research Paper No. 680. Stanford, CA.: Stanford University, Stanford Graduate School of Business, 1983.
1664. _____. *The Role of Time and Information in Bargaining.* Research Paper No. 729. Stanford, CA.: Stanford University, Stanford Graduate School of Business, 1984.B.
1665. Dagnino, Aldo, Keith W. Hipel and Niall M. Fraser. "A Decision Support System for Mediation." Paper Presented at the *International Society for General Systems Research/IIASA Symposium*, held in June 1987, in Budapest.
1666. _____. *Dynamic Analysis of an International Trade Dispute.* M.A. Thesis. Waterloo, Ont.: University of Waterloo, 1983. 195p.
1667. _____. Keith W. Hipel and Niall M. Fraser. *Dynamic Analysis of the Japanese Trade Conflict.* Technical Report No. 131-SM-111084. Waterloo, Ont.: Department of Systems Design Engineering, University of Waterloo, 1984.
1668. _____. *Modelling Strategic Interaction in Environmental Engineering.* Ph.D. Dissertation. Waterloo, Ont.: University of Waterloo, 1987. 261p.
1669. Davis, Earl E., and H. C. Triandis. *An Exploration Study of Inter-Cultural Negotiations.* Technical Report 26. Urbana, IL.: University of Illinois Group Effectiveness Research Laboratory, University of Illinois, 1965.

1670. Fang, L., Keith W. Hipel and D. Marc Kilgour. "A Decision Support System for Two Player Conflicts." In: Paper Presented at the *1985 IEEE International Conference on Systems, Man and Cybernetics*, held on November 12-15, 1985, in Tucson, AZ. pp. 998-1002.
1671. Fraser, Niall M., C. M. Benjamin and C. A. Powell. "Optimizing the Decision Process: Structure and Stability in Complex Conflict." Paper Presented at the *Society for General Systems Research International Conference Proceedings*, held on May 27-31, 1985, in Los Angeles. pp. 1061-1070.
1672. _____., and Keith W. Hipel. "Solving Complex Conflicts." In: *IEEE Transactions on Systems, Man and Cybernetics*, Vol. SMC-9.No. 2, 1979. pp. 181-185.
1673. _____. *Advances in Conflict Analysis*. M.A. Thesis. Waterloo, Ont.: University of Waterloo, 1981. 108p.
1674. _____., and Keith W. Hipel. "Computer Assistance in Multiple Participant Decision Making." Paper Presented at the *1985 IEEE International Conference on Systems, Man and Cybernetics*, held on November 12-15, 1985, in Tucson, AZ. pp. 403-410.
1675. _____. _____. "Conflict Analysis and Bargaining." Paper Presented at the *Proceedings of the 1980 International Conference on Cybernetics and Society*, held on October 8-10, 1980, in Boston, MA. pp. 225-229.
1676. _____. _____. "Conflict Analysis for Group Decision and Negotiation Support Systems." Paper Presented at the *TIMS/ORSA Joint National Meeting*, held on October 17-19, 1986, in Miami, FL.
1677. _____. _____. "Conflict Analysis in Bargaining and Negotiation." Paper Presented at the *24th Annual Convention of the International Studies Association*, held on April 5-9, 1983, in Mexico City.
1678. _____. *Conflict Analysis in Bargaining and Negotiation*. Report No. 132-SM--121084. Waterloo, Ont.: Department of Systems Design and Engineering, University of Waterloo, 1984.
1679. _____. *New Perspectives in Bargaining and Negotiation*. Ph.D. Dissertation. Waterloo, Ont.: University of Waterloo, 1983. 260p.
1680. Geisen, Martin. "Simulation of Complex Decision Situations." Paper Presented at the *25th Annual Convention of the International Studies Association*, held on March 27-31, 1984, in Atlanta, GA.
1681. Gentile, Ralph. "Bargaining and Problem Solving: Links Between Different Tasks in Negotiation." Paper Presented at the *22nd Annual Convention of the International Studies Association*, held on March 18-21, 1981, in Philadelphia, PA.
1682. Grace, William V. *The Effects of an Interactive Computer Simulator (KSIM) Upon the Resolution of Mixed Conflict in a Negotiation Situation*. Ph.D. Dissertation. Bowling Green, OH.: Bowling Green State University, 1979. 180p.
1683. Grossman, Sanford J. *Sequential Bargaining Under Asymmetric Information*. NBER Technical Paper Series, No. 56. Cambridge, MA.: National Bureau of Economic Research, 1986. 45p.
1684. Hipel, Keith W., Aldo Dagnino and Niall M. Fraser. "Modelling Misperception in Bargaining." Paper Presented at the *Proceedings of the Association of American Geographers Annual Meeting*, held on May 4-7, 1986, in Minneapolis, MN.
1685. _____., and Niall M. Fraser. "Modelling Political Uncertainty Using the Improved Metagame Analysis Algorithm: The Polish Conflict." Paper Presented at the *25th Annual Convention of the International Studies Association*, held on March 27-31, 1984, in Atlanta, GA.

1686. Ikle, Fred C., and Nathan C. Leites. *Political Negotiation as a Process of Modifying Utilities.* RAND P-2482. Santa Monica, CA.: RAND Corporation, 1962. 25p.
1687. Kahan, James P. *Experimental Studies of Bargaining as Analoques of Civil Disputes.* Rand P-6924. Santa Monica, CA.: Rand Corporation, 1983. 42p.
1688. Kaplan, Morton A. *Some Problems in the Strategic Analysis of International Politics.* Research Monograph No. 2. Princeton, NJ.: Woodrow Wilson School of Public and International Affairs, Princeton University, 1959. 37p.
1689. Kersten, Gregory E., and Tomasz Szapiro. *On Defining and Structuring Negotiations.* Ottawa: Carleton University, School of Business, 1985. 16p.
1690. _____. _____. "Decision Support Negotiations." Paper Presented at the *International Society for General Systems Research/IIASA Symposium*, held in June 1987, in Budapest.
1691. _____., et al. "Rule Based Systems to Support Negotiations." Paper Presented at the *International Society for General Systems Research/IIASA Symposium*, held in June 1987, in Budapest.
1692. Khronstalev, Mark A. "Some Methodological Problems of Diplomatic Negotiations Modeling." Paper Presented at the *First Annual Conference on the Processes of International Negotiations,* held on May 18-22, 1987, at the International Institute for Applied Systems Analysis (IIASA), in Laxenburg, Austria.
1693. Kilgour, D. Marc, Muhong De and Keith W. Hipel. "Conflict Analysis Using Staying Power." Paper Presented at the *1986 IEEE Conference on Systems, Man and Cybernetics,* held on October 14-17, 1986, in Atlanta, GA. pp. 450-459.
1694. King, Timothy D. *Bargaining and Decision Making in Arms Control and Other Foreign Policy Situations.* Columbus, OH.: Mershon Center, Ohio State University, 1981.
1695. Kuhn, J. R. D., Keith W. Hipel and Niall M. Fraser. "A Coalition Analysis Algorithm with Application to the Zimbabwe Conflict." In: *IEEE Transactions on Systems, Man and Cybernetics,* Vol. SMC-13, No. 3. (1983), 338-352.
1696. Livingstone, William G., and Dorothy Sisk. "Conflict Resolution: Start Here - Using a Simulation Game to Diagnose Negotiation Styles and Resolution Strategies III." Paper Presented at the *Tenth SIETAR International Conference,* held on May 21-25, 1984, at George Mason University, Washington, D.C.
1697. Lockhart, Charles. "A Phase Model of Bargaining in International Conflicts." Paper Presented at the *17th Annual Convention of the International Studies Association,* held on February 25-29, 1976, in Toronto.
1698. McLennan, Andrew. *A Noncooperative Definition of Two-Person Bargaining.* Working Paper No. 8303. Toronto: Department of Economics and Institute for Policy Analysis, University of Toronto, 1982. 81p.
1699. Meeker, R. J., G. H. Shure and W. Jr. Moore. "Real-Time Computer Studies of Bargaining Behavior: The Effects of Threat Upon Bargaining." Paper presented at the *American Federation of Information Processing Societies Conference,* held in 1964, pp. 115-123.
1700. Mefford, Dwayne. "Historical Analysis and the Formation of Games." Paper Presented at the *23rd Annual Convention of the International Studies Association,* held on March 24-27, 1982, in Cincinnati, OH.

1701. Mermet, L., and L. Hordijk. "On Getting Simulation Models Used in International Negotiations: A Debriefing Exercise." Paper Presented at the *First Annual Conference on the Processes of International Negotiations*, held on May 18-22, 1987 at the International Institute for Applied Systems Analysis (IIASA), in Laxenburg, Austria.

1702. Mitchell, Theodore. "A Test of the Nash Barter Solution." Paper Presented at the *25th Annual Convention of the International Studies Association*, held on March 27-31, 1984, in Atlanta, GA.

1703. Morgan, Thomas C. *Bargaining in International Crises: A Spatial Model.* Ph.D. Dissertation. Austin, TX.: University of Texas, 1986. 249p.

1704. _____. "Power Differentials, Resolve and Bargaining Concessions in International Crisis: A Spatial Model." Paper Presented at the *80th Annual Meeting of the American Political Science Association*, held on August 30 - September 2, 1984, in New Orleans.

1705. Nash, John F. "Equilibrium Points in N-Person Games." *Proceedings of the National Academy of Sciences, U.S.A.*, 36 (1950), 48-49.

1706. Nobel, J. W. "Competition and Co-operation in International Politics as a Bargaining Problem." In: *Proceedings of the International Peace Research Association Inaugural Conference.* Assen, Holland: Van Gorcum, 1966. pp. 116-139.

1707. Noble, Steven J., and Celia S. Pangalis. "A Model Conflict Resolution Workshop: A Collaborative Effort Between the International Peace Academy and Columbia University's Graduate School of International and Public Affairs." Paper Presented at *Tenth SIETAR International Conference,* held on May 21-25, 1984, at George Washington University, Washington, D.C.

1708. Nyhart, J. Daniel, and Chris Goeltner. "Computer Models as Support for Complex Negotiations." Paper Presented at the *International Society for General Systems Research/IIASA Symposium*, held in June 1987, in Budapest.

1709. _____. _____. "Computer Models as Support for Complete Negotiations." In: *Computer Support for Negotiations and Conflict Resolution.* Working Papers Series 10. Cambridge, MA.: The Program on the Processes of International Negotiations, American Academy of Arts and Science, 1987. 8p.

1710. Peyton Young, H. ""Application of "Divide and Choose" Methods to Territorial Disputes." Paper Presented at the *First Annual International Conference on the Processes of International Negotiations*, held on May 18-22, 1987, at the International Institute for Applied Systems Analysis, in Laxenburg, Austria.

1711. Powell, Charles, and Charles Benjamin. "Constructing Environments for Complex Experimentation in Foreign Policy Decision Making." Paper Presented at the *25th Annual Convention of the International Studies Association*, held on March 27-31, 1984, in Atlanta, GA.

1712. Radford, James. "Progress in Modelling Complex Decision Situations." Paper Presented at the *25th Annual Convention of the International Studies Association*, held on March 27-31, 1984, in Atlanta, GA.

1713. Riker, W. H. "Bargaining in a Three-Person Situations." Paper Presented at the *62nd Annual Meeting of the American Political Science Association*, held on September 8-10, 1966, in New York.

1714. Saraydar, Edward. *An Exploration of Unresolved Problems in Bargaining Theory.* Ph.D. Dissertation. Rochester, NY.: University of Rochester, 1968.

1715. Schelling, Thomas C. *Reinterpretation of the Solution Concept for "Non-Co-Operative" Games.* RAND P-1385. Santa Monica, CA.: RAND Corporation, 1958.
1716. _____. *For the Abandonment of Symmetry in the Theory of Co-operative Games.* RAND P-1386. Santa Monica, CA.: RAND Corporation, 1958.
1717. Seo, F., and M. Sakawa. "Effective Formation of International Concord for Conflict Solving: A Game Theoretic Approach with Risk Assessment." Paper Presented at the *First Annual Conference on the Processes of International Negotiations,* held on May 18-22, 1988 at the International Institute for Applied Systems Analysis (IIASA), in Laxenburg, Austria.
1718. Shakun, Melvin F. "Decision Support Systems for Negotiations." Paper Presented at the *Proceedings of the IEEE International Conference on Systems, Man and Cybernetics,* held on November 12-15, 1985, in Tucson, AZ. pp. 395-405.
1719. Shure, G. H., and R. J. Meeker. *Bargaining and Negotiation Behavior Technique: Progress Report.* SDC Doc. TM-2304/101/00. Santa Monica, CA.: Systems Development Corporation, 1967. 11p.
1720. _____. _____. *Bargaining and Negotiation Behavior Technique: Progress Report.* SDC Doc. TM-2304/102/00. Santa Monica, CA.: Systems Development Corporation, 1968. 10p.
1721. _____. _____. *Bargaining and Negotiation Behavior Technique: Progress Report.* SDC Doc. TM-2304/103/00. Santa Monica, CA.: Systems Development Corporation, 1968. 10p.
1722. _____. _____. *Bargaining and Negotiation Behavior Technique: Progress Report.* SDC Doc. TM-2304/104/00. Santa Monica, CA.: Systems Development Corporation, 1968. 11p.
1723. _____. _____. *Bargaining and Negotiation Behavior Technique: Progress Report.* SDC Doc. TM-2304/105/00. Santa Monica, CA.: Systems Development Corporation, 1968. 12p.
1724. _____. _____. *Bargaining and Negotiation Behavior Technique: Progress Report.* SDC Doc. TM-2304/106/00. Santa Monica, CA.: Systems Development Corporation, 1969. 8p.
1725. _____. _____. *Bargaining and Negotiation Behavior Technique: Progress Report.* SDC Doc. TM-2304/107/00. Santa Monica, CA.: Systems Development Corporation, 1969. 13p.
1726. _____. _____. *On-Line Computer Studies of Bargaining and Negotiation Behavior.* SDC Doc. TM-2304/108/00. Santa Monica, CA.: Systems Development Corporation, 1969. 112p.
1727. _____. _____. *Real-Time Computer Studies of Bargaining Behavior: The Effects of Threat Upon Bargaining.* SP-1143-000-01. Santa Monica, CA.: Systems Development Corporation, 1963. 15p.
1728. _____. W. H. Moore and H. H. Kelley. *Computer Studies of Bargaining Behavior: The Role of Threat in Bargaining.* SP-2916. Santa Monica, CA.: Systems Development Corporations, 1966.
1729. Snidal, Duncan J. *Interdependence, Regimes and International Cooperation.* Ph.D. Dissertation. New Haven, CT.: Yale University, 1981. 443p.
1730. Stokes, N. W., and Keith W. Hipel. *Simultaneous Moves in Non-Cooperative Games.* Technical Report No. 130-SM-101084. Waterloo, Ont.: Department of Systems Design Engineering, University of Waterloo, 1984.
1731. Tracy, Brian H. *Bargaining Models and Base Negotiations.* Ph.D. Dissertation. Baltimore, MD.: Johns Hopkins University, 1976.

1732. Ulvila, Jacob W., and Warren D. Snider. *Negotiation of International Oil Tanker Standards: An Application of Multiattribute Value Theory.* Boston, MA.: Harvard University, Graduate School of Business and Administration, 1978. 18p.
1733. _____. *On the Value of Assessing Tradeoffs Explicitly for Bargaining.* Boston, MA.: Division of Research, Graduate School of Business Administration, Harvard University, 1979. 43p.
1734. Wang, Muhong, Keith W. Hipel and Niall M. Fraser. "Hypergames - Flexible Mathematical Tools to Describe Misperceptions in Conflicts." Paper Presented at the *IFAC Workshop on Modelling Decision and Game Application to Social Phenomena,* held on August 11-15, 1986, in Beijing, China. pp. 368-373.
1735. _____. Niall M. Fraser and Keith W. Hipel. "Modelling Misperception in International Conflict: Applications of the Conflict Analysis Program." Paper Presented at the *27th Annual Convention of the International Studies Association,* held on March 25-29, 1986, in Los Angeles, CA.
1736. Weber, Robert J. *Negotiation and Arbitration: A Game-Theoretic Perspective.* Working Paper No. 7. Evanston, IL.: Dispute Resolution Center, Kellog Graduate School of Management, Northwestern University, 1985.
1737. Wierzbicki, Andrzej P. "Frameworks for Rational Decisions and Conflict Coefficients." Paper Presented at the *First Annual Conference on the Processes of International Negotiations,* held on May 18-22, 1987, at the International Institute for Applied Systems Analysis (IIASA), in Laxenburg, Austria.
1738. Zinnes, Dina. "An Event Model of Conflict Interaction." Paper Presented at the *12th World Congress of the International Political Science Association,* held on August 9-14, 1982, in Rio de Janeiro.

IV

Mediation

Mediation is a form of peaceful settlement procedure by which a third party is used by disputants in finding a solution to the dispute or to decrease the level of conflict. The aim of mediators is to reduce or to resolve conflict. Common to mediation is the acceptability of the role of the mediator by the partners in the conflict. The function of the mediator is to provide open communication channels, to change the images of the disputants of themselves and each other, and to provide additional ideas to enhance commonality of interest.

This first section of this chapter covers materials dealing with the growing theoretical literature on mediation with particular focus on international mediation. The second section lists case studies of international mediation.

A. MEDIATION THEORY

1. Books

1739. Bercovitch, Jacob. *Social Conflict and Third Parties: Strategies of Conflict Resolution.* Boulder, CO.: Westview Press, 1984. 163p.
1740. Bochner, Stephen, ed. *The Mediating Person: Bridges Between Cultures.* Boston, MA.: G. K. Hall, 1981. 321p.
1741. Cot, Jean Pierre. *International Conciliation.* London: Europa, 1972. 349p.
1742. Dunnigan, James F., and William Martel. *How to Stop a War: The Lessons of Two Hundred Years of War and Peace.* New York: Doubleday, 1987. 298p.
1743. Evarts, Richard W., et al. *Winning Through Accommodation: The Mediator's Handbook: The Use of New, Alternative Methods of Dispute Resolution in the Last Decades of the 20th Century.* Dubuque, IA.: Kendall,Hunt, 1983. 151p.
1744. Fisher, Roger D., and William L. Ury. *International Mediation: A Working Guide: Ideas for the Practitioner.* Cambridge, MA.: Harvard Negotiation Project, 1978. 159p.
1745. Goldberg, Stephen B., Eric D. Green and Frank E. A. Sander. *Dispute Resolution.* Boston, MA.: Little, Brown, 1985. 594p.
1746. Jackson, Elmore. *Meeting of Minds: A Way to Peace Through Mediation.* New York: McGraw-Hill, 1952. 200p.
1747. Kolb, Deborah M. *The Mediators.* Cambridge, MA.: MIT Press, 1983. 230p.
1748. Lall, Arthur S., ed. *Multilateral Negotiations and Mediation: Instruments and Methods.* New York: Pergamon Press, 1985. 206p.
1749. Mitchell, C. R. *Peacemaking and the Consultant's Role.* Farnborough: Gower, 1981. 169p.
1750. Moore, Christopher W. *The Mediation Process: Practical Strategies for Resolving Conflict.* San Francisco, CA.: Jossey-Bass, 1986. 348p.
1751. Porter, Jack N., and Ruth Taplin. *Conflict and Conflict Resolution: A Sociological Introduction with Updated Bibliography and Theory Section.* Lanham, MD.: University Press of America, 1987. 117p.
1752. Randolph, Lillian L. *Third-Party Settlement of Disputes in Theory and Practice.* Dobbs Ferry, NY.: Oceana, 1973. 335p.
1753. Stenelo, Lars G. *Mediation in International Negotiations.* Lund Political Studies, 14. Lund: Studentlitteratur, 1972. 223p.
1754. Touval, Saadia, and I. William Zartman, eds. *International Mediation in Theory and Practice.* SAIS Papers in International Affairs, 6. Boulder, CO.: Westview Press, 1985. 274p.
1755. Young, Oran R. *The Intermediaries: Third Parties in International Crises.* Princeton, NJ.: Princeton University Press, 1967. 427p.

2. Journal Articles

1756. Abrams, Nancy Ellen, and R. Stephen Berry. "Mediation: A Better Alternative to Science Courts." *The Bulletin of the Atomic Scientists,* 33:4 (April 1977), 50-53.
1757. Arnoupoulos, Paris. "Consultation and Conciliation." *International Journal,* 30:1 (1974-75), 102-126.

1758. Ascher, W., and S. R. Brown. "Technologies of Mediation: An Assessment of Methods for the Mediation of International Conflicts." In: H. Chesnut, ed. *Contributions of Technology to International Conflict Resolution*. London: Pergamon Press, 1987. pp. 95-104.
1759. Barkun, Michael. "Conflict Resolution Through Implicit Mediation." *Journal of Conflict Resolution*, 8:2 (1964), 121-130.
1760. Bartunek, Jean M., Alan A. Benton and Christopher B. Keys. "Third Party Intervention and the Bargaining Behavior of Group Representatives." *Journal of Conflict Resolution*, 19 (September 1975), 532-557.
1761. Bazerman, Max H., and Henry S. Farber. "Analyzing the Decision-Making Processes of the Third Parties." *Sloan Management Review*, (Fall 1985), 39-48.
1762. Belliveau, L. M., and Y. F. Stole. "Structure of Third Party Intervention." *Journal of Social Psychology*, 103 (December 1977), 243-250.
1763. Bercovitch, Jacob. "International Mediation: A Study of the Incidence, Strategies and Conditions of Successful Outcomes." *Cooperation and Conflict*, 21:3 (September 1986), 155-168.
1764. _____. "Third Parties in Conflict Management: The Structure and Conditions of Effective Mediation in International Relations." *International Journal*, 40:4 (1985), 736-752.
1765. Bigoness, W. J. "The Impact of Initial Bargaining Position and Alternative Modes of Third Party Intervention in Resolving Bargaining Impasses." *Organizational Behavior and Human Performance*, 17 (1976), 185-198.
1766. _____. "Effects of Locus of Control and Style of Third Party Intervention upon Bargaining Behavior." *Journal of Applied Psychology*, 61 (1976), 305-312.
1767. Bindschedler, Rudolf L. "Conciliation and Mediation." In: *Encyclopedia of Public International Law, Vol. 1. Settlement of Disputes*. Amsterdam: North-Holland, 1981. pp. 47-51.
1768. Brett, Jeanne M., Rita Drieghe and Debra L. Shapiro. "Mediator Style and Mediation Effectiveness." *Negotiation Journal*, 2:3 (July 1986), 277-285.
1769. Brookmire, David A., and Frank Sistrunk. "The Effects of Perceived Ability and Impartiality of Mediators and Time Pressure on Negotiations." *Journal of Conflict Resolution*, 24:2 (1980), 311-328.
1770. Brouillet, Alain. "Mediation as a Technique of Dispute Settlement: Appraisal and Prospects." In: R. Thakur, ed. *International Conflict Resolution*. Boulder, CO.: Westview Press, 1988. pp. 165-174.
1771. Buckingham, G. W. "Variables Affecting Mediation Outcomes." *Peace and Change*, 8:2-3 (1982), 55-64.
1772. Carnevale, Peter J. "Mediation of International Conflict." In: S. Oskamp, ed. *International Conflict and National Public Policy Issues*. Beverly Hills, CA.: Sage, 1985. pp. 87-106.
1773. _____. "Strategic Choice in Mediation." *Negotiation Journal*, 2:1 (January 1986), 41-56.
1774. _____. "An Unnecessary Neologism in Two Systems of Mediation." *Negotiation Journal*, 2 (1986), 357-361.
1775. _____., and Donald E. Conlon. "Time Pressure and Strategic Choice in Mediation." *Organizational Behavior and Human Decision Processes*, 42:1 (1988), 111-133.
1776. Cole, D. L. "Government in the Bargaining Process: The Role of Mediation." *American Academy of Political and Social Sciences, Annals*, 333 (January 1961), 42-58.
1777. Conlon, Donald E. "The Mediation - Intravention Discussion: Toward an Integrative Perspective." *Negotiation Journal*, 4:2 (April 1988), 143-148.

1778. Coulson, Robert. "Must Mediated Settlements Be Fair?" *Negotiation Journal*, 4:1 (January 1988), 15-18.
1779. Darwin, H. G. "Methods of Peaceful Settlement, B: Mediation and Good Offices." In: *International Disputes: The Legal Aspects*. London: David Davies Memorial Institute of International Studies, 1972. pp. 83-92.
1780. Davis, H. E., and M. Dugan. "Training the Mediator." *Peace and Change*, 8:2-3 (1982), 81-90.
1781. Devillers, Philippe. "Preventing the Peace: Report from an Intermediary." *Nation*, 203 (December 5, 1966), 597-603.
1782. Druckman, Daniel, and Leonard Iaquinta. "Toward Bridging the International Negotiation/Mediation Information Gap." *International Studies Notes*, 1:4 (Winter 1974), 6-14.
1783. Eckhoff, T. "The Mediator, the Judge and the Administrator in Conflict Resolution." *Acta Sociologica*, 10:2 (1967), 158-166.
1784. Edmead, Frank. "Analysis and Prediction in International Mediation." In: R. K. Venkata, ed. *Dispute Settlement Through the United Nations*. Dobbs Ferry, NJ.: Oceana, 1977. pp. 221-282.
1785. Eiseman, J. W. "A Third Party Consultation Model for Resolving Recurring Conflicts Collaboratively." *Journal of Applied Behavioral Science*, 13:3 (1977), 303-314.
1786. Firth, R. "A Note on Mediators." *Ethnology*, 4 (1965), 386-388.
1787. Fisher, Roger D. "Playing the Wrong Game?" In: J. Z. Rubin, ed. *Dynamics of Third Party Intervention*. New York: Praeger, 1981. pp. 95-121.
1788. Fisher, Ronald J. "Third Party Consultation: A Method for the Study and Resolution of Conflict." *Journal of Conflict Resolution*, 16 (1972), 67-94.
1789. _____. "Third Party Consultation as a Method of Intergroup Conflict Resolution: A Review of Studies." *Journal of Conflict Resolution*, 27 (June 1983), 301-334.
1790. _____. "Third Party Consultation: A Problem Solving Approach for De-Escalating International Conflict." In: J. P. Maas and R. A. C. Stewart, eds. *Toward a World of Peace: People Create Alternatives*. Suva, Fiji: University of South Pacific, 1986. pp. 18-33.
1791. Frei, Daniel. "Conditions Affecting the Effectiveness of International Mediation." *Peace Science Society (International) Papers*, 26 (1976), 67-84.
1792. Fuller, L. L. "Mediation - Its Forms and Functions." *Southern California Law Review*, 44 (1971), 305-339.
1793. Gazit, Mordechai. "Mediation and Mediators." *Jerusalem Journal of International Relations*, 5:4 (1981), 80-104.
1794. Gross, A. "Peaceful Settlement of International Disputes - Mediation and Conciliation." In: C. W. Jenks, et al. *International Law in a Changing World*. New York: Oceana, 1963. pp. 44-53.
1795. "Guidelines for Third Parties in International Disputes." *American Journal of International Law*, 66:4 (1972), 22-31.
1796. Harbottle, Michael. "The Strategy of Third Party Intervention in Conflict Resolution." *International Journal*, 35:1 (1979-1980), 118-131.
1797. Haynes, J. M. "The Process of Negotiation." *Mediation Quarterly*, 1 (1983), 75-92.
1798. Holmes, John W. "Mediation or Enforcement?" *International Journal*, 25:2 (1970), 388-404.
1799. Honeyman, Christopher. "Five Elements of Mediation." *Negotiation Journal*, 4:2 (April 1988), 149-160.
1800. Imai, R. "The Diplomacy of Compliance and Modern Arms Control - Problems of Third Party Participation." *International Affairs*, 62:1 (1986), 87-94.

1801. Isard, Walter, and Christine Smith. "A Dynamical System Approach to Learning Processes in Conflict Mediation and Interaction." In: W. Isard and Y. Nagao, eds. *International and Regional Conflict.* Cambridge, MA.: Balliger, 1983. pp. 11-32.
1802. Jackson, Elmore. "Mediation and Conciliation in International Law." *International Social Science Bulletin,* 10:4 (1958), 508-543.
1803. Jacobsen, Kurt. "Sponsorship Activities in the U.N. Negotiating Process." *Cooperation and Conflict,* 5:4 (1970), 241-269.
1804. Jarke, Mattias, Tawfik Jelassi and Melvin F. Shakun. "Mediator: Towards a Negotiation Support System." *European Journal of Operational Research,* 31 (1987), 314-334.
1805. Johnson, D. F., and Dean G. Pruitt. "Pre-Intervention Effects of Mediation Versus Arbitration." *Journal of Applied Psychology,* 56 (1972), 1-10.
1806. _____., and W. Fullar. "Style of Third Party Intervention, Face Saving and Bargaining Behavior." *Journal of Experimental Social Psychology,* 8 (1972), 319-330.
1807. Kaufmann, Johan. "A Methodological Summary." In: A. Lall, ed. *Multilateral Negotiation and Mediation.* New York: Pergamon Press, 1985. pp. 133-153.
1808. Kolb, Deborah M. "Strategy and the Tactics of Mediation." *Human Relations,* 36:3 (March 1983), 247-268.
1809. _____. "To Be a Mediator: Expressive Tactics in Mediation." *Journal of Social Issues,* 41:2 (Summer 1985), 11-26.
1810. Kressel, Kenneth, and Dean G. Pruitt. "Themes in the Mediation of Social Conflict." *Journal of Social Issues,* 41:2 (Summer 1985), 179-198.
1811. Lachs, Manfred. "International Law, Mediation and Negotiation." In: A. Lall, ed. *Multilateral Negotiation and Mediation.* New York: Pergamon Press, 1985. pp. 183-196.
1812. Laue, James H. "The Emergence of Institutionalization of Third Party Roles in Conflict." In: D. J. D. Sandole and I. Sandole-Staroste, eds. *Conflict Management and Problem Solving.* London: Frances Pinter, 1987. pp. 17-29.
1813. _____. "Ethical Considerations in Choosing Intervention Roles." *Peace and Change,* 8:2-3 (1982), 29-41.
1814. _____. "The Behavior of Third Parties: Roles, Rules and Ethics in Peacemaking and Conflict Resolution." In: *Coming to Terms with Conflict: Third Party Intervention and Aspects of Culture.* Amsterdam: Royal Tropical Institute, 1986. pp. 93-102.
1815. Levine, Edward P. "Mediation in International Politics." *Peace Science Society (International) Papers,* 18 (1971), 23-43.
1816. Lipstein, K. "Techniques of Mediation and Conciliation." *International Social Science Bulletin,* 10:4 (1958), 507-508, 626-628.
1817. Lloyd, William B. "Mediation: The Forgotten Approach to Peacemaking." *War/Peace Report,* 11 (October 1971), 10-11.
1818. Luard, Evan. "Conciliation and Deterrence, A Comparison of Political Strategies in the Interwar and Postwar Periods." *World Politics,* 19 (January 1967), 167-189.
1819. McGaffey, David C. "Negotiation and Mediation: A Diplomat's Perspective." In: D. J. D. Sandole and I. Sandole-Staroste, eds. *Conflict Management and Problem Solving.* London: Frances Pinter, 1987. pp. 100-103.
1820. McGillicuddy, N. B., G. L. Welton and Dean G. Pruitt. "Third-Party Intervention: A Field Experiment Comparing Three Different Models." *Journal of Personality and Social Psychology,* 1 (1987), 104-112.

1821. Metzger, S. D. "Settlement of International Disputes by Non-Judicial Methods." *American Journal of International Law,* 48 (1954), 408-420.
1822. Modelski, George. "International Settlement of Internal War." In: J. N. Rosenau, ed. *International Aspects of Civil Strife.* Princeton, NJ.: Princeton University Press, 1964. pp. 122-153.
1823. Montauer, Carlos A. "The Mediation of the Socialist International: Inconsistency, Prejudice and Ignorance." *Caribbean Review,* 11:2 (Spring 1982), 42-45, 57.
1824. Murnighan, J. K. "The Structure of Mediation and Intravention: Comments on Carnevale's Strategic Choice Model." *Negotiation Journal,* 2:4 (October 1986), 351-356.
1825. Muscari, Paul G. "The Ethical Ramifications of Mediation Theory." *The Journal of Mind and Behavior,* 6:3 (1985), 315-324.
1826. Ott, M. C. "Mediation as a Method of Conflict Resolution: Two Cases." *International Organization,* 26:4 (1972), 595-618.
1827. Parodi, Alexandre. "Pacific Settlement of Disputes." *International Conciliation,* 445 (November 1948), 616-632.
1828. Pechota, Vratislav. "Complementary Structures of Third-Party Settlement of International Disputes." In: R. K. Venkata, ed. *Dispute Settlement Through the United Nations.* Dobbs Ferry, NY.: Oceana, 1977. pp. 149-220.
1829. Podell, J. E., and W. M. Knapp. "The Effects of Mediation on the Perceived Firmness of the Opponent." *Journal of Conflict Resolution,* 13:4 (1969), 511-520.
1830. Princen, Tom. "International Mediation - The View from the Vatican." *Negotiation Journal,* 3:4 (October 1984), 347-366.
1831. _____. "Interests of the Intermediary." In: *Issues Affecting Intervenors in Disputes.* Working Paper Series 11. Cambridge MA.: The Program on the Processes of International Negotiations. American Academy of Arts and Science, 1987, 14p.
1832. Pruitt, Dean G., and D. F. Johnson. "Mediation as an Aid to Face-Saving in Negotiations." *Journal of Personality and Social Psychology,* 14 (1970), 239-246.
1833. _____. _____. "Mediation as an Aid to Face Saving in Negotiation." In: R. A. Baron and R. M. Liebert, eds. *Human Social Behavior.* Homewood, IL.: Dorsey Press, 1971. pp. 421-433.
1834. _____., and Kenneth Kressel. "The Mediation of Social Conflict: An Introduction." *Journal of Social Issues,* 41 (1985), 1-10.
1835. _____., and D. F. Johnson. "Pre-Intervention Effects of Mediation vs. Arbitration." *Journal of Applied Psychology,* 56 (1972), 1-10.
1836. _____. "Trends in the Scientific Study of Negotiation and Mediation." *Negotiation Journal,* 2:3 (July 1986), 237-244.
1837. Raiffa, Howard. "Mediation of Conflicts." *American Behavioral Scientists,* 27:2 (1983), 195-210.
1838. Raymond, Gregory A., and Charles W. Kegley, Jr. "Third Party Mediation and International Norms: A Test of Two Models." *Conflict Management and Peace Science,* 9:1 (Fall 1985), 33-52.
1839. Roehl, Janice A., and R. F. Cook. "Issues in Mediation: Rhetoric of Social Conflict." *Journal of Social Issues,* 41:2 (Summer 1985), 161-178.
1840. Rubin, A. P. "International Legal Effects on Unilateral Declarations." *American Journal of International Law,* 71 (January 1977), 10-30.
1841. Rubin, Jeffrey Z. "Experimental Research on Third Party Intervention in Conflict: Toward Some Generalizations." *Psychological Bulletin,* 87 (1980), 379-391

1842. Schwieson, Naomi. "Mediation." In: E. Luard, ed. *The International Regulation of Frontier Disputes.* London: Thames and Hudson, 1970. pp. 141-167.
1843. Shapiro, Debra L., Rita Drieghe and Jeanne Brest. "Mediator Behavior and the Outcome of Mediation." *Journal of Social Issues,* 41:2 (Summer 1985), 101-114.
1844. Singer, J. David. "Negotiation by Proxy: A Proposal." *Journal of Conflict Resolution,* 9:4 (1965), 538-541.
1845. Smith, William P. "Effectiveness of the Biased Mediator." *Negotiation Journal,* 1:4 (October 1985), 363-372.
1846. Sohn, Louis B. "The Role of Conciliation in International Disputes." *The Fine Print,* 1:2 (1981), 3-4.
1847. Stern, Louis W., Richard P. Bagozzi and Ruby Roy Dholakia. "Mediational Mechanisms in Inter-Organizational Conflict." In: D. Druckman, ed. *Negotiations: Social-Psychological Perspectives.* Beverly-Hills, CA.: Sage, 1977. pp. 367-388.
1848. Stulberg, J. "Critical Issues in Mediation." In: J. F. Power, ed. *Creative Approaches to Dispute Resolution.* Washington, D.C.: American Arbitration Association, 1983. pp. 35-39.
1849. Sullivan, C. D. "Negotiation by Proxy: A Critique." *Journal of Conflict Resolution,* 10:3 (1966), 383-385.
1850. Tandon, Yashpal. "The Peaceful Settlement of International Disputes." *International Relations,* 2:9 (April 1964), 555-587.
1851. Tener, J., T. R. Colosi and E. F. Hartfield. "Mediation and Negotiations Skills Training Workshop." In: J. F. Power, ed. *Creative Approaches to Dispute Resolution.* Washington, D.C.: American Arbitration Association, 1983. pp. 63-80.
1852. Touval, Saadia. "Biased Intermediaries: Theoretical and Historical Considerations." *Jerusalem Journal of International Relations,* 1:1 (1975), 51-69.
1853. _____. "The Context of Mediation." *Negotiation Journal,* 1:4 (October 1985), 373-378.
1854. _____., and I. William Zartman. "International Mediation: Conflict Resolution and Power Politics." *Journal of Social Issues,* 41 (Summer 1985), 27-45.
1855. Tyler, Tom R. "The Psychology of Disputant Concerns in Mediation." *Negotiation Journal,* 3:4 (October 1987), 367-374.
1856. Ury, William L. "Strengthening International Mediation." *Negotiation Journal,* 3:3 (July 1987), 225-230.
1857. Väyrynen, Raimo. "Third Parties in the Resolution of Regional Conflicts." *Bulletin of Peace Proposals,* 18:3 (1987), 293-308.
1858. Wall, James A. "Mediation: An Analysis, Review and Proposed Research." *Journal of Conflict Resolution,* 25:1 (1981), 157-180.
1859. _____. "Mediation: The Effects of Mediator Proposals, Number of Issues and Altered Negotiator Aspirations." *Journal of Management,* 10:3 (Fall/Winter 1984), 293-304.
1860. Warren, Roland L. "The Conflict Intersystem and the Change Agent." *Journal of Conflict Resolution,* 8:3 (1964), 231-241.
1861. Welton, G. L., and Dean G. Pruitt. "The Effects of Mediator Bias and Disputant Power over the Mediator on the Mediation Process." *Personality and Social Psychology Bulletin,* 13 (1987), 123-133.
1862. Westbrook, Franklin D. "Third Party Consultation, Mediation and Coercive Bargaining." *Journal of Counselling and Development,* 63:8 (April 1985), 535-536.

1863. Wierzbicki, Andrzej P. "Negotiation and Mediation in Conflicts: 1. The Role of Mathematical Approaches and Methods." In: H. Chesnut, et al. *Supplemental Ways for Improving International Stability.* Elmsford, NY.: Pergamon Press, 1984. pp. 163-178.
1864. Winham, Gilbert R. "The Mediation of Multilateral Negotiation." *Journal of World Trade Law,* 13:3 (May-June 1979), 193-208.
1865. Young, Oran R. "Anarchy and Social Choice: Reflections on the International Polity." *World Politics,* 30 (January 1978), 241-263.
1866. _____. "Intermediaries: Additional Thoughts on Third Parties." *Journal of Conflict Resolution,* 16:1 (1972), 51-65.
1867. Zartman, I. William. "Explaining Disengagement." In: J. Rubin, ed. *Dynamics of Third Party Intervention.* New York: Praeger, 1981. pp. 148-167.
1868. _____., and Saadia Touval. "International Mediation: Conflict Resolution and Power Politics." *Journal of Social Issues,* 41:2 (Summer 1985), 27-45.
1869. _____. "Ripening Conflict, Ripe Moment, Formula, and Mediation." In: D. B. Bendahmane and J. W. McDonald, eds. *Perspectives on Negotiation.* Washington, D.C.: Foreign Service Institute, 1986. pp. 205-228.

3. Documents and Reports

1870. Adler, Peter, Karen Lovaas and Neal Milner. *The Ideologies of Mediation: The Movement's Own Story.* Working Paper Series 1987-1. Honolulu, HI.: Program on Conflict Resolution, University of Hawaii at Manoa, 1986. 37p.
1871. Anson, Robert, Tawfik Jelassi and Robert Bostrom. *Negotiation Support Systems: Computer Support to Mediated Conflict Resolution.* IRMIS Working Paper #W712. Bloomington, IN.: Institute for Research on the Management of Information Systems, Indiana University, October 1987.
1872. Beattie, C. E. "Technical Skills Required in Multilateral Mediation and Negotiation to Resolve Violent or Potentially Violent Conflict." Paper Presented at the *Second Annual Meeting of the North American Council of the International Peace Academy,* held on April 20-23, 1978, in Quebec City.
1873. Bercovitch, Jacob. *Pacific Third Party Intervention at the Interpersonal, Intergroup and International Levels.* Ph.D. Dissertation. London: London University, 1980.
1874. Brookmire, David A. *The Effects of Time Pressure and Perceived Ability and Impartiality of Mediators on Negotiation.* Ph.D. Dissertation. Tampa, FL.: University of South Florida, 1978. 170p.
1875. Burton, John W. "Intervenors in International Conflicts: Diplomats, Mediators and the Media." Paper Presented at the *National Conference on Peacemaking and Conflict Resolution,* held on September 18-23, 1984, at the University of Missouri in St. Louis.
1876. Bush, Kenneth D., and Richard Price, eds. *Managing Regional Conflict: Regimes and Third Party Mediators, Part 2. Proceedings of a Workshop held in Ottawa, May 6-7, 1988.* Ottawa: Canadian Institute for International Peace and Security, 1988.
1877. Carnevale, Peter J. "Biased Mediators in International Mediation." Paper Presented at the, *Annual Meeting of the International Studies Association,* held in April, 1987, in Washington, D.C.

1878. _____, and M. Leatherwood. "Communication Processes in Mediation: A Function of Mediator Power and Bargainer Orientation." Paper Presented at the *Meeting of the Academy of Management*, held in 1984, in Boston, MA.
1879. _____. G. S. Fobian and K. Weber. "Effects of Potential Future Mediation on the Recommendations of Biased Mediators." Paper Presented at the *Annual Meeting of the American Psychological Association*, held in 1985, in Los Angeles, CA.
1880. _____. "Experiments on Mediation." Paper Presented at the *Ninth Annual Meeting of the International Society of Political Psychology*, held in July 1986, in Amsterdam.
1881. _____. A. Ebreo and A. Bauer. "The Influence of Positive Affect on Strategic Choice in Mediation." Paper Presented at the *Annual Meeting of the American Psychological Association*, held in August 1986, in Washington, D.C.
1882. _____. "A Model of Mediator Strategy and the Influence of Mediator Strategy on Negotiation." Paper Presented at the *Third National Conference on Peacemaking and Conflict Resolution*, held in June 1986, in Denver, CO.
1883. _____., and Donald E. Conlon. "Time Pressure and Strategic Choice in Mediation." Paper Presented at the *Annual Meeting of the Academy of Management*, held in August 1986, in Chicago, IL.
1884. _____., et al. "Modeling Mediator Behavior in Experimental Games." Paper Presented at the *Meeting of the Fourth Conference on Experimental Economics*, held in September 1986, in Bielefeld, West Germany.
1885. Colosi, Thomas, and Ruth M. Schimel. "Mediation Concepts and Techniques." Paper Presented at the *Tenth SIETAR International Conference*, held on May 21-25, 1984, at the George Mason University, Washington, D.C.
1886. Curle, Adam. *In the Middle: Non-Official Mediation in Violent Situations*. New York: St. Martin's Press, 1986. 57p.
1887. Doob, L. W. "Mediation and Negotiation: Personal Skills." Paper Presented at the *Second Annual Meeting of the North American Council of the International Peace Academy*, held on April 20-28, 1978, in Quebec City.
1888. Dowty, Allan. *The Role of Great Power Guarantees in International Peace Agreements*. Jerusalem Paper on Peace Problems, 3. Jerusalem: The Leonard Davis Institute for International Relations, Hebrew University, 1974. 46p.
1889. Edmead, Frank. *Analysis and Prediction in International Mediation*. New York: United Nations Institute for Training and Research (UNITAR), 1971. 50p.
1890. Faure, Guy Oliver. "Mediator as a Third Negotiator." Paper Presented at the *First Annual Conference on the Processes of International Negotiations*, held on May 18-22, 1987, at the International Institute for Applied Systems Analysis (IIASA), in Laxenburg, Austria.
1891. Fisher, Ronald J. "Third-Party Consultation: A Problem Solving Approach for De-Escalating International Conflict." Paper Presented at the *First International Conference on Conflict Resolution and Peace Studies*, held in January 1986, in Suva, Fiji.
1892. Freymond, Jacques, and Thierry Hentsch. *On Mediating Violence: Armed Political Violence and Humanitarian Principles*. Geneva: Graduate Institute of International Studies, 1973. 40p.
1893. Goldstein, Susan. *Cultural Issues in Mediation: A Literature Review*. Working Paper Series 1986-1. Honolulu, HI.: Program on Conflict Resolution, University of Hawaii at Manoa, 1986. 44p.

1894. Hamish, K., and Peter J. Carnevale. "Sex Differences in Mediator Behavior." Paper Presented at the *Meeting of the American Psychological Association*, held in August 1987, in New York City.
1895. Husbands, Jo Louise. *More Than Mediators?: Non-Major Powers in International and Regional Negotiations*. Ph.D. Dissertation. Minneapolis, MI.: University of Minnesota, 1977. 299p.
1896. Ignatieff, George. "Multilateral Mediation and Negotiation Procedures: The Mechanisms." Paper Presented at the *Second Annual Meeting of the North American Council of the International Peace Academy*, held on April 20-23, 1978, in Quebec City.
1897. Jonah, James O. "Negotiations to End Conflicts." Paper Presented at the *1979 Peacekeeping Seminar of the International Peace Academy*, held on July 25-28, 1979, in Schloss Landon, Vienna.
1898. Kaufman, Sanda. *Mediation to Resolve Conflict: Theory, Experimentation and Case Studies*. Ph.D. Dissertation. Pittsburgh, PA.: Carnegie-Mellon University, 1985. 343p.
1899. Laue, James H., and Glen H. Fisher. "Negotiation and Mediation - International Applications." Paper Presented at the *Tenth SIETAR International Conference*, held on May 21-25, 1984, at George Mason University, Washington, D.C.
1900. _____. *Sharpening the Skills of the Peacemaker*. Muscatine, IA.: The Stanley Foundation, 1986. 6p.
1901. Laylin, J. "Guidelines for Third Parties in International Disputes." Paper Presented at the *Proceedings of the 66th Annual Meeting of the American Society of International Law*, held in 1972.
1902. Levine, Edward P. *The Mediation of International Disputes*. Ph.D. Dissertation. New Haven, CT.: Yale University, 1971. 376p.
1903. Miller, Robert. *Managing Regional Conflict: Regimes and Third-Party Mediators*. CIIPS Working Paper # 8. Ottawa: Canadian Institute for International Peace and Security, 1988. 59p.
1904. Moore, Christopher W. *A General Theory of Mediation: Dynamics, Strategies and Moves*. Ph.D. Dissertation. New Brunswick, NJ.: Rutgers University, 1983. 552p.
1905. Mroz, J. E. "Third Party Roles: Peacekeeping and Mediation." Paper Presented at the *Annual Convention of the International Studies Association*, held on March 21-24, 1979, in Toronto.
1906. Neubauer, Deane E., and Michael Shapiro. "The New Politics of Mediation: Disclosing Silences." Paper Presented at the *13th World Congress of the International Political Science Association*, held on July 15-20, 1985, in Paris.
1907. Pechota, Vratislav. *Complementary Structures of Third-Party Settlement of International Disputes*. New York: United Nations Institute for Training and Research (UNITAR), 1971. 63p.
1908. Princen, Tom, Eileen Babbitt and Jim Arthur. "Assisted Negotiation: The Process of Resolving Conflict with Intermediaries." In: *Issues Affecting Intervenors in Disputes*. Working Paper Series, 11. Cambridge MA.: The Program on the Processes of International Negotiations. American Academy of Arts and Science, 1987. 9p.
1909. _____. "Intermediary's Decision Problem: Entry." In: *Issues Affecting Intervenors in Disputes*. Working Paper Series 11. Cambridge, MA.: The Program on the Processes of International Negotiations. American Academy of Arts and Science, 1987. 10p.

1910. Pruitt, Dean G. "Research and Evaluation of the Mediation Process." Paper Presented at the *PARC Theory Building Seminar*, held on April 10, 1987, at the Maxwell School of Citizenship and Public Affairs, Syracuse University.
1911. _____. *Mediation as an Aid to Face Saving in Negotiations*. Technical Report No. 7. Buffalo, NY.: SUNY at Buffalo, 1970. 21p.
1912. Ruloff, Dieter. "Mediation in International Conflicts - Computer Simulation and Some Results." *Peace Science Society (International) Papers*, 26 (1976), 22-48.
1913. Ryscavage, Richard, and Eileen Newmark. "Intercultural Conflict Mediation Workshop." Paper Presented at the *Tenth SIETAR International Conference*, held on May 21-25, 1985, at the George Mason University, Washington, D.C.
1914. Schachter, Oskar. "Mechanisms for Multilateral Mediation and Conciliation." Paper Presented at the *Second Annual Meeting of the North American Council of the International Peace Academy*, held on April 20-23, 1978, in Quebec City.
1915. Smith, Phillip C. "Fostering Conciliation Styles." Paper Presented to the *Tenth SIETAR International Conference*, held on May 21-25, 1984, at the George Mason University, Washington, D.C.
1916. Smith, William P. *Some Effects of Mediated Power in Three Person Groups*. Ph.D. Dissertation. Chapel Hills, NC.: University of North Carolina, 1963.
1917. Sohn, Louis B. "Report on Recent Developments in International Conciliation." Paper Presented at the *53rd Conference of the International Law Association*, held in 1968, in Buenos Aires. pp. 34-56.
1918. *Some Aspects of Mediation: Report of a Conference Sponsored by the Carnegie Endowment for International Peace*. Talloires, France: Carnegie Endowment for International Peace, 1970. 56p.
1919. Straus, Donald B. "Multilateral Mediation and Negotiation: Technical Skills." Paper Presented at the *Second Annual Meeting of the North American Council of the International Peace Academy*, held on April 20-23, 1978, in Quebec City.
1920. Weider-Hatfield, Deborah, William A. Dohonue and Jamie Harden. "Preliminary Results on a Theory of Mediator Communicative Competence." Paper Presented at the *National Conference on Peacemaking and Conflict Resolution*, held on September 18-23, 1984, at the University of Missouri, St.Louis, MO.
1921. Weiss-Wik, Stephen, and James Bennett. "Communicative Repertories and the Mediation of International Conflict." Paper Presented at the *21st Meeting of the International Studies Association*, held on March 18-22, 1980, in Los Angeles, CA.
1922. Winham, Gilbert R. "The Mediation of Multilateral Negotiation." Paper Presented at the *Second Annual Meeting of the North American Council of the International Peace Academy*, held on April 20-23, 1978, in Quebec City.

B. MEDIATION CASE STUDIES

1. Books

1923. Assefa, Hizkias. *Mediation of Civil Wars: Approaches and Strategies, The Sudan Conflict*. Boulder, CO.: Westview Press, 1987. 234p.

1924. Azcarate, Florez Pablo de. *Mission in Palestine, 1948-1952.* Washington, D.C.: Middle East Institute, 1966. 211p.
1925. Chopra, Surendra. *U.N. Mediation in Kashmir: A Study in Power Politics.* Kurnkshetra: Vishal, 1971. 290p.
1926. Gulhati, N. D. *Indus Water Treaty: An Exercise in International Mediation.* Bombay: Allied Publishers, 1973.
1927. Mann, P. *Ralph Bunche: UN Peacemaker.* N.Y.: Coward, McCann & Geoghegan, 1975. 384p.
1928. Rubin, Jeffrey Z., ed. *Dynamics of Third Party Intervention: Kissinger in the Middle East.* New York: Praeger, 1981. 303p.
1929. Sheehan, Edward R. F. *The Arabs, Israelis and Kissinger: A Secret History of American Diplomacy in the Middle East.* New York: Reader's Digest Press, 1976. 287p.
1930. Touval, Saadia. *The Peace Brokers: Mediators in the Arab Israeli Conflict, 1948-1979.* Princeton, NJ.: Princeton University Press, 1982. 377p.
1931. Witty, Cathie J. *Mediation and Society: Conflict Management in Lebanon.* New York: Academic Press, 1980. 156p.

2. Journal Articles

1932. Alroy, Gil. "Kissinger Delivers Another Israeli Withdrawal." *Midstream*, 21 (November 1975), 8-18.
1933. Bercovitch, Jacob. "A Case Study of Mediation as a Method of International Conflict: The Camp David Experience." *Review of International Studies*, 12 (January 1986), 43-65.
1934. _____. "Theoretical Observations on International Negotiation and Mediation: The Egyptian-Israeli Experience." In: M. Mushkat, ed. *Violence and Peace Building in the Middle East.* New York: K. G. Saur, 1981. pp. 173-183.
1935. Bourne, C. B. "Mediation, Conciliation and Adjudication in the Settlement of International Drainage Basin Disputes." *Canadian Yearbook of International Law*, 9 (1971), 114-158.
1936. Brecher, Michael. "Kashmir: A Case Study in UN Mediation." *Pacific Affairs*, 9 (1983), 195-207.
1937. Cohen, Raymond. "Twice Bitten? The European Communities 1987 Middle East Initiative." *Middle East Review*, 20 (Spring 1988), 33-40.
1938. Cormick, Gerald W. "Intervention and Self-Determination in Environmental Disputes: A Mediator's Perspective." *Resolve*, (Winter 1982), 1, 3-7.
1939. _____. "The Myth, the Reality, and the Future of Environmental Mediation." *Environment*, 24 (1982), 14-17, 36-39.
1940. Cot, Jean Pierre. "A Critical Remark on John Burton's Paper on Resolution of Conflict with Special Reference to the Cyprus Conflict." *International Studies Quarterly*, 16 (1972), 31-39.
1941. Degan, V. D. "The Commission of Mediation, Conciliation and Arbitration of the Organization of African Unity." *Revue Egyptienne de Droit International*, 20 (1964), 53-80.
1942. Dhanani, Gulshan. "Third-Party Mediation: The Role of the U.S. in the Arab-Israel Conflict." *India Quarterly*, 38:1 (1982), 78-85.
1943. Dryzek, John, and Susan Hunter. "Environmental Mediation for International Problems." *International Studies Quarterly*, 31:1 (1987), 87-102.
1944. Elias, T. O. "The Commission of Mediation, Conciliation and Arbitration of the Organization African Unity." *British Yearbook of International Law*, 40 (1964), 336-359.

1945. Fenwick, Charles. "Inter-American Regional Procedures for the Settlement of Disputes." *International Organization,* 10:1 (1956), 12-21.
1946. Fisher, Ronald J. "A Third Party Consultation Workshop on the India/Pakistan Conflict." *Journal of Social Psychology,* 112:2 (1980), 191-206.
1947. Forsythe, David P. "Humanitarian Mediation by the International Committee of the Red Cross." In: S. Touval and I. W. Zartman, eds. *International Mediation in Theory and Practice.* Boulder, CO.: Westview Press, 1985. pp. 233-249.
1948. Garfinkle, Adam M. "Negotiating by Proxy: Jordanian Foreign Policy and U.S. Options in the Middle East." *Orbis,* (Winter 1981), 847-880.
1949. Gross Stein, Janice. "Structures, Strategies, and Tactics of Mediation: Kissinger and Carter in the Middle East." *Negotiation Journal,* 1:4 (October 1985), 331-348.
1950. Kochan, Thomas A. "Step-by-Step in the Middle East from the Perspective of the Labor Mediation Process." In: J. Z. Rubin, ed. *Dynamics of Third Party Intervention.* New York: Praeger, 1981. pp. 122-147.
1951. Kostiner, Joseph. "Counterproductive Mediation: Saudi Arabia and the Iran Arms Deal." *Middle East Review,* 19:4 (Summer 1987), 41-46.
1952. Kressel, Kenneth. "Kissinger in the Middle East: An Exploratory Analysis of Role Strain in International Mediation." In: J. Z. Rubin, ed. *Dynamics of Third Party Intervention.* New York: Praeger, 1981. pp. 226-252.
1953. Lall, Arthur S. "Some Thoughts on the U.N. General Assembly as a Forum for Mediation and Negotiation." *Journal of International Affairs,* 29:1 (Spring 1975), 63-68.
1954. Levine, Herbert S. "The Mediator: Carl J. Burckhardt's Efforts to Avert a Second World War." *Journal of Modern History,* 45:3 (1973), 439-453.
1955. Levine, Steven I. "A New Look at American Mediation in the Chinese Civil War: The Marshall Mission and Nicaragua." *Diplomatic History,* 3:4 (1979), 349-375.
1956. Levy, Marc A. "Mediation of Prisoner's Dilemma Conflicts and the Importance of the Cooperation Threshold: The Case of Namibia." *Journal of Conflict Resolution,* 29:4 (December 1985), 581-604.
1957. Lieb, Diane. "Iran and Iraq at Algiers, 1975." In: S. Touval and I. W. Zartman, eds. *International Mediation in Theory and Practice.* Boulder, CO.: Westview Press, 1985. pp. 67-90.
1958. Low, Stephen. "The Zimbabwe Settlement, 1976-1979." In: S. Touval and I. W. Zartman, eds. *International Mediation in Theory and Practice.* Boulder, CO.: Westview Press, 1985. pp. 91-110.
1959. Mason, Paul E., and Thomas F. Marsteller. "U.N. Mediation: More Effective Options." *SAIS Review,* 5:2 (Summer/Fall 1985), 271-284.
1960. Pruitt, Dean G. "Kissinger as a Traditional Mediator with Power." In: J. Z. Rubin, ed. *Dynamics of Third Party Intervention: Kissinger in the Middle East.* New York: Praeger, 1981. pp. 136-147.
1961. Scheman, L. Ronald, and John W. Ford. "The Organization of American States as Mediator." In: S. Touval and I. W. Zartman, eds. *International Mediation in Theory and Practice.* Boulder, CO.: Westview Press, 1985. pp. 197-232.
1962. Sheehan, Edward R. F. "How Kissinger Did It: Step by Step in the Middle East." *Foreign Policy,* 22 (1976), 13-70.
1963. _____. "How Kissinger Did It: Step by Step in the Middle East." In: J. Z. Rubin, ed. *Dynamics of Third Party Intervention.* New York: Praeger, 1981. pp. 44-94.

1964. Sick, Gary. "The Partial Negotiator: Algeria and U.S. Hostages in Iran." In: S. Touval and I. W. Zartman, eds. *International Mediation in Theory and Practice*. Boulder, CO.: Westview Press, 1985. pp. 21-66.
1965. Spiegel, Marianne A. "The Namibia Negotiations and the Problem of Neutrality." In: S. Touval and I. W. Zartman, eds. *International Mediation in Theory and Practice*. Boulder, CO,: Westview Press, 1985. pp. 111-140.
1966. Taylor, J. R. "International Aspects of the Great Power's Mediation of the Rumanian - Bulgarian Territorial Dispute, 1912-13." *East European Quarterly*, 14:1 (Spring 1980), 23-37.
1967. Thornton, Thomas P. "The Indo-Pakistani Conflict: Soviet Mediation at Tashkent, 1966." In: S. Touval and I. W. Zartman, eds. *International Mediation in Theory and Practice*. Boulder, CO.: Westview Press, 1985.
1968. Touval, Saadia. "Mediators in the Israeli - Arab Conflict: Requisite for Success." In: A. Arian, ed. *Israel: A Developing Society*. Assen: Van Gorcum, 1980. pp. 59-93.
1969. "U.N. Mediation: More Effective Options." *SAIS Review*, 5 (Summer/Fall 1985), 271-284.
1970. Umbricht, Victor. "Some Thoughts on Preconditions Necessary for a Mediated Settlement by the United Nations in Namibia." In: *Southern Africa - Prospects for Peace and Security*. New York: International Peace Academy, 1987. pp. 45-66.
1971. Wolfers, Michael. "The Organization of African Unity as Mediator." In: S. Touval and I. W. Zartman, eds. *International Mediation in Theory and Practice*. Boulder, CO.: Westview Press, 1985. pp. 175-196.

3. Documents and Reports

1972. Al-Battah, Abdalla. *Third Party Involvement and Conflict Resolution: The U.S. Role in the Camp David Negotiations, 1977-79*. M.A. Thesis. Ottawa, Ont.: Carleton University, 1983.
1973. Amin, T. *Third Party's Role in the Resolution of Conflict: A Case Study of the Tashkent Declaration*. M.A. Thesis. Ottawa, Ont.: Carleton University, 1983.
1974. Assefa, Hizkias. *Preconditions for the Success of Mediation as a Means of Conflict Resolution: The Sudan Civil War, 1955-1972; A Case Study*. Ph.D. Dissertation. Pittsburgh, PA.: University of Pittsburgh, 1983. 382p.
1975. Azar, Edward E. "Conflict Resolution for Lebanon." Paper Presented at the *PARC Maxwell Summer Lecture Series*, held on July 1, 1986, at the Maxwell School of Citizenship and Public Affairs, Syracuse University.
1976. Badran, W. Abd el Rahman. *The Role of Third Parties in Conflict Between Small States: A Case Study of the United States and the Egyptian-Israeli Conflict, January 1967 - December 1978*. Ph.D. Dissertation. Ottawa: Carlton University, 1981.
1977. Bender, Gerald, and Witney Schneidman. *Multilateral Versus Bilateral Approaches to International Mediation: The Namibia Negotiations*. PEW Case Studies 422.0-G-88-5. Los Angeles, CA.:School of International Relations, University of Southern California, 1988.
1978. Bracey, Andrey. *Resolution of the Dominican Crisis, 1965: A Study in Mediation*. Washington, D.C.: Institute for the Study of Diplomacy, Georgetown University, 1980. 64p.
1979. Garfinkle, Adam M. "West European Peace Diplomacy in the Levant." Paper Presented at the *28th Annual Convention of the International Studies Association*, held on April 14-18, 1987, in Washington, D.C.

1980. Howe, Herbert. *Dancing on Cobwebs: The 1976 Entry of the United States into the Rhodesia Peace Process.* PEW Case Studies, 404.0-C-87-G. Washington, D.C.: School of Foreign Service, Georgetown University, 1987.
1981. Hunter, Susan, and John Dryzek. "Acid Rain: A Case for International Mediation." Paper Presented at the *28th Annual Convention of the International Studies Association,* held on April 14-18, 1987, in Washington, D.C.
1982. _____. _____. "Environmental Mediation: Can It Work for Global Problems." Paper Presented at the *25th Annual Convention of the International Studies Association,* held on March 27-31, 1984, in Atlanta, GA.
1983. Kayani, Amer. *Soviet Union as Mediator : The Tashkent Conference of 1966.* PEW Case Studies, 315.0-G-88-P. Pittsburgh, PA.: Graduate School of Public and International Affairs, University of Pittsburgh, 1988.
1984. Kostiner, Joseph. "The Role of Saudi Arabia as an Intermediary in the Arab World." Paper Presented at the *28th Annual Convention of the International Studies Association,* held on April 14-18, 1987, in Washington, D.C.
1985. Mandell, Brian S. *Mediation in the Middle East: Alternatives in American Policy and Practice, 1969-1975.* Ph.D. Dissertation. Toronto: University of Toronto, 1983.
1986. McMullen, Christopher J. *Mediation of the West New Guinea Dispute, 1962: A Case Study.* Washington, D.C.: Institute for the Study of Diplomacy, Georgetown University, 1981. 76p.
1987. _____. *Resolution of the Yemen Crisis, 1963: A Case Study in Mediation.* Washington, D.C.: Institute for the Study of Diplomacy, Georgetown University, 1980. 56p.
1988. Moses, Russell L. *Algeria and Assets: Mediation and Private Channels in the Iranian Hostage Crisis, September 1980 - January 1981.* PEW Case Studies, 316.0-F-88-P. Pittsburgh, PA.: Graduate School of Public and International Affairs, University of Pittsburgh, 1988.
1989. Pauk, Robert A. *International Mediation in Theory and Practice: U.S. Mediation in Arab-Israeli Conflicts, October 1973 - May 1980.* M.A. Thesis. Ottawa, Ont.: The Norman Paterson School of International Affairs, Carleton University, 1980.
1990. Princen, Tom. *Intermediary Intervention: A Model of Intervention and A Study of the Beagle Channel Case.* Ph.D. Dissertation. Cambridge, MA.: Harvard University, 1988. 301p.
1991. Pruitt, Dean G. "Negotiation and Mediation in the Falkland Crisis." Paper Presented at the *Meeting of the International Society of Political Psycholog,* held in July 1983, at St. Catherine's College, Oxford University, Oxford, England.
1992. Sampson, Cynthia. "International Mediation Project Progress Report." Paper Presented at the *28th Annual Convention of the International Studies Association,* held on April 14-18, 1987, in Washington, D.C.
1993. Saunders, Harold H. "The Arab-Israeli Peace Process: What Is It? Where Does It Stand?" Paper Presented at the *PARC Maxwell School Summer Lecture Series,* held on July 9, 1986, at the Maxwell School of Citizenship and Public Affairs, Syracuse University.
1994. _____., and Cecilia Albin. *Sinai II: the Politics of International Mediation.* PEW Case Studies, 421.0-F-88-J. Washington, D.C.: School of Advanced International Studies, John Hopkins University, 1988.

1995. Singer, Marshall R. *Tamil-Sinhalese Ethic Conflict in Sin Lanka: A Case Study in Efforts to Negotiate a Settlement, 1983-1987.* PEW Case Studies, 416.0-G-88-P. Pittsburgh, PA.: Graduate School for Public and International Affairs. University of Pittsburgh, 1988.
1996. Smith, William P. "Concealing Mediator Bias: The Falkland Island Case." Paper Presented at the *International Society of Political Psychology*, held in July 1983, at St.Catherine's College, Oxford University, England.
1997. Tunnicliff, Kim H. *The United Nations and the Mediation of International Conflict.* Ph.D. Dissertation. Iowa City, IA.: University of Iowa, 1984. 357p.
1998. _____. "The Impact of Situational Factors on U.N. Mediation Efforts." Paper Presented at the *26th International Studies Association Conference*, held on March 5-9, 1985, in Washington, D.C. 33p.
1999. Utter, Glen H. "International Committee of the Red Cross as a Conflict Manager." Paper Presented at the *Annual Meeting of the International Studies Association*, held on March 20-23, 1974, in St.Louis, MO.
2000. Zartman, I. William. "Formulas and Ripeness in the Israeli Border Conflicts." Paper Presented at the *PARC Maxwell Summer Lecture Series*, held on July 16, 1986, at the Maxwell School of Citizenship and Public Affairs, Syracuse University.

V

Multilateral Negotiations

Any type of negotiation process which involves more than two partners is multilateral in scope. Negotiations between states are seldom purely bilateral. There are always third parties, either as mediators or as interested parties. Since the end of World War II, our international system is moving toward an increased level of multilaterality. This is partly a function of our shrinking globe thanks to new modes of communication technology, more powerful international organizations and a tendency of players to see themselves as parts of blocs and alliances.

Since the establishment of the U.N., international organizations have become an essential part of international contacts. The U.N. is moving in the direction of a world government forum, where much of the formal interactions resemble parliamentary procedures. Multilateral contacts can also be found at the many international conferences set up by the various international bodies, state alliances or other international groupings.

This chapter is organized to reflect the various multilateral forums and to focus on aspects of international negotiations conducted through them. The first section of examines theoretical and general works dealing with multilateral negotiations as a form of negotiation. Following, the U.N. is examined as a negotiating forum. Section three examines conference diplomacy as a negotiation form, highlighting the U.N. Disarmament and World War II Conferences. The Law of the Sea Conference is one of the best covered and documented cases of multilateral negotiations available in the literature. Various aspects of the North-South issues are examined, with attention given both to the subject matter and the different international bodies active in this area. The last section covers other case studies which are of multilateral in scope.

A. GENERAL WORKS

1. Books

2001. Graham, Norman A., Richard L. Kauffman and Michael F. Oppenheimer. *The United States and Multilateral Diplomacy: A Handbook.* New York: Oceana, 1984. 266p.
2002. Haas, Ernst B., Robert L. Butterworth and Joseph S. Nye. *Conflict Management in International Organizations.* Morriston, NJ.: General Learning Press, 1972. 66p.
2003. Henrikson, Alan K., ed. *Negotiating World Order: The Artisanship and Architecture of Global Diplomacy.* Wilmington, DE.: Scholarly Resources, 1986. 265p.

2. Journal Articles

2004. Aldrich, G. H. "Establishing Legal Norms Through Multilateral Negotiation - Laws of War." *International Lawyer,* 11:1 (1977), 107-111.
2005. _____. "Establishing Legal Norms Through Multilateral Negotiation - Laws of War." *Case Western Reserve Journal of International Law,* 9:1 (1977), 9-16.
2006. Claude, Inis L. "Multilateralism." In: E. Plischke, ed. *Modern Diplomacy: The Art and the Artisans.* Washington, D.C.: American Enterprise Institute, 1979. pp. 188-198.
2007. _____. "Multilateralism - Diplomatic and Otherwise." *International Organization,* 12 (1958), 43-52.
2008. Coplin, William D. "International Organizations in the Bargaining Process: A Theoretical Projection." *Journal of International Affairs,* 25 (1971), 287-301.
2009. _____. "International Organizations in the Future Bargaining Process: A Theoretical Perspective." In: D. S. Sullivan and M. J. Satter, eds. *Change and the Future International System.* New York: Columbia University Press, 1971. pp. 81-95.
2010. Dmitriev, Timur. "The Role of Multilateral Diplomacy in the Modern World." *International Affairs (USSR),* 9 (September 1987), 96-102.
2011. Eban, Abba. "Multilateral Diplomacy in the Nuclear Age." *University of Pennsylvania Law Review,* 114 (May 1966), 984-996.
2012. Gardner, Richard N. "Foreign Policy Making in a New Era: The Challenge of Multilateral Diplomacy: Part I." *Foreign Service Journal,* 52:6 (June 1975), 10-14.
2013. "The Global Negotiation and Beyond: The Setting Discussion." In: R. D. Hansen, ed. *Global Negotiation and Beyond.* Austin, TX.: L.B.J. School of Public Affairs, University of Texas, 1981. pp. 37-64.
2014. Haas, Ernst B. "Regime Decay: Conflict Management and International Organizations." *International Organizations,* 37:2 (Spring 1983), 189-256.
2015. Haas, Michael. "International Conflict Resolution." In: M. Haas, ed. *International Systems: A Behavioral Approach.* New York: Chandler, 1974. pp. 325-350.
2016. Haq, M. V. "The Political and Economic Origins of the Global Negotiation of 1981." In: R. D. Hansen, ed. *Global Negotiation and Beyond.* Austin, TX.: L.B.J. School of Public Affairs, University of Texas, 1981. pp. 16-22.

2017. Henrikson, Alan K. "The Global Foundations for a Diplomacy of Consensus." In: A. K. Henrikson, ed. *Negotiating World Order.* Wilmington, DE.: Scholarly Resources, 1986. pp. 217-244.
2018. Kissinger, Henry A. "Coalition Diplomacy in a Nuclear Age." In: L. B. Miller, ed. *Dynamics of World Politics.* Englewood Cliffs, NJ.: Prentice-Hall, 1968. pp. 44-61.
2019. Marks, Leonard H. "International Communications and World Order." In: A. K. Henrikson, ed. *Negotiating World Orders.* Wilmington, DE.: Scholarly Resources, 1986. pp.47-58.
2020. Mautner-Markhof, Frances. "International Negotiations: Mechanisms for the Management of Complex Systems." *Cooperation and Conflict,* 23:2 (1988), 95-106.
2021. Midgaard, Knut. "Rules and Strategy in Negotiations: Notes on an Institutionalist and Internationalist Approach." *European Journal of Political Research,* 11:2 (1983), 151-166.
2022. Sanders, William. "Multilateral Diplomacy." *Department of State Bulletin,* 21 (August 8, 1949), 163-169, 199.
2023. Sohn, Louis B. "The Role of Arbitration in Recent International Multilateral Treaties." *Virginia Journal of International Law,* 23:2 (Winter 1983), 171-190.
2024. Suy, Eric. "The Meaning of Consensus in Multilateral Diplomacy." In: R. J. Akkerman, P. J. Van Krieken and C. O. Pannenborg, eds. *Declarations on Principles: A Quest for Universal Peace.* Leyden: A. W. Sijthoff, 1977. pp. 259-274.
2025. Thorsson, Inga. "Multilateral Forums." In: A. S. Lall, ed. *Multilateral Negotiation and Mediation.* New York: Pergamon Press, 1985. pp. 93-114.

3. Documents and Reports

2026. Claude, Inis L. "Problems and Possibilities of Multilateral Diplomacy." Paper Presented at the *53rd Annual Meeting of the American Political Science Association,* held in September 5-7, 1957, in New York.
2027. Durch, William J. *Information Processing and Outcome Forecasting for Multilateral Negotiations: Testing One Approach.* Arlington, VA.: Center for Naval Analysis, 1977. 58p.
2028. Erickson, Bonnie H. *International Networks - Structured Webs of Diplomacy and Trade.* Sage Professional Paper in International Studies Series, 02-036. Beverly Hills, CA.: Sage, 1975. 56p.
2029. Goudreau, Karen W. *Forecasting Outcomes of Multilateral Negotiations: Computer Programs, Vol. I.* CRC-290-Vol-1. Arlington, VA.: Institute of Naval Studies, 1977. 140p.
2030. _____. *Forecasting Outcomes of Multilateral Negotiations: Computer Programs, Vol. 2.* CRC-290-Vol-2. Alexandria, VA.: Institute of Naval Studies, 1976. 117p.
2031. Kinnas, John M. "Common Denominator of Interests: Problem or Catalyst in Multilateral Negotiations within IGOs." Paper Presented at the *28th Annual Convention of the International Studies Association,* held on April 14-18, 1987, in Washington, D.C.
2032. Lang, Winfried. "Multilateral Negotiations: The Role of Presiding Officers." Paper Presented at the *Conference on the Processes of International Negotiations,* held on May 18-22, 1987, at the International Institute for Applied Systems Analysis (IIASA) in Laxenburg, Austria.

2033. Ortona, Edigio, J. Robert Schaetzel and Nobuhito Ushiba, eds. *The Problem of International Consultations: A Report of the Trilateral Task Force on Consultative Procedures to the Trilateral Commission.* NY.: The Trilateral Commission, 1976. 21p.
2034. United States. Congress. Senate. Committee on Foreign Relations. *International Organizations and Multilateral Diplomacy: Hearings.* 99th Cong., 1st sess. Washington, D.C.: U.S. Government Printing Office, 1985. 32p.
2035. Yetimov, Gennedi. "Developing a Global Negotiating Machinery: International Organizations Experience." Paper Presented at the *Conference on the Processes of International Negotiations,* held on May 18-22, 1987, at the International Institute for Applied Systems Analysis (IIASA), in Laxenburg, Austria.

B. UNITED NATIONS

1. Books

2036. Allsebrook, Mary. *Prototypes of Peacemaking: The First Forty Years of the United Nations.* London: Longman, 1986. 160p.
2037. Azud, Jan. *The Peaceful Settlement of Disputes and the United Nations.* Bratislava: Slovak Academy of Sciences, 1970. 271p.
2038. Bailey, Sydney D. *How Wars End: The United Nations and the Termination of Armed Conflict, 1946-1964.* 2 Vols. Oxford: Clarendon Press, 1982. 404p. and 715p.
2039. _____. *Voting in the Security Council.* Bloomington, IN.: Indiana University Press, 1969. 275p.
2040. Beichman, Arnold. *The "Other" State Department: The United States Mission to the United Nations - Its Role in the Making of Foreign Policy.* New York: Basic Books, 1967. 221p.
2041. Berridge, G. R., and A. Jennings. *Diplomacy at the U.N.* London: Macmillan, 1985. 227p.
2042. Bishop, Donald G. *The Administration of United States Foreign Policy Through the United Nations.* Dobbs Ferry, NY.: Oceana, 1962. 112p.
2043. Buckley, William F. *United Nations Journal: A Delegate's Odyssey.* New York: Putman's, 1974. 280p.
2044. Claude, Inis L. *Swords into Plowshares: The Problems and Progress of International Organization.* 3rd ed. New York: Random House, 1964. 458p.
2045. Fasulo, Linda M. *Representing America: Experiences of U.S. Diplomats in the U.N.* New York: Praeger, 1984. 337p.
2046. Finger, Seymour M. *American Ambassadors at the U.N.: People, Politics and Bureaucracy in the Making of Foreign Policy.* 2nd ed. New York: Holmes & Meier, 1987. 360p.
2047. Finkelstein, Lawrence S. *Politics in the United Nations System.* Durham, NC.: Duke University Press, 1988. 500p.
2048. Forgac, Albert T. *New Diplomacy and the United Nations.* New York: Pageant, 1965. 173p.
2049. Kaufmann, Johan. *United Nations Decision Making.* 3rd ed. Alphen aan den Rijn: Sijthoff & Noordhoff, 1980. 283p.
2050. Lie, T. *In the Cause of Peace: Seven Years with the United Nations.* New York: Macmillan, 1954. 473p.
2051. Miller, Richard I. *Dag Hammarskjöld and Crisis Diplomacy.* Dobbs Ferry, NY.: Oceana, 1961. 344p.

2052. Misra, K. P. *The Role of the United Nations in the Indo-Pakistani Conflict, 1971.* Delhi: Vikas, 1973. 190p.
2053. Murphy, John F. *The United Nations and the Control of International Violence: A Legal and Political Analysis.* Totowa, NJ.: Allanheld, Osnum, 1982. 212p.
2054. Peterson, M. J. *The General Assembly in World Politics.* Boston, MA.: Allen & Unwin, 1986. 320p.
2055. Russell, Ruth B. *A History of the United Nations Charter: The Role of the United States, 1940-1945.* Washington, D.C.: Brookings Institution, 1958. 1140p.
2056. Suter, Keith. *Peace-Working: The United Nations and Disarmament.* Sydney, N.S.W.: United Nations Association of Australia, 1985. 188p.
2057. Urquhart, Brian. *A Life in Peace and War.* New York: Harper & Row, 1987. 400p.
2058. Venkata, Raman K. *Dispute Settlement Through the U.N.* Dobbs Ferry, NY.: Oceana, 1977. 749p.

2. Journal Articles

2059. Alger, Chadwick F. "Interaction and Negotiation in a Committee of the United Nations General Assembly." In: J. Rosenau, ed. *International Politics and Foreign Policy.* New York: The Free Press, 1969. pp. 483-497.
2060. _____. "Interaction in a Committee of the United Nations General Assembly." In: J. D. Singer, ed. *Quantitative International Politics: Insights and Evidence.* Chicago, IL.: The Free Press, 1968. pp. 51-84.
2061. _____. "Negotiation, Regional Groups, Interaction, and Public Debate in the Development of Consensus in the United Nations General Assembly." In: J. N. Rosenau, V. Davis and M. A. East, eds. *The Analysis of International Politics.* New York: The Free Press, 1972. pp. 278-298.
2062. _____. "Non-Resolution Consequences of the United Nations and Their Effect on International Conflict." *Journal of Conflict Resolution,* 5 (1961), 128-145.
2063. _____. "Interaction and Negotiation in a Committee of the United Nations General Assembly." *Peace Research Society (International) Papers,* 5 (1966), 141-160.
2064. Appathurai, E. R. "Permanent Missions in New York." In: G. R. Berridge and A. Jennings, eds. *Diplomacy at the U.N.* London: Macmillan, 1985. pp. 94-108.
2065. Bailey, Sydney D. "Peaceful Settlement of International Disputes: Some Proposals for Research." In: R. K. Venkata, ed. *Dispute Settlement Through the United Nations.* Dobbs Ferry, NY.: Oceana, 1977. pp. 73-148.
2066. Barratt, John. "South African Diplomacy at the UN." In: G. R. Berridge and A. Jennings, eds. *Diplomacy at the U.N.* London: Macmillan, 1985. pp. 191-203.
2067. Berridge, G. R. "'Old Diplomacy' in New York." In: G. R. Berridge and A. Jennings, eds. *Diplomacy at the U.N.* London: Macmillan, 1985. pp. 175-190.
2068. Bloomfield, Lincoln P. "United States Participation in the United Nations." In: S. D. Kertesz, ed. *American Diplomacy in a New Era.* Notre Dame, IN.: University of Notre Dame Press, 1961. pp. 459-491.

2069. Bowett, D. W. "The United Nations and Peaceful Settlement." In: *International Disputes: The Legal Aspects.* London: The David Davies Memorial Institute of International Studies, 1972. pp. 179-210.
2070. Calvocoressi, Peter. "Peace, The Security Council and the Individual." In; G. R. Berridge and A. Jennings, eds. *Diplomacy at the U.N.* London: Macmillan, 1985. pp. 17-30.
2071. Caradon, Hugh. "The Security Council as an Instrument for Peace." In: A. S. Lall, ed. *Multilateral Negotiation and Mediation.* New York: Pergamon Press, 1985. pp. 3-16.
2072. Chai, F. Y. "Consultation and Consensus in the Security Council." In: K. Venkata Raman, ed. *Dispute Settlement Through the United Nations.* Dobbs Ferry, NY.: Oceana, 1977. pp. 517-576.
2073. Coplin, William D., and J. Martin Rochester. "The Permanent Court of International Justice, the International Court of Justice, the League of Nations and the United Nations: A Comparative Empirical Survey." *American Political Science Review,* 66 (June 1972), 529-550.
2074. _____. "The World Court in the International Bargaining Process." In: R. W. Gregg and M. Barkun, ed. *The United Nations System and Its Functions.* Princeton, NJ.: Van Nostrand, 1968. pp. 317-330.
2075. Cory, Robert H. "Conflict Resolution in the United Nations: A Review of Three Studies by the Brookings Institution." *Journal of Conflict Resolution,* 2:2 (June 1958), 184-187.
2076. Dixon, Pierson. "Diplomacy at the United Nations." In: S. D. Kertesz and M. A. Fitzsimmons, eds. *Diplomacy in a Changing World.* South Bend, IN.: University of Notre Dame Press, 1959. pp. 373-385.
2077. Ernst, Manfred H. "Attitudes of Diplomats at the United Nations: The Effects of Organizational Participation on the Evaluation of the Organization." *International Organization,* 32:4 (1978), 1037-1044.
2078. Fox, William T. R. "The United Nations in the Era of Total Diplomacy." *International Organization,* 5:2 (1951), 265-273.
2079. Galloway, Eilene. "Consensus Decision-Making by the United Nations Committee on the Peaceful Uses of Outer Space." *Journal of Space Law,* 7 (1979), 3-13.
2080. Goldberg, Arthur J. "Public Diplomacy at the U.N.." *Department of State Bulletin,* 57 (August 28, 1967), 262-265.
2081. Goodwin, G. L. "Power Politics and the United Nations." In: G. R. Berridge and A. Jennings, eds. *Diplomacy at the U.N.* London: Macmillan, 1985. pp. 1-14.
2082. Goormaghtigh, John. "How an INGO Contributed to Broadening the Scope and Competence of an IGO." In: M. R. Berman and J. E. Johnson, eds. *Unofficial Diplomats.* New York: Columbia University Press, 1977. pp. 251-258.
2083. Hammarskjöld, Dag. "The Role of the United Nations." In: S. D. Kertesz and M. A. Fitzsimmons, eds. *Diplomacy in a Changing World.* South Bend, IN.: University of Notre Dame Press, 1959. pp. 367-372.
2084. _____. "The Element of Privacy in Peace-Making." *United Nations Review,* (March 1958), 10-13.
2085. _____. "The Vital Role of the United Nations in a Diplomacy of Reconciliation." *United Nations Review,* (May 1958), 6-10.
2086. _____. "New Diplomatic Techniques in a New World." In: E. Plischke, ed. *Modern Diplomacy: The Art and the Artisans.* Washington, D.C.: American Enterprise Institute, 1979. pp. 86-91.
2087. Hovet, Thomas. "United Nations Diplomacy." *Journal of International Affairs,* 17 (1963), 29-41.

2088. James, Alan M. "The Secretary General: A Comparative Analysis." In: G. R. Berridge and A. Jennings, eds. *Diplomacy at the U.N.* London: Macmillan, 1985. pp. 31-47.
2089. Jordan, W. M. "Handling of Disputes and Special Political Problems in 1950-1951." *Annual Review of United Nations Affairs,* (1951), 73-87.
2090. ____. "Handling of Disputes." *Annual Review of United Nations Affairs,* (1949), 116-131.
2091. ____. "Handling of Disputes." *Annual Review of United Nations Affairs,* (1952), 56-70.
2092. ____. "Recent Developments in the Handling of International Disputes." *Annual Review of United Nations Affairs,* (1950), 59-77.
2093. Keens-Soper, Maurice. "The General Assembly Reconsidered." In: G. R. Berridge and A. Jennings, eds. *Diplomacy at the U.N.* London: Macmillan, 1985. pp. 75-93.
2094. Kelen, Emery. "Push Button Diplomacy." *United Nations World,* 3 (March 1969), 60-62.
2095. Lachs, Manfred. "The Law and the Settlement of International Disputes." In: R. K. Venkata, ed. *Dispute Settlement Through the U.N.* Dobbs Ferry, NY.: Oceana, 1977. pp. 283-300.
2096. Lauren, Paul G. "First Principles of Racial Equality: History and the Politics and Diplomacy of Human Rights Provisions in the United Nations Charter." *Human Rights Quarterly,* 5:1 (1983), 1-27.
2097. Laves, Walter H. C. "UNESCO: Centre of Cultural Diplomacy." In: S. D. Kertesz and M. A. Fitzsimmons, eds. *Diplomacy in a Changing World.* South Bend, IN.: University of Notre Dame Press, 1959. pp.386-402.
2098. McMahon, J. F., and Michael Akehurst. "Settlement of Disputes in Special Fields." In: *International Disputes: The Legal Aspects.* London: The David Davies Memorial Institute of International Studies, 1972. pp. 211-314.
2099. Neilson, Francis. "Labyrinth of Diplomacy." *American Journal of Economics and Sociology,* 18 (October 1958), 1-14.
2100. Parsons, Anthony. "The U.N. and International Security." In: G. R. Berridge and A. Jennings, eds. *Diplomacy at the U.N.* London: Macmillan, 1985. pp. 48-58.
2101. Pechota, Vratislav. "The Quiet Approach: A Study of the Good Offices Exercised by the United Nations Secretary General in the Cause of Peace." In: K. R. Venkata, ed. *Dispute Settlement Through the United Nation.* Dobbs Ferry, NY.: Oceana, 1977. pp. 577-684.
2102. Peterson, M. J. "The Political Use of Recognition: The Influence of the International System." *World Politics,* 34:3 (1982), 324-352.
2103. Reich, Bernard, and Rosemary Holland. "The United Nations and Israel." In: G. R. Berridge and A. Jennings, eds. *Diplomacy at the U.N.* London: Macmillan, 1985. pp. 204-221.
2104. Saksena, K. P. "India and Diplomacy in the United Nations." *International Studies,* 17:3-4 (1978), 799-826.
2105. Schachter, Oskar. "The United Nations and Internal Conflict." In: R. K. Venkata, ed. *Dispute Settlement Through the United Nations.* Dobbs Ferry, NY.: Oceana, 1977. pp. 301-366.
2106. Skjelsbaek, Kjell. "Peaceful Settlement of Disputes by the United Nations and Other Intergovernmental Bodies." *Cooperation and Conflict,* 21:3 (September 1986), 139-154.
2107. Sohn, Louis B. "The Role of International Institutions as Conflict Adjusting Agencies." *University of Chicago Law Review,* 28 (1961), 205-257.

2108. _____. "Voting Procedures in United Nations Conferences for the Codification of International Law." *American Journal of International Law*, 69:2 (April 1975), 310-358.
2109. Spence, J. E. "The U.N. and the Falklands Crisis." In: G. R. Berridge and A. Jennings, eds. *Diplomacy at the U.N.* London: Macmillan, 1985. pp. 59-72.
2110. Ungerer, Werner. "The UNIDO General Conference in Lima." *Aussenpolitik*, 26:3 (1975), 326-337.
2111. "United Nations - Global Negotiations." *Journal of World Trade Law*, 17:3 (1983), 269-271.
2112. Urquhart, Brian. "The Work of Peace." *Negotiation Journal*, 1:1 (January 1985), 71-77.
2113. Väyrynen, Raimo. "Is There a Role for the United Nations in Conflict Resolution?." *Journal of Peace Research*, 22:3 (1985), 189-196.
2114. _____. "The United Nations and the Resolution of International Conflicts." *Cooperation and Conflict*, 10:3 (September 1985), 141-172.
2115. Venkata, Raman K. "A Study of the Procedural Concepts of United Nations Intermediary Assistance in the Peaceful Settlement of Disputes." In: R. K. Venkata, ed. *Dispute Settlement Through the United Nations*. Dobbs Ferry, NY.: Oceana, 1977. pp. 367-516.
2116. Vincent, Jack E. "National Attributes as Predictors of Delegate Attitude at the United Nations." *American Political Science Review*, 62 (1968), 916-981.
2117. Weintraub, Sidney. "The Role of the United Nations in Economic Negotiations." *Proceedings of the Academy of Political Science*, 32:4 (1977), 93-105.
2118. Wilkenfeld, Jonathan, and Michael Brecher. "International Crises, 1945-1975: The UN Dimension." *International Studies Quarterly*, 28:1 (March 1984), 45-68.
2119. Williamson, Richard S. "U.S. Multilateral Diplomacy at the United Nations." *Washington Quarterly*, 9:3 (1986), 5-18.
2120. Wilson, Larman C. "The Settlement of Conflicts Within the Framework of Relations Between Regional Organizations and the United Nations: The Case of Cuba, 1962-1964." *Netherlands International Law Review*, 22 (1975), 282-318.
2121. Zacher, Mark W. "The Secretary General and the United Nations Function of Peaceful Settlement." *International Organization*, 20 (1966), 724-749.

3. Documents and Reports

2122. Andemichael, Berhanykun. *Peaceful Settlement Among African States: Roles of United Nations and the Organization of African Unity*. UNITAR PS No. 5. New York: United Nations Institute for Training and Research, 1972. 68p.
2123. Bailey, Sydney D. *Peaceful Settlement of Disputes: Ideas and Proposals for Research*. UNITAR PS No. 1. New York: United Nations Institute for Training and Research, 1971. 57p.
2124. Best, Gary L. *Diplomacy in the United Nations*. Ph.D. Dissertation. Evanston, IL.: Northwestern University, 1960. 269p.
2125. Boothe, T. L. *The Negotiations at the United Nations on the Exploration and Peaceful Uses of Outer Space, 1957-1967*. M. Phil. London: King's College, London University, 1971.
2126. Branaman, Brenda M. *Namibia: U.N. Negotiations for Independence and U.S. Interests*. Washington, D.C.: Congressional Research Service, 1980. 21p.

2127. Broms, Bengt. "The Role of the United Nations in the Peaceful Settlement of Disputes." In: UNITAR, *The United Nations and the Maintenance of International Peace and Security.* Dordrecht: M. Nijhoff, 1987. pp. 73-98.
2128. Burton, John W. "International Problem Solving Organization." Paper Presented to the *24th International Studies Association Meeting,* held in 1983, Mexico City.
2129. Caradon, Hugh, et al. *U.N. Security Council Resolution 242: A Case Study in Diplomatic Ambiguity.* Washington, D.C.: Institute for the Study of Diplomacy, School of Foreign Service, Georgetown University, 1981. 54p.
2130. Cates, J. M. Jr. "The Traditional Diplomatic Function in an Untraditional Environment - The Interplay of Role and Milieu in the United Nations." Paper Presented to the *1969 Annual Meeting of the American Political Science Association,* held in 1969, in New York. Panel 2-E1.
2131. Cordovez, Diego. "Strengthening United Nations Diplomacy for Peace: The Role of the Secretary-General." In UNITAR. *The United Nations and the Maintenance of International Peace and Security.* Dordrecht: M. Nijhoff, 1987. pp. 161-176.
2132. Dedijer, Stefan. *The Failure of the 1978-9 UN Conference on Science, Technology and Development.* Offprint Series No. 2 1976. Lund, Sweden: Research Policy Program, University of Lund, 1976.
2133. Elaraby, Nabil. "The Office of the Secretary-General and the Maintenance of International Peace and Security." In: UNITAR. *The United Nations and the Maintenance of International Peace and Security.* Dordrecht: M. Nijhoff, 1987. pp. 177-212.
2134. Ernst, Manfred H. *Attitudes of Diplomats at the United Nations: Distribution and Sources of Evaluation of United Nations and Institutionalization Implications.* Ph.D. Dissertation. New Orleans, LA.: Tulane University, 1976. 315p.
2135. Haas, Ernst B. The Collective Management of International Conflict, 1945--1984." In UNITAR. *The United Nations and the Maintenance of International Peace and Security.* Dordrecht: M. Nijhoff, 1987. pp. 3-72.
2136. Hussein, Amin. *The Group of 77, the United Nations and the Quest for a New International Technological Order: Political-Economic Analysis of Issues, Processes and Evolving Policies.* Ph.D. Dissertation. Cleveland, OH.: Case Western Reserve University, 1981. 320p.
2137. Jackson, William D. *The National Conciliation in an International Organization: A United Nations Case Study.* Ph.D. Dissertation. Charlottesville, VA.: University of Virginia, 1972. 308p.
2138. Lyon-Allen, Mary M. *The United Nations Conference on Science and Technology for Development: The International Negotiation of Technological Relations.* Ph.D. Dissertation. Washington, D.C.:George Washington University, 1979. 283p.
2139. Pechota, Vratislav. *The Quiet Approach: A Study of the Good Offices Exercised by the United Nations Secretary General in the Cause of Peace.* New York: United Nations Institute for Training and Research,(UNITAR), 1976. 92p.
2140. Prudente, N. E. *Admission to Membership in the United Nations as an Instrument of Diplomacy.* Ph.D. Dissertation. Los Angeles, CA.: University of Southern California, 1959. 459p.
2141. Rikhye, Idar J. *Military Negotiations by a Peacekeeper.* PEW Case Studies, 409.0-1-88-I. New York: International Peace Academy, 1988.

2142. Serguiev, A. "Increasing Role of International Negotiations and International Organizations." Paper Presented at the *Conference on the Processes of International Negotiations*, held on May 18-22, 1987, at the International Institute for Applied Systems Analysis (IIASA), in Laxenburg, Austria.
2143. Small, Alden C. *The United Nations and South West Africa: A Study in Parliamentary Diplomacy*. Ph.D. Dissertation. Medford, MA.: Fletcher School of Law and Diplomacy, 1970. 286p.
2144. Stephenson, Carolyn M. "International Mediation." Paper Presented at the *28th Annual Convention of the International Studies Association*, held on April 14-18, 1987, in Washington, D.C.
2145. Taylor, Alastair M. *The United Nations and the Indonesian Question: An Analysis of the Role of International Mediation*. Ph.D. Dissertation. Oxford: Balliol College, 1955.
2146. Traun, Betty. *The General Committee in the Parliamentary Diplomacy of the General Assembly of the United Nations*. Ph.D. Dissertation. New York: Columbia University, 1968. 299p.
2147. United Nations Institute for Training and Research. UNITAR. *The United Nations and the Maintenance of International Peace and Security*. Dordrecht: M. Nijhoff, 1987. 431p.
2148. United Nations.Secretary General. *Review of the Multilateral Treaty-Making Process*. UN Legislative Series, 21. New York: U.N., 1985. 521p.
2149. United States.Congress.House.Committee on Foreign Affairs. *United Nations Conference on New and Renewable Sources of Energy (UNCNRSE) and U.S. Delegation Participation: Report*. 97th Cong., 2nd sess. Washington, D.C.: U.S. Government Printing Office, 1982. 45p.
2150. _____.Department of State. *United Nations Conference on Diplomatic Intercourse and Immunities, Vienna, Austria, March 2 - April 14, 1961*. Washington, D.C.: U.S. Government Printing Office, 1962. 65p.
2151. Venkata, Raman K. *The Ways of the Peacemaker: A Study of United Nations Intermediary Assistance in the Peaceful Settlement of Disputes*. New York: United Nations Institute for Training and Research, 1975. 142p.

C. CONFERENCES - GENERAL WORKS & CASES

1. Books

2152. Campbell, John C., ed. *Successful Negotiation: Trieste 1954: An Appraisal by Five Participants*. Princeton, NJ.: Princeton University Press, 1976. 181p.
2153. Dunn, Frederick S. *The Practice and Procedure of International Conferences*. Baltimore, MD.: Johns Hopkins Press, 1929. 229p.
2154. Hankey, Maurice. *Diplomacy by Conference: Studies in Public Affairs, 1920-1946*. London: Ernest Benn, 1946. 179p.
2155. Hill, Norman L. *The Public International Conferences: Its Function, Organization and Procedure*. Stanford, CA.: Stanford University Press, 1929. 267p.
2156. Kaufmann, Johan. *Conference Diplomacy: An Introductory Analysis*. Leiden: A. W. Sithoff, 1970. 222p.
2157. Pastuhov, V. D. *A Guide to the Practice of International Conference*. Washington, D.C.: Carnegie Endowment for International Peace, 1945. 275p.
2158. Shenton, Herbert N. *Cosmopolitan Conversation: The Language Problems of International Conferences*. New York: Columbia University Press, 1933. 803p.

2. Journal Articles

2159. Adamson, Peter. "The Age of the Conference." *West Africa*, 20 (December 1976), 1953-1956.
2160. Baldwin, Simeon E. "The International Congresses and Conferences of the Last Century as Forces Working Toward Solidarity of the World." *American Journal of International Law*, 1 (July/October 1907), 808-829.
2161. Bass, Charles W. "International Conference: Trends and Problems in U.S. Participation." *Department of State Newsletter*, 172 (October 1975), 17-19.
2162. Bennett, A. LeRoy. "The 1970s: A Decade of World Conferences." In: A. L. Bennett, ed. *International Organizations: Principles and Issues*. 2nd ed. Englewood Cliffs, NJ.: Prentice-Hall, 1980. pp. 310-336.
2163. Charney, Jonathan I. "Progressive Development of Public International Law Through International Conference Negotiations." In: C. L. O. Buderi and D. D. Caron, eds. *Perspectives on U.S. Policy Toward the Law of the Sea*. Honolulu, HI.: Law of the Sea Institute, 1985. pp. 88-94.
2164. Codding, G. "Influence in International Conferences." *International Organization*, 35:4 (Autumn 1981), 715-724.
2165. Graham, Norman A., and S. Haggard. "Diplomacy in Global Conferences." *UNITAR News*, 11 (1979), 14-21.
2166. Hudson, Manley O. "Procedure of International Conferences and Procedure for the Conclusion and Drafting of Treaties." *American Journal of International Law*, 20 (1926), 747-750.
2167. Kopelmanas, L. "The Technique of International Conferences and the Experience of the Economic Commission for Europe." *International Social Science Bulletin (UNESCO)*, 5:2 (1953), 343-359.
2168. Lindell, Ulf. "The Consensus Rule in Two International Conferences." *Cooperation and Conflict*, 22:2 (1987), 115-133.
2169. Midgaard, Knut, and Arild Underdal. "Multiparty Conferences." In: D. Druckman, ed. *Negotiations: Social-Psychological Perspectives*. Beverly Hills, CA.: Sage, 1977. pp. 329-346.
2170. Plischke, Elmer. "The International Conference." In: E. Plischke, ed. *Conduct of American Diplomacy*. Princeton, NJ.: Van Nostrand, 1967. pp. 469-495.
2171. _____. "International Conference Procedure." In: E. Plischke, ed. *Conduct of American Diplomacy*. Princeton, NJ.: Van Nostrand, 1967. pp. 496-523.
2172. _____. "International Conferences." In: E. Plischke, ed. *International Relations: Basic Documents*. Princeton, NJ.: Van Nostrand, 1962. pp. 38-50.
2173. Qadeer, Mohammed A. "The Futility of World Conferences." *International Development Review*, 19 (1977), 13-15.
2174. Rittberger, Volker. "Global Conference Diplomacy and International Policy Making: The Case of U.N. Sponsored World Conferences." *European Journal of Political Research*, 11:2 (1983), 167-182.
2175. Scelle, G. "The Evolution of International Conferences." *International Social Science Bulletin (UNESCO)*, 5:2 (1953), 241-256.
2176. Scott, Norman. "The Evolution of Conference Diplomacy." In: L. Dembinski, ed. *International Geneva, 1985*. Lausanne: Payot Lausanne, 1985. pp. 40-51.
2177. Sharp, Walter R. "A Checklist of Subjects for the Systematic Study of International Conferences." *International Social Science Bulletin*, 5 (1953), 311-339.
2178. _____. "The Scientific Study of International Conferences." *International Social Science Bulletin*, 2 (Spring 1950), 104-116.
2179. Spitzer, H. M. "Why the Conference Method Needs Study." *ETC.*, 15 (1957-58), 103-110.

2180. Thakore, K. "Some Recent International Codification Conferences and Cultural Interactions." In: R. P. Anand, ed. *Cultural Factors in International Relations.* New Delhi: Abhinav Publications, 1981. pp. 129-148.
2181. Weiss, Thomas G. "The United Nations Conference on the Least Developed Countries: The Relevance of Conference Diplomacy in Paris for International Negotiations." *International Affairs,* 59:4 (1983), 649-676.

3. Documents and Reports

2182. Bossi-Renaud, Claude. *The Study of International Conferences: A Method to Analyze the Interactor Patterns of Communication Exchange at the Fourth Commonwealth Youth Affairs Council.* M.Phil. Thesis. London: University of London, 1980. 182p.
2183. Brueckmann, Wolfram H. *Parliamentary Versus Private Diplomacy: A Case Study of the United Nations Conference on Trade and Development.* Ph.D. Dissertation. Washington, D.C.: The American University, 1976. 322p.
2184. Cohen, Raymond, and S. Cohen. *Peace Conferences: The Formal Aspects.* Jerusalem Papers on Peace Problems, No. 1. Jerusalem: Hebrew University, 1974. 28p.
2185. Condreu, P. L. S. *The Soviet Union and Conference Diplomacy: A Study of Soviet Attitudes and Policy Towards International Conferences in the Period, 1933-1939.* Ph.D. Dissertation. Glasgow: University of Glasgow, 1972.
2186. Graham, Norman A., and S. Haggard. "The Impact of the Ad Hoc Global Conferences: Evaluating Effects at the National and International Level." Paper Presented at the *75th Annual Meeting of the American Political Science Association,* held on August 30 - September 3, 1979 in Washington, D.C.
2187. _____. _____. "Theoretical Implications of Diplomacy in Global Conferences: A Comparative Perspective." Paper Presented at the *Annual Convention of the International Studies Association,* held on March 21-24, 1979, in Toronto.
2188. Hester, Donald C. *Practice and Procedure in Preparing for International Conferences: With Special Emphasis on United States Techniques.* Ph.D. Dissertation. College Park, MD.: University of Maryland, 1959. 541p.
2189. Luchius, David. *The United Nations Conference on the Human Environment: A Case Study of Emerging Political Alignments, 1968-1972.* Ph.D. Dissertation. New York: City University of New York, 1977. 563p.
2190. Martin, Edwin M. *Conference Diplomacy: A Case Study: The World Food Conference, Rome 1974.* Washington, D.C.: Institute for the Study of Diplomacy, School of Foreign Service, Georgetown University, 1979. 58p.
2191. Moulton, Mildred. *A Structural View of the Conferences as an Organ of International Cooperation: An Examination Emphasizing Post-War Practice as Shown in the Organization of Some Typical Conference.* Ph.D. Dissertation. New York: New York University, 1930. 126p.
2192. Pryakhin, V. "Ways to Enhance the Effectiveness of Multilateral Disarmament Forums." Paper Presented at the *Conference on the Processes of International Negotiations,* held on May 18-22, 1987, at the International Institute for Applied Systems Analysis (IIASA), in Laxenburg, Austria.
2193. Rittberger, Volker. "The New International Order and United Nations Conference Politics: Science and Technology for Development as an Issue Area." Paper Presented at the *20th Annual Convention of the International Studies Association,* held on March 21-24, 1979, in Toronto.

2194. Satow, Ernst M. *International Congresses.* London: HMSO, 1920. 168p.
2195. United States. Department of State. Office of International Conferences. *Participation of the United States Government in International Conferences.* Washington, D.C.: U.S. Government Printing Office, 1941-1960. 16 vols.
2196. Wirtz, Stepan, et al. "International Conferences - Means to Solve Intercultural Conflicts." Paper Presented at the *Tenth SIETAR International Conference,* held on May 21-25, 1984, at the George Mason University, Washington, D.C.

c1. U.N. DISARMAMENT CONFERENCES

1. Books

2197. Beker, Avi. *Disarmament Without Order: The Politics of Disarmament at the United Nations.* Westport, CT.: Greenwood Press, 1985. 212p.

2. Journal Articles

2198. Babovic, Bogdan. "The World Disarmament Conference." *Review of International Affairs,* 16 (July 5-20, 1965), 15-16.
2199. Gasteyger, Curt. "The Eighteen Nation Disarmament Conference." *Disarmament,* 12 (December 1966), 16-20.
2200. _____. "The Eighteen Nation Disarmament Conference." *Disarmament,* 16 (December 1967), 26-30.
2201. _____. "The Eighteen Nation Disarmament Conference." *Disarmament,* 10 (June 1966), 16-20.
2202. _____. "The Geneva Disarmament Conference: Report on the Negotiations." *Disarmament,* 8 (December 1965), 5-13.
2203. _____., and James Knott. "The Geneva Disarmament Conference: Some Institutional Aspects." *Disarmament,* 3 (September 1964), 1-3.
2204. Lahoda, T. "The Disarmament Problem and the Ten Nation Committee." *Review of Contemporary Literature,* 7 (1960), 311-325.
2205. Neidle, Allan F. "Peace-Keeping and Disarmament: A Report of the Discussion at the Conference of the Eighteen-Nation Committee on Disarmament." *American Journal of International Law,* 57 (January 1963), 46-72.
2206. Speidel, Helm. "The Truth About Disarmament Talks." *NATO'S Fifteen Nations,* 5 (1960), 10-19.
2207. "Summary of Developments at the Conference of the Eighteen-Nation Committee of Disarmament, Geneva, March 14-June 15, 1962." *Department of State Bulletin,* (July 23, 1962), 154-159.
2208. Tait, Richard M. "In Defence of the Big Conference." *Disarmament and Arms Control,* 2 (Summer 1964), 331-341.
2209. Tozzoli, Gian Paolo. "Geneva's Negotiations as a Constituent Assembly." *Disarmament and Arms Control,* 2 (Spring 1964), 126-135.
2210. "UN Disarmament Commission Subcommission Documents." *U.S. Department of State Bulletin,* (May 30, 1955), 892-905.
2211. Verona, Sergiu. "The Geneva Disarmament Conference: Some Considerations." *Instant Research on Peace and Violence,* 6:1-2 (1976), 62-71.

3. Documents and Reports

2212. Bougrov, Evgheny V. "Conceptual and Practical Aspects of United National Activities in the Field of Disarmament." In: UNITAR. *The United Nations and the Maintenance of International Peace and Security.* Dordrecht: M. Nijhoff, 1987. pp. 337-368.
2213. Great Britain. Foreign Office. *Further Documents Relating to the Conference of the Eighteen-Nation Committee on Disarmament.* London: H.M.S.O., 1962 -. Annual.
2214. ____.____. *Report of the Proceedings of the Sub-Committee of the United Nations Disarmament Commission Held at Lancaster House, London, May 13-June 22, 1954.* Cmnd 9240. London: H.M.S.O., 1954.
2215. ____.____. *Report of the Proceedings of the Sub-Committee of the United Nations Disarmament Commission, 1955.* Cmnd 9636. London: H.M.S.O., 1955.
2216. ____.____. *Report of the Proceedings of the Sub-Committee of the United Nations Disarmament Commission Held at Lancaster House, London, March 13-September 6, 1957.* Cmnd 333. London: H.M.S.O., 1957.
2217. ____.____. *Report of the Proceedings of the Sub-Committee of the United Nations Commission Held at Lancaster House, London, March 19-May 4, 1956.* Cmnd 9770. London: H.M.S.O., 1956.
2218. ____.____. *Report of the UN Disarmament Talks.* Cmnd 228. London: H.M.S.O., 1957.
2219. Lall, Arthur S. *Negotiating Disarmament: The Eighteen Nation Disarmament Conference, the First Two Years, 1962-64.* Ithaca, NY.: Centre for International Studies, Cornell UNiversity, 1964. 83p.
2220. Morris, Ellis. *The Verification Issue in United Nations Disarmament Negotiations.* Geneva: United Nations Institute for Disarmament Research (UNIDIR), 1987. 103p.
2221. Pullinger, Stephen. *Why Have Multilateral Negotiations Failed?: The Case of the Conference on Disarmament, 1979-1986.* Peace Research Reports. No. 18. Bradford, England: School of Peace Studies, Bradford University, 1987. 121p.
2222. United Nations. Department of Disarmament Affairs. *The United Nations Disarmament Yearbook.* New York, 1976-.
2223. ____.Department of Political and Security Council Affairs. *The United Nations and Disarmament, 1945-1970.* New York, 1970. 515p.
2224. ____.____. *The United Nations and Disarmament, 1970-1975.* New York, 1976. 267p.
2225. ____.General Assembly.Eighteen Nation Committee on Disarmament. *Documents.* ENDC/1-. Geneva, 1962-. Annual.
2226. ____.Office of Public Information. *The United Nations and Disarmament, 1945-1965.* New York: United Nations, 1967. 338p.
2227. United States.Department of State. *Struggle for Disarmament: The Record of Five Power Confidential Negotiations in London, May-June, 1954.* London: U.S. Information Service, 1955.

c2. WORLD WAR II CONFERENCES

1. Books

2228. Beitzell, Robert E., ed. *Tehran, Yalta, Potsdam: The Soviet Protocols.* Hattiesburg, MS.: Academic International, 1970. 349p.

2229. Buhite, Russell D. *Decisions at Yalta: An Appraisal of Summit Diplomacy.* Wilmington, DE.: Scholarly Resources, 1986. 156p.
2230. Churchill, Winston. *The Second World War, 6 Vols.* London: Cassell, 1948-1954.
2231. Clemens, Dianne S. *Yalta.* New York: Oxford University Press, 1970. 356p.
2232. Eubank, Keith. *Summit at Tehran: The Untold Story.* New York: Morrow, 1985. 528p.
2233. _____. *The Summit Conferences, 1919-1960.* Norman, OK.: University of Oklahoma Press, 1966. 225p.
2234. Feis, Herbert. *Between War and Peace: The Potsdam Conference.* Princeton, NJ.: Princeton University Press, 1960. 367p.
2235. _____. *Churchill - Roosevelt - Stalin: The War They Waged and the Peace They Sought.* Princeton, NJ.: Princeton University Press, 1957. 692p.
2236. Fenno, Richard F., ed. *The Yalta Conference.* Lexington, MA.: Lexington Books, 1972. 218p.
2237. Kimball, Warren F., ed. *Churchill and Roosevelt: The Complete Correspondence.* 3 Vols. Princeton, NJ.: Princeton University Press, 1984.
2238. Mayle, Paul D. *EUREKA Summit: Agreement in Principle and the Big Three at Tehran, 1943.* Newark, DE.: University of Delaware Press, 1987. 210p.
2239. Mee, Charles L. *Meeting at Potsdam.* New York: Evans, 1975. 370p.
2240. Morgan, Ted. *FDR: A Biography.* New York: Simon and Schuster, 1985. 830p.
2241. Neumann, William L. *After Victory: Churchill, Roosevelt, Stalin and the Making of the Peace.* New York: Harper & Row, 1969. 212p.
2242. Rozek, Edward J. *Allied Wartime Diplomacy: A Pattern in Poland.* New York: John Wiley, 1958. 481p.
2243. Sainsberry, K. *The Turning Point: Roosevelt, Stalin, Churchill and Chiang Kai Shek, 1943 Conferences.* Oxford: Oxford University Press, 1985. 373p.
2244. Snell, John L., et al. *The Meaning of Yalta: Big Three Diplomacy and the New Balance of Power.* Baton Rouge, LA.: Louisiana University Press, 1966. 239p.
2245. Stettinius, Edward R. *Roosevelt and the Russians: The Yalta Conference.* Garden City, NY.: Doubleday, 1948. 367p.
2246. Sulzberger, Cyrus L. *Such a Peace: The Roots and Ashes of Yalta.* New York: Continuum, 1982. 170p.
2247. Truman, Harry S. *Memoirs: Vol. 1. Years of Decision, 1945.* New York: Doubleday, 1955-56. 2 vols.
2248. Wilson, Theodore A. *The First Summit: Roosevelt and Churchill at Placenta Bay, 1941.* Boston, MA.: Houghton Mifflin, 1969. 344p.

2. Journal Articles

2249. Bates, John L. ""Eureka" Conference: A Bust Time in Teheran." *Military Review,* 66:10 (October 1986), 74-82.
2250. Bernstein, Barton J. "Truman at Potsdam: His Secret Diary." *Foreign Service Journal,* 57:7 (July-August 1980), 29-30,36.
2251. Byrnes, James F. "Yalta: High Tide of Big Three Unity." In: R. F. Fenno, ed. *The Yalta Conference.* Lexington, MA.: D. C. Heath, 1972. pp. 27-42.
2252. Charlton, Michael. "The Eagle and the Small Birds (1): The Spectre of Yalta." *Encounter,* (July 1983), 7-28.
2253. _____. "The Eagle and the Small Birds (2): The Triumph of the Commissar." *Encounter,* (July-August 1983), 39-57.

2254. _____. "The Eagle and the Small Birds (3): The Eclipse of Ideology." *Encounter*, (September-October 1983), 23-39.
2255. Churchill, Winston. "Russia and Poland: The Soviet Promise." In: R. F. Fenno, ed. *The Yalta Conference*. Lexington, MA.: D. C. Heath, 1972. pp. 11-26.
2256. Clemens, Dianne S. "The Structure of Negotiations: Dynamics and Interaction Patterns of the Crimean Conference." *Peace Research Society (International) Papers*, 11 (1969), 57-66.
2257. _____. "Yalta." In: R. F. Fenno, ed. *The Yalta Conference*. Lexington, MA.: D. C. Heath, 1972. pp. 201-214.
2258. Fluegel, Edna R. "American Preparation for the Summit." *Free World Forum*, 2:2 (April - May 1960), 17-20.
2259. Franklin, William M. "Yalta Viewed from Tehran." In: D. Beaver, ed. *Some Pathways in Twentieth Century History*. Detroit, MI.: Wayne State University Press, 1969. pp. 253-301.
2260. Kemp, Arthur. "Summit Conferences During World War II as Instruments of American Enemy." In: G. L. Anderson, ed. *Issues and Conflicts: Studies in Twentieth Century American Diplomacy*. Lawrence, KS.: University of Kansas Press, 1959. pp. 256-283.
2261. McNeill, William H. "The Yalta Conference." In: R. F. Fenno, ed. *The Yalta Conference*. Lexington, MA.: D. C. Heath, 1972. pp. 3-10.
2262. Mosely, Philip E. "Dismemberment of Germany: The Allied Negotiations from Yalta to Potsdam." *Foreign Affairs*, 28 (April 1950), 487-498.
2263. Pottserob, B. F. "Teheran - Potsdam (Conferences of the Leaders of the Three Allied Powers)." *International Affairs (Moscow)*, 10 (October 1984), 106-118.
2264. Sherwood, Robert E. "The Mood of Yalta." In: R. F. Fenno, ed. *The Yalta Conference*. Lexington, MA.: D. C. Heath, 1972. pp. 43-45.
2265. Stathis, Stephen W. "Malta: Prelude to Yalta." *Presidential Studies Quarterly*, 9:4 (Fall 1979), 469-482.
2266. Strange, Russell P. "Atlantic Conference - The First Roosevelt-Churchill Meeting." *United States Naval Institute Proceedings*, 79 (April 1953), 388-397.
2267. Theoharis, Athan. "Roosevelt and Truman on Yalta: The Origin of the Cold War." *Political Science Quarterly*, 87 (1972), 210-241.
2268. Yost, Charles W. "From Pearl Harbor to Potsdam." *Foreign Service Journal*, 57:8 (September 1980), 10-14.
2269. Zacharias, Ellis M. "The Inside Story of Yalta." *United Nations World*, (January 1949), 12-17.
2270. Zemskov, I. "The Diplomatic History of the Opening of the Second Front in Europe (1941-1944)." *International Affairs (Moscow)*, 1 (1975), 93-102; 4 (1975), 84-92.

3. Documents and Reports

2271. "ANFA Conference: Casablanca, Morocco, January 14-23, 1943." In: *Records of the Joint Chiefs of Staff, Part I: 1942-45: Meetings*. Frederick, MD.: University Publications of America, 1980. Reel I: pp. 0528-0604;Reel III: pp. 0507-0644.
2272. "ARGONAUT Conference: Malta and Yalta U.S.S.R.: January 30-February 9, 1945." In: *Records of the Joint Chiefs of Staff, Part I: 1942-1945: Meetings*. Frederick, MD.: University Publications of America, 1980. Reel II:0904-0955; Reel IV:0748-0797; Reel VI:0430-0435.

2273. Beitzell, Robert E. *Major Strategic Conferences of the Allies, 1941-1943: Quadrant, Moscow, Sextant and Eureka.* Ph.D. Dissertation. Chapell Hill, NC.: University of North Carolina, 1967. 518p.

2274. Carroce, David. *The Yalta Conference.* M.A. Thesis. New York: Columbia University, 1962.

2275. "EUREKA Conference: Tehran, Iran, November 28-30, 1943." In: *Records of the Joint Chiefs of Staff, Part I: 1942-1945: Meetings.* Frederick, MD.: University Publications of America, 1980. Reel II:0407-0417; Reel IV:031-0339.

2276. Harper, John, and Andrew Parlin. *Yalta and the Polish Question.* PEW Case Studies, 419.0-B-88-J. Washington, D.C.: School of Advanced International Studies, Johns Hopkins University, 1988.

2277. Haska, Lukas E. *Summit Diplomacy During World War II: The Conferences at Tehran, Yalta and Potsdam.* Ph.D. Dissertation. College Park, MD.: University of Maryland, 1966. 272p.

2278. "OCTAGON Conference: Quebec, Canada, September 12-16, 1944." In: *Records of the Joint Chiefs of Staff, Part I: 1942-1945: Meetings.* Frederick, MD.: University Publications of America, 1980. Reel II:0824--0852; Reel IV:0681-0717;0298-0304; Reel VII:0548-0549.

2279. Painter, David S. *Deciding Germany's Future, 1943-1945.* PEW Case Studies, 323.0-A-88-G. Washington, D.C.: School of Foreign Service, Georgetown University, 1988.

2280. _____. *Decision to Divide Germany.* PEW Case Studies, 415.0-A-88-G. Washington, D.C.: School of Foreign Service, Georgetown University, 1988.

2281. *Potsdam Conference Documents.* Frederick, MD.: University Publications of America, 1980. Two Microfilm Reels and Guide.

2282. "QUADRANT Conference: Quebec, Canada, August 12-24, 1943." In: *Record of the Joint Chiefs of Staff, Part I: 1942-1945: Meetings.* Frederick, MD.: University Publications of America, 1980. Reel II:0020-0090; Reel IV:0077-0157; Reel V:0553-0562, 0569-0570.

2283. "SEXTANT Conference: Cairo, Egypt, November 22-26, 1943 and December 2-7, 1943." In: *Records of the Joint Chiefs of Staff, Part I: 1942-1945: Meetings.* Frederick, MD.: University Publications of America, 1980. Reel II:0307-0406,0418-0459;Reel IV:0292-0330,0340-0382;Reel V:0701-0709,-0718-0724;Reel VII.

2284. Strange, Russell P. *The Atlantic and Arcadia Conferences: The First Two Wartime Meetings of Roosevelt and Churchill.* M.A. Thesis. College Park, MD.: University of Maryland, 1953. 156p.

2285. "Summit Conferences." In: *Records of the Joint Chiefs of Staff: Part I: 1942-1945: Strategic Studies.* Frederick, MD.: University Publications of America, 1983. Reel XIII: whole issue.

2286. "TERMINAL Conference: Potsdam, Germany, July 16 - August 2, 1945." In: *Reports of the Joint Chiefs of Staff, Part I: 1942-1945: Meetings.* Frederick, MD.: University Publications of America, 1980. Reel II:1028--1085; Reel IV:0841-0876; Reel VI:0683-0688.

2287. "TRIDENT Conference: Washington, D.C. May 12-25, 1943." In: *Records of the Joint Chiefs of Staff, Part I: 1942-1945: Meetings.* Frederick, MD.: University Publications of America, 1980. Reel III:0808-0931.

2288. United States. Department of State. *Conferences at Cairo and Tehran, 1943.* Washington, D.C.: U.S. Government Printing Office, 1961. 932p.

2289. _____._____. *The Conferences at Malta and Yalta, 1945.* Washington, D.C.: U.S. Government Printing Office, 1955. 1032p.

2290. _____._____. *Foreign Relations of the United States: The Conferences at Washington, 1941-1942, and Casablanca, 1943.* Washington, D.C.: U.S. Government Printing Office, 1968. 895p.
2291. _____._____. *The Conference of Berlin; The Potsdam Conference, 1945.* 2 Vols. Washington, D.C.: U.S. Government Printing Office, 1960. 1088p.; 1645p.
2292. _____._____. *Foreign Relations of the United States: The Conferences at Washington and Quebec, 1943.* Washington, D.C.: U.S. Government Printing Office, 1970. 1382p.
2293. _____._____. *Foreign Relations of the United States: The Conference at Quebec, 1944.* Washington, D.C.: U.S. Government Printing Office, 1972. 527p.
2294. Walker, Gregg B. *Franklin D. Roosevelt as Summit Negotiator at Tehran, 1943 and Yalta, 1945.* Ph.D. Dissertation. Lawrence, KS.: University of Kansas, 1983. 466p.

D. LAW OF THE SEA CONFERENCES

1. Books

2295. Adede, A. O. *The System For Settlement of Disputes Under the United Nations Convention on the Law of the Sea: A Drafting History and a Commentary.* Dordrecht: M. Nijhoff, 1987. 285p.
2296. Buzan, Barry. *Seabed Politics.* New York: Praeger, 1976. 311p.
2297. Merrills, J. G. *International Dispute Settlement.* London: Sweet & Maxwell, 1984. 211p.
2298. Sanger, Clyde. *Ordering the Oceans: The Making of the Law of the Sea.* Toronto: University of Toronto Press, 1987. 225p.
2299. Sebenius, James K. *Negotiating the Law of the Sea: Lessons in the Art and Science of Reaching Agreement.* Cambridge, MA.: Harvard University Press, 1984. 217p.

2. Journal Articles

2300. Barston, Ronald P. "The Third UN Law of the Sea Conferences." In: G. R. Berridge and A. Jennings, eds. *Diplomacy at the U.N.* London: Macmillan, 1985. pp. 152-172.
2301. _____. "The Law of the Sea." *Journal of the World Trade Law,* 17:3 (May - June 1983), 207-223.
2302. Beesley, A. "The Negotiating Strategy of UNCLOS III - A Pattern for Future Multilateral International Conferences." *Law and Contemporary Problems,* 46:2 (1983), 183-194.
2303. Bernhardt, J. P. A. "Compulsory Dispute Settlement in the Law of the Sea Negotiations: A Reassessment." *Virginia Journal of International Law,* 19:1 (1979), 69-108.
2304. Buderi, C. L. O. "Controversy and Compromise: Prelude to the Impasse in the Law of the Sea Negotiations." In: C. L. O. Buderi and D. D. Caron, eds. *Perspectives on U.S. Policy Toward the Law of the Sea.* Honolulu, HA.: Law of the Sea Institute, 1985. pp. 3-8.
2305. Bulmer, C. "Third United Nations Conference on the Law of the Sea: Some Problems in the Seabed Negotiations." *World Affairs,* 141:4 (1979), 337-346.

2306. Buzan, Barry. "Canada and the Law of the Sea." *Ocean Development*, 11:3-4 (1982), 149-180.
2307. ____. "United We Stand...Informal Negotiating Groups and UNCLOS III." *Marine Policy*, 4 (July 1980), 183-204.
2308. ____. "Negotiating by Consensus: Developments in Technique at the United Nations Conference on the Law of the Sea." *American Journal of International Law*, 75:2 (April 1981), 324-348.
2309. De Mestral, A. L. L., and L. H. J. Legault. "Multilateral Negotiation - Canada and the Law of the Sea Conference." *International Journal*, 25:1 (Winter 1979-80), 47-69.
2310. Eustis, Robert D. "Procedures and Techniques of Multinational Negotiation: The UNCLOS III Model." *Virginia Journal of International Law*, 17:2 (Winter 1977), 217-255.
2311. Friedheim, Robert L., and William J. Durch. "International Seabed Resources Agency Negotiations and the New International Economic Order." *International Organization*, 31:2 (1977), 343-384.
2312. ____. "The Third United Nations Conference on the Law of the Sea: North-South Bargaining on Ocean Issues." In: I. W. Zartman, ed. *Positive Sum*. New Brunswick, NJ.: Transaction Books, 1987. pp. 73-114.
2313. ____. "Case Study: The "Satisfied" and "Dissatisfied" States Negotiate International Law." In: L. B. Miller, ed. *Dynamics of World Politics*. Englewood Cliffs, NJ.: Prentice-Hall, 1968. pp. 168-187.
2314. ____. "Value Allocation and North-South Conflict in the Third United Nations Law of the Sea Conference." In: L. S. Finkelstein, ed. *Politics in the United Nations System*. Durham, NC.: Duke University Press, 1988. pp. 175-213.
2315. ____. "The 'Satisfied' and 'Disatisfied' States Negotiate International Law: A Case Study." *World Politics*, 18 (October 1965), 20-41.
2316. Fuandez, Julio. "The Sea-Bed Negotiations: Third World Choices." *Third World Quarterly*, 2:3 (July 1980), 487-499.
2317. Hayden, Gene. "Reopening the Negotiations on the Law of the Sea Treaty." *International Perspectives*, (July-August 1981), 8-12.
2318. Hudson, Richard. "The International Struggle for a Law of the Sea." *Bulletin of the Atomic Scientists*, 33:10 (December 1977), 14-20.
2319. Irwin, P. C. "Settlement of Maritime Boundary Disputes: An Analysis of the Law of the Sea Negotiations." *Ocean Development and International Law*, (1980), 105-148.
2320. Jacovides, Andreas J. "Peaceful Settlement of Disputes in Ocean Conflicts: Does UNCLOS III Point the Way?" In: *Contemporary Issues in International Law*. Arlington, VA.: N. P. Engle, 1984. pp.165-168.
2321. Jenisch, Uwe. "Law of the Sea Conference Before Session 7." *Aussenpolitik*, 29:1 (1978), 46-64.
2322. ____. "UN Law of the SEa Conference Before Session 9." *Aussenpolitik*, 31:1 (1980), 31-51.
2323. ____. "The UN Law of the Sea Conference Before its 11th Session." *Aussenpolitik*, 33:1 (1982), 59-73.
2324. Kildow, Judith T. "The Law of the Sea: Alliances and Divisive Issues in International Ocean Negotiations." *San Diego Law Review*, 11:3 (May 1974), 558-578.
2325. Koh, T. T. B. "Negotiating a New World Order for the Sea." In: A. K. Henrikson, ed. *Negotiating World Order*. Wilmington, DE.: Scholarly Resources, 1986. pp. 33-47.
2326. ____. "Negotiating a New World Order of the Sea." *Virginia Journal of International Law*, 24:4 (Summer 1984), 761-784.

2327. Lewis, V. A. "The Interest of the Caribbean Countries and the Law of the Sea Negotiations." In: F. Jhabvala, ed. *Maritime Issues in the Caribbean.* Gainesville, FL.: University Press of Florida, 1983. pp. 1-18.

2328. Lovald, Johan L. "In Search of an Ocean Regime: Negotiations in General Assembly's Seabed Committee, 1968-1970." *International Organization,* 29:3 (1975), 681-709.

2329. MacWhinney, B. "Law of the Sea: 9 Years of Negotiation May Be Reaching Conclusion." *International Perspectives,* (January 1978), 33-39.

2330. Miles, Edward. "Structure and Effects of the Decision Process in the Seabed Conference on the Law of the Sea." *International Organization,* 31 (Spring 1977), 159-234.

2331. Morris, Michael A. "Latin America and the Third United Nations Law of the Sea." *Ocean Development and International Law,* 9 (1981), 101-175.

2332. Oxman, Bernard H. "The Third United Nations Conference on the Law of the Sea: The Tenth Session (1981)." *American Journal of International Law,* 76:1 (January 1982), 1-23.

2333. _____. "Summary of the Law of the Sea Convention." In: B. H. Oxman, D. Caron and C. Buderi, eds. *Law of the Sea: U.S. Policy Dilemma.* San Francisco, CA.: ICS Press, 1983. pp. 147-164.

2334. _____. "The Third United Nations Conference on the Law of the Sea: The 1976 New York Sessions." *American Journal of International Law,* 71 (April 1977), 247-269.

2335. _____. "The Third United Nations Conference on the Law of the Sea: The Seventh Session (1978)." *American Journal of International Law,* 73 (January 1979), 1-41.

2336. Pardo, H. E. M. "Statement on Future Law of the Sea in Light of Current Trends in Negotiations." *Ocean Development and International Law,* 1:4 (1974), 315-335.

2337. Sebenius, James K. "The Computer as Mediator: Law of the Sea and Beyond." *Journal of Policy Analysis and Management,* 1 (1981), 77-95.

2338. Smith, J. T. "Seabed Negotiation and Law of Sea Conference - Ready for a Divorce." *Virginia Journal of International Law,* 18:1 (1978), 43-59.

2339. Stevenson, John R., and Bernard H. Oxman. "The United Nations Conference on the Law of the Sea: The 1974 Caracas Session." *American Journal of International Law,* 69:1 (January 1975), 1-30.

2340. Straus, Donald B., et al. "Computer-Assisted Negotiations - A Case History from the Law of the Sea Negotiations and Speculation Regarding Future Uses." In: H. R. Pagels, ed. *Computer Culture.* New York: New York Academy of Sciences, 1984. pp. 234-265.

2341. Tollison, Robert D., and Thomas D. Willett. "Institutional Mechanisms for Dealing with International Externalities: A Public Choice Perspective." In: R. C. Amacher and R. J. Sweeney, eds. *The Law of the Sea: U.S. Interests and Alternatives.* Washington, D.C.: American Enterprise Institute for Public Policy Research, 1976. pp. 77-102.

3. Documents and Reports

2342. Antrim, Lance. "Computer Models as an Aid to Negotiation: The Experience in the Law of the Sea Conference." In: J. D. Nyhart, ed. *Coastal Zone and Continental Shelf Conflict Resolution: Improving Ocean Use and Resource Dispute Management.* MITGS Report 85-28. Cambridge, MA.: MIT Sea Grant Program. 1985.

2343. Christy, Francis T., ed. *Law of the Sea: Problems of Conflict and Management of Fisheries in Southeast Asia.* Singapore: Institute of Southeast Asian Studies, 1980. 68p.

2344. Coll, Alberto R. *Should the Reagan Administration Have Signed the United Nations Convention on the Law of the Sea.* PEW Case Studies, 403.0-A-- 87-G. Washington, D.C.: School of Foreign Service, Georgetown University, 1987.

2345. David, Steven R., and Peter Digeser. *Law of the Sea Negotiations.* PEW Case Studies, 418.0-D-88-J. Washington, D.C.: School of Advanced International Studies, Johns Hopkins University, 1988.

2346. El Baradei, Mohamed, and Cloe Gavin. *Crowded Agendas, Crowded Rooms: Institutional Arrangements at UNCLOS III: Some Lessons in Global Negotiations.* Policy and Efficacy Studies: no. 3. New York: United Nations Institute for Training and Research (UNITAR), 1981. 27p.

2347. Friedheim, Robert L. *Packages and Tradeoffs in Negotiating a New Ocean Regime.* PEW Case Studies, 424.0-D-88-S. Los Angeles, CA.: School of International Relations, University of Southern California, 1988.

2348. _____., and Mary E. Jehn. *Anticipating Soviet Behavior at the Third U.N. Law of the Sea Conference: U.S.S.R. Positions and Dilemmas.* Arlington, VA.: Center for Naval Analysis, 1974. 48p.

2349. Hage, Robert E. *The Third U.N. Conference on the Law of the Sea: A Canadian Retrospective.* Toronto: Canadian Institute for International Affairs, 1983. 27p.

2350. Kildow, Judith T. *The Law of the Sea: Alliances and Divisive Issues in International Ocean Negotiations.* NOAA-74060507-2. Cambridge, MA.: Massachusetts Institute of Technology, Department of Ocean Engineering, 1974. 22p.

2351. Msabaha, Ibrahim S. R. *The Anatomy of Tanzania's Diplomacy in the Third United Nations Conference on the Law of the Sea: Seabed/EEZ Negotiations.* Ph.D. Dissertation. Halifax, N.S.: Dalhousie University, 1982.

2352. Nyhart, J. Daniel, ed. *Coastal Zone & Continental Shelf Conflict Resolution: Improving Ocean Use and Resource Dispute Resolution: Conference Proceedings.* MITSG-85-28. Cambridge, MA.: MIT Sea Grant College Program, Sea Grant Information Center, 1985.

2353. Schallawitz, Ronald Lee. *The Settlement of Disputes in the New Law of the Sea Convention.* Ph.D. Dissertation. Geneva: Universite de Geneve, 1986. 380p.

2354. Sebenius, James K. *Anatomy of Agreement: Negotiation Analysis and the Law of the Sea.* Ph.D. Dissertation. Cambridge, MA.: Harvard University, 1981.

2355. Tunstall, Marion D. *The Influence of International Politics on the Procedures of Multilateral Conferences: The Examples of Conferences of Human Environment and the Law of the Sea.* Ph.D. Dissertation. Charlottesville, VA.: University of Virginia, 1979. 463p.

2356. United States. Congress. House. Committee on Foreign Affairs. *The 1980 Geneva Session and Status of the Negotiations on the Law of the Sea: Hearings.* 96th Cong., 2nd sess. Washington, D.C.: U.S. Government Printing Office, 1980. 69p.

2357. _____._____.Senate.Committee on Foreign Relations.Subcommittee on Arms Control, Oceans, International Operations, and Environment. *Law of the Sea Negotiations: Hearings.* 97th Cong., 1st sess. Washington, D.C.: U.S. Government Printing Office, 1981. 301p.

2358. _____._____._____._____._____. *Law of the Sea Negotiations: Hearings.* 97th Cong., 2nd sess. Washington, D.C.: U.S. Government Printing Office, 1983. 179p.
2359. _____._____._____._____._____. *Law of the Sea Negotiations: Hearings.* 97th Cong., 1st sess. Washington, D.C.: U.S. Government Printing Office, 1981. 175p.

E. NORTH SOUTH NEGOTIATIONS

1. Books

2360. Bhagwati, Jagdish N., and John G. Ruggie. *Power, Passions, and Purpose: Prospects for North-South Negotiations.* Cambridge, MA.: MIT Press, 1984. 338p.
2361. Black, Eugene R. *The Diplomacy of Economic Development.* Cambridge, MA.: Harvard University Press, 1961. 74p.
2362. Cordovez, Diego. *UNCTAD and Development Diplomacy: From Confrontation to Strategy.* London: Headly Brothers, 1967. 167p.
2363. Hagras, Kamal. *UNCTAD: A Case Study of United Nations Diplomacy.* New York: Praeger, 1965. 171p.
2364. Hansen, Roger D. *The "Global Negotiation" and Beyond: Toward North-South Accommodation in the 1980s.* Austin, TX.: University of Texas, 1981. 230p.
2365. Helleiner, Gerald K. *For Good or Evil - Economic Theory and North-South Negotiations.* Toronto: Toronto University Press, 1982. 194p.
2366. Malloch, Theodore R. *Issues In International Trade and Development Policy.* New York: Praeger, 1987. 178p.
2367. Miljan, Toivo. *The Political Economy of North-South Relations.* Peterborough, Ont.: Broadview Press, 1987. 714p.
2368. Moore, Robert J. *Third World Diplomats in Dialogue with the First World.* London: Macmillan, 1985. 179p.
2369. O'Brien Cruise, Rita, ed. *Information, Economics and Power: The North-South Dimensions.* Boulder, CO.: Westview Press, 1983.
2370. Olson, Robert K. *United States Foreign Policy and the New International Economic Order: Negotiating Global Problems, 1974-1981.* Boulder, CO.: Westview Press, 1981. 168p.
2371. Rothstein, Robert L. *Global Bargaining: UNCTAD and the New International Economic Order.* Princeton, NJ.: Princeton University Press, 1979. 286p.
2372. Ruggie, John G., and Jagdish N. Bhagwati. *Power, Passions and Purpose: Prospects for North-South Negotiations.* Cambridge, MA.: MIT Press, 1984. 338p.
2373. Smith, D., and L. Wells. *Negotiating Third World Mineral Agreements.* Cambridge, MA.: Ballinger, 1975. 266p.
2374. Sullivan, Timothy J. *Resolving Development Disputes Through Negotiations.* New York: Plenum Publications, 1984. 222p.
2375. Weiss, Thomas G., and Robert S. Jordan. *The World Food Conference and Global Problem Solving.* New York: Praeger, 1976. 170p.
2376. _____. *Multilateral Development Diplomacy in UNCTAD: The Lessons of Group Negotiations, 1964-1984.* London: Macmillan, 1986. 187p.
2377. Zartman, I. William, ed. *Positive Sum: Improving North-South Negotiations.* New Brunswick, NJ.: Transaction Books, 1987. 314p

2. Journal Articles

2378. Al-Shaikly, Salah. "The Energy Issue and Negotiations for a New Economic Order." *Development*, 1 (1981), 12-14.
2379. _____. "The Energy Issue and Negotiations for a New Economic Order." *Development*, 2 (1981), 12-14.
2380. Amuzegar, Jahangir. "A Requiem For the North-South Conference." *Foreign Affairs*, 56 (October 1977), 136-159.
2381. Anjaria, S. J. "A New Round of Global Trade Negotiations." In: T. Miljan, ed. *The Political Economy of North-South Relations*. Lewistown, NY.: Broadview Press, 1987. pp. 197-206.
2382. Astarte, Samuel K. B. "Restructuring Transnational Mineral Agreements." *American Journal of International Law*, 73 (1979), 335-371.
2383. Azar, Edward E., and C. I. Moon. "Managing Protracted Social Conflicts in the Third-World-Facilitation and Development Diplomacy." *Millenium*, 15:3 (1986), 393-406.
2384. Behrman, J. R. "Rethinking Global Negotiations - Trade." In: J. N. Bhagwati and J. G. Ruggie, eds. *Power, Passions and Purpose: Prospects for North-South Negotiations*. Cambridge, MA.: MIT Press, 1984. pp. 231-260.
2385. Bhagwati, Jagdish N. "Rethinking Global Negotiations." In: J. N. Bhagwati and J. G. Ruggie, eds. *Power, Passions, and Purpose: Prospects for North-South Negotiations*. Cambridge, MA.: MIT Press, 1984. pp. 21-32.
2386. _____. Anne O. Krueger and Richard H. Sharpe. "The Multilateral Trade Negotiations and Developing Country Interest: Introduction." *The World Bank Economic Review*, 1:4 (September 1987), 539-548.
2387. Bressaud, A. "The Time for Painful Rethinking." In: J. N. Bhagwati and J. G. Ruggie, eds. *Power, Passions and Purpose: Prospects for North-South Negotiations*. Cambridge, MA.: MIT Press, 1984. pp. 49-64.
2388. Briggs, Wenicke. "Negotiations Between the Enlarged European Economic Community and the African, Caribbean and Pacific (ACP) States." *Nigerian Journal of International Affairs*, 1:1 (1975), 12-32.
2389. Burnett, R. "Negotiation of International Agreements in Fields of Commerce and Investment Problems of Relevance to Newly Independent States." *Journal of World Trade Law*, 9:3 (1975), 231-265.
2390. "Can Mutual Interest Agenda Evolve During the Global Negotiation - Discussion." In: R.D. Hansen, ed. *Global Negotiation and Beyond*. Austin, TX.: L.B.J. School of Public Affairs, 1981. pp.180-200.
2391. Cohen, S. D. "Forgiving Poverty - The Political Economy of the International Dept Relief Negotiations." *International Affairs*, 58:1 (1982), 59-77.
2392. Crane, Barbara B. "Policy Coordination by the Major Western Powers in Bargaining with the Third World - Dept Relief and the Common Fund." *International Organization*, 38:3 (1984), 399-428.
2393. Crawford, Vincent P., Joel Sobel and Ichiro Takahashi. "Bargaining, Strategic Reserves, and International Trade in Exhaustible Resources." *American Journal of Agricultural Economics*, 66:4 (1984), 472-480.
2394. Curry, R. L., and David Rothschild. "On Economic Bargaining Between African Governments and Multinational Companies." *Journal of Modern African Studies*, 12:2 (1974), 173-189.
2395. Desai, P. "The Soviet Union and the Third World: A Faltering Partnership." In: J. N. Bhagwati and J. G. Ruggie, eds. *Power, Passions and Purpose: Prospects for North-South Negotiations*. Cambridge, MA.: MIT Press, 1984. pp. 261-286.

2396. Diazalejandro, C. F. "Some Economic Lessons of the Early 1980s." In: J. N. Bhagwati and J. G. Ruggie, eds. *Power, Passions and Purpose: Prospects for North-South Negotiations.* Cambridge, MA.: MIT Press, 1984. pp.181--200.
2397. Dubey, Muchkund. "A Third-World Perspective." In: J. N. Bhagwati and J. G. Ruggie, eds. *Power, Passions, and Purpose: Prospects for North-South Negotiations.* Cambridge, MA.: MIT Press, 1984. pp. 65-86.
2398. _____. "The Main Forces at Work." In: A. Lall, ed. *Multilateral Negotiation and Mediation.* New York: Pergamon Press, 1985. pp. 154-182.
2399. Elgstrom, Ole. "Negotiating with the LDS's: Situation and Context. *Cooperation and Conflict,* 22:3 (1987), 135-151.
2400. "Energy and the North-South Impasse - 3 Perspectives - Discussion." In: R. D. Hansen, ed. *Global Negotiation and Beyond.* Austin, TX: L.B.J. School of Public Affairs, 1981. pp. 82-107.
2401. Erb, Guy F. "North-South 'Negotiations'." *Proceedings of the Academy of Political Science,* 32:4 (1977), 106-109.
2402. Fiallo, Fabio R. "Negotiation Strategy of Developing Countries in Field of Trade Liberalization." *Journal of World Trade Law,* 11:3 (1977), 203-212.
2403. _____. "The Negotiations Strategy of Developing Countries in the Field of Trade Liberalization." In: P. K. Ghosh, ed. *International Trade and Third World Development.* Westport, CT.: Greenwood Press, 1984. pp. 240-249.
2404. Foster, J. "A View from the North." In: R. D. Hansen, ed. *Global Negotiation and Beyond.* Austin, TX.: LBJ School of Public Affairs, University of Texas, 1981. pp. 76-81.
2405. Gregg, Robert. "Negotiating a New International Economic Order: The Issue of Venne." In: R. Jutte and A. Gross-Jutte, eds. *The Future of International Organizations.* New York: St. Martin's Press, 1981. pp. 51-69.
2406. Gruhn, Isebill. "LOME Convention Renegotiations: Litmus Test for North--South Relations." In: R. Boardman, T. M. Shaw and P. Soldatos, eds. *Europe, Africa and LOME III.* Lanham, NY.: University Press of America, 1985. pp. 13-34.
2407. Gwin, C. "Strengthening the Framework of the Global Economic Organizations." In: J. N. Bhagwati and J. G. Ruggie, eds. *Power, Passions, and Purpose: Prospects for North-South Negotiations.* Cambridge, MA.: MIT Press, 1984. pp. 125-181.
2408. Hardy, Chandra. "Dept Negotiations and the North-South Dialogue." In: I. W. Zartman, ed. *Positive Sum.* New Brunswick, NJ.: Transaction Books, 1987. pp. 259-277.
2409. Hasse, Rolf, and R. Weitz. "The Renegotiation of the LOME Convention: Experiences and Demands." *Intereconomics,* 11:12 (November-December 1978), 273-278.
2410. Helleiner, Gerald K. "The Refsues Seminar: Economic Theory and North--South Negotiations." *World Development,* 9:6 (June 1981), 539-556.
2411. _____. "The Reliance of Accepted Western Economic Theories to the Negotiations on a New International Economic Order." *International Development Review,* 22:4 (1980), 36-39.
2412. Hermes, Peter. "The UNCTAD and the North - South Dialogue." *Aussenpolitik,* 31:1 (1980), 3-15.
2413. Hopkins, Raymond F. "The Wheat Negotiations: Loss or Gain in North-South Relations?." In: I. W. Zartman, ed. *Positive Sum.* New Brunswick, NJ.: Transaction Books, 1987. pp. 115-148.
2414. Jacobson, Harald K., et al. "Revolutionaries or Bargainers?: Negotiators for a New International Economic Order?" *World Politics,* 35:3 (April 1983), 335-367.

2415. Krasner, Stephen D. "Third World Vulnerabilities and Global Negotiations." In: T. Miljan, ed. *The Political Economy of North-South Relations*. Lewistown, NY.: Broadview Books, 1987. pp. 603-608.
2416. _____. "Third World Vulnerabilities and Global Negotiations." *Review of International Studies*, 9:4 (1983), 235-250.
2417. Krishnamurti, R., and D. Cordoves. "Conciliation Procedures in UNCTAD." *Journal of World Trade Law*, 2:4 (1968),
2418. _____. "UNCTAD as a Negotiating Institution." *Journal of World Trade Law*, 15:1 (January-February 1981), 3-40.
2419. _____. "UNCTAD as a Negotiating Instrument on Trade Policy: the UNCTAD-GATT Relationship." In: M. Z. Cutajar, ed. *UNCTAD and the South-North Dialogue*. New York: Pergamon Press, 1985. pp. 33-70.
2420. _____. "Multilateral Trade Negotiations and the Developing Countries." *Third World Quarterly*, 2:2 (1980), 251-269.
2421. _____., and D. Cordoves. "Conciliation Procedures in UNCTAD." *Journal of World Trade Law*, 2:4 (1968), 445-466.
2422. Kumar, Satish. "Non-Alignment as a Diplomatic Strategy." *International Studies*, 20:1-2 (1981), 103-118.
2423. Lall, Sanjaya. "South-South Economic Cooperation and Global Negotiations." In: J. N. Bhagwati and J. B. Ruggie, eds. *Power, Passions, and Purpose*. Cambridge, MA.: MIT Press, 1984. pp.287-322.
2424. Lateef, Noll. "Parliamentary Diplomacy and the North-South Dialogue." *Georgia Journal of International and Comparative Law*, 11:1 (1981), 1-44.
2425. Lawson, Colin W. "The Soviet Union in North-South Negotiations: Revealing Preferences." In: R. Cassen, ed. *Soviet Interests in the Third World*. London: Sage, 1985. pp. 177-191.
2426. Le Paestre, Philippe. "The North-South Conflict - From Game to Debate." *World Affairs*, 142:2 (1980), 99-117.
2427. Lecraw, D. J. "Bargaining Power, Ownership, and Profitability of Trans-National Corporations in Developing Countries." *Journal of International Business Studies*, 15:1 (1984), 27-43.
2428. Marshall, Peter. "Reflections on North - South Relations and the Commonwealth." *Journal of World Trade Law*, 19:3 (May/June 1985), 191-198.
2429. May, Simon. "The Future of International Cooperation." *Development*, 3:4 (1983), 182-189.
2430. Mcphail, T. L., and B. Mcphail. "The International Politics of Telecommunications - Resolving the North-South Dilemma." *International Journal*, 42:4 (Spring 1987), 289-319.
2431. Meltzer, Ronald T. "The United Nations Committee of the Whole: Initiative and Impasse in North-South Negotiations." In: I. W. Zartman, ed. *Positive Sum*. New Brunswick, NJ.: Transaction Books, 1987. pp. 48-72.
2432. Mills, D. "A View from the Non-Oil-Exporting Developing World." In: R. D. Hansen, ed. *Global Negotiation and Beyond*. Austin, TX.: L.B.J. School of Public Affairs, 1981. pp.69-75.
2433. Navarette, J. "A View from the Oil-Exporting Developing World." In: R. D. Hansen, ed. *Global Negotiation and Beyond*. Austin, TX.: L.B.J. School of Public Affairs, University of Texas, 1981. pp.65-68.
2434. Nyerere, Julius K. "Third World Negotiating Strategy." *Third World Quarterly*, 1:2 (1979), 20-23.
2435. Ohlin, G. "Can World - Order Be Negotiated." In: A. Grahlmadsen and J. Toman, eds. *Spirit of Uppsala*. Berlin: De Gruyter, 1984. pp. 84-91.

2436. _____. "Negotiating International Order." In: M. Gersovitz, ed. *The Theory and Experience of Economic Development*. London: Allen & Unwin, 1982. pp. 215-218.
2437. Olson, Robert K. "North South: Negotiating Survival." *Foreign Service Journal*, 57:10 (November 1980), 27-30.
2438. Qadir, Shahid. "UN Conference on the Least Developed Countries: Neither Breakthrough nor Breakdown." *Third World Quarterly*, 4:1 (1982), 125-143.
2439. Ravenhill, John. "Asymmetrical Interdependence: Renegotiating the LOME Convention." *International Journal*, 25:1 (Winter 1979-80), 150-169.
2440. _____. "Negotiating the LOME Conventions: A Little is Preferable to Nothing." In: I. W. Zartmann, ed. *Positive Sum*. New Brunswick, NJ.: Transaction Books, 1987. pp.213-258.
2441. Rostow, W. "Beyond the Official Agenda - Some Crucial Issues." In: R. D. Hansen, ed. *Global Negotiation and Beyond*. Austin, TX.: L.B.J. School of Public Affairs, University of Texas, 1981. pp.31-36.
2442. Ruggie, John G. "Another Round, Another Requiem - Prospects for the Global Negotiations." In: J. N. Bhagwati and J. G. Ruggie, eds. *Power, Passions, and Purpose: Prospects for North South Negotiations*. Cambridge, MA.: MIT Press, 1984. pp. 33-48.
2443. Samuels, Nathaniel. "Dealing with the International Department Issue." In: A. K. Henrikson, ed. *Negotiating World Order*. Wilmington, DE.: Scholarly Resources, 1986. pp. 199-216.
2444. Serfaty, S. "Conciliation and Confrontation - Strategy for North-South Negotiations." *Orbis*, 22:1 (1978), 47-61.
2445. Sewell, John W., and I. William Zartman. "Global Negotiations - Path to the Future or Dead-End Street." In: J. N. Bhagwati and J. R. Ruggie, eds. *Power, Passions, and Purpose: Prospects for North-South Negotiations*. Cambridge, MA.: MIT Press, 1984. pp. 87-124.
2446. _____. _____. "Global Negotiations: Path to the Future or Dead-End Street?." *Third World Quarterly*, 6:2 (April 1984), 374-410.
2447. Singer, Hans W. "Further Thoughts on North South Negotiation: A Review of Bhagwati and Ruggie." *World Development*, 13:1 (January 1985), 255-259.
2448. Spero, J. "The Global Negotiation - Agenda, Progress, and Problems." In: R. d. Hansen, ed. *Global Negotiations and Beyond*. Austin, TX.: LBJ School of Public Affairs, University of Texas, 1981. pp. 23-30.
2449. Stern, Ernest, and Wonter Tims. "The Relative Bargaining Strength of the Developing Countries." In: R. D. Rodker, ed. *Changing Resource Problems of the Fourth World*. Washington, D.C.: Resources for the Future, 1976. pp. 6-50.
2450. Stevens, Christopher. "The Renegotiation of the Convention." In: R. Boardman, T. M. Shaw, and P. Soldatos. *Europe, Africa and LOME III*. Washington, D.C.: University Press of America, 1985. pp.59-84.
2451. Tetzlaff, Rainer. "The Lusaka Conference of Non-Aligned Nations." *Aussenpolitik*, 22:1 (1971), 44-58.
2452. Ul Haq, Mahbub. "Negotiating the Future." In: R. Falk, S. S. Kim and S. H. Mendovitz, ed. *Toward a Just World Order*. Boulder, CO.: Westview Press, 1982. pp. 326-342.
2453. _____. "Negotiating the Future." *Foreign Affairs*, 59 (Winter 1980-81), 400-401.
2454. Van Dam, Ferdinand. "North-South Negotiations." *Development and Change*, 12:4 (1981), 481-504.

2455. Weiss, Thomas G., and A. Jennings. "The Paris Conference on Least Developed Countries, 1981." In: G. R. Berridge and A. Jennings, eds. *Diplomacy at the UN.* London: Macmillan, 1985. pp. 130-151.
2456. _____. "UNCTAD: What Next?" *Journal of the World Trade Law,* 19:3 (May-June 1985), 251-268.
2457. _____. "Alternative for Multilateral Development Diplomacy: Some Suggestions." *World Development,* 13:12 (1985), 1187-1209.
2458. Wells, Louis T. "Negotiating with Third World Governments." *Harvard Business Review,* 55:1 (1977), 72-80.
2459. Whiteman, M. K. "The LOME Convention." *World Survey,* 82 (1975), 1-17.
2460. Williams, Walter L. "Transfer of Technology to Developing Countries: A Challenge to International Diplomacy." In.: M. D. Zamora, ed. *Cultural Diplomacy in the Third World.* Williamsburg, VA.: Department of Anthropology, College of William and Mary, 1981. pp.73-116.
2461. Wolf, M. "2-Edged Sword - Demands of Developing Countries and the Trading System." In: J. N. Bhagwati and J. G. Ruggie, eds. *Power, Passions and Purpose: Prospects for North-South Negotiations.* Cambridge, MA.: MIT Press, 1984. pp. 201-230.
2462. Wood, Bernard. "Canada's Views on the North-South Negotiations." *Third World Quarterly,* 3 (October 1981), 651-657.
2463. Zartman, I. William. "Conclusions: Importance of North-South Negotiations." In: I. W. Zartman, ed. *Positive Sum.* New Brunswick, NJ.: Transaction Books, 1987. pp. 278-301.
2464. _____. "Introduction: Explaining North-South Negotiations." In: I. W. Zartman, ed. *Positive Sum.* New Brunswick, NJ.: Transaction Books, 1987. pp. 1-14.
2465. _____. "Negotiating from Asymmetry: The North-South Stalemate." *Negotiation Journal,* 1:2 (April 1985), 121-138.

3. Documents and Reports

2466. Aggarwal, V. K. *International Dept Threat - Bargaining Among Creditors and Deptors in the 1980's.* Policy Papers in International Affairs. No. 29. Berkeley, CA.: University of California, Institute for International Studies, 1987. 72p.
2467. Bawa, Mahama. "Interdependence and Global Bargaining: Implications for North-South Negotiations and Strategies." Paper Presented at the *23rd Annual Convention of the International Studies Association,* held on March 24-27, 1982, in Cincinnati, OH.
2468. Bendega, Joseph T. *A Developing Country in the Search for a New International Economic Order: Nigeria's Negotiating Role in the LOME Convention and the United Nations System, 1963-1980.* Ph.D. Dissertation. New York: Columbia University, 1983. 259p.
2469. Bobrow, Davis B., Robert P. Stoker and Robert T. Kudree. "Accountability Initiatives and Accountability Constraints: Bargaining Between U.S. and the N.I.E.O." Paper Presented at the *11th World Congress of the International Political Science Association,* held on August 12-18, 1979, in Moscow.
2470. Callaghy, Thomas M. *Restructuring Zaire's Dept.* PEW Case Study 206.0--C-88-C. New York: School of International and Public Affairs, Columbia University, 1988.

2471. Castro, Fidel. *The World Economic and Social Crisis: Its Impact on the Underdeveloped Countries, Its Somber Prospects and the Need to Struggle if We Are to Survive.* Havana: Publishing Office of the Council of State, 1983. 224p.
2472. Commonwealth Group of Experts. *The North-South Dialogue: Making It Work.* London: Commonwealth Secretariat, 1982. 61p.
2473. Crane, Barbara B. *Policy Coordination by Major Western Powers in Bargaining with the Third World: Dept Relief and the Common Fund.* Ph.D. Dissertation. Ann Arbor, MI.: University of Michigan, 1984. 324p.
2474. Denton, William E. *Explaining U.S. Interactions Toward LDC Non-Fuel Mineral Resource Producers: 1960-1974.* Ph.D. Dissertation. Chapel Hill, NC.: University of North Carolina, 1980. 148p.
2475. Edidis, Wayne A. *The Hidden Agenda: Negotiations for the Generalized System of Preferences.* Ph.D. Dissertation. Waltham, MA.: Brandeis University, 1985. 551p.
2476. Gregg, Robert. "Multilateral Diplomacy and Institutional Responses to the Call for a New International Economic Order." Paper Presented at the *20th Annual Convention of the International Studies Association*, held on March 21-24, 1979, in Toronto.
2477. Hagras, Kamal. *United Nations Conference on Trade and Development: A Case Study in U.N. Diplomacy.* Ph.D. Dissertation. New York: New York University, 1965.
2478. Haji, Iqbal, and Thomas G. Weiss. *Multilateral Dept Negotiations in the General Assembly.* PEW Case Studies 203.0-D-87-I. New York: International Peace Academy, 1987.
2479. Hart, Jeffrey A. "Explaining OECD Policies Toward the New International Economic Order." Paper Presented at the *75th Annual Meeting of the American Political Science Association*, held on August 31 - September 3, 1979, in Washington, D.C.
2480. Jordan, Robert S. "The North-South Dialogue: How Effective Is It?." Paper Presented at the *23rd Annual Convention of the International Studies Association*, held on March 24-27, 1982, in Cincinnati, OH.
2481. Lancaster, Carol. *The United States and UNCTAD I.* PEW Case Studies, 108.0-D-87-G. Washington, D.C.: School of Foreign Service, Georgetown University, 1987.
2482. McDonald, John W. *The North-South Dialogue and the United Nations.* Washington, D.C.: Institute for the Study of Diplomacy, School of Foreign Service, Georgetown University, 1982. 23p.
2483. Meltzer, Ronald T. "Towards Launching Global Negotiations: The U.N. Committee of the Whole and North - South Negotiations." Paper Presented at the *79th Annual Meeting of the American Political Science Association*, held on September 1-4, 1983, in Chicago, IL.
2484. Morton, Kathryn. *Hand Worth Playing: State of Developing Countries in the International Trade and Monetary Negotiations.* London: Overseas Development Institute, 1974. 59p.
2485. Nan, Henry R. *Bargaining in the New Round: The NICs (Newly Industrialized Countries) and the United States.* FAR-112-86. Washington, D.C.: Office of External Research, U.S. Department of State, 1986. 30p.
2486. *Negotiating LOME 3: An Example of North South Bargaining.* University of Sussex. Institute of Development Studies, 1986. 23p.
2487. *The North South Negotiating Process: Report of the 16th United Nations Issues Conference, February 22-24, 1985.* Muscatine, IA.: Muscatine Foundation, 1985. 24p.

2488. Offiong, John. *The New International Economic Order: Analysis of the North-South Dialogue on the Issue of Commodity Negotiations.* Ph.D. Dissertation. Washington, D.C.: Howard University, 1983. 428p.
2489. Ravenhill, John. *Asymmetrical Interdependence: The LOME Convention and North South Relations.* Ph.D. Dissertation. Berkeley, CA.: University of Berkeley, 1981. 580p.
2490. *The Renegotiation of the LOME Convention: A Collection of Papers.* London: Catholic Institute for International Relations, 1978. 87p.
2491. Renninger, John P., and James Zech. *The 11th Special Session and the Future of Global Negotiations.* Policy & Efficacy Studies, No. 5. New York: United Nations Institute for Training and Research, 1981. 57p.
2492. Shapiro, Martin M. *The World Bank and Developing Nations: Economic Diplomacy at Work.* Ph.D. Dissertation. New York: New York University, 1967.
2493. United Nations. Department of International Economic and Social Affairs. *Manual for the Negotiation of Bilateral Tax Treaties Between Developed and Developing Countries.* New York: United Nations, 1979. 190p.
2494. United States.Congress.House.Committee on Foreign Affairs.Subcommittee on International Economic Policy and Trade. *North - South Dialog, Progress and Prospects: Hearings.* 96th Cong., 2nd sess. Washington, D.C.: U.S. Government Printing Office, 1980. 267p.
2495. _____.Department of State.Office of External Research. *Bargaining in the New Round: The NICs (New Industrial Countries) and the United States.* Washington, D.C.: U.S. Government Printing Office, 1986. 30p.
2496. Weiss, Thomas G. *International Negotiation on Aid to Least Developed Countries: The Paris Conference.* IPA Case A and B. New York: International Peace Academy, 1986. 63p.
2497. _____. *Multilateral Dept Negotiations in the 41st General Assembly: Case A.* New York: International Peace Academy, 1987.
2498. Zammit-Cutajar, Michael, ed. *UNCTAD and the South-North Dialogue: The First Twenty Years.* Oxford: Pergamon Press, 1985.

F. OTHER MULTILATERAL NEGOTIATIONS

1. Books

2499. Carroll, John E., ed. *International Environmental Diplomacy: The Management and Resolution of Transfrontier Environmental Problems.* Cambridge: Cambridge University Press, 1988. 291p.
2500. Catudal, Honore M. *A Balance Sheet of the Quadripartite Agreement on Berlin: Evaluation and Documentation.* Berlin: Berlin Verlag, 1978. 303p.
2501. _____. *The Diplomacy of the Quadripartite Agreement on Berlin: A New Era in East-West Politics.* Berlin: Berlin Verlag, 1978. 335p.
2502. Hamlin, D., ed. *Diplomacy in Evolution: 30th Couchiching Conference.* Toronto: University of Toronto Press, 1961. 127p.
2503. Ifestos, Panayiotis. *European Political Cooperation: Towards a Framework of Supranational Diplomacy.* Aldershot, England: Avebury, 1987. 635p.
2504. Jordan, Robert S. *Political Leadership in NATO: A Study in Multinational Diplomacy.* Boulder, CO.: Westview Press, 1979. 316p.
2505. Kertesz, Stephen D. *The Last European Peace Conference: Paris 1946 - Conflict of Values.* The Credibility of Institutions, Policies and Leadership, Vol X. Lanham, MD.: University Press of America, 1985. 204p.

2506. Kitzinger, Uwe. *Diplomacy and Persuasion: How Britain Joined the Common Market.* London: Thames and Hudson, 1973. 432p.
2507. Lederer, Ivo J. *Yugoslavia at the Paris Peace Conference: A Study in Frontiermaking.* New Haven, CT.: Yale University Press, 1963. 351p.
2508. O'Danover, William. *Post-War Reconstruction Conferences: The Technical Organization of International Conferences.* London: King & Staples, 1943. 166p.
2509. *Observations on International Negotiations: Transcripts of an Informal Conference, Greenwich, Connecticut, June 1971.* New York: Academy for Educational Development, 1971. 244p.
2510. Papadopoulos, Andrestinos N. *Multilateral Diplomacy Within the Commonwealth: A Decade of Expansion.* The Hague: Nijhoff, 1982. 172p.
2511. Patrick, Karen D. *International Technological Negotiations and Outer Space.* Halifax, NS.: Centre for Foreign Policy Studies, Dalhousie University, 1984. 202p.

2. Journal Articles

2512. Achilles, Theodore C. "U.S. Role in Negotiations That Led to Atlantic Alliance, Part I. and II." *NATO Review,* 27:4 (August 1979), 11-14; 27:5 (August 1979), 16-18.
2513. Alpert, Eugene J., and Samuel J. Bernstein. "International Bargaining and Political Coalitions - U.S. Foreign Aid and China's Admission to U.N.." *Western Political Quarterly,* 27:2 (1974), 314-327.
2514. Bechhoefer, Bernard G. "Negotiating the Status of the International Atomic Energy Agency." *International Organization,* 13 (Winter 1959), 38-59.
2515. Caldwell, Lynton K. "Beyond Environmental Diplomacy: The Changing Institutional Structure of International Cooperation." In: J. E. Carroll, ed. *International Environmental Diplomacy.* Cambridge: Cambridge University Press, 1988. pp. 13-28.
2516. Davidson, Lynne A. "The Helsinki Process: Multilateral Diplomacy: the Madrid Review Meeting." In: D. D. Newsom, ed. *The Diplomacy of Human Rights.* Lanham, MD.: University Press of America, 1986. pp. 167-174.
2517. Dobson, Alan P. "Economic Diplomacy at the Atlantic Conference." *Review of International Studies,* 10:2 (1984), 143-164.
2518. Doxey, Margaret. "Strategies for Multilateral Diplomacy: The Commonwealth, Southern Africa and the NIEO." *International Journal,* 35:2 (1980), 329-356.
2519. Ehrhardt, Carl A. "Lessons of the Brussels NATO Summit." *Aussenpolitik,* 26:3 (1975), 270-282.
2520. Fliess, Barbara A. "The World Administrative Radio Conference 1979 Negotiations: Toward More Equitable Sharing of the Global Radio Resources." In: I. W. Zartman, ed. *Positive Sum.* New Brunswick, NJ.: Transaction Books, 1987. pp. 171-212.
2521. Hill, Christopher, and William Wallace. "Diplomatic Trends in the European Community." *International Affairs,* 55:1 (1979), 47-66.
2522. Howe, G. "The Future of the European Community - Britain Approach to the Negotiations." *International Affairs,* 60:2 (1984), 187-192.
2523. Hull, T. N. "The Organization of African Unity and the Peaceful Resolution of Internal War: The Nigerian Case." In: D. S. Smith, ed. *From War to Peace.* New York: International Fellows Programme, Columbia University, 1974. pp. 93-124.

2524. Hume, Stephen P. "Regional Power in National Diplomacy: The Case of the US Section of the International Boundary and Water Commission." *Publius*, 14:4 (Fall 1984), 115-136.
2525. Johnston, Douglas M. "Marine Pollution Agreements: Successes and Problems." In: J. E. Carroll, ed. *International Environmental Diplomacy*. Cambridge: Cambridge University Press, 1988. pp. 199-206.
2526. Karns, Margaret P. "Ad Hoc Multilateral Diplomacy: The United States, the Contact Group and Namibia." *International Organization*, 41 (Winter 1987), 93-123.
2527. Keynes, Mary K. "The Bandung Conference." *International Relations*, 1 (October 1957), 362-376.
2528. Lyon, Peter. "The Commonwealth's Jubilee Summit." *World Today*, (July 1977), 250-258.
2529. Mayer, Jean E. "International Agreements in the Food and Health Fields." In: A. K. Henrikson, ed. *Negotiating World Order*. Wilmington, DE.: Scholarly Resources, 1986. pp. 3-18.
2530. Milensky, Edward S. "Latin America's Multilateral Diplomacy: Integration, Disintegration and Interdependence." *International Affairs*, 53 (January 1977), 73-93.
2531. Miller, J. D. B. "Commonwealth Conferences, 1945-1975." In: *Yearbook of World Affairs, 1956*. London: Steven & Sons, 1956. pp. 144-169.
2532. Morse, Edward L. "The Bargaining Structure of NATO: Multi-Issue Negotiations in an Interdependent World." In: I. W. Zartman, ed. *The Fifty Percent Solution*. Garden City, NY.: Doubleday, 1976. pp. 66-97.
2533. Mumme, Stephen P. "Regional Power in National Diplomacy - The Case of the United States Section of the International Boundary and Water Commission." *Publius*, 14:4 (1984), 115-135.
2534. Nahlik, Stanislaw E. "Belligerent Reprisals as Seen in the Light of the Diplomatic Conference on Humanitarian Law, Geneva, 1974-1977." *Law and Contemporary Problems*, 42:2 (1978), 36-66.
2535. Nau, H. R. "The Diplomacy of World Food - Goals, Capabilities, Issues and Arenas." *International Organization*, 32:3 (1978), 775-809.
2536. O'Neill, Michael. "Militancy and Accommodation: The Influence of the Heads of Government Meetings on the Commonwealth, 1960-1969." *Millenium: Journal of International Studies*, 12:3 (1983), 211-232.
2537. Quisumbing, Purification V. "International Dispute Settlement in the ASEAN Context." In: R. P. Anand, ed. *Cultural Factors in International Relations*. New Delhi: Abhinav Publications, 1981. pp. 267-286.
2538. Razvi, Mujtaba. "The Mecca Summit." *Pakistan Horizon*, 34:3 (1981), 44-55.
2539. Rose, Clive. "Political Consultation in the Alliance." *NATO Review*, 31:1 (1983), 1-5.
2540. Rush, Kenneth. "The NATO Alliance: The Basis for an Era of Negotiation." *Atlantic Community Quarterly*, 11:3 (1973), 327-334.
2541. Schrader, Rudolph. "AGARD - Model for International Cooperation." *Aussenpolitik*, 22:1 (1971), 102-114.
2542. Smith, Arnold. "Commonwealth Cross Sections: Prenegotiation to Minimize Conflict and to Develop Cooperation." In: A. S. Lall, ed. *Multilateral Negotiation and Mediation*. New York: Pergamon Press, 1985. pp. 53-76.
2543. Underdal, Arild. "Multinational Negotiation Parties: The Case of the European Community." *Cooperation and Conflict*, 8 (1973), 173-182.
2544. Von der Ropp, Klaus. "The Harare Non-Aligned Summit." *Aussenpolitik*, 38:1 (1987), 86-97.
2545. Wallace, Helen. "Negotiations and Coalition Formation in the European Community." *Government and Opposition*, 20:4 (Autumn 1985), 453-472.

2546. Wheeler-Bennett, John W., and Anthony Nicholls. "The Paris Conference and the Five Peace Treaties." In: J. W. Wheeler-Bennett and A. Nicholls, *The Semblance of Peace: The Political Settlement After the Second World War.* London; Macmillan, 1972. pp.419-464.
2547. Wiebes, C., and B. Zeeman. "The Pentagon Negotiations, March 1948 - The Launching of the North Atlantic Treaty." *International Affairs,* 59:3 (1983), 351-363.
2548. Zartman, I. William. "North Africa and the EEC: Negotiations." *Middle East Journal,* 22:1 (1968), 1-16.
2549. Zelaya-Coronado, Jorge L. "OAS Negotiations." In: A. S. Lall, ed. *Multilateral Negotiations and Mediation.* New York: Pergamon Press, 1985. pp. 17-32.

3. Documents and Reports

2550. Bingham, Gayle. "Problems and Potentials in Negotiating International Environmental Disputes." Paper Presented at the *28th Annual Convention of the International Studies Association,* held on April 14-18, 1987, in Washington, D.C.
2551. Boutros-Ghali, Boutros. *The Addis Ababa Charter; A Commentary.* New York: Carnegie Endowment for International Peace, 1964. 62p.
2552. Canada. Department of Communication. *World Administrative Radio Conference: International Negotiations and Canadian Telecommunications Policy, 1979.* Toronto: Micromedia (Microlog), 1980.
2553. Dedring, Juergen, and Raman K. Venkata. "The Role of UNITAR in International Negotiations." Paper Presented at the *15th Annual Convention of the International Studies Association,* held on March 20-23, 1974, in St.Louis.
2554. Edmunds, Sallie. "Alternative Energy Development Disputes: International Implications." Paper Presented at the *28th Annual Convention of the International Studies Association,* held on April 14-18, 1987, in Washington, D.C.
2555. Gennaro, Pietro. "An International Multiparty Negotiation: The Electrolux--Zanussi Case." Paper Presented at the *Conference on the Processes of International Negotiations,* held on May 18-22, 1987, at the International Institute for Applied Systems Analysis (IIASA), in Laxenburg, Austria.
2556. Haas, Peter. "Regional Cooperation for Pollution Control: The Mediterranean Action Plant." Paper Presented at the *25th Annual Convention of the International Studies Association,* held on March 24-31, 1984, in Atlanta, GA.
2557. Halkia, Marianna. "The Role of Superpowers in the EEC-CMEA Negotiations." Paper Presented at the *28th Annual Convention of the International Studies Association,* held on April 14-18, 1987, in Washington, D.C.
2558. Hill, Roger. *Political Consultation in NATO.* Wellesley Papers 6/1978. Toronto: Canadian Institute of International Affairs, 1978.
2559. _____. *Political Consultation in NATO: Parliamentary and Policy Aspects.* Ottawa: Operational Research and Analysis Establishment, Department of National Defence, December 1975.
2560. Hoskyns, Catherine. *The Organization of African Unity and the Congo Crisis, 1964-65; Documents.* Dar-es-Salaam: Oxford University Press, 1969. 75p.
2561. Irvine, Sally. *Baruch Plan for the International Control of Atomic Energy.* PEW Case Studies, 324.0-D-88-G. Washington, D.C.: School of Foreign Service, Georgetown University, 1988.

2562. _____. *Geneva Conference of 1954: Indochina.* PEW Case Studies, 414.0--G-88-G. Washington, D.C.: School of Foreign Service, Georgetown University, 1988.
2563. Krieg, William L. "The Peaceful Settlement of Disputes Through the Organization of American States. (1974)." In: *Latin America: Special Studies, 1962-1980.* Frederick, MD.: University Publications of America, 1982. Reel III, pp. 0389-0405.
2564. Maas, Jeannette, and Robert A. C. Stewart. *Toward a World of Peace, People Create Alternatives: Proceedings of the First Int. Conference on Conflict Resolution and Peace Studies in the United Nations Year of Peace, 1986.* Suva, Fiji: The University of The South Pacific, 1986. 600p.
2565. Mahant, E. E. *French and German Attitudes to the Negotiations about the European Economic Community, 1955-1957.* Ph.D. Dissertation. London: London School of Economics, [1970].
2566. Modelski, George. *International Conference on the Settlement of the Laotian Question, 1961-62.* Canberra: Australian National University, 1962. 156p.
2567. Morawiecki, Wojciech. "Actors and Interests in the Process of Negotiations Between CMEA and EEC." Paper Presented at the *28th Annual Convention of the International Studies Association,* held on March 14-18, 1987, in Washington, D.C.
2568. Nelkin, Dorothy. *The Role of the Media in International Environmental Negotiations.* Working Paper Series, 4. Cambridge, MA.: The Program on the Processes of International Negotiations, American Academy of Arts and Sciences, 1987. 24p.
2569. Nelson, Daniel J. *The Allied Creation of the Postwar Status of Berlin: A Study in Wartime Alliance Diplomacy.* Ph.D. Dissertation. New York: Columbia University Press, 1971. 298p.
2570. Nelson, Randall H. *Recent Developments in the Law and Practice of the United States Respecting Negotiation and Conclusion of International Agreements and Commentary on Proposed Changes.* Ph.D. Dissertation. Ann Arbor, MI.: University of Michigan, 1956. 522p.
2571. Nielsson, Gunnar P. *Institutionalized Multilateral Diplomacy: Britain's Use of International Institutions During the 1982 Falklands Crisis.* PEW Case Studies, 127.0-A-88-S. Los Angeles, CA.: School of International Relations, University of Southern California, 1988.
2572. Obaseki, Nosakhare O. *Managing Africa's Conflicts.* New York: International Peace Academy, 1982. 46p.
2573. Oluo, Samuel Lucky O. *Conflict Management of the Organization of African Unity in Intra-African Conflicts, 1963-1980.* Ph.D. Dissertation. Denton, TX.: North Texas State University, 1982. 226p.
2574. Papadopoulos, Andrestinos N. *Multilateral Diplomacy Within the Commonwealth.* Master Thesis. London: Institute of Commonwealth Studies, 1980.
2575. Patrick, Karen D. *International Technological Negotiations: A Framework for Analysis.* M.A. Thesis. Ottawa: Carleton University, 1983.
2576. Pendley, R. E. *International Safeguards on Nuclear Materials: A Study of Attitudes and Negotiations Concerning International Control over National Activities.* Ph.D. Dissertation. Evanston, IL.: Northwestern University, 1968. 245p.
2577. Segal, Brian. *The 1979 World Administrative Radio Conference: International Negotiations and Canadian Telecommunications Policy.* Ottawa: Ministry of Supply and Services Canada, 1980. 49p.
2578. Solidum, Estrella D. *Bilateral Summitry in ASEAN.* Singapore: Institute of Southeast Asian Studies, 1982. 44p.

2579. Stubblefield, Gary L. *Maximizing Negotiations over United States' National Interests with the Association of Southeast Asian Nations*. M.A. Thesis. Monterey, CA.: Naval Postgraduate School, 1980. 90p.
2580. Swagert, S. L. *International Negotiations in Support of American Air Routes*. Ph.D. Dissertation. Iowa City, IA.: University of Iowa, 1948.
2581. Thambipillai, Pushpathavi, and J. Savavanamuttu. *ASEAN Negotiations: Two Insights*. Singapore: Institute of Southeast Asian Studies, 1985. 56p.
2582. _____. *Regional Cooperations and Development: The Case of ASEAN and its External Relations*. Ph.D. Dissertation. Honolulu, HI.: University of Hawaii, 1980. 340p.
2583. United States. Congress. House. Committee on Foreign Affairs. *U.S. Participation in International Negotiations on Ozone Protocol: Hearings*. 100th Cong., 1st sess. Washington, D.C.: U.S. Government Printing Office, 1987. 24p.
2584. _____._____._____.Committee on Public Works and Transportation.Subcommittee on Aviation. *U.S. International Aviation Negotiations: Hearings*. 95th Cong., 1st sess. Washington, D.C.: U.S. Government Printing Office, 1978. 402p.
2585. _____.Department of State. *The Geneva Conference of Heads of Government, July 18-23, 1955*. Washington, D.C.: U.S. Government Printing Office, 1955.
2586. _____._____. *Making the Peace Treaties, 1941-1947: A History of the Making of the Peace Beginning with the Atlantic Charter, the Yalta and Potsdam Conferences...* Washington, D.C.: U.S. Government Printing Office, 1947. 150p.
2587. _____._____. *Foreign Ministers Meeting, May- August, 1959, Geneva*. Department of State Publication 6882. Washington, D.C.: U.S. Government Printing Office, 1959. 693p.
2588. Vaahtoranta, Tapani. "The Politics of Ozone: What Determines National Policies Towards the Protection of the Ozone." Paper Presented at the *Conference on the Processes of International Negotiations*, held on May 18-22, 1987, at the International Institute for Applied Systems Analysis (IIASA), Laxenburg, Austria.
2589. Wilkowski, Jean M. *Conference Diplomacy II: A Case Study: The UN Conference on Science and Technology for Development, Vienna, 1979*. Washington, D.C.: Institute for the Study of Diplomacy, Georgetown University, 1982. 44p.

VI

Arms Control Negotiations

Nuclear arms control has been and continues to be the central theme of superpower relations for the last two decades. The main objective of arms control is to stabilize and control certain aspects of the arms race. This chapter covers materials dealing with processes of negotiating agreements to reduce dangers of nuclear war by means of security arrangements, partial disarmament, stabilization of forces, restricting weapons testing and more. The long and arduous road to limit the arms race has bought about a number of agreements such as the Limited Test Ban Treaty, the Antiballistic Missile Treaty (ABM), the Intermediate Range Nuclear Forces Treaty (INF), Strategic Arms Limitation Talks I Agreement (SALT I) and others.

This chapter is interested in identifying and focusing on works dealing with the negotiating processes and procedures that go into the makings of nuclear arms control agreements. It is not really covering the policies, although in many of the works it is impossible to make a credible distinction.

Section one deals with arms control processes in general. Most of the other sections are identified by the type of negotiations, agreements or conferences such as Test Ban Negotiations, Strategic Arms Limitation Talks (SALT), Intermediate Range Nuclear Forces Talks (INF), Mutual and Balanced Force Reduction Talks (MBFR), Strategic Arms Reduction Talks (START), Nonproliferation Treaty Negotiations (NPT), chemical weapons and seabed arms control, Commission on Security and Cooperation in Europe Conferences (CSCE). The last section covers less distinct nuclear arms control cases.

A. GENERAL WORKS

1. Books

2590. Abt, Clark C. *A Strategy for Terminating a Nuclear War.* Boulder, CO.: Westview Press, 1985. 253p.
2591. Allan, Pierre. *Crisis Bargaining and the Arms Race: A Theoretical Model.* Cambridge, MA.: Ballinger, 1983. 155p.
2592. Alperovitz, Gar. *Atomic Diplomacy: Hiroshima and Potsdam: The Use of the Atomic Bomb and the American Confrontation with Soviet Power.* New York: Penguin, 1985. 427p.
2593. *Arms Control Chronicle.* Ottawa: Canadian Centre for Arms Control and Disarmament, 1984-. Updating Publication.
2594. *Arms Control Reporter: A Chronicle of Treaties, Negotiations, Proposals, Weapons and Policies.* Brookline, MA.: Institute for Defense and Disarmament Studies, 1982-. Monthly Publication.
2595. *Arms Control Today.* Washington, D.C.: Arms Control Association, 1972-. Monthly Publication.
2596. Aron, Raymond. *On War: Atomic Weapons and Global Diplomacy.* London: Secker & Warburg, 1958. 126p.
2597. Barton, John H., and Lawrence D. Weiler, eds. *International Arms Control: Issues and Agreements.* Stanford, CA.: Stanford University Press, 1976. 444p.
2598. Bechhoefer, Bernard G. *Postwar Negotiations for Arms Control.* Washington, D.C.: The Brookings Institute, 1961. 641p.
2599. Blacker, Coit D., and Gloria Duffy. *International Arms Control: Issues and Agreements.* 2nd ed. Stanford, CA.: Stanford University Press, 1984. 502p.
2600. _____. *Reluctant Warriors: The United States, Soviet Union and Arms Control.* New York: W. H. Freedman, 1987. 192p.
2601. Blechman, Barry M., ed. *Preventing Nuclear War: A Realistic Approach.* Bloomington, IN.: Indiana University Press, 1985. 197p.
2602. Brown, Harold, and Lynn E. Davis. *Nuclear Arms Control Choices.* Boulder, CO.: Westview Press, 1984. 55p.
2603. Carnesale, Albert, and Richard N. Haass, eds. *Superpower Arms Control: Setting the Record Straight.* Bambridge, MA.: Ballinger, 1987. 376p.
2604. Chilaty, D. *Disarmament: A Historical Review of Negotiations and Treaties.* Geneva: Impr. G. de Buren, 1978. 404p.
2605. Clarke, Duncan L. *Politics of Arms Control: The Role and Effectiveness of the U.S. Arms Control and Disarmament Agency.* New York: The Free Press, 1979. 277p.
2606. Clemens, Walter C. *The Superpowers and Arms Control: From Cold War to Independence.* Lexington, MA.: D. C. Heath, 1973. 180p.
2607. Coffey, Joseph I. *Arms Control and European Security: A Guide to East - West Negotiations.* New York: Praeger, 1977. 271p.
2608. Dahlitz, Julie. *Nuclear Arms Control: With Effective International Agreements.* London: George Allen & Unwin, 1983. 238p.
2609. Dallin, Alexander. *The Soviet Union and Disarmament: An Appraisal of Soviet Attitudes and Intentions.* New York: Praeger, 1964. 282p.
2610. *Disarmament: Negotiations and Treaties, 1946-1971: Keesing's Research Report.* New York: Scribner's, 1972. 385p.
2611. Dougherty, James E. *How to Think About Arms Control and Disarmament.* New York: Crane, Russak, 1973. 200p.
2612. Dupuy, Trevor N., and Gay M. Hammerman, ed. *A Documentary History of Arms Control and Disarmament.* New York: R. R. Bowker, 1973. 624p.

2613. Einhorn, Robert J. *Negotiating from Strength: Leverage in Arms Control Negotiations.* New York: Praeger, 1985. 129p.
2614. Feld, Werner J. *Arms Control and the Atlantic Community.* New York: Praeger, 1987. 144p.
2615. Ferraris, Luigi Vittorio, ed. *Report on a Negotiation: Helsinki - Geneva - Helsinki, 1972-1975.* Alphen aan den Rijn: Sijthoff & Noordhoff, 1979. 439p.
2616. Freedman, Lawrence. *Arms Control: Management or Reform.* Chatham House Paper; 3. London: Routledge & Kegan Paul, 1986. 102p.
2617. George, Alexander L., Philip J. Farley and Alexander Dallin, eds. *U.S. - Soviet Security Cooperation: Achievements, Failures, Lessons.* New York: Oxford University Press, 1988. 746p.
2618. Goldblat, Jozef. *Agreements on Arms Control: A Critical Survey.* London: Taylor & Francis, 1982. 387p.
2619. Jensen, Lloyd. *Bargaining for National Security: The Postwar Disarmament Negotiations.* Columbia, SC.: University of South Carolina Press, 1988. 311p.
2620. Kincade, William H., and Jeffrey D. Porro, eds. *Negotiating Security: An Arms Control Reader.* Washington, D.C.: The Carnegie Endowment for International Peace, 1979. 321p.
2621. Kraus, Max W. *They All Come to Geneva & Other Tales of a Public Diplomat.* New York: Seven Locks Press, 1988. 136p.
2622. Labrie, Roger P., ed. *SALT Handbook. Key Documents and Issues, 1972-1979.* Washington, D.C.: American Enterprise Institute for Public Policy Research, 1979. 736p.
2623. Luard, Evan, ed. *First Steps to Disarmament: A New Approach to the Problems of Arms Reductions.* London: Thames & Hudson, 1965. 277p.
2624. Mickiewicz, Ellen P., and Roman Kolkowicz, eds. *International Security and Arms Control.* New York: Praeger, 1986. 171p.
2625. Neidle, Allan F. *Nuclear Negotiations: Reassessing Arms Control Goals in U.S. - Soviet Relations.* Austin, TX.: L.B.J. School of Public Affairs, University of Texas, 1982. 166p.
2626. Nutting, Anthony. *Disarmament: An Outline of the Negotiations.* London: Oxford University Press, 1959. 52p.
2627. Nye, Joseph S., ed. *The Making of America's Soviet Policy.* New Haven, CT.: Yale University Press, 1984. 369p.
2628. Quester, George H. *Nuclear Diplomacy: The First Twenty-Five Years.* New York: Dunellen, 1978. 327p.
2629. Schwartzman, David. *Games of Chicken: Four Decades of U.S. Nuclear Policy.* New York: Praeger, 1988. 232p.
2630. Scott, Robert T. *The Race for Security: Arms and Arms Control in the Reagan Years.* Lexington, MA.: Lexington Books, 1987. 297p.
2631. Seaborg, Glenn T., and Benjamin S. Loeb. *Stemming the Tide: Arms Control in the Johnson Years.* Lexington, MA.: Lexington Books, 1987. 495p.
2632. Sherr, Alan B. *The Other Side of Arms Control: Soviet Objectives in the Gorbachev Era.* London: Allen & Unwin, 1988. 384p.
2633. Snow, Donald M. *The Necessary Peace: Nuclear Weapons and Super Power Relations.* Lexington, MA.: Lexington Books, 1987. 147p.
2634. Spanier, J. W., and J. L. Nogee. *The Politics of Disarmament: A Study in Soviet - American Gamesmanship.* New York: Praeger, 1962. 226p.
2635. Steinberg, Gerald M. *Satellite Reconnaissance: The Role of Informal Bargaining.* New York: Praeger, 1983. 200p.
2636. Stone, Jeremy J. *Strategic Persuasion: Arms Limitations Through Dialogue.* New York: Columbia University Press, 1967. 176p.
2637. Talbott, Strobe. *Deadly Gambits: The Reagan Administration and the Stalemate in Nuclear Arms Control.* New York: Knopf, 1984. 380p.

2638. Ury, William L. *Beyond the Hotline: How Crisis Control Can Prevent Nuclear War.* Boston, MA.: Houghton Mifflin, 1985. 187p.
2639. Viotti, Paul R., ed. *Conflict and Arms Control: An Uncertain Agenda.* Boulder, CO.: Westview Press, 1986. 320p.
2640. Weiberger, David. *Nuclear Dialogues.* New York: P. Lang, 1987. 226p.
2641. Weinrod, W. Bruce. *Arms Control Handbook: A Guide to the History, Arsenals and Issues of U.S. - Soviet Negotiations.* Washington, D.C.: Heritage Foundation, 1987. 175p.

2. Journal Articles

2642. "ACDA's Impact." *Foreign Service Journal,* 63:8 (September 1986), 35-41.
2643. Adelman, Kenneth L. "Arms Control With and Without Agreements." *Foreign Affairs,* 63:2 (1984-85), 240-263.
2644. ____. "Challenge of Negotiation by Democracies." *Department of State Bulletin,* 86 (January 1986), 35-38.
2645. ____. "Antisatellite Arms Control." *Department of State Bulletin,* 85:2104 (November 1985), 26-29.
2646. ____. "The Future of American - Soviet Arms Control Negotiations: The Strategic Defense Initiative Debate." In: W. G. Nichols and M. L. Boykin, ed. *Arms Control and Nuclear Weapons.* Contributions to Military Studies, 59. Westport, CT.: Greenwood Press, 1987. pp. 9-18.
2647. ____., and Charles A. Sorrels. "Negotiating with Moscow: The Case of Austria." *The National Interest,* 3 (Spring 1986), 61-65.
2648. ____. "Arms Control and Openness." *Department of State Bulletin,* 87:2122 (May 1987), 19-22.
2649. Alexandrov, V. "Western Diplomacy Zigzags on Disarmament." *International Affairs (Moscow),* 6 (August 1960), 56-60.
2650. "The Approach to Negotiations - Discussion." In: A. F. Neidle, ed. *Nuclear Negotiations.* Austin, TX.: L.B.J. School of Public Affairs, 1982. pp. 113-126.
2651. Atque, Fanzia. "Soviet - American Arms Control Negotiations." *Pakistan Horizon,* 38:2 (1985), 84-103.
2652. Azrael, Jeremy, and Stephen Sestanovich. "Superpower Balancing Acts." *Foreign Affairs,* 3 (1986), 479-498.
2653. Bargman, Abraham. "Nuclear Diplomacy." *Proceedings of the Academy of Political Science,* 32:4 (1977), 159-169.
2654. Bechhoefer, Bernard G. "Negotiating with the Soviet Union." In: D. G. Brennan, ed. *Arms Control, Disarmament and National Security.* New York: Braziller, 1961. pp. 269-281.
2655. Benoit, Emile. "The Conditions of Disarmament." *Antioch Review,* 15 (Fall 1955), 362-374.
2656. Bentley, Alvin M. "The Fate of East Central Europe and the Coming Negotiations." *Free World Forum,* 2:2 (April-May 1960), 62-69.
2657. Bertram, Christoph. "US - Soviet Nuclear Arms Control." In: *SIPRI Yearbook 1987.* Oxford: Oxford University Press, 1987. pp. 323-337.
2658. Blechman, Barry M. "Do Negotiated Arms Limitations Have a Future?" *Foreign Affairs,* 59:1 (Fall 1980), 102-125.
2659. ____. Jane E. Nolan and Alan Platt. "Negotiated Limitations on Arms Transfers: First Steps Toward Crisis Prevention?" In: A. L. George, ed. *Managing U.S. - Soviet Rivalry.* Boulder, CO.: Westview Press, 1983. pp. 255-284.
2660. ____. ____. "Reorganizing for More Effective Arms Negotiations." *Foreign Affairs,* 61 (Summer 1983), 1157-1182.

2661. _____. "Efforts to Reduce the Risk of Accidental or Inadvertent War." In: A. L. George, P. J. Farley and A Dallin, eds. *U.S. - Soviet Security Cooperation.* New York: Oxford University Press, 1988. pp. 466-481.
2662. Bobrow, Davis B. "Arms Control Through Communication and Information Regimes." *Policy Studies Journal,* 8:1 (Autumn 1979), 60-65.
2663. Bomsdorf, Falk. "Arms Control as a Process of Self-Constraint: The Workings of Western Negotiating Policy." In: U. Nerlich, ed. **Soviet Power and Western Negotiating Processes, Vol II: The Western Panacea.** Cambridge, MA.: Ballinger, 1983. pp. 67-116.
2664. Booth, Arthur. "The Disarmament Scene from Geneva." *Disarmament,* 2:2 (1979), 58-65.
2665. Boykin, Milton L. "A Critique of American - Soviet Arms Control Negotiations." In: W. G. Nichols and M. L. Boykin, eds. *Arms Control and Nuclear Weapons.* Contributions to Military Studies, 59. Westport, CT.: Greenwood Press, 1987. pp. 23-36.
2666. Brown, Harold, et al. "Negotiating with the Soviets and Prospects for Arms Control Negotiations." In: R. Kolkowicz and E. P. Mickiewick, eds. *Soviet Calculus of Nuclear War.* Lexington, MA.: Lexington Books, 1986. pp. 143-170.
2667. Brown, Scott, and Roger D. Fisher. "Building a U.S. - Soviet Working Relationship: Ideas on Process." In: R. Avenhaus, R. K. Huber and J. D. Kettelle, eds. *Modelling and Analysis of Arms Control.* Berlin: Springer Verlag, 1986. pp. 319-328.
2668. Buchheim, Robert W., and Dan Caldwell. "The U.S. - USSR Standing Consultative Commission: Description and Appraisal." In: R. B. Viotti, ed. *Conflict and Arms Control.* Boulder, CO.: Westview Press, 1986. pp. 134-145.
2669. _____., and Philip J. Farley. "The U.S. - Soviet Standing Consultative Commission." In: A. L. George, P. J. Farley and A. Dallin, eds. *U.S. Soviet Security Cooperation.* New York: Oxford University Press, 1988. pp. 254-269.
2670. Bull, Hedley. "Disarmament and International System." *Australian Journal of Politics and History,* 5:2 (1959), 41-50.
2671. Burt, Richard. "The Relevance of Arms Control in the 1980." *Daedalus,* (Winter 1981) 159-178.
2672. Byers, R. B. "The Perils of Superpower Diplomacy: Detente, Defence and Arms Control." *International Journal,* 35:3 (1980), 520-548.
2673. Clemens, Walter C., and Franklin Griffiths. "The Soviet Position on Arms Control and Disarmament: Negotiations and Propaganda, 1954-1964: An Annex to Report." In: L. P. Bloomfield, ed. *Soviet Interests in Arms Control and Disarmament.* Cambridge, MA.: Center for International Studies, MIT, 1965. 116p.
2674. Cleveland, Harland. "How to Make Peace with the Russians." *Department of State Bulletin,* 58 (May 27, 1968), 687-692.
2675. Cohen, Benjamin V. "Disarmament and Political Settlement." *New Leader,* (July 1, 1957), 16-18.
2676. Collingridge, David. "Problems of Flexibility in the Nuclear Arms Race." In: R. Avenhaus, R. K. Huber and J. D. Kettelle, eds. *Modelling and Analysis in Arms Control.* Berlin: Springer Verlag, 1986. pp. 329-335.
2677. Cooper, Henry F. "US - Soviet Defence and Space Treaty Negotiations - Important Differences Still to be Overcome." *NATO Review,* 35:6 (December 1987), 6-10.
2678. _____. "Defence and Space Talks - Two Steps Forward, One Step Back." *NATO Review,* 36:1 (February 1988), 15-18.

2679. Cooper, Mary H. "Arms Control Negotiations." *Editorial Research Report*, 8:1 (February 22, 1985), 147-170.
2680. Cory, Robert H. "Images of United States Disarmament Policy in the International Disarmament Negotiating System." *Journal of Arms Control*, 1:4 (1963), 654-663.
2681. _____. "Images of United States Disarmament Policy in International Disarmament Negotiating System." *Journal of Conflict Resolution*, 7:3 (1963), 560-568.
2682. Coser, Lewis A. "Peaceful Settlements and the Disfunctions of Secrecy." *Journal of Arms Control*, (October 1963), 340-347.
2683. Critchley, Julian. "The Three Conferences in Europe: Talking Out the Cold War?" *World Survey*, 56 (August 1973), 1-16.
2684. Dean, Arthur H. "Disarmament Negotiations and the Strategic Dialogue." In: J. E. Dougherty and J. F. Lehman, eds. *The Prospects of Arms Control*. New York: MacFadden-Bartell, 1965. pp. 131-144.
2685. Dean, Jonathan. "East West Arms Control Negotiations: The Multilateral Dimension." In: L. Sloss and M. Scott Davis, eds. *A Game for High Stakes*. Cambridge, MA.: Ballinger, 1986. pp. 79-106.
2686. _____. "East-West Conflict Management Through European Arms Control Negotiation." *International Journal*, 40:4 (1985), 716-735.
2687. _____. "The Pragmatic View." In: D. J. D. Sandole and I. Sandole-Staroste, eds. *Conflict Management and Problem Solving*. London: Frances Pinter, 1987. pp. 215-217.
2688. _____. "Gorbachev's Arms Control Moves." *Bulletin of the Atomic Scientists*, 43:5 (June 1987), 34-41.
2689. Demontbrial, T. "The French Position Vis-a-Vis NATO with Respect to Negotiations." In: M. Deperrot, ed. *European Security: Nuclear or Conventional Defense?* Elmsford, NY.: Pergamon Press, 1984. pp. 265-268.
2690. Dickinson, William B. "Struggle For Disarmament." *Editorial Research Report*, (February 25, 1960), 139-156.
2691. "Disarmament Proposal Negotiations, 1946-1955." *World Today*, 11:8 (1955), 334-348.
2692. Dobell, Peter C. "Negotiating with the United States." *International Journal*, 36 (Winter 1980-81), 17-69.
2693. Dougherty, James E. "The Status of the Arms Negotiations." *Orbis*, 9 (Spring 1965), 49-97.
2694. _____. "Soviet Arms Control Negotiations." In: E. L. Dulles and R. D. Crane, eds. *Detente: Cold War Strategies in Transition*. London: Praeger, 1965. pp. 179-200.
2695. Downs, George W., David M. Rocke and Randolph M. Silverson. "Arms Race and Cooperation." *World Politics*, 38:1 (October 1985), 118-146.
2696. Duffy, Gloria. "Conditions That Affect Arms Control Compliance." In: A. L. George, P. J. Farley and A. Dallin, eds. *U.S. - Soviet Security Cooperation*. New York: Oxford University Press, 1988. pp. 270-292.
2697. Engle, Kenneth W. "European Arms Control Negotiations: Prospects for a "Window" in the 1980's." *Air University Review*, 32 (September/October 1981), 31-39.
2698. Fallers, L. A., et al. "The Policy Proposals: A Negotiated Stalemate." *Bulletin of the Atomic Scientists*, 21 (June 1965), 42-44.
2699. Farley, Philip J. "Arms Control and U.S. - Soviet Security Cooperation." In: A. L. George, P. J. Farley and A. Dallin, eds. *U.S. - Soviet Security Cooperation*. New York: Oxford University Press, 1988. pp. 618-640.
2700. _____. "How to Negotiate a Treaty." *Bulletin of the Atomic Scientists*, 43:8 (October 1987), 33-37.

2701. _____. "Managing the Risks of Cooperation." In: A. L. George, P. J. Philip and A. Dallin, eds. *U.S. - Soviet Security Cooperation.* New York: Oxford University Press, 1988. pp. 679-691.
2702. Fartash, Manoutchehr. "The 'Disarmament Club' at Work." *Bulletin of the Atomic Scientists,* 33:1 (1977), 57-62.
2703. Ferrell, Robert H. "Disarmament Conferences: Bullets at the Brink." *American Heritage,* 22 (February 1971), 5-7, 96, 98-100.
2704. Fisher, Adrian S. "The Search for Common Ground Among the Superpowers." In: A. S. Lall, ed. *Multilateral Negotiation and Mediation.* New York: Pergamon Press, 1985. pp. 115-132.
2705. _____. "East - West Negotiations." In: D. J. D. Sandole and I. Sandole-Staroste, eds. *Conflict Management and Problem Solving.* London: Frances Pinter, 1987. pp. 203-207.
2706. Fisher, Roger D. "Getting to "Yes" in the Nuclear Age." In: B. H. Weston, ed. *Toward Nuclear Disarmament and Global Security.* Boulder, CO.: Westview Press, 1984. pp. 358-370.
2707. Foster, R. B. "Unilateral Arms Control Measures and Disarmament Negotiations." *Orbis,* 6:2 (1962), 258-280.
2708. Fox, William T. R. "Political and Diplomatic Prerequisites of Arms Control." *Daedalus,* 89 (Fall 1960), 1000-1014.
2709. Freedman, Lawrence. "Negotiations on Nuclear Forces." *Bulletin of the Atomic Scientists,* 39:10 (1983), 22-28.
2710. Gaffney, Frank J. "Arms Control Negotiations: The Rocky Road to Accord." *Defense,* (May 1984), 13-17.
2711. Garfinkle, Adam M. "Obstacles and Optimism at Geneva." *Orbis,* 29:2 (Summer 1985), 268-280.
2712. Garthoff, Raymond L. "History Confirms the Traditional Meaning." *Arms Control Today,* (September 1987), 15-19.
2713. Gellner, Charles R. "The Reagan Administration: Negotiating Arms Control with the Soviet Union." In: P. R. Viotti, ed. *Conflict and Arms Control.* Boulder, CO.: Westview Press, 1986. pp. 24-42.
2714. George, Alexander L. "Strategies for Facilitating Cooperation." In: A. L. George, P. J. Farley and A. Dallin, eds. *U.S. - Soviet Security Cooperation.* New York.: Oxford University Press, 1988. pp. 692-711.
2715. _____. "U.S. - Soviet Efforts to Cooperate in Crisis Management and Crisis Avoidance." In: A. L. George, P. J. Farley and A. Dallin, eds. *U.S. - Soviet Security Cooperation.* New York: Oxford University Press, 1988. pp. 581-600.
2716. _____. "Problems of Crisis Management and Crisis Avoidance in U.S. - Soviet Relations." In: O. Osternd, ed. *Studies of War and Peace.* Oslo: Norwegian University Press, 1986. pp. 202-226.
2717. Gerould, James. "Disarmament Negotiations." *Current History,* 26 (May 1927), 267-269.
2718. Glagolev, I. S. "Soviet Decision-Making in Arms Control Negotiations." *Orbis,* 21:4 (1978), 767-776.
2719. Glicksman, Alex. "The Other Side of Negotiations." In: D. J. D. Sandole and I. Sandole-Staroste, eds. *Conflict Management and Problem Solving.* London: Frances Pinter, 1986. pp. 210-214.
2720. Gordon, Michael R. "U.S. - Soviet Arms Control Negotiations: Nuclear and Space Weapons." *American Enterprise Institute for Policy and Defence Review,* 5:2 (1985), 21-44.
2721. Gori, Umberto. "Superpowers and Arms Negotiations: Political Climates and Optimal Strategy." In: R. Avenhaus, R. K. Huber and J. D. Kettelle, eds. *Modelling and Analysis in Arms Control.* Berlin: Springer Verlag, 1986. pp. 337-345.

2722. Gray, Colin S. "Arms Control 'The American Way'." *Wilson Quarterly*, 1:5 (1977), 94-99.
2723. _____. "Of Bargaining Chips and Building Blocks: Arms Control and Defence Policy." *International Journal*, 28 (Spring 1973), 266-296.
2724. _____. "Defence and Negotiation." *Air Force Magazine*, 57 (January 1974), 32-36.
2725. Gray, Robert C., and Robert J. Bressler. "Why Weapons Make Poor Bargaining Chips." *Bulletin of the Atomic Scientists*, 33 (September 1977), 8-9.
2726. Griffiths, Franklin. "Limits to the Tabular View of Negotiation." *International Journal*, 35:1 (Winter 1979-80), 33-46.
2727. Gross, Donald G. "Negotiated Treaty Amendment: The Solution to the SDI-ABM Treaty Conflict." *Harvard International Law Journal*, 28 (Winter 1987), 31-68.
2728. Guehenno, Jean-Marie. "Strategic Versus European Arms Negotiations: The Limits of Complementarity." In: U. Nerlich, ed. *Soviet Power and Western Negotiating Policies, Vol II: The Western Panacea: Constraining Soviet Power Through Negotiation*. Cambridge, MA.: Ballinger, 1983. pp. 361-374.
2729. Haden, Eric W. "Soviet - American Arms Negotiations." *Current History*, 46 (June 1964), 336-340.
2730. Hamilton, Andrew. "Arms Talks: In-Group Defence on the Technical Issues." *Science*, (April 10, 1970), 234-340.
2731. Hamilton, John A. "To Link or Not to Link." *Foreign Policy*, 44 (Fall 1981), 127-144.
2732. Hayden, Eric W. "Soviet - American Negotiations, 1960-1968: A Prelude for SALT." *Naval War College Review*, 24 (January 1972), 65-82.
2733. Holloway, David. "The Warshaw Pact in the Era of Negotiations." *Survival*, 14:6 (November/December 1972), 275-279.
2734. Holmes, John W. "Geneva: 1954." *International Journal*, 22:3 (Summer 1967), 457-483.
2735. Holst, Johan J. "Arms Control Revisited." In: U. Nerlich, ed. *Soviet Power and Western Negotiating Policies, Vol II: The Western Panacea: Constraining Soviet Power Through Negotiation*. Cambridge, MA.: Ballinger, 1983. pp. 153-188.
2736. Hopkins, Waring C. "An Historical Analogy: Geneva 1954 and Paris 1968." *Naval War College Review*, 21 (September 1968), 88-91.
2737. Hopmann, P. Terrence, and Charles Walcott. "The Impact of International Conflict and Detente on Bargaining in Arms Control Negotiations: An Experimental Analysis." *International Interactions*, 2 (1976), 189-206.
2738. _____. _____. "The Bargaining Process in International Arms Control Negotiations." *International Interactions*, 2:1 (1975), 63-64.
2739. Hotz, R. "U.S. Negotiation Strategy." *Strategy and Tactics*, 3:1 (1975), 57-61.
2740. Ignatieff, George. "Negotiating Arms Control." *International Journal*, 30:1 (1974-75), 92-101.
2741. Israelyan, Y. "International Detente and Disarmaments." *International Affairs (Moscow)*, 20 (May 1974), 24-29.
2742. Jack, Homer A. "Disarmament as a Career." *War/Peace Report*, 7 (January 1967), 14-16.
2743. Jacobsen, Carl G. "Soviet - American Arms Control: Hope or Hoax?" *Current History*, 84:504 (October 1985), 317-320, 342-344.
2744. Jensen, Lloyd. "Soviet - American Bargaining Behavior in the Postwar Disarmament Negotiations." *Journal of Arms Control*, 1 (1963), 616-635.
2745. _____. "Soviet - American Bargaining Behavior in the Postwar Disarmament Negotiations." *Journal of Conflict Resolution*, 7:3 (1963), 522-541.

2746. _____. "Soviet - American Behavior in Disarmament Negotiations." In: I. W. Zartman, ed. *The 50% Solution.* Garden City, NY.: Anchor Press, 1976. pp. 288-321.
2747. Kalyadin, A., and Yu Nazarkin. *Disarmament Negotiating Machinery.* Moscow: Nauka Publications, 1984. 95p.
2748. Karkoszka, Andrzej. "Conventional Arms Limitation: A Regional Approach to a Global Problem." *Disarmament,* 9:3 (Autumn 1986), 27-40.
2749. Keller, Abraham. "Ten Steps to Peace." *Bulletin of the Atomic Scientists,* 40:3 (1984), 51-52.
2750. Kettelle, John D. "Information Management in Arms Control Negotiations." In: R. Avenhaus and R. K. Huber, eds. *Quantitative Assessment in Arms Control.* New York: Plenum Press, 1984. pp. 445-462.
2751. _____. "Report of the Chairman - Negotiation Issues." In: R. Avenhaus, R. K. Huber and J. D. Kettelle, eds. *Modelling and Analysis in Arms Control.* Berlin: Springer Verlag, 1986. pp. 279-294.
2752. _____. "A Computerized Third Party." In: R. Avenhaus, R. K. Huber and J. D. Kettelle, eds. *Modelling and Analysis in Arms Control.* Berlin: Springer--Verlag, 1986. pp. 348-364.
2753. Khvostov, V. "Disarmament Negotiations." *International Affairs (Moscow),* 1 (January 1961), 92-97.
2754. _____. "Disarmament Negotiations." *International Affairs (Moscow),* 2 (February 1961), 60-67.
2755. Kincade, William H. "Thinking About Arms Control and Strategic Weapons." *World Affairs,* 136 (Spring 1974), 364-376.
2756. Kistiakowsky, G. B. "The Good and the Bad of Nuclear Arms Control Negotiations." *Bulletin of the Atomic Scientists,* 35:5 (1979), 7-9.
2757. Korhonen, Keijo T. "Disarmament Talks as an Instrument of International Politics." *Cooperation and Conflict,* 5:3 (1970), 152-167.
2758. Krickus, Richard J. "The Superpowers and Crisis Prevention: Taking Stock." In: P. R. Viotti, ed. *Conflict and Arms Control.* Boulder, CO.: Westview Press, 1986. pp. 99-117.
2759. Kruzel, Joseph J. "Arms Control and American Defence Policy: New Alternatives and Old Realities." *Daedalus,* 110:1 (Winter 1981), 137-157.
2760. _____. "What's Wrong with the Traditional Approach.?" *Washington Quarterly,* 8:2 (Spring 1985), 121-132.
2761. Lall, Arthur S. "The Nonaligned in Disarmament Negotiations." *Bulletin of the Atomic Scientists,* 20 (May 1964), 17-21.
2762. Lee, Dwight R. "Arms Negotiations, The Soviet Economy and Democratically Induced Delusions." *Contemporary Policy Issues,* 4 (October 1986), 22-37.
2763. Leitenberg, Milton. "Soviet Secrecy and Negotiations on Strategic Weapons, Arms Control and Disarmament." *Bulletin of Peace Proposals,* 4 (1974), 377-380.
2764. _____. "United States - Soviet Strategic Arms Control: The Decade of Detente 1970-1980, and a Look Ahead." *Arms Control,* 8:3 (December 1987), 213-264.
2765. Leonard, J. F., R. T. Grey and R. G. Kaiser. "Negotiations, Politics, and Prospects for the Future - Questions." In: A. F. Neidle, ed. *Nuclear Negotiations.* Austin, TX.: L.B.J. School of Public Affairs, University of Texas, 1982. pp. 150-154.
2766. Levinson, Macha. "Arms Control Negotiations at the Crossroads." In: L. Dembinski, ed. *International Geneva 1985.* Lausanne: Payot Lausanne, 1985. pp. 74-84.
2767. Lewis, Kevin N. "Negotiating a Nuclear Freeze?" *Strategic Review,* 12:1 (Winter 1984), 29-35.

2768. Luard, Evan. "The Background of the Negotiations to Date." In: E. Luard, ed. *First Steps to Disarmament.* London: Thames & Hudson, 1965. pp. 9-46.
2769. Lukes, I. "Managing United States - Soviet Arms Control Initiatives: Do We Speak the Same Language." *Comparative Strategy,* 6:2 (1987), 165-184.
2770. MacGillivray, Karen P., and Gilbert R. Winham. "Arms Control Negotiations and the Stability of Crisis Management." In: G. P. Winham, ed. *New Issues in International Crisis Management.* Boulder, CO.: Westview Press, 1988. pp. 90-120.
2771. Mackintosh, Malcolm. "The Soviet Negotiating Stance - and Goals." *The Council for Arms Control Bulletin,* 36 (February 1988), 3-5.
2772. Mann, Howard. "Resolving Disputes on Arms Control Treaties." *The Council for Arms Control Bulletin,* 22 (September 1985), 4-5.
2773. Mateesco-Matte, Mircea. "Observation on the Latest U.S. Soviet Negotiations in Geneva." In: M. Mateesco-Mate, ed. *Arms Control and Disarmament in Outer Space.* Montreal, Que.: Centre for Research of Asia and Space Law, McGill University, 1985. pp. 97-124.
2774. Mates, L. "The Big Powers and Disarmament." *Review of International Affairs (Belgrade),* (February 16, 1960), 1-3.
2775. McGeorge, Bundy. "The Unimpressive Record of Atomic Diplomacy." In: G. Prins, ed. *The Nuclear Crisis Reader.* New York: Random House, 1984. pp. 42-54.
2776. McNeill, J. H. "United States - USSR Nuclear Arms Negotiations - The Process and the Lawyer." *American Journal of International Law,* 79:1 (1985), 52-67.
2777. McVitty, Marion H. "Disarmament Negotiations, 1956-1962." *Social Education,* 26 (November 1962), 384-389, 396.
2778. Mendelsohn, Jack, and James P. Rubin. "SDI as Negotiating Leverage." *Arms Control Today,* 16 (December 1986), 6-9.
2779. Mulhall, Daniel. "Australia and Disarmament Diplomacy 1983-1985: Rhetoric or Achievement?" *Australian Outlook,* 40 (April 1986), 32-38.
2780. "Negotiation from Strength: An Interview with Eugene Rostow." *Fletcher Forum,* 7:2 (1983), 228-238.
2781. "Negotiations on Strategic Arms Reductions." *Department of State Bulletin,* 87 (October 1987), 16-18.
2782. Nerlich, Uwe. "Arms Control and the Process of Political Change in Europe: Reordering Priorities of Western Security Policies." In: U. Nerlich, ed. *Soviet Power and Western Negotiating Policies, Vol II: The Western Panacea: Constraining Soviet Power Through Negotiation.* Cambridge, MA.: Ballinger, 1983. pp. 391-408.
2783. _____. "Nuclear Weapons and East-West Negotiation." In: C. Bertram, ed. *Arms Control and Military Force.* Adelphi Library, 3. Westmead, England: Gower, 1980. pp. 31-65.
2784. Nevin, John A. "Old Dogs and New Tricks: Disarmament and Alternatives to War." *Behaviorists for Social Action Journal,* 4:2 (1984), 8-10.
2785. Niezing, Johan. "On the History of Disarmament Negotiations: Some Sociological Comments." *International Spectator,* (July 8, 1969), 1237-1250.
2786. Nitze, Paul H. "Arms Control: The First Round in Geneva." *Department of State Bulletin,* 2100 (July 1985), 44-47.
2787. _____. "The Nuclear and Space Negotiations: Translating Promise to Progress." *Department of State Bulletin,* 88:2120 (March 1987), 29-32.
2788. _____. "The Nuclear and Space Arms Talks: Where We Are After the Summit." *Department of State Bulletin,* 2107 (February 1986), 58-60.
2789. _____. "Objectives of Arms Control." *Department of State Bulletin,* 85:2098 (May 1985), 57-63.

2790. _____. "Negotiating with the Soviets." *Department of State Bulletin*, 84:2089 (August 1984), 34-37.
2791. _____. "The Strategic Balance Between Hope and Skepticism." *Foreign Policy*, 1:17 (Winter 1974/75), 136-156.
2792. Nogee, Joseph L. "The Diplomacy of Disarmament." *International Conciliation*, 526 (January 1960), 235-303.
2793. _____. "The Neutralist World and Disarmament Negotiations." *American Academy of Political and Social Science, Annals*, 362 (1965), 71-80.
2794. Nye, Joseph S., and William L. Ury. "Approaches to Nuclear Risk Reduction." In: G. R. Winham, ed. *New Issues in International Crisis Management*. Boulder, CO.: Westview Press, 1988. pp. 150-170.
2795. _____. "Restarting Arms Control." *Foreign Policy*, 47 (Summer 1982), 98-113.
2796. Oberg, J. "Why Disarmament and Arms-Control Negotiations Will Fail and What Can Be Done." *Bulletin of Peace Proposals*, 14:3 (1983), 277-282.
2797. Orwant, Jack E. "Effects of Derogatory Attacks in Soviet Arms Control Propaganda." *Journalism Quarterly*, 49 (Spring 1972), 107-115.
2798. Osgood, C. E. "A Case for Graduated Unilateral Disengagement." *Bulletin of the Atomic Scientists*, 16 (1960), 127-131.
2799. Pierre, Andrew J. "Arms Sales: The New Diplomacy." *Foreign Affairs*, 60:2 (1981-82), 266-286.
2800. _____. "Nuclear Diplomacy: Britain, France and America." *Foreign Affairs*, 49 (January 1971), 283-301.
2801. Plous, S. "Disarmament, Arms Control, and Peace in the Nuclear Age - political Objectives and Relevant Research." *Journal of Social Issues*, 44:2 (1988), 133-154.
2802. Powell, Robert. "Crisis Bargaining, Escalation and MAD." *American Political Science Review*, 81:3 (September 1987), 717-736.
2803. Price, Charles C. "A Look at Disarmament." *Bulletin of the Atomic Scientists*, 14 (June 1958), 229-231.
2804. Ranger, Robin. "Arms Control Negotiations: Progress and Prospects." *Canadian Defence Quarterly*, 4 (Winter 1974), 16-25.
2805. Rathjens, G. W. "Are Arms-Control Negotiations Worthwhile." In: P. Albrecht and N. Koshy, eds. *Before Its Too Late: The Challenge of Nuclear Disarmament*. Geneva: World Council of Churches, 1983. pp. 270-277.
2806. _____. "Unilateral Initiatives for Limiting and Reducing Arms." In: W. Epstein and B. T. Feld, eds. *New Directions in Disarmament*. New York: Praeger, 1981. pp. 173-183.
2807. Reiss, Mitchell. "Learning from GATT: Lessons for Arms Control." *Arms Control*, 4:1 (May 1983), 40-48.
2808. Rose, William M. "MX as a Bargaining Chip." *Arms Control*, 5:1 (May 1984), 60-70.
2809. Rostow, Eugene V. "When are We Going in the Nuclear Arms Talks?" *Atlantic Community Quarterly*, 20:4 (Winter 1982-83), 349-359.
2810. _____. "Nuclear Arms Talks and the Future of Soviet - American Relations." *World Affairs Journal*, 1 (Fall 1982), 32-45.
2811. Ruehl, Lothar. "German Views on Armaments Control Issues and Negotiations Approaches." In: R. Avenhaus and R. K. Huber, eds. *Quantitative Assessment in Arms Control*. New York: Plenum Press, 1984. pp. 49-67.
2812. Sakamoto, Yoshikazu. "Lessons from 'Disarmament' Negotiations." In: R. Väyrynen, D. Senghaas and C. Schmidt, eds. *The Quest for Peace*. Beverly Hills, CA.: Sage, 1987. pp. 144-162.
2813. Sandole, Dennis J. D. "Towards a New Rationality." In: D. J. D. Sandole and I. Sandole-Staroste, eds. *Conflict Management and Problem Solving*. London: Frances Pinter, 1987. pp. 218-222.

2814. Schelling, Thomas C. "Communication, Bargaining and Negotiation." *Arms Control and National Security*, 1 (1969), 63-72.

2815. _____. "Deterrence: Military Diplomacy in the Nuclear Age." *Virginia Quarterly Review*, 39:4 (1963), 531-547.

2816. _____. "The Diplomacy of Violence." In: J. A. Copps, ed. *The Cost of Conflict*. Ann Arbor, MI.: Bureau of Business Research, University of Michigan, 1969. pp. 21-34.

2817. _____. "The Importance of Agreements." In: D. Carlton and C. Schaerf, eds. *The Dynamics of the Arms Race*. London: Croom Helm, 1975. pp. 67-77.

2818. _____., and Morton H. Halperin. "Negotiation and Agreement." In: E. W. Lefever, ed. *Arms and Arms Control*. New York: Praeger, 1962. pp. 187-198.

2819. _____. "Reciprocal Measures for Arms Stabilization." In: D. G. Brennan, ed. *Arms Control, Disarmament and National Security*. New York: Braziller, 1961. pp. 167-186.

2820. _____. "Signals and Feedback in the Arms Dialogue." *Bulletin of the Atomic Scientists*, 21 (January 1965), 5-10.

2821. _____. "The Role of Communication in Arms Control." In: E. Luard, ed. *First Steps to Disarmament*. London: Thames & Hudson, 1965. pp. 201-225.

2822. _____. "What Went Wrong With Arms Control?" *Foreign Affairs*, 64:2 (1985), 219-233.

2823. _____. "What Went Wrong in Arms Control?" In: O. Osternd, ed. *Studies of War and Peace*. Oslo: Norwegian University Press, 1986. pp. 90-109.

2824. Schneider, William P. "The Road to Geneva." *Strategic Review*, 13:4 (Fall 1985), 25-31.

2825. Schulte, G. "United States - Soviet Strategic Nuclear Negotiations." In: *Strategy for Peace*. Muscatine, IA.: Stanley Foundation, 1982. pp. 50-61.

2826. Seignious, George M. "Introduction: The Recent History of American-Soviet Arms Control Negotiations." In: W. G. Nichols and M. L. Boykin, eds. *Arms Control and Nuclear Weapons*. Contributions in Military Studies. No.59. Westport, CT.: Greenwood Press, 1987. pp. 1-8.

2827. Sharp, Jane M. O. "Bargaining Chips." *Foreign Service Journal*, 61:3 (March 1984), 30-35.

2828. Sherr, Alan B. "The Languages of Arms Control." *Bulletin of the Atomic Scientists*, 41:10 (1985), 23-29.

2829. Shulman, Marshall D. "An Alternative Policy for Managing U.S.-Soviet Relations." In: A. L. Horelick, ed. *U.S. - Soviet Relations: The Next Phase*. Ithaca, NY.: Cornell University Press, 1986. pp. 259-275.

2830. Shultz, George P. "Nuclear Weapons, Arms Control, and the Future of Deterrence." *Department of State Bulletin*, 87:2118 (June 1987), 31-35.

2831. Simes, D. K. "Diplomacy and Tactics." In: A. F. Neidle. *Nuclear Negotiations*. Austin, TX.: L.B.J. School of Public Affairs, 1982. pp. 108-112.

2832. Singer, Eugene. "A Bargaining Model for Disarmament Negotiations." *Journal of Conflict Resolution*, 7:1 (1963), 21-25.

2833. Singer, J. David. "Negotiations, Initiatives, and Arms Reductions." *Bulletin of Peace Proposals*, 15:4 (1984), 317-320.

2834. Sington, D. "How the Press Covers the Geneva Negotiations." *Disarmament and Arms Control*, 2:4 (1964), 441-448.

2835. Siracusa, Joseph M. "Nuclear Diplomacy, the Arms Race and Arms Control: From Truman to Reagan." *Australian Journal of Politics and History*, 29:1 (1983), 308-317.

2836. Smith, Gerard C. "Nuclear Negotiations - Comments." In: A. F. Neidle, ed. *Nuclear Negotiations*. Austin, TX.: L.B.J. School of Public Affairs, 1982. pp. 155-160.

2837. _____. "The Arms Control and Disarmament Agency: An Unfinished History." *Bulletin of the Atomic Scientists*, 40:4 (April 1984), 13-17.
2838. Smoke, Richard, and William L. Ury. "Beyond the Hot Line: Controlling Nuclear Crises." In: R. T. Scott, ed. *The Race for Security*. Lexington, MA.: Lexington Books, 1987. pp. 252-255.
2839. Smoker, P. "Trade, Defence and the Richardson Theory of Arms Race: A Seven Nation Study." *Journal of Peace Research*, 2 (1965), 161-176.
2840. Sohn, Louis B. "The Peacemaking Process." In: *Summer Study on Arms Control: Collected Papers*. Boston, MA.: American Academy of Arts and Sciences, 1960. pp. 293-296.
2841. _____. "Peaceful Settlement of Disputes and International Security." *Negotiation Journal*, 3 (1987), 155-166.
2842. Steinberg, Gerald M. "The Role of Process in Arms Control Negotiations." *Journal of Peace Research*, 22:3 (1985), 261-272.
2843. Steinbrunner, John. "Arms and the Art of Compromise." *Brookings Review*, 1:4 (Summer 1983), 6-13.
2844. Stephenson, Carolyn M. "Alternative Methods for International Security: A Review of the Literature." In: C. M. Stephenson, ed. *Alternative Methods for International Security*. Washington, D.C.: University Press of America, 1982. pp. 203-240.
2845. Straus, Donald B. "Nuclear Arms are a Nonissue - Let's Talk About Peace." *Negotiation Journal*, 2:3 (July 1986), 273-275.
2846. Strode, Dan L., and R. V. Strode. "Diplomacy and Defence in Soviet National Security Policy." *International Security*, 8:2 (1983), 91-116.
2847. Tower, J. G. "Arms Negotiations - Areas of Convergence and Divergence." In: R. K. German, ed. *The Future of US - USSR Relations*. Austin, TX.: L.B.J. School of Public Affairs, L.B.J. Library, 1986. pp. 31-38.
2848. "U.S. Arms Control Initiatives." *Department of State Bulletin*, 88 (May 1988), 26-30.
2849. "U.S. Arms Control Initiatives: An Update." *Department of State Bulletin*, 87 (July 1987), 27-29.
2850. Ury, William L. "Reflections on a Wild Idea." *Negotiation Journal*, 2:1 (January 1986), 5-9.
2851. Van Oerdenaren, John. "The Soviet Conception of Europe and Arms Negotiations." In: U. Nerlich, ed. *Soviet Power and Western Negotiating Policies, Vol 1.: Soviet Asset: Military Power in the Competition Over Europe*. Cambridge, MA.: Ballinger, 1983. pp. 161-194.
2852. Väyrynen, Raimo. "Prospects for Arms Limitation Talks: Negotiations, Asymmetrics and Neutral Countries." *Coexistence*, 9 (March 1972), 1-15.
2853. Verona, Sergiu. "The Geneva Disarmament Negotiations as a Learning Process." *Arms Control*, 1:1 (May 1980), 99-116.
2854. _____. "Structural Negotiating Blockages to Disarmament." *Bulletin of Peace Proposals*, 9:3 (1978), 200-209.
2855. Vicas, Alex G. "Negotiating Limitations on Weapons in Outer Space as a Bargaining Problem." *Arms Control*, (1985), 159-186.
2856. _____. "Negotiating Limitations on Weapons in Outer Space as a Bargaining Problem." In: N. Mateesco Matte, ed. *Arms Control and Disarmament in Outer Space*. Montreal, Que.: Centre for Research of Air and Space Law, McGill University, 1985. pp. 159-186.
2857. Viotti, Paul R. "Berlin and Conflict Management with the USSR." In: P. R. Viotti, ed. *Conflict and Arms Control*. Boulder, CO.: Westview Press, 1986. pp. 118-133.
2858. Vonmuller, A. A. C., and A. Karkoszka. "An East - West Negotiating Proposal." *Bulletin of the Atomic Scientists*, 44:7 (September 1988), 39-41.

2859. Wallach, John P. "A Walk in the Woods: Interview with Paul Nitze." *Washingtonian,* (January 1984), 61-77.
2860. Warnke, Paul C. "Arms Control Negotiations in a Cold Climate." *Technology Review,* 83:5 (1981), 72-74.
2861. _____. "Lessons Learned in Bilateral Negotiations." In: L. Sloss and M. Scott Davis, eds. *A Game of High Stakes.* Cambridge, MA.: Ballinger, 1986. pp. 55-62.
2862. _____. "Progress and Problems in Arms Control Negotiations." *Department of State Bulletin,* 77 (November 28, 1977), 772-777.
2863. Watson, Lorna. "A Brief History of Disarmament Negotiations." *Peace Research Reviews,* 1:2 (April 1967), 16-107.
2864. Weber, Steven, and Sidney Dell. "Attempts to Regulate Military Activities in Space." In: A. L. George, P. J. Farley and A. Dallin, eds. *U.S. - Soviet Security Cooperation.* New York: Oxford University Press, 1988. pp. 373-432.
2865. Wedge, Bryant. "A Marginal Contribution to a Safer World." In: D. J. D. Sandole and I. Sandole-Staroste, eds. *Conflict Management and Problem Solving.* London: Frances Pinter, 1987. pp. 208-209.
2866. Weiler, Lawrence D. "Secrecy in Arms Control Negotiations." In: A Platt and L. Weiler, eds. *Congress and Arms Control.* Boulder, CO.: Westview Press, 1978. pp. 157-184.
2867. Wessell, Nils H. "Soviet - American Arms Control Negotiations." *Current History,* 82:484 (1983), 210-214, 228-230.
2868. Wettig, Gerhard. "Pitfalls of Journalistic Reporting on Arms Control Negotiations with the USSR." *Aussenpolitik,* 37:2 (1986), 121-133.
2869. Windsor, Philip. "German Attitudes to Arms Control Negotiations." *The Council for Arms Control Bulletin,* 32 (May 1987), 1-3.
2870. Woolsey, R. James. "Chipping Away at the Bargains." In: F. A. Long and G. W. Ratjens, eds. *Arms, Defence Policy and Arms Control.* New York: N. W. Norton, 1976. pp. 175-186.
2871. _____. "Chipping Away at the Bargains." *Daedalus,* 104 (Summer 1975), 175-186.
2872. York, Herbert F. "U.S. - Soviet Negotiations and the Arms Race: A Historical Review." In: W. F. Hanrieder, ed. *Technology, Strategy and Arms Control.* Boulder, CO.: Westview Press, 1986. pp. 1-14.
2873. _____. "Negotiating from the Bottom Up." *Bulletin of the Atomic Scientists,* 39:8 (October 1983), 54-57.
2874. _____. "Bilateral Negotiations and the Arms Race." *Scientific American,* (October 1983), 149-160.
2875. Yost, David S. "Arms Control and European Security: An Overview of START, INF, MFBR, and CSCE/CDE." In: R. Avenhaus and R. K. Huber, eds. *Quantitative Assessment in Arms Control.* New York: Plenum Press, 1984. pp. 13-48.
2876. Young, Wayland. "Disarmament: Thirty Years of Failure." *International Security,* 2:3 (1978), 33-50.

3. Documents and Reports

2877. *Achieving Effective Arms Control: Recommendations, Background and Analysis: Report.* New York: Committee on International Arms Control and Security Affairs, Association of the Bar of the City of New York, 1985. 180p.
2878. Andemichael, Berhanykun. *The Non-Aligned States and International Organization: Participation in Disarmament Negotiations, 1960-1970.* Ph.D. Dissertation. New York: Columbia University, 1975. 446p.

2879. Bailey, Terrell W. *Inspection and Control of Nuclear Armaments in a Nation-State System: United States - Russian Disarmament Negotiations, 1945-1962.* Ph.D. Dissertation. Gainesville, FL.: University of Florida, 1963. 315p.
2880. Bok-Schoettle, Enid C. *Comprehensive Negotiating Strategies for Arms Control and Disarmament: A Preliminary Draft.* Minneapolis, MN.: Harold Scott Quigley Center of International Studies, University of Minnesota, 1973. 154p.
2881. Botti, Timothy J. *Anglo-American Atomic Negotiations, 1945-1955.* Ph.D. Dissertation. Columbus, OH.: Ohio State University, 1985. 345p.
2882. *Briefing Manual: A Collection of Materials on Nuclear Weapons and Arms Control.* Cambridge, MA.: Union of Concerned Scientists, 1983. 144p.
2883. Canada. Department of External Affairs. Information Division. *Mutual Security: Negotiations in 1983.* Toronto: Microlog, 1983. 3 fiches.
2884. Carnesale, Albert, and Richard N. Haass, eds. *Learning from Experience with Arms Control: A Final Report.* Washington, D.C.: U.S. Arms Control and Disarmament Agency, 1986. 462p.
2885. *Committee on Disarmament, 1962-1984: Meetings and Documents.* Frederick, MD.: University Publications of America, 1985. 30 Microfilm Reels with Printed Guide.
2886. Congressional Quarterly Service. *History of Disarmament in the Postwar Years: A Comprehensive Chronology of International Negotiations, Events, and Organizations.* Washington, D.C.: Congressional Quarterly Service, 1964. 17p.
2887. Davy, Grant R. *Canada's Role in the Disarmament Negotiations, 1946-1957.* Ph.D. Dissertation. Medford, MA.: Fletcher School of Law and Diplomacy, Tufts University, 1962.
2888. Dellermann, Frank J. "Soviet Negotiating Techniques in Arms Control Negotiations with the United States (1979)." In: *The Soviet Union: Special Studies, 1980-1982 Supplement.* Frederick, MD.: University Press of America, 1983. Reel II. pp. 0019-0578.
2889. _____. *Soviet Negotiating Techniques in Arms Control Negotiations with the United States.* Ph.D. Dissertation. Los Angeles, CA.: University of Southern California, 1979. 2 vols. 525p.
2890. *Documents on Disarmament, 1945-1982: A Collection from United States Arms Control and Disarmament Agency.* Frederick, MD.: University Publications of America, 1985. 11 reels & guide.
2891. Epstein, William. *Disarmament: Twenty-Five Years of Efforts.* Contemporary Affairs; 45. Toronto: Canadian Institute of International Affairs, 1971. 97p.
2892. Flynn, Gregory A. *European Security and the Divided Germany in the Era of Negotiations, 1969-72.* Ph.D. Dissertation. Medford, MA.: Fletcher School of Law and Diplomacy, Tufts University, 1975.
2893. Gard, Robert G. *Arms Control Policy Formulation and Negotiation, 1945-46.* Ph.D. Dissertation. Cambridge, MA.: Harvard University, 1962. 180p.
2894. George, Alexander L. *Towards a Soviet - American Crisis Prevention Regime: History and Prospects.* ACIS Working Paper No. 28. Los Angeles, CA.: Center for International and Strategic Affairs, University of California, 1980. 27p.
2895. Giblin, J. F. "Indian Ocean Naval Arms Limitation Talks: From a Zone of Peace to the Arc of Crisis (1984)." In: *Asia: Special Studies, 1982-1985 Supplement.* Frederick, MD.: University Publications of America, 1986. 521p.
2896. Goertemiller, John C. *An Examination of the Effect of External Influences on the Soviet Negotiation Position in Past 1962 Arms Control Agreements.* Fort Leavenworth, KS.: Army Command and General Staff College, 1978. 189p.

2897. Goldblat, Jozef. "The Role of the United Nations in Arms Control: An Assessment." In: UNITAR. *The United Nations and the Maintenance of International Peace and Security.* Dordrecht: M. Nijhoff, 1987. pp. 369-386.
2898. Helms, Robert F. *A Study of U.S. - U.S.S.R. Post 1962 Arms Control Negotiations.* Ph.D. Dissertation. Lawrence, KS.: University of Kansas, 1978. 346p.
2899. Hildreth, Steven A. "Arms Control: Negotiations to Limit Defence and Space Weapons." In: *Major Studies and Issue Briefs of the Congressional Research Service, 1986-1987 Supplement.* Frederick, MD.: University Publications of America, 1987. Reel VII; pp. 0396-0410.
2900. _____. "Arms Control: Negotiations to Reduce Strategic Offensive Nuclear Weapons." In: *Major Studies and Issue Briefs of the Congressional Research Service, 1986-1987 Supplement.* Frederick, MD.: University Publications of America, 1987. Reel VII; pp. 0411-0423.
2901. Hirschfeld, Thomas J., ed. *Intelligence and Arms Control: A Marriage of Convenience.* Austin, TX.: Lyndon B. Johnson School of Public Affairs, University of Texas, 1987. 100p.
2902. Holst, Johan J. *On How to Achieve Progress in Nuclear Arms Negotiations.* Oslo: Norwegian Institute of International Affairs, 1984. 19p.
2903. Hopmann, P. Terrence, and Charles Walcott. "Bargaining in Arms Control Negotiations." Paper Presented at the *15th Annual Convention of the International Studies Association,* held on March 20-23, 1974, in St.Louis.
2904. _____. _____. "The Bargaining Process in Arms Control Negotiations: An Experimental Analysis." Paper Presented at the *Tenth Annual North American Conference of the Peace Science Society (International),* held on November 13-14, 1972, in Philadelphia, PA.
2905. Ignatieff, George. "Negotiating Arms Limitation and Disarmament." In: Paper Presented at the *Proceedings of the Thirty-First Pugwash Conference on Science and World Affairs,* held on August 28 - September 2, 1981, in Banff, Alta. pp. 205-209.
2906. Jensen, Lloyd. *Postwar Disarmament Negotiations: A Study of American - Soviet Bargaining Behavior.* Ph.D. Dissertation. Ann Arbor, MI.: University of Michigan, 1963. 266p.
2907. _____. "Bargaining Strategies and Strategic Arms Limitations." Paper Presented at the *75th Annual Meeting of the American Political Science Association,* held on August 31 - September 3, 1979, in Washington, D.C.
2908. Johansen, Robert C. *The Politics of Arms Control: American Policy Making and Negotiating in 1957.* Ph.D. Dissertation. New York: Columbia University, 1968. 537p.
2909. Kampelman, Max M. *Three Years at the East - West Divide.* Perspectives on Freedom, Number 2. New York: Freedom House, 1983. 133p.
2910. Kapur, Raj K. *The Post-War Disarmament Negotiations 1946-63: A Study of the Narrowing of Differences Between East and West.* Ph.D. Dissertation. New York: New York University, 1984. 411p.
2911. Krause, Joachim. *Prospects for Conventional Arms Control in Europe.* Occasional Paper Series, 8. New York: Institute for East - West Security Studies, 1988. 86p.
2912. Kwieciak, Stanley. "Arms Control - Past, Present and Its Potential Usefulness in the Future (1983)." In: *Nuclear Weapons, Arms Control, and the Threat of Thermonuclear War: Special Studies: Second Supplement, 1983-1984.* Frederick, MD.: University Publications of America, 1985. Reel VI; 0712-0742.

2913. Lackman, William F., and Mark E. Miller. "The Issue of Forward Based Systems in Arms Control Negotiations (1976)." In: *Nuclear Weapons, Arms Control, and the Threat of Thermonuclear War: Special Studies, 1969-1981.* Frederick, MD.: University Publications of America, 1982. Reel VII: pp. 0084-0135.
2914. Lewis, Kevin N. *Could a Nuclear Arms Freeze be Negotiated.* RAND P-6817. Santa Monica, CA.: RAND Corporation, 1982. 20p.
2915. MacFarlane, S. N. *Moscow and Theatre Nuclear Weapons: Lessons for Geneva.* Issue Brief No. 2. Ottawa: Canadian Centre for Arms Control and Disarmament, 1985. 10p.
2916. Martin, Anthony D. *Negotiation Strategies for Arms Control: Some Alternatives for the Next Decade and Beyond.* Working Paper No. 10. Los Angeles, CA.: The California Arms Control and Foreign Policy Seminar, 1972. 38p.
2917. McNamara, Robert J., and Hans A. Bethe. *Reducing the Risk of Nuclear War: Geneva Can Be a Giant Step Toward a More Secure Twenty First Century.* Washington, D.C.: The Authors, 1985. 14p.
2918. Niezing, Johan. "History of the Disarmament Negotiations." In: *International Summer School on Disarmament and Arms Control: Proceedings of the Second Pugwash Conference.* Pavia, Italy: Pugwash, 1968. pp. 191-200.
2919. *Nuclear Weapons, Arms Control, and the Threat of Thermonuclear War: Special Studies, 1969-1981. Supplements, 1981-1982, 1983-1984, 1985-1986.* Frederick, MD.: University Publications of America, 1982-1987. 17+9+11+7 Microfilm Reels and Printed Guides.
2920. Nye, Joseph S., and William L. Ury. "Approaches to Nuclear Risk Reduction." Paper Presented at the *13th World Congress of the International Political Science Association,* held on July 15-20, 1985, in Paris.
2921. Pfaltzgraff, Robert L., and Jacquelyn K. Davis. *The Cruise Missile: Bargaining Chips or Defence Bargaining.* Cambridge, MA.: Institute for Foreign Policy Analysis, 1977. 53p.
2922. Planck, C. R. *Arms Control, Disarmament and Security in Europe: An Analysis of the Negotiations, 1955-1965.* Ph.D. Dissertation. Baltimore, MD.: Johns Hopkins University, 1968. 478p.
2923. Potter, William C. *A Guide to Simulating U.S.-Soviet Arms Control Negotiations.* CISA Working Paper No. 62. Los Angeles, CA.: Centre for International and Strategic Affairs, University of California, 1988. 38p.
2924. Rathjens, G. W., Abram Chayes and J. P. Ruina. *Nuclear Arms Control Agreements: Process and Impact.* Washington,D.C.: Carnegie Endowment for International Peace, 1974. 72p.
2925. Rose, William M. *Bargaining Tactics for Arms Control: A Theoretical and Historical Analysis.* Ph.D. Dissertation. Berkeley, CA.: University of California at Berkeley, 1984. 323p.
2926. Schaefer, Henry W. *Nuclear Arms Control: The Process of Developing Positions.* Washington, D.C.: National Defence University Press, 1986. 103p.
2927. Schneider, William P. "The Soviet Military Industrial Complex and Arms Control Talks (1971)." In: *Nuclear Weapons, Arms Control, and the Threat of Thermonuclear War: Special Studies: 1969-1981.* Frederick, MD.: University Publications of America, 1982. Reel III: 0305-0331.
2928. Shipler, David K. "Soviet - American Misperceptions and Policy Implications." Paper Presented at the *28th Annual Convention of the International Studies Association,* held on April 14-18, 1987, in Washington, D.C.
2929. Sims, Jennifer E. *The Development of American Arms Control Thought, 1945-1960.* Ph.D. Dissertation. Baltimore, MD.: Johns Hopkins University, 1986. 461p.

2930. Slocombe, Walter. "Verification and Negotiation." In: *The Nuclear Weapons Freeze and Arms Control: Proceedings of a Symposium held at the American Academy of Arts and Sciences, January 13-15, 1983.* Cambridge, CA.: Center for Science and International Affairs, John F. Kennedy School of Government, Harvard University, 1983. pp. 80-87.
2931. Sohn, Louis B. *Peaceful Settlement of Disputes and International Security.* Working Paper Series - 2. Cambridge, MA.: The Program on the Processes of International Negotiation, American Academy of Arts and Sciences, 1987. 19p.
2932. "Soviet Intentions and Tactics in East-West Disarmament Negotiations (1960)." In: U.S. State Department Intelligence and Research Reports. *The Soviet Union: 1950-1961 Supplement.* Washington, D.C.: University Publications of America, 1979. Reel VI; pp. 40-62.
2933. Steinberg, Gerald M. *The Legitimization of Reconnaissance Satellites: An Example of Informal Arms Control Negotiation.* Ph.D. Dissertation. Ithaca, NY.: Cornell University, 1981. 328p.
2934. Stockholm International Peace Research Institute. SIPRI. *Arms Control: A Survey and Appraisal of Multilateral Agreements.* London: Taylor & Francis, 1978. 238p.
2935. Talbott, Strobe. *U.S. - Soviet Nuclear Arms Control: Where We Are and How We Got Here.* Santa Monica, CA.: RAND/UCLA Center for the Study of Soviet International Behavior, 1985. 15p.
2936. Tangredi, Sam J. "Negotiation from Weakness: Achieving National Security Objectives from a Position of Strategic Inferiority (1985)." In: *Nuclear Weapons, Arms Control, and the Threat of Thermonuclear War: Special Studies: Third Supplement, 1985-1986.* Frederick, MD.: University Publications of America, 1987. Reel VI;0393-0540.
2937. _____. *Negotiation from Weakness: Achieving National Security Objectives from a Position of Strategic Inferiority.* M.A. Thesis. Monterey, CA.: Naval Postgraduate School, 1985. 151p.
2938. Tucker, Michael J. *Canada's Role in the Disarmament Negotiations: 1957-1971.* Ph.D. Dissertation. Toronto: University of Toronto, 1977.
2939. "U.S.-Soviet Strategic Nuclear Negotiations." In: *Strategy for Peace: Twenty--Third Annual U.S. Foreign Policy Conference Report, October 15-17, 1982.* Muscatine, IA.: The Stanley Foundation, 1982. pp. 50-58.
2940. United Nations. General Assembly. Disarmament Commission. *Negotiations on Nuclear Disarmament: Working Paper.* New York: United Nations, 1987. 7p.
2941. United States.Arms Control and Disarmament Agency. *Arms Control and Disarmament Agreements: Texts and Histories of Negotiations, 1980.* Publication 105. Washington, D.C.: U.S. Government Printing Office, 1980. 238p.
2942. _____._____. *Arms Control and Disarmament Agreements: Texts and Histories of Negotiations, 1982.* Washington, D.C.: U.S. Government Printing Office, 1982. 289p.
2943. _____._____. *Arms Control and Disarmament Agreements: Texts and History of Negotiations.* Publication 77. Washington, D.C.: U.S. Government Printing Office, 1975. 159p.
2944. _____._____. *Arms Control: U.S. Objectives, Negotiating Efforts and Problems of Soviet Non-Compliance.* Washington, D.C.: U.S. Government Printing Office, 1984. 12p.
2945. _____.Congress.House.Committee on Armed Services. *Arms Control and Disarmament Activities: Hearings.* 98th Cong., 1st sess. Washington, D.C.: U.S. Government Printing Office, 1984. 238p.

2946. ____.____.____.____. *MX Missile and the Strategic Defence Initiative - Their Implications on Arms Control Negotiations.* 99th Cong., 1st sess. Washington, D.C.: U.S. Government Printing Office, 1985. 285p.

2947. ____.____.____.____.Subcommittee on Procurement and Military Nuclear Systems. *Review of Arms Control and Disarmament Activities: 98th Congress: Report No. 23.* 98th Cong., 2nd sess. Washington, D.C.: U.S. Government Printing Office, 1984. 65p.

2948. ____.____.____.Committee on Foreign Affairs.Subcommittee on Arms Control, International Security and Science. *Fundamentals of Nuclear Arms Control, Part 1 - Nuclear Arms Control: A Brief Historical Survey.* 99th Cong., 1st sess. Washington, D.C.: U.S. Government Printing Office, 1985. 41p.

2949. ____.____.____.____.____. *Fundamentals of Nuclear Arms Control: CRS Reports.* 99th Cong., 2nd sess. Washington, D.C.: U.S. Government Printing Office, 1986. 424p.

2950. ____.____.____.____.Subcommittee on National Security Policy and Scientific Developments. *Arms Control and Disarmament Agency: Hearings.* 93rd Cong., 2nd sess. Washington, D.C.: U.S. Government Printing Office, 1975. 241p.

2951. ____.____.Senate.Arms Control Observer Group. *Arms Control Negotiations with the Soviet Union in Geneva, Switzerland, March 9-12, 1985 - Report.* 99th Cong., 1st sess. Washington, D.C.: U.S. Government Printing Office, 1985. 42p.

2952. ____.____.____.Committee on Armed Services. *Arms Control Policy, Planning and Negotiating: Hearings.* 97th Cong., 1st sess. Washington, D.C.: U.S. Government Printing Office, 1983. 123p.

2953. ____.____.____.Committee on Foreign Relations. *Arms Control Overview: Hearings.* 98th Cong., 2nd sess. Washington, D.C.: U.S. Government Printing Office, 1984. 109p.

2954. ____.____.____.____.Subcommittee on Arms Control, Oceans, International Operations, and Environment. *Arms Control and the Militarization of Space: Hearings.* 97th Cong., 2nd sess. Washington, D.C.: U.S. Government Printing Office, 1983. 69p.

2955. ____.____.____.____.Subcommittee on Disarmament. *Control and Reduction of Armaments: A Decade of Negotiations, 1946-1956.* Staff Study, No. 3. Washington, D.C.: U.S. Government Printing Office, 1956. 22p.

2956. ____.____.____.____.____. *Disarmament and Security: A Collection of Documents, 1919-1955.* 84th Cong., 2nd sess. Washington, D.C.: U.S. Government Printing Office, 1956. 1035p.

2957. ____.____.____.Select Committee on Intelligence. *Principal Negotiations: Hearings.* 95th Cong., 1st sess. Washington, D.C.: U.S. Government Printing Office, 1977. 75p.

2958. Voas, Jeanette. "The Geneva Negotiations on Space and Nuclear Arms: Soviet Positions and Perspectives." In: *Major Studies and Issue Briefs of the Congressional Research Service, 1986-1987 Supplement.* Frederick, MD.: University Publications of America, 1987. Reel VII; pp. 0228-0268.

2959. Vogele, William B. "Negotiating Arms Control Agreements: The Conditions for Success in U.S. - Soviet Arms Control Negotiations, 1954-1980." Paper Presented at the *1986 Annual Meeting of the American Political Science Association,* held in 1986, in Washington, D.C.

2960. ____. *Negotiating Arms Control Agreements: Explaining Success in U.S. - Soviet Arms Control.* Ph.D. Dissertation. Waltham, MA.: Brandeis University, 1987. 402p.

2961. Weiler, Lawrence D. *The Arms Race, Secret Negotiations and the Congress.* Occasional Paper No. 12. Muscatine, IA.: The Stanley Foundation, 1976. 40p.

2962. Zoppo, Ciro E. *Technical and Political Aspects of Arms Control Negotiation: The 1958 Experts' Conference.* RAND RM-3286-ARPA. Santa Monica, CA.: RAND Corporation, 1962. 114p.

B. TEST BAN NEGOTIATIONS

1. Books

2963. Dean, Arthur H. *Test Ban and Disarmament: The Path of Negotiation.* New York: Harper & Row, 1966. 153p.
2964. Jacobson, Harald K., and Erick Stein. *Diplomats, Scientists, and Politicians: The United States and the Nuclear Test Ban Negotiations.* Ann Arbor, MI.: University of Michigan Press, 1966. 538p.
2965. Jönsson, Christer. *Soviet Bargaining Behavior: The Nuclear Test Ban Case.* New York: Columbia University Press, 1979. 266p.
2966. _____. *The Soviet Union and the Test Ban: A Study in Soviet Negotiating Behavior.* Lund: Studentlitteratur, 1975. 221p.
2967. Seaborg, Glenn T., and Benjamin S. Loeb. *Kennedy, Khrushchev and the Test Ban.* Berkeley, CA.: University of California of Berkeley, 1981. 320p.
2968. Terchek, Ronald J. *The Making of the Test Ban Treaty.* The Hague: Martinus Nijhoff, 1970. 211p.

2. Journal Articles

2969. Ahmed, M. Samir. "The Role of Neutrals in the Geneva Negotiations." *Disarmament and Arms Control,* 1:1 (1963), 20-32.
2970. Bargman, Abraham. "The Study of Test Ban and Disarmament Conferences: A Review." *Journal of Conflict Resolution,* 11:2 (1967), 223-234.
2971. Blechman, Barry M. "The Comprehensive Test Ban Negotiations: Can They Be Revitalized?" In: R. T. Scott, ed. *The Race for Security.* Lexington, MA.: Lexington Books, 1987. pp. 208-218.
2972. Bull, Hedley. "The Arms Race and the Banning of Nuclear Tests." *Political Quarterly,* 30 (October 1959), 344-356.
2973. Daalder, Ivo H. "The Limited Test Ban Treaty." In: A. Carnesale and R. N. Haas, eds. *Super Power Arms Control.* Cambridge, MA.: Ballinger, 1987. pp. 9-40.
2974. Doty, Paul. "A Nuclear Test Ban." *Foreign Affairs,* 65:4 (Spring 1987), 750-769.
2975. Gehron, William J. "Geneva Conference on the Discontinuance of Nuclear Weapons Tests: History of Political and Technical Developments of the Negotiations from October 31 , 1958 to August 22, 1960." *Department of State Bulletin,* (September 26, 1960), 482-497.
2976. Greb, G. A., and W. Heckrotte. "Comprehensive Test Ban Negotiations." In: D. H. Hafemeister and D. Schroeder, eds. *Physics Technology and the Arms Race.* New York: American Institute of Physics, 1983. pp. 216-229.
2977. _____. "Survey of Past Nuclear Test Ban Negotiations: Paper 6." In: J. Goldblat and D. Cox, eds. *Nuclear Weapon Tests: Prohibition and Limitation.* Stockholm: SIPRI, 1988. pp. 95-117.
2978. Harriman, W. Averell. "Negotiating a Limited Treaty for Banning Nuclear Tests." *Department of State Bulletin,* (August 19, 1963), 278-283.
2979. Hopmann, P. Terrence, and Theresa L. Smith. "An Application of a Richardson Process Model: Soviet - American Interactions in the Test Ban Negotiations, 1962-1963." *Journal of Conflict Resolution,* 21:4 (1977), 701-726.

2980. _____. "An Application of a Richardson Process Model: Soviet - American Interactions in the Test Ban Negotiations, 1962-1963." In: I. W. Zartman, ed. *The Negotiation Process.* Beverly Hills, CA.: Sage, 1978. pp. 149-174.
2981. _____., and Timothy D. King. "Interactions and Perceptions in the Test Ban Negotiations." *International Studies Quarterly,* 20 (March 1976), 105-142.
2982. _____. "Internal and External Influences on Bargaining in Arms Control Negotiations: The Partial Test Ban." In: B. M. Russett, ed. *Peace, War and Numbers.* Beverly Hills, CA.: Sage, 1972. pp. 213-237.
2983. Jack, Homer A. "Nonalignment and a Test Ban Agreement: The Role of the Nonaligned States." *Journal of Arms Control,* 1:4 (1963), 636-646.
2984. _____. "Nonalignment and A Test Ban Agreement: The Role of the Nonaligned States." *Journal of Conflict Resolution,* 7:3 (1963), 542-552.
2985. Jacobson, Harald K. "The Test Ban Negotiation: Implications for the Future." *Annals of the American Academy of Political and Social Science,* 351 (January 1964), 92-101.
2986. Jensen, Lloyd. "Approach - Avoidance Bargaining in the Test Ban Negotiations." *International Studies Quarterly,* 12 (1968), 152-160.
2987. Kapur, Ashok. "Evaluating the Progress of Test Ban Negotiations." *International Perspective,* (January 1979), 29-33.
2988. Kissinger, Henry A. "Nuclear Testing and the Problem of Peace." *Foreign Affairs,* 37 (October 1958), 1-18.
2989. Kriesberg, Louis. "Noncoercive Inducements in U.S. - Soviet Conflicts: Ending the Occupation of Austria and Nuclear Weapons Tests." *Journal of Political and Military Sociology,* 9 (1981), 1-16.
2990. Medalia, Jonathan E. "Problems in Formulating and Implementing Effective Arms Control Policy: The Nuclear Test Ban Treaty Case." *Stanford Journal of International Studies,* 7 (Spring 1972), 132-161.
2991. Neidle, Allan F. "Nuclear Test Bans: History and Future Prospects." In: A. L. George, P. J. Farley and A. Dallin, eds. *U.S. - Soviet Security Cooperation.* New York: Oxford University Press, 1988. pp. 175-214.
2992. "Nuclear Test Negotiation." *World Today,* 19:3 (1963), 95-97.
2993. Pomerance, Josephine W. "The Cuban Crisis and the Test Ban Negotiations." *Journal of Arms Control,* 1:4 (1963), 647-653.
2994. _____. "The Cuban Crisis and the Test Ban Negotiations." *Journal of Conflict Resolution,* 7:3 (1963), 553-559.
2995. Rao, M. V. Subba. "Diplomatic Background of the Test Ban Treaties." *United Asia,* 18:1 (1966), 34-41.
2996. Scott, Richard. "A Ban on Nuclear Tests: The Course of Negotiations, 1958-1962." *International Affairs (London),* 38 (October 1962), 501-510.
2997. Tucker, Michael J. "Canada and the Test Ban Negotiations, 1955-71." In: K. R. Nossal, ed. *An Acceptance of Paradox: Essays on Canadian Diplomacy in Honour of John W. Holmes.* Toronto: Canadian Institute of International Affairs, 1982. pp. 115-140.

3. Documents and Reports

2998. Ahmed, M. Samir. *The Neutrals and the Test Ban Negotiations: An Analysis of the Non-Aligned Efforts Between 1962-1963.* Occasional Paper, No. 4. New York: Carnegie Endowment for International Peace, 1967. 120p.
2999. Hsieh, Alice L. *The Chinese Genie: Peking's Role in the Nuclear Test Ban Negotiations.* RAND P-2022. Santa Monica, CA.: RAND Corporation, 1960. 21p.

3000. King, Timothy D. *Role Reversal and Problem Solving in International Negotiations: The Partial Nuclear Test Ban Case.* Ph.D. Dissertation. Minneapolis, MN.: University of Minnesota, 1978. 310p.
3001. _____. "Role Reversal in International Negotiations: The Partial Test Ban Case." Paper Presented at the *17th Annual Convention of the International Studies Association,* held in February 25-29, 1976, in Toronto.
3002. Lambert, Robert W. *Review of International Negotiations on the Cessation of Nuclear Weapons Tests, Sept. 1962 - Sept. 1965.* Publication no. 32. Washington, D.C.: U.S. Arms Control and Disarmament Agency, 1966. 103p.
3003. United States. Arms Control and Disarmament Agency. *International Negotiations on Ending Nuclear Weapons Tests, September 1961 - September 1962.* ACDA Publication No. 9. Washington, D.C.: U.S. Government Printing Office, 1962. 333p.
3004. _____.Congress.House.Committee on Armed Services.Subcommittee on Intelligence and Military Applications of Nuclear Energy. *Current Negotiations on the Comprehensive Test-Ban Treaty (CTBT): Hearings.* Committee Serial No. 95-62. 95th Cong., 2nd sess. Washington, D.C.: U.S. Government Printing Office, 1978. 146p.
3005. _____._____.Senate.Committee on Foreign Relations. *Renewed Geneva Disarmament Negotiations: Hearings.* 87th Cong., 2nd sess. Washington, D.C.: U.S. Government Printing Office, 1962.
3006. _____._____._____._____. *Strategic Arms Limitations and Comprehensive Test Ban Negotiations: A Report by Senator Frank Church.* 95th Cong., 2nd sess. Washington, D.C.: U.S. Government Printing Office, 1978. 13p.
3007. _____._____._____._____. *Test Ban Negotiations and Disarmament: Hearings.* 88th Cong., 1st sess. Washington, D.C.: U.S. Government Printing Office, 1963. 50p.
3008. _____._____._____._____. *Conference on Discontinuance of Nuclear Weapons Tests, Analysis of Progress and Positions of Participating Parties, October 1958 - August 1960: Hearings.* 86th Cong., 2nd sess. Washington, D.C.: U.S. Government Printing Office, 1960. 110p.
3009. _____._____._____._____. *Nuclear Test Ban Treaty: Hearings.* 88th Cong., 1st sess. Washington, D.C.: U.S. Government Printing Office, 1963. 1028p.
3010. _____._____._____._____. *Technical Problems and Geneva Test Ban Negotiations: Hearings.* 86th Cong., 2nd sess. Washington, D.C.: U.S. Government Printing Office, 1960. 85p.
3011. _____._____._____._____. *Testimony of John McCone on Geneva Test Ban Negotiations: Hearings.* 86th Cong., 1st sess. Washington, D.C.: U.S. Government Printing Office, 1959. 32p.
3012. _____._____._____._____.Subcommittee on Arms Control, International Law and Organization. *To Promote Negotiations for Comprehensive Test Ban Treaty: Hearing.* 93rd Cong,. 1st sess. Washington, D.C.: U.S. Government Printing Office, 1973. 155p.
3013. _____.Department of State. *Geneva Conference on the Discontinuance of Nuclear Weapons Tests: History of Political and Technical Developments of Negotiations, October 31, 1958 - August 22, 1960.* Publication 7090. Washington, D.C.: U.S. Government Printing Office, 1960. 16p.
3014. _____._____. *Geneva Conference on the Discontinuance of Nuclear Weapons Tests: History and Analysis of Negotiations.* Publication 7258. Washington, D.C.: U.S. Government Printing Office, 1961. 641p.
3015. Zoppo, Ciro E. *The Issue of Nuclear Test Cessation at the London Disarmament Conference of 1957: A Study in East - West Negotiation.* RAND RM-2821-ARPA. Santa Monica, CA.: RAND Corporation, 1961. 96p.

3016. _____. *The Test Ban: A Study in Arms Control Negotiation.* Ph.D. Dissertation. New York: Columbia University, 1963. 572p.

C. SALT NEGOTIATIONS

1. Books

3017. Calvo-Goller, Notburga K., and Michael A. Calvo. *The SALT Agreements: Content - Application - Verification.* Dordrecht: Martinus Nijhoff, 1987. 427p.
3018. Johnson, V. Alexis, and Jef O. McAllister. *The Right Hand of Power.* Englewood Cliffs, NJ.: Prentice-Hall, 1984. 634p.
3019. Kaplan, Morton A. *SALT: Problems and Prophets.* Morristown, NJ.: General Learning Press, 1973. 251p.
3020. Kintner, William R., and Robert L. Pfaltzgraff, eds. *SALT: Implications for Arms Control in the 1970's.* Pittsburgh, PA.: Pittsburgh University Press, 1973. 447p.
3021. Newhouse, John. *Cold Dawn: The Story of SALT.* New York: Holt, Rinehart and Winston, 1973. 302p.
3022. Payne, Samuel B. *The Soviet Union and SALT.* Cambridge, MA.: MIT Press, 1980. 155p.
3023. Smith, Gerard C. *DoubleTalk: The Story of SALT I.* Garden City, NY.: Doubleday, 1980. 556p.
3024. Talbott, Strobe. *Endgame: The Inside Story of SALT II.* New York: Harper & Row, 1979. 319p.
3025. Willrich, Mason, and John B. Rhinelander. *SALT: The Moscow Agreements and Beyond.* New York: The Free Press, 1974. 361p.
3026. Wolfe, Thomas W. *The SALT Experience.* Cambridge, MA.: Ballinger, 1979. 405p.

2. Journal Articles

3027. Bennett, Andrew. "The Accidents Measures Agreement." In: A. Carnesale and R. N. Haass, eds. *Superpower Arms Control.* Cambridge, MA.: Ballinger, 1987. pp. 41-64.
3028. Bertram, Christoph. "SALT II and the Dynamics of Arms Control." *International Affairs,* (October 1979), 565-573.
3029. Bloomfield, Beth. "Strategic Arms Limitations." *Proceedings of the Academy of Political Science,* 32:4 (1977), 184-194.
3030. Booth, Kenneth. "The Strategic Arms Limitation Talks: A Stocktaking." *World Survey,* 73 (January 1975), 1-17.
3031. Bowie, Robert R. "The Bargaining Aspects of Arms Control: The SALT Experience." In: W. R. Kintner and R. L. Pfaltzgraff, eds. *SALT: Implications for Arms Control in the 1970's.* Pittsburgh, PA.: Pittsburgh University Press, 1973. pp. 127-139.
3032. Brennan, D. G. "The Soviet Military Build-Up and Implications for the Negotiations of Strategic Arms Limitations." *Orbis,* 21:1 (1977), 107-120.
3033. Bressler, Robert J., and Robert C. Gray. "The Bargaining Chip and SALT." *Political Science Quarterly,* 92:1 (Spring 1977), 65-88.

3034. Bruha, Thomas. "Strategic Arms Limitation Talks (SALT)." In: R. Bernhardt, ed. *Encyclopedia of Public International Law, Instalment 9: International Relations and Legal Cooperation in General Diplomacy and Consular Relations*. Amsterdam: North-Holland, 1986. pp. 362-367.
3035. Bull, Hedley. "Strategic Arms Limitation: The Precedent of the Washington and London Naval Treaties." In: M. A. Kaplan, ed. *SALT: Problems and Prospects*. Morriston, NJ.: General Learning Process, 1973. pp. 26-52.
3036. Calogero, Francesco. "A Scenario for Effective SALT Negotiations." *Bulletin of the Atomic Scientists*, 29 (June 1973), 16-22.
3037. Clemens, Walter C. "Nicholas II to SALT II: Continuity and Change in East-West Diplomacy." *International Affairs (London)*, 49 (July 1973), 385-401.
3038. Cook, Don. "Toward a New Congress of Vienna? SALT in Old Wounds." *Encounter*, 25 (September 1970), 53-60.
3039. Costello, Mary. "Politics of Strategic Arms Negotiations." *Editorial Research Reports*, (May 13, 1977), 349-372.
3040. Cutler, Lloyd N., and Roger C. Molander. "Is There Life After Death for SALT?" *International Security*, 6:2 (Fall 1981), 3-20.
3041. Doty, Paul. "Strategic Arms Limitation After SALT I." *Daedalus*, 104:3 (June 1975), 63-74.
3042. Dougherty, James E. "SALT and the Future of International Politics." In: W. R. Kintner and R. L. Pfaltzgraff, ed. *SALT: Implications for Arms Control in the 1970's*. Pittsburgh, PA.: Pittsburgh University Press, 1973. pp. 337-367.
3043. "Dynamics of the Bargaining Process in a Bureaucratic Age (Symposium and Discussion)." In: W. R. Kintner and R. L. Pfaltzgraff, eds. *SALT: Implications for Arms Control in the 1970's*. Pittsburgh, PA.: Pittsburgh University Press, 1973. pp. 187-196.
3044. Feld, Bernard T. "The Geneva Negotiations on General and Complete Disarmament." In: S. Melman, ed. *Disarmament: Its Politics and Economics*. Boston, MA.: American Academy of Arts and Sciences, 1962. pp. 7-17.
3045. Flanagan, Stephen J. "SALT II." In: A. Carnesale and R. N. Haas, eds. *Superpower Arms Control*. Cambridge, MA.: Ballinger, 1987. pp. 105-138.
3046. Frye, A. "Decision - Making for SALT." In: M. Willrich and J. Rhinelander, eds. *SALT: The Moscow Agreements and Beyond*. New York: The Free Press, 1974. pp. 66-100.
3047. Garthoff, Raymond L. "Negotiating SALT." *Wilson Quarterly*, 1:5 (1977), 76-85.
3048. _____. "Negotiating with the Russians: Some Lessons from SALT." *International Security*, 1 (1977), 3-24.
3049. _____. "Objectives and Negotiations Strategy." In: L. Sloss and M. Scott Davis, eds. *A Game for High Stakes*. Cambridge, MA.: Ballinger, 1986. pp. 73-78.
3050. _____. "SALT and the Soviet Military." *Problem of Communism*, 24 (1975), 21-37.
3051. _____. "SALT I: An Evaluation." *World Politics*, 31 (October 1978), 1-25.
3052. Gharekhan, C. D. "Strategic Arms Limitation Talks - II." *India Quarterly*, 26 (October - December 1970), 389-411.
3053. Gray, Colin S. "The End of SALT? Purpose and Strategy in U.S. - U.S.S.R. Negotiations." *Policy Review*, 2 (Fall 1977), 31-45.
3054. _____. "SALT: Time to Quit." *Strategic Review*, 4:4 (1976), 14-22.
3055. Greb, G. A., and Gerald W. Johnson. "A History of Strategic Arms Limitation." *Bulletin of the Atomic Scientists*, 40:1 (1984), 30-37.
3056. Hampson, Fen Osler. "SALT I: Interim Agreement and ABM Treaty. In: A. Carnesale and R. N. Haass, eds. *Superpower Arms Control*. Cambridge, MA.: Ballinger, 1987. pp. 65-104.

3057. Hardt, D. Brent. "The Prophet as Statesman: Henry Kissinger, SALT and the Soviet Union." *Fletcher Forum*, 8 (Winter 1984), 117-146.
3058. Holst, Johan J. "SALT and East - West Relations in Europe." In: N. Andren and K. E. Birnbaum, eds. *Beyond Detente: Prospects for East-West Co-operation and Security in Europe.* Leyden: A. W. Sijthoff, 1976. pp. 99-122.
3059. Hoover, Robert A. "Strategic Arms Limitation Negotiations and U.S. Decision Making." In: W. F. Hanrieder, ed. *Technology, Strategy and Arms Control.* Boulder, CO.: Westview Press, 1986. pp. 93-114.
3060. Hyland, William G. "Commentary: SALT and Soviet-American Relations." *International Security*, 3 (Fall 1978), 156-162.
3061. Jensen, Lloyd. "Evaluating U.S. SALT Bargaining Strategies." *Intellect*, 106 (August 1977), 26, 28-29.
3062. _____. "Negotiating Strategic Arms Control." *Journal of Conflict Resolution*, 8:3 (July 1982), 159-170.
3063. _____. "Negotiating Strategic Arms Control, 1969-1979." *Journal of Conflict Resolution*, 28:3 (September 1984), 535-559.
3064. Jonas, Anne M. " The SALT Negotiations: Keeping Hope in Line with Reality." *Air Force and Space Digest*, 53 (March 1970), 39-42.
3065. Joshua, Wynfred. "SALT and the Middle East." In: W. R. Kintner and R. L. Pfaltzgraff, eds. *SALT: Implications for Arms Control in the 1970's.* Pittsburgh, PA.: Pittsburgh University Press, 1973. pp. 237-252.
3066. Kintner, William R. "Arms Control for a Five-Power World." In: W. R. Kintner and R. L. Pfaltzgraff, eds. *SALT: Implications for Arms Control in the 1970's.* Pittsburgh, PA.: Pittsburgh University Press, 1973. pp. 167-186.
3067. _____., and Robert L. Pfaltzgraff. "Assessing the Moscow SALT Agreements." *Orbis*, 6 (Summer 1972), 341-360.
3068. Makins, Christopher J. "The Superpower's Dilemma: Negotiating in the Nuclear Age." *Survival*, 27:4 (July/August 1985), 169-178.
3069. Muravchik, Joshua. "Expectations of SALT I: Lessons for the SALT III." *World Affairs*, 143:3 (Winter 1980-1981), 278-297.
3070. Newhouse, John. "Annals of Diplomacy: SALT I - the Labyrinth." *New Yorker*, 49 (May 5, 1973), 44-50,52,54,57-58,60,62-63,69-72,74-75,78-79.
3071. _____. "Annals of Diplomacy: SALT II - A Weapon in Search of a Role." *New Yorker*, 49 (May 12, 1973), 79-80,85-90,93-94,96,99-100,102,104-108,110,-112-117
3072. _____. "Annals of Diplomacy: SALT III - A Simple, Clear Proposal." *New Yorker*, 49 (May 19, 1973), 87-90,93-114.
3073. _____. "Annals of Diplomacy: SALT IV - The Back Channel." *New Yorker*, 49 (May 26, 1973), 76-78,80,82,84-110.
3074. _____. "Annals of Diplomacy: SALT V - at the Summit." *New Yorker*, 49 (June 2, 1973), 68,70,72-101.
3075. _____. "Talk About Talks." *New Yorker*, 60:46 (December 31, 1984), 40-52.
3076. Nitze, Paul H. "SALT: The Strategic Balance Between Hope and Skepticism." *Foreign Policy*, 17 (Winter, 1974-75), 136-156.
3077. _____. "The Vladivostok Accord and SALT II." *Review of Politics*, 37 (April 1975), 147-160.
3078. Pierre, Andrew J. "The Diplomacy of SALT." *International Security*, 5:1 (1980), 178-197.
3079. Platt, Alan. "Starting on SALT III." *Washington Quarterly*, 5:2 (Spring 1982), 17-24.
3080. Podlesni, P. T. "The Importance of the SALT Negotiations." In: P. Albrecht and N. Koshy, eds. *Before its Too Late: The Challenge of Nuclear Disarmament.* Geneva: World Council of Churches, 1983. pp. 257-263.

3081. Prince, Howard T. "SALT, National Security and International Politics." *Journal of International and Comparative Studies*, 4 (Winter 1971), 14-27.
3082. Rice, Condoleeza. "SALT and the Search for a Security Regime." In: A. L. George, P. J. Farley and A. Dallin, eds. *U.S. - Soviet Security Cooperation*. New York: Oxford University Press, 1988. pp. 293-306.
3083. Rowen, Henry S. "Objectives and Disfunctions of Arms Negotiations: The SALT Experience." In: U. Nerlich, ed. *Soviet Power and Western Negotiating Processes, Vol II.: The Western Panacea: Constraining Soviet Power Through Negotiations*. Cambridge, MA.: Ballinger, 1983. pp. 55-66.
3084. "The SALT Process and Its Use in Regulating Mobile ICBM's." *Yale Law Journal*, 84 (April 1975), 1078-1100.
3085. "The SALT Process: The Global Stakes." *Development*, 1 (1982), 21-27.
3086. Scoville, Herbert. "The SALT Negotiations." *Scientific American*, (August 1977), 24-31.
3087. Seignious, George M. "The Soviets are Though Negotiators." *Armed Forces Journal International*, 117 (August 1979), 34-40.
3088. Selin, Ivan. "Looking Ahead to SALT III." *International Security*, 5:3 (Winter 1980/81), 171-185.
3089. Sharp, Jane M. O. "Confidence Building Measures and SALT." *Arms Control*, 3:1 (May 1982), 37-61.
3090. _____. "Restructuring the SALT Dialogue." *International Security*, 6:3 (Winter 1981/82), 144-176.
3091. Smith, Gerard C. "Negotiating at SALT." *Survival*, 20 (May/June 1977), 117-120.
3092. _____. "Negotiating with the Soviets." *New York Times Magazine*, (February 27, 1977), 18-19, 26.
3093. _____. "SALT After Vladivostok." *Journal of International Affairs*, 29 (Spring 1975), 7-18.
3094. Smith, Steve. "US-Soviet Strategic Nuclear Arms Control: From SALT to START to STOP." *Arms Control*, 5:3 (December 1984), 50-74.
3095. Stakh, G. "Basic Principles of Negotiations on the Limitations of Strategic Offensive Arms." *International Affairs (Moscow)*, 11 (November 1973), 10-15.
3096. Stoll, Richard J., and William McAndrew. "Negotiating Strategic Arms Control, 1969-1979: Modelling the Bargaining Process." *Journal of Conflict Resolution*, 30:2 (June 1986), 315-326.
3097. Sullivan, David S. "The Legacy of SALT I: Soviet Deception and US Retreat." *Strategic Review*, 7 (Winter 1979), 26-41.
3098. Talbott, Strobe. "Buildup and Breakdown." *Foreign Affairs*, 62:3 (1984), 587-615.
3099. _____. "Buildup and Breakdowns." *Foreign Affairs*, 62:3 (1984), 587-615.
3100. _____. "Scrambling and Spying in SALT II." *International Security*, 4:2 (Fall 1979), 3-21.
3101. Warnke, Paul C. "Diplomacy at Home and Abroad: Paul Warnke on Negotiating SALT." *Arms Control Today*, 9 (May 1979), 3-8.
3102. _____. "The SALT Process - Why and How." *Proceedings of the American Society of International Law*, (1978), 50-56.

3. Documents and Reports

3103. Bellinger, J. B. *Decision Making in Arms Control: A Case Study of the National Security Council Interagency Group System in the Strategic Arms Limitation Negotiations*. Ph.D. Dissertation. Washington, D.C.: Georgetown University, 1977. 396p.

3104. Belsky, Don M. *Problems of Nuclear Disarmament: The Strategic Arms Limitation Talks.* MA. Thesis. Long Beach, CA.: University of California, Long Beach, 1972. 112p.
3105. Bennett, Paul R. *SALT I: Breakthrough or Deadlock.* PEW Case Study Series 303.0-B-86-C. New York: School of International and Public Affairs, Columbia University, 1987.
3106. _____. *SALT II and the Soviet First - Strike Threat.* PEW Case Studies, 330.0-B-88-C. New York: School of International and Public Affairs, Columbia University, 1988.
3107. Gellner, Charles R., and Judith A. Freedman. *SALT Negotiations: Recent Developments in U.S. and Soviet Policy.* Washington, D.C.: Congressional Research Service, 1981. 10p.
3108. Gentile, Ralph. *Stages in Negotiation: A Conceptual Structure and Some Empirical Results from SALT I.* Ph.D. Dissertation. Philadelphia, PA.: University of Pennsylvania, 1981. 310p.
3109. _____. "Tasks in Negotiation: A Conceptual Structure and Empirical Results from SALT I." Paper Presented at the *23rd Annual Convention of the International Studies Association,* held on March 24-27, 1982, in Cincinnati, OH.
3110. Gerson, M. B. *Problems of Theory and Practice: Difficulties in Formulating and Achieving American Strategic Objectives in the U.S. - Soviet Strategic Arms Limitation Talks.* M. Litt. Oxford: Oxford University, 1979.
3111. Haslam, Jonathan, and Teresa Osborne. *The SALT I Negotiations: The Limits of Arms Negotiations.* FPI Case Studies. Washington, D.C.: John Hopkins Foreign Policy Institute, 1986.
3112. Kohler, Foy D. *SALT II: How Not to Negotiate with the Russians.* Coral Gables, FL.: Advanced International Studies Institute, 1979. 34p.
3113. Mattox, Gale Ann. *The US/USSR Strategic Arms Limitation Talks: The Implications for the Security of the Federal Republic of Germany.* Ph.D. Dissertation. Charlottesville, VA.: University of Virginia, 1981. 318p.
3114. Perle, Richard N. *Superpower Postures in SALT: The Language of Arms Control.* Occasional Paper. Chicago, IL.: University of Chicago, Center for Policy Study, 1971.
3115. Rose, John P. *United States/Soviet Union Strategic Arms Limitations: A Study of Arms Control and Strategic Stability.* Fort Leavenworth, KS.: Army Command and General Staff College, 1978. 135p.
3116. *SALT and MBFR: The Next Phase: Report of a Trilateral Conference.* General Series Reprint, 302. Washington, D.C.: The Brookings Institution, 1975. 11p.
3117. Sloss, Leon. *SALT Two: An Assessment.* FAR-21349. Washington, D.C.: Office of External Research, Department of State, 1978. 26p.
3118. Sternste-Perkins, Dagnija. *SALT II: A Chronology.* Washington, D.C.: Congressional Research Service, 1978. 42p.
3119. Strong, Robert. *Bureaucracy, Statemanship, and Arms Control: The SALT I Negotiations.* Ph.D. Dissertation. Charlottesville, VA.: University of Virginia, 1980. 243p.
3120. United States. Congress. House. Committee on Armed Services. Special Subcommittee on Arms Control and Disarmament. *Review of Arms Control and Disarmament Activities: Hearings, C.S. 93-69.* 93rd Cong., 2nd sess. Washington, D.C.: U.S. Government Printing Office, 1975. 71p.
3121. _____._____._____._____._____. *Review of Arms Control and Disarmament Activities: Hearings.* 93rd Cong., 2nd sess. Washington, D.C.: U.S. Government Printing Office, 1975. 71p.
3122. _____._____._____._____.Subcommittee on Intelligence and Military Applications of Nuclear Energy. *SALT II: An Interim Assessment.* 92nd Cong., 2nd sess. Washington, D.C.: U.S. Government Printing Office, 1978. 65p.

3123. _____._____._____.Committee on Foreign Affairs.Subcommittee on International Security and Scientific Affairs. *Strategic Arms Limitation Talks: Hearings.* 95th Cong., 2nd sess. Washington, D.C.: U.S. Government Printing Office, 1979. 90p.
3124. _____._____._____._____._____. *Vladivostok Accord: Implications to U.S. Security, Arms Control and World Peace: Hearings.* 94th Cong., 1st sess. Washington, D.C.: U.S. Government Printing Office, 1975. 198p.
3125. _____.Department of State.Bureau of Public Affairs. *The Strategic Arms Limitation Talks: Special Report No. 46.* Washington, D.C.: U.S. Government Printing Office, 1978. 13p.
3126. Van Cleave, William R. "Political and Negotiating Asymmetries: Insult in SALT I." Paper Presented at the *6th International Arms Control Symposium,* held on November 2, 1973, in Philadelphia, PA.
3127. Yost, David S. *European Security and the SALT Process.* Washington Papers, No. 85. Beverly Hills, Sage, 1981. 96p.

D. INF NEGOTIATIONS

1. Journal Articles

3128. Buteux, P. "The INF Negotiations and the Prospects for Nuclear Arms Control in Europe." *International Journal,* 40:1 (1985), 42-67.
3129. Gallis, Paul E. "Intermediate Nuclear Force Talks at Geneva." *Congressional Research Service Review,* 7 (July-August 1986), 2-5.
3130. Garthoff, Raymond L. "Postmortem on INF Talks." *Bulletin of the Atomic Scientists,* 40:10 (December 1984), 7-10.
3131. George, Bruce, and John Borawski. "INF's Impact on Other Arms Limitation Negotiations." *Disarmament,* 11:1 (Winter 1987/88), 25-48.
3132. Goodby, James E., and P. C. Bobbit. "The INF Negotiation and the Relationship to Start." In: A. F. Neidle, ed. *Nuclear Negotiations.* Austin, TX.: L.B.J. School of Public Affairs, 1982. pp. 39-43.
3133. Guoxiang, Fan. "INF Negotiations and Nuclear Disarmament." *Disarmament,* 11:1 (Winter 1987/88), 18-24.
3134. Huisken, Ron. "The INF: Negotiations About What to Negotiate About." *Australian Outlook,* 38:2 (August 1984), 65-71.
3135. Kondracke, Morton M. "The Reagan Method." *The New Republic,* (November 1987), 12-14.
3136. Li, Duanben. "Brief Analysis of U.S. - Soviet Negotiations on Medium Range Missiles in Europe." *Chinese People's Institute of Foreign Affairs Journal,* 5 (September 1987), 25-34.
3137. Linebaugh, David. "INF + START = Negotiations." *Bulletin of the Atomic Scientists,* 40:4 (1984), 11-12.
3138. Marshall, Bruce D. "France and the INF Negotiations: An "American Munich"?" *Strategic Review,* 15:3 (Summer 1987), 20-30.
3139. "Negotiations on Intermediate Range Nuclear Forces." *Department of State Bulletin,* 87 (September 1987), 24-27.
3140. "Summit/INF." *Aviation Week & Space Technology,* 128 (June 6, 1988), 18-19.
3141. Wettig, Gerhard. "How the INF Negotiations in Geneva Failed." *Aussenpolitik,* 35:2 (1984), 123-139.

2. Documents and Reports

3142. Blackburn, W. R. *Influence of Soviet and American Political Culture on Negotiating Positions: The Intermediate - Range Nuclear Force Case.* MA. Thesis. Monterey, CA.: Naval Postgraduate School, 1984. 133p.
3143. Drenth, Don R. *NATO Negotiations on the Intermediate Range Nuclear Forces, 1977-1979.* PEW Case Studies, 305.0-A-88-P. Pittsburgh, PA.: Graduate School of Public and International Affairs, University of Pittsburgh, 1986.
3144. Gallis, Paul E. "Arms Control: Negotiations to Reduce INF Weapons." In: *Major Studies and Issue Briefs of the Congressional Research Service, 1986-1987 Supplement.* Frederick, MD.: University Publications of America, 1987. Reel VII; pp. 0424-1435.
3145. Gellner, Charles R. *U.S. - Soviet Negotiations to Limit Intermediate Range Nuclear Weapons.* Report No. 82-13GS. Washington, D.C.: Congressional Research Service, 1982. 52p.
3146. McKitrick, Jeffrey S. "The Intermediate Range Nuclear Force Negotiations: Problems and Prospects." Paper Presented at the *25th Annual Convention of the International Studies Association,* held on March 27-31, 1984, in Atlanta, GA.
3147. Nitze, Paul H. *INF Negotiations and European Security.* Washington, D.C.: U.S. Department of State, Bureau of Public Affairs, 1987. 3p.
3148. Rusten, Lynn F. *The Soviet Position in the Intermediate Nuclear Force (INF) Negotiations and Soviet Reaction to the U.S. INF Proposals.* Washington, D.C.: Congressional Research Service, 1983. 22p.
3149. Sigal, L. V. "The Euromissiles - Negotiating a Way Out." In: M. M. Kaplan, L. B. Kaplan and J. Rotblat, eds. *Proceedings of the Thirty-Fourth Pugwash Conference on Science and World Affairs.* London: Pugwash Council, 1984. pp. 386-406.
3150. United States. Congress. House. Committee on Foreign Affairs. Subcommittee on International Security and Scientific Affairs. *Overview of Nuclear Arms Control and Defence Strategy in NATO: Hearings.* 97th Cong., 2nd sess. Washington, D.C.: U.S. Government Printing Office, 1982. 225p.

E. MBFR NEGOTIATIONS

1. Books

3151. Keliher, John G. *The Negotiations on Mutual and Balanced Force Reductions: The Search for Arms Control in Central Europe.* New York: Pergamon Press, 1980. 203p.
3152. Klaiber, Wolfgang, et al. *Era of Negotiations: European Security and Force Reductions.* Lexington, MA.: D.C. Heath, 1973. 192p.

2. Journal Articles

3153. Bellany, Ian. "MBFR: An End and a Beginning?" *The Council for Arms Control Bulletin,* 30 (January 1987), 2-4.
3154. Blacker, Coit D. "Negotiating Security: The MBFR Experience." *Arms Control,* 7:3 (December 1986), 215-240.

3155. _____. "The MBFR Experience." In: A. L. George, P. J. Farley and A. Dallin, eds. *U.S. - Soviet Security Cooperation.* New York: Oxford University Press, 1988. pp. 123-143.
3156. Borawski, John. "Farewell to MBFR? Conventional Arms Negotiations Look for Greener Pastures." *Arms Control Today,* (May 1987), 17-19.
3157. Boss, Walter. "Aspects of the MBFR Negotiations." In: R. Avenhaus and R. K. Huber, eds. *Quantitative Assessment in Arms Control.* New York: Plenum Press, 1984. pp. 129-142.
3158. Darilek, Richard E. "Separate Processes, Converging Interest: MBFR and CBMs." In: H. G. Branch and D. L. Clark, eds. *Decision Making for Arms Limitation: Assessment and Prospects.* Cambridge, MA.: Ballinger, 1983. pp. 237-257.
3159. De Vos Van Steenwyth, W. J. "MBFR Talks." *Department of State Bulletin,* 70:203 (September 1973), 50-51.
3160. Dean, Jonathan. "MBFR: From Apathy to Accord." *International Security,* 7:4 (Spring 1983), 116-139.
3161. _____. "Will Negotiated Force Reductions Build Down the NATO - Warsaw Pact Confrontation." *Washington Quarterly,* 11:2 (Spring 1988), 69-88.
3162. Feigl, Hubert M. "Strategic Arms Control and Military Security of Western Europe." In: R. Avenhaus and R. K. Huber, eds. *Quantitative Assessment in Arms Control.* New York: Plenum Press, 1984. pp. 67-92.
3163. Freedman, Lawrence. "Negotiations on Nuclear Forces in Europe, 1969-1983." In: H. H. Holm and N. Petersen, eds. *European Missiles Crisis.* New York: St. Martins Press, 1983. pp. 118-155.
3164. Hardenbergh, Chalmers. "The Other Negotiations." *Bulletin of the Atomic Scientists,* 43:2 (March 1987), 48-49.
3165. _____. "The Other Negotiations." *Bulletin of the Atomic Scientists,* 41:6 (June/July 1985), 42-44.
3166. _____. "The Other Negotiations." *Bulletin of the Atomic Scientists,* 42:6 (June/July 1986), 42-44.
3167. Hill, Roger. "MBFR." *International Journal,* 29 (Spring 1974), 242-255.
3168. Hirschfeld, Thomas J. "MBFR in Eclipse." *Arms Control Today,* (October 1986), 7-10.
3169. Hopmann, P. Terrence. "Bridging the Gaps: Problems and Possibilities for Agreements in the Vienna Negotiations on Force Reductions in Central Europe." In: K. E. Birnbaum, ed. *Arms Control in Europe.* Laxenburg, Austria: Austrian Institute for International Affairs, 1980. pp. 65-78.
3170. _____. "Conventional Arms Control and Common Security in Europe." *Arms Control Today,* (October 1986), 10-13.
3171. Jung, Ernst F. "The Vienna MBFR Negotiations After Seven Years." *NATO Review,* 29:3 (June 1981), 6-9.
3172. _____. "Conventional Arms Control in Europe in Light of the MBFR Experience." *Aussenpolitik,* 39:2 (1988), 150-168.
3173. Kamp, Karl-Heinz. "Perspectives of Conventional Arms Control in Europe." *Aussenpolitik,* 38:4 (1987), 331-342.
3174. "Multilateral Exploratory Talks on MBFR in Vienna." *NATO Review,* 21 (January/February 1973), 3-4.
3175. Mutz, Reinhard. "MBFR: Problems and Lessons." In: R. Avenhaus and R. K. Huber, eds. *Quantitative Assessment in Arms Control.* New York: Plenum Press, 1984. pp. 93-128.

3176. Nerlich, Uwe. "Political Order and Military Stability: Changing Political Rationales for Negotiated Force Reductions in Europe." In: U. Nerlich, ed. *Soviet Power and Western Negotiating Policies, Vol II: The Western Panacea: Constraining Soviet Power Through Negotiation.* Cambridge, MA.: Ballinger, 1983. pp. 33-54.
3177. Ranger, Robin. "An Alternative Future for MFBR: A European Arms Control Conference." *Survival,* (July, August 1979), 164-179.
3178. Ruehl, Lothar. "Negotiations on Force Reductions in Central Europe." In: W. F. Hanrieder, ed. *Arms Control and Security: Current Issues.* Boulder, CO.: Westview Press, 1979. pp. 269-282.
3179. _____. "The Negotiations on Force Reductions in Central Europe." *NATO Review,* 5 (October 1976), 18-23.
3180. Sandstrom, Anders. "MBFR: A Non-Starter or a Slow Starter?" *Cooperation and Conflict,* 2 (1976), 71-94.
3181. Schilling, Walter. "New Structures in MBFR Negotiations." *Aussenpolitik,* 31:4 (1980), 407-415.
3182. Skaggs, David C. "MR Update: MBFR." *Military Review,* 67 (February 1987), 85-94.
3183. Staar, Richard F. "The MBFR and It's Prospects." *Orbis,* 27:4 (Winter 1984), 999-1009.
3184. Tassie, Lawrence R. "Can the MBFR Talks Succeed?" *Military Review,* 57:6 (1977), 3-8.
3185. "Vienna Conference Proceedings." *Bulletin of the Atomic Scientists,* 3:2 (1972), 179-184.
3186. Volten, Peter M. E. "Conventional Weapons and Measures of Conventional Arms Limitation in Europe." *Disarmament,* 9:3 (Autumn 1986), 41-52.
3187. Weickhardt, George G. "A Negotiable Euromissile Deal." *Arms Control,* 5:1 (May 1984), 54-59.

3. Documents and Reports

3188. Bertram, Christoph. *Mutual Force Reductions in Europe: The Political Aspects.* Adelphi Papers #84. London: International Institute for Strategic Studies, 1972. 34p.
3189. Blacker, Coit D. *The Soviet Union and Mutual Force Reductions: The Role of Military Detente in the European Security Policy of the USSR.* Ph.D. Dissertation. Medford, MA.: Fletcher School of Law and Diplomacy, Tuft University, 1978.
3190. Bowman, William R. *Limiting Conventional Forces in Europe: An Alternative to the Mutual and Balanced Force Reduction Negotiations.* Washington, D.C.: National Defence Union Press, 1985. 84p.
3191. Derek, Paul, and Gwen McGrenere, eds. *Defending Europe: Options for Security: The Proceedings of the Conference on European Requirements and the MBFR Talks held on May 6-7 1985 at the University of Toronto.* London: Taylor & Francis, 1985. 351p.
3192. Freedman, Lawrence. "Negotiations on Nuclear Forces in Europe." In: *Proceedings of the 33rd Pugwash Conference on Science and World Affairs.* London: Pugwash Council, 1983. pp. 147-154.
3193. Hess, Robert W. "MBFR: Problems and Prospects (1978)." In: *Europe and NATO: Special Studies, 1970-1980.* Frederick, MD.: University Publications of America, 1982. Reel II; pp. 0024-0153.
3194. Holloway, David. *The Soviet Approach to MBFR.* Waverley Papers, Session 1. Edinburgh, University of Edinburgh, Department of Politics, 1973. 36p.

Arms Control Negotiations 185

3195. Hopmann, P. Terrence. "Bargaining Within and Between Alliances on MBFR: Perceptions and Interactions." Paper Presented at the *Annual Meeting of International Studies Association,* held on March 16-20, 1977, in St.Louis, MO.
3196. _____. *Bargaining Within and Between Alliances on MBFR.* Carlisle Barracks, PA.: Army War College, Strategic Studies Institute, 1978. 54p.
3197. _____. "Detente and Security in Europe: The Vienna Force Reduction Negotiations." Paper Presented at the *11th World Congress of the International Political Science Association,* held on August 12-18, 1979, in Moscow.
3198. _____. "Bargaining Within and Between Alliances on MFBR: An Interim Report."Paper Presented at the *75th Annual Meeting of the Annual Political Science Association,* held on August 21 - September 3, 1979, in Washington D.C.
3199. Jacobson, Kenneth H. *Mutual and Balanced Force Reductions (MBFR) Negotiations and the Emerging Political - Military Balance in Europe.* Ph.D. Dissertation. Washington, D.C.: George Washington University, 1979. 251p.
3200. Ruehl, Lothar. *MBFR: Lessons and Problems.* Adelphi Paper No. 176. London: International Institute for Strategic Studies, 1982. 37p.
3201. Smart, Ian. *MBFR Assailed: A Critical View of the Proposed Negotiation on Mutual and Balanced Force Reductions in Europe.* Occasional Paper No.3. Ithaca, NY.: Peace Studies Program, Cornell University, 1973. 36p.
3202. Tassie, Lawrence R. "Can the Mutual and Balanced Force Reductions (MBFR) Talks Succeed Under Present Restrictions? (1975)." In: *Europe and NATO: Special Studies, 1970-1980.* Frederick, MD.: University Publications of America, 1982. Reel I; pp. 0741-0762.
3203. Toogood, John. *Conventional Arms Control Negotiations in Europe.* Background Papers No. 5. Ottawa: Canadian Institute for International Peace and Security, 1986. 8p.
3204. United States. Congress. House. Committee on Armed Services. Subcommittee on Intelligence and Military Applications of Nuclear Energy. *Status of MBFR Negotiations: Report.* 95th Cong., 2nd sess. Washington, D.C.: U.S. Government Printing Office, 1979. 10p.
3205. _____. _____. _____.Committee on Foreign Affairs.Subcommittee on International Security and Scientific Affairs. *East - West Troop Reductions in Europe: Is Agreement Possible.* 97th Cong., 1st sess. Washington, D.C.: U.S. Government Printing Office, 1983. 42p.
3206. _____. _____. _____. _____. *Status of Mutual and Balanced Force Reduction (MBFR) Negotiations: Hearings.* 98th Cong., 1st sess. Washington, D.C.: U.S. Government Printing Office, 1984. 88p.

F. START NEGOTIATIONS

1. Journal Articles

3207. Farley, Philip J. "Strategic Arms Control, 1967-87." In: A. L. George, P. J. Farley and A. Dallin, eds. *U.S. - Soviet Security Cooperation.* New York: Oxford University Press, 1988. pp. 215-254.
3208. George, James L. "The "Two-Track" Dilemma in the START Negotiations." *Strategic Review,* 26:1 (Winter 1988), 35-46.
3209. Lehman, Ronald. "The Strategic Arms Reduction Talks: A Treaty Takes Shape." *NATO Review,* 35:4 (August 1987), 19-23.
3210. Linebaugh, David, and Alexander Peters. "Restarting START." *Foreign Service Journal,* 60:1 (January 1983), 26-31.

3211. Lodal, Jan M. "Finishing START." *Foreign Policy*, 48 (Fall 1982), 66-81.
3212. Lodgaard, S., and F. Blackaby. "Nuclear Weapons and Arms Control." In: M. Thee, ed. *Arms and Disarmament: SIPRI Findings*. New York: Oxford University Press, 1986. pp. 325-332.
3213. Rowny, Edward L. "START in a Historical Perspective." *Department of State Bulletin*, 84 (June 1984), 44-47.
3214. Sabin, A. G. "Should INF and START be Merged? A Historical Perspective." *International Affairs*, 6:5 (Summer 1984), 419-428.
3215. Sigal, L. V. "START Nears the Finnish Line." *Bulletin of the Atomic Scientists*, 44:3 (April 1988), 14-15.
3216. "Strategic Arms Negotiations A Critical Reassessment: Panel Discussion." *New York University Journal of International Law and Politics*, 16 (Spring 1984), 655-700.

2. Documents and Reports

3217. Cox, David. *A Review of the Geneva Negotiations on Strategic Arms Reductions*. Background Paper No. 13. Ottawa: Canadian Institute for International Peace and Security, 1987. 11p.
3218. Kennedy, R. *START (Strategic Arms Reductions Talks): Problems and Prospects*. Carlisle Barracks, PA.: Army War College, 1983. 46p.
3219. Rusten, Lynn F. *The Soviet Position in the Strategic Arms Reduction Talks (START) and Soviet Reaction to the U.S. INF Proposals*. Washington, D.C.: Congressional Research Service, 1983. 13p.
3220. Warner, Edward L., Glenn A. Kent and Randall J. DeValk. *Key Issues for the Strategic Offensive Force Reduction Portion of the Nuclear and Space Talks in Geneva*. RAND N-2348-1-AF. Santa Monica, MA.: RAND Corporation, 1985. 45p.
3221. Wrenn, Harry. *Strategic Arms Reduction Talks (START)*. Washington, D.C.: Congressional Research Service, 1982. 17p.

G. CHEMICAL WEAPONS NEGOTIATIONS

1. Books

3222. Goldblat, Jozef. *The Problem of Chemical and Biological Warfare, Vol 4.: CB Disarmament Negotiations, 1920-1970*. Stockholm: SIPRI and Almquist & Wiksell, 1971. 412p.
3223. Sims, Nicholas. *The Diplomacy of Biological Disarmament: Vicissitudes of a Treaty in Force, 1975 - 1985*. New York: St. Martin's Press, 1988. 356p.

2. Journal Articles

3224. Dean, Jonathan. "Chemical Weapons in Europe." *Arms Control Today*, 16:6 (September 1986), 14-18.
3225. Feith, Douglas J. "Separating Realism from Rhetoric in Chemical Warfare Negotiations." *Defence*, (October 1985), 8-14.
3226. "Geneva Disarmament Conference Agrees on Draft Text of Bacterial Weapons Convention." *Department of State Bulletin*, (November 1, 1971), 504-512.

3227. Hardenbergh, Chalmers. "The Other Negotiations." *Bulletin of the Atomic Scientists,* 42:1 (January 1986), 45-47.
3228. Harris, Elisa D. "The Biological and Toxin Weapons Convention." In: A. Carnesale and R. N. Haass, ed. *Superpower Arms Control.* Cambridge, MA.: Ballinger, 1987. pp. 191-222.
3229. _____. "CBW Arms Control: A Regime Under Attack." *Arms Control Today,* 16:6 (September 1986), 8-13.
3230. King, John H. "The Comprehensive Chemical Weapons Ban: Problems and Possibilities." *Arms Control Today,* 16:6 (September 1986), 19-21.
3231. Leonard, J. F. "U.S. and U.S.S.R. Table Draft Biological Weapons Convention at Geneva Disarmament Conference." *Department of State Bulletin,* (August 30, 1971), 221-226.
3232. Luce, Richard. "Chemical Weapons: Negotiating a Total Ban." *NATO Review,* 33:3 (June 1985), 8-12.
3233. Miettinen, Jorma K. "Chemical Weapons and Chemical Disarmament Negotiations." In: D. Carlton and C. Schaerf, eds. *Reassessing Arms Control.* London: Macmillan, 1985. pp. 123-134.
3234. Perry Robinson, J. P. "The Negotiations on Chemical-Warfare Arms Control." *Arms Control,* 1:1 (May 1980), 30-52.
3235. Rosenhead, Jonathan. "CBW and Disarmament." *Labour Monthly,* 52 (January 1970), 15-18.
3236. Spiers, Edward. "Bargaining with Binaries." *NATO Review,* 32:5 (October 1984), 20-25.
3237. Trapp, R. "Geneva Negotiations on Chemical Weapons." In: M. Thee, ed. *Arms and Disarmament: SIPRI Findings.* New York: Oxford University Press, 1986. pp. 345-350.
3238. _____. "Geneva Negotiations on Chemical Weapons." *Bulletin on Peace Proposals,* 17:3-4 (1986), 497-500.

3. Documents and Reports

3239. Great Britain. Foreign and Commonwealth Office. *Chemical and Biological Weapons: Negotiations for an International Ban.* Background Brief: 1. London: H.M.S.O., 1986. 7p.
3240. Lambert, Robert W., and Jean E. Mayer. *International Negotiations on the Biological Weapons and Toxin Convention.* ADCA Publication 78. Washington, D.C.: U.S. Arms Control and Disarmament Agency, 1975. 324p.
3241. Lundin, S. J. "The Negotiations on a Chemical Weapons Ban." In: M. M. Kaplan and J. Rotblat, eds. *Proceedings of the Thirty-Fourth Pugwash Conference on Science and World Affairs.* London: Pugwash Council, 1984. pp. 264-279.
3242. Sims, Nicholas. *International Organization for Chemical Disarmament.* Solna: Stockholm International Peace Research Institute (SIPRI), 1987. 158p.
3243. Stockholm International Peace Research Institute. SIPRI. *Effects of Developments in Biological and Chemical Sciences on CW Disarmament Negotiations.* Stockholm: Almquist & Wiksell, 1974. 54p.
3244. United States.Congress.House.Committee on Foreign Affairs.Subcommittee on International Security and Scientific Affairs. *Foreign Policy and Arms Control Implications of Chemical Weapons: Hearings.* 97th Cong., 2nd sess. Washington, D.C.: U.S. Government Printing Office, 1983. 249p.

H. SEABED ARMS CONTROL NEGOTIATIONS

1. Books

3245. Ramberg, Bennett. *The Seabed Arms Control Negotiations: A Study of Multilateral Arms Control Conference Diplomacy.* Monograph Series in World Affairs: 15. Book Two. Denver, CO.: Graduate School of International Studies, University of Denver, 1978. 135p.

2. Journal Articles

3246. Hardenbergh, Chalmers. "The Other Negotiations." *Bulletin of the Atomic Scientists,* 43:7 (September 1987), 52-53.
3247. Hopmann, P. Terrence. "Bargaining in Arms Control Negotiations: The Seabed Denuclearization Treaty." *International Organizations,* 28 (Summer 1974), 313-343.
3248. Ramberg, Bennett. "Tactical Advantages of Opening Positioning Strategies: Lessons from the Seabed Arms Control Talks 1967-1970." In: I. W. Zartman, ed. *The Negotiation Process.* Beverly Hills, CA.: Sage, 1978. pp. 133-148.
3249. _____. "Tactical Advantages of Opening Positioning Strategies: Lessons from the Seabed Arms Control Talks, 1967-1970." *Journal of Conflict Resolution,* 21:4 (1977), 685-700.

3. Documents and Reports

3250. Bowen, Robert E. *Geopolitics and Rule Building at the International Seabed Authority.* PEW Case Studies, 420.0-D-88-S. Los Angeles, CA.: School of International Relations, University of Southern California, 1988.
3251. Lambert, Robert W., and John W. Syphax. *International Negotiations on the Seabed Arms Control Treaty.* Publication No. 68. Washington, D.C.: U.S. Arms Control and Disarmament Agency, 1973. 229p.
3252. Ramberg, Bennett. *The Seabed Arms Control Negotiation: A Study of Multilateral Arms Control Conference Diplomacy.* Ph.D. Dissertation. Baltimore, MD.: Johns Hopkins University, 1975. 206p.

I. CSCE & CSBM CONFERENCES

1. Books

3253. Andren, Nils, and Karl E. Birnbaum, eds. *Belgrade and Beyond: The CSCE Process in Perspective.* Alphen aan den Rijn: Sijthoff & Noordhoff, 1980. 179p.
3254. Berg, Rolf, and Adam D. Rotfeld. *Building Security in Europe: Confidence Building Measures and the CSCE.* East-West Monograph Series, No. 2. New York: Institute for East - West Security, 1986. 181p.
3255. Borawski, John. *From the Atlantic to the Urals: Negotiating Arms Control at the Stockholm Conference.* Elmsford, NY.: Pergamon-Brassey, 1988. 260p.

3256. Kavass, Igor I., Jacqueline P. Granier and Mary F. Dominick, eds. *Human Rights, European Politics and the Helsinki Accord: The Documentary Evolution of the Conference on Security and Cooperation in Europe, 1973-75.* Buffalo, NY.: William S. Hein, 1981. 6 vols.
3257. Maresca, John J. *To Helsinki - The Conference on Security and Cooperation in Europe, 1973-1975.* Durham, NC.: Duke University Press, 1985. 292p.
3258. Möttölä, Kari, ed. *Ten Years After Helsinki: The Making of the European Security Regime.* Boulder, CO.: Westview Press, 1986. 184p.
3259. Sizoo, Jan, and Rudolph Jurrjens. *CSCE Decision Making: The Madrid Experience.* The Hague: M. Nijhoff, 1984. 348p.
3260. Stanley, Timothy W., and Darnell M. Whitt. *Detente Diplomacy: United States and European Security in the 1970's.* New York: Dunellen, 1970. 170p.
3261. Van den Heuvel, Cornelius C., and Rio D. Praaning, eds. *The Belgrade Conference: Progress and Regression: Eastern, Western and Non-Aligned Appraisals of an Unfinished Conference.* Leiden: New Rhine Pubs, 1978. 60p.

2. Journal Articles

3262. Alting von Geusau, F. A. M. "Conflict Structures and Modes of Conflict Resolution - A Post CSCE Perspective." *Coexistence*, 14:1 (1977), 60-62.
3263. Armacost, Michael H. "CSCE Process and East - West Diplomacy." *Department of State Bulletin*, 86:2110 (May 1986), 69-72.
3264. Bacchus, William I. "Multilateral Foreign Policy Making: The Conference on Security and Cooperation in Europe." In: D. A. Caputo, ed. *The Politics of Policy Making in America.* San Francisco, CA.: W. H. Freeman, 1977. pp. 132-165.
3265. Bercovitch, Jacob. "Towards an Alternative Approach to Nuclear Arms Control: The Structure of a CBM Regime." In: A. Bernstein, ed. *Nuclear Weapons and International Law.* Geneva: Albert Meynier, 1985. pp. 101-111.
3266. Birnbaum, Karl E. "East-West Diplomacy in the Era of Multilateral Negotiations: The Case of the Conference on Security and Cooperation in Europe." In: N. Andren and K. E. Birnbaum, eds. *Beyond Detente: Prospects for East-West Cooperation and Security in Europe.* Leyden: A. W. Sijthoff, 1976. pp. 139-158.
3267. _____. "Confidence Building as an Approach to Cooperative Arms Regulations in Europe: General Considerations." In: K. E. Birnbaum, ed. *Arms Control in Europe.* Laxenburg, Austria: Austrian Institute for International Affairs, 1980. pp. 79-87.
3268. Bogdan, Corneliu. "The Process of the Conference for Security and Cooperation in Europe: A Realistic Alternative for the Emergence of a United Europe." In: M. A. Kaplan, ed. *Consolidating Peace in Europe.* New York: Paragon House, 1987. pp. 40-54.
3269. Borawski, John, Stan Weeks and Charlotte E. Thompson. "The Stockholm Agreement of September 1986." *Orbis*, 30:4 (Winter 1987), 643-662.
3270. _____. "The Stockholm CDE: Risks and Opportunities." *The Council for Arms Control Bulletin*, 29 (November 1986), 3-5.
3271. Ceska, Franz. "Confidence Building as an Approach to Cooperative Arms Regulations in Europe: Negotiating Positions." In: K. E. Birnbaum, ed. *Arms Control in Europe.* Laxenburg, Austria: Austrian Institute for International Affairs, 1980. pp. 88-94.

3272. Chossudowsky, Evgeny. "The Role of International Institutions in All-European "Extra-Political" Cooperation: ECE and CSCE." *Coexistence*, 14:1 (1977), 50-59.
3273. Cichock, Mark A. "Soviet Goal Articulations and Involvement at the European Disarmament Conference." *Coexistence*, 23:3 (1986), 189-208.
3274. Critchley, Julian. "East-West Diplomacy and the European Interest: CSCE, MBFR and SALT II." *Round Table*, 255 (July 1974), 299-306.
3275. Darilek, Richard E. "Building Confidence and Security in Europe: The Road to and From Stockholm." *Washington Quarterly*, (Winter 1985), 131-140.
3276. _____. "The Future of Conventional Arms Control in Europe; A Tale of Two Cities: Stockholm, Vienna." In: *SIPRI Yearbook 1987*. Oxford: Oxford University Press, 1987. pp. 339-354p.
3277. _____. "Reducing the Risk of Miscalculation: The Promise of the Helsinki CBMS." In: F. S. Larrabee and D. Stobbe, eds. *Confidence - Building Measures in Europe*. New York: East-West Security Studies, 1983. pp. 59-90.
3278. Edwards, Geoffrey. "The Conference on Security and Cooperation in Europe after Ten Years." *International Relations*, 8:4 (November 1985), 397-406.
3279. Farcell, Dante B. "The Madrid CSCE Meeting." *Washington Quarterly*, 5:4 (Autumn 1982), 202-208.
3280. Goodby, James E. "The Stockholm Conference: Negotiations on Reducing the Risk of War." In: R. T. Scott, ed. *The Race for Security*. Lexington, MA.: Lexington Books, 1987. pp. 255-262.
3281. _____. "Reducing the Risks of War: The Stockholm Achievement." *Disarmament*, 9:3 (Autumn 1986), 53-61.
3282. _____. "The Stockholm Conference: Negotiating a Cooperative Security System in Europe." In: A. L. George, P. J. Farley and A. Dallin, eds. *U.S. - Soviet Security Cooperation*. New York: Oxford University Press, 1988. pp. 144-172.
3283. _____. "The Stockholm Opportunity." *Arms Control Today*, 15:7 (September 1985), 2-5.
3284. Guesotto, Nicole. "Conference on Disarmament in Europe Opens in Stockholm." *NATO Review*, 31:6 (1983), 1-5.
3285. Hamed, Joseph W., et al. "Conference on Security and Cooperation in Europe and Negotiations on Mutual and Balanced Force Reductions." *Atlantic Community Quarterly*, 11 (Spring 1973), 7-54.
3286. Hardenbergh, Chalmers. "The Other Negotiations." *Bulletin of the Atomic Scientists*, 43:4 (September 1987), 52-53.
3287. Holma, Juha. "Introduction: Europe-Detente-CSCE, 1975-1985." In: K. Möttölä, ed. *Ten Years After Helsinki*. Boulder, CO.: Westview Press, 1986. pp. 1-16.
3288. Holsti, K. J. "Bargaining Theory and Diplomatic Reality: The CSCE Negotiations." *Review of International Studies*, 8:3 (July 1982), 159-170.
3289. Hopmann, P. Terrence. "Asymmetrical Bargaining in Conference on Security and Cooperation in Europe." *International Organization*, 32:1 (Winter 1978), 141-177.
3290. Jurrjens, Rudolph. "The CSCE as a Forum: How to Increase the Efficiency of Decision-Making." In: K. Möttölä, ed. *Ten Years After Helsinki*. Boulder, CO.: Westview Press, 1986. pp. 137-146.
3291. Kampelman, Max M. "The Helsinki Final Act: Peace Through Diplomacy." *Journal of International and Comparative Law, Supplement B*, (Winter 1983), 327-333.
3292. _____. "The Lessons of the Madrid CSCE Conference." In: A. K. Henrikson, ed. *Negotiating World Order*. Wilmington, DE.: Scholarly Resources, 1986. pp. 95-110.

3293. _____. "Reflections on the Madrid CSCE Review." In: L. Sloss and M. Scott Davis, eds. *A Game for High Stakes*. Cambridge, MA.: Ballinger, 1986. pp. 107-114.
3294. _____., et al. "Assessment of the Madrid CSCE Followup Meeting." *Department of State Bulletin*, 83:2078 (September 1983), 59-66.
3295. Kastl, Jorg. "The CSCE Reviews Meeting in Madrid." *NATO Review*, 31:5 (1983), 12-20.
3296. Killham, Edward L. "The Madrid CSCE Conference." *World Affairs*, 146:4 (Spring 1984), 340-357.
3297. Maresca, John J. "Helsinki Accord, 1975." In: A. L. George, P. J. Farley and A. Dallin, eds. *U.S. - Soviet Security Cooperation*. New York: Oxford University Press, 1988. pp. 106-122.
3298. Mellbin, Skjold G. "The Helsinki Process: James of Security and Confidence Building." *NATO Review*, 33:4 (August 1985), 7-13.
3299. Mertes, Alois. "Outlook for the Conference on Confidence Building and Disarmament in Europe." *Aussenpolitik*, 35:1 (1984), 18-30.
3300. "Negotiating with the Soviets in Madrid." *World Affairs*, 144:4 (Spring 1982), 299-512.
3301. Noack, Paul. "CSCE from Helsinki to Belgrade." *Problems of Communism*, 27:4 (July - August, 1978), 59-64.
3302. Notzold, Jürgen. "The Second CSCE Follow-Up Meeting in Madrid." *Aussenpolitik*, 33:2 (1982), 158-165.
3303. Palmer, Michael. "A European Security Conference: Preparation and Procedure." *The World Today*, 28:1 (January 1972), 36-46.
3304. Rachmaninov, Yuri N. "The Stockholm Conference." *Disarmament*, 10:1 (Winter 1986/87), 73-78.
3305. Racic, Obrad. "Meeting of Experts on the Conference of Security and Cooperation in Europe on the Peaceful Settlement of Disputes." *Review of International Affairs*, 35:828 (October 1984), 11-14.
3306. Rotfeld, Adam D. "The CSCE Process and European Security." In: K. Möttölä, ed. *Ten Years After Helsinki*. Boulder, CO.: Westview Press, 1986. pp. 17-30.
3307. Skilling, H. Gordon. "CSCE in Madrid." *Problems of Communism*, 30 (July-August 1981), 1-16.
3308. Velliadis, Hannibal. "The Madrid Conference and the Consensus Building Process in Decision Making." *Hellenic Review of International Relations*, 2:1 (1981), 187-198.
3309. Von Groll, Gotz. "The Geneva Final Act of the CSCE." *Aussenpolitik*, 26:3 (1975), 247-269.
3310. Von Staden, Berndt. "From Madrid to Vienna: The CSCE Process." *Aussenpolitik*, 37:4 (1986), 350-365.
3311. Wettig, Gerhard. "CSCE and the Rules of Detente." *Problems of Communism*, 26:3 (May-June 1977), 50-54.

3. Documents and Reports

3312. Antola, Esko. "The CSCE as a Collaborative Order." Paper Presented at the *Conference on the Processes of International Negotiations*, held on May 18-22, 1987, at the International Institute for Applied Systems Analysis (IIASA), in Laxenburg, Austria.
3313. Ben-Horin, Y., et al. *Building Confidence and Security in Europe: The Potential Role of Confidence and Security-Building Measures*. RAND R-3431. Santa Monica, CA.: RAND Corporation, 1986. 65p.

3314. Birnbaum, Karl E. "After Stockholm: The CSCE Process as a Framework for East - West Cooperation in Europe." In: H. Neuhold, ed. *CSCE: N+N Perspectives*. Wien: Braumüller, 1987. pp. 63-70.
3315. Boyd, William P. "European Arms Control - Issues and Prospects (1983)." In: *Nuclear Weapons, Arms Control, and the Threat to Thermonuclear War: Special Studies: Second Supplement, 1983-1984*. Frederick, MD.: University Publications of America, 1985. Reel IX; 0228-0270.
3316. Citron, Klaus. "Experiences of a Negotiator at Stockholm Conference (1984--1986)." Paper Presented at the *Conference on the Processes of International Negotiations*, held on May 18-22, 1987, at the International Institute for Applied Systems Analysis (IIASA), in Laxenburg, Austria.
3317. Holl, Otmar. "Cooperation Within The CSCE Context." In: H. Neuhold, ed. *CSCE: N+N Perspectives*. Wien: Braumüller, 1987. pp. 127-134.
3318. _____. "The CSCE Process: Basic Facts." In: H. Neuhold, ed. *CSCE: N+N Perspectives*. Wien: Braumüller, 1987. pp. 9-22.
3319. Huopaniemi, Jukka. *Parliaments and European Rapprochement: The Conference of the Inter - Parliamentary Union on European Cooperation and Security (Helsinki, January 1973)*. Geneva: Graduate Institute of International Studies, 1973. 138p.
3320. Krantz, T. A. *Moscow and the Negotiations of the Helsinki Accords, 1972-1975*. M. Litt. Oxford: Oxford University, 1981.
3321. Lawrence, M. F. *A Game Worth the Candle: The Confidence and Security Building Process in Europe - An Analysis of U.S. and Soviet Negotiating Strategies*. RAND R-7264-RGS. Santa Monica, CA.: RAND Corporation, 1987. 273p.
3322. Liedermann, Helmut. "Some Reflections on the Humanitarian Dimension of the CSCE Process." In: H. Neuhold, ed. *CSCE: N+N Perspectives*. Wien: Braumüller, 1987. pp. 135-144.
3323. Macintosh, James. *Confidence (and Security) Building Measures in the Arms Control Process: A Canadian Perspective*. Arms Control and Disarmament Studies, 1. Ottawa: Department of External Affairs, Arms Control and Disarmament Division, 1985. 136p.
3324. McClure, D. H. *Negotiations on Security and Co-operation in Europe: Helsinki to Belgrade: A Background Paper*. Occasional Paper No. 1. Braamfontein: South African Institute of International Affairs, 1978. 7p.
3325. Meissner, B. *The Soviet Conception of Coexistence and the Conference on Security and Co-operation in Europe*. The Hague: East-West Institute, 1975. 59p.
3326. Miko, Francis T. "The Madrid Conference on Security and Cooperation in Europe." In: *Major Studies and Issue Briefs of the Congressional Research Service, 1980-81 Supplement*. Frederick, MD.: University Publications of America, 1981. Reel VII. pp. 662-677.
3327. _____. "Conference on Security and Cooperation in Europe: The Soviet Approach." In: *Major Studies and Issue Briefs of the Congressional Research Service, 1975-76 Supplement*. Washington, D.C.: University Publications of America, 1977. Reel IV; 63p.
3328. Möttölä, Kari, Erki Nironen and Kalevi Ruhala. "The CSCE Process From the Finnish Viewpoint." In: H. Neuhold, ed. *CSCE: N+N Perspectives*. Wien: Braumüller, 1987. pp. 37-52.
3329. Namiesniowski, C. A. *The Stockholm Agreement: An Exercise in Confidence Building*. Background Paper No. 14. Ottawa: Canadian Institute for International Peace and Security, 1987. 8p.

3330. Neuhold, Hauspeter, ed. *CSCE: N+N Perspectives: The Process of the Conference on Security and Cooperation in Europe from the Viewpoint of the Neutral and Non-Aligned Participating States.* Laxenburg Papers; 8. Wien: Braumüller, 1987. 194p.
3331. _____. "The Group of the N+N Countries Within The CSCE Process." In: H. Neuhold, ed. *CSCE: N+N Perspectives.* Wien: Braumüller, 1987. pp. 23-36.
3332. Nimmo, Geoffrey A. *Canadian Elite Perceptions of the Canadian Role in Negotiating the Helsinki Final Act.* M.A. Thesis. Ottawa: Carleton University, 1981.
3333. Preece, Cherlotte P., et al. "The Conference of Disarmament in Europe (CDE)." In: *Major Studies and Issue Briefs of the Congressional Research Service, 1984-1985 Supplement.* Frederick, MD.: University Publications of America, 1985. Reel VI; pp. 0468-0483.
3334. Rotfeld, Adam D. "The Stockholm Conference on Confidence Building and Security Building Measures and Disarmament in Europe." In: M. M. Kaplan, L. B. Kaplan and J. Rotblat, eds. *Proceedings of the Thirty-Fourth Pugwash Conference on Science and World Affairs.* London: Pugwash Council, 1984. pp. 367-376.
3335. Schlotter, Peter. *The Madrid Conference on Security and Cooperation in Europe: A Balance Sheet.* Occasional Paper, No. 2. Ithaca, NY.: Cornell Peace Studies Program, Cornell University, 1985. 19p.
3336. United States. Congress. House. Commission on Security and Cooperation in Europe. *The Helsinki Process and East West Relations: Progress in Perspective: A Report on the Positive Aspects of the Implementation of the Helsinki Final Act, 1975-1984.* Washington, D.C.: Commission on Security and Cooperation in Europe, 1985. 252p.
3337. Vetschera, Heinz. "Effects of Basket I.: Security and Confidence - Building." In: H. Neuhold, ed. *CSCE: N+N Perspectives.* Wien: Braumüller, 1987. pp. 101-126.

J. NPT NEGOTIATIONS

1. Books

3338. Kapur, Ashok. *International Nuclear Proliferation: Multilateral Diplomacy and Regional Aspects.* New York: Praeger, 1979. 387p.

2. Journal Articles

3339. Alekseev, A. "Non-Proliferation Talks." *International Affairs (Moscow),* 15 (May 1969), 19-23.
3340. Burns, E. L. M. "The Nonproliferation Treaty: Its Negotiation and Prospect." *International Organization,* 23:4 (1969), 788-807.
3341. Dunn, Lewis A. "Standing Up for the NPT." *Arms Control Today,* 15:8 (October 1985), 6-7.
3342. Keens-Soper, Maurice. "Negotiating Non-Proliferation." *World Today,* 24 (May 1968), 189-196.
3343. Lambeth, Benjamin S. "Nuclear Proliferation and Soviet Arms Control." *Orbis,* 14 (Summer 1970), 298-325.
3344. Larson, Arthur. "Last Chance on Nuclear Non-Proliferation?" *Saturday Review,* (October 7, 1967), 21-24.

3345. Nikolayev, N., and V. Shestov. "Decisive Round at Geneva." *International Affairs (Moscow)*, 14 (March 1968), 3-7.
3346. Nye, Joseph S. "The Diplomacy of Nuclear Nonproliferation." In: A. K. Henrikson, ed. *Negotiating World Order*. Wilmington, DE.: Scholarly Resources, 1986. pp. 79-94.
3347. ____. "The Superpowers and the Non-Proliferation Treaty." In: A. Carnesale and R. N. Haass, eds. *Superpower Arms Control*. Cambridge, MA.: Ballinger, 1987. pp. 165-190.
3348. ____. "U.S. - Soviet Cooperation in a Nonproliferation Regime." In: A. L. George, P. J. Farley and A. Dallin, eds. *U.S. - Soviet Security Cooperation*. New York: Oxford University Press, 1988. pp. 336-352.
3349. Schiff, Benjamin N. "The 1985 Non-Proliferation Treaty Review Conference: Positive Steps or Damage Limitation?" In: P. R. Viotti, ed. *Conflict and Arms Control*. Boulder, CO.: Westview Press, 1986. pp. 84-98.
3350. Simpson, John. "The Non-Proliferation Treaty Review Conference: A Qualified Success?" *The Council for Arms Control Bulletin*, 25 (March 1986), 5,8.
3351. Van Doren, Charles N. "Brighter Outlook for NPT." *Arms Control Today*, 15:8 (October 1985), 8-9.
3352. ____. "The 1985 NPT Conference: Review or Showdown?" *Arms Control Today*, (July/August 1985), 5-6.
3353. Vital, David. "Double-Talk or Double-Think? A Comment on the Draft Non-Proliferation Treaty." *International Affairs*, 44 (July 1968), 419-433.

3. Documents and Reports

3354. Poulose, T. T. "The United Nations and Arms Control: Nuclear Proliferation." In: UNITAR. *The United Nations and the Maintenance of International Peace and Security*. Dordrecht: M. Nijhoff, 1987. pp. 387-406.
3355. United States. Arms Control and Disarmament Agency. *International Negotiations on Treaty on Nonproliferation of Nuclear Weapons*. Publication 48. Washington, D.C.: U.S. Government Printing Office, 1969. 183p.
3356. ____.Congress.Senate.Committee on Foreign Relations.Subcommittee on Arms Control, International Organizations and Security Agreements. *Nonproliferation Issues: Hearings*. 94th Cong., 1st and 2nd sess. Washington, D.C.: U.S. Government Printing Office, 1977. 426p.

K. OTHER NUCLEAR NEGOTIATIONS

1. Books

3357. Bass, R., B. M. Bass and Z. Shapiro. *Nuclear Site Negotiation*. LaJolla, CA.: University Associates, 1982.
3358. Heckrotte, Warren, and George C. Smith, eds. *Arms Control in Transition: Proceedings of the Livermore Arms Control Conference*. Boulder, CO.: Westview Press, 1983. 191p.
3359. Kohl, Wilfrid L. *French Nuclear Diplomacy*. Princeton, NJ.: Princeton University Press, 1971. 412p.
3360. ____. *The French Nuclear Force and Alliance Diplomacy, 1958-1967*. New York: Columbia University, 1968. 523p.

2. Journal Articles

3361. Carnesale, Albert. "On Limiting Technology by Negotiated Agreements." In: D. W. Hafemeister and D. Schroeder, eds. *Physics, Technology and the Nuclear Arms Race.* New York: American Institute of Physics, 1983. pp. 230-238.
3362. Dean, Jonathan. "Berlin in a Divided Germany: An Evolving International Regime." In: A. L. George, P. J. Farley and A. Dallin, eds. *U.S. - Soviet Security Cooperation.* New York: Oxford University Press, 1988. pp. 83-105.
3363. Gaddis, John Lewis. "The Evolving of a Reconnaissance Satellite Regime." In: A. L. George, P. J. Farley and A. Dallin, eds. *U.S. - Soviet Security Cooperation.* New York: Oxford University Press, 1988. pp. 353-372.
3364. Garthoff, Raymond L. "Brezhnev's Opening: The TNF Tangle." *Foreign Policy,* 41 (Winter 1980-81), 82-94.
3365. Gelb, Leslie H. "Indian Ocean Arms Limitation Negotiations." *Department of State Bulletin,* 78:2021 (December 1978), 5456.
3366. Haass, Richard N. "Arms Control at Sea: The United States and the Soviet Union in the Indian Ocean, 1977-78." In: A. L. George, P. J. Farley and A. Dallin, eds. *U.S. - Soviet Security Cooperation.* New York: Oxford University Press, 1988. pp. 524-539.
3367. Hall, David K. "The Laos Neutralization Agreement, 1962." In: A. L. George, P. J. Farley and A. Dallin, eds. *U.S. - Soviet Security Cooperation.* New York: Oxford University Press, 1988. pp. 435-465.
3368. Hirschfeld, Thomas J. "Arms Control in Europe: And Now the Conventional Stability Talks." *Arms Control Today,* 18 (March 1988), 13-16.
3369. Husbands, Jo Louise, and Anne Hessing Cahn. "The Conventional Arms Transfer Talks: An Experiment in Mutual Arms Trade Restraint." In: T. Ohlson, ed. *Arms Transfer Limitations and Third World Security.* Oxford: Oxford University Press, 1988. pp. 110-125.
3370. Jones, Rodney W. "Atomic Diplomacy in Developing Countries." *Journal of International Affairs,* 34:1 (1980), 89-118.
3371. Juda, Lawrence. "Negotiating a Treaty on Environmental Modification Warfare: Convention on Environmental Warfare and its Impact upon Arms-Control Negotiations." *International Organization,* 32:4 (1978), 975-991.
3372. Lynn-Jones, Sean M. "The Incidents at Sea Agreement." In: A. L. George, P. J. Farley and A. Dallin, eds. *U.S. - Soviet Security Cooperation.* New York: Oxford University Press, 1988. pp. 482-509.
3373. Nogee, Joseph L. "Propaganda and Negotiations: The Case of the Ten-Nation Disarmament Committee." *Journal of Arms Control,* 1 (1963), 604-615.
3374. _____. "Propaganda and Negotiation: The Case of the Ten-Nation Disarmament Committee." *Journal of Conflict Resolution,* 7:3 (1963), 510-521.
3375. _____. "Propaganda and Negotiation: The Ten-Nation Disarmament Committee." In: I. W. Zartman, ed. *The 50% Solution.* Garden City, NJ.: Anchor Press, 1976. pp. 322-342.
3376. Nolan, Jane E. "The U.S. - Soviet Conventional Arms Transfer Negotiations." In: A. L. George, P. J. Farley and A. Dallin, eds. *U.S. - Soviet Security Cooperation.* New York: Oxford University Press, 1988. pp. 510-523.
3377. Osborn, Frederick. "Negotiating on Atomic Energy, 1946-1947." In: R. Dennett and J. E. Johnson, eds. *Negotiating with the Russians.* Boston, MA.: World Peace Foundation, 1951. pp. 209-238.
3378. Rhinelander, John B., and James P. Rubin. "Mission Accomplished: An Insider's Account of the ABM Treaty Negotiating Record." *Arms Control Today,* (September 1987), 3-14.

3379. Schoenbaum, David. "The World War II Allied Agreement on Occupation and Administration of Postwar Germany." In: A. L. George, F. J. Farley and A. Dallin, eds. *U.S. - Soviet Security Cooperation.* New York: Oxford University Press, 1988. 21-45.
3380. Shapley, Deborah. "Antarctica: Why Success?." In: A. L. George, P. J. Farley and A. Dallin, eds. *U.S. - Soviet Security Cooperation.* New York: Oxford University Press, 1988. pp. 307-335.
3381. Strickland, Donald A. "Scientists as Negotiators: The 1958 Geneva Conference of Experts." *Midwest Journal of Political Science,* 8 (November 1964), 372-384.
3382. Towle, P. "The Montreux Convention as a Regional Arms Control Treaty Negotiation and Practice." *Military Affairs,* 45:3 (1981), 121-126.
3383. Wertheimer, John. "The Antisatellite Negotiations." In: A. Carnesale and R. N. Haass, eds. *Superpower Arms Control.* Cambridge, MA.: Balliger, 1987. pp. 139-164.

3. Documents and Reports

3384. Blechman, Barry M., and Jane E. Nolan. *The U.S. - Soviet Conventional Arms Transfer Negotiations.* FPI Case Studies, NO. 3. Washington, D.C.: Johns Hopkins Foreign Policy Institute, 1986.
3385. Giblin, J. F. *Indian Ocean Naval Arms Limitation Talks: From a Zone of Peace to the Arc of Crisis.* Ph.D. Dissertation. Medford, MA.: Fletcher School of Law and Diplomacy, 1984. 508p.
3386. Juda, Lawrence. "Negotiating a Treaty on Environmental Modification Warfare: The Convention on Environmental Warfare and its Impact on Arms Control Negotiations." In: U.S. Senate. Committee on Foreign Relations. *Environmental Modification Techniques: Hearings.* 96th Cong., 1st sess. Washington, D.C.: U.S. Government Printing Office, 1979. pp. 24-41.
3387. Mautner-Markhof, Frances. "A Study on the Processes and Impacts of the Negotiation of the Conventions on Early Notification and Emergency Assistance in the Event of Nuclear Accident." Paper Presented at the *Conference on the Processes of International Negotiations,* held on May 18-22, 1987, at the International Institute for Applied Systems Analysis (IIASA), in Laxenburg, Austria.
3388. Rusten, Lynn F., and Paul C. Stern. *Crisis Management in the Nuclear Age.* Washington, D.C.: National Academy Press, 1987. 43p.
3389. United States. Congress. House. Committee on Armed Services. Subcommittee on Intelligence and Military Applications of Nuclear Energy. *Indian Ocean Forces Limitation and Conventional Arms Transfer Limitations: Report.* 95th Cong., 2nd sess. Washington, D.C.: U.S. Government Printing Office, 1979. 15p.

VII

Summit Meetings

"Summit Diplomacy" is an old concept. It is as old as history and it means the face to face meeting of leaders. It defines the meetings of leaders of countries and governments. Summit diplomacy has a number of common aspects, such as communication, pre summit arrangements or meetings, the meetings or conferences themselves and their aftermath.

Summit meetings have become very ritualized. With the importance of superpower relations, the meetings themselves involve far more than just face to face meeting between leaders. Their public relations aspects may be more important than the agreements themselves. As public relation events, summit meetings are as important for their public relation effect as for the actual subject of the meetings. Their actual success or failure is difficult to asses in the short run. There are bilateral and multilateral summit meetings. This This chapter is focusing on the processes of negotiation at summit meetings and is not so much interested in policy issues. The first chapter covers the various superpower summit meetings from that perspective. The second chapter covers the yearly western economic summit meetings, which are multilateral in scope, and resemble classic conference diplomacy rather than the bilateral superpower summits.

This bibliography is restricted to English language materials. It will be of particular value to students and scholars working on negotiations aspects of summit diplomacy.

A. SUPERPOWER SUMMIT MEETINGS

1. Books

3390. Acheson, Dean. *Meeting at the Summit: A Study in Diplomatic Methods.* Durham, NH.: University of New Hampshire, 1958. 27p.
3391. Franck, Thomas M., and Edward Weisband. *World Politics: Verbal Strategy Among the Superpowers.* N.Y.: Oxford University Press, 1972. 176p.
3392. Mandelbaum, Michael, and Strobe Talbott. *Reagan and Gorbachev.* New York: Vintage Books, 1987. 190p.
3393. Plischke, Elmer. *Diplomat in Chief: The President at the Summit.* New York: Praeger, 1986. 518p.
3394. _____. *Summit Diplomacy: Personal Diplomacy: Personal Diplomacy of the President of the United States.* Westport, CT.: Greenwood, 1974. 125p.
3395. Pumpyansky, Alexander. *On the Way to the Summit.* Moscow: Novosti Press, 1987. 91p.
3396. Smith, A. Merriman. *The President's Odyssey.* New York: Harper, 1961. 272p.
3397. Weihmiller, Gordon. *U.S. Soviet Summits: An Account of East-West Diplomacy at the Top, 1955-1985.* Lanham, MD.: University Press of America, 1986. 211p.

2. Journal Articles

3398. Adelman, Kenneth L. "Summitry: The Historical Perspective." *Presidential Studies Quarterly,* 16:3 (Summer 1986), 435-441.
3399. _____. "What Happened at Reykjavik?" *Disarmament,* 9:3 (Autumn 1986), 1-14.
3400. Andrew, Arthur. "A View of the Summit." *International Journal,* 35:1 (1980), 21-32.
3401. "At the Summit: Avoiding Disagreements Can Sometimes Spell Genuine Victory." *National Journal,* 15 (June 4, 1983), 1171-1175.
3402. Bertsch, Gary K., and James M. Rosenbluth. "Summitry as an Instructional Tool in International Studies." *International Studies Notes,* 4:2 (June 1972), 38-47.
3403. Blacker, Coit D. "Lessons from U.S. - Soviet Summits." *Bulletin of the Atomic Scientists,* 41:10 (November 1985), 14-17.
3404. Bonafede, Dom. "Geneva Summit Shows How Diplomacy has Entered the Communications Age." *National Journal,* 17 (December 14, 1985), 2861-2864.
3405. Bouscaren, Anthony T. "Current Summit Strategy of the Soviet Union." *Free World Forum,* 2:2 (April-May 1960), 6-10.
3406. Breslauer, George W. "Do Soviet Leaders Test New Presidents?" *International Security,* 8 (Winter 1983-84), 83-107.
3407. Cooper, Mary H. "U.S. - Soviet Summitry." *Editorial Research Reports,* (November 1, 1985), 823-840.
3408. Davis, Paul C. "The New Diplomacy, The 1955 Geneva Summit Meeting." In: R. Hilsman and R. C. Good, eds. *Foreign Policy in the Sixties: Issues and Instruments.* Baltimore, MD.: Johns Hopkins University Press, 1965. pp. 159-190.
3409. De Rose, Francoise. "Brinkmanship at Reykjavik." *Atlantic Community Quarterly,* 24:4 (Winter 1986/87), 295-299.

3410. Drew, E. "Letter from Washington." *The New Yorker*, 64 (July 4, 1988), 70-80.
3411. Fairbanks, Charles H. Jr. "Reagan's Turn on Summit Diplomacy." *SAIS Review*, 8:2 (Summer - Fall 1988), 69-82.
3412. Fluegel, Edna R. "Are We Ready for the Summit?" *Free World Forum*, 1:3 (May 1959), 3-4.
3413. Freedman, Lawrence. "Star Wars and the Summit." *Government and Opposition*, 21:2 (Spring 1986), 131-145.
3414. Galtung, Johan. "Summit Meetings and International Relations." *Journal of Peace Research*, 1 (1964), 36-54.
3415. Garrity, Patrick J. "The Dubious Promise of Summitry." *Journal of Contemporary Studies*, 7 (Winter 1984), 71-79.
3416. George, Alexander L. "The Basic Principles Agreement of 1972: Origins and Expectations." In: A. L. George, eds. *Managing U.S. - Soviet Rivalry*. Boulder, CO.: Westview Press, 1983. pp. 107-118.
3417. Haley, P. Edward. "'You Could Have Said Yes': Lessons from Reykjavik." *Orbis*, 31:1 (Spring 1987), 75-98.
3418. Hamm, Manfred R. "The Umbrella Talks?" *Washington Quarterly*, 8:2 (Spring 1985), 133-146.
3419. Herbert, Wray. "Psychology at the Summit." *Psychology Today*, 22:4 (June 1988), 27-30+.
3420. Hyland, William G. "Reagan - Gorbachev III." *Foreign Affairs*, 66 (Fall 1987), 7-21.
3421. Kertesz, Stephen D. "Summit and Personal Diplomacy." In: S. D. Kertesz, ed. *The Quest for Peace Through Diplomacy*. Englewood Cliffs, NJ.: Prentice-Hall, 1967. pp. 51-61.
3422. Kissinger, Henry A. "The Vladivostock Accord: Background Briefing by Henry Kissinger, December 3, 1974." *Survival*, 17 (July/August 1975), 191-198.
3423. Kraft, Joseph. "Letter from Moscow." *New Yorker*, 48 (June 24, 1972), 54-60.
3424. Leng, Russell J. "Reagan and the Russians: Crisis Bargaining Beliefs and Historical Record." *American Political Science Review*, 78:2 (June 1984), 338-355.
3425. Lerche, Charles O. "The NATO and the Summit Negotiations." *Free World Forum*, 2:2 (April-May 1960), 44-47.
3426. Lord, Plumb. "The Need for a World Summit." *Studia Diplomatica*, 40:3-5 (1987), 651-656.
3427. Luns, Joseph M. A. H. "The Washington Summit Meeting in Perspective." *NATO Review*, 26:4 (August 1978), 3-7.
3428. Mandelbaum, Michael, and Strobe Talbott. "Reykjavik and Beyond." *Foreign Affairs*, 65:2 (Winter 1986-87), 215-235.
3429. Mates, L. "The Disarmament Problem and the Summit Meeting." *Review of International Affairs (Belgrade)*, 11:242-243 (May 1-16, 1960), 1-4.
3430. "Moscow Summit." *Department of State Bulletin*, 88:2137 (August 1988), 1-41.
3431. Nikolayev, Y. "The Vladivostok Meeting: Important Progress." *International Affairs (Moscow)*, 2 (February 1975), 3-10.
3432. Nixon, Richard M. "Superpower Summitry." *Foreign Affairs*, (Fall 1985), 1-11.
3433. _____. "Moscow Summit: New Opportunities in U.S. - Soviet Relations." *Department of State Bulletin*, 67:1733 (September 11, 1972), 275-282.
3434. Panofsky, Wolfgang K. H. "Limited Success, Limitless Prospects." *Bulletin of the Atomic Scientists*, 44:2 (March 1988), 34-35.

3435. Peterfi, William O. "Microdiplomacy and Summit Meetings." *Peace Research,* 20:2 (May 1988), 1-22.
3436. Petrovsky, Vladimir F. "What Happened at Reykjavik?" *Disarmament,* 9:3 (Autumn 1986), 15-26.
3437. Pfaltzgraff, Robert L. "Summitry, SDI, and Arms Control." *Fletcher Forum,* 10:1 (Winter 1986), 39-42.
3438. Plischke, Elmer. "The Eisenhower - Khrushchev Visits: Diplomacy at the Summit." *Maryland Magazine,* 30 (September-October 1959), 6-9.
3439. _____. "Eisenhower's Correspondence Diplomacy with the Kremlin: Case Study in Summit Diplomacy." *Journal of Politics,* 30 (February 1968), 137-159.
3440. _____. "International Conferencing and the Summit: Macro-Analysis of Presidential Participation." *Orbis,* 14 (Fall 1970), 673-713.
3441. _____. "Recent State Visits to the United States - A Technique of Summit Diplomacy." *World Affairs Quarterly,* 20 (October 1958), 223-255.
3442. _____. "Summit Conferences." In: E. Plischke, ed. *Summit Diplomacy: Personal Diplomacy of the Presidents of the United States.* College Park, MD.: Bureau of Government Research, University of Maryland, 1958. pp. 69-101.
3443. _____. "Summit Diplomacy." In: E. Plischke, ed. *Conduct of American Diplomacy.* Princeton, NJ.: Van Nostrand, 1967. pp. 43-55.
3444. _____. "Summit Diplomacy: Its Uses and Limitations." *Virginia Quarterly Review,* 48 (Summer 1972), 321-344.
3445. _____. "Summit Diplomacy - Diplomat in Chief." In: E. Plischke, ed. *Modern Diplomacy: The Art and the Artisans.* Washington, D.C.: American Enterprise Institute, 1979. pp. 169-187.
3446. Ridgway, Rozanne L. "The Geneva Summit: A Testimonial to Alliance Solidarity." *NATO Review,* 33:6 (December 1985), 1-4.
3447. Rogers, Lindsay. "Of Summits." *Foreign Affairs,* 34 (October 1955), 141-148.
3448. Rose, Clive. "The 1982 Summit and After: A Personal View." *NATO Review,* 30:4 (1982), 8-13.
3449. Rostow, Eugene V. "Of Summitry and Grand Strategy." *Strategic Review,* 14:4 (Fall 1985), 9-20.
3450. Rusk, Dean. "The Presidency and the Summit." *Coronet,* 50 (June 1961), 70-75.
3451. Schaetzel, J. Robert, and Harald B. Malmgren. "Talking Heads." *Foreign Policy,* 39 (Summer 1980), 130-142.
3452. Schlezinger, James. "Reykjavik and Revelations: A Turn of the Tide?" *Foreign Affairs,* 65:3 (1986), 426-446.
3453. Sigal, L. V. "The Reagan Compromise on ABM." *Bulletin of the Atomic Scientists,* 44 (April 1988), 10-14.
3454. Smith, Hedrick. "Geneva: A Test of Two Wills." *New York Times Magazine,* (November 17, 1985), 44-45, 74-81.
3455. _____. "Setting the Post-Summit Tone." *New York Times Magazine,* (December 8, 1985), 70,72,74,76,78,80,82.
3456. "The Soviet-American Summit 1974." *Survival,* 16 (September-October 1974), 232-246.
3457. Stefan, Charles G. "The Ups and Downs of Summitry." *Foreign Service Journal,* 64:10 (November 1987), 29-31.
3458. "The Summit Via Paris." *Round Table,* 49 (December 1959), 3-7.
3459. Tang, Peter S. H. "Moscow, Peking and the Summit Conference." *Free World Forum,* 2:2 (April-May 1960), 51-54.

3460. Thompson, William R., and George Modelski. "Global Conflict Intensity and Great Power Summitry Behavior." *Journal of Conflict Resolution*, 21 (June 1977), 339-376.
3461. Timberlake, Charles E. "The Summit Meeting as a Form of Diplomacy in American Soviet Relations in the 1970's." In: B. W. Eissenstat, ed. *The Soviet Union: The Seventies and Beyond.* Lexington, MA.: Lexington Books, 1975. pp. 93-120.
3462. Tiwari, J. N. "Moscow, Peking and the Summit Conference." *Free World Forum*, 2:2 (April-May 1960), 48-50.
3463. "The U.S. - Soviet Summit." *Congressional Quarterly Weekly Reports*, 45 (December 12, 1987), 3023-3029.
3464. Valenta, Jiri. "Soviet Foreign Policy and the Moscow Summit of 1972." *SAIS Review*, 17 (Winter 1973), 15-20.
3465. Vukadinovic, Radovan. "Brief Encounter in Reykjavik." *Review of International Affairs*, 37 (October 20, 1986), 1-3.
3466. Waples, Douglas. "Publicity Versus Diplomacy: Notes on the Reporting of the "Summit" Conferences." *Public Opinion Quarterly*, 20 (Spring 1956), 308-314.
3467. "The Washington Summit." *Department of State Bulletin*, 88:2131 (February 1988), 1-21.
3468. Weinstein, Martin E. "Japan's Defence Policy and the May 1981 Summit." *Journal of Northeast Asian Studies*, 1 (March 1983), 23-33.
3469. Wimer, Kurt. "Wilson and Eisenhower: Two Experiences in Summit Diplomacy." *Contemporary Review*, 199 (June 1961), 284-295.
3470. Worsnop, Richard L. "Head-of-State Diplomacy." *Editorial Research Report*, 2 (December 5, 1962), 873-892.
3471. _____. "Presidential Diplomacy." *Editorial Research Reports*, 11 (September 24, 1971), 737-758.
3472. Yost, David S. "The Reykjavik Summit and European Security." *SAIS Review*, 7:2 (Summer-Fall 1987), 1-22.

3. Documents and Reports

3473. Alexiev, A. R. *Of Arms Control, Summit Meetings and the Politics of Make-Believe.* RAND P-7049. Santa Monica, CA.: RAND Corporation, 1985. 6p.
3474. Ashby, Timothy, et al. *President's Reagan's Summit Meeting in Geneva, November 19-20, 1985: Briefing Book.* Washington, D.C.: Heritage Foundation, 1985. 54p.
3475. Bole, Robert D. *Summit at Holy Bush.* Glassboro, NJ.: Glassboro State College Endowment Fund, 1969. 208p.
3476. Brzezinski, Ian. *Presidential Reflections Upon U.S. - Soviet Summitry.* Significant Issues Series, Vol 7, no 8. Washington, D.C.: Center for Strategic and International Studies, Georgetown University, 1985. 22p.
3477. Cronin, P. M. *Soviet - American Summit Diplomacy.* M. Phil. Oxford: Oxford University, 1981.
3478. Franck, Thomas M., and Edward Weisband. *The Johnson-Brezhnev Doctrines: Verbal Behavior Analysis of Superpower Confrontations.* Policy Papers v.3 no.2. New York: New York University, Center for International Studies, 1970. 38p.
3479. *Geneva, The Soviet - US Summit, November 1985: Documents and Materials.* Moscow: Novosti Press Agency House, 1985. 87p.

Summit Meetings

3480. Goodby, James E. *Playing Poker in Iceland.* PEW Case Studies, 317.0-A-- 88-G. Washington, D.C.: Foreign Service Institute, Georgetown University, 1988.
3481. Great Britain. Foreign Office. *Documents Relating to the Meeting of Heads of Government of France, The United Kingdom, The Soviet Union and The United States of America, July 18-23, 1955.* Miscellaneous Pubs. No. 14. London: H.M.S.O., 1955. 31p.
3482. Haight, David. "Dwight D. Eisenhower, Nikita Khrushchev and the U.N. "Summit" Assembly of 1960." In: *The Presidency and National Security Policy.* Proceedings Vol 5; no 1. New York: Center for the Study of the Presidency, 1984. pp. 187-206; 418-423.
3483. Hill, Frederick B., and Alan K. Henrikson. "U.S. - Soviet Summitry." In: *A Fresh Look.* Washington, D.C.: Center for the Study of Foreign Affairs, 1986. 6p.
3484. McDonald, John W., ed. *U.S. - Soviet Summitry: Roosevelt Through Carter.* Washington, D.C.: Center for the Study of Foreign Affairs, Department of State, 1987. 158p.
3485. Plischke, Elmer. *Presidential Diplomacy; A Chronology of Summit Visits, Trips and Meetings.* Englewood Cliffs, NJ.: Oceana, 1986. 270p.
3486. Sears, Arthur M. *The Search for Peace Through Summit Conferences.* Ph.D. Dissertation. Boulder, CO.: University of Colorado, 1972. 967p.
3487. *U.S.S.R. - U.S. Summit: Washington, December 7-10, 1987: Documents and Materials.* Moscow: Novosti Press, 1987. 144p.
3488. "The U.S.S.R. and the Paris Summit Conference, July 25, 1960." In: O.S.S./- State Department Intelligence and Research Reports. *The Soviet Union: 1950-1961 Supplement.* Washington, D.C.: University Publications of America, 1979. Reel VI;466-493.
3489. United States. Congress. House. Committee on Armed Services. *Reykjavik and American Security.* 99th Cong., 2nd sess. Washington, D.C.: U.S. Government Printing Office, 1987. 31p.
3490. _____._____._____._____. *Reykjavik Process: Preparation For and Conduct of the Iceland Summit and its Implications for Arms Control Policy.* Committee Print No. 25. 99th Cong., 2nd sess. Washington, D.C.: U.S. Government Printing Office, 1987. 30p.
3491. _____._____._____._____.Defence Policy Panel. *Process and Implications of the Iceland Summit: Hearings.* 99th Cong., 2nd sess. Washington, D.C.: U.S. Government Printing Office, 1986. 344p.
3492. _____._____._____._____.Committee on Foreign Affairs. *The Reagan-Gorbachev Summit and Its Implications for United States-Soviet Relations: Hearing.* 99th Cong., 1st sess. Washington, D.C.: U.S. Government Printing Office, 1986. 39p.
3493. _____._____._____._____. *Reagan - Gorbachev Summit and Its Implications for U.S. - Soviet Relations.* 100th Cong., 1st sess. Washington, D.C.: U.S. Government Printing Office, 1987. 123p.
3494. _____._____._____._____.Subcommittee on Arms Control, International Security and Science. *The Reykjavik Talks: Promise or Peril: Report.* 100th Cong., 1st sess. Washington, D.C.: U.S. Government Printing Office, 1987. 201p.
3495. _____._____.Senate.Committee on Foreign Relations. *Background Documents on Events Incident to the Summit Conference.* 86th Cong., 2nd sess. Washington, D.C.: U.S. Government Printing Office, 1960. 75p.
3496. _____._____._____._____. *Events Incident to the Summit Conference: Hearings.* 86th Cong., 2nd sess. Washington, D.C.: U.S. Government Printing Office, 1960. 302p.

3497. _____._____._____._____. *Events Relating to the Summit Conference: Report.* 86th Cong., 2nd sess. Washington, D.C.: U.S. Government Printing Office, 1960. 36p.
3498. _____.Department of State. *Background of Heads of Government Conference - 1960: Principal Documents, 1955-1959, with Narrative Summary.* Washington, D.C.: U.S. Government Printing Office, 1960. 478p.
3499. _____._____. *The Washington Summit: General Secretary Brezhnev's Visit to the United States, June 18-25, 1973.* Washington, D.C.: U.S. Government Printing Office, 1973. 63p.
3500. _____._____.Office of Public Communication. *Vienna Summit: June 15-18, 1979.* Washington, D.C.: U.S. Government Printing Office, 1979. 11p.
3501. Wardall, William K. *State Visits: A Technique of United States Summit Diplomacy.* M.A. Thesis. College Park, MD.: University of Maryland, 1958. 168p.

B. ECONOMIC SUMMITS

1. Books

3502. Merlini, Cesare, ed. *Economic Summits and Western Decision-Making.* London: Croom Helm, 1984. 212p.
3503. Putnam, Robert D., and Nicholas Bayne. *Hanging Together: The Seven--Power Summits.* Cambridge, MA.: Harvard University Press, 1984. 263p.
3504. _____. _____. *Hanging Together: Cooperation and Conflict in the Seven--Power Summits.* 2nd ed. London: Sage, 1987. 293p.

2. Journal Articles

3505. "1983 Summit of Industrialized Nations: Williamsburg, Virginia, May 28-30, 1983." *Department of State Bulletin,* 83 (July 1983), 1-22.
3506. Becker, Kurt. "Between Image and Substance: The Role of the Media." In: C. Merlini, ed. *Economic Summit Meetings.* New York: St.Martin's Press, 1984. pp. 153-166.
3507. "Bonn Economic Summit." *Department of State Bulletin,* 85 (July 1985), 1-6.
3508. Bonvinici, Gianni, and Wolfgang Wessels. "The European Community and the Seven." In: C. Merlini, ed. *Economic Summit Meetings.* New York: St.Martin's Press, 1984. pp. 167-192.
3509. "The Cancun Summit." *Department of State Bulletin,* 81 (December 1981), 1-9.
3510. "Economic Summit Conference of the CMEA Countries." *International Affairs (Moscow),* 7 (July 1984), 3-18.
3511. Faleiro, Eduardo. "Africa Fund Summit." *Africa Quarterly,* 24:1-2 (1985), 1-5.
3512. Falk, Pamela S. "Whatever Happened to Cancun? The 600 Billion Dollar Question." *Caribbean Review,* 11:3 (Summer 1982), 14-17, 45-47.
3513. Garavoglia, Guido. "From Rambouillet to Williamsburg: A Historical Assessment." In: C. Merlini, ed. *Economic Summit Meetings.* New York: St.Martin's Press, 1984. pp. 1-42.
3514. Goodman, Marc B. "Cancun in Context." *Washington Quarterly,* 5:1 (Winter 1982), 155-162.
3515. Gottlieb, A. E. "Across the Western Economic Summits." *Canadian Business Review,* 8:2 (Summer 1981), 7-11.

3516. "London Economic Summit." *Department of State Bulletin*, 84 (August 1984), 1-6.
3517. Merlini, Cesare. "A Fall After the Rise? The Political Options for Europe." In: C. Merlini, ed. *Economic Summit Meetings*. New York: St.Martin's Press, 1984. pp. 193-212.
3518. Owen, H. "The World Economy: The Dollar and the Summit." *Foreign Affairs*, 63 (Winter 1984/85), 344-358.
3519. Pelkmans, Jacques. "Collective Management and Economic Cooperation." In: C. Merlini, ed. *Economic Summit Meetings*. New York: St.Martin's Press, 1984. pp. 89-136.
3520. "President Carter Attends Economic Summit Meeting in Tokyo: Symposium." *Department of State Bulletin*, 79 (August 1979), 1-11.
3521. "President Carter Attends Economic Summit in Venice." *Department of State Bulletin*, 80 (August 1980), 1-11.
3522. "President Reagan Attends Economic Summit in Canada." *Department of State Bulletin*, 81 (August 1981), 1-22.
3523. "President Reagan Attends Economic and NATO Summits." *Department of State Bulletin*, 82 (July 1982), 1-14.
3524. Putnam, Robert D. "Summit Sense." *Foreign Policy*, 55 (Summer 1984), 73-91.
3525. _____. "The Western Economic Summits: A Political Interpretation." In: C. Merlini, ed. *Economic Summit Meetings*. New York: St.Martin's Press, 1984. pp. 43-88.
3526. Sulimma, Hans Günter. "North-South Dialogue and the Cancun Summit." *Aussenpolitik*, 33:1 (1982), 46-58.
3527. Thiel, Elke. "Economic Conflicts Before and After Versailles." *Aussenpolitik*, 33 (1982), 356-369.
3528. _____. "Economic Summits from Rambouillet to Venice." *Aussenpolitik*, 32 (1981), 3-14.
3529. _____. "The World Economic Summit in Tokyo." *Aussenpolitik*, 37:3 (1986), 211-221.
3530. "Tokyo Economic Summit." *Department of State Bulletin*, 86 (July 1986), 1-14.
3531. "Toronto Economic Summit." *Department of State Bulletin.*, 88:2137 (August 1988), 46-54.
3532. Ungar, S. J. "North and South at the Summit." *Atlantic*, 249 (June 1982), 6-8+.
3533. Wallace, William. "Political Issues at the Summits: A New Concerts of Powers?" In: C. Merlini, ed. *Economic Summit Meetings*. New York: St.Martin's Press, 1984. pp. 137-152.

3. Documents and Reports

3534. Bergsten, C. Fred. *From Rambouillet to Versailles: A Symposium*. Essays in International Finance No. 149. Princeton, N.J.: Department of Economics, Princeton University, 1982.
3535. De Merril, George, and Anthony M. Solomon. *Economic Summitry*. New York: Council on Foreign Relations, 1983. 88p.
3536. Robinson, Charles, William C. Turner and Harald B. Malmgren. *Summit Meetings and Collective Leadership in the 1980's*. Washington, D.C.: The Atlantic Council, 1980. 69p.

3537. *Summit Economic Conference of the CMEA Member Countries, Moscow, 12-14, June 1984.* Moscow: Council on Mutual Economic Assistance, Secretariat, 1984. 72p.
3538. Thiel, Elke. "Cooperation and Conflict in Economic Summitry." Paper Presented at the *28th Annual Convention of the International Studies Association*, held on April 14-18, 1987, in Washington, D.C.
3539. Tooze, Roger, and Geoffrey Edwards. *Plaza Negotiations: The Attempt to Achieve Currency Re-Alignment, 1984-1985.* PEW Case Studies, 132.0--A-88-S. Los Angeles, CA.: School of International Relations, University of Southern California, 1988.
3540. United States. Congress. Joint Economic Committee. *Williamsburg Economic Summit: Hearing.* 98th Cong., 1st sess. Washington, D.C.: U.S. Government Printing Office, 1983. 68p.
3541. _____._____._____. *Venice Economic Summit: Hearing.* 100th Cong., 1st sess. Washington, D.C.: U.S. Government Printing Office, 1987. 52p.
3542. Watt, David. *Next Step for Summitry: Report of the Twentieth Century Fund International Conference on Economic Summitry.* New York: Priority Press, 1984. 61p.

VIII

International Trade Negotiations

A major part of relations between states relate to economic and trade issues. Most contacts between states relate to matters of commerce. Economic and financial issues are secondary only to matters pertaining to national security and sovereignty. This chapter focuses on negotiations between states involving finance, trade, business. The aim is to concentrate on the processes of negotiations and less on the policy issues.

The first section covers materials dealing with general aspects of international business negotiations. The second section identifies materials dealing the influence of cultural differences on international business negotiations. Sections three and four deal with oil diplomacy and commodity negotiations respectively. The fifth section covers the negotiations on GATT - General Agreement on Tariffs and Trade, and GATT's influence on international trade agreements. Section six deals with the intricacies of trade relations between the United States and Canada. The next two sections cover Soviet, Chinese and Japanese trade negotiations and their particular styles. The last chapter covers various other case studies of international business negotiations.

A. GENERAL WORKS

1. Books

3543. Adler, Nancy J. *International Dimensions of Organizational Behavior.* Boston, MA.: Kent, 1986. 242p.
3544. American Arbitration Association. *New Strategies for Peaceful Resolution of International Business Disputes.* Dobbs Ferry, NY.: Oceana, 1971. 252p.
3545. Bradlow, Daniel D. *International Borrowing: Negotiating and Structuring International Dept Transactions.* Washington, D.C.: International Law Institute, 1986. 499p.
3546. Daoudi, M. J., and M. S. Dajani. *Economic Diplomacy: Embargo Leverage and World Politics.* Boulder, CO.: Westview Press, 1985. 177p.
3547. Douglas, A. *International Industrial Peacemaking.* New York: Columbia University Press, 1962. 670p.
3548. Feketekuty, Geza. *International Trade in Services: An Overview and Blueprint for Negotiations.* Cambridge, MA.: Ballinger, 1988. 355p.
3549. Hearn, Patrick. *International Business Agreements: A Practical Guide to the Negotiation and Foundation of Agency, Distribution and Intellectual Property Licensing Agreements.* Brookfield, VT.: Gower, 1987. 222p.
3550. Hufbauer, Gary C., and Jeffrey J. Schott. *Trading for Growth: The Next Round of Trade Negotiations.* Washington, D.C.: Institute for International Economics, 1985. 110p.
3551. International Technical Information Institute. *International Business Negotiation & Contract: Encyclopedia of Terms & Conditions.* New York: Media International Promotion, 1984. 450p.
3552. Kapoor, Ashok. *Planning for International Business Negotiations.* Cambridge, MA.: Ballinger, 1975. 355p.
3553. Kennedy, Gavin. *Doing Business Abroad.* New York: Simon & Schuster, 1985. 268p.
3554. _____. *Managing Negotiations.* London: Business Books, 1980. 179p.
3555. MacBean, A. I., and P. N. Snowden. *International Institutions in Trade and Finance.* London: Allen & Unwinn, 1983. 271p.
3556. Marsh, P. D. V. *Contract Negotiation Handbook.* Aldershot, England: Gower, 1984. 412p.
3557. Snowdon, Sondra. *The Global Edge: How Your Company Can Win in the International Marketplace.* New York: Simon & Schuster, 1986. 431p.
3558. Stoever, William A. *Renegotiations in International Business Transactions: The Process of Dispute Resolution Between Multinational Investors and Host Societies.* Lexington, MA.: D. C. Heath and Lexington Books, 1981. 380p.
3559. Waldmann, Raymond J. *Managed Trade: The New Competition Between Nations.* Cambridge, MA.: Ballinger, 1986. 204p.
3560. Aggarwal, V. K., et al. "The Dynamics of Negotiated Protectionism." *American Political Science Review*, 81 (June 1987), 345-366.

2. Journal Articles

3561. Bairstow, F. "The Trend Toward Centralized Bargaining - A Patchwork Quilt of International Diversity." *Columbia Journal of World Business*, 20:1 (1985), 75-83.
3562. Bare, C. G. "Trade Policy and Atlantic Partnership - Prospects for New Negotiations." *Orbis*, 17:4 (1974), 1280-1305.

3563. Bhagwati, Jagdish N. "Trade in Services and the Multilateral Trade Negotiations." *World Bank Economic Review*, 1:4 (September 1987), 549-570.
3564. _____. "Whither the Global Negotiations." *Finance and Management*, 20 (September 1983), 34-36.
3565. "The Bretton-Woods Institutions - What Room for Accommodation - Discussion." In: R. D. Hansen, ed. *Global Negotiation and Beyond*. Austin, TX.: L.B.J. School of Public Affairs, 1981. pp. 129-159.
3566. Brock, E. William. "A Simple Plan for Negotiating Trade in Services." *World Economy*, 5 (1982), 229-240.
3567. Carmichael, W. B. "National Interest and International Trade Negotiations." *World Economy*, 9:4 (1986), 341-357.
3568. Contractor, F. J. "A Generalized Theorem for Joint Venture and Licensing Negotiations." *Journal of International Business Studies*, 16:2 (1985), 23-50.
3569. Delatorre, J. "Foreign Investment and Economic Development - Conflict and Negotiation." *Journal of International Business Studies*, 12:2 (1981), 9-32.
3570. Diebold, William, and Helena Stalson. "Negotiating Issues in International Services Transactions." In: W. Cline, ed. *Trade Policy in the 1980s*. Washington, D.C.: Institute for International Economics, 1983. pp. 581-610.
3571. Fagre, Nathan, and Louis T. Wells. "Bargaining Power of Multinational and Host Governments." *Journal of International Business Studies*, 13:2 (Fall 1982), 9-24.
3572. Gray, H. P. "A Negotiating Strategy for Trade in Services." *Journal of World Trade Law*, 5 (September-October 1983), 377-389.
3573. Hamner, F. T. "Business Investment Negotiations in Developing Countries." *Business Horizons*, (Winter 1965), 97-103.
3574. Hart, M. M. "The Mercantilists Lament - National Treatment and Modern Trade Negotiations." *Journal of World Trade Law*, 21:6 (December 1987), 37-62.
3575. Holmes, George, and Stan Glaser. "Guidelines for Commercial Negotiations." *Business Horizons*, 27 (January/February 1984), 21-25.
3576. Huntington, Samuel P. "Trade, Technology, and Leverage: Economic Diplomacy." *Foreign Policy*, 32 (Fall 1978), 63-79.
3577. Hutton, N. "Salience of Linkage in International Economic Negotiations." *Journal of Common Market Studies*, 13:1-2 (1975), 136-160.
3578. Jankowitsch, Odette. "A Round of Global Negotiations on International Economic Cooperation: A Preview." In: C. T. Saunders, ed. *East-West--South: Economic Interactions Between Three Worlds*. London: Macmillan Press, 1981. pp. 257-264.
3579. Kapoor, Ashok. "MNC Negotiations: Characteristics and Planning Implications." *Columbia Journal of World Business*, 9:4 (Winter 1974), 121-131.
3580. Kaufmann, P. J. "Commercial Exchange Relationships and the Negotiator's Dilemma." *Negotiation Journal*, 3:1 (January 1987), 73-80.
3581. Lee, Tom K. "Bilateral Trade, Dynamic Bargaining and Nonrenewable Resources." *Journal of International Economics*, 14:1-2 (1983), 169-178.
3582. Malmgren, Harald B. "Trade Policy and Trade Negotiations in the 1980s." In: J. N. Yochelson, ed. *The U.S. and the World Economy*. Boulder, CO.: Westview Press, 1985. pp. 1-14.
3583. _____. "Negotiating International Rules for Trade in Services." *World Economy*, 8:1 (March 1985), 11-27.
3584. _____. "Managing International Economic Conflicts." *Annals of International Studies*, 3 (1972), 185-198.

3585. Marks, Matthew J., and Harald B. Malmgren. "Negotiating Nontariff Distortions to Trade." *Law and Policy in International Business*, 7 (April 1975), 327-341.
3586. McLean, R. A. "Bargaining Cartels and Multinational Industrial Relations." *Columbia Journal of World Business*, 12:2 (Summer 1977), 107-111.
3587. Megna, L. L. "Outcome of the Multilateral Trade Negotiations." *Forensic Quarterly*, 53:3 (1979), 281-290.
3588. Miner, Frederick C. "International Conflict Resolution: A Business Problem Solving Strategy." In: J. P. Maas and R. A. C. Stewart, eds. *Toward a World of Peace*. Suva, Fiji: University of the South Pacific, 1986. pp. 333-48.
3589. Morse, Edward L. "Crisis Diplomacy, Interdependence, and Politics of International Economic Relations." *World Politics*, 24 (1972), 123-150.
3590. ____. "Crisis Diplomacy, Interdependence and the Politics of International Economic Relations." In: R. Tanter and R. H. Ullman, eds. *Theory and Policy in International Relations*, Princeton, NJ.: Princeton University Press, 1973. pp. 123-150.
3591. Pinder, John. "Economic Diplomacy." In: J. N. Rosenau, K. W. Thompson and G. Boyd, eds. *World Politics: An Introduction*. New York: The Free Press, 1976. pp. 312-336.
3592. ____. "Integration Groups and Trade Negotiations." *Government and Opposition*, 14:2 (Spring 1973), 149-171.
3593. Plummer, Joseph. "International Trade Negotiations." *Editorial Research Reports*, (May 14, 1976), 345-362.
3594. Rangarajan, L. N. "The Politics of International Trade." In: S. Strange, ed. *Path to International Political Economy*. London: Allen & Unwin, 1984. pp. 126-163.
3595. Renner, J. C. "Trade Barriers, Negotiations and Rules." *Columbia Journal of World Business*, 8:3 (1973), 51-58.
3596. Ribicoff, A. "Strategy for International Trade Negotiations." *Columbia Journal of World Business*, 8:3 (1973), 40-44.
3597. Rivers, Richard B., and John D. Greenwald. "The Negotiations of a Code on Subsidies and Countervailing Measures: Bridging Fundamental Policy Differences." *Law and Policy in International Business*, 2 (1979), 1447-1496.
3598. Roessler, F. "Rationale for Reciprocity in Trade Negotiations Under Floating Currencies." *Kyklos*, 31:2 (1978), 258-274.
3599. Salacuse, Jeswald W. "Making Deals in Strange Places: A Beginner's Guide to International Business Negotiations." *Negotiation Journal*, 4:1 (January 1988), 5-14.
3600. Schmidt, Robert D. "Personal Experiences in Commercial Negotiations." In: L. Sloss and M. Scott Davis, eds. *A Game for High Stakes*. Cambridge, MA.: Ballinger, 1986. pp. 115-122.
3601. Shonfield, Andrew. "International Economic Relations of the Western World: An Overall View." In: A. Shonfield, et al. *International Economic Relations of the Western World, 1959-1971: Vol 1. Politics and Trade*. London: Oxford University Press, 1976. pp. 1-142.
3602. Strange, Susan. "The Poverty of Multilateral Economic Diplomacy." In: G. R. Berridge and A. Jennings, eds. *Diplomacy at the UN*. London: Macmillan, 1985. pp. 109-129.
3603. Van Zandt, Howard F. "Comparative International Negotiating Practices." In: R. J. Lewicki and J. A. Litterer, eds. *Negotiation: Readings, Exercises and Cases*. Homewood, IL.: Irwin, 1985. pp 245-249.

3604. Wells, Louis T. "Sovereignty en Garde: Negotiating with Foreign Investors." *International Organization,* 39 (Winter 1985), 47-78.
3605. Winham, Gilbert R. "International Trade Negotiations." *International Studies Newsletter,* (1973), 30-32.

3. Documents and Reports

3606. Antrim, Lance, and David A. Lax. "Support and Analysis for International Commercial Department Negotiations." In: *Computer Support for Negotiations and Conflict Resolution.* Working Paper Series, 10. Cambridge, MA.: The Program of the Processes of International Negotiations. American Academy of Arts and Sciences, 1987. 7p.
3607. Camps, Miriam. *The Free Trade Area Negotiations.* Policy Memorandum No. 18. Princeton, NJ.: Center for International Studies, Woodrow Wilson School of Public and International Affairs, 1959. 51p.
3608. _____., and William Diebold. *The New Multilateralism: Can the World Trading System be Saved.* New York: Council on Foreign Relations, 1983. 72p.
3609. Geiger, Theodore. *International Monetary Reform Negotiations.* London: British Monetary Reform Negotiations, 1973. 14p.
3610. Ghauri, Pervez N. "International Business Negotiations." Paper Presented at the *European International Association/Academy of International Business, Joint International Conference,* held in December 17-19, 1981, in Barcelona.
3611. *International Trade: Special Studies, 1971-1981.* Frederick, MD.: University Publications of America, 1985. 12 Microfilm Reels with Printed Guide.
3612. *International Trade: Special Studies, 1982-1985.* Frederick, MD.: University Publications of America, 1986. 9 Microfilm Reels with Printed Guide.
3613. Johnson, Harry G. *Trade Negotiations and the New International Monetary System.* Leiden: A. W. Sijthoff, 1976. 37p.
3614. Kivikari, Urpo. "Joint Ventures - Joint Interests in East-West Trade." Paper Presented at the *Conference on the Processes of International Negotiations,* held on May 18-22, 1987, at the International Institute for Applied System Analysis (IIASA), in Laxenburg, Austria.
3615. Lundstedt, Sven B. "Conceptions of the Trade Negotiation Process." Paper Presented at the *Conference on the Processes of International Negotiations,* held on May 18-22, 1987, at the International Institute for Applied Systems Analysis (IIASA), in Laxenburg, Austria.
3616. Meagher, Robert F. "The Changing Bargaining Postures of Developing Countries Relating to Foreign Private Investments." Paper Presented at the *20th Annual Convention of the International Studies Association,* held on March 21-24, 1979, in Toronto.
3617. *Multinational Corporations, OPEC, Cartels, Foreign Investments and Technology Transfer: Special Studies, 1971-1981.* Frederick, MD.: University Publications of America, 1983. 10 Microfilm Reels with Printed Guide.
3618. *Multinational Corporations, OPEC, Cartels, Foreign Investments, and Technology Transfer: Special Studies, 1982-1985.* Frederick, MD.: University Publications of America, 1986. 5 Microfilm Reels and Printed Guide.
3619. Nelson, Charles G. *The Role of the OECD in International Economic Negotiations.* Ph.D. Dissertation. Bloomington, IN.: Indiana University, 1971. 459p.

International Trade Negotiations 213

3620. Nicolaidis, Kalypso. *Launching Multilateral Negotiations in Trade in Services: The Dynamics of Agenda Setting.* PIN Program Working Paper Series No. 12. Cambridge, MA.: American Academy of Arts and Sciences, 1987.
3621. Odell, John. "A Theory of International Economic Bargaining." Paper Presented at the *Annual Meeting of the American Political Science Association*, held on September 5, 1987, in Chicago, IL.
3622. Oye, Kenneth A. *Bargaining, Belief Systems, and Breakdown. International Political Economy, 1929-1936.* Ph.D. Thesis. Cambridge MA.: Harvard University, 1983. 211p.
3623. Pickering, Laurence G. *The United States and the Post-World War II International Trade Conference.* Ph.D. Dissertation. Lincoln, NB.: University of Nebraska, 1954. 570p.
3624. Schwenger, Robert B. "New Concepts and Methods in Foreign Trade Negotiations." In: U.S. Congress. House. Ways and Means Committee. *Tariff and Trade Proposals, Part 10.* 91st Cong., 2nd sess. Washington, D.C.: U.S. Government Printing Office, 1970. pp. 2735-2747.
3625. United Nations Conference on Trade and Development. UNCTAD. *The Generalized System of Preferences and the Multilateral Trade Negotiations.* New York: U.N., 1978. 44p.
3626. United States.Congress.House.Committee on Small Business.Subcommittee on General Oversight and Minority Enterprise. *Multilateral Trade Negotiations: Hearings.* 96th Cong., 1st sess. Washington, D.C.: U.S. Government Printing Office, 1979. 227p.
3627. _____._____._____.Committee on Ways and Means.Subcommittee on Trade. *Background and Status of the Multilateral Trade Negotiations.* 94th Cong., 1st sess. Washington, D.C.: U.S. Government Printing Office, 1975. 73p.
3628. _____._____._____._____. *Multilateral Trade Negotiations: Hearings.* 96th Cong., 1st sess. Washington, D.C.: U.S. Government Printing Office, 1979. 761p.
3629. _____._____.Senate.Committee on Banking, Housing and Urban Affairs.Subcommittee on International Finance and Monetary Policy. *Multilateral Trade Negotiations: Hearings.* 96th Cong., 1st sess. Washington, D.C.: U.S. Government Printing Office, 1979. 115p.
3630. _____._____._____.Committee on Foreign Relations.Joint Committee on Taxation. *Tax Treaties: Steps in the Negotiation and Ratification of Tax Treaties and Status of Proposed Tax Treaties.* Washington, D.C.: U.S. Government Printing Office, 1979. 7p.
3631. _____.Office of the Special Representative for Trade Negotiations. *1964-1967 Trade Conference: Report on United States Negotiations.* 2 Vols. Washington, D.C.: U.S. Government Printing Office, 1968.
3632. Vlachoutsicos, C. A. "Interaction Between Theory and Practice of Trade Negotiations: Experiences and Proposals of a Practitioner." Paper Presented at the *Conference on the Processes of International Negotiations*, held on May 18-22, 1987, at the International Institute for Applied Systems Analysis (IIASA), in Laxenburg, Austria.
3633. Weiss, Stephen E. "Research on Negotiation in International Business: Potential Contributions to the International Studies Literature." Paper Presented at the *28th Annual Convention of the International Studies Association*, held on April 14-18, 1987, in Washington, D.C.
3634. _____. "International Business Negotiations." Paper Presented at the *28th Annual Convention of the International Studies Association*, held on April 14-18, 1987, in Washington, D.C.

3635. Winham, Gilbert R. "Robert Strauss, the MTN and the Control of Factions." Paper Presented at the *75th Annual Meeting of the American Political Science Association,* held on August 31 - September 3, 1979, in Washington, D.C.
3636. _____. "International Trade Negotiations." Paper Presented at the *15th Annual Convention of the International Studies Association,* held on March 20-23, 1974, in St.Louis.

B. CULTURAL ASPECTS

1. Books

3637. McCall, J. B., and M. B. Warrington. *Marketing by the Agreement: A Cross-Cultural Approach to Business Negotiations.* Chichester: Wiley, 1986. 274p.

2. Journal Articles

3638. Graham, John L. "The Influence of Culture on the Process of Business Negotiations - An Exploratory Study." *Journal of Business Studies,* 16:1 (1985), 81-96.
3639. _____., and R. A. Herberger. "Negotiators Abroad - Don't Shoot from the Hip: Cross-Cultural Business Negotiations." *Harvard Business Review,* 61 (July-August 1983), 160-168.

3. Documents and Reports

3640. _____. *Cross-Cultural Sales Negotiations: A Multilevel Analysis.* Ph.D. Dissertation. Berkeley, CA.: University of California at Berkeley, 1980. 333p.
3641. Renwick, George. "Technology Transfer: Unexpected Cultural Barriers." Paper Presented at the *28th Annual Convention of the International Studies Association,* held on April 14-18, 1987, in Washington, D.C.
3642. Weiss, Stephen E., and William Stripp. *Negotiating with Foreign Businesspersons: An Introduction for Americans with Propositions on Six Cultures.* Working Paper No. 1. New York: New York University. Faculty of Business Administration, 1985. 52p.

C. OIL DIPLOMACY

1. Books

3643. Ali, Sheikh Rustan. *Saudi Arabia and Oil Diplomacy.* New York: Praeger, 1976. 197p.
3644. Chester, D. W. *United States Oil Policy and Diplomacy: A 20th Century Overview.* London: Greenwood, 1984. 399p.
3645. Chisholm, Archibald H. T. *First Kuwait Oil Concession Agreement - Record of Negotiations, 1911-1934.* London: Frank Cass, 1975. 254p.

3646. Venn, Fiona. *Oil Diplomacy in the 20th Century.* Basingstoke: Macmillan, 1986. 228p.
3647. Ward, Thomas E. *Negotiations for Oil Concessions in Bahrain, El Hasa of the Neutral Zone, Qatar and Kuwait.* New York: (the author), 1965. 296p.

2. Journal Articles

3648. Adebajo, A. "Oil and Nigerias Relations with the Great Powers - The Limits of Oil Diplomacy." In: O. Aluko, ed. *Africa and the Great Powers in the 1980s.* Lanham, MD.: University Press of America, 1987. pp. 77-98.
3649. Braden, Wythe E. "Anatomy of Failure: Japan - U.S.S.R. Negotiations on Siberian Oil Development." *Fletcher Forum,* 5:1 (Winter 1981), 74-105.
3650. Philip, G. "Limitations of Bargaining Theory - Case Study of International Petroleum Company in Peru." *World Development,* 4:3 (1976), 231-239.
3651. Schuler, G. "The International Oil Negotiations." In: I. W. Zartman, ed. *The 50% Solution.* Garden City, NY.: Anchor Press, 1976. pp. 124-207.
3652. Shafaeddin, Mehdi. "Diversification, Bargaining Power and Self-Reliance in an Oil-Exporting Country: The Case of Iran." *Development Policy Review,* 4:2 (1986), 140-160.
3653. Stivers, W. "International Politics and Iraqi Oil, 1918-1928 - A Study in Anglo-American Diplomacy." *Business History Review,* 55:4 (1981), 517-540.
3654. Walton, A. M. "Atlantic Relations: Policy Coordination and Conflict: Atlantic Bargaining over Energy." *International Affairs,* 42:2 (April 1976), 180-196.

3. Documents and Reports

3655. Adamson, David M. *Oil and North-South Negotiation: A Study of the Conference on International Economic Cooperation (CIEC), 1975-1977.* Ph.D. Dissertation. Medford, MA.: Fletcher School of Law and Diplomacy, Tuft University, 1981.
3656. Ahrari, Mohammed E. *The Dynamics of Oil Diplomacy: Conflict and Consensus.* Ph.D. Dissertation. Carbondale, IL.: Southern Illinois University at Carbondale, 1976.
3657. Kohl, Wilfrid L., and Kamal H. Shukri. *OPEC and the World Oil Market: The March 1983 London Agreement.* PEW Case Studies, 123.0-F-88-J. Washington, D.C.: School of Advanced International Studies, John Hopkins University, 1988.
3658. Kohler, Larry R. *Canadian/American Oil Diplomacy: The Adjustment of Conflicting National Oil Policies, 1975-1973.* Ph.D. Dissertation. Baltimore, MD.: Johns Hopkins University, 1985. 438p.
3659. United States. Congress. House. Committee on Foreign Affairs. Subcommittee on Foreign Economic Policy and Subcommittee on Near East and South Asia. *Oil Negotiations, OPEC and Stability of Supply: Hearings.* 93rd Cong., 1st sess. Washington, D.C.: U.S. Government Printing Office, 1973. 300p.
3660. Weisberg, Richard C. *Politics of Crude Oil Pricing in the Middle East, 1970-1975: Study in International Bargaining.* Berkeley, CA.: Institute for International Studies, 1977. 170p.

D. COMMODITY NEGOTIATIONS

1. Books

3661. Atimomo, Emiko. *Law and Diplomacy in Commodity Economics: A Study of Techniques, Cooperation and Conflict in International Public Policy Issues.* New York: Macmillan Press, 1981. 384p.
3662. Chimni, B. S. *International Commodity Agreements: A Legal Study.* Beckenham, Kent: Croom Helm, 1987. 320p.
3663. *Confrontation or Negotiation: United States Policy and European Agriculture: An Agricultural Policy Study of the Curry Foundation.* Millwood, NY.: Associated Faculty Press, 1985. 303p.
3664. Finlayson, Jock A., and Mark W. Zacher. *Managing International Markets: Developing Countries and the Community Trade Regime.* New York: Columbia University Press, 1988. 348p.
3665. Porter, Roger B. *The U.S. - U.S.S.R. Grain Agreement.* Cambridge: Cambridge University Press, 1984. 160p.
3666. Rangarajan, L. N. *Commodity Conflict: Political Economy of International Commodity Negotiations.* London: Croom Helm, 1978. 390p.
3667. Sengupta, Arjun, ed. *Commodities, Finance and Trade: Issues in North-South Negotiations.* Westport, CT.: Greenwood Press, 1980. 407p.

2. Journal Articles

3668. Ali, Liaquat. "The World Wheat Market and International Agreements." *Journal of World Trade Law,* 16:1 (January/February 1982), 59-80.
3669. Chadha, I. S. "North-South Negotiating Process in the Field of Commodities." In: A. Sengupta, ed. *Commodities, Finance and Trade.* London: Frances Pinter, 1980. pp. 3-39.
3670. Cohn, Theodore. "The 1978-79 Negotiations for an International Wheat Agreement: An Opportunity Lost?" *International Journal,* 15:1 (Winter 1979-80), 132-149.
3671. Degorter, H. "Agricultural Policies and International Trade Negotiations - Research Issues." *Canadian Journal of Agricultural Economics,* 34 (1987), 280-294.
3672. Finlayson, Jock A., and Mark W. Zacher. "The Politics of International Commodity Regulation - The Negotiation and Operation of the International Cocoa Agreements." *Third World Quarterly,* 5:2 (1983), 386-417.
3673. Gutman, G. O. "Resources Diplomacy." *Australian Quarterly,* 47:1 (1975), 36-50.
3674. Harris, Stuart. "Problems and Prospects of North-South Negotiations in the Commodity Field." In: A. Sengupta, ed. *Commodities Finance and Trade: Issues in North South Negotiations.* London: Frances Pinter, 1980. pp. 40-58.
3675. Mahler, Vincent A. "The Political Economy of North-South Commodity Bargaining: The Case of the International Sugar Agreement." *International Organization,* 38:4 (Autumn 1984), 709-732.
3676. Porter, Roger B. "The U.S. - U.S.S.R. Grain Agreement: Some Lessons for Policymakers." *Public Policy,* 29 (Fall 1981), 527-551.
3677. Rangarajan, L. N. "Commodity Conflict Revisited: From Nairobi to Belgrade." *Third World Quarterly,* 5:3 (July 1983), 586-610.

3678. Rothstein, Robert L. "Commodity Bargaining: The Political Economy of Regime Creation." In: I. W. Zartman, ed. *Positive Sum.* New Brunswick, NJ.: Transaction Books, 1987. pp. 15-47.
3679. _____. "Consensual Knowledge and International Collaboration: Some Lessons from the Commodity Negotiations." *International Negotiations,* 38:4 (Autumn 1984), 733-762.
3680. _____. "Regime-Creation by a Coalition of the Weak: Lessons from the NIEO and the Integrated Program for Commodities." *International Studies Quarterly,* 28:3 (September 1984), 307-328.
3681. Smith, Ian. "Prospects for a New International Sugar Agreement." *Journal of World Trade Law,* 17:4 (July - August 1983), 308-324.
3682. Tangermann, Stefan, T. E. Josling and Scott Pearson. "Multilateral Negotiations on Farm-Support Levels." *The World Economy: A Quarterly Journal on International Economic Affairs,* 10:3 (September 1987), 265-282.
3683. Warley, K. T. "Linkages Between Bilateral and Multilateral Negotiations in Agriculture." *American Journal of Agricultural Economics,* 69:5 (December 1987), 940-945.
3684. Worthing, H. L. "Agricultural Trade Negotiations." *Columbia Journal of World Business,* 8:3 (1973), 45-50.
3685. Zacher, Mark W., and Jock A. Finlayson. "The Politics of International Commodity Regulation: The Negotiation and Operation of the International Cocoa Agreement." *Third World Quarterly,* 5:2 (1983), 386-417.

3. Documents and Reports

3686. Harris, Simon. *EEC Trade Relations with the USA in Agricultural Products: Multilateral Tariff Negotiations.* Occasional Paper No. 3. Ashford: Centre for European Agricultural Studies, Wye College, 1977. 57p.
3687. Hudson, John F. *Report on Agricultural Concessions in the Multilateral Trade Negotiations.* FAS-M-301. Washington, D.C.: Foreign Agricultural Service, 1981. 137p.
3688. Odell, John, and Margit Matzinger. *Agricultural Trade Dispute Between the U.S. and the European Community.* PEW Case Studies, 130.0-A-88-S. Los Angeles, CA.: School of International Relations, University of Southern California, 1988.
3689. Powell, Charles, and Charles Benjamin. *Negotiating Grain Purchase Agreements: the U.S. - U.S.S.R. Experience.* PEW Case Studies, 131.0-E-88-S. Los Angeles, CA.: School of International Relations, University of Southern California, 1988.
3690. Schutjer, Wayne E., and Edward J. Ayo. *Negotiating a World Cocoa Agreement: Analysis and Prospects.* University Park, PA.: Agricultural Experimental Station, Pennsylvania State University, 1967. 53p.
3691. United States. Congress. Senate. Committee on Agriculture, Nutrition and Forestry. *International Agricultural Trade Negotiations in the Mid - 1980's: Hearings.* 99th Cong., 2nd sess. Washington, D.C.: U.S. Government Printing Office, 1986. 113p.
3692. _____._____._____.Council on International Economic Policy. *Agricultural Trade and Proposed Round of Multilateral Negotiations: Report.* 93rd Cong., 1st sess. Washington, D.C.: U.S. Government Printing Office, 1973. 241p.
3693. Vacs, Aldo C. *1980 Grain Embargo: The United States, Argentina and the U.S.S.R.* PEW Case Studies, 118.0-B-88-P. Pittsburgh, PA.: Graduate School of Public and International Affairs, 1988.

E. GATT NEGOTIATIONS

1. Books

3694. Casadio, G. P. *Transatlantic Trade: USA-EEC Confrontation in the GATT Negotiations.* Farnborough, Hants: Saxon House, 1973. 260p.
3695. Cline, William R., et al. *Trade Negotiations in the Tokyo Round: A Quantitative Assessment.* Washington, D.C.: Brookings Institution, 1978. 314p.
3696. Curtis, Thomas B., and John Robert Vastine. *The Kennedy Round and the Future of American Trade.* New York: Praeger, 1971. 239p.
3697. Curzon, Gerard. *Multilateral Commercial Diplomacy: The General Agreement on Tariffs and Trade.* London: Michael Joseph, 1965. 367p.
3698. Damm, Kenneth W. *The GATT: Law and International Economic Organization.* Chicago, IL.: University of Chicago Press, 1970. 480p.
3699. Glick, Leslie Alan. *Multilateral Trade Negotiations: World Trade After the Tokyo Round.* Totowa, NJ.: Rowman & Allanheld, 1984. 423p.
3700. Hudec, Robert E. *The GATT Legal System and World Trade Diplomacy.* New York: Praeger, 1975. 399p.
3701. Lund, Oliver. *Law and Its Limitations in the GATT Multilateral Trade System.* Dordrecht: M. Nijhoff, 1986. 145p.
3702. Twiggs, Joan E. *The Tokyo Round of Multilateral Trade Negotiations: A Case Study in Building Domestic Support for Diplomacy.* Lanham, MD.: University Press of America, 1987. 131p.
3703. Winham, Gilbert R. *International Trade and the Tokyo Round Negotiations.* Princeton, NJ.: Princeton University Press, 1986. 449p.

2. Journal Articles

3704. Ahmad, Jaleel. "Tokyo Rounds of Trade Negotiations and Generalized System of Preferences." *Economic Journal,* 88:350 (1978), 285-295.
3705. Aho, C. Michael. "The Uruguay Round: Will it Revitalize the Trading System?" *The Fletcher Forum,* 11:1 (Winter 1987), 1-12.
3706. Anjaria, S. J. "The Tokyo Round of Multilateral Trade Negotiations." *Finance and Development,* 15:1 (March 1978), 14-16.
3707. Berg, Terrence G. "Trade in Services: Toward a "Development Round" of GATT Negotiations Benefiting Both Developing and Industrialized States." *Harvard International Law Journal,* 28:1 (Winter 1987), 1-30.
3708. Chan, Kenneth S. "The International Negotiating Game: Some Evidence from the Tokyo Round." *Review of Economic and Statistics,* 67:3 (1985), 456-464.
3709. Crean, John G. "Coming Negotiations under GATT." *Behind the Headlines,* 32:3 (1973), 1-13.
3710. Culbert, Jay. "War-Time Anglo-American Talks and the Making of the GATT." *The World Economy: A Quarterly Journal on International Economic Affairs,* 10:4 (December 1987), 381-408.
3711. Curzon, Gerard, and Victoria Curzon. "The Management of Trade Relations in the GATT." In: A. Shonfield, ed. *International Economic Relations of the Western World, 1959-1971.* London: Oxford University Press, 1976. pp. 143-283.
3712. Davis, J. A. "Multilateral Trade Negotiations - The Tokyo Round." *Federal Bar News & Journal,* 29:1 (1982), 23-26.
3713. De Kieffer, D. E. "The GATT: Multilateral Trade Negotiations and Canadian--US Trade." *Canadian Council on International Law,* (1985), 133-138.

3714. Denis, J. E., and R. Poirier. "The North American Chemical Industry in the Tokyo Round Participation of Canadian and American Firms in the GATT Negotiation Process." *Journal of World Trade Law*, 19:4 (1985), 315-342.
3715. Fukui, Haruhiro. "The GATT Tokyo Round: The Bureaucratic Politics of Multilateral Diplomacy." In: M. Blaker, ed. *The Politics of Trade: U.S. and Japanese Policymaking for the GATT Negotiations.* New York: Columbia University Press, 1978. pp. 75-170.
3716. "The GATT Multilateral Trade Negotiations - Principal Results." *Bulletin for International Fiscal Documentation*, 34:4 (1980), 174-177.
3717. Graham, T. R. "Reforming the International Trading System - Tokyo Round Trade Negotiations in the Final Stage." *Cornell International Law Journal*, 12:1 (1979), 1-42.
3718. Greig, D. "The GATT and Multilateral Trade Negotiations." *Australian Quarterly*, 59:3-4 (1987), 305-321.
3719. Gundelach, Finn. "The Kennedy Round of Trade Negotiations: Results and Lessons." In: F. A. M. A. von Geusau, ed. *Economic Relations After the Kennedy Round.* Leyden: Sijthoff, 1969. pp. 146-198.
3720. Jackson, John H. "Dispute Settlement Techniques Between Nations Concerning Economic Relations - With Special Emphasis on GATT." In: *Sixth Sokol Colloquium, Resolving Transnational Disputes Through International Arbitration*, Charlottesville, VA.: University Press of Virginia, 1984. pp. 39-74.
3721. _____. "GATT Machinery and the Tokyo Round Agreements." In: W. R. Cline, ed. *Trade Policy in the 1980s.* Washington, D.C.: Institute for International Economics, 1983. pp. 159-187.
3722. _____. "Governmental Disputes in International Trade Relations: A Proposal in the Context of GATT." *Journal of World Trade Law*, 13:1 (January--February 1979), 1-21.
3723. Kalil, Michael B. "The Uruguay Round Negotiation Interview with Ambassador Michael B. Smith." *Fletcher Forum*, 11:1 (Winter 1987), 13-19.
3724. Masih, A. "Multilateral Trade Negotiations: Tokyo Round - Implications for Australia." *Australian Quarterly*, 55:1 (1983), 95-103.
3725. McRae, D. M., and J. C. Thomas. "The GATT and Multilateral Treaty Making: The Tokyo Round." *American Journal of International Law*, 77:1 (January 1983), 51-83.
3726. Meier, G. M. "The Tokyo Round of Multilateral Trade Negotiations and the Developing Countries." *Cornell International Law Journal*, 13:2 (1980), 239-256.
3727. Patterson, Gardner. "The GATT and the Negotiation of International Trade Rules." In: A. K. Henrikson, ed. *Negotiating World Order.* Wilmington, DE.: Scholarly Resources, 1986. pp. 181-198.
3728. _____., and Eliza Patterson. "Importance of a GATT Review in the New Negotiations." *The World Economy: A Quarterly Journal of International Economic Affairs*, 9:2 (June 1986), 153-170.
3729. Randhawa, P. S. "Punta del Este and After - Negotiations on Trade in Services and the Uruguay Round." *Journal of World Trade Law*, 21:4 (August 1987), 163-172.
3730. Sek, Lenore. "The Uruguay Round of GATT Negotiations." *Congressional Research Service Review*, 9:6 (June 1988), 8-9.
3731. Van Bael, Ivo. "The GATT Dispute Settlement Procedure." *Journal of World Trade*, 22:4 (1988), 67-78.
3732. Winham, Gilbert R. "Canada at Tokyo Round of Trade Negotiations." *International Perspectives*, (March 1979), 27-30.

3733. _____. "Multilateral Economic Negotiations." *Negotiation Journal*, 3 (April 1987), 175-190.
3734. _____. "The U.S. Winegallon Concession: How the Biggest Chip in the Tokyo Round was Negotiated." *International Journal*, 36:2 (1981), 851-878.

3. Documents and Reports

3735. Aronson, Jonathan D. *Negotiating to Launch the Uruguay Round of Trade Negotiations*. PEW Case Studies, 125.0-E-88-S. Los Angeles, CA.: School of International Relations, University of Southern California, 1988.
3736. Baldwin, Robert E. *The Multilateral Trade Negotiations: Toward Greater Liberalization*. Washington, D.C.: American Enterprise Institute for Public Policy Research, 1979. 30p.
3737. _____. *Beyond the Tokyo Round Negotiations*. London: Trade Policy Research Centre, 1979. 40p.
3738. Blaker, Michael, ed. *The Politics of Trade: US and Japanese Policymaking for the GATT Negotiations*. Occasional Papers of the East Asian Institute. New York: The Trustees of Columbia University, 1978. 184p.
3739. Canada. Department of External Affairs. *Multilateral Trade Negotiations, 1973-1979*. Toronto: Microlog, 1980. 132p. (Fiche No: 80-3708).
3740. Commission of the European Communities. *GATT Multilateral Trade Negotiations: Final Report on the GATT MTN (Tokyo Round) and Proposal for Council Decision*. COM(79)514 Final. Brussels: Commission of the European Communities, 1979.
3741. Curran, Timothy J. *The Politics of Trade Liberalization in Contemporary Japan: The Case of the Tokyo Round of Multilateral Trade Negotiations, 1973-1979*. Ph.D. Dissertation. New York: Columbia University, 1982. 367p.
3742. Falk, Pamela S. *Mexico's Accession to GATT: U.S. Negotiations in a Multilateral Context*. PEW Case Studies, 136.0-E-88-C. New York: School of International and Public Affairs, Columbia University, 1988.
3743. General Agreement on Tariffs and Trade. GATT. *The Tokyo Round of Multilateral Trade Negotiations II: Supplementary Report*. Geneva: GATT, 1980. 53p.
3744. _____._____. *The Tokyo Round of Multilateral Trade Negotiations: Report by the General Director of GATT. Vol I*. Geneva: GATT, 1979. 196p.
3745. Golt, Sidney. *The GATT Negotiations 1973-79: The Closing Stage and a Policy Statement*. London: British - North American Committee, 1978. 52p.
3746. _____. *The GATT Negotiations 1973-75: A Guide to the Issues*. London: British - North American Committee, 1974. 82p.
3747. Great Britain. Board of Trade. *The Kennedy Round of Trade Negotiations, 1964-67*. London: H.M.S.O., 1967. 47p.
3748. Nyerges, Janos. "Hungary's Accession to the GATT." Paper Presented at the *Conference on the Processes of International Negotiations*, held on May 18-22, 1987, at the International Institute for Applied Systems Analysis (IIASA), at Laxenburg, Austria.
3749. Pearson, Charles, and Nils Johnson. *The New GATT Trade Round*. FPI Case Studies No. 2. Washington, D.C.: Johns Hopkins Foreign Policy Institute, 1986.
3750. Preeg, Ernest H. *The Kennedy Round and World Trade*. Brookings Research Report, 103. Washington, D.C.: The Brookings Institute, 1970. 9p.

3751. _____. *Traders and Diplomats: An Analysis of the Kennedy Round of Negotiations Under the General Agreement on Tariffs and Trade.* Washington, D.C.: The Brookings Institution, 1970. 320p.
3752. Schriefer, John. *U.S.-European Negotiations to Clarify the GATT Aircraft Agreement.* PEW Case Studies, 121.0-A-88-P. Pittsburgh, PA.: Graduate School of Public and International Affairs, 1988.
3753. Stone, Frank. *Canada, the GATT and the International Trade System.* Montreal: The Institute for Research on Public Policy, 1984. 216p.
3754. United States. Congress. House. Committee on Foreign Affairs. Subcommittee on International Economic Policy and Trade. *Foreign Policy Aspects of the Kennedy Round, Part 2: GATT Negotiating Posture: Hearings.* 90th Cong., 1st sess. Washington, D.C.: U.S. Government Printing Office, 1967. 201p.
3755. _____._____.Senate.Committee on Finance.Subcommittee on International Trade. *United States/Japanese Trade Relations and the Status of the Multilateral Trade Negotiations: Hearings.* 95th Cong., 2nd sess. Washington, D.C.: U.S. Government Printing Office, 1978. 48p.
3756. _____.Congressional Budget Office. *The GATT Negotiations and the U.S. Trade Policy.* Washington, D.C.: U.S. Government Printing Office, 1987. 135p.
3757. _____.Department of State. *General Agreement on Tariffs and Trade; Analysis of United States Negotiations, 1960-61 Tariff Conference, Geneva, Switzerland.* Publications 7349-7350, 7408. Washington, D.C.: U.S. Government Printing Office, 1962. 3 Vols.
3758. _____._____. *General Agreement on Tariffs and Trade; Analysis of United States Negotiations, Sixth Protocol of Supplementary Concessions Negotiated at Geneva, Switzerland, Jan.- May 1956.* Washington, D.C.: U.S. Government Printing Office, 1956. 307p.

F. CANADA - U.S. TRADE NEGOTIATIONS

1. Books

3759. Riggs, A. R., and Tom Velk, eds. *Canadian - American Free Trade: Historical, Political and Economic Dimensions.* Montreal, Que.: Institute for Research on Public Policy, 1987. 265p.

2. Journal Articles

3760. Brock, E. William. "Canadian - United States Trade Negotiations - A Status Report." In: E. R. Fried and P. H. Trezise, eds. *U.S. - Canadian Economic Relations: Next Steps?* Washington, D.C.: Brookings Institution, 1984. pp. 65-76.
3761. Carroll, John E. "Water Resources Management as an Issue in Environmental Diplomacy." *Natural Resources Journal,* 26:2 (Spring 1986), 207-220.
3762. Cowhey, Peter H. "Trade Talks and the Informatics Sector." *International Journal,* 42:1 (Winter 1986-1987), 107-137.
3763. Curtis, John M. "Institutional Arrangements for Managing the Canada/U.S. Economic Relationship." In: D. Fretz, R. M. Stern and J. Whalley, eds. *Canada/United States Trade and Investment Issues.* Toronto: Ontario Economic Council, 1985. pp. 126-164.

3764. Feketekuty, Geza. "Negotiating Strategies for Liberalizing Trade and Investment in Services." In: R. M. Stern, ed. *Trade and Investment in Services: Canada/U.S. Perspectives.* Toronto: Ontario Economic Council, 1985. pp. 203-214.
3765. Gifford, Michael. "A Briefing by the Canadian Agricultural Negotiator." In: K. Allen and K. Macmillan, eds. *U.S. - Canadian Agricultural Trade Challenges.* Washington, D.C.: Resources for the Future, 1988. pp. 9-14.
3766. Gottlieb, A. E. "Managing Canadian - United States Interdependence." In: E. R. Fried and P. H. Trezise, eds. *U.S. Canadian Economic Relations: Next Steps?* Washington, D.C.: Brookings Institution, 1984. pp. 127-138.
3767. Grey, Rodney de C. "Negotiating About Trade and Investment in Services." In: R. M. Stern, ed. *Trade and Investment in Services: Canada/U.S. Perspectives.* Toronto: Ontario Economic Council, 1985. pp. 181-202.
3768. Henderson, Michael D. "The Negotiations: Power, Will, and Process." In: M. D. Henderson, ed. *The Future on the Table: Canada and the Free Trade Issue.* North York, Ont.: Masterpress, York University, 1987. pp. 141-168.
3769. Hocking, Brian. "Canada - U.S. Freer Trade Negotiations." *Round Table,* (October 1986), 384-394.
3770. Hudec, Robert E. "Dispute Settlement in Agricultural Trade Matters: The Lessons of the GATT Experience." In: K. Allen and K. Macmillan, eds. *U.S. - Canadian Agricultural Trade Challenges.* Washington, D.C.: Resources for the Future, 1988. pp. 145-154.
3771. Hufbauer, Gary C., and Jeffrey J. Schott. "The Role of Bilateral Investment Talks." In: D. W. Conklin and T. J. Courchene, eds. *Canadian Trade at a Crossroads: Options for New International Agreements.* Toronto: Ontario Economic Council, 1985. pp. 343-349.
3772. John, Louis B. "Dispute Settlement Mechanisms." In: T. J. Schoenbaum and D. D. Dallmeyer, eds. *How to Achieve Free and Fair Trade Between the United States and Canada.* Athens, GA.: Alan Rusk Center for International and Corporate Law, University of Georgia, 1986. pp. 93-101.
3773. Leyton Brown, David. "The Mug's Game: Automotive Investment Incentives in Canada and the United States." *International Journal,* 25:1 (Winter 1979-80), 170-184.
3774. Mayer, Leo V. "A Briefing by the Agricultural Negotiator." In: K. Allen and K. Macmillan, eds. *U.S. - Canadian Agricultural Trade Challenge.* Washington, D.C.: Resources for the Future, 1988. pp. 15-20.
3775. McLachlan, D. L., A. Apuzzo and W. Kerr. "The Canada - U.S. Free Trade Agreement: A Canadian Perspective." *Journal of World Trade,* 22:4 (1988), 9-34.
3776. Miller, Mark L., and Charles F. Broches. "United States Fishery Negotiations with Canada and Mexico." *Ocean Development and International Law,* 14:4 (1985), 417-451.
3777. _____. _____. "Treaty Talking: Observations on Canada - U.S. Salmon Negotiations." *American Review of Canadian Studies,* 12:3 (Fall 1982), 29-45.
3778. Niles, Thomas M. T. "U.S.-Canada Transboundary Air Pollution Negotiations." *Department of State Bulletin,* 82:2061 (August 1982), 50-52.
3779. Smith, Murray G. "A Canadian Perspective." In: R. M. Stern, P. H. Trezise and J. Whalley, eds. *Perspectives on a U.S. - Canadian Free Trade Agreement.* Washington, D.C.: The Brookings Institution, 1987. pp. 31-64.
3780. Stedman, Charles. "Canada - U.S. Automotive Agreement: The Sectoral Approach." *Journal of World Trade Law,* 8:2 (1974), 176-185.

3781. Steger, Debra P. "Canadian - U.S. Agricultural Trade: A Proposal for Resolving Disputes." In: K. Allen and K. Macmillan, eds. *U.S. - Canadian Agricultural Trade Challenges.* Washington, D.C.: Resources for the Future, 1988. pp. 161-168.
3782. Warley, K. T. "Linkages Between Bilateral and Multilateral Negotiations in Agriculture." In: K. Allen and K. Macmillan, eds. *U.S. - Canadian Agricultural Trade Challenges.* Washington, D.C.: Resources for the Future, 1988. pp. 169-178.
3783. Wilson, Arlene. "Update on the U.S.- Canada Free-Trade Agreement." *Congressional Research Service Review,* 9:6 (June 1988), 6-7.
3784. Winham, Gilbert R. "Bureaucratic Politics and Canadian Trade Negotiations." *International Journal,* 34:1 (1979), 64-89.
3785. Wonnacott, Ronald. "Bilateral Trade Liberalization with the United States and Multilateral Liberalization in the GATT: Selected Observations." In: D. W. Conklin and T. J. Courchene, eds. *Canadian Trade at a Crossroads: Options for New International Agreements.* Toronto: Ontario Economic Council, 1985. pp. 335-342.

3. Documents and Reports

3786. Canada. Department of External Affairs. *Canadian Trade Negotiations - Introduction - Selected Documents - Further Reading.* Ottawa, 1986. 105p.
3787. _____._____. *Trade Negotiations - Securing Canada's Future.* Ottawa: 1987. 67p.
3788. _____._____. *Canada - U.S. Trade Negotiations: A Chronology.* Ottawa, 1987. 14p.
3789. Caragata, Patrick J. *Non-Fuel Minerals and Canadian Foreign Policy: Negotiating from Strength and Weakness.* Ph.D. Dissertation. Toronto: University of Toronto, 1981.
3790. Doran, Charles F., and Timothy J. Naftali. *U.S. - Canadian Softwood Lumber: Trade Dispute Negotiations.* PEW Case Studies, 141.0-D-88-J. Washington, D.C.: School of Advanced International Studies, Johns Hopkins University, 1987.
3791. Dorcey, Anthony H. J. *Bargaining in the Governance of Pacific Coastal Resources: Research and Reform.* Vancouver, B.C.: Westwater Research Centre, Faculty of Graduate Studies, University of British Columbia, 1986. 219p.
3792. Fox, Annette Baker. *Cultural Enterprises and the Canada-United States Free Trade Negotiations.* PEW Case Studies, 137.0-D-88-C. New York: School of International and Public Affairs, Columbia University, 1988.
3793. Haffey, Neil. *Bilateral Negotiations With a More Powerful Neighbor: The Case of the Canada-U.S. Air Agreement.* PEW Case Studies, 116.0-D-88-I. New York: International Peace Academy, 1988.
3794. Maslove, Allan M., and Stanley L. Winer, eds. *Knocking on the Back Door: Canadian Perspectives on the Political Economy of Free Trade with the United States.* Montreal, Que.: Institute for Research on Public Policy, 1987. 233p.
3795. United States. Congress. House. Committee on Banking, Finance and Urban Affairs. Subcommittee on Economic Stabilization. *U.S./Canada Economic Relations: Hearings.* 99th Cong., 2nd sess. Washington, D.C.: U.S. Government Printing Office, 1986. 655p.

3796. _____._____._____.Committee on Foreign Affairs.Subcommittee on International Economic Policy and Trade and Subcommittee on Inter-American Affairs. *Issues in U.S. - Canadian Economic Relations.* 97th Cong., 1st sess. Washington, D.C.: U.S. Government Printing Office, 1982. 85p.

3797. _____._____._____.Committee on Foreign Relations.Subcommittee on International Economic Policy and Trade. *U.S. - Canada Trade Relations: Hearings.* 99th Cong., 2nd sess. Washington, D.C.: U.S. Government Printing Office, 1986. 34p.

3798. _____._____._____.Committee on Small Business. *U.S./Canada Trade Agreement: Hearing.* Committee Serial No. 100-15. 100th Cong., 1st sess. Washington, D.C.: U.S. Government Printing Office, 1987. 82p.

3799. _____._____._____.Committee on Ways and Means.Subcommittee on Trade. *Written Comments on United States - Canada Free Trade Negotiations.* 99th Cong., 2nd sess. Washington, D.C.: U.S. Government Printing Office, 1986. 351p.

3800. _____._____.Senate.Committee on Finance. *Negotiation of United States - Canada Free Trade Agreements: Hearing.* 99th Cong., 2nd sess. Washington, D.C.: U.S. Government Printing Office, 1986. 308p.

3801. _____._____._____._____. *Data and Materials Related to United States - Canada Free Trade Negotiations.* Washington, D.C.: U.S. Government Printing Office, 1987. 396p.

3802. Wang, Eric B. *Canada - United States Fisheries and Maritime Boundary Negotiations: Diplomacy in Deep Water.* Toronto: Canadian Institute of International Affairs, 1981. 23p.

3803. Winham, Gilbert R. "The Institutional Structure for Managing Canada - USA Trade Relations." In: *Proceedings of the Third International Law Seminar,* Ottawa: Department of Justice, 1985. pp. 30-38.

G. SOVIET TRADE NEGOTIATIONS

1. Books

3804. De Pauw, John W. *Soviet American Trade Negotiations.* New York: Praeger, 1979. 180p.

3805. Flagon, Alec, ed. *Soviet Foreign Trade Techniques: An Inside Guide to Soviet Foreign Trade.* London: Flagon Press, 1965. 150p.

3806. Giffen, James H. *The Legal and Practical Aspects of Trade with the Soviet Union.* New York: Praeger, 1971. 366p.

3807. Hoyt, Ronald E. *Winners and Losers in East - West Trade: A Behavioral Analysis of U.S. - Soviet Detente (1970-1980).* New York: Praeger, 1983. 238p.

3808. Pisar, Samuel. *Coexistence and Commerce: Guidelines for Transactions Between East and West.* New York: McGraw-Hill, 1970. 558p.

2. Journal Articles

3809. Beliaev, Edward, Thomas Mullen and Betty Jane Punnett. "Understanding the Cultural Environment: U.S.-U.S.S.R. Trade Negotiations." *California Management Review,* 27:2 (Winter 1985), 100-112.

3810. Bolz, Klaus. "Economic East-West Cooperation: Situation, Experience, Problems, Prospects." *Coexistence,* 14:1 (1977), 63-78.

3811. Heckrotte, Warren. "Negotiating with the Soviets." *Energy & Technology Review*, 5 (May 1983), 10-19.
3812. Kimura, Hiroshi. "Soviet and Japanese Negotiating Behavior: The Spring 1977 Fisheries Talks." In: R. P. Anand, ed. *Cultural Factors in International Relations*. New Delhi: Abhinav, 1981. pp. 33-62.
3813. _____. "Soviet and Japanese Negotiating Behavior - The Spring 1977 Fisheries Talks." *Orbis*, (1980), 43-67.
3814. Schmidt, Robert D. "Business Negotiations with the Soviet Union." In: D. D. Newsom, ed. *Private Diplomacy with the Soviet Union*. Lanham, MD.: University Press of America, 1987. pp. 73-92.
3815. Vlachoutsicos, C. A. "When the Ruble Stops in Soviet Trade." *Harvard Business Review*, 64 (September - October 1986), 82-86.

3. Documents and Reports

3816. Crawford, Beverly K. *NATO Alliance Negotiations over the Soviet Pipeline Sanctions*. PEW Case Studies, 101.0-A-86-P. Pittsburgh, PA.: University of Pittsburgh, Graduate School of Public and International Affairs, 1986.
3817. De Pauw, John W. *Soviet American Trade: A Study of Selected U.S. Commercial Negotiations with the Soviet Union*. Ph.D. Dissertation. Washington, D.C.: American University, 1977. 332p.
3818. National Science Foundation. *U.S.-U.S.S.R. Copyright Negotiations on Scientific and Technical Journals*. Washington, D.C.: National Science Foundation, 1974. 56p.
3819. Reisinger, William M. *Energy in Soviet - East European Bargaining*. Ph.D. Dissertation. Ann Arbor, MI.: University of Michigan, 1986. 251p.
3820. United States. Central Intelligence Agency. National Foreign Assessment Center. *Soviet Strategy and Tactics in Economic and Commercial Negotiations with the United States*. ER79-10276. Washington, D.C.: U.S. Government Printing Office, 1979. 19p.

H. CHINESE TRADE NEGOTIATIONS

1. Books

3821. De Pauw, John W. *U.S. - Chinese Trade Negotiations*. New York: Praeger, 1981. 231p.
3822. Lee, C. J. *China and Japan - New Economic Diplomacy*. Stanford, CA.: Hoover Institution Press, 1984. 174p.
3823. Tung, Rosalie L. *U.S. - China Trade Negotiations*. New York: Pergamon Press, 1982. 281p.

2. Journal Articles

3824. Brunner, J. A., and G. M. Taoka. "Marketing and Negotiating in the People's Republic of China: Perceptions of American Businessmen Who Attended the 1975 Canton Fair." *Journal of International Business Studies*, 8:2 (1977), 69-82.
3825. Pye, Lucien W., and S. R. Hendryx. "The China Trade: Making the Deal." *Harvard Business Review*, 64:4 (July/August 1986), 74-85.

3826. Rae, A. E. I. "Talking Business in China." *China Quarterly*, (June 1982), 271-280.
3827. Shih, Ta Lang, and Kwok Chih Tam. "A Political Analysis of Sino-Japanese Trade Negotiations." *Journal of the Chinese University of Hong Kong*, 5:1 (1979), 363-378.
3828. Tung, Rosalie L. "U.S. - China Trade Negotiations: Practices, Procedures, and Outcomes." *Journal of International Business Studies*, 13:2 (Fall 1982), 25-38.

3. Documents and Reports

3829. Crane, George. *The Sino - U.S. Textile Trade Agreement of 1983: The Anatomy of a Trade War*. PEW Case Studies, 109.0-D-87-G. Washington, D.C.: School of Foreign Service, Georgetown University, 1987.
3830. Pye, Lucien W. *Chinese Commercial Negotiating Style*. RAND R-2837-AF. Santa Monica, CA.: RAND Corporation, 1982. 109p.
3831. Verhage, William. *The Negotiations of the International Public Loans to China, 1895-1920, with Some Reference to the Theory and Practice of International Cooperation*. Ph.D. Dissertation. Minneapolis, MN.: University of Minnesota, 1940.

I. JAPANESE TRADE NEGOTIATIONS

1. Books

3832. Graham, John L. *Smart Bargaining: Doing Business with the Japanese*. Cambridge, MA.: Balliger, 1984. 164p.
3833. McCreary, Don R. *Japanese - U.S. Business Negotiations: A Cross-Cultural Study*. New York: Praeger, 1986. 115p.
3834. Moran, Robert T. *Getting You Yen's Worth: How to Negotiate With Japan, Inc.* Houston, TX.: Gulf Publications, 1985. 181p.
3835. Rothacher, Albrecht. *Economic Diplomacy Between the European Community and Japan, 1959-1981*. Aldershot, Hants: Gower, 1983. 377p.
3836. Tung, Rosalie L. *Business Negotiations with the Japanese*. Lexington, MA.: Lexington Books, 1984. 250p.
3837. Zimmerman, Mark. *How to do Business with the Japanese*. New York: Random House, 1984. 316p.

2. Journal Articles

3838. Aonuma, Y. "A Japanese Explains Japan's Business Style." *Across the Board*, 18:2 (February 1981), 41-50.
3839. Curtis, Gerald L. "The Textile Negotiations: A Failure to Communicate." *Columbia Journal of World Business*, 6 (January-February 1971), 72-78.
3840. Graham, John L. "Brazilian, Japanese and American Business Negotiations." *Journal of International Business Studies*, 14 (Spring/Summer 1983), 47-61.
3841. Guittard, Stephen W. "Negotiating and Administering an International Sales Contract with the Japanese." *International Lawyer*, 8 (1974), 822-831.

3842. Inogushi, T., and N. Miyatake. "Negotiation as Quasi-Budgeting: The Salmon Catch Negotiations Between Two World Fishery Powers." *International Organization*, 33 (1979), 229-256.
3843. _____. _____. "Politics of Decrementalism - Case of Soviet - Japanese Catch Negotiations, 1957-1977." *Behavioral Science*, 23:6 (1978), 457-469.
3844. Kuttner, R. "Zen and the Art of Trade Negotiation." *New Republic*, 193:7-8 (1985), 20-23.
3845. Miller, D. L. "The Honorable Picnic: Doing Business in Japan." *Harvard Business Review*, (November-December 1961), 79-86.
3846. Smith, Ben. "The Japanese Connection: Negotiating a Two Way Street." In: P. Hastings and A. Farran, eds. *Australia's Resource Future*. Melbourne: Thomas Nelson, 1978. pp. 108-143.
3847. Trezise, Philip H. "U.S. - Japan Trade: The Bilateral Connection." In: M. Blaker, ed. *The Politics of Trade*. New York: Columbia University, 1978. pp. 1-14.
3848. Tung, Rosalie L. "How to Negotiate with the Japanese." *California Management Review*, 26:4 (Summer 1984), 62-77.
3849. Van Zandt, Howard F. "How to Negotiate in Japan." *Harvard Business Review*, (November-December 1970), 45-56.

3. Documents and Reports

3850. Aho, C. Michael, and Jonathan D. Aronson. *Trade Talks: America Better Listen*. New York: Council on Foreign Relations, 1985. 192p.
3851. Akaha, Tsuneo. *Japanese-Russian Fisheries*. PEW Case Studies, 124.0-G--88-S. Los Angeles, CA.: School of International Relations, university of Southern California, 1988.
3852. Angel, Robert. *Dollar - Yen Negotiation of 1971*. PEW Case Studies, 135.0-G-88-C. New York: School of International and Public Affairs, Columbia University, 1988.
3853. Higashi, Chikara. *U.S. - Japanese Trade Policy Formulation and Frictions in Trade Relations: 1978-79*. D.B.A. St. Louis, MO.: The George Washington University, 1982. 594p.
3854. Kaspar, Daniel. *Holding Over Tokyo: U.S. - Japan Air Service Negotiations*. PEW Case Studies, 104.0-G-87-S. Los Angeles, CA.: School of International Relations, University of Southern California, 1987.
3855. O'Shea, Timothy J. C. *U.S. - Japan Semiconductor Agreement*. PEW Case Studies, 139.0-G-88-C. N,Y.: School of International and Public Affairs, Columbia University, 1988.
3856. United States. Congress. House. Committee on Foreign Affairs. *U.S. - Japan Economic Relations: Hearings*. 96th Cong., 2nd sess. Washington, D.C.: U.S. Government Printing Office, 1981. pp. 109-212.

K. OTHER TRADE NEGOTIATIONS

1. Books

3857. Aronson, Jonathan D., and Peter H. Cowhey. *When Countries Talk: International Trade in Telecommunications Services*. Cambridge, MA.: Ballinger, 1988. 292p.
3858. Camps, Miriam. *Britain and the European Community, 1952-1963*. London: Oxford University Press, 1964. 547p.

3859. Contractor, F. J. *International Technology Licensing - Compensation, Costs and Negotiation.* Lexington, MA.: Lexington Books, 1981. 208p.
3860. _____. *Licensing in International Strategy: A Guide for Planning and Negotiations.* London: Greenwood Press, 1985. 254p.
3861. Daddysman, J. W. *The Matamoros Trade - Confederate Commerce, Diplomacy and Intrigue.* Newark, DE.: University of Delaware Press, 1984. 215p.
3862. Fisher, Bart S. *International Coffee Agreement: A Study in Coffee Diplomacy.* New York: Praeger, 1972. 309p.
3863. Gardner, Richard N. *Sterling - Dollar Diplomacy: The Origins and the Prospects of the International Economic Order.* New York: Columbia University Press, 1980. 423p.
3864. Helmreich, Jonathan E. *Gathering Rare Ores: The Diplomacy of Uranium Acquisition, 1943-1954.* Princeton, NJ.: Princeton University Press, 1986. 303p.
3865. Kapoor, Ashok. *International Business Negotiations: A Study in India.* New York: New York University Press, 1970. 361p.
3866. Middleton, Robert. *Negotiating on Non-Tariff Distortions of Trade: The EFTA Precedents.* London: Macmillan, 1975. 195p.
3867. Noyelle, Thierry J., and Anna B. Dutka. *International Trade in Business Services: Accounting, Advertising, Law, and Management Consulting.* Cambridge, MA.: Ballinger, 1988. 138p.
3868. Peter, Wolfgang. *Arbitration and Renegotiation of International Investment Agreements: A Study with Particular Reference to Means of Conflicts Avoidance Under Natural Resources Investment Agreement.* Dordrecht: M. Nijhoff, 1986. 296p.
3869. Preeg, Ernest H., ed. *Hard Bargaining Ahead: U.S. Trade Policy and Developing Countries.* New Brunswick, NJ.: Transaction Books, 1985. 214p.
3870. Zartman, I. William. *The Politics of Trade Negotiations Between Africa and the EEC: The Weak Confront the Strong.* Princeton, NJ.: Princeton University Press, 1971. 243p.

2. Journal Articles

3871. Adamson, David M. "Multilateral Energy Negotiations: Lessons of the Conference on International Economic Cooperation." *Fletcher Forum,* 6:1 (Winter 1982), 161-169.
3872. Aggarwal, V. K. "The Unravelling of the Multi-Fiber Arrangement, 1981: An Examination of International Regime Change." *International Organization,* 37:4 (1983), 617-645.
3873. "Australia's Role in International Trade Negotiations." *Overseas Trading,* 28:23 (1976), 557-561.
3874. Bank, John C. "Negotiating International Mining Agreements: Win - Win vs Win - Lose Bargaining." *Columbia Journal of World Business,* 22:4 (Winter 1987), 67-74.
3875. Barclay, G. S. J. "Negotiation Under Threats: The Diplomacy of the Free Trade Area Discussions, 1956-1958." *Australian Outlook,* 20:1 (1966), 278-295.
3876. Bennett, Douglas C., and Kenneth E. Sharpe. "Agenda Setting and Bargaining Power: The Mexican State Versus Transnational Automobile Corporations." *World Politics,* 32:1 (October 1979), 57-89.
3877. Bilder, Richard B. "The International Coffee Agreement: A Case History in Negotiation." *Law and Contemporary Problems,* 29 (1963), 328-377.

3878. Burge, M. "Status of Tax Treaty Negotiations." *Bulletin for International Fiscal Documentation*, 34:2-3 (1980), 55-62.
3879. Cable, Vincent. "Textiles and Clothing in a New Round of Trade Negotiations." *World Bank Economic Review*, 1:4 (September 1987), 619-646.
3880. Corbett, Hugh. "Australian Commercial Diplomacy in a New Era of Negotiation." *Australian Outlook*, 26:1 (1972), 3-17.
3881. Crawford, Beverly K., and S. Lenway. "Decision Modes and International Regime Change: Western Collaboration and East West Trade." *World Politics*, 37 (1985), 375-402.
3882. Derakhshani, S. "Negotiating Transfer of Technology Agreements." *Finance and Development*, 23 (December 1986), 42-44.
3883. Eger, J. M. "United States Proposal for Progress Through Negotiations." *Journal of Communication*, 29:3 (1979), 124-128.
3884. Ghauri, Pervez N. "Negotiating Package Deals - A Case Study." In: L. Engwall and J. Johanson, eds. *Some Aspects of Control in International Business*. Upsalla: Acta Universitatis Upsaliensis, 1980. pp. 61-71.
3885. Grayson, George W. "The U.S. - Mexican Natural Gas Deal and What We Can Learn From It." *Orbis*, 24:3 (1980), 573-607.
3886. Haskel, Barbara G. "Disparities, Strategies and Opportunity Costs: The Example of Scandinavian Economic Market Negotiations." *International Studies Quarterly*, 18:2 (1974), 3-30.
3887. Henze, L. J. "United States - Philippine Economic Relations and Trade Negotiations." *Asian Survey*, 16:4 (1976), 319-337.
3888. Joyner, Christopher C. "The Antarctic Minerals Negotiating Process." *American Journal of International Law*, 81:4 (October 1987), 888-905.
3889. Kapoor, Ashok. "International Business - Government Negotiations: A Study in India." In: I. W. Zartman, ed. *The 50% Solution*. Garden City, NY.: Anchor Press, 1976. pp. 430-451.
3890. Kapur, Ashok. "Canada - India Nuclear Negotiations - Source Hypotheses and Lessons." *World Today*, 34:8 (1978), 311-320.
3891. Kramer, R. D. "Attempts to Curb Treaty Shopping in United States - Dutch Treaty Negotiations." *Bulletin for International Fiscal Documentation*, 37:3 (1983), 107-109.
3892. Lowden, S. R. "The Negotiation and Drafting of Commercial Sales Agreements in East Europe." *Business Lawyer*, 29 (April 1974), 845-860.
3893. Miller, Mark L., and Charles F. Broches. "Observations on Mexico/U.S. Fishery Negotiations." *New Scholars*, 9:1-2 (1984), 231-248.
3894. Mitchell, Bruce. "Politics, Fish, and International Resource Management: the British Icelandic Cod War." *Geographical Review*, 66 (April 1976), 127-138.
3895. Morse, D. D., and J. S. Powers. "United States Export Controls and Foreign Entities - The Unanswered Questions of Pipeline Diplomacy." *Virginia Journal of International Law*, 23:4 (1983), 537-567.
3896. Moynagh, Michael. "The Negotiation of the Commonwealth Sugar Agreement, 1949-1951." *Journal of Commonwealth and Comparative Politics*, 15:2 (July 1977), 170-190.
3897. "Multilateral/Bilateral Negotiations." *Business America*, (September 15, 1986), 9-12.
3898. Narayanan, R., and R. L. Chawla. "Global Department Renegotiations: Role of International Monetary Organizations." *International Studies*, 24:1 (January - March 1987), 1-24.
3899. Odell, John. "Latin American Trade Negotiations with the United States." *International Organization*, 34:2 (1980), 207-228.

3900. _____. "The Outcome of International Trade Conflicts: The U.S. and South Korea, 1960-1981." *International Studies Quarterly*, 29 (September 1985), 263-286.
3901. Osborn, J. E. "Re-Negotiation of the United States British Virgin Islands Tax Convention - Prelude to the End of Treaty Shopping." *Virginia Journal of International Law*, 22:2 (1982), 381-412.
3902. Pattison, J. E. "The United States - Egypt Bilateral Investment Treaty - A Prototype for Future Negotiations?" *Cornell International Law Journal*, 16:2 (1983), 305-339.
3903. Peacock, A. "Influence of Energy Resources on Australian Diplomacy and International Relations." *World Review*, 17:1 (1978), 35-37.
3904. Pelzman, Joseph. "The Multifiber Arrangement: The Third Reincarnation." In: I. W. Zartman, ed. *Positive Sum*. New Brunswick, NJ.: Transaction Books, 1987. pp. 149-170.
3905. Robinson, Glen O. "Regulating International Airwaves: the 1979 WARC." *Virginia Journal of International Law*, 21:1 (Fall 1980), 1-54.
3906. Rothstein, Robert L. "Condemned to Cooperate: U.S. Resource Diplomacy." *SAIS Review*, 5:1 (Winter/Spring 1985), 163-177.
3907. Smith, Ben. "Bilateral Monopoly and Export Price Bargaining in Resource Goods Trade." *Economic Record*, 53:141 (1977), 30-50.
3908. Stiles, K. W. "Bargaining with Bureaucrats - Dept Negotiations in the International Monetary Fund." *International Journal of Public Administration*, 9:1 (1987), 1-43.
3909. _____. "Argentina's Bargaining with the IMF." *Journal of Inter-American Studies and World Affairs*, 29:3 (Autumn 1987), 55-86.
3910. Stubbs, Richard. "The International Natural Rubber Agreement." *Journal of World Trade Law*, 18:1 (January - February 1984), 16-31.
3911. Urban, L. K. "Once More with Hindsight - German Polish Interwar Trade Negotiations." *East European Quarterly*, 17:1 (1983), 89-108.
3912. Walde, Thomas W. "Negotiating for Dispute Settlement in Transnational Mineral Contracts." *Denver Journal of International Law and Policy*, 7:1 (Fall 1977), 33-76.
3913. Winters, L. A. "Negotiating the Abolition of Non-Tariff Barriers." *Oxford Economic Papers*, 39:3 (September 1987), 465-480.
3914. Wolff, A. W. "United States Mandate for Trade Negotiations." *Virginia Journal of International Law*, 16:3 (1976), 505-564.
3915. Zeiler, Thomas. "Free-Trade Politics and Diplomacy: John F. Kennedy and Textiles." *Diplomatic History*, 11:2 (Spring 1987), 127-142.
3916. Zwass, A. "Polands Difficult Negotiations to Reschedule its Western Credits." *Soviet and Eastern European Foreign Trade*, 17:4 (1982), 14-20.

3. Documents and Reports

3917. Allen, Michael H. *The 1974 Jamaican Bauxite Negotiations as a Case Study in Bargaining*. M.S. Dissertation. Kingston, Jamaica: University of the West Indies, 1977.
3918. Antrim, Lance, and David A. Lax. "Support and Analysis for International Commercial Dept Negotiations." Paper Presented at the *International Society for General Systems Research/IIASA Symposium*, held in June 1987, in Budapest.

3919. Biersteker, Thomas J. *Reaching Agreement with the IMF: The Nigerian Negotiations, 1983-1986.* PEW Case Studies, 205.0.-C-88-S. Los Angeles, CA.: School of International Relations, University of Southern California, 1988.
3920. Borthwick, M. *Pacific Basin Approach to Trade Negotiations: A Study of Overlapping National Interests.* FAR-116-84. Washington, D.C.: Department of State, Office of External Research, 1985. 71p.
3921. Chaudhuri, Adhip. *Mexican Dept Crisis of 1982.* PEW Case Studies, 204.0--E-87-G. Washington, D.C.: School of Foreign Service, Georgetown University, 1987.
3922. Crawford, Beverly K. *Beyond Profit and Power: State Intervention and International Collaboration in East - West Technology Transfer.* Ph.D. Dissertation. Berkeley, CA.: University of California at Berkeley, 1982. 552p.
3923. Esposito, Chiarella. *The Marshall Plan in France and Italy, 1948-1950: Counterpart Fund Negotiations.* Ph.D. Dissertation. Stony Brook, NY.: State University of New York at Stony Brook, 1985. 401p.
3924. Faria, Hugo de A. *Macroeconomic Decisionmaking in a Crisis Environment: Brazil's Crusade Plan.* PEW Case Studies, 114.0-E-87-C. New York: School of International and Public Affairs, Columbia University, 1987.
3925. Friedheim, Robert L., and William J. Durch. "The International Seabed Resources Agency Negotiations and the New International Economic Order." Paper Presented at the *72nd Annual Meeting of the American Political Science Association,* held on September 2-5, 1976, in Chicago IL.
3926. Ghauri, Pervez N. *Negotiating International Package Deals: Swedish Firms and Developing Countries.* Ph.D. Dissertation. Uppsala: Acta Universitatis Upsaliensis - Studia Oeconomiae Negotiorum, 1983. 180p.
3927. Great Britain. *Negotiations for a European Free Trade Area: Documents Relating to Negotiations from July 1956 to December 1958.* Cmnd. 641. London: H.M.S.O., 1959.
3928. _____. *Negotiations for an European Free Trade Area: Report on the Course of Negotiations up to December 1958.* Cmnd. 648. London: H.M.S.O., 1959.
3929. Hooley, Richard. *Protection for the Machine Tool Industry: Domestic and International Negotiations for Voluntary Restraint Agreements.* PEW Case Studies, 120.0-G-88-P. Pittsburgh, PA.: Graduate School of Public and International Affairs, University of Pittsburgh, 1988.
3930. Hurrell, Andrew, and Ellene Felder. *U.S. - Brazilian Information Dispute.* PEW Case Studies, 122.0-E-88-J. Washington, D.C.: School of Advanced International Studies, John Hopkins University, 1988.
3931. Jönsson, Christer. *International Aviation and the Politics of Regime Change.* London: Frances Pinter, 1987. pp. 77-165.
3932. Joyner, Christopher C. *National Interests, Processes and International Negotiation: A Case Study of the Evolving Antarctic Minerals Regime.* Working Paper Series 6. Cambridge, MA.: The Program on the Processes of International Negotiations, American Academy of Arts and Sciences, 1987. 35p.
3933. Kakabadse, Mario A. *International Trade in Services: Prospects for Liberalisation in the 1980s.* Atlantic Paper No. 64. London: The Atlantic Institute for International Affairs, 1987. 88p.
3934. Kline, Harvey F. *The Coal of El Cercejon: Dependent Bargaining and Colombian Policy Making.* University Park, PA.: Pennsylvania State University Press, 1987. 227p.

3935. Lee, Hyock Sup. *The U.S. - Korean Textile Negotiations of 1969-1972: A Case Study in the Relationship Between National Sovereignty and Economic Development.* Ph.D. Dissertation. Ann Arbor, MI.: University of Michigan, 1984. 441p.
3936. Leeds, Roger S., and Gail Thompson. *The 1982 Mexican Dept Negotiation - Response to a Financial Crisis.* FPI Case Study No. 4. Washington, D.C.: Johns Hopkins Foreign Policy Institute, 1986.
3937. Linden, Ronald H. *United States - Romanian Negotiations over the Extension of Most Favored Nation Trade Status, 1983.* PEW Case Study Series 102.0-B-86-P. Pittsburgh, PA.: Graduate School of Public and International Affairs, University of Pittsburgh, 1986.
3938. McNeil, William C. *Financial Stabilization and the Rescheduling of International Dept: The Young Plan Negotiations of 1929.* PEW Case Studies, 208.0-A-88-C. New York: School of International and Public Affairs, Columbia University, 1988.
3939. Meade, James E. *Negotiations for Benelux: An Annotated Chronicle, 1945-1956.* Princeton Studies in International Finance, No.6. Princeton, NJ.: Princeton University Press, 1957. 89p.
3940. Odell, John, David Lang and Tracy Tierney. *Bilateral Trade Negotiations Between South Korea and the United States.* PEW Case Studies, 129.0-G--88-S. Los Angeles, CA.: School of International Relations, University of Southern California, 1988.
3941. _____., and Anne Dibble. *Information Negotiations Between Brazil and the U.S., 1985-1987.* PEW Case Studies, 128.0-E-88-S. Los Angeles, CA.: School of International Relations, University of Southern California, 1988.
3942. _____. "Latin American Industrial Exports and Bargaining in Trade Conflicts with the U.S." Paper Presented at the *20th Annual Convention of the International Studies Association,* held on March 21-24, 1979, in Toronto.
3943. Ozergene, Nil. *Lessons of the Pipeline Negotiations.* ACIS Working Paper No.40. Los Angeles, CA.: Center for International and Strategic Affairs, University of California, 1983. 45p.
3944. Parker, R. W. *The U.S. - Mexican Gas Dispute: A Case Study in International Bargaining.* Ph.D. Dissertation. Oxford: Oxford University, 1982.
3945. Reich, Simon. *Reagan Administration and the Auto Producers: The Case of the VER Agreement.* PEW Case Studies, 119.0-G-88-P. Pittsburgh, PA.: Graduate School of Public and International Affairs, University of Pittsburgh, 1988.
3946. United Nations. Centre on Transnational Corporations. *Issues in Negotiating International Loan Agreements with Transnational Banks.* ST/CTC/48. New York: United Nations, 1983. 103p.
3947. _____.Economic Commission for Latin America and the Caribbean.(ECLAC). *International Economic Relations and Regional Co-operation in Latin America and the Caribbean.* E.87.II.G.4. Part II. Santiago, Chile: ECLAC, 1988. pp. 207-264.
3948. Walters, Robert S. *U.S. Negotiations of Voluntary Restraint Agreements in Steel 1984: Domestic Sources of International Economic Diplomacy.* PEW Case Study Series 107.0-D-87-P. Pittsburgh, PA.: Graduate School of Public and International Affairs, University of Pittsburgh, 1987.
3949. Wasowski, Stanislaw. *Voluntary Export Restraints.* PEW Case Studies, 11.0-D-87-G. Washington, D.C.: School of Foreign Service, Georgetown University, 1987.
3950. Weiss, Thomas G. *International Negotiations on the Code of Conduct of Transnational Corporations.* PEW Case Studies, 117.0-D-88-I. New York: International Peace Academy, 1988.

3951. White, Lawrence J. *International Trade in Ocean Shipping Services: The United States and the World.* Cambridge, MA.: Ballinger, 1988. 121p.
3952. Woolcock, Stephen, Jeffrey A. Hart and Hans Van der Ven. *Interdependence in the Post-Multilateral Era: Trends in U.S. - European Trade Relations.* Cambridge, MA.: Center for International Affairs, Harvard University, 1985. 138p.
3953. Zartman, I. William, and Antonella Bassani. *Algerian Gas Negotiations.* PEW Case Studies, 103.0-C-86-J. Washington, D.C.: School of Advanced International Studies, John Hopkins University, 1986.

IX

Diplomacy

Diplomacy may be defined as the application of peaceful norms of behavior to the resolution of conflicts between states. In many instances, diplomacy may be an effective way for the conduct of relations between states. Diplomacy's principal instrument in resolution of conflicts, is the continuing process of bargaining and negotiations. The purpose always is the achievement of a common agreement between states.

This chapter focuses on diplomatic methods. I could not ignore the, for me, mainly semantic difference between diplomacy and negotiations. The terms are used in the literature separately and together or interchangeably. However, one can not get away from the fact that the negotiations and diplomacy are closely related, and that in the literature itself it is very difficult, and may be misleading do completely differentiate between the two. This is the reason for this chapter which focuses on materials identified as "diplomacy".

Section one deals with major works on diplomatic methods. The second section is a select listing on diplomatic history. Section three includes a select list of diplomatic memoirs and memoirs of statesmen who where involved in international negotiations. The fourth section examines unofficial contacts between states, which may also include contacts between non-official organizations and citizen and their influence on state relations. The last sections covers works on public diplomacy, media and propaganda.

A. DIPLOMATIC METHODS

1. Books

3954. Acheson, Dean. *Power and Diplomacy.* Cambridge, MA.: Harvard University Press, 1958. 137p.
3955. Alexandroff, Alan S. *The Logic of Diplomacy.* Beverly Hills, CA.: Sage, 1981. 240p.
3956. Bailey, Thomas A. *The Art of Diplomacy.* New York: Appleton - Century - Crofts, 1968. 303p.
3957. Barber, Peter. *Diplomacy: The World of the Honest Spy.* London: British Library, 1979. 142p.
3958. Barston, Ronald P. *Modern Diplomacy.* Harlow, England: Longman, 1988. 260p.
3959. Bell, Coral. *The Conventions of Crisis: A Study in Diplomatic Management.* London: Oxford University Press, 1971. 131p.
3960. Borisov, O. B., et al. *Modern Diplomacy of Capitalist Powers.* Elmsford, NY.: Pergamon Press, 1983. 314p.
3961. Brown, Neville, and M. Barker. *Diplomacy in an Age of Nationalism: Essays in Honor of Lynn Marshall Case.* The Hague: M. Nijhoff, 1971. 222p.
3962. Burton, John W. *Systems, States, Diplomacy and Rules.* Cambridge: Cambridge University Press, 1968. 251p.
3963. Busk, Douglas L. *The Craft of Diplomacy: How to Run a Diplomatic Service.* New York: Praeger, 1967. 293p.
3964. Butterfield, Herbert, and Martin Wright, eds. *Diplomatic Investigations, Essays in the Theory of International Politics.* Cambridge, MA.: Harvard University Press, 1966. 227p.
3965. Cable, James. *Diplomacy at Sea.* London: Macmillan Press, 1985. 191p.
3966. Cadieux, Marcel. *The Canadian Diplomat.* Toronto: University of Toronto Press, 1962. 113p.
3967. Cambon, Jules M. *The Diplomatist.* London: Allan, 1931. 151p.
3968. Cardozo, Michael H. *Diplomats in International Cooperation: Stepchildren of the Foreign Service.* Ithaca, NY.: Cornell University Press, 1962. 142p.
3969. Clark, Eric. *Diplomat: The World of International Diplomacy.* New York: Taplinger, 1974. 276p.
3970. Cohen, Raymond. *Theatre of Power: The Art of Diplomatic Signalling.* London: Longman, 1987. 229p.
3971. Cottam, Richard W. *Competitive Interference and Twentieth Century Diplomacy.* Pittsburgh, PA.: University of Pittsburgh, 1967. 243p.
3972. Craig, Gordon A., and Alexander L. George. *Force and Statecraft: Diplomatic Problems of Our Time.* New York: Oxford University Press, 1983. 288p.
3973. De Callieres, Francois. *The Art of Diplomacy.* New York: Holmes & Meier, 1983. 235p.
3974. _____. *On Manner of Negotiating with Princes.* Lanham, MD.: University Press of America, 1983. 160p.
3975. Demiashkevich, Michael J. *Shackled Diplomacy.* New York: Barnes & Noble, 1934. 244p.
3976. Der Derian, James. *On Diplomacy: A Genealogy of Western Estrangement.* Oxford: Basil Blackwell, 1987. 258p.
3977. Eayres, James. *Diplomacy and Its Discontents.* Toronto: University of Toronto Press, 1971. 198p.
3978. Eban, Abba. *The New Diplomacy: International Affairs in the Modern Age.* New York: Random House, 1983. 427p.

3979. Ekvall, Robert B. *Faithful Echo: The Role of Language in Diplomacy.* New York: Twayne, 1960. 125p.
3980. Farer, Tom J. *Toward a Humanitarian Diplomacy: A Primer for Policy.* New York: New York University Press, 1980. 228p.
3981. Franck, Thomas M., and Edward Weissband, eds. *Secrecy and Foreign Policy.* New York: Oxford University Press, 1974. 453p.
3982. Gamboa, Melquades J. *Elements of Diplomatic and Consular Practice: A Glossary.* Dobbs Ferry, NY.: Oceana, 1967. 486p.
3983. Gaselee, Stephen. *The Language of Diplomacy.* Cambridge: Bowes & Bowes, 1939. 75p.
3984. Hale, Oron J. *Publicity and Diplomacy.* New York: D. Appleton Century, 1940. 486p.
3985. Handel, Michael I. *The Diplomacy of Surprise: Hitler, Nixon, Sadat.* Cambridge, MA.: Center for International Affairs, Harvard University, 1981. 369p.
3986. Harr, John Ensor. *The Anatomy of the Foreign Service: A Statistical Profile.* New York: Carnegie Endowment, 1965. 89p.
3987. _____. *The Professional Diplomat.* Princeton, NJ.: Princeton University Press, 1969. 404p.
3988. Hayter, William. *The Diplomacy of Great Powers.* New York: Macmillan, 1961. 74p.
3989. Heatley, David P. *Diplomacy and the Study of International Relations.* Oxford: Clarendon Press, 1969. 292p.
3990. Huddleston, Sisley. *Popular Diplomacy and War.* Rindge, NH.: Smith, 1954. 285p.
3991. Iqbal, Afzal. *In Prophet's Diplomacy: The Art of Negotiation as Conceived and Developed by the Prophet of Islam.* Cape Cod, MA.: C. Stark, 1975. 142p.
3992. Jackson, Geoffrey. *Concorde Diplomacy: The Ambassador's Role in the World Today.* London: Hamilton, 1981. 254p.
3993. Johnson, Edgar A. J., ed. *The Dimensions of Diplomacy.* Baltimore, MD.: Johns Hopkins University Press, 1964. 135p.
3994. Kelly, David. *The Ruling Few: Or, the Human Background to Diplomacy.* London: Hollis and Carter, 1952. 449p.
3995. Kertész, Stephen D., and M. A. Fitzsimmons, eds. *Diplomacy in a Changing World.* Westport, CT.: Greenwood Press, 1974. 407p.
3996. _____. *The Quest for Peace Through Diplomacy.* Englewood Cliffs, NJ.: Prentice-Hall, 1967. 182p.
3997. Krishnamurty, G. V. G. *Modern Diplomacy: Dialectics and Dimensions.* New Delhi: Sagar, 1980. 554p.
3998. Lauren, Paul G., ed. *Diplomacy: New Approaches in History, Theory and Policy.* New York: Free Press, 1979. 286p.
3999. _____. *Diplomats and Bureaucrats: The First Institutional Responses to Twentieth Century Diplomacy in France and Germany.* Stanford, CA.: Hoover Institution Press, 1976. 294p.
4000. Liska, George. *Beyond Kissinger: Ways of Conservative Statecraft.* Baltimore, MD.: Johns Hopkins University Press, 1975. 159p.
4001. Macober, William B. *The Angel's Game: A Handbook of Modern Diplomacy.* New York: Stein and Day, 1975. 225p.
4002. Mayer, Martin. *The Diplomats.* Garden City, NY.: Doubleday, 1983. 417p.
4003. McCamy, James L. *Conduct of the New Diplomacy.* New York: Harper & Row, 1964. 303p.
4004. McDermott, O. *The New Diplomacy and Its Apparatus.* London: Plume Press, 1973. 208p.

4005. McGhee, George C., ed. *Diplomacy for the Future.* Lanham, MD.: University Press of America, 1987. 108p.
4006. McKenna, J. C. *Diplomatic Protest in Foreign Policy: Analysis and Case Studies.* Chicago, IL.: Loyola University Press, 1962. 222p.
4007. Mookerjee, G. K. *Diplomacy: Theory and History.* New Delhi: Trimurti, 1973. 148p.
4008. Moorhouse, Geoffrey. *The Diplomats: The Foreign Office Today.* London: Jonathan Cape, 1977. 405p.
4009. Mowat, R. B. *Diplomacy and Peace.* London: Williams and Norgate, 1935. 295p.
4010. Newsom, David D., ed. *Diplomacy Under a Foreign Flag: The Protecting Power & the Interests Section.* Washington, D.C.: Institute for the Study of Diplomacy, Georgetown University, 1988.
4011. Nicolson, Harold. *Diplomacy.* New York: Harcourt, Brace, 1939. 247p.
4012. O'Connor, Raymond G. *Force and Diplomacy: Essays Military and Diplomatic.* Coral Gables, FL.: University of Miami Press, 1972. 167p.
4013. Ostrower, A. *Language, Law and Diplomacy: A Study of Linguistic Diversity in Official International Relations and International Law.* 2 Vols. Philadelphia, PA.: University of Pennsylvania Press, 1965. 963p.
4014. Panikkar, K. M. *The Principles and Practice of Diplomacy.* Bombay: Asia Publishing House, 1956. 99p.
4015. Pearson, Lester B. *Diplomacy in the Nuclear Age.* Cambridge, MA.: Harvard University Press, 1959. 114p.
4016. Peterson, Frank A. *Hands-on Diplomacy.* New York: Enquiry Press, 1987. 220p.
4017. Plischke, Elmer. *Modern Diplomacy: The Art and the Artisans.* Washington, D.C.: American Enterprise Institute for Public Policy Research, 1979. 454p.
4018. Regala, Roberto. *The Trends in Modern Diplomatic Practice.* New York: Oceana, 1959. 209p.
4019. _____. *World Peace Through Diplomacy and Law.* Dobbs Ferry, NY.: Oceana, 1964. 270p.
4020. _____. *World Order and Diplomacy.* Dobbs Ferry, NY.: Oceana, 1969. 205p.
4021. Rondybush, Franklin. *Foreign Service Training.* Besancon: Press Comtoise, 1955. 279p.
4022. Rourke, F. E. *Secrecy and Publicity: Dilemmas of Democracy.* Baltimore, MD.: Johns Hopkins University Press, 1961. 236p.
4023. Satow, Ernst M. *A Guide to Diplomatic Practice.* London: Longmans, 1950. c.1917. 510p.
4024. Simpson, Smith. *Instruction in Diplomacy: The Liberal Arts Approach.* Philadelphia, PA.: American Academy of Political and Social Sciences, 1972. 342p.
4025. Singh, I. P. *Diplommetry.* Bombay: Somaiya Publications, 1970. 114p.
4026. Spaulding, E. W. *Ambassadors Ordinary and Extraordinary.* Washington, D.C.: Public Affairs, 1961. 302p.
4027. Steiner, Zara, ed. *The Times Survey of Foreign Ministries of the World.* London: Meckler, 1982. 624p.
4028. Strang, William. *The Diplomatic Career.* London: Deutsch, 1962. 160p.
4029. Symington, James W. *The Stately Game.* New York: Macmillan, 1971. 256p.
4030. Thayer, Charles W. *Diplomat.* New York: Harper & Brothers, 1959. 288p.
4031. Thompson, Kenneth W., ed. *Diplomacy and Values: The Life and Works of Stephen Kertész in Europe and America.* Lanham, MD.: University Press of America, 1984. 114p.
4032. Tran, Van Dinh. *Communication and Diplomacy in a Changing World.* Norwood, IL.: ABLEX, 1987. 185p.

4033. Trevalyan, Humphrey. *Diplomatic Channels.* Boston, MA.: Gambit, 1973. 157p.
4034. Vagts, Alfred. *Defence and Diplomacy: The Soldier and the Conduct of Foreign Relations.* New York: King's Crown Press, 1956. 547p.
4035. Wakelin, John. *The Roots of Diplomacy: How to Study Inter-State Relations.* London: Hutchinson Educational, 1965. 186p.
4036. Waters, Maurice. *The Ad Hoc Diplomat.* The Hague: M. Nijhoff, 1963. 233p.
4037. Watson, Adam. *Diplomacy: The Dialogue Between States.* London: Methuen, 1983. 239p.
4038. Webster, Charles. *The Act and Practice of Diplomacy.* London: Chatto and Windus, 1961. 246p.
4039. Weintal, Edward, and Charles Bartlett. *Facing the Brink: An Institute Study of Crisis Diplomacy.* N.Y: Scribner's, 1967. 248p.
4040. Wise, David. *The Politics of Lying: Government Deception, Secrecy, and Power.* New York: Random House, 1973. 415p.
4041. Wriston, Henry M. *Diplomacy in a Democracy.* New York: Harper, 1956. 115p.

2. Journal Articles

4042. Acheson, Dean. "Morality, Moralism and Diplomacy." *Yale Review,* 47 (June 1958), 481-493.
4043. Alger, Chadwick F. "The Impact of International Organizations on the Practice of Diplomacy." *Journal of Conflict Resolution,* 8:1 (1964), 79-82.
4044. Allan, Pierre. "Diplomatic Time and Climate: A Formal Model." *Journal of Peace Science,* 4:2 (1980), 133-150.
4045. Andrew, Arthur. "The Diplomat and the Manager." *International Journal,* 30:1 (1974-75), 45-51.
4046. _____. "His EX or Telex?" *International Journal,* 25:4 (1970), 676-684.
4047. Appadorai, A. "Indian Diplomacy." In: S. D. Kertész and M. A. Fitzsimmons, eds. *Diplomacy in a Changing World.* South Bend, IN.: University of Notre Dame Press, 1959. pp. 266-300.
4048. Aspaturian, V. V. "Diplomacy in the Mirror of Soviet Scholarship." In: J. Keep and L. Brisby, eds. *Contemporary History in the Soviet Mirror.* London: Allen and Unwin, 1964. pp. 243-285.
4049. Bacchus, William I. "Diplomacy for the 70's: An Afterview and Appraisal." *American Political Science Review,* (June 1974), 736-748.
4050. Bajpai, K. Shankar. "A Third World View." In: G. C. McGhee, ed. *Diplomacy for the Future.* Lanham, MD.: University Press of America, 1987. pp. 65-72.
4051. Ball, George W. "Lawyers and Diplomats." *Department of State Bulletin,* 47:1227 (1962), 987-991.
4052. _____. "The New Diplomacy." *Department of State Bulletin,* 52 (June 21, 1965), 1042-1048.
4053. _____. "The Practice of Foreign Policy." *Department of State Bulletin,* 46 (May 28, 1962), 872-877.
4054. Banerji, Arun Kumar. "Role of the Diplomat in the Decision Making Process: Some Case Studies." *India Quarterly,* 35:2 (1979), 207-222.
4055. Berding, Andrew. "Quiet vs. Unquiet Diplomacy." In: E. Plischke, ed. *Modern Diplomacy: The Art and the Artisans.* Washington, D.C.: American Enterprise Institute, 1979. pp. 115-123.

4056. Blair, William D. "Communication: The Weak Link." In: E. Plischke, ed. *Modern Diplomacy: The Art and the Artisans.* Washington, D.C.: American Enterprise Institute, 1979. pp. 136-140.
4057. Bloomfield, Lincoln P., and C. J. Gearin. "Games Foreign Policy Experts Play: The Political Exercise Comes of Age." *Orbis,* 16 (1973), 1008-1031.
4058. Bowles, Chester. "Total Diplomacy." *Department of State Bulletin,* 46 (April 23, 1962), 677-678.
4059. _____. "Toward a New Diplomacy." *Foreign Affairs,* 40 (January 1962), 244-251.
4060. Boyce, P. J. "Foreign Offices and New States." *International Journal,* 30:1 (1974-75), 141-161.
4061. Brewster, Kingman. "Advice to a New Ambassador." In: M. F. Herz, ed. *The Modern Ambassador.* Washington, D.C.: Institute for the Study of Diplomacy, School of Foreign Service, Georgetown University, 1984. pp. 28-30.
4062. Briggs, Ellis O. "Why Not Give Diplomacy Back to the Diplomats?" In: E. Plischke, ed. *Modern Diplomacy: The Art and the Artisans.* Washington, D.C.: American Enterprise Institute, 1979. pp. 292-296.
4063. _____. "Why Not Give Diplomacy Back to the Diplomats?" *Foreign Service Journal,* 46 (March 1969), 48-49, 68.
4064. Butterfield, Herbert. "The Tragic Element in Modern International Conflict." *Review of Politics,* 7:2 (1950), 147-164.
4065. Caccia, Harold. "What is Diplomacy?" *Vital Speeches,* 28 (November 1, 1961), 42-44.
4066. Callender, Harold. "Footnotes on Modern Diplomacy." *New York Times Magazine,* (December 1956), 15, 28, 30-32.
4067. Campbell, A. E. "Open Diplomacy." *Comparative Study in Society and History,* 14:4 (1972), 506-513.
4068. Carter, Alan. "The State of the Art: Communications and the Foreign Affairs." *Foreign Service Journal,* 47 (September 1970), 31-32, 46-47.
4069. Chang, King-yuh. "Diplomatic Behavior and International Crisis Management: Some Preliminary Observations." *Issues and Studies,* 17:4 (1981), 67-77.
4070. Cioffi-Revilla, Claudio A. "Diplomatic Communication Theory: Signals, Channels, Networks." *International Interactions,* 6:3 (1979), 209-266.
4071. Cleveland, Harland. "Crisis Diplomacy." *Foreign Affairs,* 41:4 (1963), 639-642.
4072. _____. "Crisis Management." In: E. Plischke, ed. *Modern Diplomacy: The Art and the Artisans.* Washington, D.C.: American Enterprise Institute, 1979. pp. 199-208.
4073. _____. "View From the Diplomatic Tightrope." *Department of State Bulletin,* 46 (May 14, 1962), 803-808.
4074. Closca, I. "Direct Diplomatic Negotiations as Means for the Peaceful Settlements of International Differences." *Revue Roumaine d'Etudes Internationales,* 12 (1971), 101-122.
4075. Cohen, Raymond. "Anthropology and Diplomacy: New Wine, or New Bottles? In: P. J. Magnarella, ed. *Anthropological Diplomacy,* Williamsburg, VA.: Department of Anthropology, College of William and Mary, 1982. pp. 1-12.
4076. _____. "International Communication: An Intercultural Approach." *Cooperation and Conflict,* 12:2 (1987), 63-80.
4077. Cordier, A. W. "Diplomacy Today." *Journal of International Affairs,* 17:1 (1963), 1-8.
4078. Crick, Bernard. "Commentary: The Diplomatic Service." *Political Quarterly,* 48:4 (1977), 389-400.

4079. De Bourbon-Busset, Jacques. "Decision-Making in Foreign Policy." In: S. D. Kertész and M. A. Fitzsimmons, eds. *Diplomacy in a Changing World.* South Bend, IN.: University of Notre Dame Press, 1959. pp. 77-100.
4080. De Margerie, Emanuel. "A European Looks at Diplomacy." In: G. C. McGhee, ed. *Diplomacy for the Future.* Lanham, MD.: University Press of America, 1987. pp. 57-64.
4081. Der Derian, James. "Mediating Estrangement: A Theory for Diplomacy." *Review of International Studies,* 13:2 (April 1987), 91-110.
4082. "Diplomacy in Transition." *Journal of International Affairs,* 17:1 (1963), 1-69.
4083. "Diplomacy." In: W. C. Olson, D. S. McLellan and F. A. Sonderman, eds. *The Theory and Practice of International Relations.* 8th ed. Englewood Cliffs, NJ.: Prentice-Hall, 1983. pp. 129-136.
4084. Durosselle, J. B. "French Diplomacy in the Postwar World." In: S. D. Kertész and M. A. Fitzsimmons, eds. *Diplomacy in a Changing World.* South Bend, IN.: University of Notre Dame Press, 1959. pp. 204-250.
4085. Eayres, James. "Farewell to Diplomacy: In the Negotiations of the 1960's, Weapons Do the Serious Talking." *Saturday Night,* 83 (December 1968), 21-25.
4086. Eban, Abba. "Scholars and Diplomats...and Some Prevailing Fallacies." *World Affairs,* 143:2 (1980), 123-135.
4087. Eilan, Arieh. "Conference Diplomacy." *Washington Quarterly,* 4:4 (Autumn 1981), 24-30.
4088. Eilts, Hermann F. "Diplomacy: Contemporary Practice." In: E. Plischke, ed. *Modern Diplomacy: The Art and the Artisans.* Washington, D.C.: American Enterprise Institute for Public Policy Research, 1979. pp. 3-18.
4089. Falk, Richard. "The Menace of the New Cycle of Interventionary Diplomacy." *Journal of Peace Research,* 17:3 (1980), 201-206.
4090. Feld, Werner J. "Diplomatic Behaviour in the European Community: Milieus and Motivations." *Journal of Common Market Studies,* 11 (1972), 18-35.
4091. Flack, M. J. "The Objectives and Purposes of Instruction in Diplomacy." In: S. Simpson, ed. *Instruction in Diplomacy: The Liberal Arts Approach.* Philadelphia, PA.: American Academy of Political and Social Sciences, 1972. pp. 77-87.
4092. Flynn, Jane. "Diplomatic Relations." *Harvard International Law Journal,* 25:2 (1984), 441-449.
4093. Fox, Annette Baker. "Small State Diplomacy." In: S. D. Kertész and M. A. Fitzsimmons, eds. *Diplomacy in a Changing World.* South Bend, IN.: University of Notre Dame Press, 1959. pp. 339-366.
4094. Fox, William T. R. "Diplomatists and Military People." In: S. D. Kertész and M. A. Fitzsimmons, eds. *Diplomacy in a Changing World.* South Bend, IN.: University of Notre Dame Press, 1959. pp. 35-54.
4095. _____. "The Varieties of Diplomacy: They Provide a Means of Adjusting Disputes Among Natives." *Worldview,* 2 (August 1959), 3-6.
4096. Frankel, Joseph. "Conventional and Theorising Diplomats: A Critique." *International Affairs,* 57:4 (1981), 537-548.
4097. Franklin, William M. "Availability of Diplomatic Information and Documents." In: E. Plischke, ed. *Modern Diplomacy: The Art and the Artisans.* Washington, D.C.: American Enterprise Institute, 1979. pp. 141-149.
4098. Gamarekian, Barbara. "Has Diplomacy Become Out of Date?." In: M. F. Herz, ed. *The Modern Ambassador.* Washington, D.C.: Institute for the Study of Diplomacy, School of Foreign Service, Georgetown University, 1984. pp. 16-18.

4099. Gavrilovic, S. "On the Science of Professional Diplomacy." *Review of International Science Association*, 26:4 (1960), 412-416.
4100. George, Alexander L. "Case Studies and Theory Development: The Method of Structure, Focused Comparison." In: P. G. Lauren, ed. *Diplomacy*. New York: The Free Press, 1979. pp. 43-68.
4101. Gerard, Andre. "Diplomacy Old and New." *Foreign Affairs*, 23 (January 1945), 256-270.
4102. Gibson, Hugh S. "Secret vs. Open Diplomacy." In: E. Plischke, ed. *Modern Diplomacy: The Art and the Artisans*. Washington, D.C.: American Enterprise Institute, 1979. pp. 124-135.
4103. Groth, Alexander J. "On the Intelligence Aspects of Personal Diplomacy." *Orbis*, 7 (Winter 1964), 833-848.
4104. Habib, P. C. "The Practice of Modern Diplomacy." *California Western International Law*, 9 (1979), 485-493.
4105. Halle, Louis J. "Morality and Contemporary Diplomacy." In: S. D. Kertész and M. A. Fitzsimmons, eds. *Diplomacy in a Changing World*. South Bend, IN.: University of Notre Dame Press, 1959. pp. 21-34.
4106. Halstead, John G. H. "Today's Ambassador." In: M. F. Herz, ed. *The Modern Ambassador*. Washington, D.C.: Institute for the Study of Diplomacy, School of Foreign Service, Georgetown University, 1984. pp. 23-27.
4107. Hambro, E. "Some Notes on Parliamentary Diplomacy." In: W. Friedman, H. Henkins and O. J. Lissitzyn, eds. *Transnational Law in a Changing Society: Essays in Honor of Philip C. Jessup*. New York: Columbia University Press, 1972. pp. 280-297.
4108. Handel, Michael I. "On Diplomatic Surprise." In: N. Oren, ed. *Images and Reality in International Politics*. Jerusalem: Magnes Press, 1984. pp. 20-33.
4109. Harr, John Ensor. "The Profession: A New Diplomacy?." In: J. E. Harr, ed. *The Professional Diplomat*. Princeton, NJ.: Princeton University Press, 1969. pp. 11-44.
4110. Hermann, Margaret G. "Commentary: A Call For a New Type of Diplomat." *Negotiation Journal*, 3:3 (July 1987), 279-282.
4111. Herter, Christian A. "New Dimensions in Diplomacy." *Department of State Bulletin*, 37 (November 25, 1957), 831-834.
4112. Herz, Martin F. "Lessons in Diplomacy." *Foreign Service Journal*, 59:9 (October 1982), 24-25.
4113. Holmes, John W. "The Study of Diplomacy: A Sermon." In: J. W. Holmes, et al. *The Changing Role of Diplomatic Function in the Making of Foreign Policy*. Halifax, NS: Centre for Foreign Policy Studies, Dalhousie University, 1973. pp. 3-17.
4114. Holsti, K. J. "A New International Politics? Diplomacy in Complex Interdependence." *International Organization*, 32:2 (1978), 513-530.
4115. _____. "The Study of Diplomacy." In: J. N. Rosenau, K. W. Thompson and G. Boyd, eds. *World Politics: An Introduction*. New York: The Free Press, 1976. pp. 293-311.
4116. Irwin, John N. "Role of Creative Diplomacy in Europe of the 1970's." *Department of State Newsletter*, 124 (August 1971), 4-7.
4117. James, Alan M. "Diplomacy in International Society." *International Relations*, 6:6 (1980), 931-948.
4118. Keens-Soper, Maurice. "Francois de Callieres and Diplomatic Theory." *Historical Journal*, 16:3 (1973), 485-508.
4119. _____. "The Liberal Disposition of Diplomacy." *International Relations*, 5:2 (1975), 908-916.

4120. Kelly, David. "British Diplomacy." In: S. D. Kertész and M. A. Fitzsimmons, eds. *Diplomacy in a Changing World*. South Bend, IN.: University of Notre Dame Press, 1959. pp. 172-203.
4121. Kennan, George F. "Diplomacy as a Profession." *Foreign Service Journal*, 38 (May 1961), 23-26.
4122. _____. "Foreign Policy and the Professional Diplomat." *Wilson Quarterly*, 1 (Winter 1977), 148-157.
4123. _____. "The Future of Our Professional Diplomacy." *Foreign Affairs*, 33 (July 1955), 566-586.
4124. _____. "History and Diplomacy as Viewed by a Diplomatist." In: S. D. Kertész and M. A. Fitzsimmons, eds. *Diplomacy in a Changing World*. South Bend, IN.: University of Notre Dame Press, 1959. pp. 101-108.
4125. _____. "Training for Statesmanship." *Atlantic Monthly*, (May 1953), 40-43.
4126. Keogh, James. "Information and Modern Diplomacy." *Department of State Bulletin*, 70 (January 1974), 57-63.
4127. Kertész, Stephen D. "Diplomacy in the Atomic Age." *Review of Politics*, 21 (January/April 1959), 151-188, 357-388.
4128. Kirkpatrick, Ivone. "As a Diplomat Sees the Art of Diplomacy." *New York Times Magazine*, (March 22, 1959), 13, 84, 86.
4129. _____. "As a Diplomat Sees the Art of Diplomacy." In: G. A. Lanyi and W. C. Mc Williams, eds. *Crisis and Continuity in World Politics*. New York: Random House, 1966. pp. 420-425.
4130. Kissinger, Henry A. "Coalition Diplomacy in a Nuclear Age." In: L. A. Miller, ed. *Dynamics of World Politics*. Englewood Cliffs, NJ.: Prentice-Hall, 1968. pp. 44-61.
4131. _____. "The Limitation of Diplomacy." *New Republic*, (May 9, 1955), 7-8.
4132. _____. "Reflections on Power and Diplomacy." In: E. A. Johnson, ed. *The Dimensions of Diplomacy*. Baltimore, MD.: Johns Hopkins University Press, 1964. pp. 17-40.
4133. Kohler, Foy D. "Reflections of a Professional Diplomat." In: M. O. Gustafson, ed. *The National Archives and Foreign Relations Research*. Athens, OH.: Ohio University Press, 1974. pp. 277-287.
4134. Kovalyova, O., and Y. Simonov. "The Outdated Recipes of the Bourgeois Theory of Diplomacy." *International Affairs (Moscow)*, 9 (September 1982), 115-126.
4135. Kruger, Herbert. "German Diplomacy." In: S. D. Kertész and M. A. Fitzsimmons, eds. *Diplomacy in a Changing World*. South Bend, IN.: University of Notre Dame Press, 1959. pp. 301-326.
4136. Lacy, William S. B. "Usefulness of Classical Diplomacy." *Department of State Bulletin*, 38 (March 3, 1958), 326-327.
4137. Laise, Carol C. "Diplomacy in a Changing Society." In: G. C. McGhee, ed. *Diplomacy for the Future*. Lanham, MD.: University Press of America, 1987. pp. 77-84.
4138. Lauren, Paul G. "Ultimata and Coercive Diplomacy." *International Studies Quarterly*, 16 (July 1972), 131-165.
4139. _____. "Theories of Bargaining with Threats of Force: Deterrence and Coercive Diplomacy." In: P. G. Lauren, ed. *Diplomacy*. New York: The Free Press, 1979. pp. 183-211.
4140. _____. "Diplomacy: History, Theory, and Policy." In: P. G. Lauren, ed. *Diplomacy*. New York: The Free Press, 1979. pp. 3-20.
4141. Lee, Robert E. "Education for the New Diplomacy." *Department of State Bulletin*, 48 (March 25, 1963), 423-427.
4142. Levi, W. "International Statecraft." In: M. Haas, ed. *International Systems: A Behavioral Approach*. New York: Chandler, 1974. pp. 151-176.

Diplomacy

4143. Litimov, N. "Socialist Diplomacy: An Instrument of Peace." *International Affairs (Moscow)*, 8 (August 1978), 85-104.
4144. London, Kurt. "Diplomatic Communication." In: K. London, ed. *How Foreign Policy is Made.* New York: Van Nostrand, 1949. pp. 194-201.
4145. Lopez, Salvador P. "Development, Diplomacy, and the Third World." In: M. D. Zamora, ed. *Culture and Diplomacy in the Third World.* Williamsburg, VA.: Department of Anthropology, College of William and Mary, 1981. pp. 63-72.
4146. Low, Maurice A. "The Vice of Secret Diplomacy." *North American Review*, 207 (February 1918), 209-220.
4147. Lubbers, Jan Hendrik. "New Horizons in Postwar Diplomacy." *Washington Quarterly*, 10 (Winter 1987), 13-22.
4148. MacDonell, John. "Secret or Constructive Diplomacy." *Contemporary Review*, 109 (January 1916), 718-724.
4149. Maechling, Charles. "The Future of Diplomacy and Diplomats." *Foreign Service Journal*, 58:1 (January 1981), 17-22.
4150. _____. "The Future of Diplomacy and Diplomats." In: W. C. Olson, D. S. McLellan and F. A. Sonderman, eds. *The Theory and Practice of International Relations.* 6th ed. Englewood Cliffs, NJ.: Prentice-Hall, 1983. pp. 140-149.
4151. Mayers, D. "Containment and the Primacy of Diplomacy - Kennan, George Views, 1947-48." *International Security*, 11:1 (1986), 124-162.
4152. McDonald, John W. "Observation of a Diplomat." In: E. E. Azar and J. W. Burton, eds. *International Conflict Resolution.* Boulder, CO.: Lynne Rienner, 1986. pp. 141-153.
4153. McGhee, George C. "The Twilight of Diplomacy." *Foreign Service Journal*, 62:4 (April 1985), 34-37.
4154. _____. "Diplomacy for the Future: A Summary." In: G. C. McGhee, ed. *Diplomacy for the Future.* Lanham, MD.: University Press of America, 1987. pp. 95-102.
4155. _____. "The State of Diplomacy." In: G. G. McGhee, ed. *Diplomacy for the Future.* Lanham, MD.: University Press of America, 1987. pp. 3-12.
4156. McInnis, Edgar. "Canadian Diplomacy." In: S. D. Kertész and M. A. Fitzsimmons, eds. *Diplomacy in a Changing World.* South Bend, IN.: University of Notre Dame Press, 1959. pp. 251-265.
4157. McLachlan, Donald. "The Death of Diplomacy." *Twentieth Century*, 149 (1951), 173-180.
4158. McMullen, Christopher J. "The Art of Diplomacy." *Foreign Service Journal*, 64:9 (October 1987), 25-30.
4159. Merchant, Livingston T. "Diplomacy and the Modern World." *Department of State Bulletin*, 43 (November 7, 1960), 707-713.
4160. _____. "New Techniques in Diplomacy." In: E. A. Johnson, ed. *The Dimensions of Diplomacy.* Baltimore, MD.: Johns Hopkins Press, 1964. pp. 117-135.
4161. Middleton, Drew. "Notes on Diplomats and Diplomacy." *New York Times Magazine*, (October 30, 1955), 14, 58, 60.
4162. Morgenthau, Hans J. "The New Diplomacy of Movement." *Encounter*, 43 (August 1974), 52-57.
4163. _____. "The Permanent Values in the Old Diplomacy." In: S. D. Kertész and M. A. Fitzsimmons, eds. *Diplomacy in a Changing World.* South Bend, IN.: University of Notre Dame Press, 1959. pp. 10-20.
4164. Mosettig, Michael D. "The Revolution in Communication and Diplomacy." *Proceedings of the Academy of Political Science*, 34:2 (1981), 190-201.

4165. Mphaisa, Chisepo J. J. "Diplomacy by Conference: Principles, Goals, and Problems of Nam." *India Quarterly*, 39:1 (1983), 23-40.
4166. Muller, Steve. "Revival of Diplomacy." *World Diplomacy*, 15 (July 1963), 647-654.
4167. Muskie, Edmund S. "A Politician Looks at Diplomacy." In: G. C. McGhee, ed. *Diplomacy for the Future*. Lanham, MD.: University Press of America, 1987. pp. 13-20.
4168. Nascimento E Silva do, G. E. "Diplomacy." In: R. Bernhardt, ed. *Encyclopedia of Public International Law, Instalment 9: International Relations and Legal Cooperation in General Diplomacy and Consular Relations*. Amsterdam: North-Holland, 1986. pp. 78-87.
4169. _____. "Secret Diplomacy." In: R. Bernhardt, ed. *Encyclopedia of Public International Law, Instalment 9: International Relations and Legal Cooperation in General Diplomacy and Consular Relations*. Amsterdam: North-Holland, 1986. pp. 87-94.
4170. Neal, F. W. "Diplomacy." In: J. Gould and W. L. Kolb, eds. *A Dictionary of the Social Sciences*. New York: The Free Press, 1964. pp. 201-202.
4171. "New Dimensions of Diplomacy." *Department of State Bulletin*, 44 (February 6, 1961), 192-193.
4172. Newsom, David D. "Leaders and Experts." *Foreign Service Journal*, 63 (June 1986), 36-37.
4173. Nicolson, Harold. "Diplomacy Then and Now." In: W. C. Olson and F. A. Sonderman, eds. *The Theory and Practice of International Relations*. 2nd ed. Englewood Cliffs, NJ.: Prentice-Hall, 1966. pp. 260-266.
4174. _____. "The Old Diplomacy." In: G. A. Lanyi and W. C. McWilliams, eds. *Crisis and Continuity in World Politics*. New York: Random House, 1966. pp. 413-416.
4175. _____. "Open Covenants Secretly Arrived At." In: I. D. Duchacek, ed. *Discord and Harmony*. Hinsdale, IL.: Dryden Press, 1972. pp. 367-370.
4176. _____. "An Open Look at Secret Diplomacy." *New York Times Magazine*, (September 13, 1953), 17, 34, 47-48.
4177. _____. "Transition from the Old to the New Diplomacy." In: E. Plischke, ed. *Modern Diplomacy: The Art and the Artisans*. Washington, D.C.: American Enterprise Institute, 1979. pp. 43-53.
4178. _____. "An Open Look at Secret Diplomacy." In: N. J. Padelford and S. L. Kriner, eds. *Contemporary International Relations Readings, Third Series*. Cambridge, MA.: Harvard University Press, 1954. pp. 301-330.
4179. Nielson, F. "Labyrinths of Diplomacy." *American Journal of Economics*, 18:1 (October 1958), 1-14.
4180. O'Donnell, Charles P. "The New Diplomacy." *Commonweal*, 69 (October 10, 1958), 43-45.
4181. Olson, William C. "Democratic Approaches to Diplomacy." In: W. C. Olson and F. A. Sonderman, eds. *The Theory and Practice of International Relations*. 2nd ed. Englewood Cliffs, NY.: Prentice-Hall, 1966. pp. 281-288.
4182. Osborne, John. "The Importance of Ambassadors." *Fortune*, (April 1957), 146-151, 184-194.
4183. Parsons, Anthony. "Vultures and Philistines - British Attitudes to Culture and Cultural Diplomacy." *International Affairs*, 61:1 (1985), 1-8.
4184. Petrie, Charles. "The Place of the Professional in Modern Diplomacy." *Quarterly Review*, 605 (July 1955), 295-308.
4185. Pfaff, William. "Computerized Diplomacy." *Commonweal*, 82 (July 23, 1965), 520-521.

4186. Plantey, A. "The European Community's Contribution to Diplomatic Method and Practices." *International Review of Administrative Studies*, 49:3 (1983), 288-291.
4187. Plischke, Elmer. "Changing Diplomatic Practice." In: E. Plischke, ed. *Modern Diplomacy: The Art and the Artisans*. Washington, D.C.: American Enterprise Institute, 1979. pp. 41-98.
4188. ____. "Democratic and Open Diplomacy." In: E. Plischke, ed. *Modern Diplomacy: The Art and the Artisans*. Washington, D.C.: American Enterprise Institute, 1979. pp. 99-149.
4189. ____. "A More Open Diplomacy vs. Greater Secrecy." *Foreign Service Journal*, 34 (April 1957), 31-34.
4190. ____. "The New Diplomacy." In: E. Plischke, ed. *Modern Diplomacy: The Art and the Artisans*. Washington, D.C.: American Enterprise Institute, 1979. pp. 54-72.
4191. ____. "The New New Diplomacy: A Changing Process." *Virginia Quarterly Review*, 49 (Summer 1973), 321-345.
4192. ____. "The Optimum Scope for Instruction in Diplomacy." In: S. Simpson, ed. *Instruction in Diplomacy: The Liberal Approach*. Philadelphia, PA.: American Academy of Political and Social Sciences, 1972. pp. 1-25.
4193. ____. "Treatment of 'Diplomacy' in International Relations Textbooks." *World Affairs*, 135 (Spring 1973), 328-344.
4194. Plumtre, T. "Diplomacy: Obsolete or Essential." *Queen's Quarterly*, 80:4 (1973), 503-520.
4195. Potter, Pitman B. "Rigid Versus Adjustable Techniques in Diplomacy." *American Journal of International Law*, 45 (October 1951), 721-723.
4196. Poullada, Leon B. "Diplomacy: The Missing Link in the Study of International Politics." In: D. S. McLellan, W. C. Olson and F. A. Sonderman, eds. *The Theory and Practice of International Relations*. 4th ed. Englewood Cliffs, NJ.: Prentice-Hall, 1974. pp. 194-202.
4197. ____. "Diplomacy: The Missing Link in the Study of International Politics." *Foreign Area Research Horizons*, 5:2 (Spring 1972), 3-7.
4198. ____. "Leaders and Experts: The Professional Solution." *Foreign Service Journal*, 63 (October 1986), 24-25.
4199. Pranger, Robert J. "Contemporary Diplomacy at Work." In: E. Plischke, ed. *Modern Diplomacy: The Art and the Artisans*. Washington, D.C.: American Enterprise Institute, 1979. pp. 73-85.
4200. Richard, I. "Diplomacy in an Interdependent World." *Academy of Political Science, Proceedings*, 32:4 (1977), 727-744.
4201. Ritchie, Charles. "What Are Diplomats Made Of?" *International Journal*, 30:1 (1974), 15-23.
4202. Rogers, William P. "The New Foreign Service and the Job of Modern Diplomacy." *Department of State Bulletin*, 65 (December 13, 1971), 675-676.
4203. Root, Elihu. "Requisite for the Success of Popular Diplomacy." In: E. Plischke, ed. *Modern Diplomacy: The Art and the Artisans*. Washington, D.C.: American Enterprise Institute, 1979. pp. 102-108.
4204. Rosencrance, Richard N. "Diplomacy in Security Systems." In: R. B. Gray, ed. *International Security Systems: Concepts and Models of World Order*. Itasca, IL.: F. E. Peacock, 1969. pp. 93-107.
4205. Rossiter, Clinton L. "The Old Conservatism and the New Diplomacy." *Virginia Quarterly Review*, 32 (Winter 1956), 28-49.
4206. Rossow, Robert. "The Professionalization of the New Diplomacy." *World Politics*, 14:4 (1962), 561-575.

4207. Rusk, Dean. "Methods of Diplomacy." *Department of State Bulletin*, 30 (February 8, 1954), 207-208.
4208. _____. "Parliamentary Diplomacy - Debate Versus Negotiation." *World Affairs Interpreter*, 26 (1955), 121-138.
4209. Russell, Francis H. "The Principal Tasks of Diplomacy." *Department of State Bulletin*, 30 (February 8, 1954), 207-208.
4210. Russett, B. M., and W. C. Lamb. "Global Patterns of Diplomatic Exchange, 1963-1964." *Journal of Peace Research*, 1 (1969), 37-55.
4211. Simpson, Smith. "Diplomacy: Some Professional and Political Perspectives." *Foreign Service Journal*, 53 (August 1976), 15-19.
4212. _____. "The Nature and Dimensions of Diplomacy." *Annals of the American Academy of Political and Social Science*, 380 (November 1968), 135-144.
4213. Singer, J. David. "Limitation of Diplomacy." *Nation*, (July 9, 1960), 26-28.
4214. _____. "The Return of Multilateral Diplomacy." *Yale Review*, 53 (October 1963), 36-48.
4215. Sofer, Sasson. "Old and New Diplomacy: A Debate Revisited: Discussions." *Review of International Studies*, 14:3 (July 1988), 195-212.
4216. Sullivan, William H. "The Transformation of Diplomacy." *Fletcher Forum*, 8:2 (1984), 291-295.
4217. Thayer, Charles W. "Case for Professional Diplomats." In: E. Plischke, ed. *Modern Diplomacy: The Art and the Artisans*. Washington, D.C.: American Enterprise Institute, 1979. pp. 323-333.
4218. _____. "Our Ambassadors: An Intimate Appraisal of the Men and the System." *Harper Magazine*, (September 1959), 29-35.
4219. Thayer, Robert H. "Cultural Diplomacy and the Development of the Mutual Understanding." *Department of State Bulletin*, 41 (August 31, 1959), 310-316.
4220. Thompson, Kenneth W. "The Ethical Dimensions of Diplomacy." *Review of Politics*, 46:3 (July 1984), 367-387.
4221. _____. "The New Diplomacy and the Quest for Peace." *International Organization*, 19:3 (1965), 394-409.
4222. _____. "Power, Force and Diplomacy." *Review of Politics*, 43:3 (1981), 410-435.
4223. _____. "The Prospects and Limitations of Diplomacy." *Review of Politics*, 36:2 (1974), 298-305.
4224. Thornton, A. P. "A Reserved Occupation." *International Journal*, 30:1 (1974-75), 1-14.
4225. Van Dyke, Vernon. "Diplomacy and the Settling of International Disputes." In: V. Van Dyke, ed. *International Politics*. 3rd ed. New York: Appleton-Century-Crofts, 1972. pp. 272-297.
4226. Vansittart, L. "The Decline of Diplomacy." *Foreign Affairs*, 28:2 (1950), 177-188.
4227. Von Staden, Berndt. "Changing Patterns and New Responsibilities." In: M. F. Herz, ed. *The Modern Ambassador*. Washington, D.C.: Institute for the Study of Diplomacy, School of Foreign Service, Georgetown University, 1984. pp. 19-22.
4228. _____. "A Diplomat Comments on His Profession." *Atlantic Community Quarterly*, 17:2 (1979), 217-220.
4229. _____. "Diplomacy in Open Societies." In: G. C. McGhee, ed. *Diplomacy for the Future*. Lanham, MD.: University Press of America, 1987. pp. 49-56.
4230. Wiethoff, William E. "A Machiavellian Paradigm for Diplomatic Communication." *Journal of Politics*, 43:4 (1981), 1090-1104.

4231. Williams, Walter L. "Discussion: Culture, Development and Diplomacy: Reflections on a Seamless Webb." In: M. D. Zamora, ed. *Culture and Diplomacy in the Third World.* Williamsburg, VA.: Department of Anthropology, College of William and Mary, 1981. pp. 117-122.
4232. Woodward, E. L. "The Old and the New Diplomacy." *The Yale Review,* 36:3 (1946/47), 405-422.
4233. Wright, Quincy. "The Decline of Classic Diplomacy." *Journal of International Affairs,* 17:1 (1963), 18-28.
4234. _____. "The Role of International Law in Contemporary Diplomacy." In: S. D. Kertész and M. A. Fitzimons, eds. *Diplomacy in a Changing World.* South Bend, IN.: University of Notre Dame Press, 1959. pp. 55-76.
4235. Wriston, Henry M. "Ministerial Diplomacy - Secretary of State Abroad." In: E. Plischke, ed. *Modern Diplomacy: The Art and the Artisans.* Washington, D.C.: American Enterprise Institute, 1979. pp. 153-168.
4236. _____. "The Special Envoy." *Foreign Affairs,* 38 (January 1960), 219-237.

3. Documents and Reports

4237. Boudreau, Tom. *A New International Diplomatic Order.* Muscatine, IA.: Stanley Foundation, 1980. 24p.
4238. Burke, Lee H. *The Ambassador at Large: A Study in Diplomatic Method.* Ph.D. Dissertation. College Park, MD.: University of Maryland, 1971.
4239. Christopher, Warren. *Diplomacy: The Neglected Imperative.* [S.1:s.n.], 1981. 77p.
4240. Claude, Inis L. *The Impact of Public Opinion Upon Foreign Policy and Diplomacy: Open Diplomacy Revisited.* The Hague: Mouton, 1965. 21p.
4241. Cottam, Richard W. "Modern Diplomacy and Intervention." Paper Presented at the *62nd Annual Meeting of the American Political Science Association,* held on September 8-10, 1966, in New York.
4242. Craig, Gordon A. *On the Diplomatic Revolution of Our Time.* Riverside, CA.: University of California Press, 1961. 64p.
4243. Creagle, John S. *Personal Qualities and Effective Diplomatic Negotiation.* Ph.D. Dissertation. College Park, MD.: University of Maryland, 1965. 320p.
4244. Der Derian, James. *The Mytho-Diplomacy and New-Diplomacy: An Inquiry into the Origins and Development of Western Diplomacy.* M.Phil. Oxford: Oxford University, 1981.
4245. Feltham, Ralph G. *Training for an International Career.* Washington, D.C.: Institute for the Study of Diplomacy, Georgetown University, 1979. 39p.
4246. Friedheim, Robert L. *Parliamentary Diplomacy.* CNA Professional Paper - 162. Arlington, VA.: Center for Naval Analyses, 1976. 115p.
4247. Geiser, Hans, Paul R. Kimmel and Alberto M. Piedra. "The Role of Diplomats in International Negotiations." Paper Presented at the *Tenth SIETAR International Conference,* held on May 21-25, 1984, at George Mason University, Washington, D.C.
4248. Harr, John Ensor. *The Professional Diplomat and the New Diplomacy.* Ph.D. Dissertation. Berkeley, CA.: University of California, 1967.
4249. Herz, Martin F., ed. *Contacts with the Opposition: A Symposium.* Washington. D.C.: Institute for the Study of Diplomacy, School of Foreign Service, Georgetown University, 1979. 72p.
4250. _____. *The Modern Ambassador: The Challenge and the Search.* Washington, D.C.: Institute for the Study of Diplomacy, School of Foreign Service, Georgetown University, 1984. 211p.

4251. _____., ed. *The Role of Embassies in Promoting Business: A Symposium.* Washington, D.C.: Institute for the Study of Diplomacy, School of Foreign Service, Georgetown University, 1981. 68p.
4252. _____. *Making the World a Less Dangerous Place: Lessons Learned from a Career in Diplomacy.* Washington, D.C.: School of Foreign Service, Georgetown University, 1981. 25p.
4253. Holmes, John W., et al. *The Changing Role of the Diplomatic Function in the Making of Foreign Policy.* Halifax, NS: Centre for Foreign Policy Studies, Dalhousie University, 1973. 83p.
4254. Kattenburg, Paul M. *Diplomatic Practices.* New York: Learning Resources in International Studies, 1975. 51p.
4255. Lankhuff, P. "Secrecy in Diplomacy." Paper Presented at the *53th Annual Meeting of the American Political Science Association,* held on September 5-7, 1957, in New York.
4256. Litman, J. M. *Role of Targeting in Coercive Diplomacy.* Maxwell AFB, AL.: Air War College, 1986. 43p.
4257. Magnarella, Paul J., ed. *Anthropological Diplomacy: Case Studies in the Applications of Anthropology to International Studies.* Studies in Third World Societies: 21. Williamsburg, VA.: Department of Anthropology, College of William and Mary, 1982. 84p.
4258. McDonald, John W. *How to Be a Delegate.* Washington, D.C.: Center for the Study of Foreign Affairs, Foreign Service Institute, 1984. 54p.
4259. Menderhausen, Horst. *The Diplomat as a National and Transnational Agent: A Problem in Multiple Loyalty.* Morristown, NJ.: General Learning Press, 1973. 19p.
4260. _____. *The Diplomat as a National and Transnational Agent: Dilemmas and Opportunities.* Santa Monica, CA.: RAND Corporation, 1969. 28p.
4261. _____. "The Diplomat as a National and Transnational Agent - Dilemmas and Opportunities." Paper Presented to the *Annual Meeting of the American Political Science Association,* held in 1969, in New York. Panel 2-E1.
4262. Menon, K. P. S. *Changing Patterns of Diplomacy.* Bombay: Bharatija Vidya Bhavan, 1977. 37p.
4263. Miller, J. D. B. *The Shape of Diplomacy.* Canberra: The Australian National University, 1963. 19p.
4264. Platig, Raymond E. "Educating Diplomats for the 21st Century." Paper Presented at the *12th World Congress of the International Political Science Association,* held on August 9-14, 1982, in Rio de Janeiro.
4265. Polk, W. R. *From Diplomacy to Politics.* Working Paper No. 7. Chicago, IL.: Adlai Stevenson Institute, 1973. 16p.
4266. Rondybush, Franklin. *Diplomatic Language.* Basel, Switzerland: Satz, 1972. 24p.
4267. Simpson, Smith. *Perspectives on the Study of Diplomacy.* Washington, D.C.: Institute for the Study of Diplomacy, Georgetown University, 1986. 31p.
4268. Spiro, Herbert J. "The Quality of Diplomacy: Patterns and Styles." Paper Presented at the *10th World Congress of the International Political Science Association,* held on August 16-21, 1976, in Edinburgh.
4269. Wilson, Clifton E. *Cold War Diplomacy: The Impact of International Conflict on Diplomatic Communications and Travel.* Institute of Government Research, International Studies, No. 1. Tucson, AR.: University of Arizona Press, 1966. 67p.

B. DIPLOMATIC HISTORY

1. Books

4270. Albrecht-Carrie, Rene. *A Diplomatic History of Europe Since the Congress of Vienna.* New York: Harper & Row, 1973. 764p.
4271. Bailey, Thomas A. *A Diplomatic History of the American People.* 9th ed. Englewood Cliffs, NJ.: Prentice-Hall, 1980. 1093p.
4272. Bemis, Samuel F. *A Diplomatic History of the United States.* New York: Holt, Rinehart and Winston, 1960. 1018p.
4273. _____., and Grace G. Griffin. *Guide to the Diplomatic History of the United States, 1775-1921.* Washington, D.C.: U.S. Government Printing Office, 1935. 979p.
4274. Craig, Gordon A., and Felix Gilbert, eds. *The Diplomats, 1919-1939.* Princeton, NJ.: Princeton University Press, 1953. 2 vols.
4275. Ferrell, Nancy W. *Passports to Peace: Embassies and the Art of Diplomacy.* Minneapolis, MI.: Lerner Publications, 1986. 87p.
4276. Findling, John E. *Dictionary of American Diplomatic History.* Westport, CT.: Greenwood Press, 1980. 622p.
4277. Fowler, Wilton R. *American Diplomatic History Since 1890.* Northbrook, IL.: AHM Publishing, 1975. 176p.
4278. Gatzke, Hans W. *European Diplomacy Between Two Wars, 1919-1939.* Chicago, IL.: Quadrangle Books, 1972. 277p.
4279. Gooch, George P. *Before the War: Studies in Diplomacy.* London: Longmans, Green, 1938. 2 vols.
4280. Grenville, J. A. S., and Bernard Wasserstein. *The Major International Treaties Since 1945: A History and Guide With Texts.* London: Methuen, 1987. 528p.
4281. Grew, Joseph C. *Turbulent Era: A Diplomatic Record of Forty Years, 1904-1945.* London: Hammond, Hammond, 1953. 2 vols.
4282. Hatton, Raynhild, and M. S. Anderson, eds. *Studies in Diplomatic History: Essays in Memory of David Bayne Horn.* London: Longman, 1970. 384p.
4283. Jones, Dorothy. *Splendid Encounters: The Thought and Conduct of Diplomacy.* Chicago, IL.: University of Chicago Library, 1984. 130p.
4284. Kennedy, A. L. *Old Diplomacy and New, 1876-1922: From Salisbury to Lloyd George.* New York: D. Appleton and Co., 1923. 414p.
4285. Kennedy, Paul, ed. *Strategy and Diplomacy, 1870-1945: 8 Studies.* London: Allen & Unwin, 1983. 254p.
4286. Launay, Jacques de. *Secret Diplomacy of World War II.* New York: Simmons-Boardman, 1953. 175p.
4287. Mattingly, Garring. *Renaissance Diplomacy.* New York: Penguin, 1973. 323p.
4288. Mayer, Arno J. *Political Origins of the New Diplomacy, 1917-1918.* New Haven, CT.: Yale University Press, 1959. 435p.
4289. Namier, Lewis B. *Diplomatic Prelude, 1938-1939.* New York: Macmillan, 1948. 502p.
4290. Nicolson, Harold. *The Evolution of Diplomatic Method.* New York: Macmillan, 1954. 93p.
4291. Numelin, Ragnar. *The Beginnings of Diplomacy: A Sociological Study of Intertribal and International Relations.* London: Oxford University Press, 1950. 372p.
4292. Petrie, Charles. *Diplomatic History, 1713-1933.* New York: Macmillan, 1949. 384p.
4293. Presseisen, Ernst L. *Germany and Japan: A Study in Totalitarian Diplomacy, 1933-1941.* The Hague: M. Nijhoff, 1958. 368p.

4294. Roetter, Charles. *The Diplomatic Art: An Informal History of World Diplomacy.* Philadelphia, PA.: Macrae Smith, 1963. 248p.
4295. Sarkissian, A. O. *Studies in Diplomatic History and Historiography in Honour of G. P. Gooch.* London: Longmans, 1961. 393p.
4296. Selby, Walford. *Diplomatic Twilight: 1930-1940.* London: John Murray, 1953. 210p.
4297. Snell, John L. *Illusion and Necessity: The Diplomacy of Global War, 1939-1945.* Boston, MA.: Houghton Mifflin, 1963. 229p.
4298. Toscano, Mario. *Design In Diplomacy: Pages from European Diplomatic History in the Twentieth Century.* Baltimore, MD.: Johns Hopkins University Press, 1970. 432p.

2. Journal Articles

4299. Boahen, A. A. "Fante Diplomacy in the Eighteen Century." In: K. Ingham, ed. *Foreign Relations of African States.* London: Butterworth, 1974. pp. 25-49.
4300. Butler, R. "Paradiplomacy." In: A. O. Sarkissian, ed. *Studies in Diplomatic History and Historiography in Honour of P. G. Gooch.* London: Longman, 1961. pp. 12-25.
4301. Butterfield, Herbert. "Diplomacy." In: R. Hatton and M. S. Anderson, ed. *Studies in Diplomatic History: Essays in Memory of David Bayne Horn.* London: Longman, 1970. pp. 357-372.
4302. _____. "The New Diplomacy and Historical Diplomacy." In: H. Butterfield and M. Wight, eds. *Diplomatic Investigations.* London: George Allen & Unwin, 1966. pp. 181-192.
4303. Craig, Gordon A. "On the Nature of Diplomatic History: The Relevance of Some Old Books." In: P. G. Lauren, ed. *Diplomacy.* New York: The Free Press, 1979. pp. 21-42.
4304. Durosselle, J. B. "Changes in Diplomacy Since Versailles." In: B. Porter, ed. *The Aberrystwyth Papers: International Politics, 1919-1969.* London: Oxford University Press, 1972. pp. 102-128.
4305. Herz, Martin F. "Patchwork-Quilt History." *Washington Quarterly*, 6:2 (1983), 209-218.
4306. Jervis, Robert. "Systems Theories and Diplomatic History." In: P. G. Lauren, ed. *Diplomacy.* New York: The Free Press, 1979. pp. 212-244.
4307. Lauren, Paul G. "Crisis Prevention in Nineteenth Century Diplomacy." In: A. L. George, ed. *Managing U.S. - Soviet Rivalry.* Boulder, CO.: Westview Press, 1983. pp. 31-64.
4308. Nicolson, Harold. "The Evolution of Diplomatic Method." In: I. D. Duchacek, ed. *Conflict and Cooperation Among Nations.* New York: Holt, Rinehart and Winston, 1960. pp. 509-517.
4309. Small, Melvin. "The Qualification of Diplomatic History." In: P. G. Lauren, ed. *Diplomacy.* New York: The Free Press, 1979. pp. 69-98.
4310. Sontag, Raymond J. "History and Diplomacy as Viewed by a Historian." In: S. D. Kertész and M. A. Fitzsimmons, eds. *Diplomacy in a Changing World.* South Bend, IN.: University of Notre Dame Press, 1959. pp. 109-116.
4311. Williamson, Samuel R., Jr. "Theories of Organizational Process and Foreign Policy." In: P. G. Lauren, ed. *Diplomacy.* New York: The Free Press, 1979. pp. 137-161.

C. DIPLOMATIC MEMOIRS

1. Books

4312. Acheson, Dean. *Present at the Creation: My Years with the State Department.* New York: W. W. Norton, 1969. 198p.
4313. Asbell, Bernard. *The F. D. R. Memoirs.* Garden City, N.Y.: Double Day, 1973. 461p.
4314. Attlee, Clement. *As It Happened.* New York: Viking, 1954. 312p.
4315. Bedell Smith, Walter. *Moscow Mission, 1946-1949.* London: Heineman, 1950. 337p.
4316. Birse, A. H. *Memoirs of an Interpreter.* London: Joseph, 1967. 254p.
4317. Bohlen, Charles E. *Witness to History, 1929-1969.* New York: W. W. Norton, 1973. 562p.
4318. Bonner, Paul H. *Ambassador Extraordinary.* New York: Scribner, 1962. 306p.
4319. Bowles, Chester. *Ambassador's Report.* New York: Harper & Row, 1954. 415p.
4320. _____. *Promises to Keep.* New York: Harper & Row, 1971. 657p.
4321. Briggs, Ellis O. *Farewell to Foggy Bottom: The Recollections of a Career Diplomat.* New York: McKay, 1964. 306p.
4322. Brzezinski, Zbigniev. *Power and Principle: Memoirs of the National Security Advisor, 1977-1981.* New York: Farrar, Straus and Giroux, 1983. 587p.
4323. Burke, Lee H. *Ambassador at Large: Diplomat Extraordinary.* The Hague: Nijhoff, 1972. 176p.
4324. Byrnes, James F. *Speaking Frankly.* New York: Harper, 1947. 324p.
4325. Davies, Joseph E. *Mission to Moscow.* New York: Simon & Schuster, 1941. 683p.
4326. Dunham, Donald C. *Envoy Unextraordinary.* New York: Day, 1944. 162p.
4327. Einstein, Lewis. *A Diplomat Looks Back.* New Haven, CT.: Yale University Press, 1968. 269p.
4328. Ford, Gerald R. *A Time to Heal.* New York: Harper & Row, 1979. 454p.
4329. Galbraith, John K. *Ambassador's Journal.* Boston, MA.: Houghton Mifflin, 1969. 656p.
4330. Gromyko, Andrei. *Memoirs.* London: Hutchinson, 1989. 2 Vols.
4331. Haig, Alexander M. *Caveat: Realism, Reason and Foreign Policy.* New York: Macmillan, 1984. 367p.
4332. Harriman, W. Averell, and Elie Abel. *Special Envoy to Churchill and Stalin, 1941 - 1946.* New York: Random House, 1975. 595p.
4333. Henderson, Loy W. *A Question of Trust: The Origins of U.S. - Soviet Diplomatic Relations: The Memoirs of Loy W. Henderson.* Stanford, CA.: Hoover Institution Press, 1986. 579p.
4334. Herz, Martin F. *215 Days in the Life of an American Ambassador: Diary Notes from Sofia, Bulgaria.* Washington, D.C.: School of Foreign Service, Georgetown University, 1981. 269p.
4335. Hull, Cordell. *Memoirs.* New York: Macmillan, 1948. 2 vols.
4336. Johnson, Lyndon B. *The Vantage Point: Perspectives of the Presidency, 1963 - 1969.* New York: Holt, Rinehart & Winston, 1971. 636p.
4337. Kennan, George F. *Memoirs, 1925-1950.* Boston, MA.: Little, Brown, 1967. 583p.
4338. _____. *Memoirs, 1950-1963.* Boston, MA.: Little, Brown, 1972. 368p.
4339. Kissinger, Henry A. *White House Years.* Boston, MA.: Little, Brown, 1979. 1521p.
4340. _____. *Years of Upheaval.* Boston, MA.: Little, Brown, 1982. 1283p.

4341. Lipski, Jozef. *Diplomat in Berlin, 1933-1939.* New York: Columbia University Press, 1968. 679p.
4342. Lukasiewicz, Juliusz. *Diplomat in Paris, 1936-1939.* New York: Columbia University Press, 1970. 408p.
4343. Maisky, Ivan. *Memoirs of a Soviet Ambassador: The War, 1939-1943.* New York: Scribner's, 1967. 408p.
4344. McGhee, George C. *Envoy to the Middle World: Adventures in Diplomacy.* New York: Harper & Row, 1983. 457p.
4345. Meyer, Armin H. *Assignment: Tokyo: An Ambassador's Journal.* Indianapolis, IN.: Bobbs - Merrill, 1974. 396p.
4346. Nixon, Richard M. *RN: The Memoirs of Richard Nixon.* New York: Grosset & Dunlap, 1978. 1120p.
4347. Ritchie, Charles. *Diplomatic Passport: More Undiplomatic Diaries, 1946-1962.* Toronto, Ont.: Macmillan of Canada, 1981. 200p.
4348. _____. *The Siren Years: A Canadian Diplomat Abroad, 1937-1945.* Toronto: Macmillan of Canada, 1974. 216p.
4349. _____. *Storm Signals: More Undiplomatic Diaries, 1962-1971.* Toronto: Macmillan of Canada, 1983. 175p.
4350. Rosen, Baron. *Forty Years of Diplomacy.* London: George Allen and Unwin, 1922. 315p.
4351. Sadat, Anwar. *In Search of Identity: An Autobiography.* New York: Harper & Row, 1978. 360p.
4352. Spain, James W. *American Diplomacy in Turkey: Memoirs of an Ambassador Extraordinary and Plenipotentiary.* New York: Praeger, 1984. 245p.
4353. Sullivan, William H. *Obbligato: Notes on a Foreign Service Career, 1939 - 1979.* New York: Norton, 1984. 279p.

2. Journal Articles

4354. Herz, Martin F. "Views from the Top. A Former Ambassador Ponders the Real Goals and Successes of a Foreign Service Career." *Foreign Service Journal,* 60 (June 1983), 26-27, 32-33.
4355. Schulzinger, Robert D. "The Naive and Sentimental Diplomat: Henry Kissinger's Memoirs." *Diplomatic History,* 4 (Summer 1980), 303-315.

D. UNOFFICIAL DIPLOMACY

1. Books

4356. Berman, Maureen R., and Joseph E. Johnson, eds. *Unofficial Diplomats.* New York: Columbia University Press, 1977. 268p.
4357. Butow, R. J. C. *The Joe Doe Associates: Backdoor Diplomacy for Peace, 1941.* Stanford, CA.: Stanford University Press, 1974. 480p.
4358. Byrnes, Robert F. *Soviet - American Academic Exchanges, 1958 - 1975.* Bloomington, IN.: Indiana University Press, 1976. 275p.
4359. Carlson, Don, and Craig Comstock. *Citizen Summitry: Keeping the Peace When It Matters Too Much to be Left to Politicians.* Los Angeles, CA.: Jeremy P. Tarcher, 1986. 396p.
4360. Newsom, David D. *Private Diplomacy with the Soviet Union.* Lanham, MD.: University Press of America, 1987. 143p.

4361. Volkan, Vanik D. *The Need to Have Enemies and Allies: From Clinical Practice to International Relationships.* Northvale, NJ.: Jason Aronson, 1988. 298p.
4362. Yarrow, C. H. M. *Quaker Experiences in International Conciliation.* New Haven, CO.: Yale University Press, 1978. 308p.

2. Journal Articles

4363. Ashmore, Harry S. "An Exercise in Demi-Diplomacy: The Case of Vietnam." In: M. R. Berman and J. E. Johnson, eds. *Unofficial Diplomats.* New York: Columbia University Press, 1977. pp. 130-141.
4364. Avneri, Uri. "Unofficial and Unrepresentative But..." *New Middle East,* 12 (September 1969), 23-28.
4365. Bailey, Sydney D. "Non-Official Mediation in Disputes: Reflections on Quaker Experience." *International Affairs,* 61:2 (Spring 1985), 205-222.
4366. Bartholomew, Sara. "A Different Summit." *Kettering Review,* (Fall 1986), 39-43.
4367. Berman, Maureen R., and Joseph E. Johnson. "The Growing Role of Unofficial Diplomacy." In: M. R. Berman and J. E. Johnson, eds. *Unofficial Diplomats.* New York: Columbia University Press, 1977. pp. 1-34.
4368. _____., and Barbara Rotenberg. "The Dartmouth Conferences: An Interview with Norman Cousins." In: M. R. Berman and J. E. Johnson, eds. *Unofficial Diplomats.* New York: Columbia University Press, 1977. pp. 45-55.
4369. Bolling, Landrum R. "Quaker Work in the Middle East Following the June 1967 War." In: M. R. Berman and J. E. Johnson, eds. *Unofficial Diplomats.* New York: Columbia University Press, 1977. pp. 80-88.
4370. _____. "Strengths and Weaknesses of Track Two: A Personal Account." In: J. W. McDonald and D. D. Bendahmane, eds. *Conflict Resolution: Track Two Diplomacy.* Washington, D.C.: Center for the Study of Foreign Affairs, Foreign Service Institute, 1987. pp. 53-64.
4371. _____. "The Dartmouth Conference Process: Subjective Reflections." In: D. D. Newsom, ed. *Private Diplomacy with the Soviet Union.* Lanham, MD.: University Press of America, 1987. pp. 39-54.
4372. Brougher, Valentina G. "Negotiating on the Academic Front." In: D. D. Newsom, ed. *Private Diplomacy with the Soviet Union.* Lanham, MD.: University Press of America, 1987. pp. 101-112.
4373. Burton, John W. "Track Two: An Alternative to Power Politics." In: J. W. McDonald and D. B. Bendahmane, eds. *Conflict Resolution: Track Two Diplomacy.* Washington, D.C.: Center for the Study of Foreign Affairs, Foreign Service Institute, 1987. pp. 65-72.
4374. Campbell, Kurt M. "Citizen Diplomacy: One Sided but Rewarding." In: D. D. Newsom, ed. *Private Diplomacy with the Soviet Union.* Lanham, MD.: University Press of America, 1987. pp. 113-116.
4375. Diekmann, Andreas. "Volunteer's Dilemma." *Journal of Conflict Resolution,* 29:4 (December 1985), 605-610.
4376. Foltz, William J. "Two Forms of Unofficial Conflict Intervention: The Problem Solving and the Process Promoting Workshops." In: M. R. Berman and J. E. Johnson, eds. *Unofficial Diplomats.* New York: Columbia University Press, 1977. pp. 201-221.
4377. Freymond, Jacques. "The International Committee of the Red Cross as a Neutral Intermediary." In: M. R. Berman and J. E. Johnson, eds. *Unofficial Diplomats.* New York: Columbia University Press, 1977. pp. 142--152.

4378. Hammer, Armand. "Private Diplomacy at the Highest Level." In: D. D. Newsom, ed. *Private Diplomacy with the Soviet Union.* Lanham, MD.: University Press of America, 1987. pp. 55-72.
4379. Kelman, Herbert C. "The Problem-Solving Workshop in Conflict Resolution." In: M. R. Berman and J. E. Johnson, eds. *Unofficial Diplomats.* New York: Columbia University Press, 1977. pp. 168-200.
4380. Kriesberg, Louis. "Non-Coercive Inducements in International Conflicts." *Peace and Change,* 7:4 (Fall 1981), 37-48.
4381. Marshall, James. "Citizen Diplomacy." *American Political Science Review,* 43 (February 1949), 83-90.
4382. Mattison, Jeanne V. "Discussing Nuclear Issues and Trade Relations." In: D. D. Newsom, ed. *Private Diplomacy with the Soviet Union.* Lanham, MD.: University Press of America, 1987. pp. 93-100.
4383. Meyer, Ernest. "The Bilateral and Multilateral Meetings of the International Press Institute." In: M. R. Berman and J. E. Johnson, eds. *Unofficial Diplomats.* New York: Columbia University Press, 1977. pp. 56-66.
4384. Montville, Joseph V. "The Arrow and the Olive Branch: A Car for Track Two Diplomacy." In: J. W. McDonald and D. B. Bendahmane, eds. *Conflict Resolution: Track Two Diplomacy.* Washington, D.C.: Center for the Study of Foreign Affairs, Foreign Service Institute, 1987. pp. 5-20.
4385. _____. "Notebook on the Psychology of the US - Soviet Relationship." *Journal of Political Psychology,* 6:2 (June 1985), 207-212.
4386. Rees, Elfan. "Exercises in Private Diplomacy: Selected Activities of the Commission of the Churches on International Affairs." In: M. R. Berman and J. E. Johnson, eds. *Unofficial Diplomats.* New York: Columbia University, 1977. pp. 111-129.
4387. Reich, Alan A. "People-to-People Diplomacy - Key to World Understanding." *Department of State Bulletin,* 67:1732 (September 4, 1972), 248-251.
4388. Roth, Lois W. "Public Diplomacy and the Past: The Search for an American Style of Propaganda (1952-1977)." *Fletcher Forum,* 8:2 (1984), 353-396.
4389. Saunders, Harold H. "When Citizens Talk: Nonofficial Dialogue in Relations Between Nations." In: J. W. McDonald and D. B. Bendahmane, eds. *Conflict Resolution: Track Two Diplomacy.* Washington, D.C.: Center for the Study of Foreign Affairs, Foreign Service Institute, 1987. pp. 81-88.
4390. _____. "The Dartmouth Conference and the Middle East." In: D. D. Newsom, ed. *Private Diplomacy in the Soviet Union.* Lanham, MD.: University Press of America, 1987. pp. 29-38.
4391. _____. "When Citizen Talk." *Kettering Review,* (Summer 1984), 49-55.
4392. Scali, John. "Backstage Mediation in the Cuban Missile Crisis." In: J. W. McDonald and D. B. Bendahmane, eds. *Conflict Resolution: Track Two Diplomacy.* Washington, D.C.: Center for the Study of Foreign Affairs, Foreign Service Institute, 1987. pp. 73-80.
4393. Sissons, D. C. S. "Private Diplomacy in the 1936 Trade Dispute with Japan." *Australian Journal of Politics and History,* 27:2 (1981), 143-159.
4394. Stewart, Philip D. "The Dartmouth Conference." In: J. W. McDonald and D. B. Bendahmane, eds. *Conflict Resolution: Track Two Diplomacy.* Washington, D.C.: Center for the Study of Foreign Affairs, Foreign Service Institute, 1987. pp. 21-26.
4395. _____. "Informal Diplomacy: The Dartmouth Conference Experience." In: D. D. Newsom, ed. *Private Diplomacy with the Soviet Union.* Lanham, MD.: University Press of America, 1987. pp. 7-28.
4396. Stoessel, Walter J. "Nonofficial Exchanges with the Soviet Union." In: D. D. Newsom, ed. *Private Diplomacy with the Soviet Union.* Lanham, MD.: University Press of America, 1987. pp. 1-6.

4397. "Unofficial Meetings." In: M. R. Berman and J. E. Johnson, eds. *Unofficial Diplomats.* New York: Columbia University Press, 1977. pp. 35-44.
4398. Volkan, Vanik D. "The Need to Have Enemies and Allies: A Developmental Approach." *Journal of Political Psychology,* 6:2 (June 1985), 219-247.
4399. Warren, Roland L. "American Friends Service Committee Mediation Efforts in Germany and Korea." In: J. W. McDonald and D. B. Bendahmane, eds. *Conflict Resolution: Track Two Diplomacy.* Washington, D.C.: Center for the Study of Foreign Affairs, Foreign Service Institute, 1987. pp. 27-34.
4400. Wedge, Bryant. "Mediating Intergroup Conflict in the Dominican Republic." In: J. W. McDonald and D. B. Bendahmane, eds. *Conflict Resolution: Track Two Diplomacy.* Washington, D.C.: Center for the Study of Foreign Affairs, Foreign Service Institute, 1987. pp. 35-52.
4401. Weinberg, Steve. "Armand Hammer's Unique Diplomacy." *The Bulletin of the Atomic Scientists,* 43:1 (August/September 1986), 50-53.
4402. Yarrow, C. H. M. "Quaker Efforts Toward Reconciliation in the India-Pakistan War of 1965." In: M. R. Berman and J. E. Johnson, eds. *Unofficial Diplomats.* New York: Columbia University Press, 1977. pp. 89-110.
4403. _____. "Unofficial Third Party Conciliation in International Conflicts." *Peace and Change,* 7:4 (Fall 1981), 49-51.
4404. _____. "Unofficial Third Party Conciliation in International Conflict." In: C. M. Stephenson, ed. *Alternative Methods for International Security.* Washington, D.C.: University Press of America, 1982. pp. 121-126.

3. Documents and Reports

4405. Juergenmeyer, John E. *Democracy's Diplomacy: The People-to-People Program - A Study of Attempts to Focus the Effects of Private Contacts in International Politics.* Ph.D. Dissertation. Princeton, NJ.: Princeton University, 1960.
4406. Llados, Jose Maria. "Second Track International Negotiations." Paper Presented at the *25th Annual Convention of the International Studies Association,* held on March 27-31, 1984, in Atlanta, GA.
4407. McDonald, John W., and Diane B. Bendahmane, eds. *Conflict Resolution: Track Two Diplomacy.* Washington, D.C.: Foreign Service Institute, Center for the Study of Foreign Affairs, 1987. 89p.
4408. Ruopp, Phillips. "Superpowers Off-the-Record: The U.S. - Soviet Dartmouth Conference." Paper Presented at the *20th Annual Convention of the International Studies Association,* held on March 21-24, 1979, in Toronto.

E. PUBLIC DIPLOMACY

1. Books

4409. Abshire, David M. *International Broadcasting: A New Dimension of Western Diplomacy.* Washington Papers, 4:35. Beverly Hills, CA.: Sage, 1976. 90p.
4410. Barghoorn, Frederick C. *Soviet Foreign Propaganda.* Princeton, NJ.: Princeton University Press, 1964. 329p.
4411. Cohen, Yoel. *Media Diplomacy: The Foreign Office in the Mass Communications Age.* London: Frank Cass, 1986. 197p.
4412. Fisher, Glen H. *Public Diplomacy and the Behavioral Sciences.* Bloomington, IN.: Indiana University Press, 1972. 180p.

4413. Hansen, Allan C. *USIA - Public Diplomacy in the Computer Age.* New York: Praeger, 1984. 250p.
4414. Henderson, Gregory, ed. *Public Diplomacy and Political Change: Four Case Studies: Okinawa, Peru, Czechoslovakia, Guinea.* New York: Praeger, 1973. 339p.
4415. Hoffman, Arthur S., ed. *International Communication and the New Diplomacy.* Bloomington, IN.: Indiana University Press, 1968. 206p.
4416. Lee, John, ed. *The Diplomatic Persuaders: New Role of the Media in International Relations.* New York: Wiley, 1968. 205p.
4417. Staar, Richard F., ed. *Public Diplomacy: USA versus USSR.* Stanford, CA.: Hoover Institution Press, 1986. 305p.

2. Journal Articles

4418. Adelman, Kenneth L. "Speaking for America: Public Diplomacy in Our Time." *Foreign Affairs,* 59:4 (1981), 913-936.
4419. Ben Eliezer, M. "Public and Instant Diplomacy." *ETC,* 36 (Winter 1979), 357-364.
4420. Bissell, Richard E. "Research on Public Diplomacy." In: R. F. Staar, ed. *Public Diplomacy: U.S.A. Versus U.S.S.R.* Stanford, CA.: Hoover Institution Press, 1986. pp. 210-244.
4421. Blitz, Mark. "Public Diplomacy and the Private Sector." In: R. F. Staar, ed. *Public Diplomacy: U.S.A. versus U.S.S.R.* Stanford, CA.: Hoover Institution Press, 1986. pp. 95-116.
4422. Carter, Jimmy, et al. "International Communication Agency and Public Diplomacy." *International Education and Cultural Exchanges,* 14:1 (June 1978), 23-31.
4423. Cavaliero, R. E. "Cultural Diplomacy: The Diplomacy of Influence." *Round Table,* (April 1986), 139-144.
4424. Cohen, Yoel. "Media Diplomacy in Britain." *Political Communication and Persuasion,* 3:3 (1986), 245-264.
4425. Davison, W. Phillips. "Mass Communication and Diplomacy." In: J. N. Rosenau, K. W. Thompson and G. Boyd, eds. *World Politics: An Introduction.* New York: The Free Press, 1976. pp. 388-403.
4426. _____. "News Media and International Negotiations." *Public Opinion Quarterly,* 38 (Summer 1974), 174-191.
4427. Delaney, Robert F. "Communications, Subversion and Public Diplomacy: The View from NATO." *Naval War College Review,* 29:3 (Winter 1977), 73-78.
4428. Dixit, J. N. "Culture as an Instrument of Diplomacy." *India Quarterly,* 35:3 (1979), 453-465.
4429. Feulner, Edwin J. "Some Issues in Public Diplomacy." In: R. F. Starr, ed. *Public Diplomacy: U.S.A. Versus U.S.S.R.* Stanford, CA.: Hoover Institution Press, 1986. pp. 119-123.
4430. Garnier-Lancon, Monique. "U.S.A./U.S.S.R.: A Diplomacy of Differences or a Difference in Diplomacies?" In: R. F. Starr, ed. *Public Diplomacy: U.S.A. Versus U.S.S.R.* Stanford, CA.: Hoover Institution Press, 1986. pp. 247-252.
4431. Hill, Frederick B. "Media Diplomacy: Crisis Management With an Eye on the TV Screen." *Washington Journalism Review,* 3:4 (May 1981), 23-27.
4432. Hoess, Friedrich. "Public Diplomacy and the Foreign Service." In: R. F. Starr, ed. *Public Diplomacy: U.S.A. Versus U.S.S.R.* Stanford, CA.: Hoover Institution Press, 1986. pp. 253-254.

4433. Karl, Patricia A. "Media Diplomacy." *Proceedings of the Academy of Political Science*, 34:4 (1982), 143-152.
4434. ____. "Prime-Time Diplomacy." *Journal of Social and Political Studies*, 3:3 (1978), 275-286.
4435. Keller, Suzanne. "Diplomacy and Communication." In: L. Kriesberg, ed. *Social Processes in International Relations*. New York: John Wiley, 1968. pp. 119-126.
4436. ____. "Diplomacy and Communication." *Public Opinion Quarterly*, 20 (September 1956), 176-182.
4437. Losev, S. "Public Diplomacy - A Doctrine of International Rape." *International Affairs (Moscow)*, 5 (1983), 88-96.
4438. Lyne, Roderic. "Making Waves: Gorbachev's Public Diplomacy, 1985-1986." *Proceedings of the Academy of Political Science*, 36:4 (1987), 235-253.
4439. ____. "Making Waves: Mr. Gorbachev's Public Diplomacy, 1985-1986." *International Affairs*, 13:2 (Spring 1987), 205-224.
4440. Malone, Gifford D. "Public Diplomacy, Challenge and Response: Managing Public Diplomacy." *Washington Quarterly*, 8 (Summer 1985), 199-216.
4441. Oseth, John M. "Repairing the Balance of Images: U.S. Public Diplomacy for the Future." *Naval War College Review*, 39:4 (July-August 1985), 52-66.
4442. Richmond, Yale. "Public Diplomacy and Other Exchanges." In: D. D. Newsom, ed. *Private Diplomacy with the Soviet Union*. Lanham, MD.: University Press of American, 1987. pp. 117-128.
4443. Scali, John, and Doder Dusko. "Diplomacy and the Media: Two Views." In: G. C. McGhee, ed. *Diplomacy in the Future*. Lanham, MD.: University Press of America, 1987. pp. 85-94.
4444. Scruter, Roger. "Public Diplomacy and the Soviet Bloc." In: R. F. Staar, ed. *Public Diplomacy: U.S.A. Versus U.S.S.R.* Stanford, CA.: Hoover Institution Press, 1986. pp. 265-272.
4445. Sugden, Scott. "Public Diplomacy and the Missiles of October." *Naval War College Review*, 24:2 (October 1971), 28-43.
4446. Von Lowis of Menar, Henning. "Radio Power in Germany: A Neglected Field of Public Diplomacy." In: R. F. Staar, ed. *Public Diplomacy: U.S.A. Versus U.S.S.R.* Stanford, CA.: Hoover Institution Press, 1986. pp. 261-264.
4447. Wedge, Bryant. "Communication Analysis and Comprehensive Diplomacy." *Social Education*, 34:1 (1970), 19-27.
4448. ____. "Communication Analysis and Comprehensive Diplomacy." In: A. S. Hoffman, ed. *International Communication and the New Diplomacy*. Bloomington, IN.: Indiana University Press, 1968. pp. 24-47.
4449. Wettig, Gerhard. "Public Diplomacy, Soviet Style." In: R. F. Starr, ed. *Public Diplomacy: U.S.A. Versus U.S.S.R.* Stanford, CA.: Hoover Institution Press, 1986. pp. 273-281.
4450. Wimmel, Kenneth. "What is Public Diplomacy?" *Foreign Service Journal*, 55:10 (October 1978), 31-34, 42-44.

3. Documents and Reports

4451. Anthony, William H. *Public Diplomacy and the Nixon Doctrine, Reaction by Foreign and American Media and the U.S. Information Agency's Role*. Ph.D. Dissertation. Washington, D.C.: George Washington University, 1976. 269p.
4452. English, Gary C. *United States Media Diplomacy: Problems in the Politics of Administration*. Ph.D. Dissertation. Atlanta, GA.: Emory University, 1968.

4453. MacDonald, Mary K. *Exploring the Concept of Public Diplomacy: Canada and the 97th United States Congress.* MA. Thesis. Kingston, Ont.: Queens University, 1982.
4454. United States. Advisory Commission on Public Diplomacy. *Public Diplomacy: Lessons from the Washington Summit: A Report.* Washington, D.C.: U.S. Government Printing Office, 1988. 11p.
4455. _____.Congress.House.Committee on Foreign Affairs. *The Future of United States Public Diplomacy.* Washington, D.C.: U.S. Government Printing Office, 1968. 175p.
4456. _____._____._____._____.Subcommittee on International Operations. *Public Diplomacy and the Future: Hearings.* 95th Cong., 1st sess. Washington, D.C.: U.S. Government Printing Office, 1978. 691p.
4457. _____._____._____._____._____. *Oversight of Public Diplomacy: Hearing.* 99th Cong., 2nd sess. Washington, D.C.: U.S. Government Printing Office, 1986. 239p.
4458. _____.General Accounting Office. *The Public Diplomacy of Other Countries: Implications for the U.S.: Report.* Washington, D.C.: U.S. Government Printing Office, 1979. 57p.

X

Soviet Diplomacy & Negotiating Behavior

Soviet diplomacy, negotiating tactics, negotiating styles and motivations have long been subject to debate, discussion and study. It is of particular importance now, at a time of major changes in Soviet leadership, the changes in Soviet domestic and foreign policies and the corresponding changes in Soviet approaches to diplomacy and negotiations, to reexamine Soviet diplomatic practices and styles. Soviet approaches to diplomacy have major implications for the foreign policies of all other states, but of particular importance for United States foreign policies.

Western scholars have concluded that Soviet diplomacy and negotiations are diametrically alien to the western traditions of compromise and cooperation. Soviet diplomacy was just another weapon in the long struggle for the supremacy of the communist system. This presumption has to be reexamined in the light of recent development inside the Soviet Union, and the corresponding shifts seen in various clash points of the globe. The recent changes in Soviet diplomatic style come under intense scrutiny after decades of suspicion.

This chapter focuses on Soviet diplomatic methods, negotiation styles and processes. It also includes case studies of negotiations. The focus is on negotiation processes rather than on policy issues.

1. Books

4459. Allard, Sven. *Russia and the Austrian State Treaty.* University Park, PA.: Pennsylvania State University Press, 1970. 248p.
4460. Barghoorn, Frederick C. *The Soviet Cultural Offensive: The Role of Cultural Diplomacy in Soviet Foreign Policy.* Princeton, NJ.: Princeton University Press, 1960. 353p.
4461. Beam, Jacob D. *Multiple Exposure: An American Ambassador's Unique Perspective on East-West Issues.* New York: W. W. Norton, 1978. 317p.
4462. Browder, Robert P. *The Origins of Soviet - American Diplomacy.* Princeton, NJ.: Princeton University Press, 1953. 256p.
4463. Dennett, Raymond, and Joseph E. Johnson, eds. *Negotiating with the Russians.* Boston, MA.: World Peace Foundation, 1951. 310p.
4464. Eran, Oded. *Mezhdunarodniki: An Assessment of Professional Expertise in the Making of Soviet Foreign Policy.* Tel Aviv: Turtledove, 1979. 331p.
4465. George, Alexander L., et al. *Managing U.S. - Soviet Rivalry: Problems of Crisis Prevention.* Boulder, CO.: Westview Press, 1983. 415p.
4466. Hingley, Ronald. *The Russian Mind.* New York: Scribner's, 1977. 247p.
4467. Joy, C. Turner. *How Communists Negotiate.* New York: Macmillan, 1955. 178p.
4468. Kaznacheev, Aleksander. *Inside a Soviet Embassy: Experiences of a Russian Diplomat in Burma.* Philadelphia, PA.: Lippincott, 1962. 250p.
4469. Kennan, George F. *Soviet Foreign Policy, 1917-1941.* Princeton, NJ.: Van Nostrand, 1960. 192p.
4470. Khrushchev, Nikita S. *Khrushchev Remembers: The Last Testament.* Boston, MA.: Little, Brown, 1974. 637p.
4471. Micunovic, Velyko. *Moscow Diary.* Garden City, NY.: Doubleday, 1980. 474p.
4472. Nerlich, Uwe, ed. *Soviet Power and Western Negotiating Policies. Vol. 1.: The Soviet Asset: Military Power in the Competition over Europe.* Cambridge, MA.: Balliger, 1983. 365p.
4473. _____., ed. *Soviet Power and Western Negotiating Policies. Vol. 2.: The Western Panacea: Constraining Soviet Power Through Negotiation.* Cambridge, MA.: Ballinger, 1983. 434p.
4474. Newsom, David D. *The Soviet Brigade in Cuba: A Study in Political Diplomacy.* Bloomington, IN.: Indiana University Press, 1987. 122p.
4475. Nogee, Joseph L. *Neither War nor Peace: The Soviets at Geneva.* Cambridge, MA.: The MIT Press, 1965. 89p.
4476. Porter, Bruce D. *The U.S.S.R. in Third World Conflicts - Soviet Arms and Diplomacy in Local Wars, 1945-1980.* Cambridge: Cambridge University Press, 1984. 248p.
4477. Samelson, Louis J. *Soviet and Chinese Negotiating Behavior: The Western World.* Sage Professional Papers in International Studies, Serial No. 02-048. Beverly Hills, CA.: Sage, 1976. 62p.
4478. Schwartz, Morton. *Soviet Perceptions of the United States.* Berkeley, CA.: University of California Press, 1978. 216p.
4479. Sloss, Leon, and M. Scott Davis, eds. *A Game for High Stakes: Lessons Learned in Negotiating with the Soviet Union.* Cambridge, MA.: Ballinger Press, 1987. 184p.
4480. Uldricks, Teddy J. *Diplomacy and Ideology: The Origins of Soviet Foreign Relations, 1917-1930.* Beverly Hills, CA.: Sage, 1979. 239p.
4481. Zimmerman, William. *Soviet Perspectives on International Relations, 1956-67.* Princeton, NJ.: Princeton University Press, 1969. 336p.

2. Journal Articles

4482. Acheson, Dean. "On Dealing with Russia: An Inside View." *New York Times Magazine,* (April 12, 1959), 27, 88-89.
4483. Adomeit, Hannes. "Negotiating, Soviet Style." *Problems of Communism,* 31:4 (July-August 1982), 57-62.
4484. Alderman, Sidney S. "Negotiating the Nuremberg Trial Agreements, 1945." In: R. Dennett and J. E. Johnson, eds. *Negotiating with the Russians.* Boston, MA.: World Peace Foundation, 1951. pp. 49-100.
4485. Aspaturian, V. V. "Dialectics and Duplicity in Soviet Diplomacy." *Journal of International Affairs,* 17:1 (1963), 42-60.
4486. _____. "Soviet Foreign Policy at the Crossroads - Conflict and/or Collaboration." *International Organization,* 23 (1969), 589-620.
4487. Barnds, William J. "Ventures in Soviet Diplomacy - Moscow and South Asia." *Problems of Communism,* 21:3 (1972), 12-31.
4488. Berton, Peter. "The Soviet and Japanese Communist Parties: Policies, Tactics, Negotiating Behavior." *Studies in Comparative Communism,* 15:3 (Autumn 1982), 266-287.
4489. Bialer, Seweryn. "Andrei Andreevich Gromyko." In: G. Simmonds, ed. *Soviet Leaders.* New York: Crowell, 1967. pp. 164-171.
4490. Billington, James. "Diplomacy and the Soviet Union." In: G. C. McGhee, ed. *Diplomacy for the Future.* Lanham, MD.: University Press of America, 1987. pp.35-48.
4491. Blakeslee, George H. "Negotiating to Establish the Far Eastern Commission, 1945." In: R. Dennett and J. E. Johnson, eds. *Negotiating with the Russians.* Boston, MA.: World Peace Foundation, 1951. pp. 119-138.
4492. Brennan, D. G. "Soviet-American Communication in Crises." *Arms Control and Society,* 1 (1974), 81-88.
4493. Brzezinski, Zbigniew. "The Problematics of Sino-Soviet Bargaining." In: K. London, ed. *Unity and Contradiction.* New York: Praeger, 1962. pp. 392-408.
4494. Campbell, John C. "Negotiations with the Soviets: Lessons of the Past." In: I. D. Duchacek, ed. *Conflict and Cooperation Among Nations.* New York: Holt, Rinehart and Winston, 1960. pp. 522-530.
4495. _____. "Negotiating with the Soviets: Some Lessons from the Past." *Foreign Affairs,* 34:1 (1956), 305-319.
4496. Chen, Shao-Hsien. "The Bilateral Talks Between the United States and the Soviet Union." *West & East,* 14 (June 1969), 1-4.
4497. Ching-Yao, Yin. "On Communist Negotiations." *Issues and Studies,* 16:2 (1980), 13-29.
4498. Cohen, Roberta. "The Soviet Union. Human Rights Diplomacy in the Communist Heartland." In: D. D. Newsom, ed. *The Diplomacy of Human Rights.* Lanham, MD.: University Press of America, 1986. pp. 175-186.
4499. Cousins, Norman. "Notes on a 1963 Visit with Khrushchev." *Saturday Review,* 47:45 (November 7, 1964), 16-21, 58-60.
4500. Craig, Gordon A. "Techniques of Negotiations." In: I. J. Lederer, ed. *Russian Foreign Policy: Essays in Historical Perspective.* New Haven, CT.: Yale University Press, 1962. pp. 351-373.
4501. _____. "Totalitarian Approaches to Diplomatic Negotiations." In: F. A. Sonderman and W. C. Olson, eds. *The Theory and Practice of International Relations.* 2nd ed. Englewood Cliffs, NJ.: Prentice-Hall, 1966. pp. 267-280.

4502. _____. "Totalitarian Approaches to Diplomatic Negotiations." In: A. D. Sarkissian, ed. *Studies in Diplomatic History and Historiography in Honour of G. P. Gooch*. London: Longmans, 1961. pp. 107-125.
4503. Crane, Robert D. "The Cuban Crisis: A Strategic Analysis of American and Soviet Policy." *Orbis*, 6:4 (Winter 1963), 528-563.
4504. Dean, Jonathan. "Negotiating by Increment." *Foreign Service Journal*, 60:7 (July/August 1983), 26-29.
4505. Deane, John R. "Negotiating on Military Assistance, 1943-1945." In: R. Dennett and J. E. Johnson, eds. *Negotiating with the Russians*. Boston, MA.: World Peace Foundation, 1951. pp. 3-30.
4506. Eckhart, William, and Ralph K. White. "A Test of the Mirror-Image Hypothesis: Kennedy and Khrushchev." *Journal of Conflict Resolution*, 11:3 (1962), 42-51.
4507. Eilan, Arieh. "Soviet Diplomacy in the Third World." In: I. W. Zartman, ed. *The Pattern of Soviet Conduct in the Third World*. New York: Praeger, 1983. pp. 42-80.
4508. Ethridge, Mark, and C. E. Black. "Negotiating on the Balkans, 1945-1947." In: R. Dennett and J. E. Johnson, eds. *Negotiating with the Russians*. Boston, MA.: World Peace Foundation, 1951. pp. 171-208.
4509. Fedder, Edwin A. "Communication and American-Soviet Negotiating Behavior." *Background*, 8 (August 1964), 105-120.
4510. Fisher, Roger D., and Scott Brown. "Building a U.S. - Soviet Working Relationship." *Negotiation Journal*, 1:4 (October 1985), 307-315.
4511. _____. "What is a "Good" U.S. - Soviet Relationship - and How Do We Build One?" *Negotiation Journal*, 3:4 (October 1987), 319-328.
4512. Floyd, David. "U.S. Negotiations with the U.S.S.R.: The Pattern of Blundering." *Survey*, 25:2 (1980), 25-31.
4513. Garthoff, Raymond L. "Soviet Views on the Interrelation of Diplomacy and Military Strategy." *Political Science Quarterly*, 94:3 (1979), 391-406.
4514. German, Robert K. "Norway and the Bear: Soviet Coercive Diplomacy and Norwegian Security Policy." *International Security*, 7:2 (1982), 55-82.
4515. Grant, Natalie. "The Russian Section: A Window on the Soviet Union." *Diplomatic History*, 2 (1978), 107-115.
4516. Graybeal, Sidney N. "Soviet Negotiating Practice." In: L. Sloss and M. Scott Davis, eds. *A Game for High Stakes*. Cambridge, MA.: Ballinger, 1986. pp. 33-42.
4517. Halle, Louis J. "The Art of Negotiating with the Russians." *New York Times Magazine*, (June 12, 1955), 9,59-60,62,64.
4518. Haven, Andrew. "The Time Factor in Soviet Foreign Policy." *Problems of Communism*, 5 (January-February, 1956), 1-8.
4519. Hazard, John N. "Negotiating Under Lend-Lease, 1942-1945." In: R. Dennett and J. E. Johnson, eds. *Negotiating with the Russians*. Boston, MA.: World Peace Foundation, 1951. pp. 31-48.
4520. Hazzard, John N. "Soviet Tactics in International Law Making." *Denver Journal of International Law and Policy*, 7 (1977), 9-32.
4521. Holmes, John W. "Negotiating with the Russians." *University of Toronto Commerce Journal*, (February 1962), 7-12.
4522. Holsti, Ole R. "Cognitive Dynamics and Images of the Enemy: Dulles and Russia." In: D. J. Findlay, O. R. Holsti and R. F. Fagen, eds. *Enemies in Politics*. Chicago, IL.: Rand-McNally, 1967. pp. 25-996.
4523. Husband, William B. "Soviet Perceptions of U.S. "Positions-of-Strength" Diplomacy in the 1970s." *World Politics*, 31:4 (1979), 495-517.
4524. Ikle, Fred C. "On Negotiating with Communist Powers." *Foreign Service Journal*, (April 1971), 21-25,55.

4525. Johansen, Elaine. "From Soviet Doctrine to Implementation: Agenda Setting in Comparable Worth." *Policy Studies Review*, 4:1 (August 1984), 71-85.
4526. Jönsson, Christer. "Soviet Political Language: The Analysis of Esoteric Communication." *Coexistence*, 24:3 (1987), 211-224.
4527. _____. "Soviet Foreign Policy and Domestic Politics: A Case Study." *Cooperation and Conflict*, 12:3 (1977), 129-148.
4528. Kampelman, Max M. "Negotiating with the Soviet Union." *World Affairs*, 148:8 (Spring 1986), 199-204.
4529. Kaplin, A. "Lenin on the Principles of Socialist Diplomacy." *International Affairs (Moscow)*, 6 (June 1969), 51-56.
4530. Kertész, Stephen D. "American and Soviet Negotiation Behavior." In: S. D. Kertész and M. A. Fitzsimmons, eds. *Diplomacy in a Changing World*. Notre Dame, IN.: University of Notre Dame Press, 1959. pp. 133-171.
4531. _____. "Reflections on Soviet and American Negotiating Behavior." *Review of Politics*, 19 (January 1957), 3-36.
4532. Kulski, Wladislav W. "Soviet Diplomatic Techniques." *Russian Review*, 19 (July 1960), 217-226.
4533. Luce, Claire Boothe. "How to Deal with the Russians: The Basis of Negotiation." *Air Force Magazine*, 62 (April 1979), 30-33.
4534. Mansbach, Richard W. "Bilateralism and Multilateralism in the Soviet Bloc." *International Organization*, 24 (1970), 371-380.
4535. McConnell, James M., and B. Dismukes. "Soviet Diplomacy of Force in the Third World." *Problems of Communism*, 28:1 (1979), 14-27.
4536. Mikesell, Raymond F. "Negotiating at Bretton Woods, 1944." In: R. Dennett and J. E. Johnson, eds. *Negotiating with the Russians*. Boston, MA.: World Peace Foundation, 1951. pp. 101-118.
4537. Molinell, Harold. "Negotiating Human Rights: The Helsinki Agreement." *World Affairs*, 141:1 (1978), 24-39.
4538. Mosely, Philip E. "The New Challenge of the Kremlin." In: S. D. Kertész and M. A. Fitzsimmons, eds *Diplomacy in a Changing World*. South Bend, IN.: University of Notre Dame Press, 1959. pp. 117-132.
4539. _____. "Some Soviet Techniques of Negotiation." In: R. Dennett and J. E. Johnson, eds. *Negotiating with the Russians*. Boston, MA.: World Peace Foundation, 1951. pp. 271-304.
4540. Mujal-Leon, Eusebio. "The Soviet and Spanish Communist Parties: Policies, Tactics, Negotiating Behavior." *Studies in Comparative Communism*, 15:3 (Autumn 1982), 236-265.
4541. "Negotiating with the Soviets." *Foreign Service Journal*, 62:10 (November 1985), 24-27.
4542. Nicolayev, A. "Soviet Diplomatic Relations in Retrospect." *International Affairs (Moscow)*, 9 (September 1982), 101-107.
4543. Nitze, Paul H. "Living with the Soviets." *Foreign Affairs*, (Winter 1984-85), 360-374.
4544. _____. "Soviet's Negotiating Style Assayed." *Aviation Week and Space Technology*, (February 19, 1975), 40-43;(February 24, 1975), 63-69;(May 12, 1975)7.
4545. Nixon, Richard M. "Dealing with Gorbachev." *New York Times Magazine*, (March 13, 1988), 26-30, 66-67, 78-79.
4546. Osgood, C. E. "Suggestions for Winning the Real War with Communism." *Journal of Conflict Resolution*, 3 (1979), 295-325.
4547. Penrose, E. F. "Negotiating on Refugees and Displaced Persons, 1946." In: R. Dennett and J. E. Johnson, eds. *Negotiating with the Russians*. Boston, MA.: World Peace Foundation, 1951. pp. 139-170.

4548. Piotrowski, Karl P. "Negotiating with the Enemy." *Air University Review*, 28:6 (1977), 53-61.
4549. Pipes, Richard. "Dealing with the Russians: The Wages of Forgetfulness." In: A. L. Horelick, ed. *U.S. - Soviet Relations: The Next Phase.* Ithaca, NY.: Cornell University Press, 1986. pp. 276-287.
4550. Raanan, Uri. "Soviet Decision Making and International Relations." *Problems of Communism*, 29:6 (1980), 41-47.
4551. Rapacki, Adam. "Socialist Diplomacy of Peace in the World Arena." *World Marxist Review*, 5 (June 1962), 12-18.
4552. Raskin, Markus G. "The McCloy - Zorin Correspondence." *Bulletin of the Atomic Scientists*, 39:2 (1983), 34-36.
4553. Reisinger, William M. "The Brezhnev Doctrine and Polish-Soviet Bargaining, 1971." *The Journal of Communist Studies*, 3:3 (September 1987), 250-- 266.
4554. Reston, James B. "Negotiating with the Russians." *Harper's*, (August 1947), 97-106.
4555. Roberts, Henry L. "Maxim Litvinov." In: G. A. Craig and F. Gilbert, eds. *The Diplomats, 1919-1939.* Princeton, NJ.: Princeton University Press, 1953. pp. 344-377.
4556. "A Round Table Discussion: Negotiating with the Soviets: Goals, Style and Method?" *Foreign Service Journal*, 62 (November 1985), 24-27.
4557. Rowny, Edward L. "How Not to Negotiate with the Russians." *Reader's Digest*, 118 (June 1981), 66-70.
4558. _____. "Negotiating with the Soviets." *Washington Quarterly*, 3:1 (Winter 1980), 58-66.
4559. _____. "Ten Commandments for Negotiating with the Soviet Union." In: L. Sloss and M. Scott Davis, eds. *A Game for High Stakes.* Cambridge. MA.: Ballinger, 1986. pp. 47-54.
4560. Rudzinski, Alexander W. "Soviet Peace Offensives." *International Conciliation*, 490 (April 1953), 175-225.
4561. Scheiding, Robert E. "A Comparison of Communist Negotiating Methods." *Military Review*, (December 1974), 79-89.
4562. Scott Davis, M. "Negotiating with Ourselves." *Foreign Service Journal*, 62:10 (November 1985), 28-33.
4563. Semenov, V. "The Leninist Principles of Soviet Diplomacy." *International Affairs (Moscow)*, 4 (1969), 3-8.
4564. Sestanovich, Stephen. "Gorbachev's Foreign Policy: A Diplomacy of Decline." *Problems of Communism*, 37 (January-February 1988), 1-15.
4565. Simmons, Ernest J. "Negotiating on Cultural Exchange, 1947." In: R. Dennett and J. E. Johnson, eds. *Negotiating with the Russians.* Boston, MA.: World Peace Foundation, 1951. pp. 239-270.
4566. Simmons, Susanne. "SDI: A Case Study in Soviet Negotiating Style." *Journal of Social, Political and Economic Studies*, 12:4 (Winter 1987), 355-376.
4567. Slocombe, Walter. "Negotiating with the Soviets: Getting Past No." In: L. Sloss and M. Scott Davis, eds. *A Game for High Stakes.* Cambridge, MA.: Ballinger, 1986. pp. 63-72.
4568. Sloss, Leon. "Chairman's Conclusions." In: L. Sloss and M. Scott Davis, eds. *A Game for High Stakes.* Cambridge, MA.: Balliger, 1986. pp. 155-160.
4569. _____. "Lessons Learned in Negotiating with the Soviet Union: Introduction and Findings." In: L. Sloss and M. Scott Davis, eds. *A Game for High Stakes.* Cambridge, MA.: Ballinger, 1986. pp. 1-20.

4570. _____., and M. Scott Davis. "The Soviet Union: The Pursuit of Power and Influence Through Negotiation." In: B. Binnendijk, ed. *National Negotiating Style*. Washington, D.C.: Foreign Service Institute, Center for the Study of Foreign Affairs, 1987. pp. 17-44.
4571. Slusser, Robert M. "The Role of the Foreign Minister." In: I. J. Lederer, ed. *Russian Foreign Policy: Essays in Historical Perspective*. New Haven, CT.: Yale University Press, 1962. pp. 197-242.
4572. Smith, Gerard C. "Negotiating with the Soviets." *The New York Times Magazine*, (February 27, 1977), 18-19, 26.
4573. Sobakin, Vadim, and Roger Fisher. "Ground Rules for Entente: Respectful Attitudes Can Improve Soviet-U.S. Relations." *Negotiation Journal*, 1:3 (July 1985), 211-212.
4574. Sonnenfeldt, Helmut. "Soviet Negotiating Concept and Style." In: L. Sloss and M. Scott Davis, eds. *A Game for High Stakes*. Cambridge, MA.: Ballinger, 1986. pp. 21-32.
4575. Steiner, Kurt. "Negotiations for an Austrian State Treaty." In: A. L. George, P. J. Farley and A. Dallin, eds. *U.S. - Soviet Security Cooperation*. New York: Oxford University Press, 1988. pp. 46-82.
4576. Stoertz, Howard. "Observations on Soviet Negotiating Practice." In: L. Sloss and M. Scott Davis, eds. *A Game for High Stakes*. Cambridge, MA.: Ballinger, 1986. pp. 53-46.
4577. Stone, W. T. "Negotiating with the Reds." *Editorial Research Reports*, (September 17, 1953), 649-655.
4578. Triska, Jan F., and D. D. Finlay. "Soviet-American Relations: A Multiple-Symmetry Model." *Journal of Conflict Resolution*, 9:2 (1965), 37-53.
4579. Ulam, Adam B. "Communist Doctrine and Soviet Diplomacy." *Survey*, 76 (Summer 1970), 3-16.
4580. Urban, Joan B. "Soviet Policies and Negotiating Behavior Toward Nonruling Communist Parties: The Case of the Italian Communist Party." *Studies in Comparative Communism*, 15:3 (Autumn 1982), 184-211.
4581. Woolsey, R. James. "The Role of Congress in U.S. - Soviet Negotiations." In: L. Sloss and M. Scott Davis, eds. *A Game for High Stakes*. Cambridge, MA.: Ballinger, 1986. pp. 133-140.
4582. Worsnop, Richard L. "East-West Negotiations." *Editorial Research Reports*, (October 11, 1961), 737-754.
4583. _____. "Negotiations with Communists." *Editorial Research Reports*, (April 21, 1965), 283-300.
4584. York, Herbert F. "Negotiating and the U.S. Bureaucracy." In: L. Sloss and M. Scott Davis, eds. *A Game for High Stakes*. Cambridge, MA.: Ballinger, 1986. pp. 123-132.

3. Documents and Reports

4585. Adomeit, Hannes. *Soviet Risk-Taking and Crisis Behavior: From Confrontation to Coexistence*. Adelphi Papers, 101. London: International Institute for Strategic Studies, 1973. 43p.
4586. Beranek, Robert E. *The Second Berlin Crisis and the Foreign Ministers' Conference at Geneva (1959): A Case Study of Soviet Diplomacy*. Ph.D. Dissertation. Pittsburgh, PA.: University of Pittsburgh, 1966.

Soviet Diplomacy

4587. Dixon, Michael J. "Soviet Attitudes and Objectives in Negotiations." In: United States. Congress. House. Committee on Foreign Affairs. Subcommittee on Arms Control, International Security, and Science. *Fundamentals of Nuclear Arms Control.* 99th Cong., 2nd sess. Washington, D.C.: U.S. Government Printing Office, 1986. pp. 247-285.
4588. Ginsburgs, George. *Theory and Practice of Neutrality in Soviet Diplomacy.* Ph.D. Dissertation. Los Angeles, CA.: University of California at Los Angeles, 1960.
4589. Gustafson, Thane. *Soviet Negotiating Strategy: The East-West Gas Pipeline Deal, 1980-1984.* RAND R-3220-FF. Santa Monica, CA.: RAND Corporation, 1985. 45p.
4590. Hupp, Alfred R. *Techniques of Soviet Diplomatic Negotiation.* USNA-TSPR-18. Annapolis, MD.: Naval Academy, 1971. 169p.
4591. Kertész, Stephen D. "Reflections on Soviet and American Negotiating Behavior." Paper Presented at the *52th Annual Meeting of the American Political Science Association*, held on September 6-8, 1956, in Washington, D.C.
4592. Kovner, Milton. *Competitive Co-Existence: The Challenge of Soviet Diplomacy.* Ph.D. Dissertation. Washington, D.C.: Georgetown University, 1960.
4593. Leites, Nathan C. *Kremlin Thoughts: Yielding, Rebuffing, Provoking, Retreating.* RAND RM-3618-ISA. Santa Monica, CA.: RAND Corporation, 1963.
4594. Meiksins, Gregory. *The Doctrine of Coexistence in Soviet Diplomacy.* Ph.D. Dissertation. New York: New School of Social Research, 1954.
4595. O'Hara, Michael N. *Negotiating with the Russians: The Case of the Austrian State Treaty.* Ph.D. Dissertation. Los Angeles, CA.: University of California at Los Angeles, 1971. 405p.
4596. Porter, Bruce D. *Soviet Military Intervention: Russian Arms and Technology in Third World Conflicts, 1958-1978.* Ph.D. Dissertation. Cambridge, MA.: Harvard University, 1980.
4597. Puryear, Edgar F. *Communist Negotiating Techniques: A Case Study of the United Nations Security Council Commission on Investigation Concerning the Greek Frontier Incidents.* Ph.D. Dissertation. Princeton, NJ.: Princeton University, 1959. 364p.
4598. Rakove, Milton. *American Attitudes Towards Negotiations with the Soviet Union.* Ph.D. Dissertation. Chicago, IL.: University of Chicago, 1956.
4599. Steibel, G. L. *How Can We Negotiate with the Communists.* New York: National Strategy Information Center, 1972. 46p.
4600. Stoeker, S. W. *Trip Report: Forum For U.S. - Soviet Dialogue: Moscow, Kishinev, Minsk, Leningrad, July 16-131, 1984.* RAND P-7011. Santa Monica, CA.: RAND Corporation, 1984. 18p.
4601. Strang, William. *The Moscow Negotiations, 1939.* London: Leeds University Press, 1968. 25p.
4602. United States. Congress. House. Committee on Foreign Affairs. *U.S. - Soviet Relations: New Promise or Peril: Report.* 99th Cong., 1st sess. Washington, D.C.: U.S. Government Printing Office, 1985. 18p.
4603. _____._____.Senate.Committee on Foreign Relations. *U.S. - Soviet Relations: Part 1: Hearings.* 98th Cong., 1st sess. Washington, D.C.: U.S. Government Printing Office, 1983. 90p.
4604. _____._____._____._____. *U.S. - Soviet Relations, Part 2.: Hearings.* 98th Cong., 1st sess. Washington, D.C.: U.S. Government Printing Office, 1983. 325p.

4605. _____._____._____._____. *U.S. - Soviet Relations: Part 3.: Hearings.* 98th Cong., 1st sess. Washington, D.C.: U.S. Government Printing Office, 1984. 144p.

4606. _____._____._____.Committee on Government Operations.Subcommittee on National Security and International Operations. *International Negotiation: American Shortcomings in Negotiation with Communist Powers, Memorandum by Fred C. Ikle.* 91st Cong., 2nd sess. Washington, D.C.: U.S. Government Printing Office, 1970. 17p.

4607. _____._____._____._____. *International Negotiation: Exchanges of Scholars with the Soviet Union. Advantages and Dilemmas: Memorandum by Robert G. Byrnes.* 91st Cong., 1st sess. Washington, D.C.: U.S. Government Printing Office, 1969. 19p.

4608. _____._____._____._____. *International Negotiations: Hearings with Robert Conquest. Part 1.* 91st Cong., 1st sess. Washington, D.C.: U.S. Government Printing Office, 1969. 28p.

4609. _____._____._____._____. *International Negotiations: Hearings with Leonard Shapiro. Part 2.* 91st Cong., 2nd sess. Washington, D.C.: U.S. Government Printing Office, 1970. pp. 29-66.

4610. _____._____._____._____. *International Negotiations: Hearings with Dirk V. Stikker. Part 3.* 92nd Cong., 1st sess. Washington, D.C.: U.S. Government Printing Office, 1971. pp. 67-90.

4611. _____._____._____._____. *International Negotiations: Hearings with Bernard Lewis. Part 4.* 92nd Cong., 2nd sess. Washington, D.C.: U.S. Government Printing Office, 1971. pp. 91-123.

4612. _____._____._____._____. *International Negotiations: Hearings with Robert F. Byrnes. Part 5.* 92nd Cong., 1st sess. Washington, D.C.: U.S. Government Printing Office, 1971. pp. 125-159.

4613. _____._____._____._____. *International Negotiations: Hearings with Robert Conquest, Part 6.* 92nd Cong., 1st sess. Washington, D.C.: U.S. Government Printing Office, 1971. pp. 161-197.

4614. _____._____._____._____. *International Negotiations: Hearings with William R. Van Cleave, Part 7.* 92nd Cong., 2nd sess. Washington, D.C.: U.S. Government Printing Office, 1973. pp. 199-246.

4615. _____._____._____._____. *International Negotiations: Impact of Changing Power Balance.* 92nd Cong., 1st sess. Washington, D.C.: U.S. Government Printing Office, 1971. 17p.

4616. _____._____._____._____. *International Negotiations: Some Operational Principles of Soviet Foreign Policy: Memorandum by Richard Pipes.* 92nd Cong., 2nd sess. Washington, D.C.: U.S. Government Printing Office, 1972. 19p.

4617. _____._____._____._____. *Soviet Approach to Negotiations: Selected Writings.* 91st Cong., 1st sess. Washington, D.C.: U.S. Government Printing Office, 1969. 92p.

4618. _____._____._____._____. *International Negotiation, Eastern Europe, Unstable Element in Soviet Empire: Memorandum by Robert F. Byrnes.* 91st Cong., 2nd sess. Washington, D.C.: U.S. Government Printing Office, 1970. 12p.

4619. _____._____._____._____. *International Negotiations: Communist Doctrine and Soviet Diplomacy: Memo by Adam Ulam.* 91st Cong., 2nd sess. Washington, D.C.: U.S. Government Printing Office, 1970. 13p.

4620. _____.Department of the Army.Institute for Advanced Russian and East European Studies. *The Soviet Union as a Negotiator.* at the 9th Soviet Affairs Symposium at Garmish-Parten Kirchen, 1975. 45p.

4621. _____.Library of Congress.Congressional Research Service.Office of Senior Specialists. *Soviet Diplomacy and Negotiating Behavior: Emerging New Context for U.S. Diplomacy: Study by Joseph G. Whelan.* Special Studies Series on Foreign Affairs, Vol 1. 96th Cong., 1st sess. No. 96-238. Washington, D.C.: U.S. Government Printing Office, 1979. 573p.

4622. Whelan, Joseph G. *Andropov and Reagan as Negotiators: Context and Styles in Contrast.* Washington, D.C.: Congressional Research Service, 1983. 135p.

4623. _____. *Brezhnev's Peace Offensive, 1981: Propaganda Ploy or U.S. Negotiating Opportunity.* Washington, D.C.: Congressional Research Report, 1982. 149p.

4624. _____. *Soviet Diplomacy and Negotiating Behavior: The Emerging New Context for U.S. Diplomacy.* Boulder, CO.: Westview Press, 1987. c.1979. 573p.

XI

American Diplomacy

This chapter covers materials dealing mainly with the processes of United States diplomacy. The focus is on processes, to differentiate from works dealing with issues of policy, although this is extremely difficult, as the two aspects of United States foreign relations are closely linked. Listed are materials dealing with the United States Department of State and the Presidency as principal agents of United States foreign relations. An effort has been made to highlight the particulars of United States diplomatic methods and to list case studies of negotiations.

1. Books

4625. Bacchus, William I. *Staffing for Foreign Affairs: Personnel Systems for the 1980's and 1990's.* Princeton, NJ.: Princeton University Press, 1983. 262p.

4626. Ball, George W. *Diplomacy in a Crowded World: An American Foreign Policy.* Boston, MA.: Little, Brown, 1976. 356p.

4627. Barnett, Vincent M., ed. *The Representatives of the United States Abroad.* New York: Praeger, 1965. 251p.

4628. Bell, Coral. *The Diplomacy of Detente: the Kissinger Era.* New York: St. Martin's Press, 1977. 278p.

4629. _____. *Negotiation from Strength: A Study in the Politics of Power.* London: Chatto & Winders, 1963. 223p.

4630. Bemis, Samuel F., and Robert H. Ferrell, eds. *The American Secretaries of State and Their Diplomacy.* New York: Alfred Knopf, 1927-. 21 volumes to date.

4631. Berding, Andrew. *Dulles of Diplomacy.* Princeton, NJ.: Van Nostrand, 1965. 184p.

4632. Briggs, Ellis O. *Anatomy of Diplomacy: The Origin and Execution of American Foreign Policy.* New York: McKay, 1968. 248p.

4633. Burns, Richard D., and Edward M. Bennett. *Diplomats in Crisis: United States - Chinese - Japanese Relations, 1919-1941.* Santa Barbara, CA.: ABC-Clio, 1974. 346p.

4634. Carroll, John M., and George C. Herring, eds. *Modern American Diplomacy.* Wilmington, DL.: Scholarly Resources, 1986. 240p.

4635. Cleveland, Harland, and Gerald J. Magnone. *The Art of Overseasmanship: Americans at Work Abroad.* Syracuse, NY.: Syracuse University Press, 1957. 150p.

4636. _____. _____. and John C. Adams. *The Overseas Americans.* New York: McGraw-Hill, 1960. 316p.

4637. Congressional Quarterly Service. *National Diplomacy, 1965-1970.* Washington, D.C.: Congressional Quarterly Service, 1970. 156p.

4638. De Santis, Hugh. *The Diplomacy of Silence: The American Foreign Service, The Soviet Union and the Cold War, 1933-1947.* Chicago, IL.: University of Chicago Press, 1979. 270p.

4639. Deane, John R. *The Strange Alliance: The Story of Our Efforts at Wartime Co-operation with Russia.* New York: Viking Press, 1947. 344p.

4640. Eagles, Keith D. *Ambassador Joseph E. Davies and American - Soviet Relations, 1937-1941.* New York: Garland, 1985. 371p.

4641. Etzold, Thomas H. *The Conduct of American Foreign Relations: The Other Side of Diplomacy.* New York: New Viewpoints, 1977. 159p.

4642. Finer, Herman. *Dulles Over Suez: The Theory and Practice of His Diplomacy.* Chicago, IL.: Quadrangle Books, 1964. 538p.

4643. Fisher, Glen H. *American Communication in a Global Society.* Norwood, NJ.: Ablex, 1979. 165p.

4644. Gerson, Louis L. *John Foster Dulles.* New York: Cooper Square Pubs., 1967. 372p.

4645. Graber, Doris A. *Crisis Diplomacy: A History of U.S. Intervention Policies and Practices.* Washington, D.C.: Public Affairs Press, 1959. 402p.

4646. Graebner, N. A. *Cold War Diplomacy: American Foreign Policy, 1945-1960.* New York: Van Nostrand, 1962. 248p.

4647. _____., ed. *An Uncertain Tradition: American Secretaries of State in the Twentieth Century.* New York: McGraw-Hill, 1961. 341p.

4648. Graham, M. W. *American Diplomacy in the International Community.* Baltimore, MD.: John Hopkins Press, 1948. 279p.

4649. Graubard, Stephen R. *Kissinger: Portrait of A Mind.* New York: Norton, 1974. 312p.
4650. Harriman, W. Averell. *America and Russia in a Changing World.* Garden City, NY.: Doubleday, 1971. 218p.
4651. Hayter, William. *The Kremlin and the Embassy.* New York: Macmillan, 1966. 160p.
4652. Heald, Morrell, and Lawrence S. Kaplan. *Culture and Diplomacy: The American Experience.* Westport, CT.: Greenwood Press, 1977. 361p.
4653. Heinrich, Waldo H. *American Ambassador: Joseph C. Grew and the Development of the United States Diplomatic Tradition.* Fairlawn, NJ.: Oxford University Press, 1986. 460p.
4654. Hersh, Seymour. *The Price of Power: Kissinger in the Nixon White House.* New York: Summit Books, 1983. 698p.
4655. Holland, Harrison M. *Managing Diplomacy: The United States and Japan.* Stanford, CA.: Hoover Institution Press, 1984, 251p.
4656. Ilchman, Warren F. *Professional Diplomacy in the United States, 1779-1939: A Study of Administrative History.* Chicago, IL.: University of Chicago Press, 1961. 254p.
4657. Isaacson, Walter, and Evan Thomas. *The Wise Men: Six Friends and the World They Made: Acheson, Bohlen, Harriman, Kennan, Lovett, McCloy.* New York: Simon & Schuster, 1986. 853p.
4658. Johnson, Loch K. *The Making of International Agreements: Congress Confronts the Executive.* New York: New York University Press, 1984. 206p.
4659. Jones, Howard. *The Course of American Diplomacy: From the Revolution to the Present.* 2nd ed. Chicago, IL.: Dorsey Press, 1988. 718p.
4660. Kalb, Marvin, and Bernard Kalb. *Kissinger.* Boston, MA.: Little Brown, 1974. 577p.
4661. Kennan, George F. *American Diplomacy, 1900-1950.* Chicago, IL.: University of Chicago Press, 1984. 154p.
4662. Kertész, Stephen D., ed. *American Diplomacy in a New Era.* Notre Dame, IN.: University of Notre Dame Press, 1961. 601p.
4663. Kimball, Warren F., ed. *American Diplomacy in the Twentieth Century.* Arlington Height, IL.: Forum Press, 1980. 177p.
4664. Kissinger, Henry A. *A World Restored.* Boston, MA.: Houghton Mifflin, 1964. 354p.
4665. _____. *American Foreign Policy: Three Essays.* New York: Norton, 1974. 304p.
4666. Marks, Frederick W. *Wind Over Sand: The Diplomacy of Franklin Roosevelt.* Athens, GA.: University of Georgia Press, 1988. 472p.
4667. McLellan, David. *Cyrus Vance.* Totowa, NJ.: Rowman and Allanheld, 1985. 194p.
4668. Mennis, Bernard. *American Foreign Policy Officials: Who Are They and What Are They.* Columbus, OH.: Ohio State University Press, 1971. 210p.
4669. Merli, Frank J., and Theodore A. Wilson. *Makers of American Diplomacy: From Theodore Roosevelt to Henry Kissinger.* New York: Scribner's, 1974. 728p.
4670. Murphy, Robert D. *Diplomats Among Warriors.* London: Collins, 1967. 467p.
4671. Newsom, David D. *Diplomacy and the American Diplomacy.* Bloomington, IL.: Indiana University Press, 1988. 226p.
4672. Ninkovich, Frank A. *The Diplomacy of Ideas: U.S. Foreign Policy and Cultural Relations, 1938 - 1950.* New York: Cambridge University Press, 1981. 253p.
4673. Nixon, Richard M. *Six Crises.* Garden City, NY.: Doubleday, 1962. 458p.

4674. Nutter, G. Warren. *Kissinger's Grand Design.* Washington, D.C.: American Enterprise Institute for Public Policy Research, 1975. 110p.
4675. Parkins, Dexter. *The Diplomacy of the New Age: Major Issues in U.S. Policy Since 1945.* Bloomington, IN.: Indiana University Press, 1967. 190p.
4676. Paulin, Charles O. *Diplomatic Negotiations of American Naval Officers, 1778-1883.* Baltimore, MD.: Johns Hopkins Press, 1912. 380p.
4677. Plischke, Elmer. *Conduct of American Diplomacy.* Princeton, NJ.: Van Nostrand, 1961. 677p.
4678. _____. *United States Diplomats and Their Missions: A Profile of American Diplomatic Emissaries since 1778.* Washington, D.C.: American Enterprise Institute, 1975. 201p.
4679. Rappaport, Armin, comp. *Essays in American Diplomacy.* New York: Macmillan, 1967. 331p.
4680. Ruddy, Thomas M. *The Cautious Diplomat: Charles E. Bohlen and the Soviet Union, 1929-1969.* Kent, OH.: Kent State University Press, 1986. 219p.
4681. Schulzinger, Robert D. *American Diplomacy in the Twentieth Century.* New York: Oxford University Press, 1984. 390p.
4682. Simpson, Smith. *The Crisis in American Diplomacy: Shots Across the Bow of the State Department.* North Quincy, MA.: Christopher Publishing, 1980. 324p.
4683. _____. *Anatomy of the State Department.* Boston, MA.: Houghton Mifflin, 1967. 285p.
4684. Siracusa, Joseph M. *The American Diplomatic Revolution: A Documentary History of the Cold War, 1941-1947.* Port Washington, NY.: Kennikat Press, 1977. 263p.
4685. Smith, Gaddis G. *Morality, Reason, and Power: American Diplomacy in the Carter Years.* New York: Hill & Wang, 1986. 296p.
4686. _____. *American Diplomacy During the Second World War, 1941-1945.* New York: Wiley, 1966. 194p.
4687. Standley, William H., and Arthur A. Ageton. *Admiral Ambassador to Russia.* Chicago, IL.: Regnery, 1955. 533p.
4688. Starr, Harvey. *Henry Kissinger: Perceptions of International Politics.* Lexington, KY.: University Press of Kentucky, 1984. 206p.
4689. Steigman, Andrew L. *The Foreign Service of the United States: First Line of Defence.* Boulder, CO.: Westview Press, 1985. 265p.
4690. Stettinius, Edward R. *The Diaries of Edward G. Stettinius.* New York: New Viewpoints, 1975. 544p.
4691. Strong, Robert. *Bureaucracy and Statesmanship: Henry Kissinger and the Making of American Foreign Policy.* Lanham, MA.: University Press of America, 1986. 109p.
4692. Thompson, Kenneth W. *American Diplomacy and Emergent Patterns.* New York: New York University Press, 1962. 273p.
4693. _____. *Traditions and Values: American Diplomacy, 1945 - to the Present.* Lanham, MD.: University Press of America, 1985. 198p.
4694. Valeriani, Richard. *Travels with Henry.* Boston, MA.: Houghton Mifflin, 1979. 400p.
4695. Vance, Cyrus. *Hard Choices: Critical Years in America's Foreign Policy.* New York: Simon & Schuster, 1983. 541p.
4696. Wriston, Henry M. *Executive Agents in American Foreign Relations.* Baltimore, MD.: Johns Hopkins Press, 1929. 874p.

2. Journal Articles

4697. Alt Powell, Eileen, Julie Salamon and Karen Elliott House. "Crisis Diplomacy: How U.S. Negotiators Saved Hostage Deal at the Eleventh Hour." In: R. J. Lewicki and J. A. Litterer, eds. *Negotiation: Readings, Exercises and Cases*. Homewood, IL.: Irwin, 1985. pp. 142-148.
4698. Aron, Raymond. "Reflections on American Diplomacy." *Daedalus*, (Fall 1962), 717-732.
4699. Bailey, Thomas A. "Qualities of American Diplomats." In: E. Plischke, ed. *Modern Diplomacy: The Art and the Artisans*. Washington, D.C.: American Enterprise Institute, 1979. pp. 211-222.
4700. Bastert, Russell H. "The Two American Diplomacies." *Yale Review*, 49 (June 1960), 518-538.
4701. Beaulac, Willard L. "U.S. Diplomacy in a Changing World." *Department of State Bulletin*, 33 (August 29, 1955), 335-338.
4702. Bell, Coral. "Kissinger in Retrospect: The Diplomacy of Power - Concert?" *International Affairs*, 53 (April 1977), 202-216.
4703. _____. "'Negotiation From Strength' - The Second Time Around." *The National Interest*, 11 (Spring 1988), 53-64.
4704. Blair, Leon B. "Amateurs in Diplomacy: The American Vice Consuls in North Africa, 1941-43." *Historian*, 35 (August 1973), 607-620.
4705. Blair, William D. "Communication: The Weak Link in Our Foreign Relations." *Department of State Bulletin*, 115 (November 1970), 580-586.
4706. Brune, Lester H. "Considerations of Force in Cordell Hull's Diplomacy, July 26 to November 26, 1941." *Diplomatic History*, 2:4 (1978), 389-405.
4707. Caldwell, Lawrence T., and G. William Benz. "Soviet - American Diplomacy at the End of an Era." *Current History*, 82:484 (1983), 205-209.
4708. Cohen, Raymond. "Problems of Intercultural Communication in Egyptian--American Diplomatic Relations." *International Journal of Intercultural Relations*, 11 (1987), 29-47.
4709. Crabb, Cecil V. "American Diplomatic Tactics and Neutralism." *Political Science Quarterly*, 78 (September 1963), 418-443.
4710. Curtis, Gerald L. "The Dulles - Yoshida Negotiations on the San Francisco Peace Treaty." In: A. W. Cordier, ed. *Columbia Essays in International Affairs, Vol II: the Deans's Papers, 1966*. New York: Columbia University Press, 1967. pp. 37-62.
4711. Gardner, Richard N. "Foreign Policy Making in a New Era: United States Missions and Conferences." *Foreign Service Journal*, 52:7 (July 1975), 8-11.
4712. _____. "Sterling Dollar Diplomacy in Current Perspective." *International Affairs*, 62:1 (1986), 21-33.
4713. Garnham, D. "Foreign Service Elitism and U.S. Foreign Affairs." *Public Administration Review*, 35 (January 1975), 44-51.
4714. Griswold, A. Whitney. "Wormwood and Gall: An Introspective Note on American Diplomacy." *Foreign Affairs*, 39 (October 1960), 27-39.
4715. Henrikson, Alan K. "The Archimedes of Diplomacy: Henry Kissinger and the Foreign Policy of Watergate America." *International Journal*, 37:4 (1982), 606-612.
4716. _____. "The Geographical 'Mental Maps' of American Foreign Policy Makers." *International Political Science Review*, 1:4 (October 1980), 495-530.
4717. Irani, Robert G. "American Diplomacy in Iran: A Review of the Literature." *Iranian Review of International Relations*, 4 (1975), 169-172.

4718. Johnson, V. Alexis. "U.S. Diplomacy in Asia." In: G. C. McGhee, ed. *Diplomacy for the Future.* Lanham, MD.: University Press of America, 1987. pp. 73-76.
4719. Johnston, Whittle. "The New Diplomacy of President Carter." *Australian Journal of Politics and History,* 24:2 (1978), 159-173.
4720. Kertész, Stephen D. "Achievements and Pitfalls of American Diplomacy, 1776-1980." *Review of Politics,* 42:2 (1980), 216-248.
4721. Kohler, Foy D. "Negotiation as an Effective Instrument of American Foreign Policy." *Department of State Bulletin,* 30 (June 2, 1958), 901-910.
4722. Krogh, Dean. "Foreign Service Should Be More Attentive to Diplomacy: It Shouldn't Try to Dominate Policy Making." *Department of State Newsletter,* (November 1977), 9-11.
4723. Lebedev, N. "Western Scholars on the Crisis of Washington's Diplomacy." *International Affairs (U.S.S.R.),* 9 (September 1981), 87-95.
4724. Lewis, Samuel W. "American Diplomacy at the United Nations: The Real Stakes." *Department of State Bulletin,* 74:1928 (June 7, 1976), 732-738.
4725. Loomis, Richard T. "The White House Telephone and Crisis Management." *U.S. Naval Institute Proceedings,* 95 (December 1969), 63-73.
4726. Mathias, Charles McC. Jr. "A View from the Congress." In: G. C. McGhee, ed. *Diplomacy for the Future.* Lanham, MD.: University Press of America, 1987. pp. 27-34.
4727. McGhee, George C. "The Changing Role of the American Ambassador." *Department of State Bulletin,* 46 (June 25, 1962), 1007-1011.
4728. Merritt, Jeffrey D. "Unilateral Human Rights Intercession: American Practice Under Nixon, Ford and Carter." In: D. D. Newsom, ed. *The Diplomacy of Human Rights.* Lanham, MD.: University Press of America, 1986. pp. 43-60
4729. Montgomery, John D. "The Education of International Affairs." *Journal of International Affairs,* 29:1 (Spring 1975), 49-62.
4730. Nicolson, Harold. "The Faults of American Diplomacy." *Harper's Magazine,* (January 1955), 52-58.
4731. Ninkovich, Frank A. "The Currents of Cultural Diplomacy: Art and the State Department, 1938-47." *Diplomatic History,* 1 (Summer, 1977), 215-237.
4732. Petrov, V. "The Search for a 'New' Diplomacy in the U.S.A." *International Affairs (Moscow),* 6 (June 1979), 92-99.
4733. Platig, Raymond E. "The Moralities of Negotiation: They Determine Our Approach and Our Objectives in the Cold War." *Worldview,* 2 (November 1959), 3-6.
4734. Plischke, Elmer. "American Ambassadors - An Obsolete Species? Some Alternatives to Traditional Diplomatic Representation." *World Affairs,* 147:1 (Summer 1984), 2-23.
4735. _____. "The President's Image as Diplomat in Chief." *Review of Politics,* 47:4 (October 1985), 544-565.
4736. _____. "The President's Right to Go Abroad." *Orbis,* 15 (Fall 1971), 755-783.
4737. _____. "Rating Presidents and Diplomats in Chief." *Presidential Studies Quarterly,* 15:4 (Fall 1985), 725-742.
4738. _____. "Research on the Conduct of United States Foreign Relations." *International Studies Quarterly,* 15 (1971), 221-250.
4739. Punke, Harold H. "Secret Diplomacy and American Diplomacy." *Social Studies,* 47 (March 1956), 83-88.
4740. Richardson, Elliot L. "The Domestic Environment." In: G. C. McGhee, ed. *Diplomacy for the Future.* Lanham, MD.: University Press of America, 1987. pp. 21-26.

4741. Rubin, Seymour J. "American Diplomacy: The Case for "Amateurism"." *Yale Review*, 45 (March 1956), 321-335.
4742. Rusk, Dean. "The Realities of Foreign Policy." *Department of State Bulletin*, 46 (March 26, 1962), 487-494.
4743. Schick, Jack M. "American Diplomacy and the Berlin Negotiations." *Western Political Quarterly*, 18 (1965), 803-820.
4744. Semmel, A. K. "Some Correlates of Attitudes to Multilateral Diplomacy in United States Department of State." *International Studies Quarterly*, 20:2 (1976), 301-324.
4745. Simpson, Smith. "Our Faltering Diplomacy." *Foreign Service Journal*, 60:8 (September 1983), 24-29.
4746. _____. "The Frontier in American Diplomacy." *Foreign Service Journal*, 57 (December 1980), 4-8, 39-40.
4747. Southerland, Daniel. "The Inscrutable Secretary." *Foreign Service Journal*, 60:4 (April 1983), 22-25.
4748. Stearns, Monteagle. "Making American Diplomacy Relevant." *Foreign Affairs*, 52 (October 1973), 153-167.
4749. Stone, I. F. "The Flowering of Henry Kissinger." *New York Review of Books*, (November 2, 1972), 19-24.
4750. Suter, Keith. "In Praise of Dr. Henry Kissinger." *Army Quarterly*, 107 (July 1977), 345-353.
4751. Vincent, R. J. "The Response of Europe and the Third World to United States Human Rights Diplomacy." In: D. D. Newsom, ed. *The Diplomacy of Human Rights*. Lanham NY.: University Press of America, 1986. pp. 31-42.
4752. Waters, Maurice. "Special Diplomatic Agents of the President." *Annals of the American Academy of Political and Social Science*, 307 (September 1956), 124-133.
4753. Watt, D. C. "Henry Kissinger: An Interim Judgement." *Political Quarterly*, 48 (January 1977), 3-13.

3. Documents and Reports

4754. Alger, Chadwick F. *The Role of the Private Expert in the Conduct of American Foreign Affairs*. Ph.D. Dissertation. Princeton, NJ.: Princeton University, 1958.
4755. Alvarez, David J. *Bureaucracy and Cold War Diplomacy: The United States and Turkey, 1943-1946*. Thessaloniki: Institute of Balkan Studies, 1980. 147p.
4756. Barnes, William, and J. H. Morgan. *The Foreign Service of the United States: Origins, Development and Functions*. Washington, D.C.: U.S. Government Printing Office, 1961. 430p.
4757. Bell, Coral. *Negotiating From Strength: A Study in American Foreign Policy, 1950-1960*. Ph.D. Dissertation. London: University of London (External), 1962.
4758. Burns, Richard D. *Cordell Hull: A Study in Diplomacy, 1933-1941*. Ph.D. Dissertation. Urbana, IL.: University of Illinois, 1960. 355p.
4759. Casmir, Fred, et al. "International Conflict Management and Negotiation: The Agencies of the United States Government." Paper Presented at the *Tenth SIETAR International Conference*, held on May 21-25, 1984, at the George Mason University, in Washington, D.C.

4760. Cheng, Peter P. C. *A Study of John Foster Dulles: Diplomatic Strategy in the Far East.* Ph.D. Dissertation. Carbondalle, IL.: Southern Illinois University, 1964. 674p.
4761. *Documents on American Foreign Relations.* Boston, MA.: World Peace Foundation, 1939 -1970. Vol I - .
4762. Grow, Mary M. *Boundaries and United States Diplomacy: Two Case Studies.* Ph.D. Dissertation. Medford, CA.: Fletcher School of Law and Diplomacy, Tufts University, 1969. 260p.
4763. Irani, Robert G. *American Diplomacy: An Option Analysis of the Azerbijan Crisis, 1945 - 1946.* Hyattsville, MA.: Institute for Middle Eastern and North African Studies, 1978. 94p.
4764. Kober, Stanley H. *From Confrontation to Negotiation: American and Soviet Interpretations of Detente.* Ph.D. Dissertation. Medford, MA.: Fletcher School of Law and Diplomacy, 1978.
4765. Lowe, Henry J. *The Planning and Negotiation of U.S. Post - War Security, 1942 - 1943.* Ph.D. Dissertation. Charlottesville, VA.: University of Virginia, 1972. 413p.
4766. *Minutes of Telephone Conversations of John Foster Dulles and of Christian Herter, (1953-1961).* Frederick, MD.: University Publications of America, 1980. 11 microfilm reels & guide.
4767. *Official Conversations and Meetings of Dean Acheson (1949-1953).* Frederick, MD.: University Publications of America, 1980. 5 microfilm reels with printed guide.
4768. Olson, Dennis. "Henry Kissinger and American Foreign Policy: Plus or Minus?" Paper Presented at the *17th Annual Convention of the International Studies Association,* held on February 25-29, 1976, in Toronto.
4769. Price, Don K. *The New Dimension of Diplomacy: The Organization of the U.S. Government for its New Role in World Affairs.* New York: Woodrow Wilson Foundation, 1951. 29p.
4770. Pruitt, Dean G. *Problem Solving in the Department of State.* Monograph Series in World Affairs, Vol 2, no 2. Denver, CO.: Department of International Relations, University of Denver, 1964. 56p.
4771. Sarros, Panayiotis P. *Congress and the New Diplomacy: The Formulation of Mutual Security Policy: 1953-1960.* Ph.D. Dissertation. Princeton, NJ.: Princeton University, 1964.
4772. Sprott, John T. "The Training of Diplomats in a World in Transition: A Case Study - the United States of America." Paper Presented at the *26th Annual International Studies Association Conference,* held on March 8, 1985, in Washington, D.C. 15p.
4773. Stebbins, Richard P., and Elaine P. Adam, eds. *American Foreign Relations: A Documentary Record.* New York: Council on Foreign Relations, 1971-78.
4774. Stupak, Ronald J., and Robert C. Hange. *Coercive Diplomacy and the Resolution of Conflict in United States Foreign Policy in the 1970's.* Buffalo, NY.: Council on International Studies, State University of New York at Buffalo, 1978. 46p.
4775. Sullivan, Michael J. III. "Kissinger's Diplomacy: The Danger of Ignoring Cultural Distinctions." Paper Presented at the *17th Annual Convention of the International Studies Association,* held on February 25-29, 1976, in Toronto.
4776. Timberlake, Charles E. *Detente: A Documentary Record.* New York: Praeger, 1978. 231p.

4777. *Top - Secret Hearings by the U.S. Senate Committee on Foreign Relations, 1959 - 1966.* Frederick, MD.: University Publications of America, 1981. 6 microfilms and guide.
4778. *Toward a Modern Diplomacy: A Report to the American Foreign Service Association.* Washington, D.C.: American Foreign Service Association, 1968. 185p.
4779. United States. Congress. House. Committee on Foreign Affairs. *Science, Technology and American Diplomacy: An Extended Study of the Interactions of Science and Technology with United States Foreign Policy.* Washington, D.C.: U.S. Government Printing Office, 1977. 3 vols.
4780. _____._____._____._____.Subcommittee on National Security Policy and Scientific Developments. *The Baruch Plan: U.S. Diplomacy Enters the Nuclear Age. by L. N. Wu.* Washington, D.C.: U.S. Government Printing Office, 1972. 67p.
4781. _____.Department of State. *Diplomacy for the 70's: Program of Management for the Department of State.* Washington, D.C.: U.S. Government Printing Office, 1970. 610p.
4782. _____._____. *Educational and Cultural Diplomacy, 1961.* Washington, D.C.: U.S. Government Printing Office, 1962. 69p.
4783. _____._____. *The Foreign Relations of the United States.* Washington, D.C.: U.S. Government Printing Office, 1961-. Yearly.
4784. _____._____. *Role of Negotiation: By J. F. Dulles.* Public Service Division No. 62. Washington, D.C.: U.S. Government Printing Office, 1958. 15p.
4785. _____._____. *A Decade of American Foreign Policy: Basic Documents, 1941-1949.* Revised Edition. Washington, D.C.: Greenwood Press, 1985. 969p.
4786. Wright, C. Ben. *George Kennan, Scholar - Diplomat, 1926-1946.* Ph.D. Dissertation. Madison, WI.: University of Wisconsin, 1972. 512p.

XII

Case Studies

This chapter lists cases studies of diplomatic negotiations, arranged by major conflicts and their accompanying negotiation processes and by a geographical or national subdivision.

The first section covers the Middle East and lists mainly negotiations dealing with the Israeli - Arab conflict, and other regional conflicts such as the Iran - Irak War. Section two covers the negotiations accompanying the Vietnam Conflict. Section three lists negotiations dealing with the Korean War and subsequent negotiations between the two Koreas. The fourth and the fifth sections cover Japanese and Chinese negotiation styles and case studies of diplomatic negotiations involving these nations. The following two sections deal with negotiations involving Latin American and African states. Section eight covers with various diplomatic negotiations involving the United States and Canada. The last section lists a wide range of negotiations which cannot be fitted into the sections listed above.

This bibliography includes English language materials only. It excludes news magazine articles. I am sure this work will be a valuable research tool for students and scholars researching various conflicts and their negotiation histories.

A. MIDDLE EAST NEGOTIATIONS

1. Books

4787. Aronson, Shlomo. *Conflict and Bargaining in the Middle East: An Israeli Perspective.* Baltimore, MD.: Johns Hopkins University Press, 1978. 448p.
4788. Rabin, Yitzhak. *The Rabin Memoirs.* Boston: Little, Brown, 1979. 344p.
4789. Al-Mani, Saleh A., and Salah Al-Shaikly, eds. *The Euro-Arab Dialogue: A Study in Associative Diplomacy.* London: St. Martin's Press, 1983. 153p.
4790. Alroy, Gil. *The Kissinger Experience: American Policy in the Middle East.* New York: Horizon Press, 1975. 189p.
4791. Bar-Zochar, Michael. *Embassies in Crisis: Diplomats and Demagogues Behind the Six Day War.* Englewood Cliffs, NJ.: Prentice-Hall, 1970. 279p.
4792. Ben-Dor, Gabriel, and David B. Dewitt, eds. *Conflict Management in the Middle East.* Lexington, MA.: Lexington Books, 1987. 320p.
4793. Ben-Gurion, David. *My Talks with Arab Leaders.* New York: Third Press, 1973. 342p.
4794. Ben-Zvi, Abraham. *The American Approach to Superpower Collaboration in the Middle East, 1973-1986.* JCSS Studies No. 5. Jerusalem: Jaffee Centre for Strategic Studies, 1986. 133p.
4795. Bradley, C. Paul. *The Camp David Peace Process: A Study of Carter Administration Policies (1977-1980).* Hamden, CT.: Shoe String Press, 1981. 79p.
4796. Brown, William R. *The Last Crusade: A Negotiator's Middle East Handbook.* Chicago, IL.: Nelson-Hall, 1980. 399p.
4797. Bryson, Thomas A. *American Diplomatic Relations with the Middle East, 1784-1975: A Survey.* Metuchen, NJ.: Scarecrow Press, 1977. 431p.
4798. Caplan, Neil. *Futile Diplomacy: Volume I - Early Arab-Zionist Negotiation Attempts, 1913-1931.* London: Frank Cass, 1983. 277p.
4799. _____. *Futile Diplomacy: Volume 2: Arab-Zionist Negotiations and the End of the Mandate.* London: Frank Cass, 1984. 358p.
4800. Carter, Jimmy. *Keeping Faith: Memoirs of a President.* London: Collins, 1982. 622p.
4801. _____. *The Blood of Abraham: Insights into the Middle East.* Boston: Houghton Mifflin, 1985. 257p.
4802. Charney, Leon H. *Special Council.* New York: Philosophical Library, 1984. 369p.
4803. Christopher, Warren, et al. *American Hostages in Iran: The Conduct of a Crisis.* New Haven, CT.: Yale University Press, 1985. 443p.
4804. Crum, Bartley C. *Behind the Silken Curtain: A Personal Account of Anglo-American Diplomacy in Palestine and the Middle East.* New York: Simon & Schuster, 1947. 297p.
4805. Dayan, Moshe. *Breakthrough: A Personal Account of Egypt-Israel Peace Negotiation.* London: Weidenfeld and Nicolson, 1981. 368p.
4806. Fahmy, Ismail. *Negotiating for Peace in the Middle East.* London: Croom Helm, 1983. 331p.
4807. Fisher, Roger D. *Dear Israelis, Dear Arabs: A Working Approach to Peace.* New York: Harper and Row, 1972. 166p.
4808. Foley, Charles, and W. I. Scobie. *The Struggle for Cyprus.* Stanford, CA.: Hoover Institution Press, 1975.
4809. Ghanayem, Ishaq I., and Alden H. Voth. *The Kissinger Legacy: American-Middle East Policy.* New York: Praeger, 1984. 237p.

4810. Golan, Mati. *The Secret Conversations of Henry Kissinger: Step-by-Step Diplomacy in the Middle East.* New York: Quadrangle, 1976. 280p.
4811. Heikal, Mohamed. *The Cairo Documents: The Inside Story of Nasser and his Relationship with World Leaders, Rebels, and Statesmen.* Garden City, NY.: Doubleday, 1973. 360p.
4812. Hurewitz, Jacob Coleman. *Diplomacy in the Near and Middle East: A Documentary Record 1916-1956.* Princeton, NJ.: Van Nostrand, 1975. 2 vols.
4813. Israeli, Raphael. *The Public Diary of President Sadat: The Road to Pragmatism, June 1975-October 1976.* Leiden: E. J. Brill, 1978. 3 vols.
4814. Kamel, Mohamed Ibrahim. *The Camp David Accords: A Testimony by Sadat's Foreign Minister.* New York: Methuen, 1987. 414p.
4815. Marantz, Paul, and Janice Gross Stein, eds. *Peacemaking in the Middle East: Problems and Prospects.* London: Croom Helm, 1985. 244p.
4816. Naveh, David, Paul Hare and Ilan Peleg. *Camp David, 1978: International Negotiations as a Drama.* Boulder, CO.: Lynne Rienner, 1989. 175p.
4817. Quandt, William B. *Camp David: Peacemaking and Politics.* Washington, D.C.: Brookings Institution, 1986. 426p.
4818. _____. *Decade of Decisions: American Policy Toward the Arab-Israeli Conflict, 1967-1976.* Berkeley, CA.: University of California Press, 1977. 313p.
4819. Riad, Mahmoud. *The Struggle for Peace in the Middle East.* Boston: Charles River Books, 1982. 365p.
4820. Salinger, Pierre. *America Held Hostage: The Secret Negotiations.* New York: Doubleday, 1981. 349p.
4821. Saunders, Harold H. *The Iranian Hostage Crisis.* New Haven, CT.: Yale University Press, 1984.
4822. Sick, Gary. *444 Days.* New York: Morrow, 1985.
4823. Sobel, Lester A. *Peace-Making in the Middle East.* New York: Facts on File, 1980. 286p.
4824. Stern, Lawrence. *The Wrong Horse: The Politics of Intervention and the Failure of American Diplomacy.* New York: Times Books, 1977. 170p.
4825. Sullivan, William H. *Mission to Iran.* New York: Norton, 1981. 296p.
4826. Weizman, Ezer. *The Battle for Peace.* New York: Bantam Books, 1981. 395p.
4827. Xydis, Stephen C. *Cyprus: Conflict and Conciliation, 1954-1958.* Columbus, OH.: Ohio State University Press, 1967. 704p.

2. Journal Articles

4828. Avineri, Shlomo. "Peacemaking: The Arab-Israeli Conflict." *Foreign Affairs,* 57:1 (1978), 51-69.
4829. Azar, Edward E. "Conflict Escalation and Conflict Reduction in an International Crisis: Suez, 1956." *Journal of Conflict Resolution,* 16:2 (1972), 183-202.
4830. Bechtoldt, Heinrich. "Middle East Between Kissinger and Geneva." *Aussenpolitik,* 26:2 (1975), 127-136.
4831. Bell, Coral. "The October Middle East War: A Case Study in Crisis Management During Detente." *International Affairs,* 50:4 (1974), 531-543.
4832. Ben-Yishai, Ron. "Israel's Move." *Foreign Policy,* 42 (Spring 1981), 43-57.
4833. Ben-Zvi, Abraham. "The Limits of Coercion in Bilateral Bargaining Situations: The Case of the American-Israeli Dyad." *Jerusalem Journal of International Relations,* 8:4 (December 1986), 68-99.

4834. ____. "The Management of Superpower Conflict in the Middle East." In: S. L. Spiegel, M. A. Heller and J. Goldberg, eds. *The Soviet-American Competition in the Middle East.* Lexington, MA.: Lexington Books, 1988. pp. 343-356.
4835. Bercovitch, Jacob. "An Analysis of Negotiation as a Successful Approach to International Conflict Management: Egyptian-Israeli Negotiations at Camp David." *Crossroads,* 17 (1985), 83-106.
4836. ____. "Conflict Management in the Middle East in Reagan's Balancing Act." *International Problems,* 24 (1984), 150-159.
4837. ____. "International Negotiations and the Middle East." *International Problems,* 25:1-2 (1986), 12-18.
4838. ____. "The Resolution of International Conflicts: A Non-Traditional Approach to the Middle East Conflict." *International Problems,* 16:1 (1977), 89-99.
4839. Brown, Neville. "The Adverse Partnership: The U.S. and Russia Learn to Talk." *New Middle East,* 23 (August 1970), 17-21.
4840. Campbell, John C. "A New Arena of Diplomacy: The Middle East." In: S. D. Kertész and M. A. Fitzsimmons, eds. *Diplomacy in a Changing World.* South Bend, IN.: University of Notre Dame Press, 1959. pp. 327-338.
4841. Caplan, Neil. "Negotiating and the Arab Israeli Conflict." *Jerusalem Quarterly,* 6 (Winter 1978), 3-19.
4842. Carter, Jimmy. "The Middle East Consultation: A Look to the Future." *Middle East Journal,* 42:2 (Spring 1988), 187-192.
4843. Chaliand, Gerard. "Kissinger's Diplomacy." *New Outlook,* 18 (March/April 1975), 11-18.
4844. Chubin, Shahram. "The Foreign Policy of the Islamic Republic of Iran." In: *Negotiations in Asia: Three Case Studies: India - Iran - Vietnam.* Geneva: Centre for Applied Studies in International Negotiations, 1984. pp. 1-29.
4845. Cohen, Michael J. "Secret Diplomacy and Rebellion in Palestine, 1936-1939." *International Journal of Middle East Studies,* 8 (1977), 379-404.
4846. Cohen, Stephen, and Harriet C. Arnone. "Conflict Resolution as the Alternative to Terrorism." *Social Issues,* 44 (Summer 1988), 175-189.
4847. Crawshaw, Nancy. "Cyprus: A Failure in Western Diplomacy." *World Today,* 40:2 (1984), 73-79.
4848. Cutler, Lloyd N. "Negotiating the Iranian Settlement." *Journal of the American Bar Association,* 67 (August 1981), 996-1000.
4849. Dinstein, Yoram. "Peace Negotiations Fatigue." *Jerusalem Quarterly,* 11 (Spring 1979), 3-14.
4850. Diskin, Abraham, and Shaul Mishal. "Spatial Models and Centrality of International Communities: Meeting between Arab Leaders 1966-1978." *Journal of Conflict Resolution,* 25:4 (December 1981), 655-676.
4851. Dowty, Allan. "Negotiations or War." *Midstream,* 14 (March 1968), 35-38.
4852. Eban, Abba. "Multilateral Diplomacy in the Arab-Israeli Conflict." In: A. Lall, ed. *Multilateral Negotiation and Mediation.* New York: Pergamon Press, 1985. pp. 40-52.
4853. Feldman, Shai. "Peacemaking in the Middle East: The Next Step." *Foreign Affairs,* 59:4 (1981), 756-780.
4854. Gross Stein, Janice. "The Alchemy of Peacemaking: The Prerequisites and Co-requisites of Progress in the Arab-Israeli Conflict." *International Journal,* 38:4 (Autumn 1983), 531-555.
4855. ____. "Conditions of Successful Arab-Israel Conflict Management." *Middle East Focus,* 9:1 (Summer/Fall 1986), 9-11.

4856. _____. "The Fundamentals of Peacemaking: A Retrospective Analysis." In: P. Marantz and J. Gross Stein, eds. *Peacemaking in the Middle East.* London: Croom Helm, 1985. pp. 218-240.
4857. _____. "Leadership in Peacemaking: 'Fate', 'Will', and 'Fortuna' in the Middle East." *International Journal,* 37:4 (Autumn 1982), 517-542.
4858. _____. "The Managed and the Managers: Crisis Prevention in the Middle East." In: G. R. Winham, ed. *New Issues in International Crisis Management.* Boulder, CO.: Westview Press, 1988. pp. 171-198.
4859. _____. "Proxy Wars - How Superpowers End Them: The Diplomacy of War Termination in the Middle East." *International Journal,* 35:3 (1980), 478-519.
4860. Grummon, S. R. "Negotiation Efforts in The Iran-Iraq War: Islam Embattled." *Washington Papers,* 10:92 (1982), 72-81.
4861. Grzybowski, Kazimierz. "The Regime of Diplomacy and the Tehran Hostages." *International and Comparative Law Quarterly,* 30:1 (1981), 42-58.
4862. Heradsveit, Daniel. "Conditions for Negotiations in the Arab-Israeli Conflict." *Bulletin for Peace Proposals,* 3 (1973), 278-285.
4863. Hopmann, P. Terrence, and Daniel Druckman. "Henry Kissinger as Strategist and Tactician in the Middle East Negotiations." In: J. Z. Rubin, ed. *Dynamics of Third Party Intervention: Kissinger in the Middle East.* New York: Praeger, 1981. pp. 197-225.
4864. Hsu, King-Yi. "Communist China's Diplomacy in the Middle East." *Issues and Studies,* 16:3 (1980), 70-93.
4865. Inbar, Michael, and Yuchtman-Yaar Ephraim. "Some Cognitive Dimensions of the Israeli-Arab Conflict: A Preliminary Report." *Journal of Conflict Resolution,* 29:4 (December 1985), 699-725.
4866. Indyck, Martin. *Reagan and the Middle East: Learning the Art of the Possible.*
4867. Jacobsen, Dan. "Intraparty Dissensus and Interparty Conflict Resolution: A Laboratory Experiment in the Context of the Middle East Conflict." *Journal of Conflict Resolution,* 25:3 (September 1981), 471-494.
4868. Kaplan, Morton A. "Negotiations in the Middle East Dispute." *Armed Forces and Society,* 1:4 (1975), 505-513.
4869. Kelman, Herbert C. "Creating the Conditions for Israeli-Palestinian Negotiations." *Journal of Conflict Resolution,* 26:1 (1982), 39-76.
4870. _____. "Creating the Conditions for Israeli-Palestinian Negotiations." In: S. F. Wells and M. A. Druzowsky, eds. *Security in the Middle East.* Boulder, CO.: Westview Press, 1987. pp. 139-157.
4871. _____. "An International Approach to Conflict Resolution and its Application to Israeli-Palestinian Relations." *International Interactions,* 6 (1979), 99-122.
4872. _____. "Overcoming the Barriers to Negotiation of the Israeli-Palestinian Conflict." *Journal of Palestine Studies,* 16:1 (Autumn 1986), 13-28.
4873. Khuri, F. "The Etiquette of Bargaining in the Middle East." *American Anthropologist,* 70 (1968), 698-706.
4874. Kimche, Jon. "Kissinger Diplomacy and the Art of Limited War." *Midstream,* 20 (November 1974), 3-12.
4875. Lapidoth, Ruth. "The Autonomy Negotiations: A Stocktaking." *Middle East Review,* 15:3/4 (Spring/Summer 1983), 35-43.
4876. Lawson, Fred H. "Positive Sanctions and the Managing of International Conflict: Five Middle Eastern Cases." *International Journal,* 40:4 (1985), 628-654.
4877. Lee, William. "Faced with Breakdown." *Middle East International,* 171 (March 26, 1982), 3-4.

4878. Magnarella, Paul J. "Iranian Diplomacy and The Khomeini Era." In: M. D. Zamora, ed. *Culture and Diplomacy in the Third World.* Williamsburg, VA.: Dept. of Anthropology, College of William and Mary, 1981. pp. 1-16.
4879. Maksoud, Clovis. "Arab League Negotiations." In: A. Lall, ed. *Multilateral Negotiations and Mediation.* New York: Pergamon Press, 1985. pp. 32-40.
4880. McTague, John J. Jr. "Anglo-French Negotiations over the Boundaries of Palestine, 1919-1920." *Journal of Palestine Studies,* 11:2 (1982), 100-112.
4881. Monroe, Elisabeth. "Camp David: Prelude to Peace? Efforts Towards a Middle East Settlement and the Problem of Palestine." *Round Table,* 273 (1979), 75-80.
4882. Newsom, David D. "Miracle and Mirage: Reflections on U.S. Diplomacy and the Arabs." *Middle East Journal,* 35:3 (1981), 299-314.
4883. Park Teter, Daniel. "West-Bank Negotiations." *Editorial Research Reports,* 2:3 (July 20, 1979), 521-540.
4884. Perlmutter, Amos. "Begin's Strategy and Dayan's Tactics: The Conduct of Israeli Foreign Policy." *Foreign Affairs,* 56 (January 1978), 357-372.
4885. _____. "Crisis Management: Kissinger's Middle East Negotiations (October 1973-June 1974)." *International Studies Quarterly,* 19:3 (1975), 316-343.
4886. _____. "Race Against Time - Egyptian-Israeli Negotiations over the Future of Palestine." *Foreign Affairs,* 57:5 (1979), 987-1004.
4887. "Prospects for Negotiation: An Interview with Ambassador Sol M. Linowitz." *Fletcher Forum,* 8:1 (1984), 9-18.
4888. Quandt, William B. "Camp David and Peacemaking in the Middle East." *Political Science Quarterly,* 101:3 (1986), 357-377.
4889. _____. "Egypt: A Strong Sense of National Identity." In: H. Binnendijk, ed. *National Negotiating Style.* Washington, D.C.: Foreign Service Institute, Center for the Study of Foreign Affairs, 1987. pp. 105-124.
4890. _____. "Kissinger and the Arab-Israeli Disengagement Negotiations." *Journal of International Affairs,* 29:1 (Spring 1975), 33-48.
4891. _____. "Menachem Begin: A Past Master at Negotiation." *Brookings Review,* 2:2 (Winter 1983), 12-18.
4892. Reich, Bernard. "The Jarring Mission and the Search for Peace in the Middle East." *Wiener Library Bulletin,* 26 (1972), 13-20.
4893. _____. "The Middle East Autonomy Talks." *Current History,* 80:462 (1981), 14-18.
4894. Rodman, Peter W. "The Hostage Crisis: How Not to Negotiate." *Washington Quarterly,* 4:3 (1981), 9-24.
4895. Rumpf, Helmut. "Cyprus as a Model Case of International Conflict." *Aussenpolitik,* 32:2 (1981), 174-186.
4896. Saunders, Harold H. "American Diplomacy and Arab-Israel-Palestinian Peace Since 1967." In: S. F. Wells and M. A. Bruzonsky, eds. *Security in the Middle East.* Boulder, CO.: Westview Press, 1987. pp. 280-305.
4897. _____. "The Psychology of Negotiations." *American-Arab Affairs,* 15 (Winter 1985/86), 10-18.
4898. _____. "Regulating Soviet - U.S. Competition and Cooperation in the Arab - Israeli Arena, 1967-86." In: A. L. George, P. J. Farley and A. Dallin, eds. *U.S. - Soviet Security Cooperation.* New York: Oxford University Press, 1988. pp. 540-580.
4899. Sharabi, H. "The Palestinian Approach to Negotiations." In: M. C. Hudson, ed. *Alternative Approaches to the Arab-Israeli Conflict: A Comparative Analysis of the Principal Actors.* Washington, D.C: Center for Contemporary Arab Studies, 1984. pp. 63-74.

4900. Spiegel, Steven L. "The American Approach to Middle East Conflict Management." *International Interactions,* 13:2 (1987), 145-170.
4901. _____. "The U.S. Approach to Conflict Resolution in the Middle East." In: G. Ben-Dor and D. B. Dewitt, eds. *Conflict Management in the Middle East.* Lexington, MA.: Lexington Books, 1987. pp. 155-186.
4902. Stoddard, Philip H. "U.S. Policy and the Arab-Israeli Conflict: Observations on the Current Science." *Annals of the American Academy of Political and Social Science,* 482 (November 1985), 19-39.
4903. Touval, Saadia. "Frameworks for Arab-Israeli Negotiations - What Difference Do They Make?" *Negotiation Journal,* 3:1 (January 1987), 37-52.
4904. Vigny, G. "Superpower Diplomacy Limited After Sadat Visit to Israel." *International Perspectives,* (March 1978), 32-35.
4905. Von Dornoch, Alex. "Iran's Violent Diplomacy." *Survival,* 30:3 (May/June 1988), 252-266.
4906. Watt, D. C. "Towards a Middle East Settlement? The Policy of Ambiguity." *Political Quarterly,* 49 (January 1978), 13-24.
4907. Wilkenfeld, Jonathan, V. L. Lussier and Dale Tahtinen. "Conflict Interactions in the Middle East, 1949-1967." *Journal of Conflict Resolution,* 16:2 (1971), 135-154.
4908. Yevseyev, Y. "Israel's Diplomacy and Propaganda of Aggression." *International Affairs (USSR),* 9 (September 1979), 113-127.
4909. Zak, Moshe. "Israeli-Jordanian Negotiations." *Washington Quarterly,* 8:1 (Winter 1985), 167-176p.
4910. Zartman, I. William. "The Middle East - The Ripe Moment?" In: G. Ben-Dor and D. B. Dewitt, eds. *Conflict Management in the Middle East.* Lexington, MA.: Lexington Books, 1987. pp. 283-296.

3. Documents and Reports

4911. Al-Abib, Ibrahim. *Israel and Negotiations.* Palestine Essays, 20. Beirut: Palestine Liberation Organization Research Centre, 1970. 29p.
4912. Becker, Abraham S. *Moscow and the Middle East Settlement: A Role for Soviet Bureaucracy.* RAND P-5532. Santa Monica, CA.: RAND Corporation, 1975. 13p.
4913. Ben-Gurion, David. *Negotiations with Nasser.* Jerusalem: Israel Information Center, 1973. 64p.
4914. Bobrow, Davis B. "The Autonomy Talks and the Camp David Framework." Paper Presented at the *14th Annual Meeting of the Middle East Studies Association of North America,* held on November 7, 1980, in Washington D.C.
4915. Chaibane, Antoine. *Crisis Diplomacy: America's Decision for Failure in the Middle East.* Ph.D. Dissertation. Tallahassee, FL.: Florida State University, 1980. 344p.
4916. Cohen, Herbert A. "Negotiating the Iran Crisis." In: U.S. Congress. House. Committee of Post Office and Civil Service. *Unauthorized Transfers of Nonpublic Information During the 1980 Presidential Election, Part 2.* 98th Cong.,2nd sess. Washington, D.C.: U.S. Government Printing Office, 1984. pp. 1542-1605.
4917. Creighton, John J. *Egypt's Role in the Middle East Peace Process.* Washington, D.C.: Defence Intelligence College, 1986. 46p.
4918. Elazar, David J. *The Camp David Framework for Peace.* Washington, D.C.: American Enterprise Institute, 1979. 20p.

4919. Freedman, Matthew C., and Henry A. Kissinger. *After Camp David: The Role of Autonomy Negotiations in Furthering Middle East Peace.* Washington, D.C.: Georgetown University Press, 1979. 49p.

4920. Friedlander, Melvin A. *The Management of Peace-Making in Egypt and Israel, 1977-1979.* Ph.D. Dissertation. Washington, D.C.: The American University, 1982. 629p.

4921. Fry, Michael G. *Suez Canal.* PEW Case Studies, 126.0-F-88-S. Los Angeles, CA.: School of International Relations, University of Southern California, 1988.

4922. Garfinkle, Adam M. *Western Europe Middle East Diplomacy and the United States.* Philadelphia, PA.: Foreign Policy Research Institute, 1983. 118p.

4923. Ghanayem, Ishaq I. *The Nixon - Kissinger Middle East Strategy, 1969-1974.* Ph.D. Dissertation. Santa Barbara, CA.: University of California at Santa Barbara, 1980. 315p.

4924. Gomaa, Salwa, and Joseph Kechkeméthy. *Henry Kissinger and the Sinai Disengagement Agreements of 1974 and 1975.* PEW Case Studies, 412.0-F-88-P. Pittsburgh, PA.: Graduate School of Public and International Affairs, University of Pittsburgh, 1988.

4925. Gottheil, Diane Levitt. *National Capital Diplomacy: A Study of Diplomats and the Diplomatic Community in Israel.* Ph.D. Dissertation. Urbana, IL.: University of Illinois, 1973.

4926. Gromoll, Robert H. *The May 17 Accord: Studies of Diplomacy and Negotiations on Troop Withdrawals from Lebanon.* PEW Case Studies, 310.0-F--87-P. Pittsburgh, PA.: Graduate School of Public and International Affairs, University of Pittsburgh, 1987.

4927. Haley, P. Edward. *Carter's Lonesome Road to Peace: Perception, Bargaining, and the Limits of Multilateral Diplomacy in the Middle East.* Research Note, No. 6. Los Angeles, Ca.: Center for International and Strategic Affairs, 1981. 69p.

4928. Hand, Robert D. *Arab Negotiation. Not No, but Hell No.* AD-761439. Carlisle Barracks, PA.: U.S. Army War College, 1973. 39p.

4929. Hayaki, I. *The Arab-Israeli Conflict: International Efforts to Negotiate a Permanent Political Settlement, 1967-1973.* B. Litt. Oxford: Oxford, University. [1975].

4930. Kern, Montague. *Television and Middle-East Diplomacy - Carter Fall 1977 Peace Initiative.* Washington, D.C.: Centre for Contemporary Arab Studies, Georgetown University, 1985. 58p.

4931. Kiewe, Amos. *An Analysis by Rhetorical Models of the Sadat - Begin Peace Negotiation from Inception to Completion.* Ph.D. Dissertation. Athens, OH.: Ohio University, 1984. 268p.

4932. Klieman, Aharon. *Statecraft in the Dark: Israel's Practice of Quiet Diplomacy.* JCSS Study no. 10. Tel Aviv: Jaffee Center for Strategic Studies, Tel Aviv University, 1988. 156p.

4933. Kriesberg, Louis. *Strategies of Negotiating Agreements: U.S.-Soviet and Arab-Israeli Cases.* PARK Working Paper #1. Syracuse, NY.: The Program on the Analysis and Resolution of Conflict, Maxwell School of Citizenship and Public Affairs, Syracuse University, 1987.

4934. _____. "Transforming Intractable Conflicts: Cases from the Middle East and Central Europe." Paper Presented at the *PARC Workshop on Intractable Conflicts*, held on October 23, 1987, at the Maxwell School of Citizenship and Public Affairs, Syracuse University.

4935. Le Blanc, James L. *Superpower Risk-Taking in the Context of International Crisis Bargaining: The Middle East, 1967-73.* M.A. Thesis. Ottawa: Carleton University, 1984.

4936. Lieb, Diane. *Conflict Resolution Theory and Practice: A Case Study of the Egyptian Israeli Peace Treaty, 1973-1979*. Ph.D. Dissertation. New York: New York University, 1982. 331p.
4937. Magnes, Ralph H. *Documents on the Middle East*. Washington, D.C.: American Enterprise Institute for Public Policy Research, 1969. 232p.
4938. Mark, Clyde R. "Arab-Israeli Peace: Sadat-Begin Negotiations." In: *Major Studies and Issue Briefs of the Congressional Research Service, 1978-79 Supplement*. Washington, D.C.: University Publications of America, 1979. Reel VI; pp. 883-915.
4939. O'Brien, William. *U.S. Diplomacy in the 1982 Lebanon War*. PEW Case Studies, 308.0-F-87-G. Washington, D.C.: School of Foreign Service, Georgetown University, 1987.
4940. Parker, Thomas R. *U.S. Negotiating Strategy Towards the Arab - Israeli Conflict, 1967-1979*. Ph.D. Dissertation. New York: City University of New York, 1985. 261p.
4941. Reich, Bernard. *Israel's Foreign Policy: A Case Study of Small State Diplomacy*. Ph.D. Dissertation. Charlottesville, VA.: University of Virginia, 1964. 542p.
4942. Rosenthal, Yemima. *Documents on the Foreign Policy of Israel, Vol. 1, May 15-September 30, 1948; Vol. 2, October 48-April 49; Vol. 3, December 1948-July 1949. Armistice Negotiations with the Arab St*. Jerusalem: Israel State Archives, 1981-84.
4943. Rubin, Barry, and Laura Blum. *The May 1983 Agreement over Lebanon*. FPI Case Studies. Washington, D.C.: Johns Hopkins Foreign Policy Institute, 1987.
4944. Saleh, Hamdi A. W. *Egypt and the Superpowers, 1967-1977: A Study of Bargaining Strategy of a Small State in Conflict, Crisis and Peace - Making*. Ph.D. Dissertation. Cambridge, MA.: Harvard University, 1987.
4945. Saunders, Harold H. *The Other Walls: The Politics of the Arab-Israeli Peace Process*. Washington, D.C.: American Enterprise Institute for Public Policy Research, 1985. 179p.
4946. Schwartz, Richard. "Transformation of Intractable Conflicts in the Middle East." Paper Presented at the *PARC Workshop on Intractable Conflicts*, held on October 23, 1987, at the Maxwell School of Citizenship and Public Affairs, Syracuse University.
4947. Sicherman, Harvey. *Broker or Advocate? The U.S. Role in the Arab-Israeli Dispute, 1973-1978*. Monograph No.25. Philadelphia, PA.: Foreign Policy Research Institute, 1978. 120p.
4948. Sisco, Joseph J. *Middle East Negotiations: A Conversation with Joseph Sisco, with Basic Documents*. Washington, D.C.: American Enterprise Institute for Public Policy Research, 1980. 35p.
4949. Siverson, Randolph M. *Inter-Nation Conflict, Dyadic and Mediated: Egypt, Israel and the United Nations, 1956-1957*. Ph.D. Dissertation. Stanford, CA.: Stanford University, 1969. 240p.
4950. Tarr, David W. *American Power and Diplomacy in the Middle East*. Ph.D. Dissertation. Chicago, IL.: University of Chicago, 1961.
4951. Telhami, Shibley. *International Bargaining and the Level of Analysis Problem: The Case of Camp David*. Ph.D. Dissertation. Berkeley, CA.: University of California, 1986. 488p.
4952. _____. *International Crisis Bargaining: The Case of Camp David*. PEW Case Studies, 339.0-F-88-S. Los Angeles, CA.: School of International Relations, University of Southern California, 1988.
4953. *Toward Arab - Israeli Peace: Report of a Study Group*. Washington, D.C.: The Brookings Institution, 1988. 42p.

Case Studies 293

4954. United States. Congress. House. Committee on Foreign Affairs. Subcommittee on Europe and the Middle East. *An Assessment of the West Bank and Gaza Autonomy Talks, November 1980.* 96th Cong., 2nd sess. Washington, D.C.: U.S. Government Printing Office, 1980. 40p.

4955. ____.____.____.____.____. *Documents and Statements on Middle East Peace, 1979-82.* 97th Cong., 2nd sess. Washington, D.C.: U.S. Government Printing Office, 1982. 337p.

4956. ____.____.____.____.____. *Perspectives on the Middle East Peace Process, December 1, 1981: Hearings.* 97th Cong., 1st sess. Washington, D.C.: U.S. Government Printing Office, 1982. 145p.

4957. ____.____.____.____.____. *The Search for Peace in the Middle East: Documents and Statements, 1967-79: Report.* 96th Cong., 1st sess. Washington, D.C.: U.S. Government Printing Office, 1979. 306p.

4958. ____.____.____.____.____. *Status of Middle East Peace Talks Regarding The West Bank and Gaza, October 1979: Hearings.* 96th Cong., 1st sess. Washington, D.C.: U.S. Government Printing Office, 1980. 34p.

4959. ____.____.____.____.____. *Status of Negotiations on the Cyprus Dispute and Recent Developments in Cyprus: Hearings.* 98th Cong., 1st sess. Washington, D.C.: U.S. Government Printing Office, 1984. 33p.

4960. ____.____.____.____.____. *Assessment of the 1978 Middle East Camp David Agreements: Hearings.* 95th Cong., 2nd sess. Washington, D.C.: U.S. Government Printing Office, 1979. 126p.

4961. ____.____.____.____.Subcommittee on International Economic Policy and Trade. *The Iran Hostage Crisis: A Chronology of Daily Developments: Report.* 99th Cong., 1st sess. Washington, D.C.: U.S. Government Printing Office, 1981. 421p.

4962. ____.____.Senate.Committee on Foreign Relations.Subcommittee on Near Eastern and South Asian Affairs. *Middle East Peace Process: Hearings.* 95th Cong., 2nd sess. Washington, D.C.: U.S. Government Printing Office, 1978. 34p.

4963. ____.Department of State. *The Camp David Summit.* Washington, D.C.: U.S. Government Printing Office, 1978. 19p.

4964. ____.____. *The Quest for Peace: Principal United States Public Statements and Documents Relating to the Arab - Israeli Peace Process, 1967-1983.* Washington, D.C.: U.S. Government Printing Office, 1984. 145p.

4965. ____.Secretary of Defence. "Current Negotiations for Extension of U.S. Military Rights at Ibabran, Saudi Arabia, May 1947." In: *Records of the Joint Chiefs of Staff, Part II: 1946-1953: The Middle East.* Washington, D.C.: University Publications of America, 1979. Reel II. pp. 202-212.

B. VIETNAM WAR NEGOTIATIONS

1. Books

4966. Ashmore, Harry S., and William C. Baggs. *Mission to Hanoi: A Chronicle of Double-Dealing in High Places.* New York: Putnam, 1963. 369p.

4967. Cable, James. *The Geneva Conference of 1954 on Indochina.* New York: St. Martin's Press, 1986. 179p.

4968. Fifield, Russell H. *The Diplomacy of Southeast Asia: 1954-1958.* New York: Harper, 1958. 587p.

4969. Goodman, Allan E. *The Lost Peace: America's Search for A Negotiated Settlement of the Vietnam War.* Stanford, CA.: Hoover Institution Press, 1978. 298p.

4970. Kraslow, David, and Stuart H. Loory. *The Secret Search for Peace in Vietnam.* New York: Vintage, 1969. 247p.
4971. Porter, Gareth. *A Peace Denied: The United States, Vietnam, and the Paris Agreement.* Bloomington, IN.: Indiana University Press, 1975. 357p.
4972. Radványi, János. *Delusion and Reality: Gambits, Hoaxes and Diplomatic One-Upmanship in Vietnam.* South Bend, IN.: Gateway, 1978. 295p.
4973. Randle, Robert. *Geneva 1954: The Settlement of the Indochinese War.* Princeton, NJ.: Princeton University Press, 1969. 639p.
4974. _____. *Origins of Peace: A Study of Peace-Making and the Structure of Peace Settlements.* New York: Free Press, 1973. 550p.
4975. Thies, Wallace J. *When Governments Collide: Coercion and Diplomacy in the Vietnam Conflict, 1964-1968.* Berkeley: University of California Press, 1979. 446p.

2. Journal Articles

4976. Baral, J. K. "Paris Talks on Vietnam and American Diplomacy," *International Studies (India),* 14 (April-June 1975), 375-396.
4977. Browne, M. W. "Are Negotiations Possible? No." *War/Peace Report,* 7 (January 1967), 6-7.
4978. Burchett, Wilfred G. "Negotiations on Vietnam? How It Looks from the Other Side." *War/Peace Report,* 6 (November 1966), 3-5.
4979. _____. "The Paris Talks and the War." *Liberation,* 13:5 (1968), 29-31.
4980. _____. "Vietnam: One Year of the Peace Talks." *New World Review,* 37:2 (1969), 2-9.
4981. _____. "Why North Vietnam Rejects Unconditional Negotiations." *War/Peace Report,* 5 (December 1965), 7-9.
4982. Buttinger, Joseph. "Toward Peace at Paris?" *Dissent,* 16 (March/April 1969), 108-112.
4983. _____. "Can the Negotiations Bring Peace to Vietnam?" *Dissent,* (July/August 1968), 296-300.
4984. Coletta, Paolo E. "The Peace Negotiations and the Treaty of Paris." In: P.E. Coletta, ed. *Threshold to American Internationalism.* New York: Exposition Press, 1970. pp. 121-176.
4985. Cooper, C. L. "The Complexities of Negotiation." *Foreign Affairs,* 46:3 (1968), 454-466.
4986. Cousins, Norman. "Vietnam: The Spurned Peace." *Saturday Review,* 52 (July 16, 1969), 12-16.
4987. Devillers, Philippe. "The Paris Negotiations on Vietnam." *World Today,* 25:8 (1969), 339-350.
4988. Donnelly, Dorothy C. "A Settlement of Sorts: Henry Kissinger's Negotiations and America's Extrication from Vietnam." *Peace and Change,* 9:2-3 (Summer 1983), 55-79.
4989. Downs, Hunton. "Diplomacy: Saigon in Retrospect." *Ramparts,* 6 (December 1967), 12-19, 22.
4990. Draper, Theodore. "Vietnam: How Not to Negotiate: A Special Supplement." *New York Review of Books,* 8 (May 4, 1967), 17-29.
4991. Dubrow, Elbridge. "Negotiating with the Communists: Firmness is the Key." *Air Force and Space Digest,* 51:9 (1968), 48-52.
4992. Fall, Bernard B. "That Geneva Agreement: How the French Got Out of Vietnam." *New York Times Magazine,* (May 2, 1965), 28-29, 113-119.
4993. Gittings, John. "Vietnam: The Record of Proposals to Negotiate." *World Today (London),* 21 (December 1965), 503-506.

Case Studies

4994. Goodman, Allan E. "Diplomatic and Strategic Outcomes of the Conflict." *Peace Research Society (International) Papers*, 10 (1969), 115-125.
4995. Grinter, Lawrence E. "Bargaining Between Saigon and Washington: Dilemmas of Linkage Policies During War." *Orbis*, 18 (Fall 1974), 837-868.
4996. Halberstam, David. "Bargaining with Hanoi." *New Republic*, 159 (December 21, 1968), 15-17.
4997. ____. "Bargaining with Hanoi." *New Republic*, 158 (May 11, 1968), 14-16.
4998. Haney, Patrick J. "North Vietnam and Peace Negotiations." *China News Analysis*, 726 (September 20, 1968), 1-7.
4999. Hannon, John S. "A Political Settlement for Vietnam: The 1954 Geneva Conference and Its Current Implications." *Virginia Journal of International Law*, 8 (December 1967), 20-65.
5000. Hayden, Tom. "The Impasse in Paris." *Ramparts*, (August 27, 1968), 18-21.
5001. Herring, George C., and Richard H. Immerman. "Eisenhower, Dulles and Dienbienphu: 'The Way We Didn't Go to War' Revisited." *Journal of American History*, 71:2 (September 1984), 343-363.
5002. Hunter, R. E. "U.S. Dilemma on Vietnam Negotiations." *World Today*, 24 (May 1968), 173-176.
5003. Ikle, Fred C. "The Real Negotiations on South Vietnam." *Reporter*, 32 (June 3, 1965), 15-19.
5004. Joiner, C. A. "South Vietnam: The Politics of Peace." *Asian Survey*, 9 (February 1969), 138-155.
5005. Kahin, George M. "Impasse at Paris." *New Republic*, 159 (October 12, 1968), 23-26.
5006. ____. "Negotiations: The View from Hanoi." *New Republic*, 165 (November 6, 1971), 13-16.
5007. Kahn, Herman. "If Negotiations Fail." *Foreign Affairs*, 46:4 (1968), 627-641.
5008. Kissinger, Henry A. "Dr. Kissinger Discusses Status of Negotiations Toward Vietnam Peace - A Transcript of October 30 News Conference." *Department of State Bulletin*, 67 (November 13, 1972), 549-558.
5009. ____. "The Vietnam Negotiations." *Foreign Affairs*, 47:2 (1968), 211-234.
5010. Koch, K. F. "10th Anniversary of the Paris Table Talks Dilemma - Some Thoughts and an Experiment on the Management of Symbolic Conflicts through Negotiation." *Et Cetera*, 35:4 (1978), 383-397.
5011. Kraft, Joseph. "In Search of Kissinger." *Harper's*, (January 1971), 54-61.
5012. Lacouture, Jean. "How to Talk to Mr. Ho." *Ramparts*, 5 (October 1966), 42-46.
5013. Lieurance, Peter R. "Negotiation Now! The National Committee for a Political Settlement in Vietnam." In: D. S. Smith, ed. *From War to Peace: Essays in Peacemaking and War Termination*. New York: Columbia Press, 1974. pp. 171-201.
5014. McCullouch, Frank. "Peace Feelers: This Frail Dance of the Seven Veils." *Life*, 64 (March 22, 1968), 32-38.
5015. Morgenthau, Hans J. "Henry Kissinger, Secretary of State." *Encounter*, 3 (November 1974), 57-61.
5016. Mustafa, Zubeida. "The Paris Peace Talks." *Pakistan Horizon*, 22:1 (1969), 29-38.
5017. Nguyen, Van Ba. "Bases for a Valid Settlement." *Vietnamese Studies*, 18/19 (September 1968), 303-335.
5018. Nicolson, Nigel. "Diplomatic Initiative on Vietnam." *Listener*, 74 (July 22, 1965), 111-112, 142.
5019. Osborne, John. "Kissinger's Course." *New Republic*, 167 (November 11, 1972), 13-14.

5020. _____. "Vietnam Scoreboard: U.S. and North Vietnamese Proposals." *New Republic*, 166 (February 12, 1972), 10-12.
5021. Palmer, Joe M. "Political Initiatives on Vietnam." *Military Revie*, 46:9 (1966), 62-69.
5022. Radványi, János. "Vietnam War Diplomacy: Reflections of a Former Iron Curtain Official." *Parameters: Journal of the U.S. Army War College*, 10:3 (1980), 8-15.
5023. Rimalfo, Robert. "A Report on the Paris Peace Talks." *Journal of Contemporary Revolutions*, 3 (Winter 1970-71), 75-84.
5024. Roberts, Adam. "Hanoi's Offer to Talk." *World Affairs*, 24 (May 1968), 176-178.
5025. Roche, John P. "The Vietnam Negotiations: A Case Study in Communist Political Warfare." In: J. P. Roche, ed. *Sentenced to Life*. New York: Macmillan, 1974. pp. 108-131.
5026. Shapleau, Robert. "A Reporter at Large: the Peace Talks." *New Yorker*, 46 (October 17, 1970), 162.
5027. _____. "Seats at the Table." *New Yorker*, 44 (November 16, 1968), 193-206.
5028. _____. "Until the Chains Rot." *New Yorker*, 45 (July 5, 1969), 36-57.
5029. Swoly, J. M. Jr. "Peace Negotiations and President Johnson." *Minority of One*, 10:9 (1968), 10-12.
5030. Szulc, Tad. "Behind the Vietnam Ceasefire Agreement: How Kissinger Did It." *Foreign Policy*, 15 (Summer 1974), 21-69.
5031. Terrill, Ross. "Making Peace at Paris: A Special Report on the Negotiations." *Atlantic Monthly*, 222 (December 1968), 4-33.
5032. _____. "The Paris Negotiations." *Atlantic Monthly*, 223 (May 1969), 18-22.
5033. Thee, Marek. "Vietnam: The Subtle Art of Negotiations." *Bulletin of Peace Proposals*, 3:2 (1972), 163-171.
5034. Thies, Wallace J. "Searching for Peace: Vietnam and the Question of How Wars End." *Polity*, (Spring 1975), 304-333.
5035. Tombough, William W. "Some Thoughts on Negotiations with the North Vietnamese." *Forum*, 22 (Spring=Summer 1975), 49-58.
5036. Trager, F. N. "Back to Geneva '54? An Act of Political Folly!" *Vietnam Perspectives*, 1:1 (1965), 1-7.
5037. Tran, Van Dinh. "The Other Side of the Table." *Washington Monthly*, 1:1 (January 1970), 74-80.
5038. Wainwright, W. H. "The Paris Peace Talks: Diplomacy and Stagecraft." *Antioch Review*, 29:4 (1969), 505-514.
5039. Walker, Stephen G. "The Interface Between Beliefs and Behaviour: Henry Kissinger's Operational Code and the Vietnam War." *Journal of Conflict Resolution*, 21:1 (1977), 129-168.
5040. Williams, G. "America Seeks to Negotiate." *Contemporary Review*, 213 (August 1968), 84-88.
5041. Zartman, I. William. "Reality, Image and Detail: The Paris Negotiations, 1969-1973." In: W. Zartman, ed. *The 50% Solution*. Garden City, NY.: Anchor Press, 1976. pp. 372-398.
5042. Zasloff, Joseph J. "Laos 1972: The War, Politics and Peace Negotiations." *Asian Survey*, 13:1 (1973), 60-75.

3. Documents and Reports

5043. "Chronology of Negotiations Between the Royal Lao Government and the Communist Pathet Lao, July 20, 1954-August 15, 1957, (September 26, 1957). In: O.S.S./State Department Intelligence and Research Re *Japan, Korea, Southeast Asia, and the Far East Generally: 1950-1961 Supplement.* Washington, D.C.: University Publications of America, 1979. Reel VI. pp. 118-199.

5044. Critchley, Julian, and Betty Hunt. *The Vietnam War Negotiations.* London: World and School Crisis Papers, 1968.

5045. Dam, Nguyen Cao. *The Use of Verbal Influence Strategies in International Negotiations with Special Reference to the Vietnam Peace Talks in Paris, 1968-1973. A Study in Purposive Communication.* Ph.D. Dissertation. Minneapolis, MN.: University of Minnesota, 1977. 243p.

5046. Duff, Peggy. *The Credibility Gap: A Chronological Record of Attempts to Achieve a Political Solution Leading to Peace in Vietnam from 1954--1967.* London: International Confederation for Disarmament and Peace, 1967. 29p.

5047. Geipel, Gary. *U.S. and Vietnam: Negotiations During the Nixon Years.* PEW Case Studies, 337.0-G-88-C. New York: School of International and Public Affairs, Columbia University, 1988.

5048. Goodman, Allan E. *The Vietnam Negotiations, October-December, 1972.* Case Study Series. Washington, D.C.: School of Foreign Service, Georgetown University, 1987.

5049. Gurtov, Melvin. *Negotiations and Vietnam: A Case Study of the 1954 Geneva Conference. Part 2. A Fully Documented Account.* Santa Monica, CA.: RAND Co., 1968. 185p.

5050. Herring, George C., ed. *The Secret Diplomacy of the Vietnam War: The Negotiating Volumes of the Pentagon Papers.* Austin, TX.: University of Texas Press, 1983. 873p.

5051. Lawrence, Stewart. *U.S. Negotiations with South Vietnam, 1961.* PEW Case Studies, 338.0-G-88-C. New York: School of International and Public Affairs, Columbia University, 1988.

5052. Mark, Clyde R. "The Geneva Conference on Laos, 1961-62." In: *Major Studies of the Legislative Reference Service/Congressional Research Service.* Arlington, VA.: University Publications of America, 1975. Reel I; 19p.

5053. Thai, V. V. *Fighting and Negotiating in Vietnam: A Strategy.* RAND RM-5997-ARAA. Santa Monica, CA.: RAND Co., 1969. 82p.

5054. Thee, Marek, ed. *Vietnam Peace Proposals, Documents, 1954-1968.* Oslo: International Peace Research Institute, 1969.

5055. Thieu, Ton That. "Negotiation Strategy and Tactics of the Vietnamese Communists." In: *Negotiations in Asia. Three Case Studies: India - Iran - Vietnam.* Geneva: Centre for Applied Studies in International Negotiations, 1984. pp. 72-102.

5056. Thomas, John T. *Negotiating with the North Vietnamese: A Military Perspective.* Fort Leavenworth, KS.: Army Command and General Staff College, 1975. 134p.

5057. *Transcripts and Files of the Paris Peace Talks on Vietnam, 1968-1973.* Frederick, MD.: University Publication of America, 1982. 12 microfilm reels + guide.

5058. United States. Congress. House. *United States - Vietnam Relations, 1945-- 1967. Settlement of the Conflict, Book 12. Part VI. Parts A and B. Negotiations, 1965-67.* 92nd Cong., 1st sess. Washington, D.C.: U.S. Government Printing Office, 1971. 353p.
5059. ____.____.____.Committee on Foreign Affairs. *Selected Executive Session Hearings of the Committee 1951-56; Vol. XVII:U.S. Policy in the Far East, Part I: U.S. Policy and Japan; Korean War and Peace Negotiations.* Washington, D.C.: U.S. Government Printing Office, 1981. pp. 1-249.
5060. ____.____.Senate.Committee on Foreign Relations. *Briefing on Vietnam: Vietnam Conflict Combat Policies and Negotiation Policies: Review.* 91st Cong., 1st sess. Washington, D.C.: U.S. Government Printing Office, 1969. 167p.
5061. ____.____.____.____. *Vietnam and Paris Negotiations, Situation in Czechoslovakia and U.S. Forces in Europe: Report of Mike Mansfield.* 90th Cong., 2nd sess. Washington, D.C.: U.S. Government Printing Office, 1968. 60p.
5062. Waito, Robert. *Vietnam Peace Proposals.* Berkeley, CA.: World Without War Council, 1967. 52p.
5063. Zartman, I. William. "Power, Formula, Concession, Convergence: Alternative Hypothesis and Approaches to the Analysis of the Vietnam Negotiations." Paper Presented at the *17th Annual Convention of the International Studies Association,* held on February 25-29, 1976, in Toronto.
5064. Zagare, Frank C. "The Geneva Conference of 1954: A Case Study of Tacit Deception." *International Studies Quarterly,* 23 (September 1979), 390-411.

C. KOREAN NEGOTIATIONS

1. Books

5065. Cheng, Peter P. C. *Truce Negotiations Over Korea and Quemoy.* Washington, D.C.: University Press of America, 1977. 164p.
5066. Joy, C. Turner. *Negotiating While Fighting: The Diary of Admiral C. Turner Joy at the Korean Armistice Conference.* Stanford, CA.: Hoover Institution Press, 1978. 476p.
5067. Vatcher, William H. *Panmunjon: The Story of the Korean Military Armistice Negotiations.* Westport, CT.: Greenwood Press, 1958. 322p.

2. Journal Articles

5068. Bacchus, Wilfred A. "The Relationship between Combat and Peace Negotiations: Fighting While Talking in Korea, 1951-1953." *Orbis,* 17 (Summer 1973), 545-574.
5069. Gleysteen, William H. Jr. "Korea - A Special Target of American Concern." In: D. D. Newsom, ed. *The Diplomacy of Human Rights.* Lanham, MD.: University Press of America, 1986. pp. 85-100.
5070. Heo, Mane. "Peace Build-up on the Korean Peninsula: With Special Reference to "North-Diplomacy." *Korea and World Affairs,* 11:2 (Summer 1987), 286-303.
5071. Holmes, William D. "Communications in the DMZ." *Army Communicator,* 9:2 (Spring 1984), 52-55.

5072. Kihl, Y. W. "Conflict Issues in North-Korea South-Korea Negotiation - Analysis of Expert Generated Data. *International Journal of Group Tensions*, 7:1-2 (1977), 50-65.
5073. Kim, Hak-Joon. "Present and Future of the South-North Talks: As Viewed from Korea." *Korea and World Affairs*, 3:2 (Summer 1979), 209-222.
5074. Kindermann, Gottfried-Karl. "The New South-North Dialogue: As Viewed from Abroad." *Korea and World Affairs*, 3:2 (Summer 1979), 223-234.
5075. Lee, Ki-Tak. "Structure of Korean Partition and Problems of National Integration: The Phases and Logic of South-North Korea Negotiations." *Korea and World Affairs*, 6:2 (Summer 1982), 312-333.
5076. Rodenberg, Klaus. "South Korea's Past Experience with Dialogue and Its Unification Formula for the 1980s." *Korea and World Affairs*, 6:1 (Spring 1983), 96-111.
5077. Song, Jong-Hwan. "How the North Korean Communists Negotiate: A Case Study of the South-North Dialogue of the Early 1970s." *Korea and World Affairs*, 8:3 (Fall 1984), 610-664.
5078. "South-North Dialogue in Korea: Proposals for Reaching the Bargaining Table." *Korea and World Affairs*, 8:1 (1981), 161-171.
5079. Toner, James H. "Exceptional War, Exceptional Peace: The 1953 Cease-Fire in Korea." *Military Review*, 56:7 (1976), 3-13.

3. Documents and Reports

5080. *The 1954 Geneva Conference: Indo-China and Korea*. New York: Greenwood Press, 1968. 210p.
5081. Chung, Chong Wook. *Triangular Diplomacy and the Inter-Korean Dialogue*. Essays on Strategy and Diplomacy, 6. Claremont, CA.: The Keck Center for International Strategic Studies, 1986. 26p.
5082. Great Britain. Foreign Office. *Korea: A Summary of Developments in the Armistice Negotiations...* CMND 8793. London: H.M.S.O., 1952. 27p.
5083. Niksch, Larry A. "The Korean Armistice Negotiations." In: *Major Studies of the Legislative Reference Service/Congressional Research Service*. Arlington, VA.: University Publications of America, 1975. Reel 1; 18p.
5084. Probst, Reed R. *Negotiating with the North Koreans: The U.S. Experience at Panmunjon*. Carlisle Barracks, PA.: Army War College, 1977. 25p.
5085. "R.O.K./Japanese Negotiations and Prospects of Improved Relations, July 1953." In: O.S.S./State Department Intelligence and Research Reports. *Japan, Korea, Southeast Asia, and the Far East Generally: 1950-1961 Supplement*. Washington, D.C.: University Publications of America, 1979. Reel V. pp. 621-632.

D. JAPANESE NEGOTIATIONS

1. Books

5086. Blaker, Michael. *Japanese International Negotiating Style*. New York: Columbia University Press, 1977. 253p.
5087. Cohen, Bernard C. *The Political Process and Foreign Policy: The Making of the Japanese Peace Settlement*. Princeton, NJ.: Princeton University Press, 1957. 293p.
5088. Yoshitsu, Michael M. *Japan and the San Francisco Peace Settlement*. New York: Columbia University Press, 1982. 124p.

2. Journal Articles

5089. Abelson, Donald S. "Experiencing the Japanese Negotiating Style." In: D. B. Bendahmane and L. Moser, eds. *Toward a Better Understanding: U.S. - Japan Relations*. Washington, D.C.: Foreign Service Institute, 1986. pp. 39-42.
5090. Emmerson, J. K., and Michael Blaker. "Japanese International Negotiating Style." *Political Science Quarterly*, 93:2 (1978), 364-365.
5091. Glazer, Herbert. "Understanding Japanese Decision Making." In: D. B. Bendahmane and L. Moser, eds. *Toward a Better Understanding: U.S. - Japan Relations*. Washington, D.C.: Foreign Service Institute, 1986. pp. 39-42.
5092. Hahn, E. J. "Negotiating with the Japanese." *California Lawyer*, 2 (1982), 21-59.
5093. Holdsworth, Richard. "Japanese Peace Treaty Negotiations with the Soviet Union and China, January to April, 1975." *Millenium*, 5:1 (1976), 41-57.
5094. McCreary, Don R., and Robert A. Blanchfield. "The Art of Japanese Negotiation." In: N. Schweda Nicolson, ed. *Languages in International Perspective*. Norwood, NJ.: Ablex, 1986. pp. 301-350.
5095. Mushakoji, Kinhide. "The Strategies of Negotiation: An American-Japanese Comparison." In: J. A. Laponce, ed. *Experimentation and Simulation in Political Science*. Toronto: University of Toronto Press, 1972. pp. 109-131.
5096. _____. "The Cultural Premises of Japanese Diplomacy." *Trilateral Commission Papers: Social and Political Issues in Japan*, (1975), 17-29.
5097. Strazan, Marie D. "The San Francisco Peace Treaty: Cross-Cultural Elements in the Interaction between the Americans and the Japanese." In: R. P. Anand, ed. *Cultural Factors in International Relations*. New Delhi: Abhinav, 1981. pp. 63-76.
5098. Suttmeier, R. P. "Japanese Reactions to U.S. Nuclear Policy: The Domestic Origins of an International Negotiating Position." *Orbis*, 22:3 (1978), 651-680.
5099. Van de Velde, James R. "The Influence of Culture on Japanese-American Negotiations." *Fletcher Forum*, 7:2 (1983), 395-400.
5100. Wang, Robert S. "Talking Turkey with Tokyo: To Have Successful Discussions with the Japanese, the United States Must Pay More Attention to its Ally's Negotiating Style." *Foreign Service Journal*, 62 (November 1985), 34-37.

3. Documents and Reports

5101. Bendahmane, Diane B., and Leo Moser, eds. *Toward a Better Understanding: U.S.-Japan Relations*. Washington, D.C.: Foreign Service Institute, Center for the Study of Foreign Affairs, 1985. 142p.
5102. Blaker, Michael. *Patterns of Japan's International Negotiating Behavior Before World War II*. Ph.D. Dissertation. New York: Columbia University, 1973.
5103. Leng, Shoa-Chuan. *United States - Japanese Negotiations in 1941*. Ph.D. Dissertation. Philadelphia, PA.: University of Pennsylvania, 1950. 301p.
5104. McCreary, Don R. *Communicative Strategies in Japanese - American Negotiations*. Ph.D. Dissertation. Newark, DE.: University of Delaware, 1984. 211p.
5105. Murakami, Yoshio. *Japanese - American Negotiations, 1940-1941*. Ph.D. Dissertation. Medford, MA.: Fletcher School of Law and Diplomacy, 1965.

5106. Mushakoji, Kinhide. *The Strategies of Negotiation: An American - Japanese Comparison.* Tokyo: Sophia University, 1970. 42p.
5107. Ohno, K. *The Japanese Attempts to Negotiate Peace Between 1937-1945, and an Analysis of the Reasons for their Failure.* B. Litt. Oxford: St. Anthony's, 1960.
5108. Thayer, Nathaniel B., and Stephen E. Weiss. "Japan: The Changing Logic of a Former Minor Power." In: H. Binnendijk, ed. *National Negotiating Style.* Washington, D.C.: Foreign Service Institute, Centre for the Study of Foreign Affairs, 1987. pp. 45-74.
5109. Unterberg, Betty M., Irvine H. Anderson and James H. Herzog. *Closing the Open Door: American - Japanese Diplomatic Negotiations, 1936-1941.* Annapolis, MD.: U.S. Naval Institution Press, 1973. 235p.

E. CHINESE NEGOTIATIONS

1. Books

5110. Kapp, Robert A., ed. *Communicating with China.* Chicago, IL.: Intercultural Press, 1983. 80p.
5111. Lall, Arthur S. *How Communist China Negotiates.* New York: Columbia University Press, 1968. 291p.
5112. Lauren, Paul G., ed. *The China Hands' Legacy: Ethics and Diplomacy.* Boulder, CO.: Westview Press, 1987. 196p.
5113. Young, Kenneth T. *Negotiating with the Chinese Communists: The United States Experience, 1953-1967.* New York: McGraw-Hill, 1968. 461p.
5114. Yu, Peter K. *A Strategic Model of Chinese Checkers: Power and Exchange in Beijing's Interactions with Washington and Moscow.* New York: P. Lang, 1984. 221p.

2. Journal Articles

5115. Berris, Jan Carol. "The Art of Interpreting." In: R. A. Kapp, ed. *Communicating with China.* Chicago, IL.: Intercultural Press, 1983. pp. 41-59.
5116. Bloom, Alfred. "Linguistic Impediments to Cross-Cultural Communication: Chinese Hassles with the Hypothetical." *Journal of Peace Science,* 2:2 (1977), 205-214.
5117. Chan, Kenneth C. "The Anglo-Chinese Loan Negotiations (1941-1944): A Study of Britain's Relations with China During the Pacific War." *Paper on Far Eastern History,* 9 (1974), 101-135.
5118. Chang, David W. "A Case Study on Unconventional Diplomacy: The Republic of China's Relations with the U.S. and Other Western Nations." *Asian Forum,* 10:3 (1981), 1-26.
5119. Chang, Pao Min. "Beijing versus Hanoi: The Diplomacy over Kampuchea." *Asian Survey,* 23:5 (1983), 598-618.
5120. Chin, H. D. "The Use of International Law in Communist Chinese Treaty Negotiation and Implementation - 4 Case Studies with the United States." *Issues and Studies,* 20:2 (1984), 37-56.
5121. Copithorue, M. D. "The Settlement of International Claims Between Canada and China: A Status Report." *Pacific Affairs,* 48:2 (1975), 230-237.
5122. Dean, Arthur H. "What It Is Like to Negotiate with the Chinese." *New York Times Magazine,* (October 30, 1966), 44-46, 47, 49, 52, 54, 57, 59.

5123. Kazuo, Ogura. "How the 'Inscrutables' Negotiate with the 'Inscrutables': Chinese Negotiating Tactics vis-a-vis the Japanese." *China Quarterly*, (Summer 1979), 529-552.
5124. Klein, David H. "Chou En Lai - Henry Kissinger Talks: Continuity, Revolution and 'Pacific' Diplomacy." *Peace and Change*, 1 (Fall 1972), 63-66.
5125. Lien, Chan. "Negotiation in Communist China's Foreign Policy Toward the United States." *Issues and Studies*, 11:2 (1975), 27-49.
5126. Lubmann, Stanley B. "Negotiations in China: Observations of a Lawyer." In: R. A. Kapp, ed. *Communicating with China*. Chicago, IL.: Intercultural Press, 1983. pp. 59-70.
5127. Ross, Robert S. "International Bargaining and Domestic Politics: U.S.-China Relations Since 1972." *World Politics*, 38:2 (January 1986), 255-287.
5128. Schroeder, Paul E. "The Ohio-Hubei Agreement: Clues to Chinese Negotiating Practices." *China Quarterly*, 91 (1982), 486-491.
5129. Scott, Gary L., and Takashi Shinobu. "Reassessing the Japan-China Peace and Friendship Treaty Negotiations: A Comparative Foreign Policy Perspective." *Journal of Northeast Asia Studies*, 2:4 (1983), 51-68.
5130. Shenkar, O., and S. Ronen. "The Cultural Context of Negotiations: the Implications of Chinese Interpersonal Norms." *Journal of Applied Behavioral Science*, 23:2 (1987), 263-275.
5131. Solomon, Richard H. "China: Friendship and Obligation in Chinese Negotiating Style." In: H. Binnendijk, ed. *National Negotiating Styles*. Washington, D.C.: Foreign Service Institute, Center for the Study of Foreign Affairs, 1987. pp. 1-16.
5132. Stuart, Douglas T., and William T. Tow. "China's New Diplomacy: The New European Connection." *NATO Review*, 28:1 (1980), 25-29.
5133. Thompson, James C. "China's New Diplomacy: A Symposium." *Problems of Communism*, 21:1 (January - February 1972), 48-70.
5134. Wang, Jen-Huong. "Some Cultural Factors Affecting Chinese in Treaty Negotiation." In: R. P. Anand, ed. *Cultural Factors in International Relations*. New Delhi: Abhinav, 1981. pp. 97-112.
5135. Wang, Yu. "The Maoist 'Peace Talks' - Chinese Experience in Negotiating with the C.C.P." *Issues and Studies*, 8:5 (1972), 50-63.
5136. Weiss, J. "The Negotiating Style of the People's-Republic-of-China - The Future of Hong-Kong and Macao." *Journal of Social Political and Economic Studies*, 13:2 (Summer 1988), 175-194.
5137. White, Nathan. "People's Diplomacy: Its Use by China to Influence Japan, 1949-1976." *Contemporary China*, 3:3 (1979), 24-40.
5138. Whiting, Allen S. "Conflict Resolution in the Sino-Soviet Alliance." In: K. London, ed. *Unity and Cooperation: Major Aspects of Sino-Soviet Relations*." New York: Praeger, 1962. pp. 375-391.
5139. Yin, Ching-Yao. "On Communist Negotiations." *Issues and Studies (Taiwan)*, 16:2 (1980), 13-29.
5140. Young, Kenneth T. "Comparative Approaches to Negotiations with the People's Republic of China." *American Journal of International Law*, 66:4 (1972), 108-121.
5141. Yu, George T. "Peking's African Diplomacy." *Problems of Communism*, 21:2 (March - April 1972), 16-24.

3. Documents and Reports

5142. Bernstein, Thomas P. *Negotiations to Normalize U.S. - China Relations, 1978.* PEW Case Studies, 426.0-G-88-C. New York: School of International and Public Affairs, Columbia University, 1988.
5143. Brenner, Michael J. *The U.S./China Bilateral Accord.* PEW Case Study Series 106.0-G-87-P. Pittsburgh, PA.: Graduate School of Public and International Affairs, University of Pittsburgh, 1987.
5144. Byrnes, Robert F. "When the Academic Door to Peking Opens." In: U.S. Congress. Senate. Committee on Government Operations. Subcommittee on National Security and International Operations. *International Negotiations.* 91st Cong., 2nd sess. Washington, D.C. U.S. Government Printing Office, 1870. 30p.
5145. Carde, Freeland H. III. *The Making of Chinese Foreign Policy: Action and Processes.* Ph.D. Dissertation. Monterey, CA.: Naval Postgraduate School, 1979. 219p.
5146. Chang, Jaw-ling Joanne. *Peking's Negotiating Style: A Case Study of U.S. - PRC Normalization.* Occasional Paper No. 5. Baltimore, MD.: School of Law, University of Maryland, 1985. 22p.
5147. "Communist China's "People's Diplomacy" January 1955 through June 1956." [February 7, 1957]. In: O.S.S./State Department Intelligence and Research Department. *China and India 1950-1961 Supplement.* Washington, D.C.: University Publications of America, 1979. 261p.
5148. Freeman, Charles W. Jr. *Notes on Chinese Negotiating Styles.* Cambridge, MA.: East Asian Legal Studies, Harvard Law School, 1975.
5149. Reardon-Anderson, James. *U.S.-China Agreement on Peaceful Nuclear Cooperation.* PEW Case Studies, 110.0-G-87-G. Washington, D.C.: School of Foreign Service, Georgetown University Press, 1987.
5150. Scalopino, Robert A., and Allen S. Whiting. "Communist Chinese Attitudes Toward Negotiating with U.S." In: U.S. Congress. House. Committee on Foreign Affairs. Subcommittee on Asian and Pacific Affairs. *United States-China Relations: A Strategy for the Future: Hearings.* 91st Cong., 2nd sess. Washington, D.C.: U.S. Government Printing Office, 1970. pp. 178-182.
5151. Stanisland, Martin. *Negotiations Between the United Kingdom and the People's Republic of China over the Future Status of Hong Kong, 1982-1984.* PEW Case Studies, 411.0-G-88-P. Pittsburgh, PA.: Graduate School of Public and International Affairs, 1988.
5152. Solomon, Richard H. *Chinese Political Negotiating Behaviour: A Briefing Analysis.* RAND R-3295. Santa Monica, CA.: RAND Corporation, 1985. 31p.
5153. United States. Congress. Senate. Committee on Government Operations. *International Negotiations: When the Academic Door to Peking Opens: Memo by Robert F. Byrnes.* 91st Cong., 2nd sess. Washington, D.C.: U.S. Government Printing Office, 1970. 30p.
5154. ____.____.____.____.Subcommittee on National Security and International Operations. *Peking's Approach to Negotiation: Selected Writings.* 91st Cong., 1st sess. Washington, D.C.: U.S. Government Printing Office, 1969. 94p.
5155. Weakland, John H. *Chinese Communist Patterns of Strategy and Negotiation.* TR-6. Palo Alto, CA.: Mental Research Institute, 1970. 47p.
5156. Wilhelm, Alfred D. *Sino - American Negotiations: The Chinese Approach.* Ph.D. Dissertation. Lawrence, KA.: University of Kansas, 1986. 336p.

5157. Wolverton, George D. *The Meetings at the Ambassadorial Level Between the Governments of the People's Republic of China and the United States as a Form of Diplomacy.* M.A. Thesis. Fullerton, CA.: California State University at Fullerton, 1969. 130p.

5158. Wu, Fu Mei Chiu. *The China Policy of Richard M. Nixon: From Confrontation to Negotiation.* Ph.D. Dissertation. Salt Lake City, UT.: University of Utah, 1976. 259p.

5159. Yin, Ching-Yao. *Negotiations in an Era of Negotiation.* Pamphlet No. 171. Taipei: Asia Peoples Anti-Communist League, 1973. 69p.

5160. Young, Kenneth T. *Diplomacy and Power in Washington-Peking Dealings: 1953-1967.* Chicago, IL.: University of Chicago. Centre for Policy Studies, 1967. 42p.

F. AFRICAN NEGOTIATIONS

1. Books

5161. Davidow, Jeffrey. *A Peace in Southern Africa: The Lancaster House Conference on Rhodesia.* Boulder, CO.: Westview Press, 1984. 143p.

5162. Goldenhuys, Deon. *The Diplomacy of Isolation: South African Foreign Policy Making.* Johannesburg: Macmillan South Africa, 1984. 295p.

5163. Hoskyns, Catherine, ed. *Case Studies in African Diplomacy: The Ethiopia--Somalia-Kenya Dispute 1960-67.* Nairobi: Oxford University Press, 1969. 91p.

5164. Makinda, Samuel M. *Superpower Diplomacy in the Horn of Africa.* London: Croom Helm, 1987. 241p.

5165. McKay, Vernon, ed. *African Diplomacy: Studies in the Determinants of Foreign Policy.* London: Pall Mall Press, 1966. 210p.

5166. Verrier, Anthony. *The Road to Zimbabwe: 1890-1980.* London: Cape, 1986. 364p.

5167. Wiseman, Harry, and Alastair M. Taylor. *From Rhodesia to Zimbabwe: The Politics of Transition.* New York: Pergamon Press, 1981. 170p.

5168. Zartman, I. William. *Ripe for Resolution: Conflict and Intervention in Africa.* Oxford: Oxford University Press, 1985. 260p.

2. Journal Articles

5169. Austin, D. "A South-African Policy - 6 Percepts in Search of a Diplomacy." *International Affairs,* 62:3 (1986), 391-403.

5170. Blake, Cecil A. "Developing Diplomatic Communication Models and Strategies for Africa: Some Key Issues." *Journal of Black Studies,* 14:3 (March 1984), 267-293.

5171. Fisher, Roger D. "Negotiating South Africa's Future." *Negotiating Journal,* 3:3 (July 1987), 231-234.

5172. _____. "The Power of Looking at Their Choice: The South African Case." *Negotiation Journal,* 2:2 (April 1986), 129-133.

5173. Libby, Ronald T. "Anglo-American Diplomacy and the Rhodesian Settlement: A Loss of Impetus." *Orbis,* 23:1 (1979), 185-212.

5174. Matthews, R. D. "Talking Without Negotiating - The Case of Rhodesia." *International Journal,* (1980), 91-117.

5175. Mayall, J. "Battle for the Horn - Somali Irredentism and International Diplomacy." *World Today,* 34:9 (1978), 336-345.

5176. Minter, W., and E. Schmidt. "When Sanctions Worked - The Case of Rhodesia Reexamined." *African Affairs*, 87:347 (1988), 207-237.
5177. Redekop, Clarence G. "The Limits of Diplomacy: The Case of Namibia." *International Journal*, 35:1 (1980), 70-90.
5178. Richardson, H. J. "Constitutive Questions in the Negotiations for Namibian Independence." *American Journal of International Law*, 78:1 (1984), 76-120.
5179. Rothschild, David. "Racial Stratification and Bargaining: The Kenya Experience." In: I. W. Zartman, ed. *The 50% Solution.* Garden City, NY.: Doubleday, 1976. pp. 235-254.
5180. Shaw, Malcolm. "Dispute Settlement in Africa." *Yearbook of World Affairs*, 37 (1983), 149-167.
5181. Soames, Christopher. "Rhodesia to Zimbabwe." *International Affairs*, (Summer 1980), 405-419.
5182. "South Africa: The View from the Embassy/Pretoria: An Interview with Ambassador William B. Edmondson." In: D. P. Newsom, ed. *The Diplomacy of Human Rights.* Lanham, MD.: University Press of America, 1986. pp. 141-166.
5183. Van der Merwe, Hendrik W. "Prospects for Negotiation in South Africa." In: *Southern Africa: Prospects for Peace and Security.* New York: International Peace Academy, 1987. pp. 157-174.
5184. Zartman, I. William. "Issues in African Diplomacy in the 1980s." *Orbis*, 25:4 (Winter 1982), 1025-1043.
5185. _____. "The Moroccan - American Base Negotiations." *Middle East Journal*, 18:1 (1964), 27-40.

3. Documents and Reports

5186. Branaman, Brenda M. "Namibia: U.N. Negotiations for Independence and U.S. Interests." In: *Major Studies and Issue Briefs of the Congressional Research Service, 1980-81 Supplement.* Frederick, MD.: University Publications of America, 1981. Reel VII. pp. 815-835.
5187. _____. "Namibia: United Nations Negotiations for Independence/U.S. Interests." In: *Major Studies and Issue Briefs of the Congressional Research Service, 1984-1985 Supplement.* Frederick, MD.: University Publications of America, 1985. Reel VIII; pp. 0131-0154.
5188. Culora, Thomas J. *Conflict Resolution: A Comparative Analysis of Three African Studies.* M.A. Thesis. Monterey, CA.: Naval Postgraduate School, 1986. 197p.
5189. D'Amato, James V. "Coercive Bargaining and its Role in the Rhodesian Peace Process." Paper. Presented at the *22nd Annual Convention of the International Studies Association*, held on March 18-21, 1981, in Philadelphia, PA.
5190. Davidow, Jeffrey. *Dealing with International Crises: Lessons from Zimbabwe.* Occasional Paper No. 34. Muscatine, IA.: The Stanley Foundation, 1983. 23p.
5191. Falk, Pamela S. *The U.S., U.S.S.R., and Cuba in Angola: Superpower Negotiations and U.S. Policy in Southern Africa, 1974-1987; Part A: Negotiator's Nightmare; Diplomat's Dilemma.* PEW Case Studies, 405.0-C-87-C. New York: School of International and Public Affairs, Columbia University, 1987.

5192. Galaydh, Ali Khalif. *Intragovernmental Negotiation: Soviet - Somali Relations and the Ogaden War, 1978-79.* New York: International Peace Academy, 1986. 41p.
5193. Great Britain. Foreign and Commonwealth Office. *A History of the Namibia Negotiations to 1981.* (Foreign Policy Documents; 87). (1983), (1 microfiche).
5194. Nzomo, Maria. "What is Wrong with the Present Negotiations? " Paper Presented at the *Women's International Peace Conference,* held on June 5-9, 1985, at Mount St. Vincent.
5195. Pangalis, Celia S., and Ali Khalif Galaydh. *Zanaka and Lugbala Simulation.* PEW Case Studies, 112.0-C-87-I. New York: International Peace Academy, 1987.
5196. Rikhye, Bhalinder. *Negotiating the End of Conflicts II: Namibia and Zimbabwe: Report of IPA's November 1979 and April 1980 Conference.* New York: International Peace Academy, 1980. 128p.
5197. Stedman, Stephen. *Henry Kissinger and the Geneva Conference on Rhodesia.* PEW Case Studies, 329.0-C-88-S. Los Angeles, CA.: School of International Relations, University of Southern California, 1988.
5198. United States. Congress. House. Committee on Foreign Affairs. Subcommittee on Africa. *Angola: Intervention or Negotiation: Hearings.* 99th Cong., 1st sess. Washington, D.C.: U.S. Government Printing Office, 1985. 200p.
5199. Zartman, I. William. "Negotiation, Intervention and Crisis Management in Africa." Paper Presented at the *20th Annual Convention of the International Studies Association,* held on March 21-24, 1979, in Toronto.

G. LATIN AMERICAN NEGOTIATIONS

1. Books

5200. Bagley, Bruce M., ed. *Contadora and the Diplomacy of Peace in Central America: Vol. I: The United States, Central America and Contadora.* Boulder, CO.: Westview Press, 1987. 275p.
5201. _____., ed. *Contadora and Diplomacy of Peace in Central America: Vol. 2: The Contadora Process.* Boulder, CO.: Westview Press, 1987. 288p.
5202. Furlong, William L., and Margaret E. Scranton. *The Dynamics of Foreign Policy Making: The President, The Congress and the Panama Canal Treaties.* Boulder, CO.: Westview Press, 1984. 263p.
5203. Garner, William R. *The Chaco Dispute: A Study of Prestige Diplomacy.* Washington, D.C.: Public Affairs Press, 1966. 151p.
5204. Jorden, William J. *Panama Canal Odyssey.* Austin, TX.: University of Texas Press, 1984. 746p.
5205. Lamborn, Alac C., and Stephen P. Mumme. *Statecraft, Domestic Politics, and Foreign Policy Making: The EL Chamizai Dispute.* Boulder, CO.: Westview Press, 1988. 200p.
5206. Metford, J. C. J. *The Struggle for the Falkland Islands: A Study in Legal and Diplomatic History.* New Haven, CT.: Yale University Press, 1982. 482p.
5207. Slater, Jerome. *Intervention and Negotiation: The United States and the Dominican Revolution.* New York: Harper & Row, 1970. 254p.

2. Journal Articles

5208. "Argentina - Chile: Negotiation and Conclusion of Border Dispute Agreement." *International Legal Materials,* 24 (January 1985), 1-31.
5209. Axline, W. A. "Integration and Development in Commonwealth Caribbean - Politics of Regional Negotiations." *International Organization,* 32:4 (1978), 953-973.
5210. Bagley, Bruce M. "Contadora; The Failure of Diplomacy." *Journal of Inter-American Studies and World Affairs,* 28:3 (fall 1986), 1-32.
5211. Bunker, Ellsworth. "New Panama Canal Treaties: A Negotiator's View." *Department of State Bulletin,* 77:1999 (October 17, 1977), 506-509.
5212. Charlton, M. L. "Making of United States Policy Toward Panama Canal Treaty Negotiations, 1964-1976." *Journal of International Affairs,* 32:1 (1978), 135-138.
5213. Child, Jack. "War in the South Atlantic." In: J. D. Martz, ed. *United States Policy in Latin America.* Lincoln, NB.: University of Nebraska Press, 1988. pp. 202-236.
5214. Claude, Inis L. "The Use of the United Nations in the Falkland Crisis." *Global Perspectives,* 1:1 (Spring 1983), 64-71.
5215. De Hoyos, Ruben. "Islas Malvinas or Falkland Islands: The Negotiation of a Conflict, 1945-1982." In: M. A. Morris and V. Millan, eds. *Controlling Latin American Conflicts.* Boulder, CO.: Westview Press, 1983. pp. 185-198.
5216. De Shazo, F. A. "The Inter-American Peace Committee as an Instrument for the Pacific Settlement of Disputes." *International Review of History and Political Science,* 7:4 (November 1970), 1-36.
5217. Dickson, H. M. "Negotiation and Cooperation as a Strategy for Development in the Caribbean Basin." In: J. Child, ed. *Conflict in Central America.* New York: St. Martins Press, 1986. pp. 132-141.
5218. Flood, Patrick J. "U.S. Human Rights Initiatives Concerning Argentina." In: D. D. Newsom, ed. *The Diplomacy of Human Rights.* Lanham, MD.: University Press of America, 1986. pp. 129-140.
5219. Garrett, James C. "The Beagle Channel Dispute: Confrontation and Negotiation in the Southern Cone." *Journal of Inter-American Studies and World Affairs,* 27:3 (Fall 1985), 81-109.
5220. Grayson, George W. "Mexico: A Love-Hate Relationship with North America." In: H. Binnendijk, ed. *National Negotiating Style.* Washington, D.C.: Foreign Service Institute, Centre for the Study of Foreign Affairs, 1987. pp. 125-147.
5221. Holsti, Ole R., Richard A. Brody and Robert C. North. "Measuring Affect and Action: The 1962 Cuban Crisis." In: I. W. Zartman, ed. *The 50% Solution.* Garden City, NY.: Anchor Press, 1976. pp. 261-287.
5222. Kryzanek, Michael J. "The Dominican Intervention Revisited: An Attitudinal and Operational Analysis." In: J. D. Martz, ed. *United State Policy in Latin America.* Lincoln, NB.: University of Nebraska Press, 1988. pp. 135-156.
5223. Lad, Richard L. "Dilemma over Panama: Negotiation of the Thompson-Unutia Treaty." *Mid-America,* 61:1 (1979), 35-45.
5224. Lopez, Guerara, and Carlos Alfredo. "Negotiating a Peaceful Solution to the Panama Canal Question." *New York University Journal of International Law and Politics,* (Spring 1976), 3-14.
5225. McEachrane Dickson, Helen. "Negotiation and Cooperation as a Strategy for Development in the Caribbean Basin." In: J. Child, ed. *Conflict in Central America.* London: Hurst, 1986. pp. 132-141.

5226. Merritt, Jeffrey D. "The Ford Administration Response to Human Rights Violations in Brazil." In: D. D. Newsom, ed. *The Diplomacy of Human Rights*. Lanham, MD.: University Press of America, 1986. pp. 111-128.

5227. Neimeier, J. G. "Panama as I See It." *United States Naval Institute Proceedings*, 103:1 (1977), 35-42.

5228. Osborne, Alfred I. Jr. "On the Economic Cost to Panama of Negotiating a Peaceful Solution to the Panama Canal Question." *Journal of Inter-American Studies and World Affairs*, 19:4 (1977), 509-521.

5229. Parsons, Anthony. "The Falklands Crisis in the United Nations, 31 March - 14 June 1982." *International Affairs*, 59:2 (Spring 1983), 169-178.

5230. Ropp, Steven C. "Negotiating the 1978 Panama Canal Treaties: Contending Theoretical Perspectives." In: J. D. Martz, ed. *United States Policy in Latin America*. Lincoln, NB.: University of Nebraska Press, 1988. pp. 175-201.

5231. Rosenfeld, Stephen S. "The Panama Negotiations - A Close Run Thing." *Foreign Affairs*, 54:1 (October 1975), 5-6.

5232. Segal, Aron. "Dance and Diplomacy: The Cuban National Ballet." *Caribbean Studies*, 9:1 (1980), 30-32.

5233. Smith, Wayne S. "Dateline Havana: Myopic Diplomacy." *Foreign Policy*, 48 (Fall 1982), 157-174.

5234. Stemplowski, Ryszard. "Latin America, the United States, and Diplomacy: New Books, Old Problems." *Latin American Research Review*, 15:1 (1980), 206-210.

5235. "U.S. and Panama Agree on Principles for Canal Negotiations." *Department of State Bulletin*, 70 (February 25, 1974), 184-185.

5236. Valero, Ricardo. "Contadora: The Search for Peace in Central America." *Washington Quarterly*, 9:3 (Summer 1986), 19-32.

5237. Wilson, Larman C. "The Settlement of Boundary Disputes: Mexico, the United States, and the International Boundary Commission." *International and Comparative Law Journal*, 29 (January 1980), 38-53.

5238. Windsor, Philip. "Diplomatic Dimensions of the Falkland Crisis." *Millennium: Journal of International Studies*, 12:1 (1983), 88-96.

5239. Wohlstetter, Albert, and Roberta Wohlstetter. "Case Study: Controlling the Risks in Cuba." In: L. B. Miller, ed. *Dynamics of World Politics*. Englewood Cliffs, NJ.: Prentice-Hall, 1968. pp. 62-97.

5240. Zinser, Adolfo Aquilar. "Obstacles to Negotiated Peace in the Region." In: J. Child, ed. *Conflict in Central America*. London: C. Hurst and Co., 1986. pp. 55-68.

5241. _____. "Negotiation in Conflict - Central America and Contadora." In: N. Hamilton, et al. *Crisis in Central America*. Boulder, CO.: Westview Press, 1988. pp. 97-118.

3. Documents and Reports

5242. Bagley, Bruce M., and Juan Gabriel Tokatlian. *Contadora: The Limits of Negotiations*. PEW Case Studies, 309.0-E-87-J. Washington, D.C.: School of Advanced International Studies, Johns Hopkins University, 1987.

5243. Barros, Jose Miguel. *Chilean - Argentine Relations: The Beagle Channel Controversy*. 2nd ed. Geneva: (Government of Chile), 1979.

5244. Burns, Robert A. *Diplomacy, War and Parliamentary Democracy: Further Lessons from the Falklands or Advice from Academe*. Lanham, MD.: University Press of America, 1985. 52p.

5245. Chalmers, Douglas. *United States and Anastasio Somoza.* PEW Case Studies, 105.0-E-87-C. New York: School of International and public Affairs, University of Columbia, 1987.
5246. Child, Jack, ed. *Regional Cooperation for Development and the Peaceful Settlement of Disputes in Latin America.* New York: International Peace Academy, 1987. 151p.
5247. De Wind, Adrian. *U.S. and Haiti: Encouragement of Stability and Democracy in a Third World Country.* PEW Case Studies, 427.0-E-88-C. New York: School of International and Public Affairs, Columbia University, 1988.
5248. Downs, Charles. *Negotiating Development Assistance Implementation: USAID and the Choice Between Public and Private Agencies in the Case of Haiti.* PEW Case Studies, 207.0-E-88-C. New York: School of International and Public Affairs, Columbia University, 1988.
5249. Fontaine, Roger W. *On Negotiating with Cuba.* Foreign Affairs Studies 28. Washington, D.C.: American Enterprise Institute for Public Policy Research, 1975. 99p.
5250. Gordenker, Leon. *Human Rights in Chile.* PEW Case Studies, 408.0-E-87-I. New York: International Peace Academy, 1987.
5251. Great Britain. *The Falkland Islands: Negotiations for a Peaceful Settlement.* White Paper. London: H.M.S.O., 1982.
5252. Gustafson, Lowell S. *The Sovereignty Dispute over the Falkland (Malvinas) Islands.* Ph.D. Dissertation. Charlottesville, VA.: University of Virginia, 1984. 415p.
5253. Habeeb, William M., and I. William Zartman. *The Panama Canal Negotiations.* Case Studies, no. 1. Washington, D.C.: Johns Hopkins Foreign Policy Institute, 1986.
5254. Horelick, Arnold L. *The Cuban Missile Crisis: An Analysis of Soviet Calculations and Behavior.* Santa Barbara, CA.: RAND Corp., 1963. 60p.
5255. Hybel, Alex R. *United States and Nicaragua: Anatomy of a Failed Negotiation for Regime Change, 1978-1979.* PEW Case Studies, 327.0-E-88-S. Los Angeles, CA.: School of International Relations, University of Southern California, 1988.
5256. Jacobini, H. B. "Settlement of the Chamizal Tract Dispute." Paper Presented at the *17th Annual Convention of the International Studies Association*, held on February 25-29, 1976, in Toronto.
5257. Jenks, Carl M. *The Structure of Diplomacy: An Analysis of Brazilian Foreign Relations in the Twentieth Century.* Ph.D. Dissertation. Durham, NC.: Duke University, 1979. 317p.
5258. Lowenthal, Abraham, and Pamela Starr. *United States and the Cuban Revolution, 1958-1960.* PEW Case Studies, 328.0-E-88-S. Los Angeles, CA.: School of International Relations, University of Southern California, 1988.
5259. McCreary, Scott, and Francisco Szekely. *Applying the Principles of Environmental Dispute Resolution to International Transboundary Conflicts: The Case of a U.S. - Mexico Border Environmental Issue.* Working Paper Series 5. Cambridge, MA.: The Program on the Processes of International Negotiations, American Academy of Arts and Sciences, 1987. 41p.
5260. Naughton, William A. *Panama Versus the United States: A Case Study in Small State Diplomacy.* Ph.D. Dissertation. Washington, D.C.: The American University Press, 1972. 367p.
5261. North, Lisa, Steven Baranyi and Julie Leonard. *Measures for Peace in Central America.* Ottawa, Ont.: The Canadian Institute for International Peace and Security, 1987. 76p.

5262. _____. *Negotiations for Peace in Central Amrica: A Conference Report: Proceedings of the Round Table on Negotiations for Peace in Central America, Ottawa, September 27-8, 1985.* Ottawa, Ont.: Canadian Institute for International Peace and Security, 1985. 59p.

5263. Petrash, Vilma, and Martin Stanisland. *Arias Initiative and Peace Negotiations in Central America, 1987-1988.* PEW Case Studies, 314.0-E-88-P. Pittsburgh, PA.: Graduate School of Public and International Affairs, University of Pittsburgh, 1988.

5264. Raiffa, Howard, and Tom Princen. *The Beagle Channel Dispute.* PEW Case Studies, 401.0-E-87-H. Cambridge, MA.: Kennedy School of Government, Harvard University, 1987.

5265. Rivas-Gallant, Ernesto, et al. *Negotiating with Marxists in Central America.* New York: CAUSA Publications, 1985.

5266. Roett, Riordan, and Frank Smyth. *Dialogue and Armed Conflict: Negotiating the Civil War in El Salvador.* PEW Case Studies, 321.0-E-88-J. Washington, D.C.: School of Advanced International Studies, Johns Hopkins University, 1988.

5267. Scranton, Margaret E. *Changing United States Foreign Policy: Negotiating New Panama Canal Treaties, 1958-1978.* Ph.D. Dissertation. Pittsburgh, PA.: University of Pittsburgh, 1980.

5268. Sims, Harold, et al. *Contadora Group and Negotiations for Peace in Central America, 1983-1984.* PEW Case Studies, 410.0-E-88-P. Pittsburgh, PA.: Graduate School of Public and International Affairs, University of Pittsburgh, 1988.

5269. Treverton, Gregory, and Donald Lippincott. *Negotiations Concerning the Falklands/Malvinas Dispute (A) - Breakdown of Negotiations.* PEW Case Studies, 406.0-E-87-H. Cambridge, MA.: Kennedy School of Government, Harvard University, 1987.

5270. _____. _____. *Negotiations Concerning the Falklands/Malvinas Dispute (B): The Haig Mediation Effort.* PEW Case Studies, 406.0-E-87-H. Cambridge, MA.: Kennedy School of Government, Harvard University, 1987.

5271. Tyler, M. *Dreams to Ashes: The Negotiation and Conclusion of the ANZUS Pact, 1947-1952.* M.A. Thesis. Keele, England: University of Keele, 1983.

5272. Wilson, Larman C. "U.S. - Mexican Boundary Disputes." Paper Presented at the *17th Annual Convention of the International Studies Association,* held on February 25-29, 1976, in Toronto.

H. CANADA - U.S. NEGOTIATIONS

1. Books

5273. Chacko, C. J. *The International Joint Commission Between the United States and the Dominion of Canada.* New York: AMS Press, 1968. 431p.

5274. Corbett, P. E. *The Settlement of Canadian-American Disputes: A Critical Study of Methods and Results.* New Haven, CT.: Yale University Press, 1937. 134p.

5275. Savelle, Max. *The Diplomatic History of the Canadian Boundary, 1749-1763.* New Haven, CT.: Yale University Press, 1940. 172p.

5276. Swainson, Neil A. *Conflict Over the Columbia: The Canadian Background to an Historic Treaty.* Montreal: McGill-Queen's University Press, 1979. 476p.

2. Journal Articles

5277. Cooper, Catharine A. "The Management of International Environmental Disputes in the Context of Canada-United States Relations: A Survey and Evaluation of Techniques and Mechanisms." In: *The Canadian Yearbook of International Law, 1986.* Vancouver, B.C.: University of British Columbia, 1987. pp. 247-311.
5278. Holsti, K. J., and Thomas A. Levy. "Bilateral Institutions and Transgovernmental Relations Between Canada and the Unites States." In: A. B. Fox, A. O. Hero, and J. S. Nye, eds. *Canada and the United States: Transnational and Transgovernmental Relations.* New York: Columbia University Press, 1976. pp. 283-309.
5279. Jockel, Joseph T. "The Canada-United States Relationship after the Third Round: The Emergence of Semi-Institutionalized Management." *International Journal,* 40:4 (1985), 689-715.
5280. Kim, Jackie K., and Marion E. Marts. "The Skagit-High Ross Dam Controversy: Negotiation and Settlement." *Natural Resources Journal,* 26:2 (Spring 1986), 261-290.
5281. Le Marquand, David G. "Preconditions to Cooperation in Canada-United States Boundary Waters." *Natural Resources Journal,* 26:2 (Spring 1986), 221-242.
5282. Roberts, John. "The Diplomacy of Acid Rain: The North American Experience in Global Perspective." In: A. K. Henrikson, ed. *Negotiating World Order.* Wilmington, DE.: Scholarly Resources, 1986. pp. 19-32.
5283. Sadler, Barry. "The Management of Canada-U.S. Boundary Waters: Retrospect and Prospect." *Natural Resources Journal,* 26:2 (Spring 1986), 359-376.
5284. Sewell, W. R. D., and Albert E. Utton. "'Getting to Yes' in United States-Canadian Water Disputes." *Natural Resources Journal,* 26:2 (Spring 1986), 201-206.
5285. Sullivan, J. L. "Beyond the Bargaining Table - Canada's Use of Section 115 of the United States Clean Air Act Prevent Acid-Rain." *Cornell International Law Journal,* 16:1 (1983), 193-227.
5286. Swainson, Neil A. "The Columbia River Treaty - Where Do We Go From Here?" *Natural Resources Journal,* 26:2 (Spring 1986), 243-260.

3. Documents and Reports

5287. Bilder, Richard B. *When Neighbors Quarrel: Canada-U.S. Dispute Settlement Experience.* DPRP Working Paper 8-4. Madison, WI.: Disputes Processing Research Program, University of Wisconsin, 1987. 95p.
5288. Clute, Robert. "Why Negotiations Sometimes Fail: A Study of US - Canadian Arbitrations." Paper Presented at the *17th Annual Convention of the International Studies Association,* held on February 25-27, 1976, in Toronto.
5289. Munton, Don. "Conflict Management in Canada-U.S. Relations." Paper Presented at the *11th World Congress of the International Political Science Association,* held on August 12-18, 1979, in Moscow.
5290. Sonto, Maior J. *The Analysis of Complex Decision-Making: Negotiation of the Saint John River Basin Agreement (Canada-U.S.A.).* Ph.D. Dissertation. Vancouver, B.C.: University of British Columbia, 1981.
5291. Swanson, Roger F. *Canadian-American Summit Diplomacy, 1923-1973: Selected Speeches and Documents.* Toronto: McClelland and Stewart, 1975. 314p.

5292. United States. Congress. Senate. Committee on Energy and Natural Resources. *Acid Precipitation and the Use of Fossil Fuels: Hearings.* 97th Cong., 2nd sess. Washington, D.C.: U.S. Government Printing Office, 1982. pp. 1219-1474.
5293. ____.____.____.Committee on Foreign Relations.Subcommittee on Arms Control, Oceans, International Operations, and Environment. *Acid Rain: Hearing.* 97th Cong., 2nd sess. Washington, D.C.: U.S. Government Printing Office, 1982. pp. 16-72, 98-111.

I. OTHER CASE STUDIES

1. Books

5294. Abel, Elie. *The Missile Crisis.* Philadelphia, PA.: Lippincott, 1966. 220p.
5295. Alison, Graham T. *The Essence of Decision: Explaining the Cuban Missile Crisis.* Boston, MA.: Little, Brown, 1971. 338p.
5296. Berkes, Ross N., and Mohinder S. Bedi. *The Diplomacy of India.* Stanford, CA.: Stanford University Press, 1958. 221p.
5297. Boardman, Robert, and A. J. R. Groom. *The Management of Britain's External Relations.* London: Macmillan, 1973. 362p.
5298. Domingo, Benjamin E., ed. *Marco's Diplomacy: Guide to Philippine Bilateral Relations.* Manila: Foreign Service Institute, 1983. 554p.
5299. Frei, Daniel, and Dieter Ruloff. *East-West Relations: Volume I: A Systematic Survey.* Cambridge, MA.: Oelgeschlager, Gunn & Hain, 1983. 297p.
5300. ____. ____. *East-West Relations: Volume 2: Methodology and Data.* Cambridge MA.: Oelgeschlager, Gunn & Hain, 1983. 331p.
5301. Garthoff, Raymond L. *Reflections on the Cuban Missile Crisis.* Washington, D.C.: Brookings Institution, 1988. 159p.
5302. George, Alexander L., et al. *The Limits of Coercive Diplomacy: Laos, Cuba, Vietnam.* Boston. MA: Little, Brown, 1971. 286p.
5303. Graham, Robert. *Vatican Diplomacy: A Study of Church and State on the International Plane.* Princeton, NY.: Princeton University Press, 1959. 442p.
5304. Henderson, William. *West New Guinea: The Dispute and Its Settlement.* South Orange, NY.: Seton Hall University Press, 1972. 281p.
5305. Holmes, John W. *The Better Part of Valour: Essays on Canadian Diplomacy.* Toronto: McClelland, 1970. 239p.
5306. Kennedy, Robert F. *Thirteen Days: A Memoir of the Cuban Missile Crisis.* New York: Norton, 1971. 224p.
5307. Kratochwil, Friedrich, Paul Rohrlich and Harpreet Mahajan. *Peace and Disputed Sovereignty: Reflections on Conflict over Territory.* Lanham, MD.: University Press of America, 1985. 158p.
5308. Leiss, Amelia C., and Dennett Raymond, eds. *European Peace Treaties after World War II: Negotiations and Texts with Italy, Hungary, Rumania and Finland.* Boston, MA.: World Peace Foundation, 1954. 341p.
5309. Myhre, Jeffrey D. *The Antarctic Treaty System: Politics, Law and Diplomacy.* Boulder, CO.: Westview Press, 1986. 162p.
5310. Newsom, David D., ed. *The Diplomacy of Human Rights.* Lanham, MD.: University Press of America, 1986. 240p.
5311. Sagi, Nava. *German Reparations: A History of the Negotiations.* Jerusalem: Magnes Press, 1980. 256p.
5312. Schick, Jack M. *The Berlin Crisis, 1958-1962.* Philadelphia, PA.: University of Pennsylvania Press, 1971. 266p.

5313. Spender, Sir Percy. *Exercises in Diplomacy: The ANZUS Treaty and the Colombo Plan.* New York: New York University Press, 1969. 303p.
5314. Tanter, Raymond. *Modelling and Managing International Conflicts: The Berlin Crisis.* Beverly Hills, CA.: Sage, 1974. 272p.
5315. Wagner, Wolfgang. *The Genesis of the Oder - Neisse Line; A Study in the Diplomatic Negotiations During World War II.* Stuttgart: Brentano Verlag, 1964. 192p.
5316. Wheeler-Bennett, John W. *The Semblance of Peace: the Political Settlement after the Second World War.* London: Macmillan, 1972. 878p.

2. Journal Articles

5317. Armstrong, A. J. "The Negotiations for the Future Political Status of Micronesia." *American Journal of International Law,* 74:3 (1980), 689-693.
5318. _____., and H. L. Hills. "The Negotiations for the Future Political Status of Micronesia, 1980-1984." *American Journal of International Law,* 78:2 (1984), 484-497.
5319. Banerjee, Jyotirmoy. "Hot and Cold Diplomacy in Indo - Pakistani Relations." *Asian Survey,* 23:3 (1983), 280-301.
5320. Baral, J. K. "From Simla to Delhi: A Case Study of a Sub-System Diplomacy." *Indian Journal of Political Science,* 38:2 (1977), 218-236.
5321. _____. "Indo-Pak Diplomacy Since 1981: Motivations, Strategies and Prospects." *Foreign Affairs Reports,* 35:4-5 (April-May 1986), 29-47.
5322. Bjorkbom, Lars. "Resolution of Environmental Problems: The Use of Diplomacy." In: J. E. Carroll, ed. *International Environmental Diplomacy.* Cambridge: Cambridge University Press, 1988. pp. 123-137.
5323. Bos, M. "The Franco-Italian Conciliation Commission." *Acta Scandinavia Juris Geutium,* 22 (1952), 133-159.
5324. Bothwell, Robert, and John English. "The View from Inside Out: Canadian Diplomats and Their Public." *International Journal,* 39:1 (1983-84), 47-67.
5325. Brady, Linda P., and Dieter Fleck. "Transatlantic Military Co-operation in Times of Crisis: The United States-German Agreement on Support for United States Forces in the Federal Republic of Germany." *Atlantic Quarterly,* 2:1 (Spring 1984), 88-96.
5326. Buszinski, Leszek. "Vietnam's ASEAN Diplomacy: Recent Moves." *World Today,* 39:3 (1983), 98-105.
5327. _____. "Vietnam's ASEAN Diplomacy: Incentives for Change." *World Today,* 40:1 (1984), 29-36.
5328. Carpi, David. "The Diplomatic Negotiations over the Transfer of Jewish Children from Croatia to Turkey and Palestine in 1943." *Yad Vashem Studies on the European Jewish Catastrophe and Resistance,* 12 (1977), 109-124.
5329. Conway, John S. "Vatican Diplomacy Today: The Legacy of Paul VI." *International Journal,* 34:3 (1979), 457-474.
5330. Cundick, Ronald P. "Oil Pollution - Negotiation - Alternative to Intervention." *International Lawyer,* 6:1 (1972), 34-41.
5331. Davidson, Lynne A. "The Tools of Human Rights Diplomacy with Eastern Europe." In: D. D. Newsom, ed. *The Diplomacy of Human Rights.* Lanham, MD.: University Press of America, 1986. pp. 21-30.
5332. Druckman, Daniel, et al. "Cultural Differences in Bargaining Behavior: India, Argentina and the United States." *Journal of Conflict Resolution,* 20:3 (1976), 413-452.

5333. _____. "Stages, Turning Points and Crisis: Negotiating Military Base Rights, Spain and the United States." *Journal of Conflict Resolution*, 30:2 (June 1986), 327-360.
5334. Eiland, Michael. "Cambodia in 1985: From Stalemate to Ambiguity." *Asian Survey*, 26:1 (January 1986), 118-125.
5335. Elkin, Jerrold F., and Brian Fredericks. "Sino-Indian Border Talks: The View from New Delhi." *Asian Survey*, 23:10 (October 1983), 1128-1139.
5336. Elliott, David W. P. "Vietnam in Asia: Strategy and Diplomacy in a New Context." *International Journal*, 38:2 (1983), 287-315.
5337. Fentress, Marvin A. "Maritime Boundary Dispute Settlement: The Nonconvergence of Guiding Principles." *Georgia Journal of International and Comparative Law*, 15:3 (1986), 591-626.
5338. Giesbert, Franz-Olivier. "French Diplomacy: A Two-Headed Sphinx." *SAIS Review*, 4 (Summer 1982), 93-98.
5339. Harrison, Selig S. "Inside the Afghan Talks." *Foreign Policy*, 72 (Autumn 1988), 31-60.
5340. Hartman, Frederick H. "Case Studies in the Settlement of Disputes." In: F. H. Hartman. *The Relations of Nations*. 5th ed. New York: Macmillan, 1978. pp. 211-231.
5341. Jessup, Philip C. "Park Avenue Diplomacy - Ending the Berlin Blockade." *Political Science Quarterly*, 87:3 (1972), 377-400.
5342. Johnston, Douglas M. "Marginal Diplomacy in East Asia." *International Journal*, 26:3 (1971), 469-506.
5343. Kriesberg, Louis. "Strategies of Negotiating Agreements: Arab-Israeli and American-Soviet Case." *Negotiation Journal*, 4:1 (January 1988), 19-30.
5344. Leutze, James R. "Technology and Bargaining in Anglo-American Naval Relations: 1938-1946." *United States Naval Institute Proceedings*, 103:6/-892 (June 1977), 50-61.
5345. Levine, Stephen. "Nuclear-Free Zones and Alliance Diplomacy: The New Zealand Experience." *Jerusalem Journal of International Relations*, 9:4 (December 1987), 1-34.
5346. Makeig, Douglas C. "War, No-War, and India-Pakistan Negotiating Process." *Pacific Affairs*, 60:2 (Summer 1987), 271-294.
5347. Marwah, Onkar. "Negotiating Development in a Changing Environment: India's Administrative Elites." In: *Negotiations in Asia. Three Case Studies: India-Iran-Vietnam*. Geneva: Centre for Applied Studies in International Negotiations, 1984. pp. 31-71.
5348. Maurer, John Henry. "Sea Power and Crisis Diplomacy." *Orbis*, 26:3 (1982), 569-572.
5349. McGaffey, David C. "Policy and Practice: Human Rights in Shah's Iran." In D. D. Newsom, ed. *The Diplomacy of Human Rights*. Lanham, MD.: University Press of America, 1986. pp. 69-79.
5350. McRae, D. M. "The Negotiation of Article 234." In: F. Griffiths, ed. *Politics of the Northwest Passage*. Kingston: McGill-Queen's University Press, 1987. pp. 98-114.
5351. Micholus, Edward F. "Negotiating For Hostages: A Policy Dilemma." *Orbis*, 19:4 (1976), 1309-1325.
5352. Mikus, Joseph A. "Man, Tactics and Issues in East-West Negotiations." *Free Will Forum*, 1:2 (May 1959), 5-9.
5353. Mohd, Tan Sri Datuk Haj, and Salleh Bin Abbas. "Cultural Problems in Treaty Negotiations: A Case Study." In:R. P. Anand, ed. *Cultural Factors in International Relations*. New Delhi: Abhinav, 1981. pp. 149-162.

5354. Newsom, David D. "Indonesia: Release in Indonesia." In: D. D. Newsom, ed. *Diplomacy of Human Rights.* Lanham, MD.: University Press of America, 1986. pp. 101-110.
5355. Noorani, Munawar. "Afghanistan Negotiations: Implications for the U.S. of an Impasse." *Journal of South Asian and Middle Eastern Studies,* 9:3 (1986), 3-18.
5356. Page, Don. "Unlocking Canada's Diplomatic Record." *International Journal,* 34:2 (1979), 251-280.
5357. Painchaud, P. "Canadian Cultural Diplomacy - Its Illusions and Problems." *International Perspectives,* (May 1977), 34-38.
5358. Parimal, Kumar Das. "The Indo - Chinese Crisis and India's Efforts Toward Peace Making, 1959-1966." *International Studies (India),* 10 (January 1969), 303-320.
5359. Porter, Gareth. "The Decline of U.S. Diplomacy in Southeast Asia." *SAIS Review,* (Winter 1981), 149-159.
5360. Poullada, Leon B. "The Failure of American Diplomacy in Afghanistan." *World Affairs,* 145:3 (1982-83), 230-252.
5361. Quester, George H. "Bargaining and Bombing During World War II in Europe." *World Politics,* 15 (1963), 417-437.
5362. Reid, Escott. "Comparing Notes with the British on Negotiating the Atlantic Pact." *International Perspectives,* (September/October 1981), 16-19.
5363. Salzberg, John P. "The Carter Administration and Human Rights." In: D. D. Newsom, ed. *The Diplomacy of Human Rights.* Lanham, MD.: University Press of America, 1986. pp. 61-66.
5364. Samuelson, William F. "Dividing Coastal Waters." *Journal of Conflict Resolution,* 29:1 (March 1985), 83-111.
5365. Scherer, Michael F. "Peter Buell Porter and the Development of the Joint Commission Approach to Diplomacy in the North Atlantic Triangle." *American Review of Canadian Studies,* 12:1 (1982), 65-73.
5366. Schmidt, Helmut. "Germany in the Era of Negotiation." *Foreign Affairs,* (October 1970), 40-50.
5367. Stepancic, D. "The Rapacki Plan - A Case Study of East European Diplomacy." *East European Quarterly,* 21:4 (Winter 1987), 401-412.
5368. Tarling, Nicholas. "Rice and Reconciliation: The Anglo - Thai Peace Negotiations of 1945." *Journal of the Siam Society,* 66:2 (1978), 59-111.
5369. Tracy, Brian H. "Bargaining as Trial and Error: The Case of the Spanish Base Negotiations 1963-1970." In: I. W. Zartman, ed. *The Negotiation Process.* Beverly Hills, CA.: Sage, 1978. pp. 183-224.
5370. Ury, William L., and Richard Smoke. "Anatomy of a Crisis." *Negotiation Journal,* 1:1 (January 1985), 93-101.
5371. Vogelgesang, Sandy. "The Diplomacy of Human Rights." *International Studies Quarterly,* 23:2 (1979), 216-245.
5372. Washburn, John Nelson. "People's Republic of Albania - Shall We Now Enter an Era of Negotiation with It After 25 Years of Confrontation." *International Lawyer,* 6:4 (1972), 718-741.
5373. Wiklund, C. "The Zig-Zag Course of the Nordek Negotiations." *Scandinavian Political Studies,* 5 (1970), 307-335.
5374. Willheim, Ernst. "Cultural Problems in Treaty Negotiation: A Case Study of the International Convention on the Conservation of Nature in the South Pacific, Apia, 1976." In: R. P. Anand, ed. *Cultural Factors in International Relations.* New Delhi: Abhinav, 1981. pp. 77-96.

5375. Wittkamper, Gerhard W., and Jurgen Bellers. "The Press and Foreign-Policy Decision Making: An Analysis of German - Polish Negotiations in 1969-1970." *International Political Science Review*, 7:4 (October 1986), 400-414.
5376. Wriggins, W. Howard. "Up For Auction: Malta Bargains with Great Britain." In: I. W. Zartman, ed. *The 50% Solution*. Garden City, NY.: Anchor Press, 1976. pp. 208-234.
5377. Zartman, I. William. "The Strategy of Preventive Diplomacy in Third World Conflicts." In: A. L. George, ed. *Managing U.S. - Soviet Rivalry*. Boulder, CO.: Westview Press, 1983. pp. 341-364.

3. Documents and Reports

5378. Akers, Albert B. *The Cuban Missile Crisis: A Study in Multilateral Diplomacy*. MA. Thesis. Washington, D.C.: The American University, 1966. 114p.
5379. Andrews, Richard. "Report of the U.S. Environment and Natural Resources Task Group, Processes of International Negotiation Program." Paper Presented at the *Conference on the Processes of International Negotiations*, held on May 18-22, 1987, at the International Institute for Applied Systems Analysis (IIASA), in Laxenburg, Austria.
5380. Baehr, Peter R. "Building Agreement: The Role of the Netherlands in the Realization of the International Convention Against Torture." Paper Presented at the *28th Annual Convention of the International Studies Association*, held on April 14-18, 1987, in Washington, D.C.
5381. Bark, Dennis L. *Agreement on Berlin: A Study of the 1970-72 Quadripartite Negotiations*. American Enterprise Institute Policy Study 10. Washington, D.C.: American Enterprise Institute for public Policy Research, 1974. 131p.
5382. Berry, William E. *American Military Bases in the Philippines, Base Negotiations and Philippine - American Relations: Past, Present and Future*. Ph.D. Dissertation. Ithaca, NY.: Cornell University, 1981. 539p.
5383. Blanchette, Arthur E., ed. *Canadian Foreign Policy, 1955-1965: Selected Speeches and Documents*. Toronto: McClelland & Stewart, 1977. 424p.
5384. _____., ed. *Canadian Foreign Policy, 1966-1976: Selected Speeches and Documents*. Toronto: Gage, 1980. 366p.
5385. Bokil, S. V., and R. M. Honavar. *India's Principal Concerns in International Negotiations in the Eighties*. Working Paper, 34. New Delhi: Indian Council for Research on International Economic Relations, 1985. 134p.
5386. Brussel, Gabrielle S. *U.S. Deliberations During the Cuban Missile Crisis: Balance of Resolve*. PEW Case Studies, 334.0-E-88-L. New York: School of International and Public Affairs, Columbia University, 1988.
5387. Carnes, Mark C. *American-British Negotiations on Sharing Atomic Energy, July 1943*. PEW Case Studies, 335.0-A-88-C. New York: School of International and Public Affairs, Columbia University, 1988.
5388. *The Control of Local Conflict: A Design Study on Arms Control and Limited War in the Developing Areas*. ACDA/WEC-98. Washington D.C.: U.S. Arms Control and Disarmament Agency, 1967. 4 vols.
5389. Coulter, Edwin M. *The Diplomacy of the Sino-Indian Border Dispute: 1950-1962*. Ph.D. Dissertation. Charlottesville, VA.: University of Virginia, 1965. 336p.

5390. Cronin, Richard D. "Afghanistan: United Nations - Sponsored Negotiations, An Annotated Chronology and Analysis." In: *Major Studies and Issue Briefs of the Congressional Research Service, 1986-1987 Supplement.* Frederick, MD.: University Publications of America, 1987. Reel VIII. pp. 0139-0169.
5391. Goldstein, Donald. *United States-Philippine Negotiations over United States Bases, 1988.* PEW Case Studies, 325.0-G-88-P. Pittsburgh, PA.: Graduate School for Public and International Affairs, University of Pittsburgh, 1988.
5392. Harrison, Michael. "France: The Diplomacy of a Self-Assured Middle Power." In: H. Binnendijk, ed. *National Negotiating Style.* Washington, D.C.: Foreign Service Institute, Centre for the Study of Foreign Affairs, 1987. pp. 75-104.
5393. _____., and Mark McDonough. *The Negotiations Leading to the French Withdrawal from NATO.* PEW Case Studies, 301.0-A-87-J. Washington, D.C.: School of Advanced International Studies, John Hopkins University, 1987.
5394. Henderson, William. *Pacific Settlement of Disputes: The Indonesian Question, 1946-1949.* New York: Woodrow Wilson Foundation, 1954. 89p.
5395. Jabber, Fuad. *The Politics of Arms Transfer and Control: The United States and Egypt's Quest for Arms, 1950-1955.* Working Paper No.16. Los Angeles, CA.: The California Arms Control and Foreign Policy Seminar, 1972. 46p.
5396. Kumar, Satish. "Challenges in Contemporary Diplomacy with Special Reference to the Indian Subcontinent." Paper Presented at the, *12th World Congress of the International Political Science Association*, held on August 9-14, 1982 in Rio do Janerio. 4: 1-27.
5397. Lampson, Edward T., and Pauline Mian. "Current U.S.-Spanish Negotiations." In: *Major Studies and Issue Briefs of the Congressional Research Service, 1975-76 Supplement.* Washington, D.C.: University Publications of America, 1977. Reel IV. 46p.
5398. McDonald, John W., and Diane B. Bendahmane, eds. *Perspectives on Negotiation: Four Case Studies and Interpretations.* Washington, D.C.: Foreign Service Institute, Centre for the Study of Foreign Affairs, 1986. 315p.
5399. Nazem, Nurul Islam. *Indo - Bangladesh Common Rivers and Water Diplomacy.* Dhaka: Bangladesh Institute of International and Strategic Studies, 1986. 51p.
5400. Nossal, Kim Richard. *An Acceptance of Paradox: Essays on Canadian Diplomacy in Honour of John W. Holmes.* Contemporary Affairs; 49. Toronto: Canadian Institute of International Affairs, 1982. 202p.
5401. Paalberg, Robert L., E. Y. Park and Donald L. Wyman. *Diplomatic Dispute: U.S. Conflict with Iran, Japan, and Mexico.* Harvard Studies in International Affairs, 39. Cambridge, MA.: Center for International Affairs, Harvard University, 1984. 174p.
5402. Pakistan. Ministry of Kashmir Affairs. *Negotiations Between the Prime Ministers of Pakistan and India Regarding the Kashmir Dispute, June 1953 - September 1954.* Pakistan: (1954), 104p.
5403. *Philippine Diplomacy: Chronology and Documents, 1972-1981.* Manila: Foreign Service Institute, 1981. 456p.
5404. Pruitt, Dean G., and J. Holland. *Settlement in the Berlin Crisis, 1958-1962.* Special Studies No. 18. Buffalo, NY.: Council on International Studies, State University of New York at Buffalo, 1971. 23p.

5405. Randolph, Sean R. *Diplomacy and National Interest: Thai-American Security Cooperation in the Vietnam Era.* Ph.D. Dissertation. Medford, MA.: Fletcher School of Law and Diplomacy, 1978. 476p.
5406. Satawedin, Dhanasarit. *Thai-American Alliance During the Laotian Crisis, 1959-1962: A Case Study of the Bargaining Power of a Small State.* Ph.D. Dissertation. DeKalb, IL.: Northern Illinois University, 1984. 435p.
5407. Sharfman, Peter. *The International Negotiations Preceding West German Rearmament, 1949-1955.* Ph.D. Dissertation. Chicago, IL.: University of Chicago, 1972.
5408. Thornton, Thomas P., and Imtiaz Bokhari. *Negotiating the Aftermath of the 1971 War Between India and Pakistan.* PEW Case Studies, 420.0-F-88-J. Washington, D.C.: School of Advanced International Studies, Johns Hopkins University, 1988.
5409. Tow, William T. *Disintegration Of the ANZUS Alliance, 1984-1986.* PEW Case Studies, 331.0-G-88-S. Los Angeles, CA.: School of International Relations, University of Southern California, 1988.
5410. United States. Congress. Joint Postwar Committee. "Negotiations for the Retention of American Bases in the Philippines after Independence." In: *Records of the Joint Chiefs of Staff, Part I: 1942-1945: The Pacific Theater.* Frederick, MD.: University Publications of America, 1981. Reel 12; pp. 0591-0594; 0596-0607.
5411. _____._____.Senate.Committee on Foreign Relations.Subcommittee on East Asia and Pacific Affairs. *Micronesia Status Negotiations.* 97th Cong., 2nd sess. Washington, D.C.: U.S. Government Printing Office, 1973. 22p.
5412. _____.Department of State. *The Austrian State Treaty; An Account of the Postwar Negotiations Together with the Text of the Treaty and Related Documents.* Washington, D.C.: U.S. Government Printing Office, 1957. 99p.
5413. _____._____. *The Berlin Crisis: A Report on the Moscow Discussions, 1948.* European and British Commonwealth Series 1. Publ. 3298. Washington, D.C.: U.S. Government Printing Office, 1948. 61p.
5414. Vogt, Erich. *The Role of Berlin and the Four Power Negotiations in the Foreign Policy Process of the Nixon Administration.* Ph.D. Dissertation. Berlin: The Free University, 1980. 323p.
5415. Walker, Penelope. *Political Crisis and Dept Negotiation: The Case of the Philippines, 1983-1986.* PEW Case Studies, 133.0-G-88-S. Los Angeles, CA.: School of International Relations, University of Southern California, 1988.
5416. Westermeyer, William, and Christopher C. Joyner. *Negotiating a Minerals Regime for Antarctica.* PEW Case Studies, 134.0-E-88-S. Los Angeles, CA.: School of International Relations, University of Southern California, 1988.
5417. Wright, Marcia. *U.S. Decision Whether or Not to Recognize the MPLA Government of Angola, 1976 - 1985.* PEW Case Studies, 140.0-C-88-C. New York: School of International and Public Affairs, Columbia University, 1988.
5418. Wu, Jiajing. *The Marshall Mission and the KMT-CCP Negotiations after World War II.* M.A. Thesis. East Lansing, MI.: Michigan State University, 1984. 88p.
5419. Zasloff, Joseph J. *United States and Vietnam: The Question of Diplomatic Relations, 1975-1979.* PEW Case Studies, 417.0-G-88-G. Pittsburgh, PA.: Graduate School of Public and International Affairs, University of Pittsburgh, 1988.

Author Index

Abdennur, Alexander, 500
Abel, Elie, 4332, 5294
Abelson, Donald S., 5089
Abrams, Nancy Ellen, 1756
Abshire, David M., 4409
Abt, Clark C., 2590
Acheson, Dean, 3390, 3954, 4042, 4312, 4482
Achilles, Theodore C., 2512
Ackoff, Russell L., 1332
Acuff, Frank L., 548
Adam, Elaine P., 4773
Adams, J. S., 679
Adams, John C., 4636
Adamson, David M., 3655, 3871
Adamson, Peter, 2159
Adebajo, A., 3648
Adede, A. O., 2295
Adelman, Kenneth L., 2643-2648, 3398-3399, 4418
Adler, Nancy J., 3543
Adler, Peter, 1870
Adomeit, Hannes, 4483, 4585
Adra, Jawad, 1594
Ageton, Arthur A., 4687
Aggarwal, Lalit, 1647
Aggarwal, V. K., 405, 2466, 3560, 3872
Ahmad, Jaleel, 3704
Ahmed, M. Samir, 2969, 2998
Aho, C. Michael, 3705, 3850
Ahrari, Mohammed E., 3656
Akaha, Tsuneo, 3851
Akehurst, Michael, 2098
Akers, Albert B., 5378

Al-Abib, Ibrahim, 4911
Al-Battah, Abdalla, 1972
Al-Mani, Saleh A., 4789
Al-Shaikly, Salah, 2378-2379, 4789
Albers, Wulf, 1230-1231, 1648
Albin, Cecilia, 1994
Albrecht-Carrie, Rene, 4270
Alcock, James E., 549-550, 1288
Alderman, Sidney S., 4484
Aldrich, G. H., 2004-2005
Alekseev, A., 3339
Alevy, Daniel I., 551
Alexander, C. N., 1232
Alexander, Elmore R., 552
Alexandroff, Alan S., 3955
Alexandrov, V., 2649
Alexiev, A. R., 3473
Alfredo, Carlos, 5224
Alger, Chadwick F., 553, 2059-2063, 4043, 4754
Ali, Liaquat, 3668
Ali, Sheikh Rustan, 3643
Alison, Graham T., 5295
Alker, H. R., 1233, 1649
Allan, Pierre, 406, 2591, 4044
Allard, Sven, 4459
Allen, Michael H., 117, 3917
Allen, Thomas, 745
Allsebrook, Mary, 2036
Alperovitz, Gar, 2592
Alpert, Eugene J., 2513
Alroy, Gil, 1932, 4790
Alt Powell, Eileen, 4697
Altfeld, Michael F., 118
Alting von Geusau, F. A. M., 3262

Alvarez, David J., 4755
American Arbitration Association., 3544
Amin, T., 1973
Amuzegar, Jahangir, 2380
Anand, R. P., 1
Andemichael, Berhanykun, 2122, 2878
Andersen, Kenneth E., 501
Anderson, A. J., 975
Anderson, Irvine H., 5109
Anderson, M. S., 4282
Anderson, R. E., 554
Andren, Nils, 3253
Andrew, Arthur, 3400, 4045-4046
Andrews, Richard, 5379
Angel, Robert, 3852
Anjaria, S. J., 2381, 3706
Anson, Robert, 1871
Anthony, William H., 4451
Antola, Esko, 3312
Antrim, Lance, 407, 1650, 2342, 3606, 3918
Aonuma, Y., 3838
Apfelbaum, E., 555
Appadorai, A., 4047
Appathurai, E. R., 2064
Apuzzo, A., 3775
Archibald, Kathleen, 1182
Arend, Anthony Clark, 119
Argyle, Michael, 502, 556
Armacost, Michael H., 3263
Armstrong, A. J., 5317-5318
Arnone, Harriet C., 4846
Arnoupoulos, Paris, 1757
Aron, Raymond, 2, 2596, 4698
Aronson, Jonathan D., 3735, 3850, 3857
Aronson, Shlomo, 4787
Arthur, Jim, 1908
Asbell, Bernard, 4313
Ascher, W., 1758
Ash, Ronald A., 773
Ashby, Timothy, 3474
Ashmore, Harry S., 4363, 4966
Aspaturian, V. V., 4048, 4485-4486
Assefa, Hizkias, 1923, 1974
Astarte, Samuel K. B., 2382
Atimomo, Emiko, 3661
Atque, Fanzia, 2651
Atthowe, J. M., 557
Attlee, Clement, 4314
Atwater, Elton, 3
Aumann, R. J., 1183
Austin, D., 5169

Avenhaus, Rudolf, 1184-1185
Avineri, Shlomo, 4828
Avneri, Uri, 4364
Avruch, K., 120-121
Axelrod, Robert, 4, 122-123, 1065, 1186-1187, 1234-1240
Axline, W. A., 5209
Ayling, K., 991
Ayo, Edward J., 3690
Azar, Edward E., 5-7, 124, 1975, 2383, 4829
Azcarate, Florez Pablo de, 1924
Azrael, Jeremy, 2652
Azud, Jan, 2037

Babbitt, Eileen, 408-409, 1908
Babovic, Bogdan, 2198
Bacchus, Wilfred A., 5068
Bacchus, William I., 3264, 4049, 4625
Bacharach, Samuel B., 8, 125, 503
Bachner, Dave, 410
Bacon, Francis, 126
Bacon, Lawrence S., 127
Badirach, S. B., 856
Badran, W. Abd el Rahman, 1976
Baehr, Peter R., 5380
Baggs, William C., 4966
Bagley, Bruce M., 5200-5201, 5210, 5242
Bagozzi, Richard P., 1847
Bailey, Sydney D., 2038-2039, 2065, 2123, 4365
Bailey, Terrell W., 2879
Bailey, Thomas A., 3956, 4271, 4699
Baird, S. L., 607-608, 1373
Bairstow, F., 3561
Bajpai, K. Shankar, 4050
Baldwin, Robert E., 1241, 3736-3737
Baldwin, Simeon E., 2160
Ball, George W., 4051-4053, 4626
Ball, M. Margaret, 128
Banerjee, Jyotirmoy, 5319
Banerji, Arun Kumar, 4054
Bank, John C., 3874
Banks, M. H., 1242
Banks, Michael, 9
Bar-Yaacov, Nissim, 10
Bar-Zochar, Michael, 4791
Baral, J. K., 4976, 5320-5321
Baranyi, Steven, 5261
Barber, Peter, 3957
Barclay, G. S. J., 3875
Barclay, S., 1651

Author Index

Bare, C. G., 3562
Barghoorn, Frederick C., 4410, 4460
Bargman, Abraham, 2653, 2970
Bark, Dennis L., 5381
Barker, M., 3961
Barkun, Michael, 1759
Barnds, William J., 4487
Barnes, M., 784
Barnes, William, 4756
Barnett, Bruce, 1278
Barnett, Lester W., 1299
Barnett, Vincent M., 4627
Barratt, John, 2066
Barros, Jose Miguel, 5243
Barston, Ronald P., 129, 2300-2301, 3958
Bartholdi, John J., 130
Bartholomew, Sara, 4366
Bartlett, Charles, 4039
Barton, John H., 2597
Bartos, Otomar J., 11, 131-132, 558-562, 1243-1246, 1605, 1652
Bartunek, Jean M., 1760
Bass, B. M., 411, 563, 3357
Bass, Charles W., 2161
Bass, R., 3357
Bassani, Antonella, 3953
Bastert, Russell H., 4700
Bates, John L., 2249
Baudier, Edmond, 1247
Bauer, A., 1881
Bawa, Mahama, 2467
Bayne, Nicholas, 3503-3504
Bazerman, Max H., 12, 133-134, 564-569, 605, 877, 881, 1019, 1248, 1550, 1761
Beal, Richard S., 1188
Beam, Jacob D., 4461
Beattie, C. E., 1872
Beaulac, Willard L., 4701
Bechhoefer, Bernard G., 2514, 2598, 2654
Bechtoldt, Heinrich, 4830
Becker, Abraham S., 4912
Becker, Josef, 135
Becker, Kurt, 3506
Becker, Otwin, 1249
Beckman, L. L., 757
Beckmann, Neal W., 13
Bedell Smith, Walter, 4315
Bedi, Mohinder S., 5296
Beesley, A., 2302
Beggan, J. K., 847
Behrman, J. R., 2384

Behue, August, 412
Beichman, Arnold, 2040
Beitzell, Robert E., 2228, 2273
Beker, Avi, 2197
Beliaev, Edward, 3809
Bell, Coral, 3959, 4628-4629, 4702-4703, 4757, 4831
Bell, David V. J., 136
Bellany, Ian, 3153
Bellers, Jurgen, 5375
Bellinger, J. B., 3103
Belliveau, L. M., 1762
Belsky, Don M., 3104
Bemis, Samuel F., 4272-4273, 4630
Ben Eliezer, M., 4419
Ben Yoav, Orly, 570-571, 1066-1068
Ben-Dak, Joseph D., 7, 1250
Ben-Dor, Gabriel, 4792
Ben-Gurion, David, 4793, 4913
Ben-Horin, Y., 3313
Ben-Yishai, Ron, 4832
Ben-Zvi, Abraham, 4794, 4833-4834
Bendahmane, Diane B., 413, 4407, 5101, 5398
Bendega, Joseph T., 2468
Bender, Gerald, 1977
Benjamin, A., 288
Benjamin, C. M., 1671
Benjamin, Charles, 1653, 1711, 3689
Benne, Kenneth D., 137
Bennett, A. LeRoy, 2162
Bennett, Andrew, 3027
Bennett, Douglas C., 3876
Bennett, Edward M., 4633
Bennett, James, 1921
Bennett, P. G., 1189
Bennett, Paul R., 3105-3106
Bennett, R., 825
Benoit, Emile, 2655
Benson, J., 1069
Benson, Oliver, 1251-1252, 1654
Bentley, Alvin M., 2656
Benton, A. A., 572-575, 1070, 1655, 1760
Bentrup, A., 1568
Benz, G. William, 4707
Beranek, Robert E., 4586
Bercovitch, Jacob, 138-139, 414-415, 1739, 1763-1764, 1873, 1933-1934, 3265, 4835-4838
Berding, Andrew, 4055, 4631
Berg, Rolf, 3254
Berg, Terrence G., 3707
Bergsten, C. Fred, 3534

Berkes, Ross N., 5296
Berl, Janet E., 1253
Berman, Maureen R., 4356, 4367-4368
Bernhardt, J. P. A., 2303
Bernhardt, R. G., 1254
Bernstein, Barton J., 2250
Bernstein, Samuel J., 2513
Bernstein, Thomas P., 5142
Berridge, G. R., 2041, 2067
Berris, Jan Carol, 5115
Berry, R. Stephen, 1756
Berry, William E., 5382
Berton, Peter, 4488
Bertram, Christoph, 2657, 3028, 3188
Bertsch, Gary K., 3402
Best, Gary L., 2124
Bethe, Hans A., 2917
Betts, George C., 1656
Bhagwati, Jagdish N., 2360, 2372, 2385-2386, 3563-3564
Bialer, Severyn, 4489
Biersteker, Thomas J., 3919
Bigoness, W. J., 695, 1255, 1765-1766
Bilder, Richard B., 140, 504, 3877, 5287
Billington, James, 4490
Bin Abbas, Salleh, 5353
Bindschedler, Rudolf L., 1767
Bingham, Gayle, 2550
Binmore, K. G., 1190, 1256-1258
Binnendijk, Hans, 416
Birnbaum, Karl E., 3253, 3266-3267, 3314
Birse, A. H., 4316
Bishop, Donald G., 2042
Bishop, Robert L., 1259-1262
Bissell, Richard E., 4420
Bixenstine, V. E., 576-578, 1263-1264, 1494, 1629-1630
Bjorkbom, Lars, 5322
Black, C. E., 4508
Black, Eugene R., 2361
Black, J., 1265
Black, P. W., 120-121
Blackaby, F., 3212
Blackburn, W. R., 3142
Blacker, Coit D., 2599-2600, 3154-3155, 3189, 3403
Blair, Leon B., 4704
Blair, William D., 4056, 4705
Blake, Cecil A., 5170
Blake, Robert R., 579
Blaker, Michael, 3738, 5086, 5090, 5102
Blakeslee, George H., 4491
Blalack, Richard, 1280
Blanchette, Arthur E., 5383-5384
Blanchfield, Robert A., 5094
Blass, Asher, 417
Blechman, Barry M., 2601, 2658-2661, 2971, 3384
Blitz, Mark, 4421
Blix, H., 141
Bloom, Alfred, 5116
Bloomfield, Beth, 3029
Bloomfield, Lincoln P., 14, 1266-1267, 2068, 4057
Blum, Laura, 4943
Blundell, H., 1264
Boahen, A. A., 4299
Boardman, Robert, 5297
Bobbit, P. C., 3132
Bobrow, Davis B., 1268, 2469, 2662, 4914
Bochner, Stephen, 1740
Boehringer, G. H., 580
Bogdan, Corneliu, 3268
Bohlen, Charles E., 4317
Bok, Sissela, 15
Bok-Schoettle, Enid C., 2880
Bokhari, Imtiaz, 5408
Bokil, S. V., 5385
Bole, Robert D., 3475
Bolling, Landrum R., 4369-4371
Bolz, Klaus, 3810
Bomsdorf, Falk, 2663
Bonacich, Phillip, 1269-1270
Bonafede, Dom, 3404
Bonham, Matthew G., 581, 1271
Bonner, Paul H., 4318
Bonoma, Thomas V., 582, 646, 832, 1006-1007, 1009-1010, 1071, 1565
Bontadini, Pier Luigi, 418
Bonvinici, Gianni, 3508
Booth, Arthur, 2664
Booth, Kenneth, 3030
Boothe, T. L., 2125
Borah, L. A.,Jr., 583, 1072
Borawski, John, 3131, 3156, 3255, 3269-3270
Borgatta, E. F., 584
Borgatta, M. L., 584-585
Borisov, O. B., 3960
Borthwick, M., 3920
Bos, M., 5323
Boss, Walter, 3157
Bossi-Renaud, Claude, 2182

Author Index

Bostrom, Robert, 1871
Bothwell, Robert, 5324
Botti, Timothy J., 2881
Boudreau, Tom, 4237
Bougrov, Evgheny V., 2212
Boulding, Kenneth E., 16, 1272
Bourne, C. B., 1935
Bouscaren, Anthony T., 3405
Boutros-Ghali, Boutros, 2551
Bovis, H. E., 1633-1634
Bowen, Robert E., 3250
Bowett, D. W., 17, 2069
Bowie, Robert R., 3031
Bowles, Chester, 4058-4059, 4319-4320
Bowman, William R., 3190
Boyce, P. J., 4060
Boyd, Norman K., 1073
Boyd, William P., 3315
Boykin, Milton L., 2665
Bracey, Andrey, 1978
Braden, Wythe E., 3649
Bradley, C. Paul, 4795
Bradlow, Daniel D., 3545
Brady, Linda P., 24, 720, 5325
Brams, Steven J., 1191-1194, 1273-1276, 1657
Branaman, Brenda M., 2126, 5186-5187
Brandstatter, H., 586
Braunstein, Yale, 1277
Braver, L. S., 789
Braver, Sanford, 1278
Breaugh, James A., 587-588
Brecher, Michael, 18, 109, 142, 1936, 2118
Bredemeier, M. E., 1279
Brehmer, Berndt, 589, 705
Brenenstuhl, Daniel C., 1280
Brennan, D. G., 3032, 4492
Brenner, A. R., 777
Brenner, Michael J., 5143
Breslauer, George W., 3406
Bressaud, A., 2387
Bressler, Robert J., 2725, 3033
Brest, Jeanne, 1843
Brett, Jeanne M., 1768
Brew, J. S., 1281
Brewster, Kingman, 4061
Briggs, Ellis O., 4062-4063, 4321, 4632
Briggs, Wenicke, 2388
Britton, S. D., 603, 914
Broches, Charles F., 3776-3777, 3893
Brock, E. William, 3566, 3760

Brockner, Joel, 505, 590-592
Brody, Richard A., 143, 5221
Brohmer, B., 593
Broms, Bengt, 2127
Bronisz, Piotr, 1658-1659
Brookmire, David A., 1769, 1874
Broskowski, A. T., 1074
Brotherton, C. J., 988
Brougher, Valentina G., 4372
Brouillet, Alain, 1770
Browder, Robert P., 4462
Brown, B. R., 537, 594-597, 1075
Brown, E. H. P., 144
Brown, Harold, 2602, 2666
Brown, Neville, 3961, 4839
Brown, R. C., 1010
Brown, S. N., 145
Brown, S. R., 1758
Brown, Scott, 201, 1282, 2667, 4510
Brown, William A., 19
Brown, William R., 4796
Brown, Winthrop A., 146
Browne, E. C., 147
Browne, M. W., 4977
Brueckmann, Wolfram H., 2183
Bruehl, M. E., 86
Bruha, Thomas, 3034
Brune, Lester H., 4706
Brunner, J. A., 3824
Brunner, R. D., 1233
Brussel, Gabrielle S., 5386
Bryant, Jim, 1283
Bryson, Thomas A., 4797
Brzezinski, Ian, 3476
Brzezinski, Zbigniev, 4322, 4493
Buchan, Alastair, 419
Buchheim, Robert W., 2668-2669
Buckingham, G. W., 1771
Buckley, G., 1265
Buckley, James J., 1284-1285
Buckley, William F., 2043
Buderi, C. L. O., 2304
Buhite, Russell D., 2229
Bull, Hedley, 2670, 2972, 3035
Bulmer, C., 2305
Bunker, Ellsworth, 5211
Burchett, Wilfred G., 4978-4981
Burge, M., 3878
Burke, Lee H., 4238, 4323
Burnett, R., 2389
Burns, E. L. M., 20, 3340
Burns, Richard D., 4633, 4758
Burns, Robert A., 5244
Burns, T., 1286

Burt, Richard, 2671
Burton, John W., 5, 21-22, 148-154, 420, 1875, 2128, 3962, 4373
Bush, Kenneth D., 1876
Busk, Douglas L., 3963
Buszinski, Leszek, 5326-5327
Buteux, P., 3128
Butler, C. Allen, 130
Butler, R., 4300
Butow, R. J. C., 4357
Butterfield, Herbert, 3964, 4064, 4301-4302
Butterworth, Robert L., 23, 155, 2002
Buttinger, Joseph, 4982-4983
Buzan, Barry, 2296, 2306-2308
Byers, R. B., 2672
Byrnes, James F., 2251, 4324
Byrnes, Robert F., 4358, 5144

Cable, James, 3965, 4967
Cable, Vincent, 3879
Caccia, Harold, 4065
Cadieux, Marcel, 3966
Caldarelli, Cesare, 1076
Caldwell, Dan, 2668
Caldwell, Lawrence T., 4707
Caldwell, Lynton K., 2515
Callaghy, Thomas M., 2470
Callahan, Patrick, 24
Callen, J. L., 156
Callender, Harold, 4066
Calogero, Francesco, 3036
Calvo, Michael A., 3017
Calvo-Goller, Notburga K., 3017
Calvocoressi, Peter, 2070
Cambon, Jules M., 3967
Campbell, A. E., 4067
Campbell, John C., 2152, 4494-4495, 4840
Campbell, Kurt M., 4374
Campion, Douglas E., 939
Camps, Miriam, 3607-3608, 3858
Canada. Department of Communication. , 2552
_____. Department of External Affairs., 3739, 3786-3788
_____._____. Information Division., 2883
Canavan, D., 624
Cann, Arnie, 598, 1077
Caplan, Neil, 4798-4799, 4841
Caradon, Hugh, 2071, 2129
Caragata, Patrick J., 3789

Carde, Freeland H. III, 5145
Cardozo, Michael H., 3968
Carling, Alan H., 1287
Carlisle, J., 934
Carlson, Don, 4359
Carment, D. W., 1288
Carmichael, W. B., 3567
Carnes, Mark C., 5387
Carnesale, Albert, 2603, 2884, 3361
Carnevale, Peter J., 599-604, 907, 914, 971, 1078-1082, 1165-1166, 1168, 1289, 1772-1775, 1877-1884, 1894
Carpi, David, 5328
Carroce, David, 2274
Carroll, Berenice A., 157
Carroll, John E., 2499, 3761
Carroll, John M., 4634
Carroll, John S., 568, 605
Carter, Alan, 4068
Carter, Jimmy, 158, 421, 4422, 4800-4801, 4842
Casadio, G. P., 3694
Casmir, Fred, 4759
Casse, Pierre, 422-423
Castles, Alex, 1083
Castore, C. H., 993
Castro, Fidel, 2471
Cates, J. M. Jr., 2130
Catudal, Honore M., 2500-2501
Cavaliero, R. E., 4423
Cave, J. K., 1660
Ceska, Franz, 3271
Chacko, C. J., 5273
Chadha, I. S., 3669
Chai, F. Y., 2072
Chaibane, Antoine, 4915
Chaliand, Gerard, 4843
Chalmers, Douglas, 5245
Chammah, Albert M., 1215, 1511-1512
Chan, Kenneth C., 5117
Chan, Kenneth S., 3708
Chang, David W., 5118
Chang, Jaw-ling Joanne, 5146
Chang, King-yuh, 4069
Chang, Pao Min, 5119
Charell, Ralph, 25
Charlton, M. L., 5212
Charlton, Michael, 2252-2254
Charney, Jonathan I., 159, 2163
Charney, Leon H., 4802
Charny, Israel W., 26
Chatterjee, Kalyan, 1290-1293, 1661
Chaudhuri, Adhip, 3921

Author Index

Chawla, R. L., 3898
Chayes, Abram, 2924
Chen, Shao-Hsien, 4496
Cheney, John, 606, 1084
Cheng, Peter P. C., 4760, 5065
Chertkoff, J. M., 607-610, 779, 1294
Chesnut, H., 27
Chester, D. W., 3644
Chester, E. R., 208
Chilaty, D., 2604
Child, Jack, 5213, 5246
Chimni, B. S., 3662
Chin, H. D., 5120
Ching-Yao, Yin, 4497
Chisholm, Archibald H. T., 3645
Chopra, Surendra, 1925
Chossudowsky, Evgeny, 3272
Christopher, Warren, 4239, 4803
Christy, Francis T., 2343
Chubin, Shahram, 4844
Chung, Chong Wook, 5081
Churchill, Winston, 2230, 2255
Cialdini, R. B., 611
Cichock, Mark A., 3273
Cicourel, Aaron V., 160
Cioffi-Revilla, Claudio A., 28, 4070
Citron, Klaus, 3316
Clark, Eric, 3969
Clark, Marian F., 1085
Clark, R. D., 612
Clarke, Duncan L., 2605
Clarke, Richard N., 1241
Clarke, Sarah, 462
Claude, Inis L., 2006-2007, 2026, 2044, 4240, 5214
Clemens, Dianne S., 2231, 2256-2257
Clemens, Walter C., 2606, 2673, 3037
Cleveland, Harland, 2674, 4071-4073, 4635-4636
Cline, William R., 3695
Closca, I., 4074
Clute, Robert, 5288
Coady, H., 999
Codding, G., 2164
Coddington, Alan H., 1195, 1295-1298
Coffey, Joseph I., 2607
Coffin, Royce A., 424
Cohen, Benjamin V., 2675
Cohen, Bernard C., 5087
Cohen, Eugene D., 854, 1086
Cohen, Herb, 29
Cohen, Herbert A., 4916
Cohen, M. D., 682-683
Cohen, Michael J., 4845

Cohen, Raymond, 30, 161, 506, 1937, 2184, 3970, 4075-4076, 4708
Cohen, Roberta, 4498
Cohen, S., 2184
Cohen, S. D., 2391
Cohen, S. P., 766
Cohen, Stephen, 425, 613, 4846
Cohen, Yoel, 4411, 4424
Cohn, Theodore, 3670
Cole, D. L., 1776
Cole, Steven G., 614, 1299, 1397
Coletta, Paolo E., 4984
Coll, Alberto R., 2344
Collingridge, David, 2676
Collins, M. G., 827
Colman, Andrew M., 1196
Colosi, Thomas, 162-165, 1851, 1885
Commission of the European Communities., 3740
Commonwealth Group of Experts., 2472
Comstock, Craig, 4359
Condreu, P. L. S., 2185
Congressional Quarterly Service., 2886, 4637
Conlon, Donald E., 1775, 1777, 1883
Conner, Thomas L., 473
Conrath, David W., 1300-1301
Contini, Bruno, 427, 1302
Contractor, F. J., 3568, 3859-3860
Conway, John S., 5329
Cook, Don, 1662, 3038
Cook, R. F., 1839
Cooper, C. L., 166, 4985
Cooper, Catharine A., 5277
Cooper, Henry F., 2677-2678
Cooper, Mary H., 2679, 3407
Copithorue, M. D., 5121
Coplin, William D., 1303, 2008-2009, 2073-2074
Corbett, Hugh, 3880
Corbett, P. E., 5274
Cordier, A. W., 4077
Cordoves, D., 2417, 2421
Cordovez, Diego, 2131, 2362
Cormick, Gerald W., 1938-1939
Cory, Robert H., 2075, 2680-2681
Coser, Lewis A., 167, 2682
Costello, Mary, 3039
Cot, Jean Pierre, 1741, 1940
Cottam, Martha L., 507, 615, 1087
Cottam, Richard W., 428, 3971, 4241
Coudry, S. C., 1088
Coulson, Robert, 168, 1778

Coulter, Edwin M., 5389
Cousins, Norman, 4499, 4986
Cowhey, Peter H., 3762, 3857
Cowley, M., 609
Cox, David, 3217
Crabb, Cecil V., 4709
Craig, Gordon A., 3972, 4242, 4274, 4303, 4500-4502
Crampton, Peter C., 1304, 1663-1664
Crane, Barbara B., 2392, 2473
Crane, George, 3829
Crane, Robert D., 4503
Crawford, Beverly K., 169, 3816, 3881, 3922
Crawford, Vincent P., 1305-1307, 2393
Crawshaw, Nancy, 4847
Creagle, John S., 4243
Crean, John G., 3709
Creighton, John J., 4917
Crick, Bernard, 4078
Critchley, Julian, 2683, 3274, 5044
Croce, Cynthia, 170
Cronin, P. M., 3477
Cronin, Richard D., 5390
Cross, John G., 429, 1197, 1308-1312
Crott, Helmut W., 616, 802, 1313-1314
Crow, W. J., 617
Crowne, D. P., 618
Crum, Bartley C., 4804
Crumbaugh, C., 619, 667
Culbert, Jay, 3710
Culora, Thomas J., 5188
Cummings, B. L., 1378
Cummings, L. L., 514, 713-714
Cundick, Ronald P., 5330
Curle, Adam, 31, 1886
Curran, Timothy J., 3741
Curry, R. L., 1036, 2394
Curtis, Gerald L., 3839, 4710
Curtis, John M., 3763
Curtis, Thomas B., 3696
Curwurah, A. O., 32
Curzon, Gerard, 3697, 3711
Curzon, Victoria, 3711
Cutler, Lloyd N., 3040, 4848

D'Amato, James V., 5189
Daalder, Ivo H., 2973
Daddysman, J. W., 3861
Dagnino, Aldo, 1315, 1665-1668, 1684
Dahl, Robert A., 171
Dahlitz, Julie, 2608

Dajani, M. S., 3546
Dale, Phillip S., 1513, 1521
Dallin, Alexander, 2609, 2617
Dam, Nguyen Cao, 5045
Damm, Kenneth W., 3698
Daniels, W., 620
Daoudi, M. J., 3546
Darilek, Richard E., 3158, 3275-3277
Darwin, H. G., 172, 1779
Dasgupta, Partha, 1190
David, Steven R., 2345
Davidow, Jeffrey, 5161, 5190
Davidson, Lynne A., 2516, 5331
Davies, Joseph E., 4325
Davis, Diana K., 1089
Davis, Earl E., 1090, 1669
Davis, H. E., 1780
Davis, J. A., 3712
Davis, Jacquelyn K., 2921
Davis, Lillian J., 1091
Davis, Lynn E., 2602
Davis, Morton D., 1198
Davis, Paul C., 3408
Davison, W. Phillips, 33, 4425-4426
Davy, Grant R., 2887
Day, J., 621
Day, R., 621, 1069
Dayan, Moshe, 4805
De Bourbon-Busset, Jacques, 4079
de Calliéres, François, 3973-3974
de Felice, Fortune-Barthelemy, 173
De Hoyos, Ruben, 5215
De Kieffer, D. E., 3713
De Margerie, Emanuel, 4080
De Merril, George, 3535
De Mestral, A. L. L., 2309
De Pauw, John W., 3804, 3817, 3821
De Renck, Anthony, 1092
De Rivera, Joseph H., 508
De Rose, Francoise, 3409
De Santis, Hugh, 4638
De Shazo, F. A., 5216
De Vos Van Steenwyth, W. J., 3159
De Waart, P. J. I. M., 34
De Wind, Adrian, 5247
De, Muhong, 1693
DeValk, Randall J., 3220
Dean, Arthur H., 2684, 2963, 5122
Dean, Jonathan, 556, 2685-2688, 3160-3161, 3224, 3362, 4504
Deane, John R., 4505, 4639
Dedijer, Stefan, 2132
Dedring, Juergen, 35, 2553
Degan, V. D., 1941

Author Index

Degorter, H., 3671
Del Monte, J. R., 1346-1347
Delaney, Robert F., 4427
Delano, Juno Lee, 1093
Delatorre, J., 3569
Dell, Sidney, 2864
Dellermann, Frank J., 2888-2889
Demiashkevich, Michael J., 3975
Demontbrial, T., 2689
Denis, J. E., 3714
Dennett, Raymond, 4463
Denton, William E., 2474
Deol, Surinder, 422
Der Derian, James, 3976, 4081, 4244
Derakhshani, S., 622, 3882
Derek, Paul, 3191
Desai, P., 2395
Deutsch, Karl W., 1316
Deutsch, Morton, 509, 623-631, 687, 699, 792, 872, 1317-1322
Devillers, Philippe, 1781, 4987
Dewitt, David B., 4792
Dhanani, Gulshan, 1942
Dholakia, Ruby Roy, 1847
Di Matteo, M. R., 943
Diazalejandro, C. F., 2396
Dibble, Anne, 3941
Dickinson, William B., 2690
Dickson, H. M., 5217
Diebold, William, 3570, 3608
Diekmann, Andreas, 4375
Diesing, Paul, 99, 369
Diez, Mary E., 177, 1094
Digeser, Peter, 2345
Dinstein, Yoram, 4849
Diskin, Abraham, 1338, 4850
Dismukes, B., 4535
Dixit, J. N., 4428
Dixon, Michael J., 4587
Dixon, Pierson, 2076
Dmitriev, Timur, 2010
Dobell, Peter C., 2692
Dobson, Alan P., 2517
Dohonue, William A., 1920
Dolbear, F. Trenery, 1323-1324
Domingo, Benjamin E., 5298
Dominick, Mary F., 174, 3256
Donelan, M. D., 77
Donnelly, Dorothy C., 4988
Donohue, William A., 175-178
Doob, A. N., 841
Doob, L. W., 36, 510, 632-639, 1887
Doran, Charles F., 3790
Dorcey, Anthony H. J., 3791

Doty, Paul, 2974, 3041
Douchin, E., 648
Dougherty, James E., 2611, 2693-2694, 3042
Douglas, A., 3547
Douval, B., 966
Downs, Charles, 5248
Downs, George W., 1325, 2695
Downs, Hunton, 4989
Dowty, Allan, 1888, 4851
Doxey, Margaret, 2518
Draper, Theodore, 4990
Drecos, J. L., 910
Drenth, Don R., 3143
Drew, E., 3410
Drews, Julie L., 1139
Drieghe, Rita, 1768, 1843
Driver, M. J., 640
Dror, Yehezkel, 179
Druckman, Daniel, 180-183, 430, 511-512, 573, 575, 641-656, 1095, 1127, 1326-1327, 1555, 1644, 1782, 4863, 5332-5333
Dryzek, John, 1943, 1981-1982
Du Toit, Pierre, 184
Dubey, Muchkund, 2397-2398
Dubrow, Elbridge, 4991
Duff, Peggy, 5046
Duffy, Gloria, 2599, 2696
Duffy, John F., 657-658
Dugan, Maire A., 185, 659, 1780
Dulles, John Foster, 186
Dunham, Donald C., 4326
Dunlop, John T., 37
Dunn, Frederick S., 38, 2153
Dunn, L., 1146
Dunn, Lewis A., 3341
Dunnigan, James F., 1742
Dupont, Christophe, 431
Dupuy, Trevor N., 2612
Durch, William J., 2027, 2311, 3925
Durosselle, J. B., 4084, 4304
Dusko, Doder, 4443
Dutka, Anna B., 3867
Dutton, William B., 1199

Eagles, Keith D., 4640
Eayres, James, 3977, 4085
Eban, Abba, 2011, 3978, 4086, 4852
Ebreo, A., 1881
Eckhart, William, 4506
Eckhoff, T., 1783
Edidis, Wayne A., 2475
Edmead, Frank, 1784, 1889

Edmunds, Sallie, 2554
Edwards, Geoffrey, 3278, 3539
Egea, Marcel, 1466
Eger, J. M., 3883
Ehrhardt, Carl A., 2519
Eilan, Arieh, 4087, 4507
Eiland, Michael, 5334
Eilts, Hermann F., 4088
Einhorn, Robert J., 2613
Einstein, Lewis, 4327
Eiseman, J. W., 1785
Eisenberg, M. A., 660
Ekvall, Robert B., 3979
El Baradei, Mohamed, 2346
Elaraby, Nabil, 2133
Elazar, David J., 4918
Eldridge, Albert F., 39
Elgstrom, Ole, 2399
Elias, T. O., 1944
Elkes, Roy, 598
Elkin, Jerrold F., 5335
Elliott, David W. P., 5336
Ellis, William F., 1096
Ells, J. G., 1328
Ellsberg, Daniel, 1329-1331
Emerson, R. M., 661
Emmerson, J. K., 5090
Emmons, Timothy D., 976
Emshoff, J. R., 1332
England, J. Lynn, 1333-1336
Engle, Kenneth W., 2697
English, Gary C., 4452
English, John, 5324
Engram, P. S., 1097
Ephraim, Yuchtman-Yaar, 4865
Epstein, William, 2891
Epstein, Y., 699
Eran, Oded, 4464
Erb, Guy F., 2401
Erickson, Bonnie H., 2028
Ernst, Manfred H., 2077, 2134
Esposito, Chiarella, 3923
Esser, James K., 610, 662, 785, 790, 1077
Etheredge, Lloyd S., 663-664
Ethridge, Mark, 4508
Etzioni, Amitai, 665
Etzold, Thomas H., 4641
Eubank, Keith, 2232-2233
Eustis, Robert D., 2310
Evans, G., 619, 666-667
Evarts, Richard W., 1743

Faber, Jan, 188

Faerstein, Paul H., 1098
Fagre, Nathan, 3571
Fahmy, Ismail, 4806
Fairbanks, Charles H. Jr., 3411
Faleiro, Eduardo, 3511
Faley, T., 668
Falk, Pamela S., 3512, 3742, 5191
Falk, Richard, 189, 4089
Fall, Bernard B., 4992
Fallers, L. A., 2698
Fang, L., 1337, 1432, 1670
Farber, D. C., 190
Farber, Henry S., 1761
Farcell, Dante B., 3279
Farer, Tom J., 3980
Faria, Hugo de A., 3924
Farley, Philip J., 2617, 2669, 2699-2701, 3207
Farrands, C., 191
Fartash, Manoutchehr, 2702
Fasulo, Linda M., 2045
Faucheux, C., 1016
Faure, Guy Oliver, 1890
Fedder, Edwin A., 192, 4509
Feigl, Hubert M., 3162
Feis, Herbert, 2234-2235
Feith, Douglas J., 3225
Feketekuty, Geza, 3548, 3764
Feld, Bernard T., 3044
Feld, Werner J., 2614, 4090
Felder, Ellene, 3930
Feldman, Shai, 4853
Fells, R. E., 669
Felsenthal, Dan S., 840, 1338-1339
Feltham, Ralph G., 4245
Fenno, Richard F., 2236
Fentress, Marvin A., 5337
Fenwick, Charles, 1945
Ferraris, Luigi Vittorio, 2615
Ferrell, Nancy W., 4275
Ferrell, Robert H., 2703, 4630
Festinger, L., 727
Festinger, Leon, 1200
Feulner, Edwin J., 4429
Fiallo, Fabio R., 2402-2403
Fifield, Russell H., 4968
Finch, M. L., 829
Findling, John E., 4276
Fine, Gary A., 670
Finer, Herman, 4642
Finger, Seymour M., 2046
Finkelstein, Lawrence S., 2047
Finlay, D. D., 4578
Finlayson, Jock A., 3685

Author Index

Finlayson, Jock A., 3664, 3672
Firestone, J. M., 1163
Firth, R., 1786
Fischoff, Stuart P., 1090, 1099
Fisher, Adrian S., 2704-2705
Fisher, Bart S., 3862
Fisher, C. S., 757
Fisher, Glen H., 40, 432, 671, 1899, 4412, 4643
Fisher, M. L., 672
Fisher, Roger D., 41-44, 193-201, 433-434, 673-674, 1744, 1787, 2667, 2706, 4510-4511, 4573, 4807, 5171-5172
Fisher, Ronald J., 1788-1790, 1891, 1946
Fitzgerald, Mark, 435
Fitzmaurice, H., 202
Fitzsimmons, M. A., 3995
Flack, M. J., 4091
Flagon, Alec, 3805
Flanagan, Stephen J., 3045
Fleck, Dieter, 5325
Fleischer, A., 1568
Fleischhauer, Carl August, 203
Fleishman, J. A., 857
Fliess, Barbara A., 2520
Flood, Patrick J., 5218
Floyd, David, 4512
Fluegel, Edna R., 2258, 3412
Flynn, Gregory A., 2892
Flynn, Jane, 4092
Fobian, G. S., 1879
Foddy, Margaret, 675
Fogelman, S. F., 1340
Fogg, Richard W., 204-205
Foley, Charles, 4808
Foltz, William J., 632, 635-636, 4376
Fontaine, Roger W., 5249
Forcey, B., 1100
Ford, David L., 676
Ford, Gerald R., 4328
Ford, John W., 1961
Forgac, Albert T., 2048
Forkosch, Joel A., 206
Forsythe, David P., 1947
Foster, J., 2404
Foster, K., 3
Foster, R. B., 2707
Fouraker, Lawrence E., 1201, 1224, 1582
Fowler, Wilton R., 4277
Fox, Annette Baker, 3792, 4093

Fox, John, 1341-1344, 1372
Fox, William T. R., 2078, 2708, 4094-4095
Francis, C., 207
Franck, Thomas M., 208, 3391, 3478, 3981
Frank, Jerome D., 677-678
Frankel, Joseph, 4096
Franklin, William M., 2259, 4097
Fraser, Niall M., 1202, 1315, 1345-1349, 1403-1405, 1554, 1665, 1667, 1671-1679, 1684-1685, 1695, 1734-1735
Fredericks, Brian, 5335
Freedman, Judith A., 3107
Freedman, Lawrence, 2616, 2709, 3163, 3192, 3413
Freedman, Matthew C., 4919
Freedman, Stuart C., 1075, 1101
Freeman, Charles W. Jr., 5148
Frei, Daniel, 45, 209-210, 350, 1791, 5299-5300
Freimer, M., 1350
Frey, Robert L., 679
Freymond, Jacques, 1892, 4377
Fried, K. E., 211
Friedheim, Robert L., 2311-2315, 2347-2348, 3925, 4246
Friedland, Nehemia, 680
Friedlander, Melvin A., 4920
Friedman, Myles I., 681
Friend, Kenneth E., 1351
Froman, L. A., Jr., 682-683
Fry, Michael G., 4921
Fry, William R., 684, 817
Frye, A., 3046
Fuandez, Julio, 2316
Fudenberg, Drew, 1352
Fukui, Haruhiro, 3715
Fullar, W., 1806
Fuller, L. L., 1792
Furlong, William L., 5202

Gaddis, John Lewis, 3363
Gaebelein, J. W., 578
Gaffney, Frank J., 2710
Gahagan, J. P., 685, 1353
Galaydh, Ali Khalif, 5192, 5195
Galbraith, John K., 4329
Gale, Basya, 212
Gale, Stephen, 212
Gallis, Paul E., 3129, 3144
Gallo, Philip S., 686, 959, 1354
Galloway, Eilene, 2079

Galtung, Johan, 213, 3414
Gamarekian, Barbara, 4098
Gamboa, Melquades J., 3982
Garavoglia, Guido, 3513
Gard, Robert G., 2893
Gardner, Richard N., 2012, 3863, 4711-4712
Garfinkle, Adam M., 1948, 1979, 2711, 4922
Garland, H., 1075
Garner, Katherine, 687
Garner, William R., 5203
Garnham, D., 4713
Garnier-Lancon, Monique, 4430
Garrett, James C., 5219
Garrison, James L., 724
Garrity, Patrick J., 3415
Garthoff, Raymond L., 2712, 3047-3051, 3130, 3364, 4513, 5301
Gaselee, Stephen, 3983
Gasteyger, Curt, 2199-2203
Gatzke, Hans W., 4278
Gavin, Cloe, 2346
Gavrilovic, S., 4099
Gazit, Mordechai, 1793
Gearin, C. J., 4057
Gehron, William J., 2975
Geiger, Theodore, 3609
Geipel, Gary, 5047
Geis, Florence, 688
Geisen, Martin, 1680
Geiser, Hans, 4247
Geisleker, Stephen B., 1459
Geiwitz, P. J., 1024
Gelb, Leslie H., 3365
Gellner, Charles R., 2713, 3107, 3145
General Agreement on Tariffs and Trade. GATT., 3743-3744
Gennaro, Pietro, 2555
Gentile, Ralph, 1355, 1681, 3108-3109
George, Alexander L., 2617, 2714-2716, 2894, 3416, 3972, 4100, 4465, 5302
George, Bruce, 3131
George, James L., 3208
Gerard, Andre, 4101
Gergen, K. J., 841
German, Robert K., 4514
Gerould, James, 2717
Gerson, Louis L., 4644
Gerson, M. B., 3110
Ghanayem, Ishaq I., 4809, 4923

Gharekhan, C. D., 3052
Ghauri, Pervez N., 3610, 3884, 3926
Giblin, J. F., 2895, 3385
Gibson, Hugh S., 4102
Giesbert, Franz-Olivier, 5338
Giffen, James H., 3806
Giffin, K., 533
Gifford, Michael, 3765
Gilbert, Felix, 4274
Gilkey, Roderick W., 689, 692
Gillette, Paul, 58
Gillis, John S., 1356
Ginsberg, I. J., 1458
Ginsburgs, George, 4588
Gittings, John, 4993
Gladwin, T. N., 690
Glagolev, I. S., 2718
Glaser, Stan, 3575
Glazer, Herbert, 5091
Glenn, E.S., 214
Gleysteen, William H. Jr., 5069
Glick, Leslie Alan, 3699
Glicksman, Alex, 2719
Gochman, C. S., 285
Goehring, Dwight J., 1357
Goeltner, Chris, 1708-1709
Goertemiller, John C., 2896
Golan, Mati, 4810
Goldberg, Andrew, 1358
Goldberg, Arthur J., 2080
Goldberg, Stephen B., 1745
Goldblat, Jozef, 2618, 2897, 3222
Goldenhuys, Deon, 5162
Goldhamer, H., 1359-1360
Goldstein, Donald, 5391
Goldstein, Susan, 1893
Golt, Sidney, 3745-3746
Gomaa, Salwa, 4924
Gooch, George P., 4279
Goodby, James E., 3132, 3280-3283, 3480
Goodman, Allan E., 4969, 4994, 5048
Goodman, Marc B., 3514
Goodrich, L. M., 215
Goodwin, G. L., 2081
Goormaghtigh, John, 2082
Gordenker, Leon, 5250
Gordon, David G., 1216
Gordon, Michael R., 2720
Gorecki, H., 216
Gori, Umberto, 2721
Goryachev, A., 1361
Gottheil, Diane Levitt, 4925
Gottlieb, A. E., 3515, 3766

Goudreau, Karen W., 2029-2030
Gould, W. L., 217
Graber, Doris A., 4645
Grace, William V., 1682
Graebner, N. A., 4646-4647
Graeven, D. B., 1102
Graham, John L., 3638-3640, 3832, 3840
Graham, M. W., 4648
Graham, Norman A., 2001, 2165, 2186-2187
Graham, Robert, 5303
Graham, T. R., 3717
Granier, Jacqueline P., 3256
Grant, D. F., 986
Grant, Natalie, 4515
Graubard, Stephen R., 4649
Gray, Colin S., 2722-2724, 3053-3054
Gray, H. P., 3572
Gray, Robert C., 2725, 3033
Gray, S. H., 691
Graybeal, Sidney N., 4516
Grayson, George W., 3885, 5220
Great Britain., 3927-3928, 5251
_____. Board of Trade., 3747
_____. Foreign Office., 2213-2218, 3481, 5082
_____. Foreign and Commonwealth Office., 3239, 5193
Greb, G. A., 2976-2977, 3055
Green, Eric D., 1745
Greene, Fred, 218
Greenhalgh, Leonard, 219, 689, 692-694, 1046
Greensburger, Francis, 46
Greenwald, John D., 3597
Gregg, Robert, 2405, 2476
Greig, D., 3718
Grenville, J. A. S., 4280
Grew, Joseph C., 4281
Grey, R. T., 2765
Grey, Rodney de C., 3767
Griesinger, D., 1362
Griffin, Grace G., 4273
Griffith, J., 858
Griffiths, Franklin, 2673, 2726
Grigsby, D. W., 695, 1255
Grinter, Lawrence E., 4995
Griswold, A. Whitney, 4714
Gromoll, Robert H., 4926
Gromyko, Andrei, 4330
Groom, A. J. R., 220, 5297
Gross Stein, Janice, 221-223, 1949, 4815, 4854-4859

Gross, A., 1794
Gross, Donald G., 2727
Grossman, Sanford J., 1363, 1683
Groth, Alexander J., 4103
Groux, Jean, 224
Grow, Mary M., 4762
Gruder, C. L., 696-698, 1018, 1103
Gruder, George W., 1364
Gruhn, Isebill, 2406
Grummon, S. R., 4860
Grunert, Horst, 436
Grzelak, Janusz, 1608
Grzybowski, Kazimierz, 4861
Guehenno, Jean-Marie, 2728
Guesotto, Nicole, 3284
Guetzkow, H., 225, 951, 1365-1366
Guittard, Stephen W., 3841
Gulhati, N. D., 1926
Gulliver, Philip H., 226-227
Gumpert, P., 437, 699
Gundelach, Finn, 3719
Guoxiang, Fan, 3133
Gurtov, Melvin, 5049
Gustafson, Lowell S., 5252
Gustafson, Thane, 4589
Güth, Werner, 1367-1368
Gutman, G. O., 3673
Guyer, Melvin J., 1216, 1341, 1343-1344, 1369-1372, 1517
Gwin, C., 2407
Gwom, A. J. R., 1242

Haas, Ernst B., 228, 2002, 2014, 2135
Haas, Michael, 229, 513, 2015
Haas, Peter, 2556
Haass, Richard N., 230, 2603, 2884, 3366
Habeeb, William M., 47, 438, 5253
Habib, P. C., 4104
Haccoun, R. R., 700, 775, 1104
Haden, Eric W., 2729
Haffey, Neil, 3793
Hage, Robert E., 2349
Haggard, S., 2165, 2186-2187
Hagras, Kamal, 2363, 2477
Hagva, V., 701
Hahn, E. J., 5092
Haig, Alexander M., 4331
Haight, David, 3482
Haines, Y. Y., 231
Haji, Iqbal, 2478
Halberstam, David, 4996-4997
Hale, Oron J., 3984

Haley, P. Edward, 3417, 4927
Halkia, Marianna, 2557
Hall, David K., 3367
Halle, Louis J., 4105, 4517
Halperin, Morton H., 2818
Halstead, John G. H., 4106
Hamblin, Robert L., 702-703
Hambro, E., 4107
Hamburger, Henry, 1372
Hamed, Joseph W., 3285
Hamel, Peter L., 1314
Hamilton, Andrew, 2730
Hamilton, John A., 2731
Hamilton, T., 704, 783
Hamilton, William D., 1239
Hamish, K., 1894
Hamlin, D., 2502
Hamm, Manfred R., 3418
Hammarskjöld, Dag, 2083-2086
Hammer, Armand, 4378
Hammerman, Gay M., 2612
Hammond, Kenneth R., 232, 589, 705-706
Hamner, F. T., 3573
Hamner, W. C., 707-710, 714, 1105, 1373, 1380, 1402
Hampson, Fen Osler, 3056
Han, Gyuseog, 834
Hand, Robert D., 4928
Handel, Michael I., 439, 3985, 4108
Haney, Patrick J., 4998
Hange, Robert C., 4774
Hankey, Maurice, 2154
Hannon, John S., 4999
Hansen, Allan C., 4413
Hansen, Richard E., 233
Hansen, Roger D., 2364
Hansford, E. A., 962-963, 1580
Haq, M. V., 2016
Harbottle, Michael, 1374, 1796
Harden, Jamie, 1920
Hardenbergh, Chalmers, 3164-3166, 3227, 3246, 3286
Hardford, Thomas, 606
Hardt, D. Brent, 3057
Hardy, Chandra, 2408
Hare, Paul, 711, 4816
Harf, J. E., 712
Harford, J. C., 1375
Harman, Willis, 98
Harnett, D. L., 514, 708, 713-714, 1376-1380
Harper, John, 2276
Harr, John Ensor, 3986-3987, 4109, 4248
Harral, H. B., 344
Harriman, W. Averell, 234, 2978, 4332, 4650
Harris, Elisa D., 3228-3229
Harris, Simon, 3686
Harris, Stuart, 3674
Harrison, Michael, 5392-5393
Harrison, Selig S., 5339
Harsanyi, John C., 715-716, 1203-1204, 1381-1396
Hart, Jeffrey A., 2479, 3952
Hart, M. M., 3574
Hartfield, E. F., 1851
Hartman, E. Alan, 1397
Hartman, Frederick H., 5340
Harvey, Jerry, 717
Haska, Lukas E., 2277
Haskel, Barbara G., 3886
Haslam, Jonathan, 3111
Hasse, Rolf, 2409
Hassner, Pierre, 440
Hatton, Raynhild, 4282
Haven, Andrew, 4518
Hayaki, I., 4929
Hayden, Eric W., 2732
Hayden, Gene, 2317
Hayden, Tom, 5000
Hayles, Robert, 441
Haynes, J. M., 1797
Hayter, William, 3988, 4651
Hazard, John N., 4519
Hazleton, William A., 1398
Hazzard, John N., 4520
Heald, Morrell, 4652
Hearn, Patrick, 3549
Heatley, David P., 3989
Heckathorn, Douglas, 718-719
Heckrotte, W., 2976
Heckrotte, Warren, 3358, 3811
Heeler, Roger, 861
Heikal, Mohamed, 4811
Heinrich, Waldo H., 4653
Helleiner, Gerald K., 2365, 2410-2411
Helmreich, Jonathan E., 3864
Helms, Robert F., 2898
Henderson, Bruce D., 235
Henderson, Gregory, 4414
Henderson, Loy W., 4333
Henderson, Michael D., 3768
Henderson, William, 5304, 5394
Hendriks, Erwin C., 1136
Hendryx, S. R., 3825

Author Index

Henkin, Louis, 48
Henrikson, Alan K., 2003, 2017, 3483, 4715-4716
Henss, Ronald, 1399
Hentsch, Thierry, 1892
Henze, L. J., 3887
Heo, Mane, 5070
Heradsveit, Daniel, 4862
Herberger, R. A., 3639
Herbert, Wray, 3419
Herman, Charles F., 515, 720, 1400
Hermann, Margaret G., 24, 516, 721-722, 4110
Hermes, Peter, 2412
Herrero, M. J., 1258
Herring, George C., 4634, 5001, 5050
Hersh, Seymour, 4654
Herter, Christian A., 4111
Herz, Martin F., 4112, 4249-4252, 4305, 4334, 4354
Herzog, Jaames H., 5109
Hess, Robert W., 3193
Hessel, Marek, 723, 1401
Hessing Cahn, Anne, 3369
Hester, Donald C., 2188
Hickman, James L., 724
Higashi, Chikara, 3853
Higgins, R. C., 978
Hildreth, Steven A., 2899-2900
Hill, Barbara J., 236
Hill, Christopher, 2521
Hill, Frederick B., 3483, 4431
Hill, Norman L., 2155
Hill, Roger, 2558-2559, 3167
Hills, H. L., 5318
Hiltrop, Jean M., 725-726
Himes, J. S., 517
Hingley, Ronald, 4466
Hinton, B. L., 1402
Hipel, Keith W., 1202, 1315, 1337, 1346-1349, 1403-1405, 1432, 1554, 1590-1592, 1665, 1667, 1670, 1672, 1674-1677, 1684-1685, 1693, 1695, 1730, 1734-1735
Hirschfeld, Thomas J., 2901, 3168, 3368
Hocking, Brian, 3769
Hoedemaker, Edward D., 237
Hoess, Friedrich, 4432
Hoffman, Arthur S., 4415
Hoffman, P. J., 727
Hofstede, Geert, 442
Hoggatt, Austin, 1406-1407
Hoglund, B., 49

Holder, William E., 238
Holdsworth, Richard, 5093
Holl, Otmar, 3317-3318
Holland, Harrison M., 4655
Holland, J., 5404
Holland, Rosemary, 2103
Holloway, David, 2733, 3194
Holma, Juha, 3287
Holmes, George, 3575
Holmes, J. G., 728
Holmes, John W., 1798, 2734, 4113, 4253, 4521, 5305
Holmes, William D., 5071
Holst, Johan J., 2735, 2902, 3058
Holsti, K. J., 50, 239, 729-730, 3288, 4114-4115, 5278
Holsti, Ole R., 731-732, 4522, 5221
Honavar, R. M., 5385
Honeyman, Christopher, 240, 1799
Hooley, Richard, 3929
Hoover, Robert A., 3059
Hopkins, Raymond F., 2413
Hopkins, Waring C., 2736
Hopmann, P. Terrence, 443, 733, 1038, 2737-2738, 2903-2904, 2979-2982, 3169-3170, 3195-3198, 3247, 3289, 4863
Hopple, Gerald W., 518, 1106
Horai, J., 734
Hordijk, L., 1701
Horelick, Arnold L., 5254
Hornstein, H. A., 735-736
Horowitz, Abraham D., 1408-1409
Horowitz, Irving Lewis, 241
Hoskyns, Catherine, 2560, 5163
Hotz, R., 2739
Houlden, P., 737
House, Karen Elliott, 4697
Hovet, Thomas, 2087
Howard, Nigel, 1410
Howe, G., 2522
Howe, Herbert, 1980
Hoyt, Ronald E., 3807
Hsieh, Alice L., 2999
Hsu, King-Yi, 4864
Huber, Reiner K., 1184-1185
Huber, Vandra L., 738-739, 880
Huddleston, Sisley, 3990
Hudec, Robert E., 3700, 3770
Hudson, John F., 3687
Hudson, Manley O., 2166
Hudson, Richard, 2318
Hufbauer, Gary C., 3550, 3771
Hughes, G. D., 713

Huisken, Ron, 3134
Hull, Cordell, 4335
Hull, T. N., 2523
Hume, Stephen P., 2524
Hunsaker, J. S., 1411
Hunsaker, P. L., 1411
Hunt, Betty, 5044
Hunter, R. E., 5002
Hunter, Susan, 1943, 1981-1982
Huntington, Samuel P., 3576
Huopaniemi, Jukka, 3319
Hupp, Alfred R., 4590
Hurewitz, Jacob Coleman, 4812
Hurrell, Andrew, 3930
Hurwitz, Alan, 444
Husband, William B., 4523
Husbands, Jo Louise, 1895, 3369
Huschens, Stephan, 1249
Hussein, Amin, 2136
Huston, T. L., 1023
Hutton, N., 3577
Hybel, Alex R., 5255
Hyland, William G., 3060, 3420

Iaquinta, Leonard, 445, 1782
Ifestos, Panayiotis, 2503
Ignatieff, George, 1896, 2740, 2905
Ikle, Fred C., 51-52, 242-248, 1412-1413, 1686, 4524, 5003
Ilchman, Warren F., 4656
Ilich, John, 53-54
Imai, R., 1800
Immerman, Richard H., 5001
Inbar, Michael, 4865
Indyck, Martin, 4866
Inogushi, T., 3842-3843
International Technical Information Institute., 3551
Intriligator, Michael D., 250
Iqbal, Afzal, 3991
Irani, Robert G., 4717, 4763
Irvine, Sally, 2561-2562
Irwin, John N., 4116
Irwin, P. C., 2319
Isaacson, Walter, 4657
Isard, Walter, 55-56, 251, 1801
Isen, Alice M., 600-601, 1080
Israeli, Raphael, 4813
Israelyan, Y., 2741

Jabber, Fuad, 5395
Jack, Homer A., 2742, 2983-2984
Jacks, M. E., 681
Jackson, Conrad N., 1107
Jackson, Elmore, 1746, 1802
Jackson, Geoffrey, 3992
Jackson, John H., 3720-3722
Jackson, William D., 2137
Jacob, James E., 1398
Jacobini, H. B., 5256
Jacobs, David C., 252
Jacobsen, Carl G., 2743
Jacobsen, Dan, 4867
Jacobsen, Kurt, 1803
Jacobson, Harald K., 2414, 2964, 2985
Jacobson, Kenneth H., 3199
Jacovides, Andreas J., 2320
James, Alan M., 2088, 4117
Jandt, Fred E., 57-58
Janis, Irving L., 519, 740
Jankowitsch, Odette, 3578
Janosik, Robert J., 253, 446-447
Jarke, Mattias, 1804
Jefferson, Gail, 741
Jehn, Mary E., 2348
Jelassi, Tawfik, 1804, 1871
Jenisch, Uwe, 2321-2323
Jenkins, Frank W., 1414
Jenks, Carl M., 5257
Jennings, A., 2041, 2455
Jensen, Lloyd, 742, 2619, 2744-2746, 2906-2907, 2986, 3061-3063
Jervis, Robert, 59, 254, 743-744, 1415, 4306
Jessup, Philip C., 5341
Jockel, Joseph T., 5279
Johansen, Elaine, 4525
Johansen, Robert C., 2908
John, Louis B., 3772
Johnson, D. F., 1805-1806, 1832-1833, 1835
Johnson, D. W., 736
Johnson, David W., 745, 1021
Johnson, Edgar A. J., 3993
Johnson, Gerald W., 3055
Johnson, Harry G., 3613
Johnson, Joseph E., 4356, 4367, 4463
Johnson, Loch K., 4658
Johnson, Lyndon B., 4336
Johnson, Nils, 3749
Johnson, Roger, 1021
Johnson, V. Alexis, 3018, 4718
Johnston, Douglas M., 2525, 5342
Johnston, Robert W., 255
Johnston, Whittle, 4719
Joiner, C. A., 5004
Joiner, Harry, 448

Author Index

Jonah, James O., 1897
Jonas, Anne M., 3064
Jones, A. J., 1205
Jones, Dorothy, 4283
Jones, Howard, 4659
Jones, Rodney W., 3370
Jones, T., 932
Jönsson, Christer, 256-258, 520, 746, 1108, 2965-2966, 3931, 4526-4527
Jordan, Robert S., 2375, 2480, 2504
Jordan, W. M., 2089-2092
Jorden, William J., 5204
Joseph, M. L., 747
Joseph, Myron L., 1054
Joshua, Wynfred, 3065
Josling, T. E., 3682
Joy, C. Turner, 4467, 5066
Joyner, Christopher C., 3888, 3932, 5416
Juda, Lawrence, 3371, 3386
Juergenmeyer, John E., 4405
Julian, J. W., 851, 1122-1123
Jung, Ernst F., 3171-3172
Jurrjens, Rudolph, 3259, 3290

Kahan, James P., 748, 1357, 1416-1418, 1504-1505, 1687
Kahin, George M., 5005-5006
Kahn, A. S., 749
Kahn, Herman, 5007
Kaiser, R. G., 2765
Kakabadse, Mario A., 3933
Kalai, Ehud, 1419-1421
Kalb, Bernard, 4660
Kalb, Marvin, 4660
Kalil, Michael B., 3723
Kalyadin, A., 2747
Kambalov, S., 449
Kamel, Mohamed Ibrahim, 4814
Kamp, Karl-Heinz, 3173
Kampelman, Max M., 2909, 3291-3294, 4528
Kaplan, Lawrence S., 4652
Kaplan, Morton A., 259, 1422, 1688, 3019, 4868
Kaplin, A., 4529
Kaplowitz, Noel, 750
Kapoor, Ashok, 3552, 3579, 3865, 3889
Kapp, Robert A., 5110
Kapur, Ashok, 2987, 3338, 3890
Kapur, Raj K., 2910
Karis, D., 648
Karkoszka, Andrzej, 2748, 2858

Karl, Patricia A., 4433-4434
Karns, Margaret P., 2526
Karrass, Chester L., 60-61, 1109
Kaspar, Daniel, 3854
Kastl, Jorg, 3295
Kattenburg, Paul M., 4254
Katz, Daniel, 260
Katz, E., 261
Katz, Marsha, 1423
Katz, Neil, 262, 1110
Kauffman, Richard L., 2001
Kaufman, Sanda, 1898
Kaufmann, Johan, 450, 1807, 2049, 2156
Kaufmann, P. J., 3580
Kavanagh, Michael J., 657-658
Kavass, Igor I., 3256
Kayani, Amer, 1983
Kayser, E., 616, 799, 802
Kaznacheev, Aleksander, 4468
Kazuo, Ogura, 5123
Kechkeméthy, Joseph, 4924
Kee, Herbert W., 751, 1111
Keeney, Ralph L, 1206
Keens-Soper, Maurice, 2093, 3342, 4118-4119
Kegley, Charles W., 1838
Keiffer, M. G., 1112
Keil, Linda J., 848
Kelen, Emery, 2094
Keliher, John G., 3151
Keller, Abraham, 2749
Keller, Suzanne, 4435-4436
Kellerman, Barbara, 263
Kelley, Harold H., 574, 752-759, 1424, 1728
Kelly, David, 3994, 4120
Kelman, Herbert C., 521, 760-767, 4379, 4869-4872
Kemp, Arthur, 2260
Kennan, George F., 4121-4125, 4337-4338, 4469, 4661
Kennedy, A. L., 4284
Kennedy, Gavin, 3553-3554
Kennedy, Paul, 4285
Kennedy, R., 3218
Kennedy, Robert F., 5306
Kent, George, 264, 522
Kent, Glenn A., 3220
Keogh, James, 4126
Keohane, Robert O., 122, 1236
Kern, Montague, 4930
Kerr, W., 3775
Kersten, Gregory E., 1425-1429, 1689-

1691
Kertész, Stephen D., 2505, 3421, 3995-3996, 4127, 4530-4531, 4591, 4662, 4720
Kette, G., 586
Kettelle, John D., 1185, 2750-2752
Keynes, Mary K., 2527
Keys, Christopher B., 1760
Khronstalev, Mark A., 1692
Khrushchev, Nikita S., 4470
Khuri, F., 4873
Khvostov, V., 2753-2754
Kiernan, Thomas, 46
Kiewe, Amos, 4931
Kihl, Y. W., 5072
Kildow, Judith T., 2324, 2350
Kilgour, D. Marc, 1193, 1276, 1337, 1430-1433, 1670, 1693
Killham, Edward L., 3296
Killough, Hugh B., 128
Kilmann, R. H., 768
Kim, Hak-Joon, 5073
Kim, Jackie K., 5280
Kimball, Warren F., 2237, 4663
Kimche, Jon, 4874
Kimmel, M. J., 769, 930
Kimmel, Paul R., 451, 4247
Kimura, Hiroshi, 3812-3813
Kincade, William H., 2620, 2755
Kinder, D., 770
Kindermann, Gottfried-Karl, 5074
King, F. P., 875
King, John H., 3230
King, Timothy D., 1694, 2981, 3000-3001
Kinnas, John M., 2031
Kintner, William R., 3020, 3066-3067
Kirkpatrick, Ivone, 4128-4129
Kissinger, Henry A., 62, 265-267, 2018, 2988, 3422, 4130-4132, 4339-4340, 4664-4665, 4919, 5008-5009
Kistiakowsky, G. B., 2756
Kite, W. R., 1034
Kitzinger, Uwe, 2506
Kivikari, Urpo, 1434, 3614
Klaiber, Wolfgang, 3152
Klauss, R., 771
Klein, David H., 5124
Kleinke, C., 772, 889
Klieman, Aharon, 4932
Klimoski, Richard J., 587-588, 700, 773-775, 1113, 1435
Kline, Harvey F., 3934

Klineberg, Otto, 523
Kloepzig, R., 452
Knapp, W. M., 1829
Kniveton, B. K., 990
Knott, James, 2203
Knouse, Stephen B., 1113-1114
Knox, Robert E., 751
Kober, Stanley H., 4764
Koch, K. F., 5010
Kochan, Thomas A., 268, 1950
Kofoed-Hansen, Otto, 524
Kogan, Nathan, 721-722, 776, 806
Koh, T. T. B., 2325-2326
Kohl, Wilfrid L., 3359-3360, 3657
Kohler, Foy D., 3112, 4133, 4721
Kohler, Larry R., 3658
Kohls, J. W., 749
Kolb, Deborah M., 1747, 1808-1809
Kolkowicz, Roman, 2624
Komorita, S. S., 662, 777-791, 1077, 1115, 1436
Kondracke, Morton M., 3135
Kopelmanas, L., 2167
Kordonski, William M., 842
Korhonen, Keijo T., 2757
Kostiner, Joseph, 1951, 1984
Kotik, Paul, 1320
Kovalyova, O., 4134
Kovner, Milton, 4592
Koziej, R., 1115
Kraemer, Kenneth L., 1199, 1437
Kraft, Joseph, 3423, 5011
Kramer, R. D., 3891
Krantz, T. A., 3320
Kraslow, David, 4970
Krasner, Stephen D., 2415-2416
Kratochwil, Friedrich, 5307
Kraus, Max W., 2621
Krause, Joachim, 2911
Krauss, Robert M., 625-626, 792-793, 1319, 1322
Kravitz, David A., 782, 1436
Kremenyuk, Victor A., 269, 453
Kressel, Kenneth, 1810, 1834, 1952
Krickus, Richard J., 2758
Krieg, William L., 2563
Kriesberg, Louis, 270-273, 454, 525, 794-795, 2989, 4380, 4933-4934, 5343
Krishnamurti, R., 2417-2421
Krishnamurty, G. V. G., 3997
Kritzer, Herbert M., 291
Krogh, Dean, 4722
Krueger, Anne O., 2386

Kruger, Herbert, 4135
Kruglanski, Arie W., 343
Krus, Lech, 1658-1659
Kruzel, Joseph J., 2759-2760
Kryzanek, Michael J., 5222
Kudree, Robert T., 2469
Kuhlman, D. M., 796
Kuhn, Alfred, 797
Kuhn, Harold W., 1438
Kuhn, J. R. D., 1695
Kulski, Wladislav W., 4532
Kumar, R., 690
Kumar, Satish, 2422, 5396
Kumar, U., 1135
Kuttner, R., 3844
Kwieciak, Stanley, 2912

Labrie, Roger P., 2622
Lachs, Manfred, 1811, 2095
Lackman, William F., 2913
Lacouture, Jean, 5012
Lacy, William S. B., 798, 4136
Lad, Richard L., 5223
Ladner, Robert, 1439
Lahoda, T., 2204
Laing, James D., 1351, 1440
Laise, Carol C., 4137
Lake, D. G., 1116
Lall, Arthur S., 63, 1748, 1953, 2219, 2761, 5111
Lall, Sanjaya, 2423
Lamb, W. C., 4210
Lambert, Robert W., 3002, 3240, 3251
Lambeth, Benjamin S., 3343
Lamborn, Alac C., 5205
Lamm, Helmut, 616, 776, 799-807
Lampson, Edward T., 5397
Lancaster, Carol, 2481
Landi, Dale M., 274, 455
Lang, David, 3940
Lang, E., 590
Lang, Winfried, 2032
Lange, R., 783
Langmeyer, David, 1583
Lankhuff, P., 4255
Lanto, S., 1117
Lapidoth, Ruth, 4875
Larson, Arthur, 3344
Larson, Deborah W., 808
Lateef, Noll, 2424
Latour, Stephen, 809
Laue, James H., 275, 456-457, 810, 1812-1814, 1899-1900
Laue, Lynn L., 1294

Launay, Jacques de, 4286
Lauren, Paul G., 276, 2096, 3998-3999, 4138-4140, 4307, 5112
Lave, Lester B., 811, 1324
Laver, Michael, 277-278
Laves, Walter H. C., 2097
Lawler, Edward J., 8, 125, 503, 604, 812-813, 856
Lawrence, D., 727
Lawrence, M. F., 3321
Lawrence, Stewart, 5051
Lawson, Colin W., 2425
Lawson, Fred H., 4876
Lax, David A., 64, 279-282, 458-460, 1650, 3606, 3918
Laylin, J., 1901
Le Blanc, James L., 4935
Le Marquand, David G., 5281
Le Paestre, Philippe, 2426
Leap, T. L., 887
Leap, Terry L., 1484
Leatherwood, M., 1878
Lebedev, N., 4723
Lebow, Richard Ned, 283
Lechy, William A., 435
Lecraw, D. J., 2427
Lederer, Ivo J., 2507
Lee, C. J., 3822
Lee, Dwight R., 2762
Lee, Hyock Sup, 3935
Lee, John, 4416
Lee, Ki-Tak, 5075
Lee, Robert E., 4141
Lee, Tom K., 3581
Lee, William, 4877
Leeds, Roger S., 3936
Legault, L. H. J., 2309
Leginski, W. A., 974
Lehman, Ronald, 3209
Leiss, Amelia C., 5308
Leitenberg, Milton, 2763-2764
Leites, Nathan C., 1412-1413, 1686, 4593
Leng, Russell J., 284-287, 1441, 3424
Leng, Shoa-Chuan, 5103
Lensberg, Terje, 1227
Lenway, S., 3881
Leonard, J. F., 2765, 3231
Leonard, Julie, 5261
Lerche, Charles O., 3425
Leung, K., 814-815
Leutze, James R., 5344
Levi, A., 288

Levi, W., 289, 4142
Levin, Edward P., 65
Levine, Edward P., 1815, 1902
Levine, Herbert S., 1954
Levine, Stephen, 5345
Levine, Steven I., 1955
Levinsohn, Jay R., 1442
Levinson, Macha, 2766
Levitt, C. A., 1263
Levy, Marc A., 1956
Levy, Thomas A., 5278
Lewicki, Roy J., 12, 66-67, 133, 290, 816, 946, 1118, 1146, 1318
Lewis, David V., 68
Lewis, Kevin N., 2767, 2914
Lewis, Samuel W., 4724
Lewis, Steven A., 817, 908, 920
Lewis, V. A., 2327
Leyton Brown, David, 3773
Li, Chia Yiu, 479
Li, Duanben, 3136
Libby, Ronald T., 5173
Lie, T., 2050
Lieb, Diane, 1957, 4936
Lieberman, B., 818-819, 839
Liebert, Robert M., 820-821
Liebling, B., 574
Liebrand, Wim B. G., 822
Liedermann, Helmut, 3322
Lien, Chan, 5125
Lieurance, Peter R., 5013
Lifshitz, Michaela N., 823, 1119, 1135
Light, Margot, 1443
Lilien, Gary L., 1292
Lind, E. A., 824
Lindell, Ulf, 2168
Linden, Ronald H., 3937
Lindskold, Svenn, 825-831, 832-834, 1007, 1120
Linebaugh, David, 3137, 3210
Lipe, Dewey, 835
Lippincott, Donald, 5269-5270
Lipsitz, Lewis, 291
Lipski, Jozef, 4341
Lipstein, K., 1816
Liska, George, 4000
Litimov, N., 4143
Litman, J. M., 4256
Litterer, Joseph A., 66-67
Livingston, D., 1362
Livingstone, William G., 1696
Livne, Zvi, 461, 1444
Llados, Jose Maria, 4406

Lloyd, William B., 1817
Lockhart, Charles, 69, 292-293, 526, 836, 1697
Lodal, Jan M., 3211
Lodgaard, S., 3212
Loeb, Benjamin S., 2631, 2967
London, Kurt, 4144
Look, J. D., 967
Loomis, J. L., 837
Loomis, Richard T., 4725
Loory, Stuart H., 4970
Lopez, George A., 294
Lopez, Guerara, 5224
Lopez, Salvador P., 4145
Lord, Plumb, 3426
Losev, S., 4437
Lovaas, Karen, 1870
Lovald, Johan L., 2328
Low, Maurice A., 4146
Low, Stephen, 1958
Lowden, S. R., 3892
Lowe, Henry J., 4765
Lowenthal, Abraham, 5258
Luard, Evan, 70, 1818, 2623, 2768
Luban, David, 295
Lubbers, Jan Hendrik, 4147
Lubmann, Stanley B., 5126
Luce, Claire Boothe, 4533
Luce, R. Duncan, 1207
Luce, Richard, 3232
Luchius, David, 2189
Ludwig, L. D., 644
Luhr, R., 1313
Lukasiewicz, Juliusz, 4342
Lukes, I., 2769
Lukov, Vadim B., 296-297
Lumsden, Malvern, 1445
Lund, Oliver, 3701
Lundgren, David, 1583
Lundin, S. J., 3241
Lundstedt, Sven B., 3615
Luns, Joseph M. A. H., 3427
Lupfer, Michael, 1446
Lupworth, C. William, 787
Lussier, V. L., 4907
Lutzker, D. R., 1447
Lyne, Roderic, 4438-4439
Lynn-Jones, Sean M., 3372
Lyon, Peter, 2528
Lyon-Allen, Mary M., 2138

M'Bow, Amadou M., 298
Maas, Jeannette, 2564
Mabry, Bebars DuPre, 299

MacBean, A. I., 3555
MacDonald, Mary K., 4453
MacDonell, John, 4148
MacFarlane, S. N., 2915
MacGillivray, Karen P., 2770
MacMurray, B. K., 812
MacWhinney, B., 2329
Macintosh, James, 3323
Mackintosh, Malcolm, 2771
Macober, William B., 4001
Maechling, Charles, 4149-4150
Magenau, J. M., 838, 1121
Magnarella, Paul J., 4257, 4878
Magnes, Ralph H., 4937
Magnone, Gerald J., 4635-4636
Magnusson, Ulla, 91
Mahajan, Harpreet, 5307
Mahant, E. E., 2565
Mahler, Vincent A., 3675
Mahoney, Robert, 182, 653
Mainland, Edward A., 300
Maisky, Ivan, 4343
Makeig, Douglas C., 5346
Makinda, Samuel M., 5164
Makins, Christopher J., 3068
Maksoud, Clovis, 4879
Malcolm, D., 839
Malitza, Mircea, 301
Malloch, Theodore R., 2366
Malmgren, Harald B., 3451, 3536, 3582-3585
Malone, Gifford D., 4440
Malouf, M. W. K., 1448, 1530, 1540, 1544
Mandel, Robert, 302, 462
Mandelbaum, Michael, 3392, 3428
Mandell, Brian S., 463, 1985
Mann, Howard, 2772
Mann, P., 1927
Mannix, E. A., 1019
Mansbach, Richard W., 4534
Mansell, Diana, 550
Maoz, Zeev, 840, 1449
Marais, N., 464
Marantz, Paul, 4815
Maresca, John J., 3257, 3297
Marin, Gerardo, 1450
Mark, Clyde R., 4938, 5052
Marks, Frederick W., 4666
Marks, Leonard H., 2019
Marks, Matthew J., 3585
Marlowe, D., 841
Marsh, P. D. V., 3556
Marshall, Bruce D., 3138

Marshall, Charles Burton, 303
Marshall, James, 4381
Marshall, Peter, 2428
Marshello, A. F. J., 796
Marsteller, Thomas F., 1959
Martel, William, 1742
Martin, Anthony D., 2916
Martin, Edwin M., 2190
Martin, Geoffrey R., 304
Martinez, Oscar J., 71
Marts, Marion E., 5280
Martz, M. J. R., 305
Marwah, Onkar, 5347
Maschler, Michael, 1451
Masih, A., 3724
Maslove, Allan M., 3794
Mason, Paul E., 1959
Mastenbrock, Willem F. G., 306, 465
Mateesco-Matte, Mircea, 2773
Mates, L., 2774, 3429
Mathias, Charles McC. Jr., 4726
Matthews, Byron A., 842
Matthews, R. D., 5174
Mattingly, Garring, 4287
Mattison, Jeanne V., 4382
Mattox, Gale Ann, 3113
Matzinger, Margit, 3688
Maurer, John Henry, 5348
Maury, Robin, 605
Mautner-Markhof, Frances, 2020, 3387
May, Simon, 2429
Mayall, J., 5175
Mayer, Andrew C., 466
Mayer, Arno J., 4288
Mayer, Jean E., 2529, 3240
Mayer, Leo V., 3774
Mayer, Martin, 4002
Mayers, D., 4151
Mayle, Paul D., 2238
Mazur, Allan, 843
McAllister, Jef O., 3018
McAndrew, William, 3096
McCall, J. B., 3637
McCamy, James L., 4003
McCarthy, Kenneth, 745
McClintock, Charles G., 844-848, 987
McClintock, Robert, 307
McClure, D. H., 3324
McConnell, James M., 4535
McCreary, Don R., 3833, 5094, 5104
McCreary, Scott, 5259
McCullouch, Frank, 5014
McCullough, George B., 308
McDermott, O., 4004

McDonald, Alan, 409
McDonald, John D., 1208
McDonald, John W., 413, 467, 2482, 3484, 4152, 4258, 4407, 5398
McDonough, Mark, 5393
McEachrane Dickson, Helen, 5225
McGaffey, David C., 300, 1819, 5349
McGeorge, Bundy, 2775
McGhee, George C., 4005, 4153-4155, 4344, 4727
McGillicuddy, N. B., 849, 1820
McGinnis, Michael D., 309
McGrath, J. E., 850-852, 1122-1123, 1170-1171
McGrenere, Gwen, 3191
McInnis, Edgar, 4156
McKay, Vernon, 5165
McKenna, J. C., 4006
McKersie, Robert B., 310, 543
McKitrick, Jeffrey S., 3146
McLachlan, Donald, 3775, 4157
McLaren, Virginia, 1124
McLean, C., 1246
McLean, R. A., 3586
McLellan, David, 4667
McLennan, Andrew, 1698
McMahon, J. F., 2098
McMullen, Christopher J., 1986-1987, 4158
McNamara, Robert J., 2917
McNeel, S. P., 844
McNeil, William C., 3938
McNeill, J. H., 2776
McNeill, William H., 2261
McRae, D. M., 3725, 5350
McTague, John J. Jr., 4880
McVitty, Marion H., 2777
Mcphail, B., 2430
Mcphail, T. L., 2430
Meade, James E., 3939
Meagher, Robert F., 3616
Mechling, J., 780
Medalia, Jonathan E., 2990
Medford, Robert E., 1125
Mee, Charles L., 2239
Meeker, L. D., 1286
Meeker, R. J., 962-963, 1452, 1580-1581, 1699, 1719-1727
Meeks, Kenneth W., 311
Mefford, Dwayne, 1700
Megna, L. L., 3587
Meier, G. M., 3726
Meiksins, Gregory, 4594
Meissner, B., 3325

Mellbin, Skjold G., 3298
Meltzer, Ronald T., 2431, 2483
Mendelsohn, Jack, 2778
Menderhausen, Horst, 4259-4261
Mennis, Bernard, 4668
Menon, K. P. S., 4262
Merchant, Livingston T., 4159-4160
Merle, Mercel, 468
Merli, Frank J., 4669
Merlini, Cesare, 3502, 3517
Mermet, L., 1701
Merrills, J. G., 2297
Merritt, Jeffrey D., 4728, 5226
Merritt, Richard L., 527
Mertes, Alois, 3299
Mese, L. A., 853
Messinger, S. L., 661
Metford, J. C. J., 5206
Metzger, S. D., 1821
Meyer, Armin H., 4345
Meyer, Ernest, 4383
Mian, Pauline, 5397
Michelini, Ronald L., 1453
Michener, H. A., 854-858, 1454-1459
Micholus, Edward F., 5351
Mickiewicz, Ellen P., 2624
Micunovic, Velyko, 4471
Middleton, Drew, 4161
Middleton, Robert, 3866
Midgaard, Knut, 312-313, 1460-1461, 2021, 2169
Miettinen, Jorma K., 3233
Mikesell, Raymond F., 4536
Miko, Francis T., 3326-3327
Mikus, Joseph A., 5352
Milburn, Thomas W., 528
Milensky, Edward S., 2530
Miles, Edward, 2330
Miljan, Toivo, 2367
Miller, C. E., 778, 791
Miller, Clyde R., 529
Miller, D. L., 3845
Miller, G. H., 859
Miller, Gary J., 118
Miller, J. D. B., 2531, 4263
Miller, Linda B., 72
Miller, Mark E., 2913
Miller, Mark L., 3776-3777, 3893
Miller, Ralph R., 860
Miller, Richard I., 2051
Miller, Robert, 1903
Millhauser, M., 314
Mills, D., 2432
Milner, Neal, 1870

Author Index

Minas, J. Sayer, 1462
Miner, Frederick C., 3588
Minter, W., 5176
Mishal, Shaul, 4850
Misra, K. P., 2052
Mitchell, Bruce, 3894
Mitchell, C. R., 315-316, 1749
Mitchell, Ted J., 861, 1126
Mitchell, Terence R., 862
Mitchell, Theodore, 1702
Mittelmark, M., 1127
Miyatake, N., 3842-3843
Modelski, George, 1822, 2566, 3460
Mogy, R. B., 863, 909
Mohd, Tan Sri Datuk Haj, 5353
Molander, Peter, 864
Molander, Roger C., 3040
Molinell, Harold, 4537
Monroe, Elisabeth, 4881
Montauer, Carlos A., 1823
Montgomery, John D., 4729
Montville, Joseph V., 4384-4385
Mookerjee, G. K., 4007
Moon, C. I., 2383
Moore, Christopher W., 1750, 1904
Moore, Robert J., 2368
Moore, Sally F., 865
Moore, W. H., 1728
Moore, W. Jr., 1699
Moorhouse, Geoffrey, 4008
Moran, Robert T., 3834
Morawiecki, Wojciech, 2567
Moreaux, Michel, 1463
Morehouse, L. G., 1464
Morgan, J. H., 4756
Morgan, Ted, 2240
Morgan, Thomas C., 1465, 1703-1704
Morgan, W. R., 866
Morgenstern, Oskar, 1229
Morgenthau, Hans J., 73, 317-318, 4162-4163, 5015
Morley, Ian E., 530, 867-869, 1128-1129
Morris, Ellis, 2220
Morris, Michael A., 2331
Morrison, Bruce J., 870
Morrison, Richard J., 1351, 1440
Morse, D. D., 3895
Morse, Edward L., 2532, 3589-3590
Morse, Oliver, 319
Morton, Kathryn, 2484
Mosely, Philip E., 2262, 4538-4539
Moser, Leo, 5101
Moser, Sheila, 18, 109

Moses, Russell L., 1988
Mosettig, Michael D., 4164
Moss, Barry F., 987
Möttölä, Kari, 3258, 3328
Moulton, Mildred, 2191
Mowat, R. B., 4009
Mowshovitz, A., 1503
Moynagh, Michael, 3896
Mphaisa, Chisepo J. J., 4165
Mroz, J. E., 1905
Msabaha, Ibrahim S. R., 2351
Mudd, Stuart D., 74
Mugny, Gabriel, 871
Mujal-Leon, Eusebio, 4540
Mulhall, Daniel, 2779
Mullen, Thomas, 3809
Muller, Gunter F., 1314
Muller, Steve, 4166
Mumme, Stephen P., 2533, 5205
Muney, B. F., 872
Munier, Bertrand R., 1209, 1340, 1466
Munton, Don, 5289
Murakami, Yoshio, 5105
Muravchik, Joshua, 3069
Murdoch, P., 873
Murnighan, J. K., 874, 1467-1470, 1534, 1539, 1544, 1824
Muromcew, Cyril, 1050
Murphy, J. L., 1471
Murphy, John F., 2053
Murphy, Robert D., 4670
Murray, John S., 320
Muscari, Paul G., 1825
Mushakoji, Kinhide, 5095-5096, 5106
Muskie, Edmund S., 4167
Mustafa, Zubeida, 5016
Mutz, Reinhard, 3175
Myers, A. E., 875
Myerson, R. M., 1472-1474
Myhre, Jeffrey D., 5309
Mytelka, Lynn K., 1475

Naftali, Timothy J., 3790
Nagao, Yoshimi, 56
Nahlik, Stanislaw E., 2534
Nail, P., 614
Namier, Lewis B., 4289
Namiesniowski, C. A., 3329
Nan, Henry R., 2485
Narayanan, R., 3898
Nardin, T., 876
Nascimento E Silva do, G. E., 4168-4169

Nash, John F., 1476-1479, 1705
National Science Foundation., 3818
Nau, H. R., 2535
Naughton, William A., 5260
Navarette, J., 2433
Naveh, David, 711, 4816
Nazarkin, Yu, 2747
Nazem, Nurul Islam, 5399
Neal, F. W., 4170
Neale, Margaret A., 75, 134, 564, 738-739, 877-881, 1130-1131
Neidle, Allan F., 2205, 2625, 2991
Neilson, Francis, 2099
Neimeier, J. G., 5227
Nelkin, Dorothy, 2568
Nelson, Charles G., 3619
Nelson, Daniel J., 2569
Nelson, Randall H., 2570
Nemeth, C., 882-883
Nerlich, Uwe, 2782-2783, 3176, 4472-4473
Neslin, Scott A., 692, 694
Neubauer, Deane E., 1906
Neuhold, Hauspeter, 3330-3331
Neumann, William L., 2241
Nevin, John A., 2784
Newcomb, T. M., 884
Newhouse, John, 3021, 3070-3075
Newmark, Eileen, 441, 1913
Newsom, David D., 321, 4010, 4172, 4360, 4474, 4671, 4882, 5310, 5354
Nguyen, Van Ba, 5017
Nicholls, Anthony, 2546
Nicholson, M. B., 322-323
Nicolaidis, Kalypso, 3620
Nicolayev, A., 4542
Nicolson, Harold, 4011, 4173-4178, 4290, 4308, 4730
Nicolson, Nigel, 5018
Nielson, F., 4179
Nielsson, Gunnar P., 2571
Nierenberg, Gerald I., 76, 324-325, 531-532
Niezing, Johan, 2785, 2918
Nikolayev, N., 3345
Nikolayev, Y., 3431
Niksch, Larry A., 5083
Niles, Thomas M. T., 3778
Nimmo, Geoffrey A., 3332
Ninkovich, Frank A., 4672, 4731
Nironen, Erki, 3328
Nitz, Lawrence H., 898, 1480
Nitze, Paul H., 2786-2791, 3076-3077, 3147, 4543-4544
Nixon, Richard M., 3432-3433, 4346, 4545, 4673
Noack, Paul, 3301
Nobel, J. W., 1706
Noble, Steven J., 1707
Nochajski, T. H., 1132
Noel, R. C., 617
Nogee, Joseph L., 2634, 2792-2793, 3373-3375, 4475
Nolan, Jane E., 2659-2660, 3376, 3384
Noorani, Munawar, 5355
North, Lisa, 5261-5262
North, Robert C., 5221
Northcraft, Gregory B., 75, 879-880, 1131
Northedge, F. S., 77, 326
Nossal, Kim Richard, 5400
Notzold, Jurgen, 3302
Novison, N., 1009
Noyelle, Thierry J., 3867
Numelin, Ragnar, 4291
Nurmi, Harmu, 1434
Nutter, G. Warren, 4674
Nutting, Anthony, 2626
Nydegger, Rudy V., 1481-1482
Nye, Joseph S., 2002, 2627, 2794-2795, 2920, 3346-3348
Nyerere, Julius K., 2434
Nyerges, Janos, 327, 469, 3748
Nyhart, J. Daniel, 1650, 1708-1709, 2352
Nzomo, Maria, 5194

O'Brien Cruise, Rita, 2369
O'Brien, G. M., 1133
O'Brien, William, 4939
O'Connor, Raymond G., 4012
O'Danover, William, 2508
O'Donnell, Charles P., 4180
O'Hara, Michael N., 4595
O'Keefe, David, 78
O'Neill, Michael, 2536
O'Shea, Timothy J. C., 3855
Obaseki, Nosakhare O., 2572
Oberg, J., 2796
Odell, John, 3621, 3688, 3899-3900, 3940-3942
Offiong, John, 2488
Ofshe, Richard, 885, 1483
Ofshe, S. L., 885
Ohlin, G., 2435-2436
Ohlman, H., 414

Author Index

Ohno, K., 5107
Oliva, Terence A., 1484
Oliver, Pamela, 886
Oliver, Robert T., 79
Olivia, T. A., 887
Olson, Dennis, 4768
Olson, Robert K., 2370, 2437
Olson, William C., 4181
Oluo, Samuel Lucky O., 2573
Opie, R., 80
Oppenheim, A. N., 1242
Oppenheimer, Michael F., 2001
Ordeshook, Peter C., 1210
Oren, Nissan, 81
Orion, White, Jr., 328
Orkin, Michael, 1485
Ortona, Edigio, 2033
Orwant, Carol J., 1486, 1509
Orwant, Jack E., 1486, 2797
Osborn, Frederick, 3377
Osborn, J. E., 3901
Osborne, Alfred I. Jr., 5228
Osborne, John, 4182, 5019-5020
Osborne, Teresa, 3111
Oseth, John M., 4441
Osgood, C. E., 82, 470, 2798, 4546
Oskamp, Stuart, 888-892
Ostrower, A., 4013
Ott, M. C., 1826
Overstreet, R. E., 893
Owen, G., 1482
Owen, H., 3518
Oxman, Bernard H., 2332-2335, 2339
Oye, Kenneth A., 3622
Ozergene, Nil, 3943

Paalberg, Robert L., 5401
Pace, Roger C., 1134
Page, Don, 5356
Paige, Michael R., 410
Painchaud, P., 5357
Painter, David S., 2279-2280
Pakistan. Ministry of Kashmir Affairs., 5402
Palmer, Joe M., 5021
Palmer, Michael, 3303
Palmer, R. L., 858
Pangalis, Celia S., 1707, 5195
Panikkar, K. M., 4014
Panofsky, Wolfgang K. H., 3434
Pantev, Plamen, 471
Paone, Rocco M., 472
Papadopoulos, Andrestinos N., 2510, 2574

Pardo, H. E. M., 2336
Parimal, Kumar Das, 5358
Park Teter, Daniel, 4883
Park, E. Y., 5401
Parker, R. W., 3944
Parker, Thomas R., 4940
Parkins, Dexter, 4675
Parlin, Andrew, 2276
Parodi, Alexandre, 1827
Parsons, Anthony, 2100, 4183, 5229
Pastuhov, V. D., 2157
Patch, M. E., 660
Patchen, Martin, 83, 894-895
Patrick, Karen D., 2511, 2575
Patterson, Eliza, 3728
Patterson, Gardner, 3727-3728
Pattison, J. E., 3902
Patton, Bobby R., 533
Pauk, Robert A., 1989
Paulin, Charles O., 4676
Payne, Samuel B., 3022
Peacock, A., 3903
Pearson, Charles, 3749
Pearson, Lester B., 4015
Pearson, Scott, 3682
Peay, Marilyn Y., 896
Pechota, Vratislav, 1828, 1907, 2101, 2139
Pedler, Mike J., 329-332
Peleg, Ilan, 4816
Pelkmans, Jacques, 3519
Pelzman, Joseph, 3904
Pen, Jan, 1487-1489
Pendley, R. E., 2576
Penrose, E. F., 4547
Pepinsky, Harold B., 1135
Perle, Richard N., 3114
Perlmutter, Amos, 4884-4886
Perner, J., 1518
Perry Robinson, J. P., 3234
Perry, Motty, 1363
Perry, S. E., 897
Peter, Wolfgang, 3868
Peterfi, William O., 3435
Peters, Alexander, 3210
Peterson, C., 1651
Peterson, Frank A., 4016
Peterson, M. J., 2054, 2102
Petrash, Vilma, 5263
Petrie, Charles, 4184, 4292
Petrov, V., 4732
Petrovsky, Vladimir F., 3436
Peyton Young, H., 1710
Pfaff, William, 4185

Pfaltzgraff, Robert L., 2921, 3020, 3067, 3437
Philip, G., 3650
Phillips, James L., 473, 898, 1397, 1480
Phillips, Thomas E., 899
Phillips, Warren R., 900
Picard, Louis A., 1490
Pickering, Laurence G., 3623
Piedra, Alberto M., 4247
Pierre, Allan, 405
Pierre, Andrew J., 2799-2800, 3078
Pilisuk, Mark, 901-902, 1491-1493
Pillar, Paul R., 84, 474
Pilsworth, M., 261
Pincus, J., 1494
Pinder, John, 3591-3592
Piotrowski, Karl P., 4548
Pipes, Richard, 4549
Pirages, Dennis, 85
Pisar, Samuel, 3808
Planck, C. R., 2922
Plantey, A., 333, 4186
Platig, Raymond E., 4264, 4733
Platt, Alan, 2659, 3079
Plischke, Elmer, 2170-2172, 3393-3394, 3438-3445, 3485, 4017, 4187-4193, 4677-4678, 4734-4738
Plous, S., 2801
Plummer, Joseph, 3593
Plumtre, T., 4194
Pneuman, R. W., 86
Podell, J. E., 1829
Podlesni, P. T., 3080
Pohlan, P. D., 772
Pohlen, M. F., 1402
Poirier, R., 3714
Polk, W. R., 4265
Pomerance, Josephine W., 2993-2994
Poon, Byron, 1579
Poortinga, Ype H., 1136
Porro, Jeffrey D., 2620
Porshalt, Lars, 334
Porter, Bruce D., 4476, 4596
Porter, Gareth, 4971, 5359
Porter, Jack N., 1751
Porter, Roger B., 3665, 3676
Posses, Frederick, 87
Potash, H. M., 576
Potter, K., 1455
Potter, Pitman B., 4195
Potter, William C., 2923
Pottserob, B. F., 2263
Poullada, Leon B., 4196-4198, 5360

Poulose, T. T., 3354
Poussard, Jean-Pierre, 1463
Powell, Charles, 1671, 1711, 3689
Powell, G. B., 903
Powell, Robert, 1495, 2802
Powers, J. S., 3895
Praaning, Rio D., 3261
Pranger, Robert J., 4199
Preece, Cherlotte P., 3333
Preeg, Ernest H., 3750-3751, 3869
Presseisen, Ernst L., 4293
Price, Charles C., 2803
Price, D., 145
Price, Don K., 4769
Price, Richard, 1876
Price, Thomas J., 1301
Prince, Howard T., 3081
Princen, Tom, 1830-1831, 1908-1909, 1990, 5264
Probst, Reed R., 5084
Prudente, N. E., 2140
Pruitt, Dean G., 88, 335-337, 534-535, 570-571, 602-603, 838, 849, 863, 904-930, 971, 1066, 1068, 1079, 1081, 1137-1143, 1165-1166, 1168, 1496-1498, 1805, 1810, 1820, 1832-1836, 1861, 1910-1911, 1960, 1991, 4770, 5404
Pryakhin, V., 2192
Prybyla, J. S., 3
Psathas, G., 931
Pullinger, Stephen, 2221
Pumpyansky, Alexander, 3395
Punke, Harold H., 4739
Punnett, Betty Jane, 3809
Puryear, Edgar F., 4597
Putnam, L., 932
Putnam, Robert D., 3503-3504, 3524-3525
Pye, Lucien W., 3825, 3830
Pyke, S. W., 859

Qadeer, Mohammed A., 2173
Qadir, Shahid, 2438
Quandt, R. E., 1499
Quandt, William B., 4817-4818, 4888-4891
Quester, George H., 2628, 5361
Quisumbing, Purification V., 2537

Raanan, Uri, 4550
Rabbie, Jacob M., 933
Rabin, Yitzhak, 4788
Rachmaninov, Yuri N., 3304

Author Index

Racic, Obrad, 3305
Racklam, N., 934
Radford, James, 1712
Radlow, Robert, 1500-1501
Radványi, János, 4972, 5022
Rae, A. E. I., 3826
Raichur, S., 145
Raider, Ellen, 484
Raiffa, Howard, 89, 338-339, 417, 475, 1206-1207, 1502, 1837, 5264
Rakove, Milton, 4598
Ramberg, Bennett, 3245, 3248-3249, 3252
Ramsey, George H. Jr., 1144
Ramsey, James A., 340
Randhawa, P. S., 3729
Randle, Robert, 4973-4974
Randolph, Lillian L., 341, 476, 1752
Randolph, Sean R., 5405
Rangarajan, L. N., 90, 3594, 3666, 3677
Ranger, Robin, 2804, 3177
Rao, G. A., 342
Rao, M. V. Subba, 2995
Rapacki, Adam, 4551
Rapoport, Amnon, 1211, 1409, 1416-1418, 1442, 1503-1505
Rapoport, Anatol, 1212-1217, 1370-1371, 1492, 1506-1522
Rappaport, Armin, 4679
Raskin, Markus G., 4552
Rathjens, G. W., 2805-2806, 2924
Raven, Bertram H., 343, 935
Ravenhill, John, 2439-2440, 2489
Ray, P., 964
Raymond, Dennett, 5308
Raymond, Gregory A., 1838
Razvi, Mujtaba, 2538
Reardon-Anderson, James, 5149
Redekop, Clarence G., 5177
Rees, Elfan, 4386
Regala, Roberto, 4018-4020
Reich, Alan A., 4387
Reich, Bernard, 2103, 4892-4893, 4941
Reich, Simon, 3945
Reiches, N. A., 344
Reid, Escott, 5362
Reisinger, William M., 3819, 4553
Reiss, Mitchell, 2807
Renner, J. C., 3595
Renninger, John P., 2491
Renwick, George, 3641
Reston, James B., 4554

Rey, Patrick, 1463
Reychler, Luc, 536, 936
Rhinelander, John B., 3025, 3378
Riad, Mahmoud, 4819
Ribicoff, A., 3596
Rice, Condoleeza, 3082
Rice, Peter, 147, 1523
Richard, I., 4200
Richardson, Elliot L., 4740
Richardson, H. J., 5178
Richardson, V. A., 452
Richmond, Yale, 4442
Ridgway, Rozanne L., 3446
Rieger, Hans Christoph, 1524
Riggs, A. R., 3759
Riker, W. H., 1525, 1713
Rikhye, Bhalinder, 5196
Rikhye, Idar J., 2141
Rimalfo, Robert, 5023
Ritchie, Charles, 4201, 4347-4349
Rittberger, Volker, 2174, 2193
Rivas-Gallant, Ernesto, 5265
Rivers, Richard B., 3597
Roberts, Adam, 5024
Roberts, Henry L., 4555
Roberts, John, 5282
Robinson, Charles, 3536
Robinson, Glen O., 3905
Roche, John P., 5025
Rochester, J. Martin, 2073
Rochet, J. C., 1526
Rocke, David M., 1325, 2695
Rodenberg, Klaus, 5076
Roderick, Hilliard, 91
Rodman, Peter W., 4894
Roe, P. H., 1591
Roehl, Janice A., 1839
Roering, K. Y., 368
Roessler, F., 3598
Roett, Riordan, 5266
Roetter, Charles, 4294
Rogers, John P., 1145
Rogers, Lindsay, 3447
Rogers, Rita M., 937-938
Rogers, William P., 4202
Rohrl, Vivian J., 345
Rohrlich, Paul, 5307
Roloff, Michael E., 939
Rombach, C., 1313
Rondybush, Franklin, 4021, 4266
Ronen, S., 5130
Roos, L. L., 156, 940
Root, Elihu, 4203
Ropp, Steven C., 5230

Rosch, E., 804
Rose, Clive, 2539, 3448
Rose, John P., 3115
Rose, William M., 2808, 2925
Rosen, Baron, 4350
Rosen, N., 696
Rosenbluth, James M., 3402
Rosencrance, Richard N., 347, 4204
Rosenfeld, P., 1005
Rosenfeld, Stephen S., 5231
Rosenhead, Jonathan, 3235
Rosenthal, Donald B., 348
Rosenthal, Robert W., 941, 1527
Rosenthal, Yemima, 4942
Ross, G. L., 368
Ross, Robert S., 5127
Rossiter, Cliton L., 4205
Rossow, Robert, 4206
Rostow, Eugene V., 2809-2810, 3449
Rostow, W., 2441
Rotenberg, Barbara, 4368
Rotfeld, Adam D., 3254, 3306, 3334
Roth, Alvin E., 1218-1219, 1448, 1467-1470, 1528-1546
Roth, Lois W., 4388
Rothacher, Albrecht, 3835
Rothaus, Paul, 1045
Rothschild, David, 2394, 5179
Rothschild, K. W., 349
Rothstein, Robert L., 2371, 3678-3680, 3906
Roucek, Joseph S., 942
Rourke, F. E., 4022
Rowen, Henry S., 3083
Rowny, Edward L., 3213, 4557-4559
Rozek, Edward J., 2242
Rozelle, Richard, 643, 1127
Rubin, A. P., 1840
Rubin, Barry, 4943
Rubin, James P., 2778, 3378
Rubin, Jeffrey Z., 356, 505, 535, 537, 590, 592, 624, 704, 725-726, 935, 943-949, 998, 1118, 1146-1147, 1841, 1928
Rubin, Seymour J., 4741
Rubinstein, Ariel, 1256, 1547-1548
Ruddy, Thomas M., 4680
Rudzinski, Alexander W., 4560
Ruehl, Lothar, 2811, 3178-3179, 3200
Ruggie, John G., 2360, 2372, 2442
Ruhala, Kalevi, 3328
Ruina, J. P., 2924
Ruloff, Dieter, 350, 1912, 5299-5300
Rummel, R. J., 351-352

Rumpf, Helmut, 4895
Ruopp, Phillips, 4408
Rush, Kenneth, 2540
Rush, Thomas A., 353
Rusk, Dean, 3450, 4207-4208, 4742
Russ, Lee E., 566
Russell, Francis H., 4209
Russell, Ruth B., 2055
Russett, B. M., 4210
Rusten, Lynn F., 3148, 3219, 3388
Rutter, D. R., 991
Ryscavage, Richard, 1913

Saaty, Thomas, 1220
Sabin, A. G., 3214
Sadat, Anwar, 4351
Sadler, Barry, 5283
Sageder, J., 586
Sagi, Nava, 5311
Sainsberry, K., 2243
Sakamoto, Yoshikazu, 2812
Sakawa, M., 1717
Saksena, K. P., 2104
Salacuse, Jeswald W., 3599
Salamon, Julie, 4697
Saleh, Hamdi A. W., 4944
Salinger, Pierre, 4820
Salleh Bin Abas, Haji Mohammed Tan, 354
Salzberg, John P., 5363
Samelson, Louis J., 4477
Sampson, Cynthia, 1992
Sampson, Martin W. III, 355
Samuels, Nathaniel, 2443
Samuelson, L., 1291
Samuelson, William F., 1248, 1549-1550, 5364
Sander, Frank E. A., 356, 1745
Sanders, William, 2022
Sandler, S. I., 994
Sandole, Dennis J. D., 92, 148-149, 478, 2813
Sandole-Staroste, Ingrid, 92
Sandstrom, Anders, 3180
Saner, Raymond, 479
Sanger, Clyde, 2298
Saraydar, Edward, 1551-1553, 1714
Sarkissian, A. O., 4295
Sarros, Panayiotis P., 4771
Satawedin, Dhanasarit, 5406
Satow, Ernst M., 2194, 4023
Sauer, C., 800
Sauermann, Heinz, 1221
Saunders, Harold H., 357-359, 950,

Author Index

1993-1994, 4389-4391, 4821, 4896-4898, 4945
Savavanamuttu, J., 2581
Savelle, Max, 5275
Savery, L. K., 669
Savich, P., 1554
Sawyer, J., 866, 951
Scali, John, 4392, 4443
Scalopino, Robert A., 5150
Scelle, G., 2175
Schachter, Oskar, 1914, 2105
Schaefer, Henry W., 2926
Schaetzel, J. Robert, 2033, 3451
Schallawitz, Ronald Lee, 2353
Scheff, T., 952
Scheiding, Robert E., 4561
Scheinitzki, D. P., 752
Schellenberg, James A., 93, 1555-1556
Schelling, Thomas C., 94, 360-362, 1557-1563, 1715-1716, 2814-2823
Scheman, L. Ronald, 1961
Schemitzki, D. P., 1148
Scherer, Michael F., 5365
Schermers, Henry G., 78
Schick, Jack M., 4743, 5312
Schiff, Benjamin N., 3349
Schilling, Walter, 3181
Schimel, Ruth M., 1885
Schleicher, Heinz, 1564
Schlenker, Barry R., 953, 1565
Schlezinger, James, 3452
Schlotter, Peter, 3335
Schmidt, Christian, 105
Schmidt, E., 5176
Schmidt, Helmut, 5366
Schmidt, Robert D., 3600, 3814
Schmittberger, R., 1368
Schneider, William P., 2824, 2927
Schneidman, Witney, 1977
Schoenbaum, David, 3379
Schofield, Michael, 1566
Schofield, Norman, 954, 1567
Scholz, R. W., 1568
Schott, Jeffrey J., 3550, 3771
Schotter, Andrew, 1277
Schoumaker, F., 1529
Schrader, Rudolph, 2541
Schriefer, John, 3752
Schroeder, Paul E., 5128
Schuler, Douglas, 480
Schuler, G., 3651
Schulte, G., 2825
Schulzinger, Robert D., 4355, 4681
Schutjer, Wayne E., 3690
Schwartz, H., 363
Schwartz, Morton, 4478
Schwartz, Richard, 4946
Schwartzman, David, 2629
Schwarze, B., 1368
Schwenger, Robert B., 3624
Schwerin, E. W., 1615
Schwieson, Naomi, 1842
Scobie, W. I., 4808
Scodel, A., 1569-1570
Scott Davis, M., 4479, 4562, 4570
Scott, A. Neslin, 219
Scott, Andrew M., 364-365
Scott, Bill, 95
Scott, Gary L., 5129
Scott, Norman, 2176
Scott, Richard, 2996
Scott, Robert T., 2630
Scoville, Herbert, 3086
Scranton, Margaret E., 5202, 5267
Scruter, Roger, 4444
Seaborg, Glenn T., 2631, 2967
Sears, Arthur M., 3486
Sebenius, James K., 64, 279, 281-282, 366, 459-460, 475, 481, 2299, 2337, 2354
Sechrest, L. B., 612
Segal, Aron, 5232
Segal, Brian, 2577
Seignious, George M., 2826, 3087
Seilheinner, S. D., 602, 1079
Seitz, Steven T., 1571
Sek, Lenore, 3730
Selby, Walford, 4296
Selin, Ivan, 3088
Selten, R., 1390
Semenov, V., 4563
Semmel, A. K., 4744
Senghaas, Dieter, 105
Sengupta, Arjun, 3667
Seo, F., 1717
Serfaty, S., 2444
Sergeev, Victor M., 297, 1361
Serguiev, A., 482, 2142
Sermat, V., 955-956, 1328
Sestanovich, Stephen, 2652, 4564
Sewell, John W., 2445-2446
Sewell, W. R. D., 5284
Shafaeddin, Mehdi, 3652
Shaked, A., 1257
Shakun, Melvin F., 342, 1209, 1340, 1718, 1804
Shapiro, Debra L., 1149, 1768, 1843

Shapiro, Martin M., 2492
Shapiro, Michael, 1906
Shapiro, Mitchell B., 588
Shapiro, Z., 3357
Shapleau, Robert, 5026-5028
Shapley, Deborah, 3380
Sharabi, H., 4899
Sharfman, Peter, 5407
Sharp, Jane M. O., 2827, 3089-3090
Sharp, Walter R., 2177-2178
Sharpe, Kenneth E., 3876
Sharpe, Richard H., 2386
Shaver, Kelly G., 1026-1027
Shaw, Jerry I., 957-958, 1150
Shaw, M. C., 592
Shaw, Malcolm, 5180
Shea, Gordon F., 96
Shea, Gregory P., 367
Sheehan, Edward R. F., 1929, 1962-1963
Shenkar, O., 5130
Shenton, Herbert N., 2158
Sheposh, J. P., 789, 959
Sher, Jordan M., 960
Sherer, P., 1081
Sherman, Allen W., 1151
Sherman, Steven J., 598
Sherr, Alan B., 2632, 2828
Sherwood, Robert E., 2264
Shestov, V., 3345
Shih, Ta Lang, 3827
Shimoff, Eliot, 842
Shinobu, Takashi, 5129
Shinotsuka, Hiromi, 1607
Shipler, David K., 2928
Shonfield, Andrew, 3601
Short, J. A., 961
Shubik, Martin, 1222-1223, 1572-1579
Shukri, Kamal H., 3657
Shulman, Marshall D., 2829
Shultz, George P., 2830
Shure, G. H., 962-963, 1117, 1452, 1580-1581, 1699, 1719-1728
Sicherman, Harvey, 4947
Sick, Gary, 1964, 4822
Siegel, Sidney, 1201, 1224, 1582
Sigal, L. V., 3149, 3215, 3453
Silver, R. B., 1152
Silverson, Randolph M., 2695
Simes, D. K., 2831
Simmons, Ernest J., 4565
Simmons, Susanne, 4566
Simonov, Y., 4134
Simpson, John, 3350

Simpson, Smith, 4024, 4211-4212, 4267, 4682-4683, 4745-4746
Sims, Harold, 5268
Sims, Jennifer E., 2929
Sims, Nicholas, 3223, 3242
Singer, Eugene, 2832
Singer, Hans W., 2447
Singer, J. David, 483, 538, 964-965, 1844, 2833, 4213-4214
Singer, Marshall R., 1995
Singh, I. P., 4025
Sington, D., 2834
Siracusa, Joseph M., 2835, 4684
Sirois, P., 966
Sisco, Joseph J., 4948
Sisk, Dorothy, 1696
Sissons, D. C. S., 4393
Sistrunk, Frank, 1769
Siverson, Randolph M., 4949
Sizoo, Jan, 3259
Skaggs, David C., 3182
Skilling, H. Gordon, 3307
Skinner, M., 988
Skjelsbaek, Kjell, 2106
Skotko, Vincent, 1583
Slack, B. D., 967
Slater, Jerome, 5207
Slocombe, Walter, 2930, 4567
Sloss, Leon, 3117, 4479, 4568-4570
Slusher, E. Allen, 368, 968
Slusser, Robert M., 4571
Small, Alden C., 2143
Small, Melvin, 4309
Smart, Ian, 3201
Smart, Reginald, 484
Smith, A. Merriman, 3396
Smith, Arnold, 2542
Smith, Ben, 3846, 3907
Smith, Christine, 55, 251, 1801
Smith, Clagett G., 539, 969
Smith, D., 2373
Smith, D. F., 970
Smith, D. Leasel, 912, 971
Smith, David H., 972-973, 1153
Smith, David S., 97
Smith, Gaddis G., 4685-4686
Smith, George C., 3358
Smith, Gerard C., 2836-2837, 3023, 3091-3093, 4572
Smith, Hedrick, 3454-3455
Smith, Ian, 3681
Smith, J. T., 2338
Smith, Murray G., 3779
Smith, Phillip C., 1915

Author Index

Smith, Steve, 3094
Smith, Theresa L., 2979
Smith, Wayne S., 5233
Smith, William P., 974-977, 1845, 1916, 1996
Smoke, Richard, 98, 2838, 5370
Smoker, P., 2839
Smorodinsky, M., 1420
Smyth, Frank, 5266
Snell, John L., 2244, 4297
Snidal, Duncan J., 1584-1585, 1729
Snider, Warren D., 1609-1610, 1732
Snow, Donald M., 2633
Snowden, P. N., 3555
Snowdon, Sondra, 3557
Snyder, C. R., 978
Snyder, Glenn H., 99, 369, 485, 979-980, 1154
Snyder, Jack L., 981
Snyder, R. C., 88
Soames, Christopher, 5181
Sobakin, Vadim, 4573
Sobel, Joel, 1586, 2393
Sobel, Lester A., 4823
Sofer, Sasson, 4215
Sohn, Louis B., 100, 1846, 1917, 2023, 2107-2108, 2840-2841, 2931
Solidum, Estrella D., 2578
Solomon, Anthony M., 3535
Solomon, Daniel, 645
Solomon, Leonard, 606, 1375
Solomon, Richard H., 5131, 5152
Solomon-Ravich, Rachel, 1155
Sondak, Harris, 569
Song, Jong-Hwan, 5077
Sonnenfeldt, Helmut, 4574
Sontag, Raymond J., 4310
Sonto, Maior J., 5290
Soriano, L. J., 992
Sorrels, Charles A., 2647
Southerland, Daniel, 4747
Spain, James W., 4352
Spanier, J. W., 2634
Sparks, Donald B., 101
Spaulding, E. W., 4026
Spector, Bertram I., 982-984, 1156-1158
Speidel, Helm, 2206
Speier, H., 1359-1360
Spence, J. E., 2109
Spender, Sir Percy, 5313
Spero, J., 2448
Spiegel, Marianne A., 1965
Spiegel, Steven L., 4900-4901

Spiers, Edward, 3236
Spiro, Herbert J., 4268
Spitzer, H. M., 2179
Sprott, John T., 4772
Staar, Richard F., 3183, 4417
Stagner, Ross, 985
Stahelski, A. J., 755, 758
Stahl, Ingolf, 1225
Stakh, G., 3095
Stalson, Helena, 3570
Standley, William H., 4687
Stanisland, Martin, 5151, 5263
Stanley, Timothy W., 3260
Starbuck, W., 986
Starr, Harvey, 4688
Starr, Pamela, 5258
Stathis, Stephen W., 2265
Steach, Frank J., 848
Stearns, Monteagle, 4748
Stebbins, Richard P., 4773
Stech, Frank J., 847, 987, 1159
Stedman, Charles, 3780
Stedman, Stephen, 5197
Steele, M. W., 1587
Stefan, Charles G., 3457
Steger, Debra P., 3781
Steibel, G. L., 4599
Steigman, Andrew L., 4689
Stein, Erick, 2964
Steinberg, Gerald M., 2635, 2842, 2933
Steinbrunner, John, 2843
Steiner, Kurt, 4575
Steiner, Zara, 4027
Stemplowski, Ryszard, 5234
Stenelo, Lars G., 1753
Stepancic, D., 5367
Stephenson, Carolyn M., 2144, 2844
Stephenson, G. M., 869, 988-991, 1160
Stern, Ernest, 2449
Stern, Lawrence, 4824
Stern, Louis W., 1847
Stern, Paul C., 3388
Sternberg, R. J., 992
Sternste-Perkins, Dagnija, 3118
Stettinius, Edward R., 2245, 4690
Stevens, Carl M., 102, 1588
Stevens, Christopher, 2450
Stevens, R. B., 635
Stevenson, John R., 2339
Stevenson, V. A., 214
Stewart, Philip D., 4394-4395
Stewart, Robert A. C., 2564

Stifbold, R. P., 903
Stiles, K. W., 3908-3909
Stivers, W., 3653
Stockholm International Peace Research Institute. SIPRI., 2934, 3243
Stoddard, Philip H., 4902
Stoecker, Rolf, 1589
Stoeker, S. W., 4600
Stoertz, Howard, 4576
Stoessel, Walter J., 4396
Stoever, William A., 3558
Stoker, Robert P., 2469
Stokes, N. W., 1590-1592, 1730
Stole, Y. F., 1762
Stoll, Richard J., 3096
Stone, Frank, 3753
Stone, I. F., 4749
Stone, Jeremy J., 1593, 2636
Stone, W. T., 4577
Stover, William J., 1594
Strang, William, 4028, 4601
Strange, Russell P., 2266, 2284
Strange, Susan, 3602
Straus, Donald B., 1919, 2340, 2845
Strauss, Anselm, 540
Strazan, Marie D., 5097
Streufert, S., 993-995
Streufert, S. C., 993
Strickland, Donald A., 3381
Strickland, L. H., 728
Strickland, Lloyd H., 1026-1027
Stripp, William, 3642
Strode, Dan L., 2846
Strode, R. V., 2846
Strong, Robert, 3119, 4691
Stryker, S., 931
Stuart, Douglas T., 5132
Stubblefield, Gary L., 2579
Stubbs, Richard, 3910
Stulberg, J., 1848
Stupak, Ronald J., 4774
Suefeld, Peter, 370
Sugden, Robert, 1595
Sugden, Scott, 4445
Sulimma, Hans Guuter, 3526
Sullivan, C. D., 1849
Sullivan, David S., 3097
Sullivan, J. L., 5285
Sullivan, Michael J. III., 4775
Sullivan, Michael P., 996
Sullivan, Timothy J., 2374
Sullivan, William H., 4216, 4353, 4825

Sulzberger, Cyrus L., 2246
Summers, D. A., 997
Susskind, Lawrence, 371, 998
Suter, Keith, 2056, 4750
Suttmeier, R. P., 372, 5098
Sutton, John, 1257, 1596-1597
Suy, Eric, 2024
Swagert, S. L., 2580
Swainson, Neil A., 5276, 5286
Swanson, Roger F., 5291
Swap, W. C., 704
Swenson, R. G., 1598
Swingle, Paul G., 373, 541, 999-1003, 1161
Swinth, R. L., 1004, 1599
Swoly, J. M. Jr., 5029
Symington, James W., 4029
Syna, Helena, 849, 916, 927
Syphax, John W., 3251
Szajkowski, E., 874
Szapiro, Tomasz, 1425, 1427, 1689-1690
Szekely, Francisco, 5259
Szulc, Tad, 5030

Tabory, Mala, 103
Tahtinen, Dale, 4907
Tait, Richard M., 2208
Takahashi, Ichiro, 1586, 2393
Talbot, Phillips, 1600
Talbott, Strobe, 2637, 2935, 3024, 3098-3100, 3392, 3428
Tam, Kwok Chih, 3827
Tandon, Yashpal, 1850
Tang, Peter S. H., 3459
Tangermann, Stefan, 3682
Tangredi, Sam J., 2936-2937
Tanter, Raymond, 5314
Taoka, G. M., 3824
Taplin, Ruth, 1751
Tarling, Nicholas, 5368
Tarr, David W., 4950
Tassie, Lawrence R., 3184, 3202
Taylor, Alastair M., 2145, 5167
Taylor, J. R., 1966
Taylor, Michael, 1226
Tedeschi, James T., 668, 734, 832-833, 1005-1010, 1353, 1587
Teger, A. I., 1011
Teja, J. S., 374
Telhami, Shibley, 4951-4952
Tener, J., 1851
Terchek, Ronald J., 2968
Terhune, Kenneth W., 1012-1014, 1162-

1163, 1601
Terrill, Ross, 5031-5032
Tetlock, Philip, 370, 1015
Tetzlaff, Rainer, 2451
Thai, V. V., 5053
Thakore, K., 2180
Thakur, Ramesh, 104
Thambipillai, Pushpathavi, 2581-2582
Thayer, Charles W., 4030, 4217-4218
Thayer, Nathaniel B., 5108
Thayer, Robert H., 4219
Thee, Marek, 5033, 5054
Theoharis, Athan, 2267
Thibault, J., 1016-1018
Thiel, Elke, 3527-3529, 3538
Thies, Wallace J., 4975, 5034
Thieu, Ton That, 5055
Thomas, Evan, 4657
Thomas, J. C., 3725
Thomas, John T., 5056
Thomas, K. W., 768
Thompson, Charlotte E., 3269
Thompson, Gail, 3936
Thompson, James C., 5133
Thompson, Kenneth W., 4031, 4220-4223, 4692-4693
Thompson, L. L., 1019
Thompson, William R., 3460
Thomson, William, 1227
Thornton, A. P., 4224
Thornton, Thomas P., 1967, 5408
Thorp, W. F., 728
Thorslund, Christer, 958
Thorson, Stuart, 262
Thorsson, Inga, 2025
Tierney, Tracy, 3940
Tietz, Reinhard, 1228, 1246, 1367, 1602-1606, 1625-1626
Timberlake, Charles E., 3461, 4776
Tims, Wonter, 2449
Tindell, J. O., 1614
Tirole, Jean, 1352
Tiwari, J. N., 3462
Tjosvold, Dean, 1020-1023
Tobias, Andrew, 375
Toda, Masanao, 1607
Tokatlian, Juan Gabriel, 5242
Tollison, Robert D., 376, 2341
Tombough, William W., 5035
Toner, James H., 5079
Toogood, John, 3203
Tooze, Roger, 3539
Tornatzky, L., 1024
Torre, Motram, 1025

Toscano, Mario, 4298
Touval, Saadia, 377, 1754, 1852-1854, 1868, 1930, 1968, 4903
Tow, William T., 5132, 5409
Tower, J. G., 2847
Towle, P., 3382
Tozzoli, Gian Paolo, 2209
Tracy, Brian H., 1731, 5369
Trager, F. N., 5036
Tran, Van Dinh, 4032, 5037
Trapp, R., 3237-3238
Traun, Betty, 2146
Trevalyan, Humphrey, 4033
Treverton, Gregory, 5269-5270
Trezise, Philip H., 3847
Triandis, H. C., 1669
Trick, Michael A., 130
Triska, Jan F., 4578
Trommsdorff, G., 776
Trubowitz, Peter, 486
Truman, Harry S., 2247
Tucker, Michael J., 2938, 2997
Tung, Rosalie L., 3823, 3828, 3836, 3848
Tunnicliff, Kim H., 1997-1998
Tunstall, Marion D., 2355
Turkington, D. J., 970
Turnbull, Allen A., 1026-1027
Turner, William C., 3536
Tutzauer, Frank, 1028
Twiggs, Joan E., 3702
Tyler, M., 5271
Tyler, Tom R., 1855
Tysoe, Maryon, 1029
Tyszka, Tadeusz, 1608
Tyulin, Ivan G., 297

Ul Haq, Mahbub, 2452-2453
Ulam, Adam B., 4579
Uldricks, Teddy J., 4480
Ulrich, J. W., 49
Ulvila, Jacob W., 1609-1610, 1732-1733
Umbricht, Victor, 1970
Umeoka, Yoshitaka, 1611
Underdal, Arild, 378, 2169, 2543
Underhill, J., 277
Ungar, S. J., 3532
Ungerer, Werner, 2110
United Nations Conference on Trade and Development. UNCTAD., 3625
United Nations Institute for Training and Research. UNITAR., 2147

United Nations. Centre on Transnational Corporations., 3946
———. Department of Disarmament Affairs., 2222
———. Department of International Economic and Social Affairs., 2493
———. Department of Political and Security Council Affairs., 2223-2224
———. Economic Commission for Latin America and the Carribean. (ECLAC)., 3947
———. General Assembly. Disarmament Commission., 2940
———.———. Eighteen Nation Committee on Disarmament., 2225
———. Office of Public Information., 2226
———. Secretary General., 2148
United States. Advisory Commission on Public Diplomacy., 4454
———. Arms Control and Disarmament Agency., 2941-2944, 3003, 3355
———. Central Intelligence Agency. National Foreign Assessment Center., 3820
———. Congress. House., 5058
———.———. Commission on Security and Cooperation in Europe., 3336
———.———. Committee on Armed Services., 2945-2946, 3489-3490
———.———.———. Defence Policy Panel., 3491
———.———.———. Special Subcommittee on Arms Control and Disarmament., 3120-3121
———.———.———. Subcommittee on Intelligence and Military Applications of Nuclear Energy., 3004, 3122, 3204, 3389
———.———.———. Subcommittee on Procurement and Military Nuclear Systems., 2947
———.———. Committee on Banking, Finance and Urban Affairs. Subcommittee on Economic Stabilization., 3795
———.———. Committee on Foreign Affairs., 2149, 2356, 2583, 3492-3493, 3856, 4455, 4602, 4779, 5059
———.———.———. Subcommittee on Africa., 5198
———.———.———. Subcommittee on Arms Control, International Security and Science., 2948-2949, 3494
———.———.———. Subcommittee on Europe and the Middle East., 4954-4960
———.———.———. Subcommittee on Foreign Economic Policy and Subcommittee on Near East and South Asia., 3659
———.———.———. Subcommittee on International Economic Policy and Trade and Subcommittee on Inter-American Affairs., 3796
———.———.———. Subcommittee on International Economic Policy and Trade., 2494, 3754, 4961
———.———.———. Subcommittee on International Operations., 4456-4457
———.———.———. Subcommittee on International Security and Scientific Affairs., 3123-3124, 3150, 3205-3206, 3244
———.———.———. Subcommittee on National Security Policy and Scientific Developments., 2950, 4780
———.———. Committee on Foreign Relations. Subcommittee on International Economic Policy and Trade., 3797
———.———. Committee on Public Works and Transportation. Subcommittee on Aviation., 2584
———.———. Committee on Small Business., 3798
———.———.———. Subcommittee on General Oversight and Minority Enterprise., 3626
———.———. Committee on Ways and Means. Subcommittee on Trade. , 3627-3628, 3799
———.———. Joint Economic Committee., 3540-3541
———.———. Joint Postwar Committee. , 5410

Author Index

_____._____. Senate. Arms Control Observer Group., 2951
_____._____._____. Committee on Agriculture, Nutrition and Forestry., 3691
_____._____._____._____. Council on International Economic Policy., 3692
_____._____._____. Committee on Armed Services., 2952
_____._____._____. Committee on Banking, Housing and Urban Affairs. Subcommittee on International Finance and Monetary Policy., 3629
_____._____._____. Committee on Energy and Natural Resources., 5292
_____._____._____. Committee on Finance., 3800-3801
_____._____._____._____. Subcommittee on International Trade., 3755
_____._____._____. Committee on Foreign Relations., 1164, 2034, 2953, 3005-3011, 3495-3497, 4603-4605, 5060-5061
_____._____._____._____. Joint Committee on Taxation., 3630
_____._____._____._____. Subcommittee on Arms Control, International Law and Organization., 3012
_____._____._____._____. Subcommittee on Arms Control, International Organizations and Security Agreements., 3356
_____._____._____._____. Subcommittee on Arms Control, Oceans, International Operations, and Environment., 2357-2359, 2954, 5293
_____._____._____._____. Subcommittee on Disarmament., 2955-2956
_____._____._____._____. Subcommittee on East Asia and Pacific Affairs., 5411
_____._____._____._____. Subcommittee on Near Eastern and South Asian Affairs., 4962
_____._____._____. Committee on Government Operations., 5153
_____._____._____._____. Permanent Subcommittee on Investigations., 487-490
_____._____._____._____. Subcommittee on National Security and International Operations., 491-492, 4606-4619, 5154
_____._____._____. Select Committee on Intelligence., 2957
_____. Congressional Budget Office., 3756
_____. Department of State., 2150, 2227, 2288-2293, 2585-2587, 3013-3014, 3498-3499, 3757-3758, 4781-4785, 4963-4964, 5412-5413
_____._____. Bureau of Public Affairs., 3125
_____._____. Office of External Research., 2495
_____._____. Office of International Conferences., 2195
_____._____. Office of Public Communication., 3500
_____. Department of the Army. Institute for Advanced Russian and East European Studies., 4620
_____. General Accounting Office., 4458
_____. Library of Congress. Congressional Research Service. Office of Senior Specialists., 4621
_____. Office of the Special Representative for Trade Negotiations., 3631
_____. Secretary of Defence., 4965
Unterberg, Betty M., 5109
Unterman, Israel, 379
Urban, Joan B., 4580
Urban, L. K., 3911
Uren, Emmanuel, 902
Urquhart, Brian, 2057, 2112
Ury, William L., 42, 1744, 1856, 2638, 2794, 2838, 2850, 2920, 5370
Ushiba, Nobuhito, 2033
Utter, Glen H., 1999
Utton, Albert E., 5284

Vaahtoranta, Tapani, 2588
Vacs, Aldo C., 3693
Vagts, Alfred, 4034
Valavanis, Stephan, 1612
Valenta, Jiri, 3464

Valeriani, Richard, 4694
Valero, Ricardo, 5236
Van Bael, Ivo, 3731
Van Cleave, William R., 3126
Van Dam, Ferdinand, 2454
Van Damme, Eric, 1613
Van Doren, Charles N., 3351-3352
Van Dyke, Vernon, 4225
Van Oerdenaren, John, 2851
Van Opstal, Debra, 1358
Van Slyck, M. R., 1165-1168
Van Zandt, Howard F., 3603, 3849
Van de Velde, James R., 5099
Van de Velde, Kenneth J., 380
Van den Heuvel, Cornelius C., 3261
Van der Merwe, Hendrik W., 5183
Van der Ven, Hans, 3952
Vance, Cyrus, 4695
Vansittart, L., 4226
Varis, Tapio, 381
Vaske, J. J., 857
Vastine, John Robert, 3696
Vatcher, William H., 5067
Väyrynen, Raimo, 105, 1857, 2113-2114, 2852
Velk, Tom, 3759
Velliadis, Hannibal, 3308
Venkata, Raman K., 2058, 2115, 2151, 2553
Venn, Fiona, 3646
Verhage, William, 3831
Verma, Anil, 268
Verona, Sergiu, 2211, 2853-2854
Verrier, Anthony, 5166
Vetschera, Heinz, 3337
Vetschera, Rudolf, 493
Vicas, Alex G., 2855-2856
Vidmar, N. J., 850, 1030-1031, 1169-1171
Vigny, G., 4904
Villere, Maurice, 548
Vinacke, W. Edgar, 1032-1033
Vincelette, L. P., 1379
Vincent, Jack E., 1614-1615, 2116
Vincent, R. J., 4751
Viotti, Paul R., 2639, 2857
Visser, Lieuwe, 933
Vital, David, 3353
Vitz, P. C., 1034
Vlachoutsicos, C. A., 3632, 3815
Voas, Jeanette, 2958
Vogele, William B., 2959-2960
Vogelgesang, Sandy, 5371
Vogt, Erich, 5414

Volkan, Vanik D., 1035, 4361, 4398
Volten, Peter M. E., 3186
Von Dornoch, Alex, 4905
Von Groll, Gotz, 3309
Von Lowis of Menar, Henning, 4446
Von Neumann, John, 1229
Von Staden, Berndt, 3310, 4227-4229
Von der Ropp, Klaus, 2544
Vonmuller, A. A. C., 2858
Voth, Alden H., 4809
Vukadinovic, Radovan, 3465

Wade, L. L., 1036
Wadington, J., 1037
Wagner, Harvey M., 1616-1618
Wagner, R. Harrison, 382, 1619-1623
Wagner, Wolfgang, 5315
Wainhouse, David W., 106
Wainwright, W. H., 5038
Waito, Robert, 5062
Wakelin, John, 4035
Walcott, Charles, 733, 1038, 2737-2738, 2903-2904
Walde, Thomas W., 3912
Waldmann, Raymond J., 3559
Walker, Gregg B., 2294
Walker, Penelope, 5415
Walker, Stephen G., 284, 5039
Wall, James A., 107, 1039-1044, 1376, 1624, 1858-1859
Wallace, Donnel, 1045
Wallace, Helen, 2545
Wallace, Samuel P., 1172
Wallace, William, 2521, 3533
Wallach, John P., 2859
Wallsten, Thomas S., 1505
Walsh, J. P., 1046
Walters, Robert S., 3948
Walther, Regis, 542
Walton, A. M., 3654
Walton, Richard E., 543-545, 1047
Wang, Eric B., 3802
Wang, Jen-Huong, 5134
Wang, Muhong, 1405, 1734-1735
Wang, Robert S., 5100
Wang, Yu, 5135
Waples, Douglas, 3466
Ward, Hugh D., 1048, 1173
Ward, M. D., 1049
Ward, Thomas E., 3647
Wardall, William K., 3501
Warley, K. T., 3683, 3782
Warner, Edward L., 3220
Warnke, Paul C., 2860-2862, 3101-

Author Index

3102
Warren, Roland L., 1860, 4399
Warrington, M. B., 3637
Warschaw, Tessa A., 108
Washburn, John Nelson, 5372
Wasowski, Stanislaw, 3949
Wasserstein, Bernard, 4280
Waters, Maurice, 4036, 4752
Watman, Kenneth H., 528
Watson, Adam, 4037
Watson, Lorna, 2863
Watt, D. C., 4753, 4906
Watt, David, 3542
Ways, Max, 383-385
Weakland, John H., 5155
Weber, Hans-Jürgen, 1602, 1604, 1625
Weber, K., 1879
Weber, Robert J., 1736
Weber, Steven, 2864
Webster, Charles, 4038
Wedge, Bryant, 1050, 2865, 4400, 4447-4448
Weeks, Stan, 3269
Weiberger, David, 2640
Weickhardt, George G., 3187
Weider-Hatfield, Deborah, 1920
Weidner, Marianna F., 1501
Weihmiller, Gordon, 3397
Weil, H. G., 1232
Weiler, Lawrence D., 2597, 2866, 2961
Weinberg, Steve, 4401
Weinrod, W. Bruce, 2641
Weinstein, Martin E., 3468
Weintal, Edward, 4039
Weintraub, Sidney, 2117
Weisband, Edward, 3391, 3478
Weisberg, Richard C., 3660
Weiss, J., 770, 5136
Weiss, Stephen E., 1174-1175, 3633-3634, 3642, 5108
Weiss, Thomas G., 2181, 2375-2376, 2455-2457, 2478, 2496-2497, 3950
Weiss-Wik, Stephen, 494, 1051, 1176, 1921
Weissband, Edward, 3981
Weitz, R., 2409
Weizman, Ezer, 4826
Wells, L., 2373
Wells, Louis T., 2458, 3571, 3604
Wells, R. B., 1177
Welton, G. L., 1820, 1861
Werner, T., 1626
Wertheimer, John, 3383

Wessell, Nils H., 2867
Wessels, Wolfgang, 3508
Westbrook, Franklin D., 1862
Westen, T. Edward, 1284-1285
Westermeyer, William, 5416
Wettig, Gerhard, 2868, 3141, 3311, 4449
Wheeler, H. G., 286
Wheeler, M., 127
Wheeler-Bennett, John W., 2546, 5316
Whelan, Joseph G., 4622-4624
White, Lawrence J., 3951
White, Nathan, 5137
White, Ralph K., 546, 1052, 4506
Whiteman, M. K., 2459
Whiting, Allen S., 5138, 5150
Whitney, G. G., 1411
Whitt, Darnell M., 3260
Wiberg, Hakan, 1627
Wichman, H., 1053
Wiebes, C., 2547
Wierzbicki, Andrzej P., 1628, 1737, 1863
Wiethoff, William E., 4230
Wiklund, C., 5373
Wilhelm, Alfred D., 5156
Wilkenfeld, Jonathan, 18, 109, 2118, 4907
Wilkowski, Jean M., 2589
Willett, Thomas D., 376, 2341
Willheim, Ernst, 5374
Williams, G., 5040
Williams, Philip Maynard, 110, 386
Williams, R. M., 387
Williams, Walter L., 2460, 4231
Williamson, Richard S., 2119
Williamson, Samuel R., Jr., 4311
Willis, Richard H., 747, 1054
Willrich, Mason, 3025
Wilson, Arlene, 3783
Wilson, Clifton E., 4269
Wilson, Kellog V., 576-577, 1263, 1629-1630
Wilson, Larman C., 2120, 5237, 5272
Wilson, Theodore A., 2248, 4669
Wilson, W., 1055, 1631-1632
Wimer, Kurt, 3469
Wimmel, Kenneth, 4450
Windsor, Philip, 2869, 5238
Winer, Stanley L., 3794
Winham, Gilbert R., 111, 388-392, 495, 1056, 1633-1634, 1864, 1922, 2770, 3605, 3635-3636, 3703, 3732-3734, 3784, 3803

Winkenfeld, Jonathan, 1106
Winters, L. A., 3913
Wirtz, Stepan, 2196
Wise, David, 4040
Wiseman, Harry, 5167
Witmeyer, D., 214
Wittkamper, Gerhard W., 5375
Wittman, Donald, 393, 1274
Witty, Cathie J., 1931
Wohlstetter, Albert, 5239
Wohlstetter, Roberta, 5239
Wolf, Gerrit, 1579
Wolf, M., 2461
Wolfe, Thomas W., 3026
Wolfers, Arnold, 394
Wolfers, Michael, 1971
Wolff, A. W., 3914
Wolinsky, A., 1256
Wollman, Neil, 547
Wolverton, George D., 5157
Womack, Deanna F., 1178
Wong, J., 1055
Wonnacott, Ronald, 3785
Wood, Bernard, 2462
Woods, George T., 1356
Woodward, E. L., 4232
Woolcock, Stephen, 3952
Woolsey, R. James, 2870-2871, 4581
Worchel, Philip, 1635
Worchel, Stephen, 1057
Worsnop, Richard L., 3470-3471, 4582-4583
Worthing, H. L., 3684
Wrenn, Harry, 3221
Wriggins, W. Howard, 5376
Wright, C. Ben, 4786
Wright, Marcia, 5417
Wright, Martin, 3964
Wright, Quincy, 4233-4234
Wriston, Henry M., 4041, 4235-4236, 4696
Wu, Fu Mei Chiu, 5158
Wu, Jiajing, 5418
Wyer, R., 1058-1059
Wyman, Donald L., 5401

Xydis, Stephen C., 4827

Yakurra, Elaine, 566
Yalem, R., 1060
Yarrow, C. H. M., 4362, 4402-4404
Yetimov, Gennedi, 2035
Yevseyev, Y., 4908
Yin, Ching-Yao, 5139, 5159

York, Herbert F., 2872-2874, 4584
Yoshitsu, Michael M., 5088
Yost, Charles W., 2268
Yost, David S., 2875, 3127, 3472
Young, Allan R., 1179
Young, Jerald W., 1636
Young, Kenneth T., 5113, 5140, 5160
Young, Oran R., 112-113, 395, 1637-1638, 1755, 1865-1866
Young, Wayland, 2876
Yu, George T., 5141
Yu, P. L., 1350
Yu, Peter K., 5114
Yuen, K., 1457-1459
Yukl, Gary A., 710, 1061-1063, 1180

Zacharias, Ellis M., 2269
Zacher, Mark W., 2121, 3664, 3672, 3685
Zagare, Frank C., 1181, 1639-1643, 5064
Zagare, Marc A., 1433
Zak, Moshe, 4909
Zammit-Cutajar, Michael, 2498
Zartman, I. William, 114-116, 396-403, 496-499, 1754, 1854, 1867-1869, 2000, 2377, 2445-2446, 2463-2465, 2548, 3870, 3953, 4910, 5041, 5063, 5168, 5184-5185, 5199, 5253, 5377
Zasloff, Joseph J., 5042, 5419
Zech, James, 2491
Zechmeister, Kathleen, 641-643, 645, 1644
Zeeman, B., 2547
Zeiler, Thomas, 3915
Zelaya-Coronado, Jorge L., 2549
Zellner, A., 1645
Zemke, Ron, 404
Zemskov, I., 2270
Zeuthen, Frederick, 1646
Zimbardo, Phillip G., 1064
Zimmerman, Mark, 3837
Zimmerman, William, 4481
Zinnes, Dina, 1738
Zinser, Adolfo Aquilar, 5240-5241
Zoppo, Ciro E., 2962, 3015-3016
Zwass, A., 3916

Subject Index

ABM Treaty, 2712, 3378
Academic Exchanges
 U.S./Soviet Union, 4358, 4372
Acceptable Outcomes
 psychological aspects, 861
Accidental War Reduction, 2661
Accountability, 939, 1070
 bargaining outcome, 1079
 behavioral aspects, 1067
 dissertation, 1067, 1114
 group representatives, 599
 integrative bargaining, 1496
 negotiator behavior, 570, 700, 773, 1127
 negotiator status, 775
Acheson Dean
 memoirs, 4312
 official conversations, 4767
Achieved Power
 coalition formation behavior, 1299
Achievement Needs
 game theory, 1255
Acid Rain
 mediation, 1981
 U.S. Senate Hearings, 5292-5293
 U.S./Canada negotiations, 5282, 5285
Ad Hoc Diplomat, 4036
Addis Ababa Summit, 2551
Aerospace Research Negotiations, 2541
Afghanistan War, 5339, 5355
 U.N. negotiations, 5390
 U.S. diplomacy, 5360
Africa

Chinese diplomacy, 5141
conflict resolution, 5180, 5188, 5199
diplomacy, 4299, 5165, 5168, 5170, 5184
EEC Trade Negotiations, 3870
multinationals, 2394
North South negotiations, 5199
simulation, 5195
U.N. negotiations, 2122
Africa Fund
 economic summits, 3511
AGARD Negotiations, 2541
Age Factor
 bargaining behavior, 1046
Aggressive Behavior, 1006
Agreement Pressure
 psychological aspects, 784
 stalemated negotiation, 1105
Agricultural Trade
 negotiations, 2393, 3671, 3683-3684, 3687, 3692
 U.S./Canada negotiations, 3765, 3774, 3781-3782
 U.S./EEC, 3686, 3688
 See also Commodity Negotiations
Air Service
 U.S./Japan Negotiations, 3854
Air Transport Routes
 multilateral negotiations, 2580
Alaskan Gas Pipeline Conflict
 game theory, 1554
Albania
 diplomatic aspects, 5372
Algeria

Iran hostage crisis, 1988
natural gas negotiations, 3953
Alliance Formation, 473
Alliance Negotiations
  psychological aspects, 1034
Altruism
  game theory, 1320
Amateur Negotiators, 879
Ambassadors, 3992, 4026, 4218
  function of, 4182
  responsibilities, 4227
  role analysis, 4106, 4250
  training, 4061
  See also Diplomacy, Diplomats
American Friends Service Committee
  mediation, 4399
Andropov
  negotiating style, 4622
  See also Soviet Negotiating Behavior
ANFA Conference
  Casablanca 1943, 2271
Anger
  elite behavior, 903
Angola, 5191
  historical analysis, 5191
  U.S. House Hearings, 5198
  U.S. policies, 5417
Antarctic Minerals Negotiations, 3380, 3888, 3932, 5416
Antarctic Treaty System, 5309
Anthropological Aspects, 227
Anthropological Diplomacy, 4075, 4257
Anti Ballistic Missile Treaty
  See ABM Treaty
Antisatellite Negotiations, 2645, 3383
ANZUS Alliance
  disintegration, 5409
ANZUS PACT
  negotiations, 5271, 5313
Apex Games
  bloc formation, 1231
Arab Leaders' Meetings
  spatial models, 4850
Arab League Negotiations, 4879
Arab Rebellion (1936-39)
  secret diplomacy, 4845
Arab/European Diplomacy, 4789
  See also Middle East Conflict
Arab/Israeli Conflict *See* Middle East Conflict
Arbitration
  costs, 878

pre intervention effects, 1805, 1835
Arcadia Conference
  World War II, 2284
Argentina
  cultural aspects, 5332
  IMF negotiations, 3909
  human rights issues, 5218
Argentina/Chile
  Beagle Channel Dispute, 5243, 5264
  boundary negotiations, 5208
ARGONAUT Conference
  Malta, 2272
  Yalta, 2272
Argumentation Analysis
  case studies, 1238
  game theory, 1240
Arias Plan
  Central American negotiations, 5262
  See also Contadora Negotiations
Armand Hammer
  unofficial diplomacy, 4401
Armistice Negotiations
  dissertation, 474
Arms Control Agreements, 2597, 2599, 2924
  assessment, 2934
  compliance, 2696
  effectiveness, 2608
  survey, 2618, 2934
  texts, 2941-2942
Arms Control Negotiations, 2025, 2590, 2592, 2598, 2600-2603, 2610-2611, 2613, 2616, 2620-2621, 2623-2624, 2626, 2633, 2636, 2639-2640, 2643-2644, 2648, 2650-2655, 2666-2667, 2670-2672, 2674-2675, 2677-2679, 2684, 2690, 2692, 2695, 2702-2703, 2705-2706, 2710, 2717, 2719-2720, 2728-2729, 2735, 2738, 2740, 2743, 2747, 2749, 2755-2756, 2764, 2766, 2768-2769, 2774, 2777, 2781, 2783-2784, 2789-2792, 2801, 2803-2805, 2809-2810, 2816, 2822-2823, 2825, 2831, 2833, 2835-2836, 2840-2842, 2845, 2861-2862, 2870-2871, 2873-2874, 2877, 2880, 2883-2884, 2902-2903, 2905, 2907, 2909, 2916-2917, 2919, 2925, 2931, 2935, 2937, 2939
1945/46, 2893
1946/55, 2691

Subject Index

1987 update, 2657
agreements, 2817-2818
alternatives, 2829
assessment, 2625, 2634, 2665, 2751, 2760, 2775, 2787-2788, 2795, 2812, 2865, 2912
Austria, 2647
bargaining chips, 2723, 2725, 2808, 2827
bargaining models, 2832
behavioral aspects, 2744-2746
briefing manual, 2882
CRS Reports, 2949
Canada, 2887, 2938
chemical weapons, 3222, 3229-3230
chronology, 2848
cold climate, 2860
common grounds, 2704
communication, 2662, 2814, 2821
compromises, 2843
computer models, 2752
conventional weapons, 2748, 2911, 3368
converging views, 2847, 2910
cooperation, 2699, 2701, 2714
crisis management, 2591, 2686, 2758, 2770, 2794, 2802
defence policy, 2723
detente, 2737
diplomacy, 2596, 2708
dissertation, 2879, 2906, 2960
documentary history, 2612
documents, 2885, 2890, 2943, 2956
Eastern Europe, 2656
environmental issues, 3371, 3386
European security, 2607, 2697, 2728, 2782, 2922
experimental analysis, 2904
failure of, 2796
feedback, 2820
flexibility, 2676
forward based systems, 2913
French diplomacy, 2689, 3359
future expectations, 2658, 2765
GATT examples, 2807
game theory, 1345, 1577
Geneva, 2615, 2664, 2711, 2773, 2786, 2824
Geneva 1954, 2734
German policies, 2811, 2869
Gorbachev, 2688
guide, 2641
Helsinki, 2615
historical analysis, 2604, 2606, 2628, 2826, 2863, 2867, 2872, 2876, 2886, 2891, 2898, 2918, 2941-2942, 2948, 2955, 3207
Indian Ocean, 3365-3366
information management, 2750
intelligence aspects, 2901
Johnson presidency, 2631
language aspects, 2828
learning process, 2853
legal aspects, 2772, 2776
linkages, 2731
MX missiles, 2946
mathematical models, 1184-1185, 1220
media coverage, 2868
mediation, 1800
military diplomacy, 2815
misperceptions, 2928
modelling, 1694
Montreux Convention, 3382
multilateral aspects, 2685
NATO, 2614
national security, 2619
neutral countries, 2793, 2852
nonaligned states, 2761, 2878
optimal strategy, 2721
organization, 2660
periodical, 2595
policy development, 2926
political aspects, 2708, 2721, 2757, 2962
pragmatism, 2687
proposals, 2858
psychological aspects, 546, 678, 1050, 1052
rationality, 2813
Reagan Administration, 2630, 2637, 2713
reciprocal measures, 2819
regional approaches, 2748
Richardson Theory, 2839
SDI, 2646, 2946
satellites, 2933
secrecy, 2682, 2866, 2961
self constraint policy, 2663
signals, 2820
simulation, 1184, 1271, 1414, 1491, 1514, 2923
sociological aspects, 795, 2785
Soviet decision making, 2718
Soviet economy, 2762
Soviet industry, 2927
Soviet policies, 2609, 2632, 2649, 2673, 2694, 2741, 2753-2754,

2771, 2851, 2896, 2958
Soviet propaganda, 2797
Soviet secrecy, 2763
Soviet techniques, 2888-2889, 2932
space weapons, 2855-2856, 2899, 2954
Standing Commission, 2668
status report, 2693
structural blocks, 2854
success conditions, 2959-2960
tabular aspects, 2726
technical aspects, 2730, 2962
U.N. role, 2226, 2897, 2940
U.S. Congress, 2961
U.S. House Hearings, 2945
U.S. House Report, 2947
U.S. Senate Hearings, 2952-2953, 2957
U.S. policies, 2627, 2629, 2698, 2722, 2739, 2759, 2780, 2830, 2849, 2908, 2929, 2936, 2944, 4695
unilateral disarmament, 2798
unilateral initiatives, 2707, 2806
updating service, 2593-2594
verifications, 2930
Warsaw Pact, 2733
western powers, 2800
Arms Control Negotiator
career aspect, 2742
Arms Control and Disarmament Agency
assessment, 2605, 2642
Arms Trade
negotiations, 2659, 2799, 3369
Arms Transfer
Soviet diplomacy, 4596
ASEAN, 2581
conflict resolution, 2537
dissertation, 2582
regional cooperation, 2582
summitry, 2578
U.S. diplomacy, 2579
Vietnamese policies, 5326-5327
Aspiration
negotiation behavior, 769, 1132
Aspiration Level, 1066
balancing of, 1605
bargaining behavior, 614, 618, 708, 1314
bargaining toughness, 812
coalition bargaining, 783
direct experience, 614
experimental bargaining, 748
game theory, 1228, 1313, 1603

social learning, 614
Aswan Dam Negotiations
psychological aspects, 984
Asymmetric Initiation, 986
Asymmetric Negotiation, 47
communication, 616, 802
motivation, 549
dissertation, 438
Atlantic Conference
economic diplomacy, 2517
Roosevelt/Churchill, 2266
World War II, 2284
Atlantic Energy Negotiations, 3654
Atomic Energy Negotiations, 3377
Attention Focus, 1167
Attitudes
gender differences, 572
international interactions, 760
Attlee Clement
memoirs, 4314
Attraction
cooperation, 1057
interpersonal bargaining, 1024
interpersonal conflicts, 833
Australia
disarmament negotiations, 2779
energy resource diplomacy, 3903
GATT negotiations, 3724
trade diplomacy, 3873, 3875, 3880
Australia/Japan Negotiations, 3846
Austria
arms control negotiations, 2647
U.S./Soviet cooperation, 2989
Austrian State Treaty
negotiations, 4575, 4595, 5412
Soviet Union, 4459
Authoritarian Behavior, 967
Automobile Industry
U.S./Japan agreement, 3945
Autonomy Negotiations
West Bank, 4875, 4893, 4919
Axiomatic Models
game theory, 1218
Azerbijan Crisis (1945/46)
U.S. diplomacy, 4763

Bahrain
oil concession negotiations, 3647
Balkans
negotiations with Soviets, 4508
Bandung Conference, 2527
Bargaining
definitions, 144
public good theory, 145

Subject Index

research, 171
Bargaining Behavior
  social psychological aspects, 530, 838
  arbitration costs, 878
  aspiration level, 614, 708
  bilateral monopoly, 645-646
  coalitions, 156, 931
  computer studies, 1726-1727
  game theory, 1201, 1528, 1719-1725
  information, 708
  international studies, 514
  mediation simulation, 695
  military capability, 742
  mutual perceptions, 723
  overconfidence, 877
  psychological aspects, 739, 752, 782, 1373
  relative power, 1373
  risk taking, 713
  stalemated negotiation, 707
  threats, 847
  See also Negotiation Behavior, Psychological Aspects
Bargaining Chips
  arms control negotiations, 2827
Bargaining Costs
  game theory, 1401
Bargaining Efficiency
  threats, 683
Bargaining Expectations, 1529
Bargaining Experience
  bargaining outcome, 1314
Bargaining Games, 1558-1559
  pacifist strategies, 962-963
  social responsibility, 873
  status, 554
  unified treatment, 1617
Bargaining Groups
  success factors, 850
Bargaining Models, 718, 887, 1551-1552, 1586
  arms control negotiations, 2832
  asymmetric information, 1549
  dissertation, 1731
  perfect equilibrium, 1548
  SALT negotiations, 3096
  time and information, 1663-1664
  time preferences, 1547
  value of time, 427
Bargaining Outcomes
  limit salience, 1165
  personal controls, 676
  structural aspects, 709

visual access, 684
Bargaining Ploys
  helplessness, 680
Bargaining Power, 382, 786
  aspiration level, 812
  democracies, 184
  interpersonal relationships, 797
  military capability, 486
Bargaining Processes
  efficiency, 682
  game theory, 1310-1312
  See also Negotiating Processes
Bargaining Results
  concession rate, 574
Bargaining Set Theory, 1284
Bargaining Styles
  bargaining payoff, 714
  dissertation, 1103
  Soviet, 4482
Bargaining Tactics
  arms control negotiations, 2925
  psychological aspects, 688
Bargaining Theory, 19, 299
  coalition formation, 147, 779
  coercive diplomacy, 276
  diplomacy, 4139
  economic aspects, 435
  Peru oil diplomacy, 3650
Bargaining Uncertainty, 1293
Baruch Plan
  U.S. diplomacy, 4780
Beagle Channel Negotiations, 1990, 5219, 5243, 5264
Bedell Smith
  memoirs, 4315
Begin
  negotiation assessment, 4891
Begin/Sadat Negotiations, 4938
  See also Camp David Summit, Middle East Conflict
Behavioral Analysis, 513, 534, 586, 996, 998, 1095, 1106
  conflict resolution, 539, 729
  international conflicts, 969
  mediation, 1760
  two person game, 1058
  See also Bargaining Behavior, Psychological Aspects
Behavioral Models, 1048
Behavioral Research
  crises, 515
Behavioral Styles
  diplomats, 542
Behavioral Tactics

mediation, 1809
Behavioral Theories
  comparative studies, 970
  labor negotiations, 543
Belfast Workshop
  grassroots leaders, 636
  group techniques, 632
Belgrade Conference
  CSCE negotiations, 3253, 3261
Bellex Bellagio Mini Game, 1266
Ben Gurion, 4793
  negotiating with Nasser, 4913
  See also Middle East Conflict
Benelux Financial Negotiations, 3939
Berlin
  conflict management, 2857
  U.S. policies, 5414
  U.S./Soviet cooperation, 3362
Berlin Agreement Negotiations, 5381
Berlin Crisis (1948), 5341
  Moscow negotiations, 5413
Berlin Crisis (1958-62), 5312, 5404
  chronology, 5314
  U.S. diplomacy, 4743
Berlin Crisis (1959)
  Soviet diplomacy, 4586
Berlin Quadripartite Agreement, 2501
  documents, 2500
Berlin Status
  World War II Diplomacy, 2569
Bertrand Duopoly Experiments
  altruism, 1589
Betrayal
  two person game, 780
Biased Mediators, 1845, 1852, 1877
  future mediations, 1879
Big Lie Technique, 607
Bilateral Coercion
  U.S./Israel, 4833
Bilateral Monopoly
  aspiration levels, 1582
  bargaining behavior, 645-646
  concession making, 777, 1075
  concession rate, 645-646
  constituency feedback, 1075
  game theory, 1377-1378
Biological Weapons Negotiations, 3223
  See also Chemical Weapons
Bivariate Negotiations, 1340
Blackmail
  game theory, 1329
Bloc Formation
  apex games, 1231

Bluffing
  experiments, 1126
Bohlen Charles
  biography, 4680
  memoirs, 4317
Bonn Economic Summit, 3448, 3507, 3518
  See also Economic Summits
Boundary Conflicts, 70, 180-181
  Chile/Argentina, 5208
  Fermeda Workshop, 635
  legal aspects, 32
  mediation, 1842
  U.S./Mexico, 5272
Boundary Water Disputes
  Canada/U.S., 5281, 5283-5284
Bounded Rational Bargaining Theories, 1249, 1606
Bowles Chester
  memoirs, 4319
Braithwaite Arbitration Scheme, 1430
Brazil
  dept relief, 3924
  diplomatic analysis, 5257
  human rights issues, 5226
  trade negotiations, 3840
Bretton Woods, 3565, 4536
Brezhnev Peace Offensive 1981, 4623
Briggs Ellis
  memoirs, 4321
British Mandate
  Arab/British negotiations, 4798
  Arab/Zionist negotiations, 4799
British/Chinese Loan Negotiations, 5117
British/French Negotiations
  Palestine 1919-1920, 4880
British/Icelandic Cod Wars, 47, 3894
British/Soviet Negotiations (1939), 4601
British/Thai Peace Negotiations (1945), 5368
British/U.S. Diplomacy
  Iraqi Oil 1918/1928, 3653
Brzezinski Zbigniew
  memoirs, 4322
Bureaucratic Influences, 118
Burke Lee
  memoirs, 4323
Burma
  Soviet diplomats, 4468
Byrnes James
  memoirs, 4324

Subject Index

Cairo Conference 1943, 2288
  SEXTANT Conference, 2283
Cambodia Negotiations, 5334
Camp David Accords, 4881, 4918
  assessment, 4960
  autonomy talks, 4919
  Egyptian testimony, 4814
Camp David Summit, 4816-4817, 4835, 4888, 4963
  autonomy talks, 4914
  behavioral aspects, 711
  crisis bargaining, 4952
  dissertation, 4951
  mediation, 1933, 1972
  negotiation theory, 4951
  U.S. policies, 4795
  See also Middle East Conflict
Canada
  arms control negotiations, 2887, 2938
  cultural diplomacy, 5357
  diplomacy, 4156, 5305, 5324, 5356, 5400
  foreign policy documents, 5383-5384
  GATT negotiations, 3732, 3739, 3753
  Law of the Sea Conferences, 2306, 2309, 2349
  non fuel mineral negotiations, 3789
  test ban negotiations, 2997
  diplomacy, 3966
Canada/China Negotiations, 5121
Canada/India
  nuclear power negotiations, 3890
Canada/U.S.
  acid rain hearings, 5293
  acid rain negotiations, 5285, 5292
  air agreement negotiations, 3793
  auto agreement, 3773, 3780
  bilateral institutions, 5278-5279
  boundary water disputes, 5281, 5283-5284, 5286
  conflict resolution, 5274, 5287, 5289
  diplomatic history, 5275
  environmental disputes, 5277
  fisheries negotiations, 3802
  GATT role, 3785
  International Joint Commission, 5273
  investment negotiations, 3771
  oil diplomacy, 3658
  salmon negotiations, 3777
  summit diplomacy, 5291
  trade negotiations, 3713, 3760, 3762-3764, 3766-3767, 3784, 3786-3787, 3796, 3803
  water management talks, 5280
Canada/U.S. Free Trade
  negotiations, 3759, 3768, 3794
  U.S. House Report, 3799
  U.S. Senate Hearings, 3800
Canada/U.S. Trade
  U.S. House Hearings, 3797
Canada/U.S./Mexico
  fisheries negotiations, 3776
Cancun Economic Summit, 3509, 3512, 3514, 3532
  North South negotiations, 3526
Caribbean Basin Negotiations, 5217, 5225
Caribbean Commonwealth Negotiations, 5209
Caribbean States
  Law of the Sea, 2327
Cartels
  negotiations, 3586
Carter Jimmy
  diplomacy, 4719
  Middle East Conflict, 4927
  memoirs, 4800
Casablanca Conference 1943, 2271, 2290
Causes of War, 88, 289
CBM Negotiations
  assessment, 3265
  Europe, 3267
CDE Negotiations, 3227
  Europe, 3333
  Stockholm, 3284
Central America, 5261
  Contadora diplomacy, 5200-5201
  peace negotiations, 5240, 5262, 5265
Central Europe
  intractability, 4934
  MBFR negotiations, 3178-3179
Chaco War Diplomacy, 5203
Chamizal Tract Dispute, 5256
Chemical Industry
  GATT negotiations, 3714
Chemical Weapons, 3165, 3222, 3224-3227, 3229, 3232-3236, 3240-3241
  British policies, 3239
  conventions, 3228
  draft treaties, 3231

Geneva negotiations, 3237-3238
international organization, 3242
negotiations update, 3166, 3286
scientific aspects, 3243
U.S. House Hearings, 3244
U.S. policies, 3244
Children Transfer
Palestine 1943, 5328
Chile
human rights issues, 5250
China
African diplomacy, 5141
Canada negotiations, 5121
communication aspects, 5110
economic diplomacy, 3822
foreign policy, 5145
foreign relations, 5114
international exchanges, 5144
Marshall Mission, 5418
Middle East diplomacy, 4864
negotiation aspects, 5153
policy towards U.S., 5125
Soviet negotiations, 4493
trade negotiations, 3824-3826
U.N. admission, 2513
China/Japan Trade Negotiations, 3827
China/Soviet Alliance
conflict resolution, 5138
China/U.S. Agreements
case study, 5143
nuclear energy, 5149
China/U.S. Negotiations, 5112
assessment, 5113
domestic aspects, 5127
China/U.S. Trade Negotiations, 3821
Chinese Civil War
American mediation, 1955
Chinese Diplomacy, 5118, 5133
Europe, 5132
influence on Japan, 5137
Kampuchea, 5119
linguistic aspects, 5116
Soviet Union, 5138
Chinese Foreign Policy
dissertation, 5145
Chinese Loan Negotiations
dissertation, 3831
Chinese Negotiating Style, 4477,
  5111, 5122, 5126, 5135, 5139-
  5140, 5146-5148, 5150-5151, 5154-
  5155, 5159
business aspects, 3830
case studies, 5120
cultural aspects, 5130, 5134

friendship, 5131
Hongkong, 5136
international law, 5120
interpersonal norms, 5130
Korea, 5122
obligation, 5131
Ohio/Hubei Agreement, 5128
translation aspects, 5115
treaty agreements, 5120
Chronology
arms control negotiations, 2848
Churchill/Roosevelt Correspondence,
  2237
Civil Wars
mediation, 1822, 1923
Clausewitz
negotiation theory, 495
Coal Bargaining
Colombia, 3934
Coalition Bargaining, 278, 2018,
  4130
advantages, 277
aspiration levels, 783
behavioral aspects, 156, 885
outcomes, 791
Coalition Formation
achieved power, 1299
bargaining behavior, 931
bargaining theory, 147
four person games, 857
game theory, 1436
psychological aspects, 779
success probability, 608
three person games, 1442, 1607
Coalition Outcomes
game theory, 1351
Coalitions
psychological aspects, 778
three person groups, 584-585
Coastal Water Negotiations, 5364
Cocoa Agreement
analysis, 3690
Coercive Diplomacy, 276, 1006
Cuba, 5302
Laos, 5302
mediation, 1862
targeting, 4256
U.S. foreign policy, 4774
Vietnam, 5302
Coercive Power
analysis, 1010
Coffee Diplomacy, 3862
Cognition Theory
analysis, 1065

Subject Index

research project, 1108
Cognitive Aspects, 160, 520, 552, 581, 593, 746
  crisis bargaining, 1145
  deterrence failure, 981
  dissertation, 1145
  foreign policy decisions, 1087
  interpersonal conflicts, 589
Cognitive Structure
  Munich 1938, 412
Cold War Diplomacy, 4269
  memoirs, 4315
  U.S. foreign policy, 4646
Collective Bargaining
  behavioral aspects, 550
  models, 208
  theories, 102
Colombia
  coal bargaining, 3934
Columbia River Treaty, 5276, 5286
Commercial Dept Negotiations, 3918
Commission of Churches
  unofficial diplomacy, 4386
Commitment
  assessment, 1170
  international relations, 836
Committee on Disarmament
  documents, 2885
Commodity Negotiations, 3666, 3673
  collaboration, 3679
  conflicts, 3677
  North South negotiations, 3667, 3669, 3674-3675, 3680
  policy issues, 3661
  political economy, 3678
  U.S. Senate Hearings, 3691
  U.S. Senate Report, 3692
  legal aspects, 3662
  See also North South Negotiations
Commonwealth Diplomacy, 2510, 2518, 2528, 2531, 2536
  Masters Thesis, 2574
  north south issues, 2428
  prenegotiations, 2542
Commonwealth Sugar Agreement Negotiations, 3896
Commonwealth Youth Conference
  analysis, 2182
Communication, 28, 177, 361, 600, 741, 828, 932, 973, 975, 1005, 1060, 4068, 4705
  arms control negotiations, 2662, 2814, 2821
  asymmetric negotiations, 802
  bargaining power, 1084
  bargaining structures, 425
  behavioral aspects, 620, 792, 837, 884
  bilateral negotiations, 600
  China, 5110
  conflict resolution, 57, 154, 315
  controlled, 1092
  crisis decision making, 731
  crisis management, 370
  cultural aspects, 79, 379, 4076
  diplomacy, 4032, 4056, 4070, 4144, 4164, 4230, 4435-4436, 4447-4448
  dissertation, 1084, 1153
  experimental negotiations, 961
  experimental studies, 1321
  flow studies, 381
  indirect, 913
  influence, 848
  international relations, 21, 527, 900
  language aspects, 1175
  mediation, 1878, 1921
  multilateral negotiations, 2019
  negotiation outcomes, 972, 1153
  negotiation success, 1026-1027
  negotiation theory, 242-243
  peace aspects, 135
  prisoner dilemma game, 1045, 1115
  research, 261, 261
  Sadat/Begin negotiations, 4931
  strategic interaction, 876
  U.S. policies, 3883
  U.S./Japanese negotiations, 5104
  U.S./Soviet negotiations, 4509
Communication Competence
  dissertation, 1174
  mediators, 1920
Communist Diplomacy
  Lenin, 4529
Communist Ideology
  Soviet diplomacy, 4579, 4619
Communist Negotiating Techniques, 4467, 4497, 4503, 4582-4583, 4606
  comparisons, 4561
  Greek issues, 4597
  U.S. policies, 4599
  See also Soviet Negotiating Behavior
Community Trade Regime
  developing countries, 3664
Competence Perception
  dissertation, 1120
Competitive Dyads

risk taking, 1446
Competitive Tests, 1458
Competitiveness
   interpersonal bargaining, 976
Compliance
   second request timing, 598
Compliance Inducement
   reciprocal concessions, 611
Compliance to Threats, 863, 953
   dissertation, 1101
Comprehensive Test Ban, 3006, 2971, 2976
   U.S. House Hearings, 3004
   U.S. Senate Hearings, 3012
   See also Test Ban Negotiations, Test Ban Treaty
Compromises
   social aspects, 1023
   game theory, 1209, 1426
Computer Analysis, 417
   threats, 1728
Computer Applications, 480
   conflict resolution, 414
Computer Assisted Research, 426
Computer Forecasting
   multilateral negotiations, 2029-2030
Computer Industry
   U.S./Brazil negotiations, 3930, 3941
Computer Mediation
   Law of the Sea, 2337
Computer Models, 1437
   Law of the Sea, 2342
   negotiation support, 1708-1709
   policy processes, 1199
Computer Simulation
   dissertation, 1682
Computer Studies
   bargaining behavior, 1726-1727
   effects of threat, 1699
Computer Support Systems
   mediation, 1871
Concession Making, 648, 662, 1077
   bilateral monopoly, 777, 1075
   conflict resolution, 781
   experimental negotiations, 558
   frequency, 609, 790
   psychological aspects, 1044
   reciprocity, 785
Concession Rate, 1081
   bargaining behavior, 1062
   bargaining outcomes, 574
   bilateral monopoly, 645-646

games, 1402
time pressure, 971
toughness, 971
Conciliation
   international, 1741
   power capability, 825
   psychological effects, 830
   style of, 829, 1915
Confederate Behavior
   payoff effects, 1480
Conference Diplomacy, 2156, 2159, 4032, 4087, 4165
   decision making, 225
   evolution, 2176
   North South aspects, 2424, 2589
   seabed arms control, 3245, 3252
   studies, 2154
   U.N. role, 2181
   See also International Conferences
Conference on Security and Cooperation in Europe *See* CSCE Negotiations
Confidence and Security Building Measures
   See CSBM Negotiations
Confidence Building Measures
   CSCE, 3254
   SALT, 3089
   See also CSCE Conferences
Conflict Analysis, 94, 137, 1404, 1673, 1675, 1677-1678
   game theory, 1202
   international misperceptions, 1735
   models, 1571
   negotiation support system, 1349, 1676
   staying power, 1693
   strategic choice, 1348
   trade disputes, 1590
Conflict Avoidance, 815
Conflict Behavior, 285, 352, 367
   historical analysis, 351
   measurements, 768
Conflict Coefficients, 1737
Conflict Data Bank Project, 124
Conflict Deescalation, 454
Conflict Escalation
   compliance aspects, 582
   cooperation, 1011
   withdrawal factors, 592
Conflict Misperceptions
   hypergames, 1734
Conflict Modelling, 1432
   algorithms, 1346
   nuclear confrontation, 1347

Subject Index

Conflict Orientation
  dissertation, 1178
Conflict Resolution, 10, 14, 34, 37, 72, 77, 80, 86, 92-93, 104, 128, 152, 167, 183, 204, 215, 218, 221, 271, 283, 291, 305, 316, 319, 322-323, 334, 343, 347, 353, 387, 456, 463, 473, 5340
  abjudicated, 824
  axiomatic approach, 123
  behavioral aspects, 539, 729-730
  coercion, 83
  cognitive aspects, 706
  communication aspects, 57, 154, 315, 494
  complex systems, 249
  computers, 414
  concessions, 781
  conciliation, 83
  conflict control, 49
  cultural aspects, 478
  curricula, 75
  decision making, 99
  dissertation, 1121
  education, 74
  effectiveness, 134, 936
  empathy, 209
  empirical assessments, 155
  flexibility, 288
  game theory, 1213, 1507
  generic theory, 120-121, 148-149
  handbook, 22
  historical analysis, 23, 23, 150
  intercultural aspects, 457
  intragroup factors, 774
  institutionalized, 213
  Janus quality, 356
  legal aspects, 238
  management aspects, 55, 251, 293
  mathematical analysis, 1189
  mediation, 1751
  Middle East, 4834, 4876
  mode preference, 809
  model, 712
  nationalism, 260
  noncoersive inducements, 273
  ocean use, 2352
  private initiatives, 168
  problem solving, 220, 236, 420
  procedures, 151
  psychological aspects, 500, 509, 517, 545, 638, 860
  reaction models, 814
  research, 35, 232, 443, 2123
  resistance to, 314
  simulation, 1250
  small states, 301
  social psychological aspects, 764-765, 4379
  stabilizing factors, 169
  technological aspects, 27
  theories, 5, 141, 185, 239, 629
  timing, 230
  U.N., 2037, 2069, 2098, 2114, 2127, 2151
  U.S. Government Agencies, 4759
  war termination, 157, 222
  workshop, 1110
  workshops, 764, 1707, 4379
  See also Crisis Management
Conflict Theory, 9, 16
  non rational approach, 843
  research, 250
  theory of divergent goals, 4
Conflict of Interest
  dispute resolution, 725
  social aspects, 915
  sociology of conflict, 642
  value dissensus, 641-643
Congo Crisis
  O.A.U., 2560
Conjoint Analysis
  personal preferences, 694
Consensus Diplomacy, 2017
  international conferences, 2168
Consensus Formation Communication
  dissertation, 1134
Constituent Pressure
  simulation, 968
Constituent Surveillance
  psychological aspects, 603, 914
Consular Practices
  glossary, 3982
Consultation, 452
  legal aspects, 174
Contadora Negotiations, 5200-5201, 5236, 5241-5242, 5263, 5268
  failure of, 5210
  update, 3166
Containment Policy
  diplomatic aspects, 4151
Contextual Variation Effects
  dissertation, 1085
Contract Negotiations
  handbook, 3556
Contractual Agreements
  unequal power parties, 1018
Contractual Norms, 1017

stress aspects, 1016
Conventional Arms Transfer
  Negotiations, 3376, 3384, 3389
Cooperation, 122, 130, 956, 960,
  1447
  arms control negotiations, 2701,
    2714
  behavioral aspects, 687
  communication aspects, 837
  conflict escalation, 1011
  experimental studies, 1014
  facial aspects, 1078
  foreign policy behavior, 1049
  game theory, 1186, 1226, 1236-1237,
    1239, 1415, 1623, 1729
  gaze patterns, 675
  inducement to, 628, 827, 895
  integrative bargaining, 1497
  issue linkages, 309
  mixed motive game, 955
  models, 894
  non cooperative games, 1463
  non zero sum game, 940
  nonverbal communication, 745
  personality aspects, 1162, 1012
  prisoner dilemma game, 619, 667,
    699, 811, 923
  rewards, 666
  social aspects, 754, 840
  theory, 623
  trust, 837
  two person games, 772
  unilateral promises, 666
  verbal communication, 745
  See also Communication
Cooperative Choice
  two person game, 789
Cooperative Dyads
  risk taking, 1446
Cooperative Games, 1394, 1408, 1431,
  1567, 1572, 1631
  game theory, 1386, 1393, 1395,
    1614
  N Person games, 1564
  Nash solution, 1518
  symmetry, 1716
Copyright Negotiations, 3818
Cordell Hull
  dissertation, 4758
  force in diplomacy, 4706
Costs
  effects on bargaining, 1647
Couchiching Conference
  diplomacy, 2502

Crisis Bargaining, 4039, 4071
  arms control negotiations, 2591,
    2802
  behavioral aspects, 979
  cognitive factors, 1145
  Reagan, 3424
  social psychological aspects, 690
  Soviets, 4492, 4585
  spatial model, 1465, 1703
  U.S. intervention policies, 4645
Crisis Communication
  telephone hotline, 274, 455
Crisis Learning Games, 1441
Crisis Management, 45, 85, 91, 99,
  110, 210, 386, 396, 485, 496,
  2716, 2758, 2894, 3388
  arms control negotiations, 2770
  coercion, 287
  communication aspects, 370
  diplomacy, 419, 4069, 4072-4073
  empathy, 209
  historical aspects, 483
  Middle East, 4792, 4858
  nuclear risk reduction, 2794, 2920
  reciprocal assurances, 360
  simulation, 1267, 1566
  studies, 111
  telephone hotline, 2638, 2838,
    4725
  U.S./Soviet cooperation, 2715
  war termination, 377
  Yom Kippur war, 4831
Crisis Prevention
  19 century diplomacy, 4307
  U.S./Soviet negotiations, 4465
Cross Cultural Analysis, 40, 345,
  549
  See also Cultural Aspects, Cultural
    Diplomacy
Cross Cultural Communication, 379
Cross Cultural Negotiations
  technology transfer, 3641
Cross Cultural Sales Negotiations
  dissertation, 3640
Cross Cultural Training, 423
Cross/Coddington Model
  unified solution, 1287
CRS Reports
  arms control, 2949
Cruise Missiles
  bargaining chips, 2921
CSBM Negotiations, 3334
  assessment, 3313
  Canadian perspectives, 3323

Subject Index

European cooperation, 3271
Soviet negotiating strategies, 3321
Stockholm Agreement, 3329
Stockholm Conference, 3275-3276, 3280, 3304
U.S. negotiating strategies, 3321
CSCE Conferences, 2909, 3257, 3263, 3266, 3268-3270, 3274, 3278, 3285, 3291, 3294, 3298-3299, 3303, 3305-3306, 3311, 3315, 3318, 3324, 3336-3337
assessment, 3281
asymmetrical bargaining, 3289
Belgrade, 3253, 3261
Canadian perceptions, 3332
confidence building measures, 3254
conflict structures, 3262
cooperation, 3312, 3314, 3317
decision making, 3290
detente, 3260
documents, 3256
Finnish views, 3328
Geneva final act, 3309
Helsinki, 3297, 3319
Helsinki Accords, 3258, 3277, 3320
historical analysis, 3287, 3301, 3310
humanitarian aspects, 3322
institutional role, 3272
Madrid, 3259, 3279, 3292-3293, 3295-3296, 3300, 3302, 3307-3308, 3326, 3335
multilateral diplomacy, 3264
negotiation theory, 3288
negotiator experience, 3316
neutrals, 3330-3331
nonaligned views, 3330-3331
overview, 2875
Soviet policies, 3273, 3325, 3327
Stockholm, 3255, 3283
update, 3286
Cuba
cultural diplomacy, 5232
diplomatic aspects, 5233, 5239
Soviet diplomacy, 4474
U.N. negotiations, 2120
U.S. policies, 5249
Cuban Missile Crisis, 4503, 5294-5295, 5301, 5306, 5370
diplomatic aspects, 5221, 5378
public diplomacy, 4445
Soviet behavior analysis, 5254
test ban negotiations, 2993-2994
U.S. policies, 5386
unofficial mediation, 4392
Cuban Revolution 1958/60
U.S. policies, 5258
Cultural Aspects, 333, 432, 5332, 5353
experience, 447
international conferences, 2196
international relations, 1
international trade, 3637, 3640
Japanese trade negotiations, 3639, 3833
persuasion, 214
psychological aspects, 1136
research proposals, 1136
trade negotiations, 3638
treaty negotiations, 354
Cultural Diplomacy, 4219, 4423, 4428
British views, 4183
Canada, 5357
Soviet Union, 4460
U.S., 4652
U.S. (1938/47), 4731
U.S. (1938/50), 4672
UNESCO, 2097
Cultural Exchange Negotiations
Soviets, 4565
Cyprus Conflict, 4808, 4847, 4895, 5398
historical analysis, 4827
mediation, 1940
prisoner dilemma game, 1445
U.S. House Hearings, 4959
U.S. diplomacy, 4824
Cyprus Seminar
simulation, 1600
Cyprus Workshop
intervention methodology, 633-634

Dartmouth Conference
Middle East aspects, 4390
unofficial diplomacy, 4368, 4371, 4394-4395, 4408
See also Unofficial Diplomacy
Davies Joseph
memoirs, 4325
Dayan Moshe
Israeli/Egyptian negotiations, 4805
negotiating tactics, 4884
See also Camp David Summit, Middle East Conflict
Deception
behavioral aspects, 816

game theory, 1657
Geneva 1954, 5064
three person game simulations, 1181
Deceptive Communication
  dissertation, 1149
Decision Integration Analysis, 995
Decision Making, 127, 270, 374, 732, 964, 1295
  bargaining models, 737
  CSCE Negotiations, 3290
  cognitive aspects, 569
  communication patterns, 731
  conferences, 225
  dissertation, 1130
  foreign policy, 4079
  game theory, 1427, 1602, 1711
  interpersonal, 557
  Japanese negotiations, 5091
  mediation, 1761
  theories, 1449
  models, 1712
  political elites, 1187
  psychological aspects, 732, 770, 997
  Saint John River Basin Talks, 5290
  simulation, 617, 1254, 1644, 1680
  theories, 740
  See also Psychological Aspects
Decision Support Systems, 1428, 1690, 1718
  mediation, 1665
  two player conflicts, 1670
Deescalation
  compliance aspects, 582
  influence aspects, 1071
  social aspects, 794
Definitions
  mediation, 1767
  negotiation, 928-929
Demand Increases
  psychological aspects, 800
Democracy, 4041, 4739
  bargaining aspects, 184
Dept Relief Negotiations, 2391, 2466, 3545
  Brazil, 3924
  developing countries, 2391
  Mexico, 3936
  north south negotiation, 2408
  Philippines, 5415
  Poland, 3916
  U.N., 2478, 2497
  western policies, 2473

Young Plan, 3938
Zaire, 2470
See also North South Negotiations
Detente Diplomacy, 3260, 4628
  documents, 4776
  Soviet policies, 4764
  U.S. policies, 4764
Deterrence Games, 241
Deterrence Hypothesis, 854
Deterrence Theories, 813
Developing Countries, 2399
  dept relief negotiations, 2391
  diplomacy, 2368, 4145
  economic diplomacy, 2361, 2389
  energy negotiations, 2379
  investment negotiations, 3573, 3616
  limited wars, 5388
  multinationals negotiations, 2458
  negotiating power, 2427
  nonmineral trade with U.S., 2474
  nuclear diplomacy, 3370
  Soviet diplomacy, 4507, 4535
  trade negotiations, 2386, 2402-2403, 2420, 2461, 2484
  U.N. Conference, 2438
  World Bank diplomacy, 2492
  See also North South Negotiations
Development Diplomacy, 2383
  UNCTAD, 2376
Dialectics
  diplomacy, 3997
Dictionary
  U.S. diplomatic history, 4276
Different Offer Strategies
  effectiveness, 710
Diplomacy, 189, 3954, 3956-3957, 3962, 3964, 3969, 3971-3974, 3976-3978, 3988-3990, 3993, 3995, 3998, 4005, 4008, 4010-4012, 4014-4016, 4019-4020, 4024-4025, 4029-4030, 4035, 4037-4038, 4046, 4049, 4053, 4055, 4057-4060, 4063-4064, 4067, 4077, 4082, 4089, 4095, 4098-4100, 4112-4115, 4117, 4128-4129, 4132-4133, 4137, 4142, 4152, 4155, 4158, 4161, 4173, 4179, 4194-4197, 4199-4200, 4207, 4209-4210, 4212, 4214-4216, 4222, 4225, 4231, 4237-4239, 4252-4254, 4263, 4265, 4267-4268
  Africa, 5184
  ambassador's role, 3992, 3994
  anthropological analysis, 4075,

Subject Index

4257
bargaining theory, 276, 4139
classic, 4136, 4163, 4174, 4232-4233
communication, 4032-4033, 4056, 4068, 4070, 4144, 4230, 4269, 4435-4436, 4447-4448, 5170
computers, 4185
conservatism, 4205
containment, 4151
Couchiching conference, 2502
crisis management, 419, 4069, 4072-4073, 4307
de Callieres, 4118
decision making, 4054
decline of, 4157, 4226
definition, 4065, 4083, 4168, 4170
delegates, 4258
democracies, 4041, 4181, 4188, 4229
developing countries, 4050, 4145
diplomatic service, 3963
direct, 4074
EEC, 4090, 4186
education, 4192
effectiveness, 4243
environmental aspects, 5322
ethical aspects, 4042, 4105, 4220
Europe, 4080
evolution of, 4187, 4290, 4308
formal models, 4044
France, 4084
future of, 4149-4150, 4154
game theory, 1252, 1654
glossary, 3982
government deception, 4040
guide, 4023
human rights, 5310
humanitarian, 3980
India, 4047, 5296
information availability, 4097
intelligence aspects, 4103
international conferences, 2165
international law, 4234
international organizations, 4043
intervention, 4241
Islamic, 3991
Kissinger's Influence, 4000
language aspects, 3979, 3983, 4013, 4266
leadership, 4153
legal aspects, 4092
limitation of, 4131
limitations of, 4213, 4223

management aspects, 3959, 4045
media aspects, 3984, 4022, 4425, 4443
ministerial level, 4235
modelling, 1692
modern, 3958, 4003-4004, 4052, 4066, 4088, 4101, 4104, 4111, 4126-4127, 4147, 4159-4160, 4162, 4166, 4171, 4180, 4190-4191, 4232, 4242, 4262
nationalism, 3961
naval, 3965
nonalignment, 2422
old, 4163
open, 4102, 4189
parliamentary, 4107, 4208, 4246
peace, 3996, 4009, 4221
popular, 4203
professional aspects, 4028, 4109, 4121-4123, 4206, 4211, 4224, 4228
psychological aspects, 938
public opinion, 4240
rituals, 3970
sea power, 5348
secret, 4022, 4040, 4102, 4148, 4169, 4175-4176, 4178, 4189, 4255, 4286
security systems, 4204
signals, 3970
simulation, 1251, 1358
small states, 4093
social psychological aspects, 536
sociological aspects, 942
Soviet policies, 3960, 4134, 4143, 4513, 4542
Soviet scholarship, 4048
special envoy, 4236
Stephen Kertesz, 4031
summit meetings, 3411
surprise, 3985, 4108
symposium, 4249
textbook treatment, 4193
theory, 3955, 4081, 4119, 4124, 4140
threats, 4139
totalitarian approaches, 4501-4502
training, 4091, 4125, 4141
U.N., 2087, 2093-2094
ultimatums, 4138
unofficial, 4055
World Food Conference, 2190
World War II, 4297
See also Negotiation Processes

Diplomatic History, 4007, 4140, 4244,
    4279, 4281-4283, 4285, 4289,
    4292, 4295-4296, 4301, 4303,
    4305-4306, 4309-4310
  Africa, 4299
  Britain, 4285
  changes in, 4304
  embassies, 4275
  Europe, 4270, 4278, 4298
  evolution of, 4294
  new diplomacy, 4288, 4302
  organizational processes, 4311
  sociological aspects, 4291
  U.S., 4271-4273, 4277
Diplomatic Memoirs
  Charles Ritchie, 4348-4349
  Chester Bowles, 4320
  Henderson Loy, 4333
  Martin Herz, 4354
  McGhee George, 4344
  Meyer Armin, 4345
  Sullivan William, 4353
  See also Memoirs
Diplomatic Protest, 4006
Diplomatic Service, 4078
  management of, 3963
Diplomatic Travel
  U.S. diplomats, 4716
Diplomats, 3967-3968, 4002, 4086,
    4096, 4149-4150, 4172, 4198
  behavioral aspects, 542, 671
  education, 4264
  interwar diplomacy, 4274
  lawyers, 4051
  loyalties, 4259-4260
  mental illness, 1025
  military persons, 4094
  new demands, 4110
  personal qualities, 4201
  professionalism, 3987, 4217
  physical illness, 1025
  role of, 4062, 4247, 4261
  soldiers, 4034
  training, 4021, 4245
  unofficial, 4356
  See also Ambassadors, Memoirs
Direct Negotiations, 229
  linguistic aspects, 1176
Disagreement Theory
  game theory, 1307, 1448
Disarmament *See* Arms Control
Negotiations
Disarmament Activities
  U.N., 2197, 2212, 2223-2224

Disarmament Conferences
  effectiveness, 2192
  Europe, 2683
  multilateral negotiation, 2221
  U.N., 2056, 2198
Disruptive Behavior Control
  dissertation, 1177
Dissertation
  ASEAN cooperation, 2582
  accountability, 1114
  ambiguity tolerance, 1091
  armistice negotiations, 474
  arms control negotiations, 2879,
    2906, 2960
  asymmetric negotiations, 438
  bargaining models, 1703, 1731
  bargaining styles, 1103
  behavioral aspects, 1073, 1172
  Brazilian diplomacy, 5257
  Camp David Summit, 4951
  Canada/U.S. oil diplomacy, 3658
  Canadian minerals negotiations,
    3789
  Chinese foreign policy, 5145
  commodities negotiations, 2488
  communication aspects, 1084, 1153
  competence perception, 1120
  compliance to threats, 1101
  computer simulation, 1682
  conflict orientation, 1178
  conflict resolution, 1121
  conflict simulation, 1096
  consensus formation, 1134
  contextual variation effects, 1085
  Cordell Hull, 4758
  cross cultural sales negotiations,
    3640
  deceptive communication, 1149
  decision making, 1130
  diplomatic effectiveness, 4243
  disruptive behavior control, 1177
  duopoly bargaining, 1159
  dyadic interaction, 1097
  effect of suspicion, 1111
  effect of trust, 1111
  Egyptian negotiations, 4944
  energy negotiations, 3819
  environmental disputes, 1668
  experimental social interactions,
    1129
  Falkland Islands Crisis, 5252
  foreign policy decisions, 1087
  GATT negotiations, 3741
  game theory, 1679, 1714

Subject Index

gender influence, 1093
group decision making, 1148
impression formation, 1116
India/China boundary dispute, 5389
intergroup simulation, 1099
international conferences, 2188, 2191
international trade conference, 3623
international trade negotiations, 3619
interpersonal perceptions, 1133
Israel/Egypt negotiations, 4920, 4936
Israeli diplomacy, 4925, 4941
Japanese negotiating behavior, 5102
Kennan's diplomacy, 4786
LOME Convention negotiations, 2489, 2468
language aspects, 1174
Laotian Crisis, 5406
Law of the Sea, 2351, 2353-2355
leadership, 1169
locus of control, 1119
mandate base, 1104
Marshall Plan negotiations, 3923
mediation, 1873, 1898, 1902, 1904, 1916, 1974
Middle East mediation, 1976, 1985
motivation, 1089, 1155
negotiating skills, 476, 1094, 1098, 1109
negotiation outcomes, 476
negotiation theory, 406, 446
negotiator accountability, 1067
negotiator motivation, 1125
North South negotiations, 2475
O.A.U. in Africa, 2573
oil negotiations, 3655
open negotiation behavior, 1076
Panama, 5260
Panama Canal Negotiations, 5267
Paris Peace Talks (Vietnam), 5045
personality aspects, 1158
power relations, 1102
psychological advantages, 1150
reciprocity, 1074
relinquishing power, 1152
risk taking, 1179
SALT negotiations, 3103, 3108, 3119
Saint John River Basin Agreement, 5290
satellites negotiations, 2933
seabed arms control negotiations, 3252
South West African diplomacy, 2143
Soviet diplomacy, 4596, 2185, 2889, 4586, 4588, 4592, 4594
stalemated negotiation, 1105
subjective power models, 1173
summit conferences, 3486
test ban negotiations, 3000, 3016
Thai/U.S. diplomacy, 5405
theoretical model, 448
threat effects, 1072, 1112
time analysis, 461
two person bargaining, 1088
U.N. Conference on Human Environment, 2189
U.N. Membership Admission Factor, 2140
U.N. Science and Technology Conf., 2138
U.N. diplomacy, 2124, 2134, 2136-2137, 2146
U.S. arms control policies, 2929
U.S. diplomacy, 4762
U.S. nonmineral trade, 2474
U.S./British nuclear negotiations, 2881
U.S./Chinese negotiations, 5156-5158
U.S./Japanese negotiations, 5103-5105
U.S./Middle East diplomacy, 4950
U.S./Middle East policies, 4940
U.S./Philippine negotiations, 5382
U.S./Soviet trade negotiations, 3817
UNCTAD, 2477
unofficial diplomacy, 4405
Vietnam misrepresentation, 1181
West German rearmament negotiations, 5407
See also Masters Thesis
Distributive Tactics, 1081
Distrust Analysis, 237, 705
Dogmatism
    dyadic behavior, 647
Dollar Auction Game, 1573
Dominican Crisis 1965
    analysis, 5222
    mediation, 1978
    U.S. role, 5207
Dominican Republic
    mediation, 4400

unofficial diplomacy, 4400
Door in the Face Technique, 611
Dulles
  biography, 4644
  Far East diplomacy, 4760
  negotiating with Soviets, 4522
  negotiation analysis, 4631, 4784
  Suez Canal Crisis, 4642
  telephone conversations, 4766
  See also U.S. Diplomacy, U.S. Foreign Policy
Dunham Donald
  memoirs, 4326
Duopoly Bargaining
  dissertation, 1159
  dyadic outcomes, 987
  threat effects, 1471
Dyadic Bargaining
  asymmetric conditions, 801
  dissertation, 1097
  integrative, 1097
  prenegotiation experience, 647, 652
  resolution of, 557
  toughness, 749

East African Border Conflicts
  workshop, 1047
East Asian Diplomacy, 5342
East/West Negotiations, 2557, 2567, 5352
  arms control, 2607
East/West Relations
  data, 5300
  survey, 5299
East/West Technology Transfer, 3922
East/West Trade, 3810
  behavioral analysis, 3807
  decision modes, 3881
  game theoretic analysis, 1434
  guidelines, 3808
  joint ventures, 3614
  See also Trade Negotiations
Eastern Europe
  arms control negotiations, 2656
  commercial negotiations, 3892
  diplomacy, 5367
  economic summit meetings, 3510
  human rights negotiations, 5331
  political assessment, 4618
Economic Analysis, 376
  game theory, 1197
  interdependence, 382
Economic Diplomacy, 2361, 3546, 3576, 3578, 3589-3591, 3601-3602, 3622
  Atlantic Conference, 2517
  China, 3822
  dissertation, 3619
  Japan, 3822
  linkages, 3577
  OECD, 3619
  theories, 3621
  U.N., 2117
  See also Trade Negotiations
Economic Models
  bargaining, 1036
  Nash bargaining game, 1256
Economic Summits, 1237, 3503-3504, 3515, 3524, 3534-3536, 3538, 3542
  Africa Fund, 3511
  Bonn, 3507, 3518
  Cancun, 3509, 3512, 3514, 3532
  cooperation, 3519
  currency negotiations, 3539
  decision making aspects, 3502
  EEC, 3508
  Eastern Europe, 3510, 3537
  European issues, 3517
  historical analysis, 3513, 3528
  London, 3516
  media role, 3506
  nonaligned countries, 2471
  Ottawa, 3522
  political aspects, 3525, 3533
  Tokyo, 3520, 3529-3530
  Toronto (1988), 3531
  Venice, 3521
  Versailles, 3523, 3527
  Williamsburg, 3505, 3540
EEC
  agricultural policies, 3663
  British negotiations, 3858
  British policies, 2506, 2522
  diplomacy, 2503, 2521, 2543, 2545, 4090, 4186
  French attitudes, 2565
  German attitudes, 2565
  international conferences, 2167
  Japanese economic diplomacy, 3835
  North Africa negotiations, 2548
  North South negotiations, 2388
  seven economic summit members, 3508
  U.S. trade negotiations, 3694
Effectiveness, 1171
  bargaining processes, 682
  behavioral aspects, 1122

Subject Index

training, 564
EFTA Negotiations, 3866
Ego Involvement
   simulation, 1099
Egypt
   dissertation, 4944
   negotiating style, 4889
   negotiation analysis, 4944
   U.S. 1950/55 arms transfer, 5395
   U.S. communication aspects, 4708
Egyptian/Israeli Negotiations
   Ezer Weizman, 4826
   Palestine issue, 4886
   See also Middle East Conflict
Egyptian/Israeli Peace
   psychological aspects, 762
Eisenhower
   1960 Summit, 3496
   summit meetings, 3396, 3469
Eisenhower/Khrushchev
   summit diplomacy, 3438, 3482
El Chamizai Dispute, 5205
Electrolux Zanussi Negotiations, 2555
Elite Behavior, 903
   foreign policy crises, 518
Embassies
   business promotion, 4251
   diplomatic history, 4275
   See also Oil Diplomacy
Empirical Models, 560
Empirical Research, 484
Energy Negotiations, 2554, 3871
   Australia, 3903
   developing countries, 2379
   North Atlantic Area, 3654
   Soviet Union/Eastern Europe, 3819
   developing countries, 2400
   See also Oil Diplomacy
Entrapment
   face saving aspects, 590
   social psychological aspects, 505
   timing, 591
Environmental Issues
   negotiation research, 472
Environmental Modification Treaty, 3371
   arms control, 3386
Environmental Negotiations, 2374, 2499, 2515, 2550
   diplomacy, 5322
   media role, 2568
   mediation, 1938-1939, 1943, 1982
   strategic models, 1668

U.S., 5379
U.S./Canada, 5277
U.S./Mexico, 5259
Epstein Louis
   memoirs, 4327
Equality Preference
   psychological aspects, 866
Escalation
   game theory, 1577
   influence aspects, 1071
Ethical Aspects, 282
   diplomacy, 4042, 4105
   mediation theory, 1825
   U.S. diplomacy, 4733
Ethiopia/Somalia/Kenya Dispute, 5163
Ethnic Aspects
   interpersonal bargaining, 1000
EUREKA Conference, 2275
   Tehran, 2238
   Tehran 1943, 2275
Europe
   arms control negotiations, 2683, 2607, 2922
   CBM negotiations, 3267
   CSBM negotiations, 3271
   diplomacy, 440, 4116
   diplomatic history, 4270, 4278, 4298
   MBFR negotiations, 3162, 3186, 3192, 3199, 3203, 3205
   Middle East Mediation, 1937, 1979
   peace treaties, 5308
European Free Trade Area
   negotiations, 3927-3928
Event Model Analysis, 1738
Events Interaction Analysis, 6
   measurements, 143
Events Research Analysis, 7
Excuses
   psychological aspects, 978
Executive Skills Development, 418
Expectations
   coordination of, 362
   future negotiations, 571, 1066
Experience
   social psychological aspects, 875
Experimental Games, 1560
   critique, 930
   experience, 1300
Experimental Negotiations
   communication effects, 961
   concession making, 558
   formality, 867
   social interactions, 1128

Experimental Social Interactions
  dissertation, 1129
Expert Negotiators, 879
Experts' Conference (1958), 2962
Explicit Bargaining
  psychological experiments, 610
Export Restraints
  steel industry, 3949
External Stresses, 733
Eye Contact Analysis, 556

F Scale
  trust, 631
Face Saving, 595, 597
  entrapment, 590
  induced embarrassment, 596
  interpersonal bargaining, 594
  low power persons strategies, 1022
  mediation, 1806, 1832-1833
  See also Bargaining Behavior,
  Negotiation Behavior, Psychological
  Aspects
Facial Expressions
  cooperation expectations, 1078
Fahmy Ismail
  Middle East negotiations, 4806
Failure in Negotiations, 378
  psychological aspects, 567
Fairness Model, 1246
Fairness Principle Balancing, 1605
Falkland Islands Crisis, 1991, 5206,
    5213, 5215, 5238, 5244, 5251,
    5398
  dissertation, 5252
  hypergame analysis, 1405
  mediation, 1991, 5270
  mediator bias, 1996
  negotiation failures, 5269
  U.N. diplomacy, 2109, 2571, 5214,
    5229
Family Orientation
  interpersonal bargaining, 618
Fante Diplomacy, 4299
Far East Diplomacy
  John Foster Dulles, 4760
Far Eastern Commission Negotiations
  Soviets, 4491
Farm Support Systems
  multilateral negotiations, 3682
Feedback Analysis, 1131
Fermeda Workshop, 510, 639
  boundary conflict experiment, 635
  Horn of Africa conflicts, 637
Final Offer Arbitration
  effectiveness, 564
Firmness
  impression management, 912
  psychological perceptions, 849
Fisheries Negotiations
  Canada/U.S., 3777, 3802
  Canada/U.S./Mexico, 3776
  Japan/Soviet Union, 3851
  Southeast Asia, 2343
  U.S./Mexico, 3893
Five Person Games, 1409
  symmetric solution, 1285
Flexibility
  international relations, 836
Focal Point Theory, 1541, 1545
Food Agreements, 2529
Force Ratio
  game theory, 1615
Ford Gerald
  memoirs, 4328
Forecasting
  diplomatic models, 350
Foreign Investments
  negotiations, 3569, 3604
Foreign Ministries
  guide, 4027
  Soviet Union, 4571
Foreign Policy
  cognitive aspects, 507
  decision making aspects, 4079
  dissertation, 1087
  handbook, 109
  psychological aspects, 24, 508,
    519, 770
  secrecy, 3981
Foreign Service Profile
  statistics, 3986
Formality
  experimental negotiations, 867
Forward Based Systems
  arms control negotiations, 2913
Four Person Bargaining
  influence attempts, 944
Four Person Games, 1409
  coalition bargaining, 874
  coalition formation theory, 857
  sources of power, 1505
Framing of Negotiations, 880
France
  diplomatic analysis, 3999, 4084,
    5338, 5392
  INF negotiations, 3138
  nuclear diplomacy, 3359-3360
  withdrawal from NATO, 5393

Subject Index

France/Italian Conciliation
  Commission, 5323
Free Trade Area Negotiations, 3607
  Australia, 3875
Free Trade Negotiations
  Canada/U.S., 3759, 3769, 3794
  See also Canada/U.S. Free Trade
  Negotiations, U.S./Canada
Function Games
  large groups, 1470

Galbraith John
  memoirs, 4329
Game Behavior
  reward level, 844
Game Formation
  historical analysis, 1700
Game Theory, 312, 1183, 1186, 1191,
    1193, 1198, 1203, 1205-1208,
    1212, 1216, 1221, 1223-1225,
    1243, 1259-1260, 1268, 1317,
    1335, 1359-1360, 1371, 1381-1383,
    1392, 1396, 1422, 1439, 1449,
    1476-1477, 1487-1489, 1493, 1508-
    1509, 1526, 1542-1543, 1555,
    1557-1558, 1574, 1585, 1588,
    1616, 1627, 1638, 1645, 1655,
    1660, 1687-1688
  achievement, 1255
  Alaska gas pipeline conflict, 1554
  altruism, 1320
  arbitration, 1736
  argumentation, 1238, 1240
  arms control negotiations, 1345,
    1577
  aspiration level, 1603, 1228, 1313-
    1314
  axiomatic theory, 1218, 1227
  balance of power, 1622
  bargaining analysis, 1195, 1247,
    1297, 1310-1312, 1384, 1528,
    1556, 1593, 1637, 1706
  bargaining behavior, 1319, 1322,
    1373, 1448, 1719-1725
  bargaining costs, 1401
  bargaining effectiveness, 1379
  bargaining theory, 1201, 1298
  bilateral monopoly, 1378, 1582
  bivariate negotiations, 1340
  blackmail, 1329
  coalition formation, 1211, 1436
  coalition outcomes, 1351
  cognitive dissonance, 1200
  competitive tests, 1454

  complex conflicts, 1672
  compromise proposals, 1350, 1426
  conflict analysis, 1202, 1404,
    1671
  conflict resolution, 1213, 1507,
    1561
  cooperation, 1226, 1236-1237, 1239,
    1415, 1614, 1631
  cooperative games, 1386, 1393,
    1395
  cooperative opponents, 1001
  crisis learning games, 1441
  cultural aspects, 1669
  deception, 1273
  decision making, 1295, 1427, 1602,
    1711-1712
  deterrence, 1620
  diplomacy, 1252, 1654
  disagreement theory, 1307
  dissertation, 1679, 1714
  duopology bargaining, 1369
  dynamic games, 1305
  economic analysis, 1190, 1197,
    1229, 1646
  economic summits, 1237
  effects of costs, 1647
  efficiency study, 1292
  environmental disputes, 1668
  escalation, 1577
  expectations, 1453
  experimental games, 1196, 1563,
    1596
  finite negotiation problem, 1523
  focal point theory, 1541
  game of chicken, 1318, 1328
  group decision making, 1429, 1599
  incomplete information, 1290-1291,
    1352
  infinite horizon model, 1304
  information, 1265, 1380, 1530,
    1539
  international cooperation, 1623,
    1729
  international relations, 1388,
    1400, 1499, 1584
  Japanese trade conflicts, 1667
  justice aspects, 1245
  KRESKO game, 1604
  kernel test, 1409
  Korean Unification, 1662
  laboratory studies, 658
  Lancaster House Conference, 1656
  learning process, 1308-1309
  linear models, 1333-1334

mediation, 1376, 1628
Middle East Conflict (1967), 1643
minimum utility point, 1338
mixed motive games, 1377
modelling, 1219, 1244, 1283, 1425, 1438, 1484, 1576, 1689
modifying utilities, 1413, 1686
motivation, 1362
n person games, 1214, 1416
Nash bargaining problem, 1420
Nash bargaining solution, 1518
New York Subway Car Dispute, 1591
non constant sum games, 1456
non cooperative games, 1597
non zero sum game, 1569
nonlinear models, 1333
pacifist strategies, 1452, 1580
peace research, 1506
policy simulations, 1279
political applications, 1316
political science, 1210
prisoner dilemma game, 667, 1328, 1353, 1598
problem solving, 1681
profits and loses, 1339
proportional solutions, 1419, 1537
ratio of force, 1615
rational behavior, 1204, 1389
rational politics, 1194
renegotiations, 1466, 1527
responsiveness, 1326, 1498
risk assessment, 1717
SALT I negotiations, 1490
security equilibrium, 1258
sequential bargaining, 1363, 1683
simulation, 1327, 1365-1366
social behavior, 1222
strategic interaction, 1182
strategic reasoning, 1296
strategic studies, 1516
superpower conflicts, 1192
suspicion, 1510, 1522
tacit games, 1461
territorial conflicts, 1581
theory of the reluctant duelist, 1330-1331
threats, 1272
three person bargaining, 1713
time studies, 1302
trade negotiations, 1241, 1666
trade protectionism, 1524
trust, 1510, 1522
two person games, 1217, 1390-1391, 1619
two x two games, 1274
U.S./Soviet negotiations, 1282
ultimatum bargaining, 1367-1368
uncertain outcome, 1444
unified treatment, 1617
utility function, 1385
validity of, 1565
Vietnam War negotiations, 1639-1641
water contamination dispute, 1315
winning aspects, 1248
zero sum games, 1341-1342
Zeuthen's principle, 1460
Game of Chicken, 1511-1512, 1562
cooperation, 1301
game theory, 1318, 1328
models, 980
sex roles, 1301
stable strategies, 1595
Gas Negotiations
U.S./Mexico, 3944
Gas Pipeline Deal
Soviet negotiating strategy, 4589
GATT
1973/75 negotiations, 3746
1973/79 negotiations, 3745
aircraft agreement, 3752
Australia, 3724
Canada, 3739, 3753
Canada/U.S. trade negotiations, 3713
chemical industry, 3714
conflict resolution procedures, 3731
developing countries, 3726
dissertation, 3741
historical aspects, 3710
Hungary, 3748
international organizations, 3698
international trade rules, 3722, 3727
Japanese trade policies, 3738
Kennedy Round Negotiations, 3696, 3719, 3747, 3750-3751, 3754
legal aspects, 3698, 3700-3701
Mexico, 3742
negotiations analysis, 3720, 3728, 3733, 3749
Tokyo Round Negotiations, 3695, 3702-3704, 3706, 3708, 3712, 3715, 3717, 3721, 3725, 3732, 3737, 3740, 3743-3744
trade negotiations, 3697, 3699, 3707, 3709, 3711, 3716, 3718,

Subject Index

3736
U.S. House Hearings, 3754
U.S. negotiations (1956), 3758
U.S. negotiations (1960/61), 3757
U.S. trade policies, 3738, 3756
U.S. wine issue, 3734
U.S./Canada agricultural trade talks, 3770
U.S./EEC trade negotiations, 3694
U.S./Japan relations, 3755
UNCTAD as negotiator, 2419
Uruguay Round Negotiations, 3705, 3723, 3730, 3735
Gaza Strip Autonomy Talks
assessment, 4954
See also Middle East Conflict
Gaze Patterns
competitive negotiations, 675
cooperative negotiations, 675
emotional responses, 772
See also Bargaining Behavior, Negotiation Behavior, Psychological Aspects
Gender Aspects, 1624
dissertation, 1093
intergroup bargaining, 1042
mediator behavior, 1894
negotiation behavior, 572
negotiation outcome, 1093
negotiation tactics, 769
negotiation behavior, 911
General Agreement on Tariffs and Trade
See GATT
General Systems Research, 1650
Generalized System of Preferences Negotiations, 2475
Generosity Level
psychological aspects, 864
Geneva (1955)
Heads of Government Conference, 2585
Geneva Conferences
arms control negotiations, 2209, 2615, 2711, 2773, 2786, 2824, 2951
Conference of Experts, 3381
consensus rule, 2168
humanitarian law, 2534
Indochina 1954, 2562, 4967, 4974, 4992, 4999, 5080
Laos (1961-62), 5052
press coverage, 2834
Soviet negotiating techniques, 4475

Soviet policies, 2915
test ban negotiations, 3013-3014
Geneva Conferences (1954), 2734, 2736
deception analysis, 5064
dissertation, 4586
Indochina, 4973
Korea, 5080
U.S. diplomacy, 5001
documents, 5049
Geneva Conferences (1955), 3408, 3481
Geneva Conferences (1959), 2587
Geneva Conferences (1985), 3454-3455
communication, 3404
documents, 3479
Reagan's briefing book, 3474
Soviet policies, 3479
See also Arms Control Negotiations, Conference Diplomacy, Disarmament Conferences
German Polish Negotiations (1969/70)
media issue, 5375
Germany
arms control negotiations, 2892
arms control policies, 2869
diplomacy, 3999, 4135, 5366
dissertation, 2892
Israel Reparation Negotiations, 5311
Polish interwar trade, 3911
SALT negotiations, 3113
World War II agreements, 3379
Glassboro Summit, 3475
Global Negotiations
trade negotiations, 3564, 3578
See also Multilateral Negotiations, North South Negotiations
Global Radio Conference, 2520
Gorbachev
arms control negotiations, 2688
arms control objectives, 2632
diplomacy, 4439, 4564
public diplomacy, 4438
U.S. policies, 4545
See also Soviet Negotiating Behavior, Soviet Union
Grain Embargo Negotiations (1980), 3693
Grain Purchase Agreements
U.S./Soviet Union, 3689
See also Commodity Negotiations
Great Britain
diplomacy, 4120

diplomatic history, 4284
EEC negotiations, 2506
foreign office management, 5297
public diplomacy, 4411, 4424
Greek Frontier Incidents
communist negotiations, 4597
Grew Joseph
U.S. diplomatic tradition, 4653
Gromyko
biography, 4489
memoirs, 4330
See also Soviet Foreign Policy, Soviet Negotiating Behavior
Group Cohesiveness
intergroup negotiation, 681
negative effects, 681
Group Comparability
bargaining behavior, 727
Group Conflicts, 696
crisis situations, 702-703
problem solving aspects, 533
psychological aspects, 679, 1019
Group Decision Making
dissertation, 1148
Group Loyalty
prisoner dilemma game, 1045
Group Participation
experimental groups, 988
Group Polarization, 933
research experiments, 807
Group Representation
accountability, 599
choice of, 587
psychological effects, 650
Group Status
age factor, 1046
Group Strength, 933
Group of Five Negotiations
currency negotiations, 3539

Haig Alexander
memoirs, 4331
Haiti
development negotiations, 5248
U.S. negotiations, 5247
Hammarskjold
crisis diplomacy, 2051
Harare Nonaligned Summit Conference, 2544
Harriman W. Averell
memoirs, 4332
views on negotiating, 234
Harsanyi Theory of Bargaining, 1306
See also Game Theory

Helplessness
bargaining ploy, 680
Helsinki Accords, 3277, 3297
arms control negotiations, 2615
CSCE Negotiations, 3320
Canadian Role, 3332
documents, 3256
human rights, 4537
Helsinki Final Act
implementation, 3336
Henderson Loy
diplomatic memoirs, 4333
Herter
telephone conversations, 4766
Herz Martin
memoirs, 4334, 4354
Heuristics, 134
Hitler
surprise diplomacy, 3985
Holland
torture agreement, 5380
Hongkong
Chinese negotiating style, 5136
Hongkong Status Negotiations, 5152
Hopeless Conflict
resolution, 899
Horn of Africa
diplomacy, 5175
U.S./Soviet diplomacy, 5164
Hostage Negotiations
policy aspects, 5351
House Hearings *See* U.S. House Hearings
Hull Cordell
memoirs, 4335
Human Rights Diplomacy, 2516, 4751, 5310, 5371
Argentina, 5218
Carter Administration, 5363
Chile, 5250
Eastern Europe, 5331
Helsinki Accords, 4537
Indonesia, 5354
Korea, 5069
South Africa, 5182
Soviet Union, 4498
See also Madrid Conference
Humanitarian Law
Geneva conference, 2534
Hungary
GATT negotiations, 3748
Hypergame Analysis
conflict misperceptions, 1734
Falkland Islands Crisis, 1405

Subject Index 381

Image Loss
  bargaining behavior, 726
Image of Other
  psychological aspects, 871
IMF Negotiations, 3613, 3898
  Argentina, 3909
  bureaucracy, 3908
  Nigeria, 3919
  reforms, 3609
  See also Dept Relief Negotiations, North South Negotiations, Trade Negotiations
Implicit Mediation, 1759
Impression Formation
  dissertation, 1116
Impression Management
  firmness, 912
  trustworthiness, 912
Incentives
  compatibility, 1472
  threats, 686
Incidents at Sea Negotiations, 3372
Incomplete Information, 757
  game theory, 1304, 1406
India
  cultural aspects, 5332
  development negotiations, 5347
  diplomacy, 4047, 5296, 5396
  negotiation issues, 5385
  trade negotiations, 3865, 3889
  U.N. diplomacy, 2104
India/Bangladesh
  waterways negotiations, 5399
India/China Boundary Dispute
  dissertation, 5389
India/China Negotiations, 5335
  historical analysis, 5358
India/Pakistan Conflict, 5321, 5408
  diplomacy, 5319-5320, 5346
  Kashmir Crisis, 5402
  mediation workshop, 1946
  Quaker mediation, 4402
  Soviet mediation, 1967
  U.N. diplomacy, 2052
Indian Ocean
  arms control negotiations, 3365-3366
Indian Ocean Forces Limitations, 3389
Indian Ocean Naval Arms Limitation Talks, 2895, 3385
Indirect Communication, 913
Indochina
  Geneva Conference 1954, 2562, 4967, 4973-4974, 4992, 4999, 5049, 5080
Indonesia
  conflict settlement, 5394
  human rights diplomacy, 5354
  U.N. mediation, 2145
Induced Embarrassment
  face saving, 596
Indus Water Treaty
  mediation, 1926
Industrial Conflicts
  negotiations, 3547
INF Negotiations, 2875, 3130-3131, 3133-3134, 3137, 3139-3140, 3144-3146, 3149, 3212, 3315
  Chinese analysis, 3136
  Europe, 3128
  failure of, 3141
  France, 3138
  Geneva, 3129
  NATO, 3143, 3150
  negotiating positions, 3142
  START negotiations relationship, 3132
  Soviet policies, 3148
  Soviet political culture, 3142
  U.S. policies, 3135, 3147
  U.S. political culture, 3142
  See also Arms Control Negotiations
Infinite Horizon Model, 1291
Influence
  cooperative contexts, 1021
  deescalation, 1071
  escalation, 1071
  psychological studies, 944
Informal Bargaining
  Law of the Sea, 2307
  satellite reconnaissance, 2635
  social status, 1387
Information
  asymmetric negotiations, 616, 802
  bargaining behavior, 708, 820-821
  game theory, 1530, 1539
  performance in negotiation, 801
Information Gap Problems, 1782
Information Management
  arms control negotiations, 2750
  game theory, 1265
  opponent concession, 648
Initial Offer
  bargaining behavior, 820-821, 1062
Instability
  international relations, 921
Integrative Agreements, 604

Integrative Bargaining, 205, 335,
    834, 904-905, 1475
  accountability, 602, 1068, 1496
  bilateral negotiations, 601, 604
  cooperation incentives, 1497
  dyadic interaction, 1097
  psychological aspects, 920
  social conflicts, 907
  time pressure, 1063
  visual access, 602, 817
Integrative Solutions, 601, 908
Intelligence Aspects
  personal diplomacy, 4103
Inter American Peace Committee, 5216
Inter Nation Simulation, 1303
  aggression determinants, 640
Interaction Analysis, 1038
  dissertation, 1172
  dyadic negotiations, 1172
Interactive Choice Behavior
  explanatory models, 1332
Intercultural Communication
  Egypt/U.S. diplomacy, 4708
Intercultural Mediation Workshop,
  1913
Intercultural Negotiations, 410
  training guidelines, 422
  See also Cross Cultural Analysis,
  Cultural Aspects, Cultural Diplomacy
Intergovernmental Organizations
  personal contact, 553
Intergroup Cooperation
  attraction, 1057
Intergroup Negotiations
  dynamics, 717
  group cohesiveness, 681
  psychological aspects, 805
  risk taking, 806
  behavioral aspects, 573
Intergroup Simulation
  dissertation, 1099
Intermediate Range Nuclear Forces
  Negotiations *See* INF Negotiations
International Abjudication
  legal aspects, 140
International Agreements, 78
  risk management, 504
  theories, 429
  U.S. negotiations, 2570
International Airwaves Agreement
  1979, 3905
International Atomic Energy
  Commission, 2514
International Aviation Negotiations,
    3931
  U.S. House H, 2584
International Boundary and Water
  Commission, 2524, 2533
International Business Services
  Negotiations, 3867
International Cocoa Agreement, 3672,
  3685
International Coffee Agreement, 3862,
  3877
International Conciliation, 1802,
  1846, 1917
  Quakers, 4362
International Conferences, 2153,
  2155, 2162, 2166, 2171-2172,
  2177-2178, 2509
  19th Century, 2160
  codification aspects, 2180
  consensus aspects, 2168
  cultural conflicts, 2196
  diplomacy, 2165, 2176, 2194
  dissertation, 2188, 2191
  EEC experience, 2167
  evaluation of, 2186
  evolution of, 2175
  futility of, 2173
  guide, 2157
  influence, 2164
  interaction patterns, 2182
  international law, 2163
  language aspects, 2158, 2179
  organization, 2155, 2179
  psychological aspects, 2169
  Soviet attitudes, 2185
  structural analysis, 2191
  technical organization, 2508
  theories, 2187
  treaty drafting, 2166
  U.N. sponsorship, 2174
  U.S. diplomacy, 2170, 2188
  U.S. participation, 2161, 2195
  World Food Conference, 2190
  See also Conference Diplomacy
International Crises
  behavioral research, 515
  behavioral theories, 142
  handbook, 18
  models, 720
  negotiation processes, 99, 113
  systems analysis, 1188
  threat perception, 506
  U.N. role, 2118
  See also Crisis Management
International Drainage Disputes

Subject Index

mediation, 1935
International Economic Organizations, 2407
International Law, 337
  diplomacy, 4234
  international conferences, 2163
  mediation, 1802, 1811, 1840
  Soviet negotiating techniques, 4520
International Loan Agreements
  banks, 3946
International Marketing
  cultural aspects, 3637
International Mining Negotiations, 3874
International Natural Rubber Agreement, 3910
International Negotiations *See* Multilateral Negotiations, Negotiation Processes
International Organizations, 2008-2009, 2021, 2034, 2142
  comparative survey, 2073
  conflict management, 2002, 2014-2015, 2020, 2106-2107
  consultations, 452
  diplomacy, 4043
  GATT, 3698
  global negotiations, 2035
  North South issues, 2443
  See also U.N. Diplomacy
International Policy Coordination, 355
International Press Institute
  unofficial talks, 4383
International Red Cross
  mediation, 1947, 1999, 4377
International Relations
  accommodation aspects, 3
  analysis, 48
  communication, 33, 527
  cultural factors, 1
  decision making, 964
  forecasting, 471
  human factors, 523
  peaceful change, 38
  principles, 30, 161
  psychological aspects, 767, 951
  social aspects, 767
  social psychology aspect, 665
  theory, 2, 73
International Rivers Disputes
  negotiations, 409
International Seabed Authority, 3250

International Seabed Resources
  negotiations, 3925
International Security
  literature review, 2844
International Service Transaction Negotiations, 3570
International Sugar Agreement, 3681
  negotiations, 3675
International Technology Negotiations, 2511, 2575
International Trade Conference
  dissertation, 3623
International Trade in Services, 3583, 3933
International Treaties
  guide, 4280
International Wheat Agreement Negotiations, 3670
Internationalism
  cooperative behavior, 1447
  two person game, 846
Interorganization Theory, 256
Interpersonal Attitudes
  negotiation outcomes, 1090
Interpersonal Bargaining, 1322
  aspiration level, 618
  attitudinal factors, 771, 793
  bargaining power, 797
  classroom studies, 1424
  cognitive factors, 589
  communication, 620
  competitiveness, 976
  conflict magnitude, 624
  ethnic factors, 1000
  expectations, 941
  face saving, 594
  family orientation, 618
  game theory, 1319
  gender aspects, 624
  personality aspects, 841
  promises, 1118
  psychological aspects, 502, 820-821
  social power, 697
  structural factors, 771, 793
  threats, 625-626, 1118
  See also Bargaining Behavior, Behavioral Analysis, Negotiation Behavior, Psychological Aspects
Interpersonal Generalization Theory, 664
Interpersonal Influences, 1147
Interpersonal Mediation

psychological aspects, 701
Interpersonal Perception
　dissertation, 1133
　information access, 1133
Intervenor Role
　psychological aspects, 659
Intervention
　conflict resolution, 725
　modern diplomacy, 4241
　U.S. diplomacy, 4646
Intervention Methodology
　Cyprus workshop, 633-634
Interwar Diplomacy, 3975
　diplomats, 4274
Intractable Conflicts
　Middle East, 4934
　resolution, 899
Investment Negotiations, 3868
　Canada/U.S., 3771
　See also Trade Negotiations
Iran
　diplomacy, 4878, 4905
　human rights, 5349
　negotiation behavior, 4844
　oil diplomacy, 3652
　U.S. diplomacy, 4825, 4717
Iran Arms Deal
　Saudi mediation, 1951
Iran Hostage Crisis, 4803, 4820-4822, 4848, 4861, 4894, 4916
　Algerian Mediation, 1964, 1988
　chronology, 4961
　metagame analysis, 1653
　public diplomacy, 4431
Iran/Iraq War
　negotiation efforts, 4860
Islamic Diplomacy, 3991
Isolationism
　two person game, 846
Israel
　Armistice Negotiations 1948/49
　　documents, 4942
　diplomatic aspects, 4941
　German reparation negotiations, 5311
　secret diplomacy, 4932
　U.N. aspects, 2103
Israel/Egypt Negotiations
　Dayan's account, 4805
　dissertation, 4920, 4936
　Kissinger, 1932
　mediation, 1934
　See also Middle East Conflict
Israeli Diplomacy
　dissertation, 4925
　Soviet views, 4908
Israeli Palestinian Conflict
　psychological aspects, 763
　See also Middle East Conflict
Israeli Palestinian Pilot Workshop, 613
Issue Linkages, 228
Italian Communist Party
　Soviet negotiating style, 4580

Jamaican Bauxite Negotiations, 3917
Japan/China Peace Treaty
　Negotiations, 5129
Japan/Soviet
　fisheries negotiations, 3851
　Siberian oil negotiations, 3649
Japanese Communist Party
　negotiating behavior, 4488
Japanese Currency Negotiations, 3852
Japanese Defence Policy, 3468
Japanese Diplomacy
　decision making, 5091
Japanese Negotiating Policies
　nuclear issues, 5098
Japanese Negotiating Style, 3837, 3848-3849, 5086, 5089-5090, 5092, 5094-5095, 5106, 5108, 5123
　cultural aspects, 3812-3813, 5096, 5099
　dissertation, 5102
　pre WWII, 5102
　U.S. adjustments, 5100
Japanese Peace Negotiations
　World War II, 5087, 5107
Japanese Peace Treaty
　China, 5093
　Soviet Union, 5093
Japanese Sales Contracts
　legal aspects, 3841
Japanese Trade Negotiations, 3822, 3840, 3845
　cultural aspects, 3639
　EEC, 3835
　GATT, 3741
　game theory, 1667
　style, 3834, 3838
　textiles, 3839
Jarring's Diplomacy
　Middle East, 4892
　See also Middle East Conflict, U.S. Diplomacy
John Doe Associates
　unofficial diplomacy 1941, 4357

Subject Index

Johnson L.B.
  memoirs, 4336
Johnson Presidency
  arms control negotiations, 2631
Johnson/Kossygin
  summit meeting, 3475
Joint Decision Making Process, 400-401
Joint Development Program
  experimental support, 1658
Jordan
  mediation, 1948
Jordan/Israeli Negotiations, 4909
  See also Middle East Conflict
Judgmental Processes
  negotiations, 881

Kamel Mohamed
  Camp David Accords, 4814
Kampuchea
  Chinese diplomacy, 5119
Kashmir
  India/Pakistan negotiations, 5402
  U.N. mediation, 1925, 1936
Kennan George
  containment policies, 4151
  dissertation, 4786
  memoirs, 4337-4338
  See also U.S. Diplomacy, U.S. Foreign Policy
Kennedy Round Negotiations
  GATT, 3747, 3750-3751
  See also GATT
Kennedy/Khrushchev Negotiations, 4506
  See also Summit Meetings
Kenya Negotiations
  racial aspects, 5179
Kertész Stephen
  diplomacy, 4031
Khrushchev
  interview, 4499
  memoirs, 4470
Kissinger
  analysis, 266-267, 4649, 4688, 4694, 4729, 4753
  biography, 4660
  diplomacy, 4000, 4630, 4702, 4749-4750, 4775
  Israeli withdrawal, 1932
  mediation, 1949
  memoirs, 4339-4340, 4355
  Middle East diplomacy, 1928, 4790, 4796, 4810, 4830, 4843, 4863, 4874, 4885, 4890
  Middle East mediation, 1929, 1952, 1960, 1962-1963
  Middle East policies, 4809
  observations, 62, 265
  Paris Peace talks, 5030
  Rhodesia conference, 5197
  SALT negotiations, 3057
  Sinai Disengagement Agreement, 4924
  U.S. foreign policy, 4654, 4665, 4674, 4691, 4715, 4768
  Vietnam War negotiations, 4988, 5008-5009, 5011, 5015, 5019, 5039
  See also Memoirs, Middle East Conflict, Middle East Mediation, Paris Peace Talks, U.S. Foreign Policy, Vietnam War Negotiations
Korea
  armistice negotiations, 5066-5068, 5075, 5079, 5082-5084, 5122
  communist negotiations, 4582
  DMZ negotiations, 5071
  diplomatic aspects, 5070, 5081
  game theory, 1662
  Geneva Conference 1954, 5080
  human rights diplomacy, 5069
  Japanese negotiations, 5085
  negotiation issues, 5065, 5072, 5078
  North Korean negotiating style, 5077
  North/South Korea dialogue, 5074
  unification talks, 5073, 5076
KRESKO Game
  game theory, 1604
Kuwait Oil Concession Agreement
  negotiations, 3645, 3647
  See also Oil Diplomacy

Labor Negotiations
  behavioral theories, 543
Lancaster House Conference
  game theory, 1656
  Zimbabwe, 5161
  See also Rhodesia Negotiations, Zimbabwe
Language
  analysis, 136, 160, 212
  arms control negotiations, 2828
  Chinese communications, 5116
  diplomacy, 3979, 4013, 4268
  direct negotiations, 1176

dissertation, 1174
interaction sequences, 902
international conferences, 2158
international law, 103
political aspects, 136
semiotics, 212
simulation, 1175
Soviet communication, 4526
Laos
  dissertation, 5406
  Geneva Conference 1961-62, 2566, 5052
  negotiations chronology, 5043
  Neutralization Agreement 1962, 3367
  peace negotiations 1972, 5042
Last Clear Chance Doctrine, 607
Latin America
  conflict resolution, 5246
  Law of the Sea, 2331
  multilateral diplomacy, 2530
  U.S. diplomacy, 5234
  regional cooperation, 3947
Law of the Sea Conferences, 2296, 2298-2299, 2301-2302, 2311, 2313, 2315-2316, 2318, 2321-2326, 2329, 2332, 2335-2336, 2345-2347, 2350 1976, 2334
  boundary disputes, 2319
  Canada, 2306, 2309, 2349
  Caracas Session, 2339
  Caribbean States, 2327
  compromises, 2304
  compulsory processes, 2303
  computer mediation, 2337
  computer models, 2340, 2342
  conflict resolution, 2295, 2353
  consensus techniques, 2308
  decision processes, 2330
  dissertation, 2354-2355
  informal groups, 2307
  international law, 2163
  Latin America, 2331
  legal aspects, 2297
  North South aspects, 2312, 2314
  renegotiations, 2317
  seabed negotiations, 2305, 2338
  South Asian Fisheries, 2343
  Soviet policies, 2348
  Tanzanian diplomacy, 2351
  U.N. diplomacy, 2297, 2300, 2328
  U.S. House Hearings, 2356
  U.S. policy, 2356
  U.S. Senate Hearings, 2357-2359

U.S. policies, 2341
UNCLOS III, 2310, 2320
Law of the Sea Convention, 2333
  U.S. policies, 2344
Laws of War
  multilateral negotiations, 2004-2005
Lawyers
  diplomats, 4051
Leadership, 1171
  diplomacy, 4153
  dissertation, 1169
  negotiation groups, 722
  negotiation outcome, 669
  productive strategy, 669
  psychological aspects, 993
Learning Process
  game theory, 1309
Least Developed Countries Conference
  Paris 1981, 2455, 2496
Lebanon
  1983 agreement, 4943
  mediation, 1931, 1975
  troop withdrawal negotiations, 4926
  U.S. diplomacy, 4939
  See also Middle East Conflict
Legal Aspects, 202
  GATT, 3698, 3700-3701
Lend Lease Negotiations, 4519
Leninist Principles
  communist diplomacy, 4529
  Soviet diplomacy, 4563
  See also Communist Negotiating Techniques
Licensing Negotiations, 3860
  generalized theorem, 3568
Limited Test Ban Negotiations, 2978
  See also Test Ban Negotiations
Limited Test Ban Treaty, 2973
  See also Test Ban Negotiations, Test Ban Treaty
Limited War
  negotiations, 361
Linear Bargaining Models, 1336
Linowitz Sol
  interview, 187
  Middle East negotiations, 4887
Lipski Jozef
  memoirs, 4341
Literature Analysis, 294, 300, 304
Literature Review
  international security, 2844
Litvinov

Subject Index 387

Soviet interwar diplomacy, 4555
Livermore Arms Control Conference, 3358
Location Games
  aspirations, 1648
Locus of Control, 823, 1041, 1043
  bargaining behavior, 1766
  dissertation, 1119
  See also Psychological Aspects
LOME Convention Negotiations, 2440, 2459, 2486, 2490
  dissertation, 2489
  Nigeria's role, 2468
  U.N. system, 2468
  See also North South Negotiations
LOME Convention Renegotiation, 2406, 2409, 2439, 2450
London Economic Summit, 3516
Low Power Persons Strategies, 1022
Lukasiewicz Juliusz
  memoirs, 4342
Lusaka Conference
  nonaligned states, 2451
Lying
  behavioral aspects, 816
  ethical aspects, 15

Machiavellianism Dyad
  bargaining outcomes, 684
Madrid Conference
  CSCE negotiations, 3259, 3292-3293, 3296, 3300
  decision making aspects, 3259
  human rights, 2516, 2909
  See also Human Rights Diplomacy
Maisky Ivan
  memoirs, 4343
Malta Conference 1945, 2265, 2289
  military aspects, 2272
Malta/Great Britain
  negotiations, 5376
Mandate Base Factor
  dissertation, 1104
Marcos
  diplomacy, 5298
Marine Pollution Agreements, 2525
Maritime Boundary Disputes, 2319, 5337
Marshall Mission
  Chinese civil war, 1955
  Chinese negotiations, 5418
Marshall Plan Negotiations
  dissertation, 3923
Masters Thesis
  Commonwealth diplomacy, 2574
  social psychological aspects, 1151
  U.N. negotiations, 2125
  See also Dissertation
Matamoros Trade, 3861
Mathematical Analysis
  conflict resolution, 1189
Mathematical Models, 1325, 1361, 1652
  arms control negotiations, 1184-1185, 1220
  nuclear confrontation, 1495
Maximizing Difference Game
  impression formation, 1354
MBFR Negotiations, 3152-3155, 3157-3159, 3163-3165, 3167-3168, 3170, 3172-3174, 3182-3184, 3187, 3191-3193, 3195-3196, 3198, 3200, 3274, 3285, 3315
  alternatives, 3177
  assessment, 3156, 3160-3161, 3175, 3180, 3201-3202
  Central Europe, 3151, 3178-3179
  conventional forces, 3190
  European security, 3162, 3186, 3199, 3203
  military stability, 3176
  overview, 2875
  political aspects, 3176, 3188
  Soviet policies, 3189, 3194
  status report, 3204, 3206
  structural changes, 3181
  trilateral conference, 3116
  troop reductions, 3205
  update, 3166
  Vienna Conference, 3169, 3171, 3185, 3197, 3276
  See also Arms Control Negotiations
McCloy/Zorin Correspondence, 4552
McGhee George
  diplomatic memoirs, 4344
Mecca Summit, 2538
Media
  diplomacy, 4409, 4416, 4433-4434
  Geneva negotiations, 2834
  international negotiations, 4426
  public diplomacy, 4411, 4424
Mediation, 1745, 1750, 1752-1757, 1770, 1774, 1776, 1779, 1781, 1784-1785, 1787-1788, 1790, 1792-1794, 1796-1798, 1808, 1815-1817, 1821, 1826-1827, 1831, 1836, 1844, 1846, 1848-1850, 1853-1854, 1856, 1858-1859, 1864-1869, 1872,

1885, 1889, 1899, 1906, 1908, 1917-1918, 1922, 1992
acid rain, 1981
American Friends Service Committee, 4399
arms control negotiations, 1800
behavioral aspects, 695, 1760, 1766, 1809, 1814, 1837
boundary conflicts, 1842
Camp David Summit, 1933, 1972
Chinese civil war, 1955
civil wars, 1822, 1923
coercive bargaining, 1862
communication processes, 1878, 1921
computer simulation, 1912
computer support systems, 1871
conciliation, 1915
consultant's role, 1749
cultural aspects, 1740, 1893
Cyprus conflict, 1940
decision making, 1761, 1909
decision support system, 1665
definitions, 1767
diplomatic perspective, 1819
dissertation, 1873, 1898, 1902, 1904, 1974
Dominican Crisis 1965, 1978, 4400
effectiveness, 1764, 1791, 1900, 1990
environmental disputes, 1938-1939, 1943, 1982
ethical aspects, 1825
experiments, 1880
face saving aspects, 1806, 1832-1833, 1911
fairness, 1778
Falkland Islands Crisis, 1991, 5270
field experiments, 1820
game theory, 1376, 1628
guidelines, 1744, 1795, 1901
handbook, 1743
historical analysis, 1742, 1818
ideologies, 1870
Indus Water Treaty, 1926
information gap problems, 1782
initial bargaining position, 1765
institutionalization, 1812
Inter American region, 1945
inter organizational aspects, 1847
International Red Cross, 1947, 1999, 4377
international arbitration, 1746

international drainage disputes, 1935
international law, 1802, 1811, 1840
intravention issue, 1777
Iran Hostage Crisis 1975, 1957
Israel/Egypt negotiations, 1934
Kissinger, 1949, 1960
learning processes, 1801
Lebanon, 1931, 1975
mathematical methods, 1863
methodology, 1807
Middle East Conflict, 1928, 1930, 1942, 1949-1950, 1968, 1976, 1985, 1989, 1993, 2000, 4842, 4927
models, 163-164, 1838, 1882
multilateral, 1748, 1896, 1914, 1919
Namibia, 1956, 1965, 1977
negotiator aspirations, 1859
O.A.U., 1941, 1944, 1971
opponents firmness, 1829
outcomes of, 1763, 1771
Palestine 1948, 1924
peacekeeping, 1905
personal skills, 1887
pre intervention effects, 1805, 1835
problem solving, 1891
problem solving workshops, 4376
process promoting workshops, 4376
psychological aspects, 544-545, 701, 704, 1841, 1855
regional conflicts, 1857, 1876, 1903
research, 1910
Rhodesia, 1980
Rumania/Bulgaria disputes, 1966
Saudi Arabia, 1951, 1984
Sinai II agreement, 1994
social conflicts, 1739, 1810, 1834, 1839
social psychological aspects, 1762, 1772, 1820
Socialist International, 1823
sociological aspects, 1751, 1783
Sri Lanka, 1995
strategic choice, 1773, 1824, 1881, 1883
studies review, 1789
Sudan civil war, 1923, 1974
support system, 1804
Tashkent Declaration, 1973

Subject Index

technological methods, 1758
theory, 1799, 1892
three person groups, 1916
time pressure, 1775, 1883
training, 1851
U.N., 1803, 1828, 1897, 1907, 1953, 1959, 1969, 1997-1998, 2115, 2144, 2151
U.N. and Indonesia, 2145
U.S./Middle East options, 1948, 1976
unofficial, 4376, 4403-4404
Vatican Attitudes, 1830
West New Guinea Dispute, 1986
Yemen Crisis 1963, 1987
Zimbabwe Settlement, 1958
Mediation Workshop
India/Pakistan Conflict, 1946
Mediator
as third negotiator, 1890
Carl Burckhardt, 1954
Mediator Behavior, 1786, 588
experimental games, 1884
gender differences, 1894
models, 1289
outcome, 1843
time pressure, 1769, 1874
Mediator Bias, 1861
effectiveness, 1845
Falkland Islands Crisis, 1996
Mediators, 1747, 1793, 1860
ability of, 1769, 1874
bias effects, 1861
biased, 1877
communication, 1878
communication competence, 1920
effectiveness, 1768
ethical aspects, 1813
media aspects, 1875
medium powers, 1895
O.A.S., 1961
psychological aspects, 1030, 1040
Quakers, 4365
training, 1780
unofficial, 1886
Mediterranean Action Plant
regional cooperation, 2556
Medium Powers
mediators, 1895
Memoirs
Anwar Sadat, 4351
Baron Rosen, 4350
Bohlen Charles, 4317
Bonner Paul, 4318

Bowles Chester, 4319
Briggs Ellis, 4321
Burke Lee, 4323
Byrnes James, 4324
Clement Attlee, 4314
Davies Joseph, 4325
Dean Acheson, 4312
Dunham Donald, 4326
Epstein Louis, 4327
Ford Gerald, 4328
Galbraith John, 4329
Gromyko, 4330
Herz Martin, 4334
Hull Cordell, 4335
Kennan George, 4337-4338
Lipski Jozef, 4341
Lukasiewicz Juliusz, 4342
Maisky Ivan, 4343
Nixon, 4346
Ritchie Charles, 4347
Spain James, 4352
See also Diplomatic Memoirs, Diplomats
Mental Illness
diplomats, 1025
Metagame Analysis, 1410
Polish Conflict, 1685
Mexican Natural Gas Case
psychological aspects, 615
Mexico
accession to GATT, 3742
dept crisis 1982, 3921
dept relief negotiations, 3936
negotiating style, 5220
transnational automobile negotiations, 3876
U.S. boundary negotiations, 5237
Micronesia Status Negotiations, 5317-5318, 5411
Middle East Conflict, 4798-4799, 4815, 4840-4841, 4841, 4849, 4851, 4853, 4868, 4871, 4876, 4906, 4910, 4929, 4933, 4953, 5343
Arab policies, 4928
autonomy negotiations, 4875, 4893, 4954
Begin's negotiating style, 4884, 4891
Begin/Sadat negotiations, 4938
Ben Gurion/Nasser talks, 4913
Chinese diplomacy, 4864
chronology, 4823
cognitive aspects, 4865

conflict management, 4834, 4838, 4846, 4855-4856
crisis management, 4792, 4858, 4858, 4915
crisis modelling, 1594
Dayan's tactics, 4884
documents, 4937, 4955, 4957
Egypt's role, 4917
Egyptian negotiating style, 4889
European mediation, 1937, 1979
European policies, 4789, 4922
game theory, 1643
Gaza, 4958
Gunnar Jarring, 4892
historical analysis, 4812, 4907
intractability, 4934, 4946
Ismail Fahmy, 4806
Israeli policies, 4787, 4832, 4911
Jimmy Carter, 4800-4801
Joseph Sisco, 4948
Kissinger, 1928, 4775, 4790, 4796, 4809-4810, 4830, 4843, 4863, 4874, 4885, 4890
lab experiment, 4867
leadership aspects, 4857
media influence, 4930
mediation, 1928, 1930, 1949-1950, 1968, 1976, 1989, 1993, 2000, 4828, 4842, 4927
multilateral negotiations, 4837, 4852
negotiation barriers, 4872
negotiation breakdown, 4877
negotiation conditions, 4862
negotiation framework, 4903
negotiation model, 4807
negotiation preconditions, 4869
negotiations etiquette, 4873
Palestinian policies, 4899
peace simulation, 1374
political analysis, 4945
preconditions, 4870
prerequisites, 4854
psychological aspects, 750, 761-763, 950, 4897
Rabin's memoirs, 4788
Reagan's policies, 4836
Riad's memoirs, 4819
Six Day War diplomacy, 4791
socio psychological aspects, 4896
Soviet role, 4912
superpowers influence, 4904, 4935
U.S. House Hearings, 4956
U.S. policies, 1985

U.S. Senate Hearings, 4962
U.S. diplomacy, 4797, 4802, 4804, 4882, 4896, 4900-4901, 4930
U.S. documents, 4964
U.S. mediation, 1942, 4947
U.S. policies, 4790, 4794, 4809, 4818, 4866, 4887, 4902, 4915, 4923, 4940, 4949, 4962
U.S./Soviet competition, 4898
U.S./Soviet negotiations, 4839
unofficial diplomacy, 4364, 4390
war termination, 4859
West Bank, 4883, 4958
Middle East Mediation
Kissinger, 1929, 1952, 1962-1963
Militarization of Space
arms control, 2954
Military Capability
bargaining power, 486
Military Diplomacy
arms control negotiations, 2815
Military Persons
diplomats, 4094
Mineral Agreements
renegotiations, 2382
Minority Influence
psychological aspects, 871
Misperceptions, 743-744
conflict analysis, 1735
Mixed Conflict Negotiation
simulation, 1682
Mixed Motive Bargaining
opponent interaction, 698
partner interaction, 698
Mixed Motive Games, 1370, 1423, 1486
cooperation, 1278, 1364, 955
intentions, 755
opponent motive perception, 1278
personality effects, 859
sex variations, 859
strategy choices, 1587
Modelling, 1208, 1283, 1355
arms control negotiations, 1694
misperceptions, 1684
Modern Diplomacy, 4003-4004, 4017-4018, 4085, 4088, 4104, 4126-4127, 4147, 4162, 4202
dialectics, 3997
handbook, 4001
professionalism, 4184
transition to, 4177
See also Diplomacy, Diplomatic History
Modifying Utilities, 1412

Subject Index

Montreux Convention
  regional arms control, 3382
Moscow Summit 1972
  Soviet foreign policy, 3464
  See also Summit Meetings
Most Favored Nation Trade Status
  Romanian Talks, 3937
Motivation
  asymmetric bargaining, 549
  dissertation, 1089, 1125, 1155
  game theory, 1362
  prisoner dilemma game, 796, 917
  professional negotiator, 1125
Multi Fiber Agreement, 3872, 3904
Multiattribute Utility Models, 1651
Multiattribute Value Theory
  oil tanker standards, 1610, 1732
Multilateral Diplomacy, 4214
Multilateral Environmental Diplomacy, 2499, 2515
Multilateral Negotiations, 1748, 2003, 2006-2007, 2011, 2013, 2015-2016, 2018, 2022, 2026, 2028, 2032, 2441, 2457, 2564
  ASEAN, 2537
  air transport routes, 2580
  CSCE conferences, 3264
  Commonwealth, 2510, 2518
  communications, 2019
  computer forecasting, 2029-2030
  consensus in, 2024
  disarmament, 2025, 2221
  EEC, 2543, 2545
  Electrolux case, 2555
  forecasting, 2027
  handbook, 2001
  human rights, 2516
  international bodies, 2021, 2031, 2034
  Latin America, 2530
  Law of the Sea, 2299, 2311, 2346
  laws of war, 2004-2005
  media aspects, 4426
  Middle East Conflict, 4837, 4852
  mutual interests, 2390
  nuclear proliferation, 3338
  nuclear safeguards, 2576
  O.A.S., 2549
  Southern Africa, 2518
  Soviet policies, 2010
  U.N., 2119
  U.S. Department of State, 4745
  U.S. and Namibia, 2526
  U.S. foreign policy, 2012
Multilateral Treaties
  arbitration, 2023
  U.N., 2148
Multinationals, 3579
  African negotiations, 2394
  bargaining cartels, 3586
  bargaining power, 3571
  code of conduct, 3950
  developing countries negotiations, 2458
  negotiating power, 2427
  See also Trade Negotiations
Multiobjective Decision Making, 231
Multiple Players Decision Making
  computer models, 1674
Munich 1938 Negotiations
  cognitive analysis, 412
Mutual and Balanced Force Reduction
  See MBFR Negotiations
Mutual Perceptions
  quantitative aspects, 723
MX Missiles
  arms control negotiations, 2946

N Person Games, 1214, 1253, 1451, 1455
  cooperation, 1269
  equilibrium, 1705
  group size, 1269, 1343
  impossibility result, 1531
  matrix experiments, 1416
  prisoner dilemma game, 1357
  sidepayment games, 1459
  theory absorbtion, 1277
Namibia, 5177, 5196
  constitutional aspects, 5178
  historical analysis, 5193
  mediation, 1956, 1965, 1977
  multilateral diplomacy, 2526
  U.N. mediation, 1970, 2126, 5186-5187
Nash Bargaining Model, 1256, 1420
  two person game, 1482
  utility scaling, 1481
Nash Bargaining Solution, 1532, 1535-1536, 1613, 1702
  rationality, 1533
  risk aversion, 1538
  two person games, 1390
Nasser
  diplomacy, 4811
  negotiating with Ben Gurion, 4913
  See also Middle East Conflict
National Cooperation

measurements, 188
National Evaluations
  social psychology, 644
National Negotiating Styles, 416
  cultural aspects, 442
National Power
  psychological aspects, 918
Nationalism
  conflict resolution, 260
  diplomacy, 3961
NATO
  1948 negotiations, 2547
  alliance diplomacy, 2504, 2532, 2539-2540, 5362
  arms control negotiations, 2614
  INF negotiations, 3143, 3150
  Joint Commission diplomacy, 5365
  political consultations, 2558-2559
  political leadership, 2504
  Soviet Pipeline Negotiations, 3816
  summit meetings, 2519, 3425
  U.S. role, 2512
Natural Gas Negotiations
  Algeria, 3953
  U.S./Mexico, 3885
  See also Oil Diplomacy
Nature Conservation Treaty
  cultural aspects, 5374
  South Pacific, 5374
  See also Environmental Negotiations
Naval Diplomacy, 3965
Negotiated Order Theory, 621, 1069
Negotiation Behavior, 246, 1123, 1140
  accountability, 700, 773
  concession rates, 1139
  dissertation, 1098
  evaluation, 672
  experimental studies, 753
  group influences, 803
  operant conditioning, 1113
  personality, 721
  power use, 437
  reaction systems, 1141
  research studies, 862
  self awareness, 1166
  simulated conflict, 1096
  status, 700
  study groups, 411
  time pressure aspects, 1139
  topic change, 966
  training, 404, 1851
  See also Bargaining Behavior, Behavioral Aspects, Psychological Aspects
Negotiation Breakdown
  simulation, 1633
Negotiation Competence
  dissertation, 1094
Negotiation Constraints
  partner observations, 776
Negotiation Experiments
  psychological aspects, 851
Negotiation Failure, 378
Negotiation Groups
  experimental studies, 1160
Negotiation Interaction System, 175
Negotiation Mandate, 612
Negotiation Manual
  bilateral tax treaties, 2493
Negotiation Models, 163-164, 341
  behavioral aspects, 622
  development, 176
  See also Game Theory
Negotiation Outcomes, 264
  assessments, 219
  communication, 972, 1153
  dissertation, 476
  empirical assessment, 178
  gender influence, 1093
  negotiator attitude, 736
  negotiator skill, 1109
  prior helping experience, 1100
  prominence, 660
Negotiation Processes, 11, 13, 61, 64, 68-69, 76, 95, 170, 179, 182, 186, 193, 217, 235, 254-255, 257, 266, 269, 298, 317-318, 324, 327-328, 373, 375, 430, 433, 469, 492, 60
  arms control, 2667
  B. Lewis's testimony, 489
  case studies, 114
  coalition aspects, 211
  common elements, 398, 497
  comparative studies, 284
  creativity, 336
  crisis management, 111
  cultural aspects, 253, 444
  deescalation aspects, 272
  direct, 229
  dissertation, 476
  domestic examples, 321
  domestic origins, 372
  effectiveness, 101, 244-245
  empirical assessment, 178
  friendly nations, 340
  GATT, 3720

Subject Index

game theory, 1247, 1706
gender influence, 769
Harriman's views, 234
historical analysis, 479
influence strategies, 286
integral analysis, 450
international crises, 113
international system, 453
intractability, 462
L. Labedz's testimony, 488
limited retaliation, 259
Linowitz Sol, 187
longterm impacts, 292
multicultural analysis, 451
multiobjective approach, 216
political aspects, 449
practitioners' views, 392
professional aspects, 200
questions, 325
reflective model, 297
training, 329-332, 339
training guidelines, 423
transborder aspects, 71
U.S. Senate Hearings, 488-490
war termination, 84
alternative models, 199
Negotiation Research, 133
communication, 941
environmental aspects, 472
Negotiation Styles, 467, 561
Chinese, 3830
cultural aspects, 442
national, 416
simulation, 1696
video tape modeling, 657
Negotiation Success
communication medium, 1026
psychological aspects, 1031
Negotiation Support Systems, 493, 1691
computer models, 1709
conflict analysis, 1349, 1676
future needs, 407
Negotiation Theory, 8, 17, 20, 25, 29, 39, 41-43, 46, 50, 52-54, 58, 63, 65-67, 82, 87, 89-90, 94, 96, 107-108, 112, 115-116, 126, 129, 139, 146, 153, 158, 166, 172-173, 190, 194-198, 201, 206-207, 224, 262-263, 265, 267, 279-281, 295-296, 307-308, 310-311, 313, 320, 344, 348-349, 357, 364-366, 368-369, 383-385, 388, 391, 397, 399, 402, 405, 413, 415, 421, 429,
434, 459, 468, 481, 491, 498-499, 1704
academic contributions, 428
adversary participation, 252
ambiguity, 240
CSCE conferences, 3288
Camp David Summit, 4951
Clausewitz, 495
collective bargaining, 102, 208
communication, 242-243
conceptual model, 306
core model, 162
cultural aspects, 479
decision making, 270
dissertation, 406, 446
ethical aspects, 282
external bargaining, 369
guide, 44
historical analysis, 479
incompatible purposes, 303
Japanese cases, 446
literature analysis, 192, 304
management aspects, 389-390, 460
models, 226
optimal search, 458
political analysis, 403
power analysis, 258, 312
prenegotiation, 358-359
semantics, 363
U.S. Senate Hearings, 487
U.S. cases, 446
Negotiation Winding Down
game theory, 1276
Negotiations
definitions, 203, 247-248, 326, 928-929
multidisciplinary analysis, 223
Negotiator Attitude
negotiation outcome, 736
Negotiator Cognition, 568, 605
Negotiator Judgement
arbitration, 878
rationality, 565
Negotiator Moods
barrier effects, 1080
Negotiator Skill
dissertation, 1109
negotiation outcome, 1109
Negotiator Status
accountability, 775
Negotiator Success
empirical research, 1051
Neutral Countries
arms control negotiations, 2793,

2852
test ban negotiations, 2969
Neutrality
Soviet diplomacy, 4588
U.S. diplomacy, 4709
New York Subway Car Dispute
game theory, 1591
New Zealand
nuclear free zone negotiation, 5345
Newcomb's Paradox, 1520
Newcomb's Problem
prisoner dilemma game, 1275
Nicaragua
U.S. negotiations 1978/79, 5255
U.S. policies, 5245
See also Contadora Negotiations
Nigeria
IMF negotiations, 3919
oil diplomacy, 3648
Nigerian War Negotiations
O.A.U. role, 2523
Nitze Paul
interview, 2859
Nixon
China policy, 5158
crisis analysis, 4673
memoirs, 4346
surprise diplomacy, 3985
Nixon/Brezhnev Summit, 3456
See also Summit Meetings
Non Constant Sum Games, 1456, 1608
Non Cooperative Bargaining Theory, 1257
Non Cooperative Games, 1394, 1592, 1597, 1698, 1730
cooperation, 1463
solutions, 1715
Non Profit Treaty, 3341
Non Representatives
behavioral aspects, 575
Non Tariff Trade Negotiations, 3913
distortions, 3585
Non Zero Sum Games, 1462, 1519, 1570
cooperation, 940
exploitative behavior, 1003
illusory powers, 1002
induced cooperation, 1569
information, 1575
threats, 1635
warning effects, 870
Nonaligned States
disarmament negotiations, 2761, 2878

economic summit, 2471
Lusaka Conference, 2451
test ban negotiations, 2983-2984, 2998
Noncoercive Inducements
conflict resolution, 273
Nonlinear Bargaining Models, 1336
Nonprofessional Bargainers
aspiration levels, 1568
Non-Proliferation Treaty See NPT Treaty Negotiations
Nonrenewable Resources
trade negotiations, 3581
Nonverbal Communication, 941
bargaining outcome, 1079
cooperation, 745
Nonviolent Strategies, 26
Nordek Negotiations, 5373
Normative Models, 342
North Africa
EEC Negotiations, 2548
North Korea
negotiating style, 5077
See also Korea
North South Negotiations, 2360, 2364, 2369, 2372, 2380, 2387, 2396-2398, 2401, 2405, 2414, 2416, 2426, 2429, 2432, 2434-2437, 2443-2448, 2452-2454, 2463-2465, 2467, 2469, 2476, 2483, 2487, 2495
Africa, 5199
aid issues, 2496
assessment, 2385
Canadian views, 2462
Cancun Summit, 3526
commodities, 2488, 3667, 3669, 3674-3675
Commonwealth, 2428, 2472
conference diplomacy, 2424
dept relief negotiation, 2392, 2408
development, 2362, 2374
dissertation, 2475
EEC, 2388
economic aspects, 2365, 2410-2411
effectiveness, 2480
energy issues, 2378, 2400
future prospects, 2442
improvements, 2377
international trade, 2381, 2384
LOME Convention, 2406, 2440, 2450, 2486, 2489-2490
LOME renegotiation, 2439

Subject Index

Law of the Sea, 2312, 2314
northern perspective, 2404
OECD policies, 2479
oil producing negotiations, 2433, 3655
organizations, 2407
policy coordination, 2392
political economy, 2367
power issues, 2449
South South aspects, 2423
Soviet policies, 2395, 2425
technology transfer, 2460
telecommunications, 2430
Third World weaknesses, 2415
trade aspects, 2366, 3616
U.N., 2431, 2482, 2491
U.N. conferences, 2193
U.S. House Hearings, 2494
U.S. policies, 2370, 2485
UNCTAD, 2371, 2412, 2498
wheat negotiations, 2413
Northwest Passage Negotiations, 5350
Norway
Soviet. diplomacy, 4514
NPT Review Conference, 3349-3350
NPT Treaty Negotiations, 3165, 3339-3340, 3342-3348, 3351-3353, 3355
multilateral diplomacy, 3338
U.N., 3354
U.S. Senate Hearings, 3356
Nuclear Accident Notification Negotiations, 3387
Nuclear Accidents Measures Agreement SALT I, 3027
Nuclear Arms Freeze
negotiations, 2914
Nuclear Forces
negotiations, 2709
Nuclear Free Zones
New Zealand, 5346
Nuclear Freeze
negotiations, 2767
Nuclear Power
Canada/India negotiations, 3890
U.S./China agreement, 5149
Nuclear Risk Reduction
crisis management, 2794, 2920
Nuclear Safeguards
multilateral negotiations, 2576
Nuclear Site Negotiations, 3357
Nuclear War Termination
strategies, 2590
Nuremberg Trial Agreements
negotiations, 4484

O.A.S.
dispute settlements, 2563
mediation, 1961
multilateral negotiations, 2549
O.A.U.
Addis Ababa Summit Conference, 2551
conflict resolution, 2122, 2572
Congo Crisis, 2560
dissertation, 2573
mediation, 1941, 1944, 1971
Nigerian War negotiations, 2523
Ocean Shipping Services Talks, 3951
Ocean Use
conflict resolution, 2352
OCTAGON Conference
Quebec 1944, 2278
OECD
international economic
negotiations, 3619
North South negotiations, 2479
Ogaden War Negotiations, 5192
Ohio/Hubei Agreement
Chinese negotiating styles, 5128
Oil Diplomacy, 3651, 3656
Canada/U.S., 3658
concession negotiations, 3647
dissertation, 3655
historical analysis, 3646
Iraq 1918/1928, 3653
Nigeria, 3648
North South negotiations, 3655
pricing negotiations, 3660
Saudi Arabia, 3643
U.S. House Hearings, 3659
U.S. policies, 3644
Oil Pollution Negotiation, 5330
Oil Tanker Standards
multiattribute value theory, 1609-1610, 1732
One Stage Distributive Bargaining Game, 1661
OPEC
special studies, 3617-3618
diplomacy, 3657
Open Diplomacy, 4102, 4188
dissertation, 1076
public opinion, 4240
Opening Offer
bargaining strategy, 609
Opponent Concession
psychological aspects, 1061, 1180
time pressure, 910
Opponent Offers, 916

Opposing Representative
  locus of control, 1043
Organization of American States
  See O.A.S.
Organization of African Unity
  See O.A.U.
Organization for Economic Cooperation
  and Development See OECD
Organization of Petroleum Exporting
  Countries See OPEC
Organizational Aspects, 160
Organizational Conflicts
  psychological factors, 503
Organizational Culture, 670
Organizational Negotiations, 12, 268
Osgood's GRIT Strategy
  cooperation inducement, 827
Ottawa Economic Summit, 3522
  See also Economic Summits
Outcome Information
  competitiveness, 976
Outcome of Games
  prominence factor, 1054
Outcome of Negotiation
  interpersonal attitudes, 1090
  process analysis, 736
  representative's power, 1107
Overconfidence, 877
  behavioral aspects, 877
Ozone Negotiations, 2588
  U.S. participation, 2583
  See also Environmental Negotiations

Pacific Basin Trade Negotiations
  interests, 3920
Pacific Coastal Resources
  negotiations aspects, 3791
Pacifist Strategies
  bargaining games, 962-963
  effectiveness, 1483, 1580
  game theory, 1452
Palestine 1919-1920
  British/French negotiations, 4880
Palestine 1943
  children's transfer, 5328
Palestine 1948
  mediation, 1924
Palestinian Policies
  Middle East negotiations, 4899
  See also Middle East Conflict
Panama Canal Negotiations, 47, 5202,
  5204, 5211, 5223-5224, 5227,
  5230-5231, 5235, 5253, 5398
  dissertation, 5260, 5267

economic issues, 5228
U.S. policies, 5212
Paradiplomacy, 4300
Paris Peace Conference (1946), 2505,
  2546
  Yugoslavia, 2507
Paris Peace Talks, 5010
  agreement assessment, 4971
  diplomatic aspects, 5038
  dissertation, 5045
  documents, 5057
  Kissinger, 5030
  U.S. diplomacy, 4976
  verbal influence, 5045
  Vietnam War, 4979-4980, 4982, 4984,
    4987, 5000, 5005, 5016, 5023,
    5026-5028, 5031-5032, 5037, 5041
  See also Kissinger, Vietnam War
    Negotiations,
Paris Summit Conference (1960), 3488
Parliamentary Diplomacy, 4107, 4208,
  4246
Partial Test Ban Negotiations
  dissertation, 3000
  external influence, 2982
  internal influence, 2982
  role reversal, 3001
  See also Test Ban Negotiations
Peace
  communication aspects, 135, 381
  historical aspects, 106
Peace Agreements
  superpower guarantees, 1888
Peace Conditions, 289
Peace Conferences
  legal aspects, 2184
Peace Negotiations, 31, 36, 394
  psychological aspects, 547
Peace Proposals
  Vietnam, 5054
  See also Vietnam War Negotiations
Peace Research, 98
  game theory, 1506
  theories, 138
Peace Studies, 105
Peace Treaties 1941/47
  historical analysis, 2586
Peacekeeping Negotiations, 2141
  See also U.N. Diplomacy
Pentagon Papers
  negotiation aspects, 5050
  See also Vietnam War Negotiations
Perception
  mixed motive games, 755

Subject Index

success of opponent, 994
Performance
  cognitive heuristics, 738
  goal settings, 738
Periodical
  arms control, 2595
Personal Contacts
  intergovernmental organization, 553
Personal Controls
  bargaining outcomes, 676
Personal Interdependence, 935
Personal Preferences
  business negotiations, 692
Personal Qualities
  diplomatic effectiveness, 4243
Personal Relationships
  negotiation processes, 693
Personality, 561
  business negotiations, 692
  cooperation, 1012
  decisions, 1088
  dissertation, 1158
  foreign policy, 663
  influence, 721
  psychological aspects, 663, 841
  simulation, 1158
  successful negotiations, 689
  See also Bargaining Behavior, Psychological Aspects
Persuasion
  cultural aspects, 214
  theory, 501
  ethics, 1064
  psychological aspects, 529
  tactics, 1064
Peru Oil Diplomacy
  bargaining theory, 3650
  See also Oil Diplomacy
Phase Model Analysis, 1697
Philippine Diplomacy
  chronology, 5403
  dept relief, 5415
  documents, 5403
  Marcos, 5298
  military bases, 5382
Physical Illness
  diplomats, 1025
PIN Program, 475, 477, 482
Pipeline Diplomacy
  analysis, 3943
  U.S. export controls, 3895
Poland
  dept rescheduling negotiations, 3916
  World War II Diplomacy, 2242
Polish Conflict
  metagame analysis, 1685
Political Communication, 33
Political Conflicts
  crisis management, 85
Political Elites
  decision making, 1187
Political Forecasting, 471
Political Leaders
  psychological aspects, 516
Political Misperceptions, 59
Political Perception, 59
Political Science
  mathematical models, 1210
Political Uncertainty
  metagame analysis, 1403
Popular Diplomacy, 4203
Position Loss, 726
Position Modification
  Aswan Dam negotiations, 984
Positive Inducements
  psychological aspects, 826
Positive Mood, 1132
Post Settlements, 338, 566, 1546
Potsdam Conference, 2234, 2239, 2247, 2263, 2277, 2291
  documents, 2281
  Soviet protocols, 2228
  TERMINAL Conference, 2286
  Truman's diary, 2250
  See also Summit Meetings, World War II
Power
  analysis, 312, 952
  dissertation, 1102
  perception of, 856
  psychological aspects, 849, 919
Power Balance
  Soviet negotiations, 4615
Power Dependency
  negotiations, 125
Power Negotiation
  use of influence, 674
Power Sources
  four person apex games, 1505
Power Structure
  coalitions, 1397
  three person groups, 585
Predictability, 131-132
  bargaining, 691
Prenegotiation, 358-359
  Commonwealth diplomacy, 2542

dyadic behavior, 647
dyadic conflict, 652
expectations, 728
needs assessment, 441
payoff size, 1117
psychological aspects, 868
reality of rewards, 1117
research project, 431
SALT, 2732
simulation, 1099
transchannel case study, 431
Presidential Diplomacy, 3471
See also Summit Meetings
Primitive Power
  bargaining strategy, 974
Prisoner Dilemma Game, 759, 980, 999, 1215, 1232, 1234-1235, 1263, 1270, 1286, 1294, 1323, 1375, 1421, 1464, 1494, 1503, 1513, 1515, 1521, 1601
  altruistic parameter, 1281
  balanced strategies, 1485
  communication, 1045, 1115, 1598
  competitive opponent, 1055
  cooperation, 619, 667, 699, 811, 923, 959, 1055, 1142-1143, 1269, 1344, 1450, 1500, 1598, 1632
  cooperative choice, 576-578, 788
  Cyprus conflict, 1445
  format effects, 1372
  game theory, 1328, 1353
  gender differences, 1583
  initial strategies, 890
  interpersonal conflict, 1013
  motivation, 796, 917
  n person game, 1357
  Newcomb's Problem, 1275
  payoff structure, 959
  performance indicator, 1356
  personality, 1450
  programmed strategies, 891
  public choice, 1344
  reciprocity, 1632
  reward cooperation, 958
  reward structure, 889, 923, 1142-1143
  risk orientation, 1324
  sequential variables, 892
  simultaneous variables, 892
  solutions, 1578
  stable strategies, 1595
  trustworthiness, 831
  vulnerability, 831
Prisoner Dilemma Paradigm, 883

Prisoner Dilemma Research
  sex effects factors, 798
Private Experts
  U.S. Foreign Relations, 4754
Problem Solving
  psychological aspects, 927
Problem Solving Workshops, 765
  East African Conflict, 1047
  simulation, 1443
Professional Airmen
  negotiators, 233
Professional Diplomats, 4217, 4248
  See also Diplomacy, Diplomats
Professional Negotiator
  aspiration levels, 1568
  motivation, 1125
Program on International Negotiations
  See PIN Program
Prominence
  negotiation outcome, 660, 1054
Promises
  effects of, 606
  interpersonal bargaining, 1118
  psychological aspects, 1008
  three factor analysis, 946
Promisors
  perception off, 1146
Propaganda
  Soviet Union, 4410
  ten nation disarmament committee, 3373-3375
  See also Public Diplomacy
Protectionism
  negotiations, 3560
Proxy Wars
  Middle East, 4859
Psychiatry
  international conciliation, 937
Psychological Advantages, 957
  dissertation, 1150
Psychological Aspects, 524, 531-532, 534, 540-541, 548, 579, 651, 653, 673, 677-678, 688, 743-744, 747, 752, 799, 835, 853, 881, 899, 906, 945, 977, 982-983, 985, 989, 1028, 1041, 1124, 1137, 1154, 1156, 1161
  bargaining alternatives, 782
  bargaining performance, 739
  conflict resolution, 638, 1083
  cultural factors, 1136
  definitions, 928-929
  diplomacy, 938
  disarmament negotiations, 1050

Subject Index

elite behavior, 518
empirical analysis, 1157
foreign policy, 508, 519
group conflicts, 679
integrative bargaining, 920
international negotiations, 511
mediation, 544, 701, 704, 1855
Mexican Natural Gas Case, 615
Middle East Conflict, 750, 950
negotiator cognition, 568
nuclear war prevention, 546, 1052
opponents offer, 916
political leaders, 516
power, 919
summit meetings, 3419
threats, 858
U.S. Senate Hearings, 1164
U.S. policies, 4728
unofficial diplomacy, 1035, 4385
See also Bargaining Behavior, Behavioral Aspects
Psychological Research
  mediation, 1841
Psychological Traps, 947-948
Public Diplomacy, 4419, 4421, 4425, 4429, 4432-4434, 4440, 4442, 4450, 4458
  behavioral aspects, 4412
  Canada/U.S., 4453
  Cuban missile crisis, 4445
  dissertation, 4451
  European views, 4430
  German radio, 4446
  Gorbachev, 4438
  Great Britain, 4411, 4424
  international communication, 4415, 4422
  Iran hostage crisis, 4431
  mass media, 4416
  NATO views, 4427
  political change, 4414
  research, 4420
  Soviet Union, 4437, 4444, 4449
  summit meetings, 4454
  U.N., 2080
  U.S., 4388, 4418, 4441, 4452, 4455
  U.S. House Hearings, 4457, 4456
  U.S. Information Agency, 4413
  U.S. vs U.S.S.R., 4417
  See also Media, Propaganda
Public Good Theory
  bargaining, 145
Public Opinion
  open diplomacy, 4240

Publicity
  diplomacy, 3984
Punishment
  magnitude of, 1086
  psychological reactions, 685

Qatar
  oil concession negotiations, 3647
QUADRANT Conference
  Quebec 1944, 2282
Quaker Mediation
  India/Pakistan Conflict, 4402
Quakers
  international conciliation, 4362
  non official mediators, 4365
  unofficial diplomacy, 4369
  See also Unofficial Diplomacy
Quebec Conference (1943), 2229
Quebec Conference (1944), 2293
  OCTAGON Conference, 2278
  QUADRANT Conference, 2282
Quemoy
  negotiations, 5065

Rabin
  memoirs, 4788
  See also Middle East Conflict
Rapacki Plan
  East European diplomacy, 5367
Rational Behavior
  game theory, 1204, 1389
Rational Choice
  behavioral aspects, 569
Rational Decision Making
  foreign policies, 770
  framework, 1737
Rational Empirical Models, 560
Rational Politics
  game theory, 1194
Reaction Systems
  international relations, 921
Reagan
  attitude to summit meetings, 3411
  negotiating style, 4622
Reagan Administration
  arms control negotiations, 2713
Reagan/Gorbachev Summits, 3420
  Geneva (1985), 3404
  U.S. House Hearing, 3492
  See also Summit Meetings
Reciprocity, 662, 922
  compliance inducement, 611
  dissertation, 1074
  psychological aspects, 808, 882

toughness, 812
Reconnaissance Satellites
　U.S./Soviet cooperation, 3363
Reconstruction Conferences, 2508
Refugee Negotiations (1946), 4547
Regime Change
　negotiations, 191
Regional Conflicts, 56
　mediation, 1857, 1876
　mediators, 1903
　Soviet military, 4476
Regional Cooperation
　Mediterranean actions, 2556
Related Matrix Games
　payoff structure, 1579
Renaissance Diplomacy, 4287
Renegotiations, 466
　aspiration behavior, 1603
　education aspects, 1527
　game theory, 1466
　international trade, 3558
Representative Behavior, 575
　dissertation, 1073
Representative Orientation, 1039
Representative's Power
　negotiation outcome, 1107
Research
　experimental, 445
　international business
　　negotiations, 3633
Research Materials
　development of, 408
Resource Trade Negotiations, 2393, 3907
Revolutionary Wars
　political settlement phase, 464
Rewards
　incentives, 886
　interpersonal conflicts, 833
　negotiation games, 1402
　prisoner dilemma game, 923
　psychological aspects, 844
　conflict resolution, 828
Reykjavik Summit, 3399, 3409, 3417, 3428, 3432, 3436, 3452, 3465, 3480, 3493
　European security, 3472
　Soviet preparations, 3395
　U.S. House Hearings, 3491
　U.S. House Report, 3494
　U.S. policies, 3489-3490
　See also Summit Meetings
Rhodesia Negotiations, 5174
　coercive bargaining, 5189

sanctions, 5176
U.S. role, 1980
Western diplomacy, 5173
See also Lancaster House Conference, Zimbabwe
Riad Mahmoud
　memoirs, 4819
Richardson Process Model
　test ban negotiations, 2979-2980
Risk Assessment
　game theory, 1717
Risk Management, 231
　international agreements, 504
Risk Orientation
　prisoner dilemma game, 1324
Risk Taking
　bargaining behavior, 713
　dissertation, 1179
　intergroup negotiations, 806
Ritchie Charles
　memoirs, 4347-4349
Robots
　simulation studies, 1407
Role Assignment, 1170
Role Reversals
　opposing viewpoints, 872
Roosevelt
　biography, 2240
　diplomacy, 4666
　memoirs, 4313
　negotiator assessment, 2294
　Yalta Conference, 2245
Roosevelt/Churchill
　Atlantic Conference, 2266
　Placenta Bay Summit, 2248
　World War II conferences, 2284
　See also Summit Meetings
Rumania/Bulgaria Disputes
　mediation, 1966

Sadat
　diaries, 4813
　memoirs, 4351
　surprise diplomacy, 3985
Sadat/Begin
　communication aspects, 4931
　speech patterns, 4931
Saint John River Basin Agreement
　dissertation, 5290
Salmon Catch Negotiations, 3842-3843
　Canada/U.S., 3777
SALT Agreements, 3017, 3025
　assessment, 3067, 3069
SALT I Negotiations, 3105, 3111

Subject Index

ABM treaty, 3056
Accidents Measures Agreement, 3027
bureaucracy, 3119
dissertation, 3108, 3119
evaluation, 3051
game theory, 1490, 3109
history of, 3023
interim agreement, 3056
political asymmetries, 3126
Soviet deceptions, 3097
SALT II Agreement
defence aspects, 2724
SALT II Negotiations, 3024, 3028, 3045, 3112, 3274
assessment, 3117, 3122
chronology, 3118
Soviet first strike threat, 3106
Soviet negotiators, 3087
spying, 3100
Vladivostock Accords, 3077
SALT III Negotiations
recommendations, 3079
SALT Negotiations, 3018-3019, 3026, 3029-3031, 3034, 3036-3038, 3040-3043, 3047, 3049, 3052-3054, 3060, 3062, 3064, 3066, 3068, 3070-3072, 3075-3076, 3078, 3080, 3082-3083, 3085-3086, 3090-3092, 3094-3095, 3098-3099, 3101-3102, 3104
bargaining chips, 3033
bargaining models, 3096
bibliography, 2622
confidence building measures, 3089
decision making, 3046
dissertation, 3103
documents, 2622
European security, 3058, 3127
future negotiations, 3088
Geneva, 3044
historical analysis, 2941, 3021, 3055, 3063
Kissinger, 3057
Middle East, 3065
mobile ICBMs, 3084
objectives, 3049, 3083, 3110
policy aspects, 3107
political aspects, 3020, 3039
postures, 3114
precedents, 3035
prenegotiations, 2732
security aspects, 3081
Soviet Union, 3022, 3048, 4543
Soviet military, 3032, 3050

strategic stability, 3115
trilateral conference, 3116
U.S. Dept. of State Report, 3125
U.S. House Hearings, 3120-3121, 3123
U.S. decision making, 3059, 3103
U.S. policies, 3061
unofficial diplomacy, 3073
Vladivostock Summit, 3074, 3093
West German security, 3113
See also Arms Control Negotiations
Salvador Civil War Negotiations, 5266
San Francisco Peace Treaty, 5088
cultural aspects, 5097
Satellite Reconnaissance
arms control, 2933
informal bargaining, 2635
Saudi Arabia
failed mediation, 1951
mediation, 1984
oil diplomacy, 3643
U.S. military rights negotiations, 4965
See also Middle East Conflict, Oil Diplomacy
Scandinavian Economic Market Negotiations, 3886
SDI
arms control negotiations, 2646, 2850, 2946
bargaining problems, 2855-2856
negotiating leverage, 2778
Soviet negotiating style, 4566
summit diplomacy, 3413, 3437
SDI/ABM Treaty Conflicts, 2727
See also Arms Control Negotiations
Sea Power
diplomacy, 5348
Seabed Arms Control Negotiations, 3246-3249, 3251
conferences, 3245, 3252
dissertation, 3252
Seabed Negotiations
Law of the Sea Conferences, 2316, 2338
Seating Position
negotiation outcome, 990
Second Request Timing
compliance, 598
Secrecy, 165
arms control negotiations, 2682, 2866, 2961
diplomacy, 4255

foreign policy, 346, 3981
Secret Diplomacy, 4022, 4102, 4146, 4148, 4175-4176, 4178, 4189
  Arab Rebellion (1936-39), 4845
  definition, 4169
  Israel, 4932
  World War II, 4286
Security Systems
  diplomacy, 4204
Self Awareness
  effect on negotiations, 1168
  negotiation behavior, 1166
Semiconductor Agreement
  U.S./Japan, 3855
Senate Hearings *See* U.S. Senate Hearings
Sequential Bargaining
  asymmetric information, 1363, 1683
  experiments, 1249
Sequential Games
  power aspects, 1433
SEXTANT Conference
  Cairo Conferences 1943, 2283
Shared Information
  game theory, 1540
Siberian Oil
  Japan/Soviet negotiations, 3649
Sidepayment Games, 1457, 1459
Simulation, 1649
  aggression determinants, 640
  arms control negotiations, 1184, 1271, 1414, 1514, 2923
  arms race, 1491
  benefit distribution, 1634
  communication language, 1175
  conflict analysis, 1233
  constituent pressure, 968
  counterpart strategy, 968
  crisis management, 1267, 1566
  Cyprus seminar, 1600
  decision making, 1254, 1680
  diplomacy, 1251, 1358
  dissertation, 1096
  dyadic behavior, 647
  international negotiations, 1701
  international relations, 1242, 1365-1366
  Israeli Palestinian Workshop, 613
  mediation, 1912
  methodologies, 1435
  Middle East Conflict, 1374
  negotiation agreements, 1633
  negotiation breakdown, 1633
  negotiation styles, 1696

negotiation training, 1411
  personality effects, 1158
  political decision making, 617, 1644
  problem solving workshops, 1443
  robots, 1407
  role preference, 1280
  social exchange, 1250
  social psychological aspects, 869
  social systems, 1327
  surrogate disputants, 1502
  U.N. diplomacy, 1398
  See also Game Theory
Sinai Disengagement Agreement
  Kissinger, 4924
  See also Israel/Egypt Negotiations, Kissinger
Sinai II Agreement
  mediation, 1994
Sisco Joseph
  Middle East negotiations, 4948
Situational Influences, 656
Six Day War
  diplomacy, 4791
  Quaker unofficial diplomacy, 4369
  See also Israel/Egypt Negotiations, Kissinger, Middle East Conflict
Skagit High Ross Dam Negotiations, 5280
Small States
  conflict resolution, 301
  diplomacy, 4093
Social Aspects, 525, 661, 865, 1029
  Cooperation, 840
Social Conflicts, 535, 627
  integrative agreements, 907
  mediation, 1810, 1834, 1839
Social Control
  two person games, 1630
Social Dilemma Games, 822, 1469
Social Dilemmas
  alternative choice, 787
Social Interactions
  cooperation, 758
  experimental negotiations, 1128
  psychological studies, 1163
  three person games, 893
Social Motivation, 845
Social Power
  interpersonal bargaining, 697
  measurement of, 715
  two person game, 716
  two person games, 1391
Social Psychological Aspects, 503,

Subject Index

511-512, 521, 530, 537-538, 555, 649, 654-655, 665, 766, 838, 852, 888, 897, 984, 992, 1056, 1083
  crisis bargaining, 690
  diplomacy, 536
  masters thesis, 1151
  threats, 528
Social Responsibility
  bargaining games, 873
Social Status
  bargaining models, 1387
Social Theory
  deescalation, 794
Socialist Diplomacy, 4143
Socialist International
  mediation, 1823
Sociological Aspects, 562, 810, 1033
  conflict resolution, 1083
  game theory, 1544
Sociology of Conflict
  conflict of interest, 642
Softwood Lumber Negotiations
  U.S./Canada Talks, 3790
  See also Canada/U.S. Free Trade, U.S./Canada
Somalia
  diplomacy, 5175
  Ogaden War, 5192
South Africa
  diplomacy, 5169
  human rights issues, 5182
  negotiations, 5162, 5171-5172, 5183, 5194
  U.N. diplomacy, 2066
South Asia
  Soviet diplomacy, 4487
South Pacific
  Nature Conservation Treaty, 5374
South South Cooperation, 2423
South West Africa
  U.N. diplomacy, 2143
Southeast Asia
  diplomatic analysis, 4968
  Kissinger diplomacy, 4775
  U.S. diplomacy, 5359
Sovereignty Disputes
  case studies, 5307
Soviet Bloc Negotiations, 4534
Soviet Conference Diplomacy
  dissertation, 2185
Soviet Decision Making, 4550
  Arms Control Negotiations, 2718
Soviet Diplomacy, 3970, 4461, 4542
  arms transfer, 4596

Austrian state treaty, 4459
coexistence, 4592, 4594
communist doctrine, 4579
developing countries, 4507, 4535
dissertation, 4592, 4594
Geneva Conference (1959), 4586
Gorbachev, 4439, 4564
ideological aspects, 4619
Leninist principles, 4563
Litvinov, 4555
military strategy, 4513
neutrality theory, 4588
Norway, 4514
origins of, 4480
peace issues, 4551
South Asia, 4487
Soviet troops in Cuba, 4474
U.S. Senate Hearings, 4619
Soviet Economy
  arms control negotiations, 2762
Soviet First Strike Threat
  SALT II, 3106
Soviet Foreign Policy, 4481, 4486
  domestic factors, 4527
  history of, 4469
  ideological aspects, 4480
  Moscow Summit 1972, 3464
  professional aspects, 4464
  rhetoric, 1015
  time factors, 4518
  U.S. Senate Hearings, 4616
Soviet Gas Pipeline
  NATO negotiations, 3816
Soviet Japanese Fisheries Talks
  cultural aspects, 3812-3813
Soviet Japanese Salmon Negotiations, 3843
Soviet Mediation
  India/Pakistan Conflict, 1967
  Tashkent conference, 1983
Soviet Military
  SALT negotiations, 3032, 3050
Soviet Military Industrial Complex
  arms control, 2927
Soviet National Characteristics, 4466
Soviet Negotiating Behavior, 2666, 4463, 4467, 4477, 4479, 4482-4483, 4488-4489, 4491-4492, 4495, 4500-4502, 4504-4506, 4512, 4516, 4520-4521, 4523, 4528, 4530-4533, 4538-4541, 4544, 4546, 4548-4549, 4554, 4562, 4567-4570, 4572, 4574, 4576-4577, 4585, 4590-4591,

4593, 4617, 4621-4622, 4624
  agenda setting, 4525
  arms control, 2888
  attitudes, 4587
  Brezhnev, 4623
  communication, 4509
  cultural aspects, 3812-3813
  dialectics, 4485
  dissertation, 2889
  duplicity, 4485
  gas pipeline deal, 4589
  Geneva, 4475
  historical aspects, 4494
  Italian Communists, 4580
  Khrushchev, 4499
  Nuremberg Trials, 4484
  objectives, 4587
  SALT negotiations, 3048, 4543
  SDI issue, 4566
  test ban negotiation, 2965-2966
  U.S. Senate Hearings, 4608-4615
  U.S. policies, 4557-4559, 4598
  U.S. views, 4461
Soviet Negotiating Style, 4556
Soviet Negotiating Policies
  external influences, 2896
Soviet Negotiators
  SALT II, 3087
Soviet Peace Offensives, 4560
Soviet Perceptions of U.S., 4478, 4523
Soviet Political Language
  communication, 4526
Soviet Power
  U.S. policies, 4472-4473
Soviet Propaganda
  arms control negotiations, 2797
  See also Public Diplomacy
Soviet Scholars Exchanges
  negotiations, 4607
Soviet Secrecy
  arms control negotiations, 2763
Soviet Security Policy, 2846
  MBFR negotiations, 3189
Soviet Trade Negotiations, 3805
  legal aspects, 3806
  style, 3811, 3815
  tactics, 3820
Soviet Union
  academic exchanges, 4372
  arms control policies, 2609, 2673, 2915
  Austrian State Treaty, 4595
  Balkans, 4508
  Bretton Woods 1944, 4536
  British negotiations (1939), 4601
  Chinese negotiations, 4493
  cultural diplomacy, 4460, 4565
  Foreign Minister's role, 4571
  human rights, 4498
  Lend Lease, 4519
  negotiation style, 4620
  North South negotiations, 2425
  Polish negotiations (1971), 4553
  propaganda, 4410
  public diplomacy, 4417
  SALT negotiations, 3022
  summit strategy, 3405
  unofficial diplomacy, 724, 4360
Soviet/Eastern Europe
  energy negotiations, 3819
Soviet/U.S. Diplomacy
  historical analysis, 4462
Space Military Activities
  Regulations, 2864
Space Weapons
  arms control negotiations, 2855-2856, 2899
Spain James
  memoirs, 4352
Spanish Communist Party
  negotiating behavior, 4540
Spanish Military Base Negotiations, 5333, 5369
Special Envoy, 4236
Sri Lanka Conflict
  mediation, 1995
Stability
  international relations, 924-925
  psychological aspects, 924-925
Stalemated Negotiation
  agreement pressure, 707
  dissertation, 1105
  pressure for agreement, 1105
Standing Consultative Commission
  arms control, 2668
START Negotiations, 2900, 3094, 3137, 3208-3212, 3216, 3218, 3220-3221
  Geneva meetings, 3217
  historical aspects, 3213
  INF merge, 3214
  overview, 2875
  Soviet positions, 3219
  update, 3215
  See also Arms Control Negotiations
State Visits
  U.S. summit diplomacy, 3501
Statistical Analysis

Subject Index

foreign service, 3986
Status
  coalition games, 554
  negotiator behavior, 700, 775
Steel Industry
  export restraints, 3949
Sterling Dollar Diplomacy, 3863
Stettinius
  diaries, 4690
Stirling Workshop
  applications, 580
  role relations, 551
Stockholm Agreement
  CSBM negotiations, 3329
Stockholm Conference, 3282
  CDE Negotiations, 3284
  CSBM Negotiations, 3275-3276, 3304
  consensus rule, 2168
  European disarmament, 3255
  See also CSCE Conferences
Strategic Arms Limitation Talks
  See SALT Negotiations
Strategic Arms Reduction Talks
  See START Negotiations
Strategic Choice, 926
  mediation structure, 1824
Strategic Conceptualization, 1131
Strategic Defence Initiative
  See SDI
Strategic Interaction, 395
Stress Impact, 733
Structural Aspects
  bargaining outcomes, 709
Subjective Power Models
  dissertation, 1173
Subjective Utility Parameters, 943
Successful Negotiations
  behavioral aspects, 934
  coalition formation, 608
  groups, 850
  Israel/Egypt, 4835
  personality aspects, 689
Sudan Civil War
  mediation, 1923, 1974
Sudden Changes
  international relations, 924-925
Suez Canal Crisis, 4921
  conflict reduction, 4829
  U.S. diplomacy, 4642
  U.S. mediation, 4949
  nationalization, 4921
  See also Middle East Conflict, Nasser
Sugar Agreement

Commonwealth negotiations, 3896
Sullivan William
  diplomatic memoirs, 4353
Summit Meetings, 3400, 3403, 3407, 3407, 3426, 3429, 3434, 3442, 3449, 3457, 3459, 3462, 3473, 3476-3477, 3483
  ABM compromise (1987), 3453
  background documents (1960), 3495
  Canada/U.S., 5291
  chronology, 3485
  conflict intensity, 3460
  diplomacy, 3394, 3414-3416, 3418, 3421, 3443-3444, 3447, 3451, 3458, 3470-3471, 4032
  diplomatic methods, 3390, 3411, 3461
  disagreement avoidance, 3401
  dissertation, 3486
  documents, 3498
  education aspects, 3402
  Eisenhower, 3396, 3439, 3469
  Eisenhower/Khrushchev, 3438
  Eisenhower/Khrushchev 1960, 3482
  Geneva 1955, 3408, 3481
  Geneva 1985, 3446, 3454-3455
  historical analysis, 2233, 3397-3398, 3484
  Japan's defence policy, 3468
  Khrushchev, 3441
  macro analysis, 3440
  media aspects, 3466
  microdiplomacy, 3435
  Moscow (1971), 3433
  Moscow (1988), 3430
  Moscow 1972, 3423
  NATO, 3425
  Placenta Bay 1941, 2248
  Potsdam Conference, 2234
  public diplomacy, 4454
  Reagan/Gorbachev, 3392, 3420
  Reykjavik, 3428
  Roosevelt, 2240
  SDI, 3413
  SDI issues, 3437
  Soviet strategy, 3405
  Soviet tests, 3406
  state visits, 3501
  Tehran conference, 2232
  U.S. Presidential diplomacy, 3450
  U.S. Presidential diplomacy, 3393, 3445
  U.S. Senate Report, 3497
  U.S. preparation, 3412

verbal communication, 3478
Washington (1988), 3467
Washington 1978, 3427
Wilsonian diplomacy, 3469
World War II, 2235, 2241, 2243, 2259-2260, 2262, 2268, 2273, 2277, 2285
Yalta Conference, 2229
Superpower Collaboration
  Middle East conflict, 4794
Superpower Conflicts
  game theory, 1192
Superpower Influence
  Middle East negotiations, 4904
Suspicion
  dissertation, 1111
  game theory, 1510
  methodological studies, 751
  psychological aspects, 630
Sweden
  developing countries negotiations, 3926
Symbolic Aspects, 865
Systems Analysis, 1188

Tacit Games
  game theory, 1461
Tanzanian Diplomacy
  Law of the Sea, 2351
Tashkent Conference
  Soviet mediation, 1983
Tashkent Declaration
  mediation, 1973
Tax Treaties
  negotiation manual, 2493
Tax Treaty Negotiations, 3878
  U.S. Senate Hearings, 3630
  See also Trade Negotiations
Teaching Methods, 290, 339
  development, 408
  See also Training
Technological Aspects, 159
Technology Licensing
  negotiations, 3859
Technology Transfer, 3361, 3882
  cross cultural aspects, 3641
  North South negotiations, 2460
  special studies, 3617-3618
Tehran Conference, 2232, 2238, 2249, 2263, 2277, 2288
  EUREKA Conference, 2275
  Roosevelt, 2294
  Soviet protocols, 2228
Telecommunications, 3857

North South talks, 2430
Telephone Hotline, 2838
  crisis management, 274, 455, 2638, 4725
Ten Nation Disarmament Committee
  propaganda, 3373-3375
Tensions Reduction
  reciprocity, 470
TERMINAL Conference
  Potsdam Conference, 2286
Territorial Conflicts
  game theory, 1581, 1710
Test Ban Negotiations, 2963, 2968, 2972-2974, 2976, 2978, 2982, 2986, 2988, 2992, 2995-2996, 3002-3003, 4582
  Canada, 2997
  Chinese policies, 2999
  conference, 3008
  Cuban missile crisis, 2993-2994
  dissertation, 3016
  evaluation, 2987
  future, 2985
  Geneva Conference, 3013-3014
  historical analysis, 2975, 2977, 2991
  Khrushchev and Kennedy, 2967
  London Conference, 3015
  McCone Senate Hearing, 3011
  neutral countries, 2969, 2998
  nonaligned countries, 2983-2984
  perceptions, 2981
  problem solving, 3000
  review, 2970
  revitalization, 2971
  Richardson Process Model, 2979-2980
  role reversal, 3001
  Soviet bargaining behavior, 2965-2966
  technical issues, 3010
  U.S. Senate Hearings, 3005, 3007, 3010-3011
  U.S. role, 2964
  U.S./Soviet cooperation, 2989
Test Ban Treaty
  policy formulation, 2990
  U.S. House Hearings, 3004
  U.S. Senate Hearings, 3009
Textile Negotiations, 3879, 3915
  Japan, 3839
  U.S./China, 3829
  U.S./Korea, 3935
Thai/U.S. Diplomacy

Subject Index 407

dissertation, 5405
Theater Nuclear Forces Negotiations
    See TNF Negotiations
Theoretical Model
    dissertation, 448
Theory of the Reluctant Duelist
    game theory, 1330-1331
Third Party Characteristics, 588
Third Party Influences
    negotiation behavior, 1625
Third World Conflicts
    preventive diplomacy, 5377
Third World Mineral Agreements
    negotiations, 2373
Threat Compliance, 953
    credibility, 734
    motive attribution, 1101
Threat Credibility
    compliance, 909
    psychological aspects, 863
Threat Perception, 965
    international crises, 506
Threat Research
    social psychology aspects, 1144
Threats, 855, 975, 1086, 1230, 1272
    bargaining behavior, 583, 625-626,
        847, 1007, 1024, 1072, 1112,
        1118
    bargaining efficiency, 683
    bilateral conflicts, 854-855
    bilateral negotiations, 1086
    compliance to, 863
    computer analysis, 1699, 1728
    diplomacy, 4139
    dissertation, 1072, 1112
    duopoly bargaining, 1471
    enforcement costs, 909
    experimental studies, 756, 1321
    fixed opportunity costs, 1009
    incentives in bargaining, 686
    influence of, 606
    international negotiations, 337,
        756
    magnitude of, 735
    non zero sum games, 1635
    perception off, 1146
    psychological aspects, 522, 526,
        668, 685, 858, 1008
    punishment magnitude, 854
    reaction to, 668
    relative costs, 832
    social psychological analysis, 528
    strategic interaction, 876
    three factor analysis, 946

    See also Bargaining Behavior,
        Negotiation
        Behavior, Psychological Aspects
Three Factor Analysis, 946
Three Person Bargaining
    game theory, 1713
Three Person Games, 1399, 1417, 1519,
    1525
    accommodative strategy, 1032
    coalition formation, 1440, 1442,
        1504, 1607
    communication, 1467
    deception, 1181
    guaranteed payoffs, 1418
    social exchange, 893
    trust, 818
Three Person Groups
    coalition behavior, 584
    coalitions, 585
    power structure, 585
    social aspects, 898
Three x Three Game
    behavioral aspects, 819
Time Pressure, 604
    bilateral negotiations, 604
    integrative bargaining, 1063
    mediation, 1775, 1883
    opponent's concession rate, 910
Time Studies
    dissertation, 461
    game theory, 1302
TNF Negotiations, 3364
Tokyo Economic Summit, 3529-3530
    symposium, 3520
Tokyo Round Negotiations
    developing countries, 3726
    GATT, 3702-3704, 3717, 3721, 3725
    Japanese trade, 3741
    See also GATT
Tolerance of Ambiguity
    dissertation, 1091
Torture Agreement
    role of Holland, 5380
Totalitarian Diplomacy
    Germany 1933/41, 4293
    Japan 1933/41, 4293
Toughness, 1246
    dyadic bargaining, 749
    game theory, 1243
    psychological aspects, 559, 603
Trade Barriers
    negotiations, 3560, 3595
Trade Conferences
    U.S. negotiations, 3631

Trade Distortions
  negotiations, 3585
Trade Liberalization
  developing countries, 2402-2403
Trade Negotiations, 76, 2381, 2384,
    2420, 3543-3544, 3549-3550, 3553-
    3554, 3557, 3559, 3561, 3567,
    3574-3575, 3580, 3582, 3588,
    3593-3594, 3596, 3605-3606, 3608,
    3610-3612, 3615, 3617-3618, 3624,
    3634-3636
  Africa/EEC, 3870
  agriculture, 3671
  Australia, 3873
  case study, 3884
  conflict analysis, 1590
  cultural aspect, 3640
  cultural aspects, 3638
  definitions, 3551
  developing countries, 2386, 2389,
    2484
  Eastern Europe, 3892
  foreign cultural aspects, 3642
  GATT, 3697, 3699
  game models, 1241
  game theory, 1666
  guide, 3599
  India, 3865
  integration groups, 3592
  international, 3603
  international institutions, 3555
  international monetary system,
    3613
  nonrenewable resources, 3581
  outcomes, 3587
  personal experience, 3600
  personality aspects, 692
  planning, 3552
  policy issues, 3597
  practical experiences, 3632
  reciprocity, 3598
  renegotiations, 3558
  research, 3633
  services, 3563
  theory and practice, 3632
  U.N., 2111
  U.S. Congress Hearings, 3626-3627
  U.S. House Hearings, 3628
  U.S. Senate Hearings, 3629
  U.S. mandate, 3914
  U.S. options, 3850
  U.S./Europe, 3562
  U.S./Latin America, 3899
  U.S./South Korea, 3900, 3940

UNCTAD, 3625
  conflict analysis, 3584
Trade Promotion
  embassies role, 4251
Trade Protectionism
  game theory, 1524
Trade in Services, 3548, 3566, 3572,
    3620
  GATT, 3707
  Uruguay Round Negotiations, 3729
Tradeoff Value Assessment, 1733
Training Manual, 424
Training Methods, 290, 371, 465
  diplomacy, 4091
  negotiation skills, 404
  U.S. diplomats, 4772
Translator's Memoirs
  World War II Conferences, 4316
Transnational Mineral Agreements,
    2382, 3912
Treaties
  historical analysis, 100
Treaty Interpretation
  negotiator perspective, 380
Treaty Negotiations
  cultural aspects, 354, 5353
  procedures, 2700
TRIDENT Conference
  Washington 1943, 2287
Trieste 1954 Conference Negotiations,
    2152
Trilateral Commission Negotiations,
    2033
Trilateral Conference
  MBFR negotiations, 3116
  SALT negotiations, 3116
Trivial Games
  predictors, 1423
Truman
  Potsdam Conference, 2247, 2250
Trust
  bargaining behavior, 1039, 1135
  cooperative behavior, 837
  development of, 830
  dissertation, 1111
  F scale, 631
  game theory, 1510
  maintenance of, 842
  methodological studies, 751
  negotiation behavior, 769
  Osgood proposal, 901
  prisoner dilemma game, 831, 1045
  psychological aspects, 630, 825
  theoretical studies, 623

Subject Index

three person game, 818
unilateral promise, 666
See also Bargaining Behavior, Psychological Aspects
Trust Relationship, 1004
Trustworthiness
  F scale, 631
  impression management, 912
Turkey
  U.S. diplomacy, 4352, 4755
Two Party Negotiations
  behavioral aspects, 747
  compliance aspects, 582
  decision support systems, 1670
  dissertation, 1088
  settlements, 566
Two Person Games, 1217, 1230, 1264, 1462, 1478-1479, 1492, 1698
  aspirations, 1534
  attitude change, 896
  bargaining problems, 1474
  behavioral aspects, 1058-1059, 1636
  betrayal, 780
  communication, 1053
  cooperation, 772
  cooperative choice, 789
  game theory, 1619
  internationalism, 846
  isolation, 846, 1053
  Nash solution, 1390
  Nash theorem, 1482
  non constant sum game, 1501
  non zero sum games, 1570
  noncooperative solutions, 1621
  opportunity costs, 716
  reconciliation, 780
  social control, 1629-1630
  social decisions, 1037
  social power, 716, 1391
  solution, 1659
  utility of, 1473
Two Person Negotiation
  competitiveness, 804
  decision support, 1337
  information factors, 804
  representation factors, 803
Two Person Power Games, 1288
Two x Two Games, 1216, 1274, 1430, 1517, 1611
  deception, 1657
  equilibria, 1642

U.N. Atomic Energy Controls
  Baruch Plan, 2561
U.N. Charter Negotiations
  U.S. role, 2055
U.N. Conference on Human Environment
  dissertation, 2189
U.N. Conference on Science
  failure, 2132
U.N. Delegates
  national attributes, 2116
U.N. Diplomacy, 1803, 2041, 2048, 2064, 2067, 2070, 2076, 2078, 2080-2082, 2087, 2094, 2099-2100, 2105, 2130, 2150
  Africa, 2122, 2572
  arms control negotiations, 2226, 2897
  conference diplomacy, 2108, 2181
  conflict management, 2058, 2065, 2069, 2075, 2089-2092, 2098, 2106, 2113-2114, 2127-2128, 2135, 2151, 2037
  Dag Hammarskjöld, 2051
  decision making, 2049
  dept relief negotiations, 2478, 2497
  developing countries, 2136
  disarmament activities, 2147, 2197, 2212, 2223-2224
  disarmament conferences, 2056, 2198
  dissertation, 2124, 2134
  economic negotiations, 2117
  Falkland Islands Crisis, 2109, 5214, 5229
  General Assembly, 2059-2061, 2061, 2063, 2093
  General Secretary's Role, 2121
  global role, 2083
  human rights, 2096
  India, 2104
  India/Pakistan Conflict, 2052
  international conferences, 2174
  international crises, 2118
  international trade, 2111
  Israel issues, 2103
  Law of the Sea Conferences, 2297, 2300, 2328
  legal aspects, 2053, 2095
  memoirs, 2057
  modern, 2086
  multilateral, 2119
  NPT negotiations, 3354
  Namibia negotiations, 2126
  non resolution of conflicts, 2062

North South negotiations, 2193, 2431, 2482, 2491
organizational analysis, 2044
peacemaking, 2036, 2112
political aspects, 2047
privacy aspects, 2084
recognition aspects, 2102
reconciliation aspects, 2085
Secretary General's role, 2131, 2133, 2088, 2101, 2139
Security Council, 2039, 2071-2072
simulation, 1398
South Africa, 2066
South West Africa, 2143
space negotiations, 2079, 2125
termination of wars, 2038
Trade and Development Conference, 2183
treaty making processes, 2148
U.S. diplomacy, 2068, 4724
U.S. diplomats, 2045-2046
U.S. foreign policy, 2042
U.N. Diplomats
attitudes, 2077, 2134
memoirs, 2043, 2050
U.N. Disarmament Negotiations
verification, 2220
U.N. Disarmament Yearbook, 2222
U.N. Eighteen Nation Disarmament Conference, 2200-2203, 2205, 2207-2208, 2211, 2213, 2219, 2225, 2199
U.N. Five Power Subcommittee, 2218, 2227
documents, 2210, 2214-2217
U.N. General Assembly
diplomacy, 2054
dissertation, 2146
U.N. Mediation, 1828, 1897, 1907, 1953, 1959, 1969, 1997-1998, 2115, 2137, 2144, 2151
dissertation, 2137
Indonesian Question, 2145
Kashmir, 1925, 1936
Namibia, 1970
Ralph Bunche, 1927
U.N. Membership Admission
dissertation, 2140
U.N. Resource Conference
U.S. participation, 2149
U.N. Science and Technology Conf.
dissertation, 2138
U.N. Security Council Resolution 242, 2129

U.N. Ten Nation Disarmament Committee, 2204, 2206
U.S. Ambassadors, 4734
role of, 4727
U.S. Arms Control & Disarmament Agency
hearings, 2950
history, 2837
U.S. Arms Control Initiatives
chronology, 2849
U.S. Arms Control Policies
dissertation, 2929
U.S. Asian Policies
U.S. House Hearings, 5059
U.S. Boundary Diplomacy
dissertation, 4762
U.S. Bureaucracy
negotiating with Soviets, 4584
U.S. Congress
arms control negotiations, 2961
diplomatic aspects, 4771
U.S. Congress Hearings
trade negotiations, 3626-3627
Venice Economic Summit, 3541
U.S. Cultural Diplomacy
historical analysis, 4672, 4731
U.S. Defence Policies
arms control, 2759
U.S. Department of State
multilateral diplomacy, 4744
problem solving, 1138, 4770
reforms, 4781
U.S. Diplomacy, 4626, 4632, 4634-4635, 4637, 4641, 4648, 4662, 4671, 4675, 4677, 4679, 4692, 4698, 4700-4701, 4709, 4712, 4714, 4722, 4742, 4745-4746, 4778
Afghanistan, 5360
amateurism, 4741
army bases in Philippines, 5410
Asia, 4718
Azerbijan Crisis (1945/46), 4763
Baruch Plan, 4780
Berlin Crisis (1958/62), 4743
Bohlen Charles, 4680
boundary issues, 4762
Carter, 4685, 4719
China, 5112
cold war period, 4638, 4684
communication, 4644
communication, 4705
cultural aspects, 4652, 4782, 5332
Cyprus Conflict, 4824

Subject Index

Cyrus Vance, 4667
disarmament policy, 2680-2681
domestic aspects, 4740
ethical aspects, 4685, 4733
faults of, 4730
Geneva Conference (1954), 5001
historical analysis, 4661, 4663, 4681, 4693, 4720, 4659
hostage negotiations, 4697
human rights, 4751
Indochina War, 5001
international conferences, 2170, 2195
Iran, 4717
Japan, 4655
Joseph Grew, 4653
Kissinger, 4660, 4664
Lebanon War (1982), 4939
Middle East Conflict, 4797, 4804, 4836, 4896, 4940
Moroccan military bases, 5185
multilateral negotiations, 2001
naval officers, 4676
negotiation strategies, 5106
neutralism, 4709
North South relations, 2469
organization aspects, 4769
Paris Peace talks, 4976
presidential rating, 4737
reforms, 4781
relevance of, 4748
research, 4738
Roosevelt, 4666
SALT negotiations, 3059
science and technology, 4779
secret diplomacy, 4739
Secretaries of State, 4669
Southeast Asia, 5359
Soviet Union, 4490
Soviet analysis, 4723, 4732
special envoys, 4752
steel agreement, 3948
Turkey, 4352, 4755
U.N., 2068, 4724
U.S. Congress, 4726
U.S. State Department, 4682
wine negotiations, 3734
World War II, 4686, 4765
U.S. Diplomatic History, 4271-4273, 4277
dictionary, 4276
U.S. Diplomatic Missions
policy making, 4711
U.S. Diplomats, 4627, 4636, 4657, 4670
administrative history, 4656
executive agents, 4696
historical analysis, 4678
North Africa (1941/43), 4704
personal qualities, 4699
profiles, 4668
psychological aspects, 4716
training, 4772
U.N., 2045-2046
U.S. Foreign Policy, 4695
Berlin issues, 5414
coercive diplomacy, 4774
cold war diplomacy, 4646
congressional influence, 4658
documents, 4785
effectiveness, 4721
Kissinger, 4654, 4691, 4715, 4768
multilateral diplomacy, 2012
personality aspects, 664
rhetoric, 1015
U.N., 2040, 2042
U.S. Foreign Relations
documents, 4761, 4773, 4783
private experts, 4754
U.S. Foreign Service, 4689, 4756
elitism, 4713
staffing, 4625
U.S. Government Agencies
conflict management, 4759
U.S. House Hearings
Angola negotiations, 5198
arms control negotiations, 2945
Canada/U.S. trade relations, 3797
chemical weapons, 3244
comprehensive test ban, 3004
Cyprus conflict, 4959
GATT negotiations, 3754
international aviation, 2584
Law of the Sea, 2356
Middle East negotiations, 4956
North South negotiations, 2494
oil negotiations, 3659
public diplomacy, 4456-4457
Reagan/Gorbachev Summit, 3492
Reykjavik Summit, 3491
SALT negotiations, 3120-3121, 3123
trade negotiations, 3628
U.S. Arms Control Agency, 2950
U.S. Asian policies, 5059
U.S./Canada Trade, 3795, 3798
U.S./Japan economic relation, 3856
Vietnam War talks, 5059
Vladivostock Accords, 3124

U.S. House Report
  Canada/U.S. Free Trade, 3799
U.S. INF Proposals
  Soviet positions, 3219
U.S. Information Agency
  Nixon Doctrine, 4451
  public diplomacy, 4413
U.S. Institute for Peace
  research activities, 275
U.S. Machine Tool Industry
  international talks, 3929
U.S. Mediation
  Middle East Conflict, 1989, 4794, 4947
U.S. Negotiating Techniques, 4530-4531, 4591
  communication, 4511
  communist powers, 4524
  cultural aspects, 5099
  failures, 4512
  with Soviets, 4517, 4528
U.S. Negotiation Shortcomings
  with communists, 4606
U.S. Oil Diplomacy, 3644
U.S. Pipeline Diplomacy, 3895
U.S. Presidential Summit Diplomacy, 3445
U.S. Presidents
  diplomacy, 4737
  diplomatic image, 4735
  foreign visits, 4736
U.S. Public Diplomacy, 4388, 4417-4418, 4441, 4452, 4455-4456
U.S. Resource Diplomacy, 3906
U.S. Secretaries of State, 4669, 4747
  diplomatic analysis, 4630
  history, 4647
U.S. Senate Hearings
  acid rain, 5292-5293
  arms control negotiations, 2953, 2957
  arms control policies, 2952
  Canada/U.S. Free Trade Talk, 3800
  commodity negotiations, 3691
  communist negotiations, 4606
  comprehensive test ban, 3012
  Law of the Sea, 2357-2359
  Middle East negotiations, 4962
  negotiation processes, 488-490
  negotiation theory, 487
  nonproliferation issues, 3356
  psychological aspects, 1164
  scholarly exchanges, 4607
  secret, 4777
  Soviet foreign policy, 4616
  Soviet negotiating behavior, 4608-4615, 4619
  Summit Conference 1960, 3496
  tax treaty negotiations, 3630
  test ban negotiations, 3005, 3007, 3009-3011
  trade negotiations, 3629
  U.S./Soviet relations, 4603-4605
U.S. Senate Report
  commodity negotiations, 3692
  Vietnam War negotiations, 5060
U.S. State Department, 4683
  memoirs, 4312
  Russian Section, 4515
  training simulation, 1633-1634
U.S. Trade Negotiations, 3897
  developing countries, 3869
  GATT, 3696, 3756-3758
U.S./Brazil Negotiations
  computer industry, 3941
  computer markets, 3930
U.S./British Atomic Negotiations (1943), 5387
U.S./British Naval Relations, 5344
U.S./British Nuclear Negotiations
  dissertation, 2881
U.S./Canada
  acid rain, 5282, 5285, 5292
  acid rain hearings, 5293
  agricultural trade talks, 3770, 3765, 3774, 3781-3782
  air pollution negotiations, 3778
  bilateral institutions, 5278-5279
  boundary water disputes, 5281, 5283-5284, 5286
  Columbia River Treaty negotiations, 5276
  conflict resolution, 5289, 5274, 5287
  environmental disputes, 5277
  free trade agreement, 3775
  free trade negotiations, 3769, 3779, 3783, 3792, 3801
  International Joint Commission, 5273
  negotiation failure, 5288
  softwood lumber negotiations, 3790
  summit diplomacy, 5291
  trade negotiations, 3760, 3762, 3772, 3795
  water resources diplomacy, 5280, 3761

Subject Index

U.S./Canada Free Trade Negotiations
  chronology, 3788
U.S./Canada Trade Agreement
  U.S. House Hearings, 3798
U.S./China Agreements
  case study, 5143
  nuclear energy, 5149
U.S./China Negotiations, 5124, 5142, 5160
  assessment, 5113
  dissertation, 5156-5158
  domestic aspects, 5127
  textiles, 3829
U.S./China Trade Negotiations, 3821, 3823, 3828
U.S./Chinese/Japanese Diplomacy, 4633
U.S./EEC
  agricultural tariff negotiations, 3686
U.S./Egypt
  bilateral negotiations, 3902
U.S./Europe
  trade relations, 3952
U.S./Germany
  military cooperation talks, 5325
U.S./Holland
  financial negotiations, 3891
U.S./Iran Diplomacy, 5401
U.S./Japan
  negotiation comparison, 5095
  semiconductor agreement, 3855
U.S./Japan Economic Relations
  U.S. House Hearing, 3856
U.S./Japan Negotiations, 5101
U.S./Japanese Air Service Negotiations, 3854
U.S./Japanese Negotiations, 5401
  communication, 5104
  cultural aspects, 5097
  dissertation, 5104
  GATT, 3755
U.S./Japanese Negotiations (1939-41), 5109
U.S./Japanese Negotiations (1941)
  dissertation, 5103, 5105
U.S./Japanese Peace Negotiations, 4710
U.S./Japanese Trade Negotiations, 3832-3833, 3836, 3840, 3844, 3847, 3850, 3853
U.S./Korea
  textile negotiations, 3935
  trade negotiations, 3900, 3940

U.S./Latin America
  diplomatic aspects, 5234
  trade negotiations, 3899, 3942
U.S./Mexico
  boundary disputes, 5272
  Chamizal Tract dispute, 5256
  diplomatic aspects, 5401
  environmental negotiations, 5259
  fisheries negotiations, 3893
  gas negotiations, 507
  legal aspects, 5256
  natural gas negotiations, 3885, 3944
U.S./Middle East Diplomacy
  dissertation, 4950
U.S./Morocco
  military bases negotiations, 5185
U.S./Nicaragua
  negotiations 1978/79, 5255
U.S./Philippines
  trade negotiations, 3887
  U.S. military base negotiations, 5391
U.S./Rumania
  most favored nation trade status, 3937
U.S./Soviet Academic Exchanges, 4358
U.S./Soviet Copyright Negotiations, 3818
U.S./Soviet Diplomacy
  ambassador's study, 4687
  Moscow Embassy, 4651
  origins, 4333
  pre World War II, 4640
  report, 4600
  World War II, 4639
U.S./Soviet Grain Purchase Agreements, 3665, 3676, 3689
U.S./Soviet Negotiations, 4496, 4510, 4629, 4650, 4703, 4707, 4757, 5343
  attitudes, 4573
  crisis management, 2716, 2894
U.S./Soviet Negotiations
  future issues, 4511
  game theory, 1282
  Horn of Africa, 5164
  Middle East Conflict, 4839, 4898
  multiple symmetry model, 4578
  refugee negotiations, 4547
  strategies, 4933
  U.S. Congress, 4581
U.S./Soviet Relations
  U.S. House Report, 4602

U.S. Senate Hearings, 4603-4605
U.S./Soviet Security Cooperation, 2617
U.S./Soviet Standing Consultative Commission, 2669
U.S./Soviet Trade Negotiations, 3804, 3814
  behavioral aspect, 3807
  cultural aspects, 3809
  dissertation, 3817
  Soviet tactics, 3820
U.S./Soviet Unofficial Diplomacy, 4385
U.S./Spanish Negotiations, 5397
  military bases, 47
U.S./Vietnam Diplomatic Relations, 5419
Ultimatums
  diplomacy, 4138
  game theory, 1367-1368
Uncertain Outcomes
  game theory, 1444
UNCLOS III
  law of the sea negotiations, 2310, 2320
UNCTAD
  conciliation procedures, 2417, 2421
  development diplomacy, 2362, 2376
  diplomatic aspects, 2363, 2477
  diplomatic history, 2376
  dissertation, 2477
  future assessment, 2456
  GATT negotiations, 2419
  institutional analysis, 2418
  North South negotiations, 2362, 2371, 2412, 2498
  trade negotiations, 3625
  U.S. policies, 2481
Unequal Status Groups
  negotiator's presentation, 1020
UNESCO
  cultural diplomacy, 2097
UNIDO Conference, 2110
Unified Bargaining Model, 719
Unified Treatment
  bargaining theory, 1618
Unilateral Disarmament, 2707, 2798
UNITAR Negotiations, 2553
United Nations *See* U.N. Diplomacy
United Nations Conference on the Law of the Sea *See* UNCLOS
United Nations Conference on Trade and Development *See* UNCTAD
United Nations Educational, Scientific, and Cultural Organization *See* UNESCO
United Nations Industrial Development Organization *See* UNIDO
United Nations Institute for Training and Research *See* UNITAR
United States of America *See* U.S.
Unofficial Diplomacy, 4359, 4361, 4366-4367, 4370, 4380-4381, 4384, 4387, 4391, 4397-4398, 4404, 4406-4407
  alternative system, 4373
  Armand Hammer, 4401
  citizen diplomacy, 4389
  Commission of Churches, 4386
  Dartmouth Conference, 4368, 4371, 4394-4395, 4408
  dissertation, 4405
  Dominican Republic, 4400
  Germany, 4399
  International Red Cross, 4377
  Japanese trade dispute, 4393
  John Doe Associates, 4357
  Korea, 4399
  media aspects, 4383
  Middle East, 4364, 4390
  psychological aspects, 724, 1035, 4385
  Quakers, 4362, 4369, 4402-4403
  SALT negotiations, 3073
  simulation, 1266, 1374, 1600
  Soviet Union, 4360, 4374, 4378, 4382, 4396
  Soviet academic exchanges, 4372
  U.N., 2084
  U.S./Soviet relations, 4385
  Vietnam, 4363
  volunteers, 4375
  workshops, 4376, 4379
Unofficial Diplomats, 4356
Unofficial Mediation, 1886, 4403-4404
  Cuban missile crisis, 4392
Update Service
  arms control negotiations, 2594
Uranium Diplomacy, 3864
Urquhart Brian
  memoirs, 2057
Uruguay Round of Trade Negotiations, 3729
  See also GATT
Utility Interaction

Subject Index

conflict resolution, 1612
Utility Measurements, 1183

Value of Time in Bargaining, 427
Vatican Diplomacy, 5303, 5329
  mediation, 1830
Venice Economic Summit, 3521
  U.S. Congress Hearing, 3541
  See also Economic Summits
Verbal Communication, 3391
  cooperation, 745
  summit meetings, 3478
Verification
  U.N. disarmament negotiations, 2220
Versailles Economic Summit, 3523, 3527
  See also Economic Summits
Veto Games
  communication, 1468
  group size, 1468
Video Tape Modeling
  negotiation styles, 657
Vienna
  MBFR Negotiations, 3169, 3171, 3197
Vienna Summit 1979, 3500
Vietnam
  U.S. relations, 1945-67, 5058
  unofficial diplomacy, 4363
  diplomacy (1983), 5336
  Vietnam War Negotiations, 4583, 4966, 4970, 4972, 4975, 4977, 4983, 4985-4986, 4989-4990, 4993-4994, 4996-4998, 5003-5004, 5007, 5012-5013, 5022, 5025, 5033, 5035, 5040, 5044, 5048, 5053, 5061, 5063
  chronology, 5046
  diplomatic initiatives, 5018
  game theory, 1639-1641
  Hanoi, 5006, 5024
  historical assessment, 5036
  Johnson's policies, 5029
  Kissinger, 4988, 5008-5009, 5011, 5015, 5019, 5039
  linkage issues, 4995
  military aspects, 5056
  Nixon term, 5047
  North Vietnamese policies, 4978, 4981
  Paris Peace Agreement, 4971
  Paris Peace talks, 4979-4980, 4982, 4984, 4987, 5000, 5005, 5016, 5023, 5026-5028, 5031-5032, 5037-5038, 5041
  peace proposals, 5020, 5054, 5062
  Pentagon papers, 5050
  political options, 5021
  secrecy, 5014
  settlement options, 5017
  South Vietnam 1961, 5051
  U.S. House Hearings, 5059
  U.S. Senate Report, 5060
  U.S. policies, 4969, 4991, 5002
  war termination, 5034
Vietnamese Communists
  negotiation strategies, 5055
Vietnamese Diplomacy
  ASEAN countries, 5326-5327
Virgin Islands Tax Convention, 3901
Visibility
  group representatives, 572
Visual Access, 601
  bargaining outcomes, 684
  bilateral negotiations, 601
  integrative bargaining, 817
Visual Communication, 991
  bilateral negotiations, 1082
Visual Interactions, 1082
Vladivostock Accords, 3422
  SALT negotiations, 3077
  U.S. House Hearings, 3124
Vladivostock Summit, 4328
  SALT negotiations, 3074, 3093
  Soviet policies, 3431
  See also Summit Meetings
Voluntary Restraint Agreement (Steel), 3948
Voting Games, 954
Vulnerability
  prisoner dilemma game, 831

War Termination, 51, 81, 97, 157, 439
  adversary expectations, 302
  conflict resolution, 222, 377
  Middle East, 4859
  negotiation processes, 84
  rational models, 393
  U.N., 2038
Wars
  causes of, 88
Warsaw Pact
  arms control negotiations, 2733
Wartime Negotiations
  legal aspects, 119
Washington Conference (1943), 2292

TRIDENT Conference, 2287
Washington Conferences (1941/42), 2290
Washington Summit (1973), 3499
Washington Summit (1987), 3420, 3463
  documents, 3487
Washington Summit (1988)
  assessment, 3410
  psychological aspects, 3419
  See also Summit Meetings
Water Contamination Dispute
  game theory, 1315
Water Resources Diplomacy
  Canada/U.S., 3761
Weakness
  bargaining tactic, 949
Weizman Ezer
  Egypt/Israeli peace, 4826
  See also Camp David Summit, Middle East Conflict
West Bank Negotiations, 4883, 4958
  assessment, 4954
  See also Middle East Conflict
West German Rearmament Negotiations
  dissertation, 5407
West New Guinea Dispute, 5304
  mediation, 1986
Wheat Negotiations, 3668
  North South aspects, 2413
  See also Commodity Negotiations
Williamsburg Economic Summit, 3505, 3540
  See also Economic Summits
Wilson
  summit diplomacy, 3469
Winner's Curse, 1550
Winning, 117
  game theory aspects, 1248
World Administrative Radio Conference, 2552
World Bank Diplomacy
  developing countries, 2492
World Court
  negotiations, 2074
World Food Conference, 2375
  diplomacy, 2190, 2535
World Radio Conference
  negotiations (1979), 2577
World War II
  Berlin status, 2569
  diplomacy, 4297, 5361
  division of Germany, 5315
  Germany's partition decision, 2280
  Malta Conference, 2265

military assistance negotiations, 4505
peace settlement, 5316
Poland, 2242
second front negotiations, 2271
secret diplomacy, 4286
summit conferences, 2230, 2235, 2260, 2262-2263, 2268, 2273
U.S. diplomacy, 4686
World War II Agreements
  postwar Germany, 3379
World War II Conferences
  Germany's future, 2279
  interpreter's memoirs, 4316
  See also Summit Meetings

Yalta Conference, 2229, 2231, 2236, 2252-2254, 2256-2257, 2259, 2261, 2264, 2269, 2274, 2277, 2289
  allied unity, 2251
  balance of power, 2244
  military aspects, 2272
  Polish question, 2255, 2276
  results, 2246
  Roosevelt, 2245, 2267, 2294
  Soviet promise on Poland, 2255
  Soviet protocols, 2228
  Truman, 2267
  U.S. preparations, 2258
Yemen Crisis
  mediation, 1987
Yom Kippur War
  crisis management, 4831
  See also Middle East Conflict
Yugoslavia
  Paris Peace Conference, 2507
Yugoslavian Ambassador
  Moscow diary, 4471

Zaire
  dept restructuring, 2470
Zero Sum Games, 1341-1342
  behavioral aspects, 839
Zeuthen Theory of Bargaining, 1306, 1460, 1553
Zeuthen-Hicks Theory of Bargaining, 1261-1262
  See also Game Theory
Zimbabwe
  coalition analysis algorithm, 1695
  independence negotiations, 5166-5167, 5181, 5190, 5196-5197, 5398
  Lancaster House Conference, 5161

mediation, 1958
See also Rhodesia Negotiations